AF581009

# Double Vision

# Double Vision

## The Cinema of Robert Beavers

Rebekah Rutkoff

The MIT Press
Cambridge, Massachusetts
London, England

The MIT Press would like to thank the anonymous peer reviewers who provided comments on drafts of this book. The generous work of academic experts is essential for establishing the authority and quality of our publications. We acknowledge with gratitude the contributions of these otherwise uncredited readers.



This book was set in New Frank by The MIT Press. Printed and bound in the United States of America.

Library of Congress Cataloging-in-Publication Data

Names: Rutkoff, Rebekah, author.

Title: Double vision : the cinema of Robert Beavers / Rebekah Rutkoff.
Description: Cambridge, Massachusetts : The MIT Press, 2024. | Includes bibliographical references and index.
Identifiers: LCCN 2023024650 (print) | ISBN 9780262048767 (hardcover) | ISBN 9780262377713 (pdf)
Subjects: LCSH: Beavers, Robert—Criticism and interpretation. | Experimental films—United States—History and criticism. | LCGFT: Film criticism.
Classification: LCC PN1998.3.B424 R88 2024 (print) | DDC 791.4302/33092—dc23/eng/20230919

LC record available at https://lccn.loc.gov/2023024650

10 9 8 7 6 5 4 3 2 1

In memory of Maja Naef (1973–2021) and Jonathan Schwartz (1973–2018)

# Contents

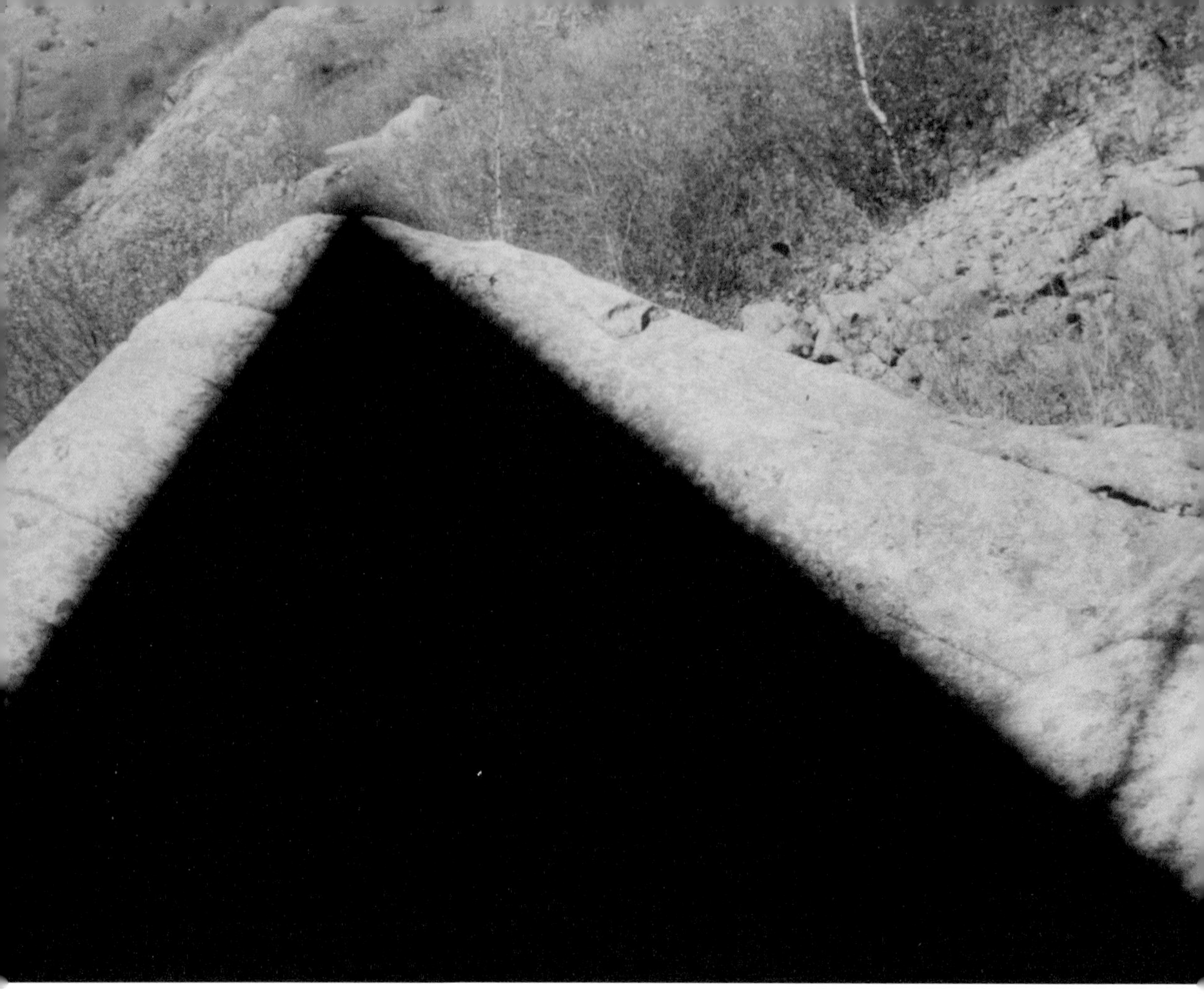

*Ruskin* (1975/1997)

# Prologue: The Prismatic Way

> The image is always one side until it becomes more.
> **Robert Beavers, notes for *Sotiros*[1]**

In the long game of telephone that has transmitted contemplative practice into the twenty-first century, thinking itself has emerged as the apparent enemy of stillness. In the fantasy of pure presence, the evacuation of thought is imagined as cure-all, spacious foil to discursive preoccupation and contracted, neurotic mind. But thinking has infinite faces, and the composure of awareness and the generative kinetics of thought are not inherently at odds.

For Robert Beavers, the making of films and the disciplined cultivation of awareness have developed as interdependent practices for more than half a century. Beavers left high school after his junior year, in 1965, and began to pursue filmmaking the following year. From the start, his autodidacticism manifested as a structured reception to experience. Attention itself served as an itinerant school where thinking and feeling, mind and body, were not at odds. It was a multidisciplinary undertaking marked by formal rigor and anchored in writing. Tuned to stimuli both ordinary and elevated, Beavers embraced a formal note-making method, transcribing thought-shards (observations, pleasures, intuitions, aphorisms, self-instructions) on a regular basis.

In Rome in the summer of 1967, having recently eloped to Europe with his new partner, Greek American filmmaker Gregory Markopoulos (1928–1992), eighteen-year-old Beavers regularly deposited 100 lire at the church of San Luigi dei Francesi to light up Caravaggio's paintings of Saint Matthew the Evangelist. In the two volumes of the filmmaker's first notes, made in 1967–1968 while he was in Greece, Italy, and Belgium, painting plays a primary role. Beavers collects models for narrative plurality, transparent color, and the compositional distribution of eros from the pigment of Hieronymus Bosch, Vittore Carpaccio, Lucas Cranach, Antonello da Messina, Albrecht Dürer, El Greco, Francisco Goya, Andrea Mantegna, Peter Paul Rubens, Jean-Baptiste-Camille Corot, Jean-Auguste-Dominique Ingres, Pieter Bruegel the Elder, and Rogier van der Weyden.[2] And he searches for "clues to the correct composition"—coexistent figuration and abstraction, fracture and grace, movement and fixity, line and form—in decorative objects, mosaic floors, and ancient stelae. Beavers's art observations rotate with receptivity to the multiplicity available in any moment when awareness is turned on: a single tea bubble holds two views ("I see a wide-angle view of myself with the steam of the tea rising at the same time"); when observed through a goblet of water, a knife surface casts back a kaleidoscopic Roman cityscape ("Every window moves rhythmically with prismatic color"). His motion studies draw on air patterns, dreams, and the facial display of unconscious affect.

In his first notes, Beavers is as interested in mediations as in objects—and attuned to instruments beyond the optical: what can be known somatically.

> **The sensual perceived with the eye,**
> **the sensual perceived with the body.**

## BEHIND SEEING

Beavers's filmmaking tools changed shape in tandem with the expansion of his own awareness. In the autumn of 1967, he enlarged his 16mm Bolex camera by attaching a compendium, or matte box, to its front. The metal frame generated two new planes in which he could insert shaped mattes and colored gelatin filters. His lens was now trained on more than the usual world; "the shot" became a multidimensional composite, the view interrupted by graphic ornamentation or flooded by color. He remade the camera as an observational transitional object composed of distinct spaces in which awareness could reside and also be seen. "I found it was like going behind how one is seeing," he said. As the compendium renovated the front of his instrument, nonoptical forces reshaped its back. "In the moment of filming you are surrounding the camera as much as actually looking through it. You're thinking in a searching way [about] what you want to reveal—you're not necessarily seeing [it]."[3]

"Going behind seeing" resides as a value in multiple sites. It is ground into the language of contemplative practice and traditions of attentional cultivation with spiritual aim. Awareness—the present-tense knowing of phenomena as they occur—is conceived of as larger than the discrete mind-objects (thoughts, feelings, sensory information) it stands behind and aerates. (Awareness is infinitely expandable: more can always be brought into its surround.) And although self-conscious seeing in the history of Western art has no single start date, "going behind seeing" was a distinctly modernist concern: the frame in the foreground, Clement Greenberg's self-critical painting, Marcel Duchamp's "looking at seeing."[4] Beavers's double vision unites deconditioning pursuits and representational orientations we've learned to separate.

If camera/eye kinship makes photographic media hospitable "going behind seeing" territory, avant-garde filmmakers have historically exploited this potential. West Coast film curator Susan Oxtoby identifies Beavers as "occupying a noble position *between* structural and lyrical filmmaking traditions"—the two major American avant-garde film cultures of the 1960s.[5] Neither constitutes a pure category, but the stripped-down demystification of imagistic illusionism of structural film (apparatus as content) and the subjectivity-driven enactment of nonnarrative seeing of lyricism (film as poetic pathway to mystery and perspective enlargement that exceeds the visual world) represent distinct alternatives to the real of classical film. In Beavers's films, rigorous semiotic shake-up catalyzed by material/processual self-reflexivity interfaces with intimate soul-balancing priorities. The death of filmic illusionism does not rule. Apparatus theatrics and investments in figurative beauty coexist, as do indexical stability (image tethered comfortably to object) and signification oriented to mindedness itself (and beyond). At the heart of Beavers's approach, the limitless space of awareness serves as a model for the construction of vision-bound cinematic space. Dualistic and nondualistic reality registers refuse to cancel each other out.

Beavers rejects most affiliations: "I'm put in this category—experimental or avant-garde film—but I myself don't think in this category," he said.[6] He embraces a sui generis art historical language: "Am I in the strong main tradition of Hellenism (associated with Greece, Catholicism and the figurative) that ends with Matisse? Or am I in the ascetic tradition of Klee, Northern Europe and poetry?" But every opposition produces a new limit, so he quickly adds: "Then again, Matisse and Klee were also both musicians." He sometimes invokes Marianne Moore's formulation—"I can see no reason for calling my work poetry except that there is no other category in which to put it"—to express his allergy to professional guilds.[7]

In the late 1960s and early 1970s, as writers on Beavers's first works remarked on the unfamiliarity of his dialect (Jonas Mekas called it "a completely new philosophy of life and reality"; "Beavers offers us a *new vision*," Belgian critic René Micha wrote), they frequently turned to two-at-once formulations.[8] "Any image may be an abstraction both of the form and idea represented," filmmaker Tom Chomont wrote.[9] Finding it "impossible to say which is the language and which is the content" in Beavers's films, Mekas embraced the precision of poetry instead: "Gregory Markopoulos has described Beavers' film language most accurately, I think, when he called it 'the language of diamonds,' in a recent essay in *Film Culture* magazine. Robert Beavers' film language is curiously close to the crystalline qualities of stones and minerals—in shapes, in tones, in feeling, in quality."[10]

## CAUSES AND CONDITIONS

Beavers considered the 1967 trip a visit, but it inaugurated five decades of European itineracy (and ultimately extreme isolation) with Markopoulos and the development of an original filmmaking language spun from the physical environments and cultural atmospheres of his new home. Between 1967 and 1999, Beavers shot films in Greece, Italy, England, Switzerland, and Germany. They are complex poems marked by subtle spiritual priorities and a preoccupation with the vicissitudes of colored light. Many stage dialogues between the working and representational conditions of 16mm filmmaking and those of six centuries of European art and craft. Beavers's interlocutors include famous artists (Leonardo da Vinci, Francesco Borromini, John Ruskin, il Sassetta) and anonymous manual artisans (an Athenian candlemaker, a Florentine bookbinder, a Roman tailor), but the inspiring makers—and their labors, materials, and object-outcomes—are less his films' subjects than their causes. Architecture, sewing, writing, drawing, stone-carving—and illustrated book, religious triptych, baroque dome, ancient vase: all become identificatory allies—agents of potential—in the construction of cinematic space. Beavers has said that "the goal is for the projected image to have the same force of awakening sight as any other great image."[11] But the goal is also, it would seem, to resist the object-fixity that accrues around "great images" and to use film to protect the present-tense life-form of imaginative work.

Beavers's films are slanted odes to having been moved (touched) by the work of others, and his exploration of optical sensuality—"How we see is like a hand reaching into space," he said—makes his a cinema of multivalent touch. I had never heard of Beavers when I first saw a handful of his films in 2008 and 2009—*Pitcher of Colored Light* (2007), *Ruskin* (1975/1997), and *AMOR* (1980)—and was myself moved by their intersubjective matrixes and unfamiliar angle of address to spectators. Images fused by lushness and asceticism registered as provocations rather than arrests of pleasure; the films entreated a response and stymied language. In the following years, opportunities to see retrospectives of Beavers's films at Pacific Film Archives and the Austrian Film Museum confirmed my wish to study his work.

The unusual conditions of Beavers's secluded partnership with Markopoulos in Europe account for the extremity of his intellectual and psychic investments in his art as well as its relative obscurity. Beavers had just begun to establish a name for himself as a young artist when he and Markopoulos dramatically exited film culture and withdrew—themselves into self-enclosure and their films from circulation. That story can overwhelm study of the films themselves, and I have been tempted to distance Beavers's work from the Markopoulos narrative by setting it into intertextual dialogue with any number of philosophical formations (including depth psychology, pragmatism, phenomenology, Zen thought) with which it resonates. But wrapping his work in discursive unity, no matter how spacious the discourse is, goes against the variegated textual grain of Beavers's films (which are so frequently balanced on the edge of language itself). The intricacy and diversity of Beavers's films have led me to turn to the artist's own language—a decade's worth of conversations with the artist, as well as his own notebooks and writings—as primary context for considering his work. The sporadic presence of my own first-person voice is meant to acknowledge, rather than neutralize, the impress of my own interests. Beavers's films have been so little seen that the range of uses to be made of them is still to be determined. The acuity of his engagement with the "otherness" of the spectator requires multiple responses.

## THINKING OBJECT

As a child growing up near Boston, Beavers watched up to four movies a week. His mother drove him to the Cameo Theater in South Weymouth and the Victor Theater in East Weymouth to see Douglas Sirk's *Imitation of Life* (1959), Robert Pirosh's Eastmancolor adventure *Valley of the Kings* (1954), and Cecil B. DeMille's *The Ten Commandments* (1956). On special occasions, he saw Margaret O'Brien, Shirley Temple, Jane Withers, Judy Garland, and Mickey Rooney in 35mm at the Boston Children's Museum, in Jamaica Plain. "It was magical. I left the cinema captured by a dream," he said. It was one of only two times I've heard him use the word *magic* in connection to cinema. The aura of the projected film image ushered him out of ordinary life, but this early magical impress didn't become his model.

"When I began to make films, I didn't want that absorption, I didn't want to make the kind of film that places you inside it or captures you that other way," he said. "I want conscious seeing for the spectator." Sometimes he calls it "direct seeing."

Conventional film spectatorship runs on the willingness to swap awareness of impossibility for the sake of immersive pleasure: what Samuel Taylor Coleridge called "suspension of disbelief." Beavers, like most avant-garde film practitioners, has pursued an alternate belief system. "My belief in the camera as a thinking object is central," he said. "The camera reflects thought."

When Beavers recounted first sliding a glass plate—on top of which he had mounted a red filter fragment—into the compendium frame in 1967, the word *magic* came up again. "Having something suspended in front of you is a kind of visual magic," he said of seeing the landscape suddenly stamped by a luminous foreign shape. This was not absorptive Hollywood magic—nor was the floating shape a spectacle to freeze for a future spectator. It was a momentary glimpse of creation amid the flux that arises from approaching the camera as a "thinking object": an awareness theater for motions of mind, hands, and eyes as they move in and out of consciousness of one another. As he turned the Bolex exposure knob, the graphic surprise of red lost its edge and the entire frame was washed by pink; shape became tint. A moment later, the compendium removed, the filter was a shard of transparent gelatin resting on a table.

When Beavers shot *Winged Dialogue* (1967/2000) on Hydra in 1967, he inserted multicolored filter combinations *inside* the camera, using the slot between prism and lens, designed for corrective filters, as a compositional palette for additive color instead.[12] (Later, when the film was projected, he discovered that chroma was more subtly integrated into the image, as if "breathing" through it, when it originated behind the lens rather than in front of it.) "I saw that after I'd place the filters inside the camera, the prism reversed the order of colors in the viewfinder," which corresponds to what the spectator will see on-screen. A red-over-green filter combination inside the camera appeared in the viewfinder as green-over-red. "I thought, *aha*! . . . This prism is like the eye-mind connection; I want to show this—it's like what happens in sight." The convex lens of eye and camera bends light and projects an incoming image upside down before another medium flips it right side up. In a human being, that medium is the brain. In the Bolex reflex camera, it's a glass prism between lens and film.[13]

The color reversal was a glimpse behind the optical curtain and introduced the camera as analogy generator (here: prism-as-mind). But it was also a reminder of the eventful distance traveled by a film image. The elegant unity of analog filmmaking—the full circumference of celluloid transit from camera to projector to screen—is, at closer range, a dotted line of discrepancy and difference, an interconnected chain of distinct views, frames, and image registrations. Chief among them is the difference between minds at both ends of the filmmaking process—filmmaker and spectator, front and back. "The act of filming should be a source of thought and discovery," Beavers insists—but the mind inhabited by the artist amid creative process cannot be transferred directly to the spectator.[14] "Beavers is engaged, and would engage us, in the 'work' of film-making and film-viewing. . . . The viewer must be prepared to perform an analogous creative act when 'entering' the film," P. Adams Sitney writes.[15]

## TWO SIDES

As Beavers has negotiated this analog ecology of totality and difference, the representation of divided unities has played a central role. "I have returned several times to the question of how to show the 'reverse side' of an object in film, how to give the full sense of it and other facets of prismatic space in film. This retains a fascination for me, whether it is the two sides of a hand or the turning of a page or the dialogue between two figures," he writes.[16] Seeing Dürer's two-sided *Portrait of a Young Man* (1507) at the Vienna Kunsthistorisches Museum in 1968 first inspired him. In *AMOR*, set in Salzburg and Rome amid the rhyming labors of sewing, architecture, and filmmaking, Beavers's performances in front of and behind the camera bring first- and third-person perspectives into contact. In *From the Notebook of . . .* (1971/1998), spurred by French poet Paul Valéry's essay on da Vinci's notebooks, complex matting simulates turning pages on a vertically divided screen. And views shot from both sides of Athenian industrial arcades construct "a shape of emptiness" in *The Stoas* (1991–1997).[17] Depolarizing material sides produces space larger than the sum of its two parts.

Sidedness is speculative: "Every sense organ has two directions within it," Beavers writes.[18] It is also structural: Beavers's two-part films include *Still Light* (1970/2001), *Ruskin*, *Sotiros* (1976–1978/1996), and *The Hedge Theater* (1986–1990/2002). When, in the 1990s, Beavers took on the decade-long labor of producing *My Hand Outstretched to the Winged Distance and Sightless Measure* (1967–2002), a cycle of eighteen films made since 1967, he radically altered his originals; his revised films acquired two production dates (e.g., 1971/1998) and the originals became "first versions."[19] In making the cycle, Beavers placed the transitional sound of fluttering bird wings between individual films—a replacement for titles—thus bringing *My Hand Outstretched* into analogical resonance with a page-turning object.

Writing constitutes one half of Beavers's process. "I am always doing both. Moving back and forth between the writing and the filmmaking," he said. Neither diaristic nor meant for an audience, note-making is Beavers's primary means of protecting his filmmaking from the controls of intention. "Beginning with a few notes, I continue to write while the filming progresses, and I see my notebook as a place to be patient and sustain the continuity of the work while remaining open to unforeseen additions or deletions," he writes.[20] Rather than direct or dictate his filming, the notes color the climate in which it happens. Beavers's note-making method was influenced by Valéry's pursuit of writing modes that resisted the hardening of thinking into language. Valéry ultimately forsook poetry in favor of the early morning note, producing more than 250 notebooks—never meant for public consumption—before he died.

As Beavers travels between sides, his notes bear witness to diverse events of turning, drawn from inner and outer worlds, as they interact. The turning over of object (hand, page) coexists with the turns of association (*x* is like *y*), awareness (the turn of attention toward an object), apparatus/body (the turning, by hand, of apparatus parts: lens, turret, tripod). Beavers identifies his two-sided investigations as an ambition to multidimensionalize materiality and mind in filmic form—an effort to "give the full sense of [an object] and other facets of prismatic space."

The filmmaking field—its simultaneous views and the spaces between them—is an opportunity to think and feel according to prismatic awareness and to pursue the making of art anchored in that full potential. The prism, the small glass element inside the Bolex camera, is an emblem for this fullness.

## RESONANCE AND OTHER MAGICS

A prism (beam-splitter, image-reverser, rainbow-maker) is also an emblem of release. Beavers takes a vitalist view of his filmmaking—"I hold an almost biological object in my hands, what I am making, and try not to deform or deny its life," he writes[21]—and conceives of events of energetic transit, conversion, and release at every stage: from shooting ("The energy released by the moving camera changes the meaning of the film cut")[22] to editing ("The simple unwinding and rewinding of film rolls . . . can help to release an insight leading to the film's distinct form").[23] At the center of this energetic economy is the release of the film image from the paradoxical soil of nonretinal "intuition and feeling" and optical rigor ("I hold to the discipline of composing the individual image").[24] "Tentative searching" coexists with a readiness to "reach . . . the truth in an instant."[25] While shooting, Beavers sometimes turns the camera on himself as he releases spontaneous gesture: he reaches, holds, strikes.[26]

Beavers extends the value of sudden knowing to the audience. "The spectator must discover why an image was chosen, and the silence of such a discovery is a moment of release."[27] The viewer's sense-making of a single image might release affect (the unlikely appearance of a loaf of golden bread in a rocky Saronic island landscape clears the climate of intractable grief in *The Ground* [1993–2001]) or language (when a backlit Italian banknote in *AMOR* reveals two portraits at once, the phrase "two men" erupts in my mind and crystallizes the racing erotic energy of the film). Release might take somatic form: "Despite their restraint, [Beavers's films] have an immediate kinetic impact—they go right to your solar plexus and change the rate of your breathing," Amy Taubin writes.[28] The spectator's discoveries occur at degrees of intuited proximity to/distance from those of the filmmaker. One could say this about any experience of art; Beavers's films promote a dilated space of spectatorial self-witnessing that highlights the "fort-da" game by which one seeks and abandons the presence of the artist's mind.

Release, for Beavers, is a multimotion figure; it combines letting go and arrival. Don Daniels names "birth itself—an act of creative forthcoming, primal aesthetic generation" at the thematic heart of Beavers's films.[29] Micha calls Beavers's approach "closer to the act of creation than of the thing created."[30] In *From the Notebook of . . .*, "the act of creation" is distributed among processes seen and suggested—from filmmaking, notebook assembly, and Renaissance space-construction to depth perception, erotic sublimation, and the act that binds them all inside the dynamic notebook space: analogical thinking. As the spectator acclimates to the role of participant-observer in a field of nonstop associative rhyme (a leaf recalls a wing, the shutters of camera and Florentine pension room collide, the split screen reminds the eyes of their binocular intake, fragments of Beavers's own notes magnetize film images and sounds), object orientation gradually softens. As her attentional field opens, the spectator comes close to Valéry's wide-view position when he transcribes his own mind's drive to draw far-flung objects into generative relation: "I recognize it in myself by this: that all possible objects of the ordinary world, external or internal, beings, events, feelings, and actions, while keeping their usual appearance . . . somehow change in value. They attract one another, they are connected in ways quite different from the ordinary; they become . . . musicalized, resonant, and as it were, harmonically related."[31] Resonance, for Valéry, is a form of magic—but one whose generativity-in-time is more primary than its spectacle-display, than the shapes of its evanescent fruits.[32] "The form . . . does not last . . . it dissolves into the light; it has acted; it has done its work; it has lived."[33]

When, like Valéry, the *Notebook* spectator sees the charged gestalt script of poetic transit (the film no longer an assembly of Beavers's notes but an ecstatic enactment of imaginative thought), the frame that holds the continuous script—her own awareness—might also descend into view. "The point from which to begin . . . is with the eye of the spectator, the first sense, and proceed to the others, as he recognizes the presence which becomes awareness," Beavers writes.[34] When "awareness becomes silently transparent," accessible to direct experience, its role among the many creative and semiotic agencies involved in the making or viewing of a film is potentiated.[35] "Attention creates a different tense," Beavers writes.[36] In *Ruskin*, the falling pages of an open book produce an arc through space: a rectangle has become round. Such alchemy vocalizes not only apparatus conditions (image intake through a circle and export as a rectangle) but awareness itself, which speaks below concept, in a poetic tongue.[37] In Beavers's cinema of relations between the compositions of image and mind, awareness, like a prism, is both a source of fleeting release and the unified ground of full presence.

—

Unlike resonance, "magic" as conventionally understood—the kind that produces a rabbit from a hat, captures cinema spectators (like Beavers as a child) in a dense and directed dream state, or casts a ritual spell—*intends* on release, concretizes it as repeatable spectacle. Magic is the display of effects without causes: hat and rabbit are highly legible, but the transit between them is out of sight, under the magician's command. When French anthropologist Marcel Mauss searched for the essence of magic at the turn of the twentieth century, he identified the missing material as the associative chain along which the current of magic passes. Magic, for the spectacle-receiver, excises the movements of thought.[38]

Beavers's work brings to mind an alternate vision of magic—magic as born not of redacted transit but of transition itself. The British psychoanalyst Donald Winnicott saw magic as a shifting potential inside a moving sequence. Winnicott is famous for theorizing the infant's "magical thinking"—the illusion that her own wail instantly *creates* the breast. But a few psychic steps away from one-noted omnipotent creation, he identified a second magic that emerges as the infant begins to perceive an attuned caregiver as both "me" and "not-me." In this intermediate relational space, she develops a psycho-imaginative capacity to cope with distance and difference by blending primary magical creation and "control of the actual"—by mixing illusion and reality, subjective and objective impressions, inner and outer objects. She develops the capacity, one might say, to pursue experiential "resonance." "This is the precariousness of magic itself, magic that arises in intimacy," Winnicott writes.[39] Such magic is the seed of aliveness, the crucial kernel of all creative capacities to come. If official magic relies on forms of coercion and extreme imbalances of power (one party must be blind), Beavers's flims generate a space of transitional magic that allows for the possibility of two seeing-subjects.

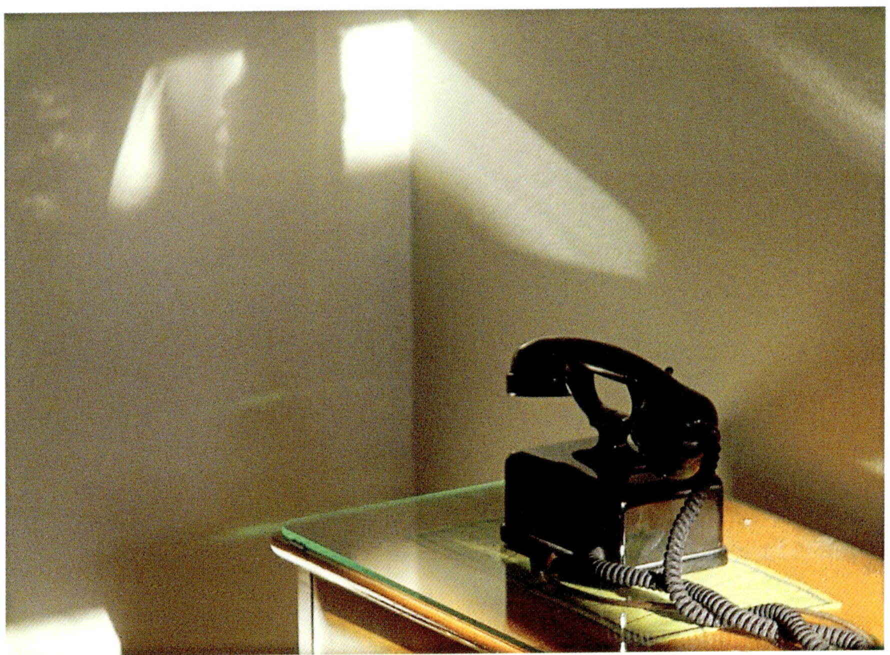

*Sotiros* (1976–1978/1996)

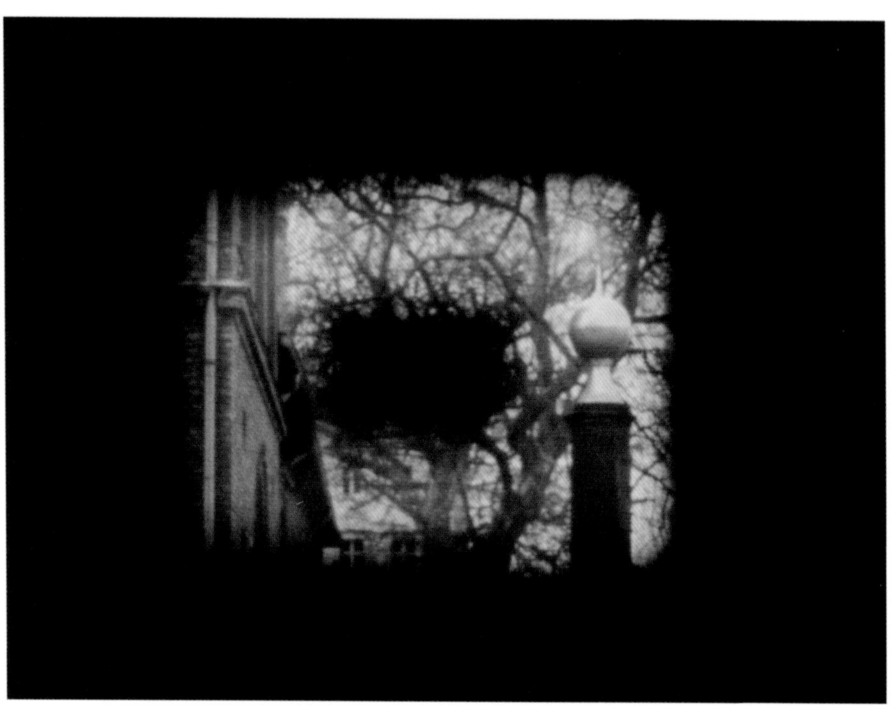

*Diminished Frame* (1970/2001)

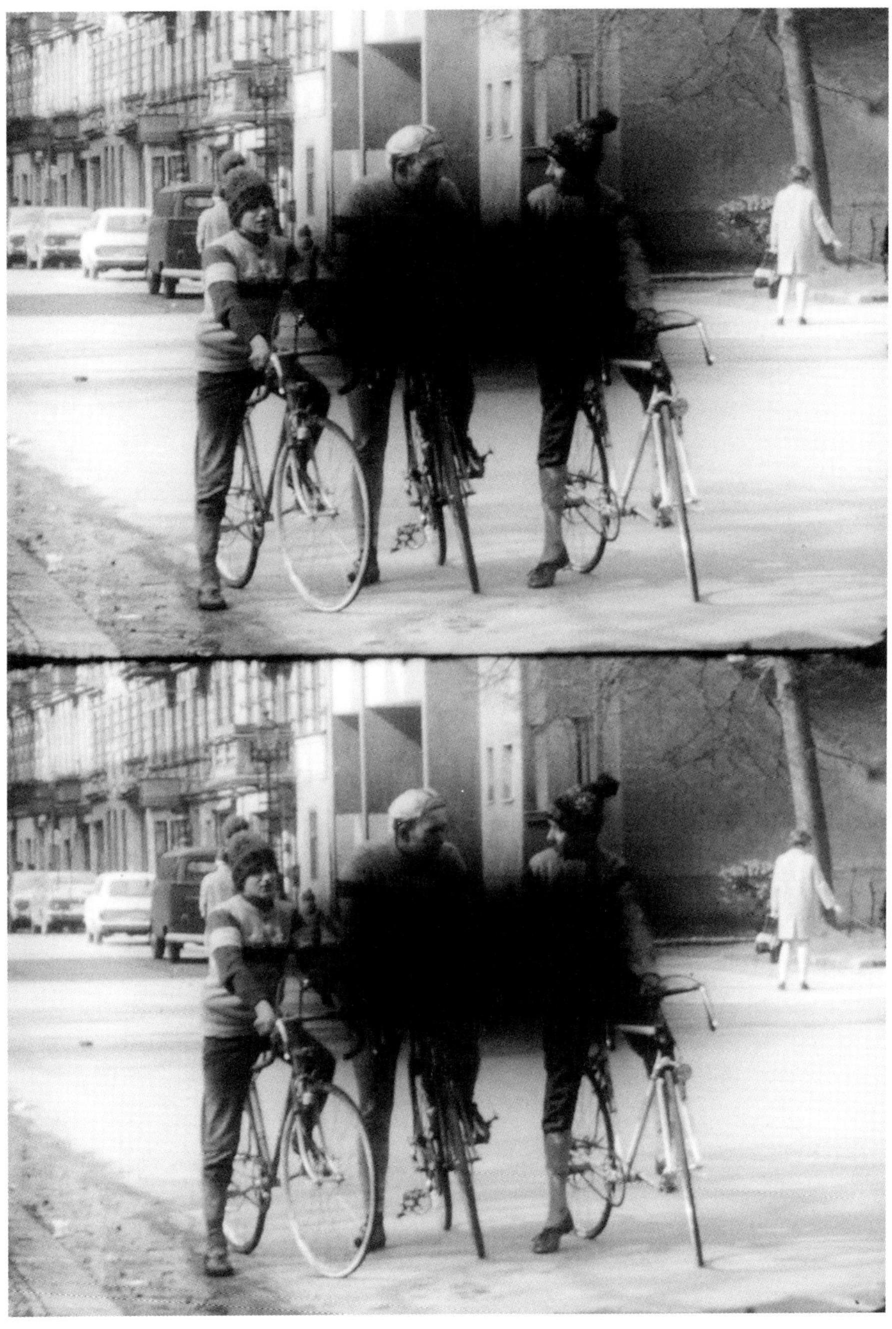

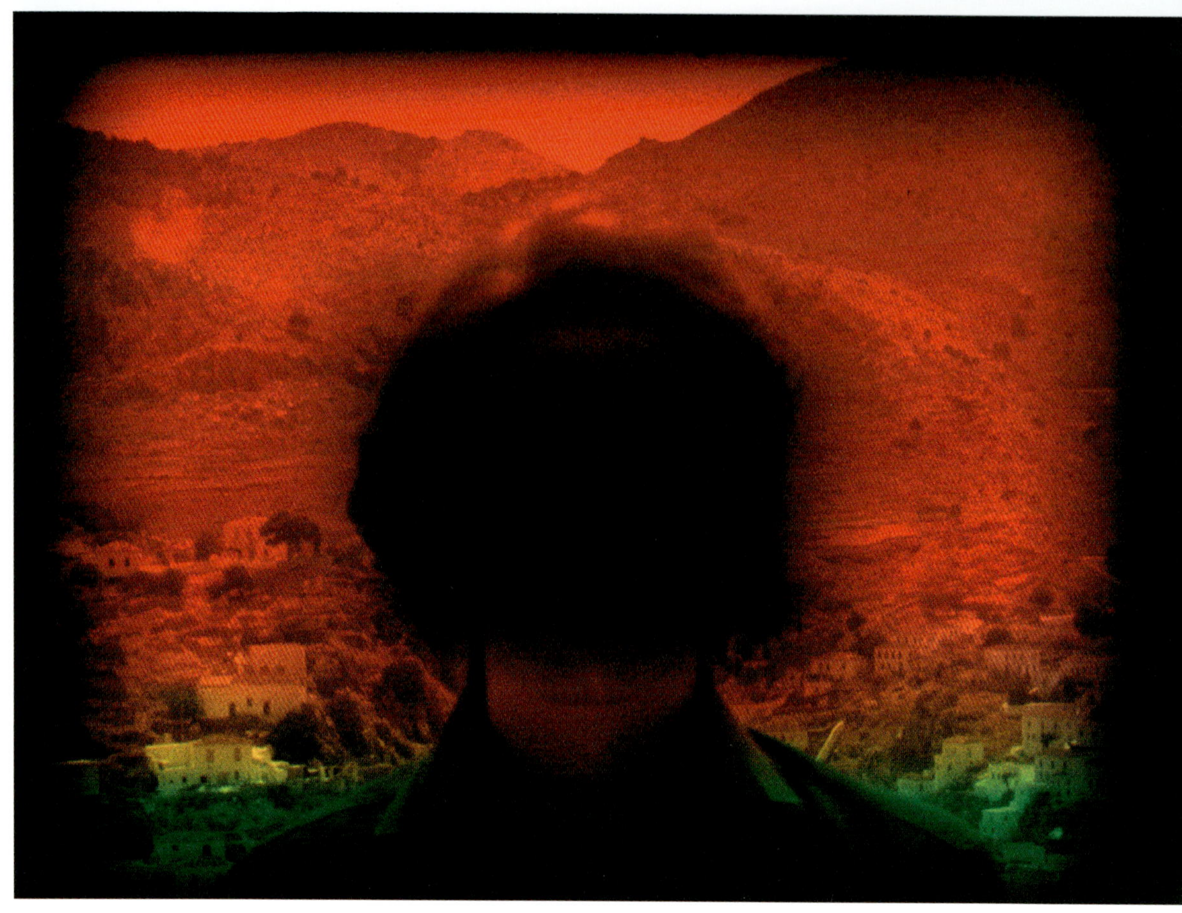

*Still Light* (1970/2001)

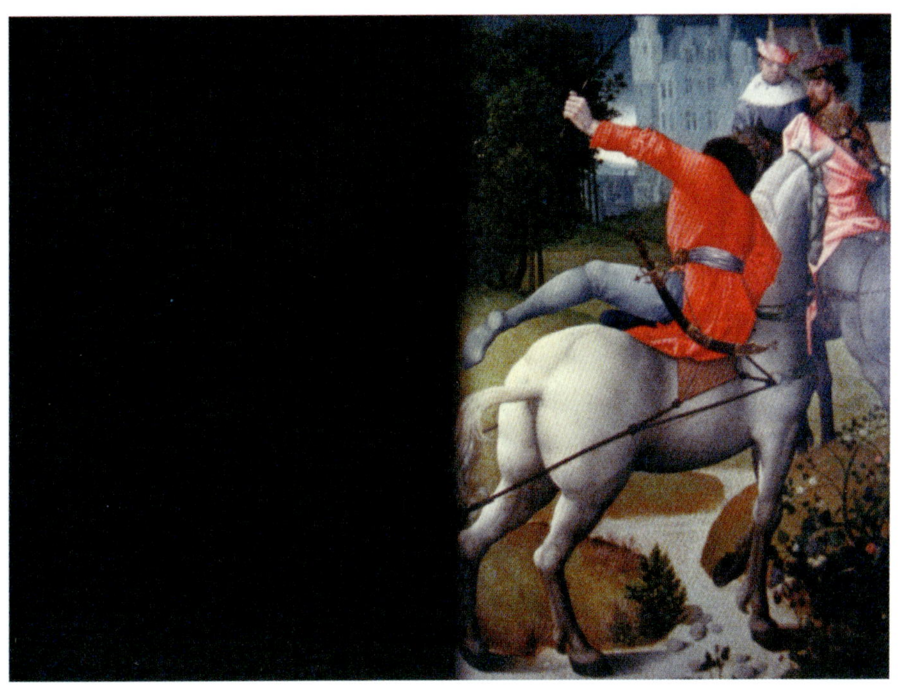

*The Painting* (1972/1999)

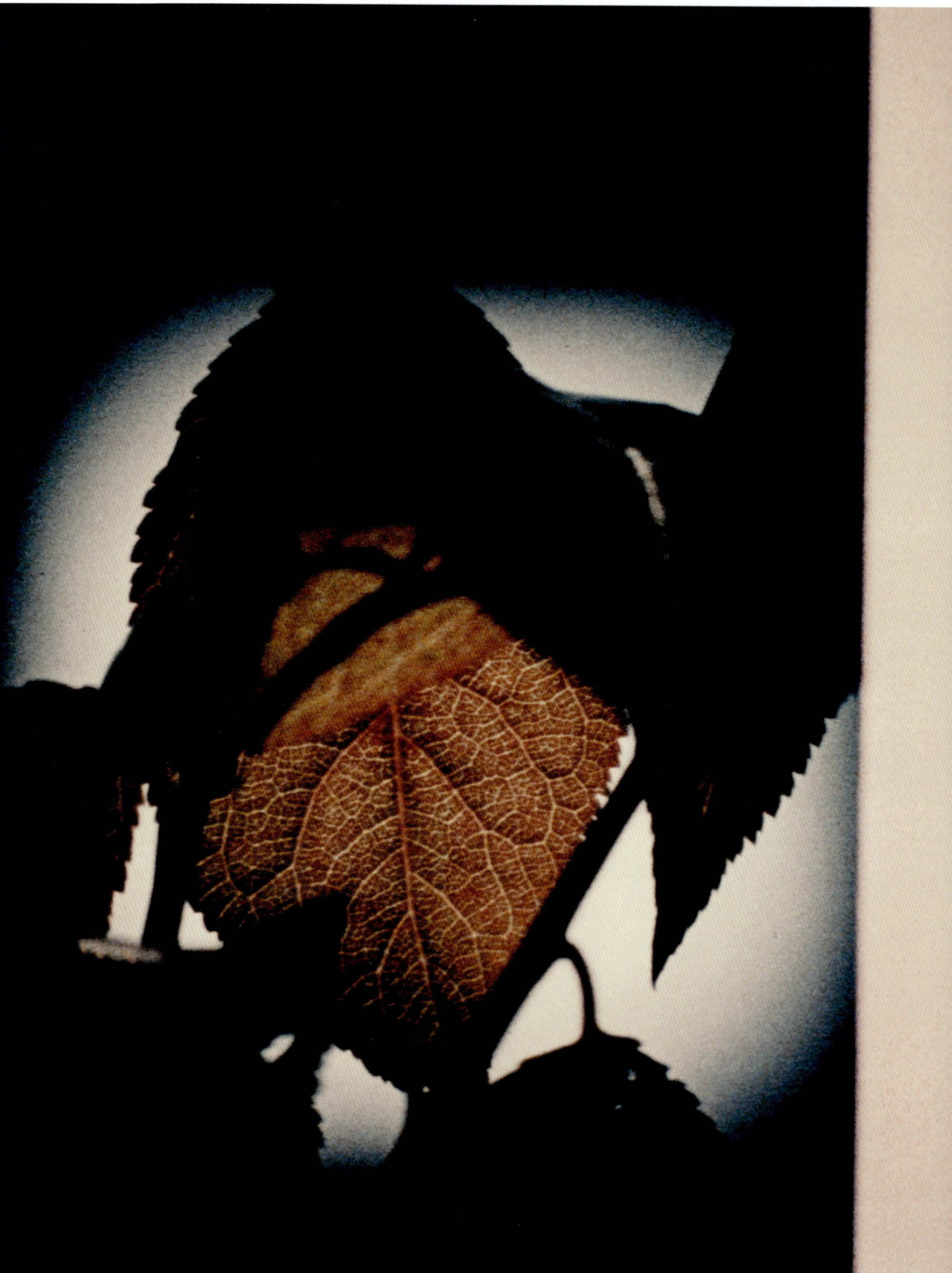

*From the Notebook of . . .* (1971/1998)

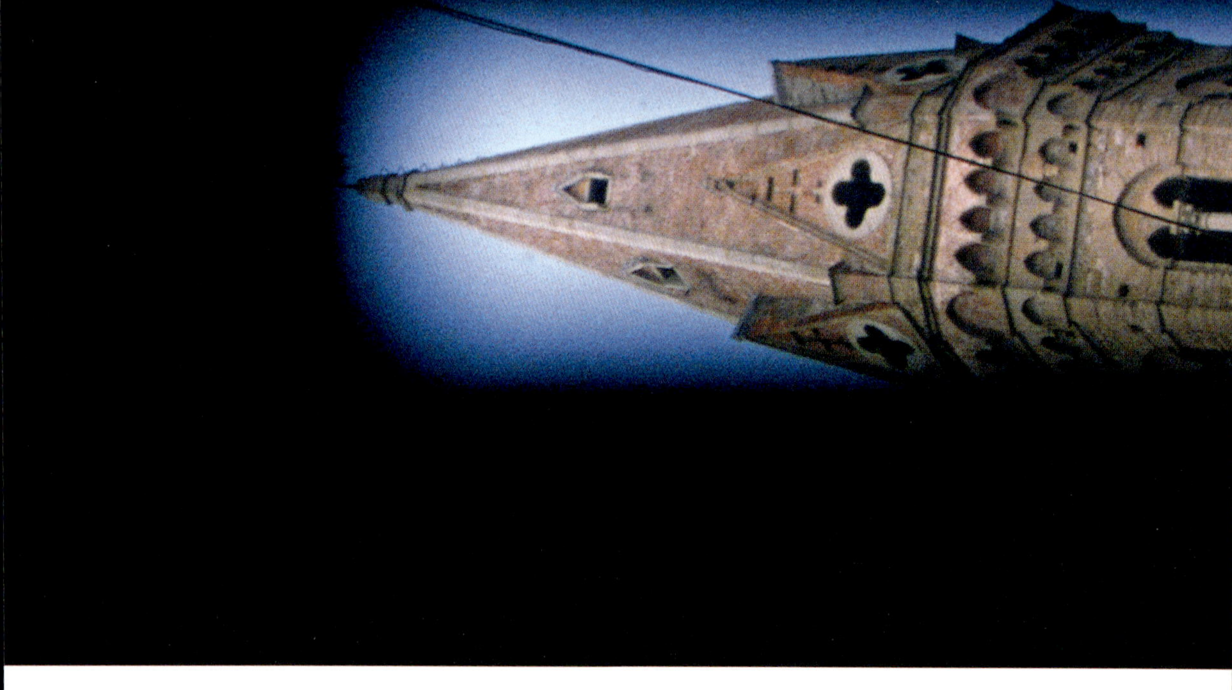

*From the Notebook of . . .* (1971/1998)

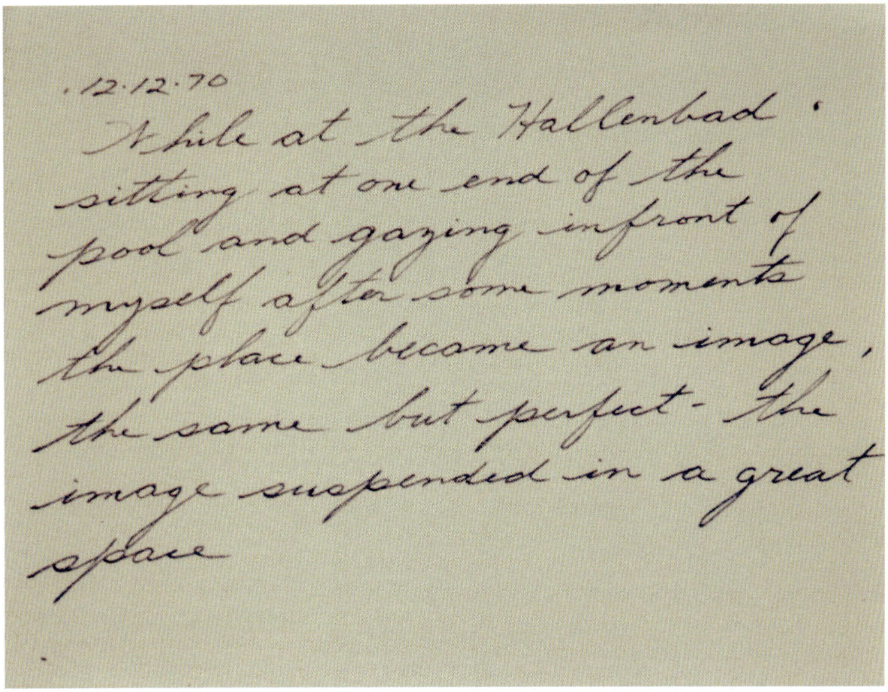

12·12·70
While at the Hallenbad:
sitting at one end of the
pool and gazing infront of
myself after some moments
the place became an image,
the same but perfect - the
image suspended in a great
space

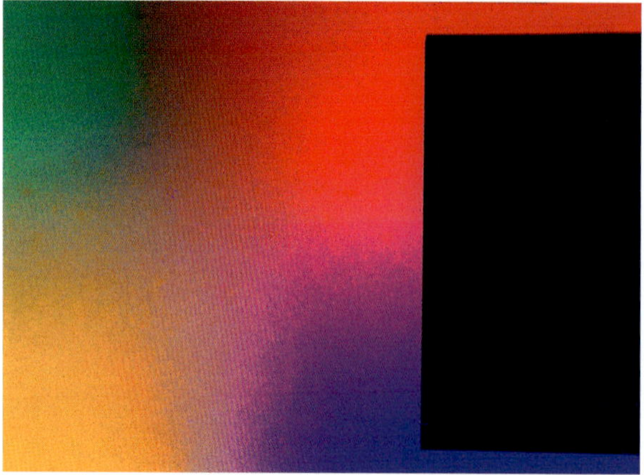

*Plan of Brussels* (1968/2000)

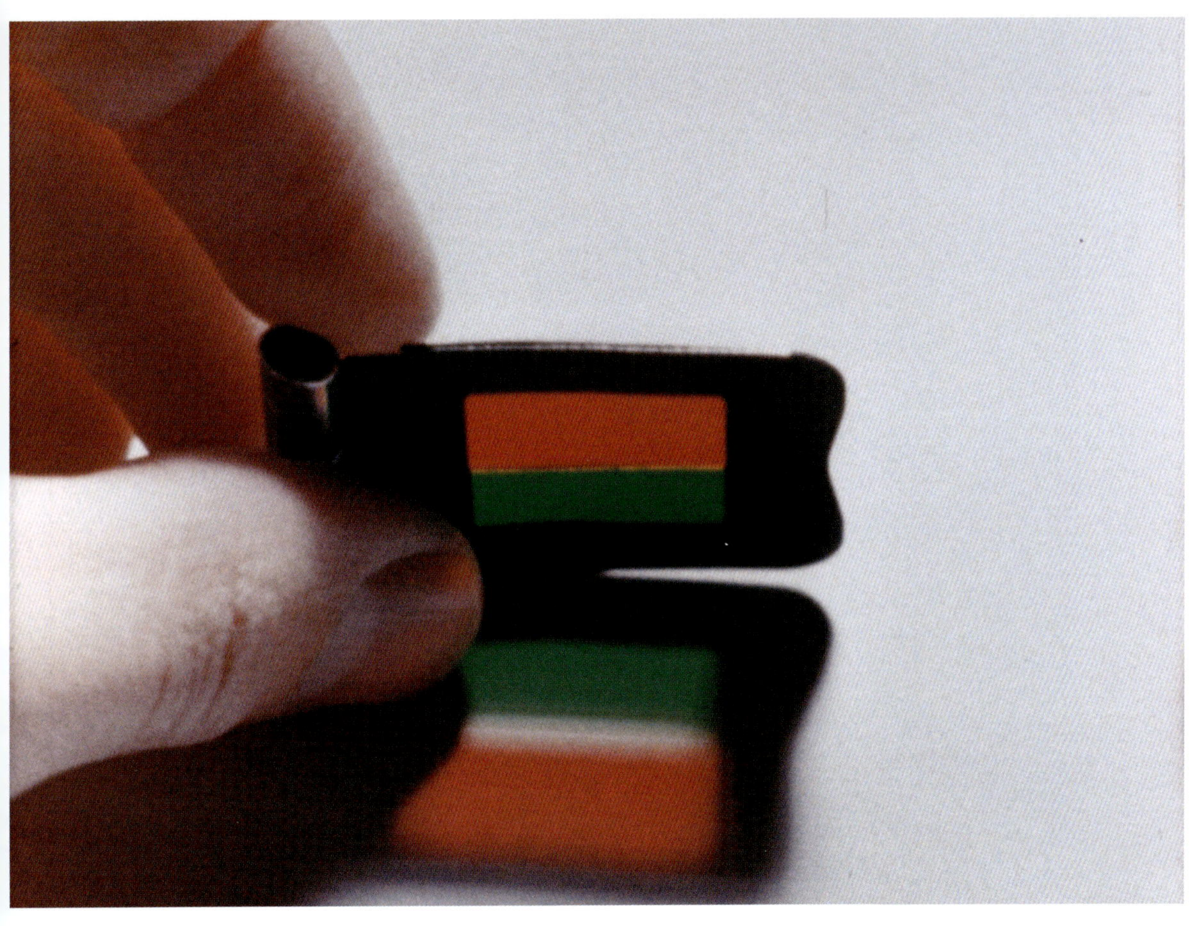

*Diminished Frame* (1970/2001)

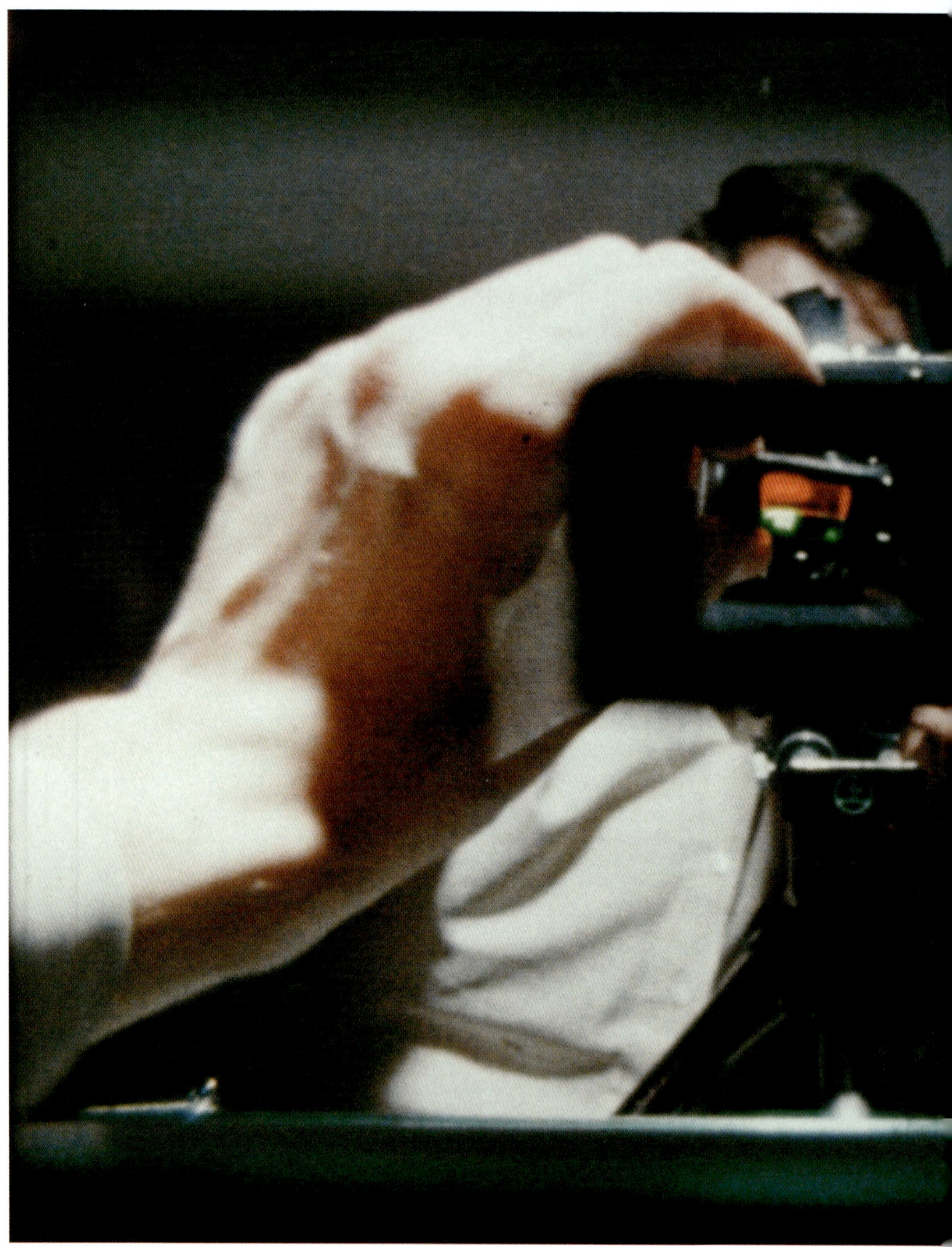

*Diminished Frame* (1970/2001)

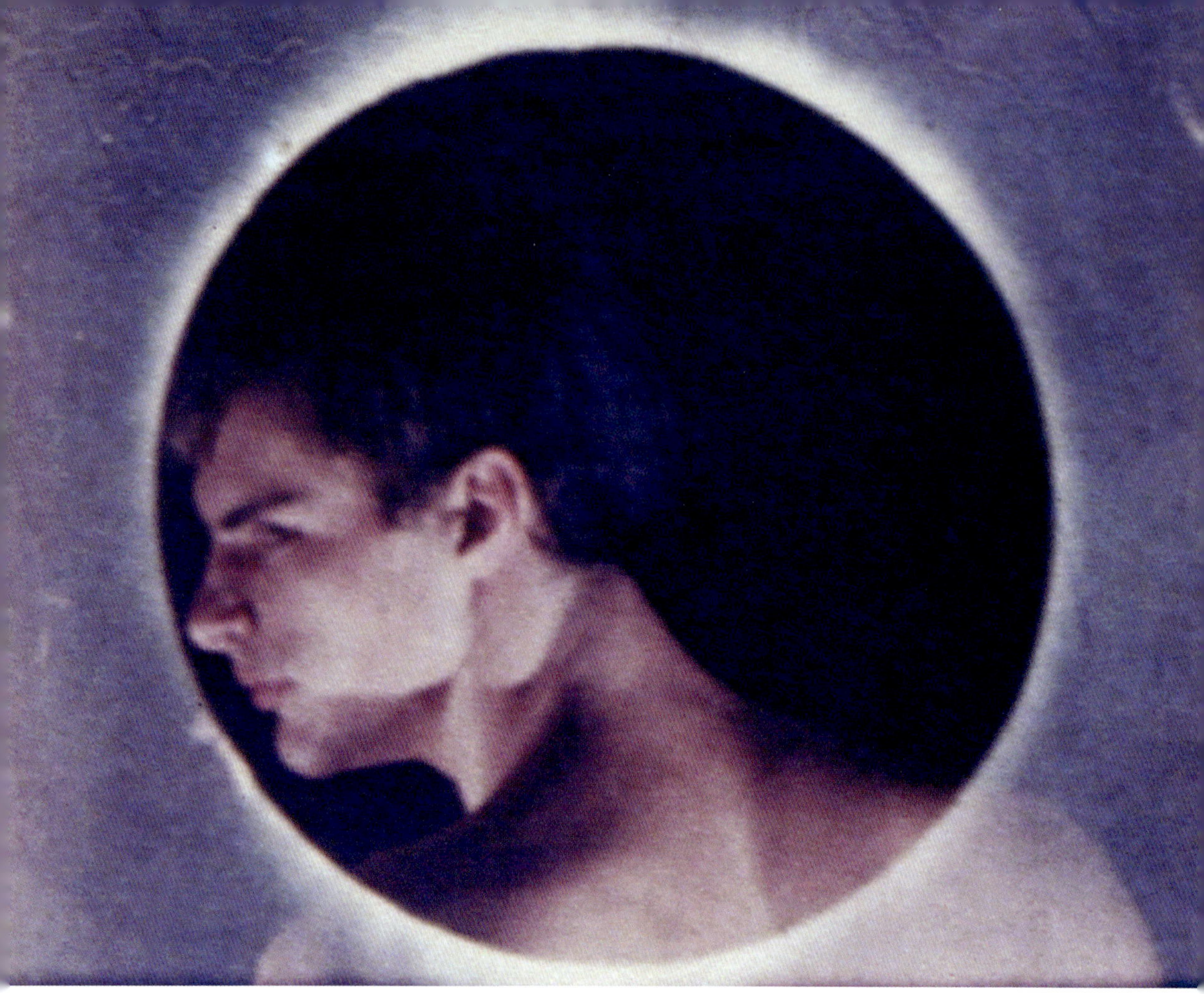

Gregory Markopoulos, *Twice a Man* (1963)

# EARLY SEQUENCES

# 1

## FIRST CONTACT

In February 1967, eighteen-year-old Beavers took Icelandic Air's New York to Reykjavík flight, the cheapest direct route between North America and Europe, and then flew to Luxembourg City. On a train to Brussels the next morning, a student initiated a brief conversation: he asked Beavers if he believed in God. The young man accidentally left his multicolored scarf behind, and Beavers kept it for many years—a memento of a disarming exchange with a stranger in a foreign place. The memory of first contact with Europe was sealed by color.

In Brussels, Beavers submitted a film précis to Jacques Ledoux, the Belgian Royal Film Archive curator, for a competition connected to the upcoming edition of the Knokke-le-Zoute experimental film festival (also called EXPRMNTL), the sporadic international event founded in 1949 by Ledoux and held at a Flemish seaside casino between Christmas and New Year's.[1] Agfa-Gevaert, the Belgian-German celluloid producer, was offering five rolls of color film to selected young filmmakers; the resulting films would screen at the festival. The following day, Beavers met Ledoux and René Micha, the Belgian poet, critic, and screenwriter, for lunch, where Ledoux shared Beavers's film proposal—a study of bourgeoning sexuality that climaxed in ejaculation—with Micha. "Ah, yes, alas," he sighed in response.

Even if Beavers's proposal struck the two men as pubescent, they swiftly became advocates. Ledoux selected *Spiracle* (1966), Beavers's first film, for the 1967 Knokke-le-Zoute competition and purchased an answer print for the Royal Film Archive of Belgium; he and Micha appeared in Beavers's *Plan of Brussels* the following year.[2] In a 1973 essay for *Art International*, Micha assigned Beavers an essential spot in the evolution of film language, following Louis Lumière and D. W. Griffith, as the creator of an integrated, absolute cinema. "[His films] do not speak of motion. They are motion. They do not speak of light. They are light. They are nothing but themselves. Maybe we could call them 'anti-films.' Do they destroy the image of the cinema as we know it?"[3]

In Brussels, Beavers toured the display of precinematic instruments at the Film Archive's Musée du Cinéma. He met Baron Leon Lambert, a banker, art collector, and patron of his new partner, filmmaker Gregory Markopoulos, in his apartment above the Banque Lambert on Avenue Marnix.[4] The white marble and glass facade of Gordon Bunshaft's modernist building belied a Florentine shape. "It was like going to a Renaissance palace," Beavers recalled. A monumental group of Giacometti women flanked Lambert's penthouse entrance.

Beavers was en route to Greece—first Athens and then the Saronic island Hydra, where, in June, he made his second film and Markopoulos joined him. A dramatic narrative of lives entwined and devoted to filmmaking began to unfold. The two men had met in the foyer of the Film-Makers' Cinematheque in New York two years earlier;

Beavers was sixteen and Markopoulos, a filmmaker and critic with an international reputation, thirty-seven. For Markopoulos, departure from the United States was energized by rising discontent with American screening and distribution conditions, the stifling of artists' intentions by the "bad monies and grim politicizing" of institutional interests and curatorial egos, and a wish for greater control over the presentation of his work.[5] Once in Europe, Beavers and Markopoulos gradually consolidated as a society of two. They stopped showing work in the United States in 1974 (and screened it only sporadically in Europe), halted distribution, and devoted their energies to making films. Markopoulos stopped printing the films he made and edited after 1971. The narrative peaks in Markopoulos's vision of a Bayreuth-like cinematic sanctuary called the Temenos (ancient Greek for "a place set apart for the worship of a god" or "sacred grove"): a site devoted to the screening and study of his and Beavers's films in remote Arcadia. The Temenos was a dream of hybrid enclosure and freedom as well as an effort of genealogical redefinition; Markopoulos set film in dialogue with ancient Greek religion and tied spectatorship to cure-seeking pilgrimage. He spent the final decade of his life reediting his previous films into a silent eighty-hour magnum opus. The film, *Eniaios* (1948–1990), was designed for exclusive screening at the Temenos location: a field near Lyssarea, his ancestral village in the Peloponnese.[6] The film was fully edited but unprinted when he died in 1992. He never saw it projected.

Beavers began to distribute his films regularly again after Markopoulos's death. His 2005 Whitney Museum of American Art retrospective initiated a new phase of visibility; retrospectives at the Tate Modern, Austrian Film Museum, and Pacific Film Archive followed. At the time of the Whitney screenings, Roberta Smith lauded Beavers's "astounding achievement": "Mr. Beavers has spent his career being precociously ahead of schedule and also somewhat outside his time."[7] After five decades of nonstop filmmaking, a combination of the work's intrinsic qualities and the historical trajectory of its circulation seems to make Beavers's films feel persistently new.

## THREE GUIDES

A decisive event—Beavers's coming together with Markopoulos—joined a sequence of desires and ambitions already in motion. Greek American Markopoulos was older, charismatic, supremely proud, and a self-identified visionary, and it is tempting to situate Beavers's achievements exclusively in the container of their relationship and the ancient story of pedagogical love. Markopoulos was undeniably an essential guide and influence, obsessively dedicated to his singular vision, ceaseless in his pursuit of the unplumbed reparative potentials of cinema. He provided Beavers with protective encouragement to pursue his vocation no matter the material costs (which were severe: the two men often lived on the brink of poverty). "He taught me to invest in solitude," Beavers said.

But the story of Beavers's origins needs refinement. Markopoulos was not the first but the last of three figures in a sequence: "guiding personalities who brought me freedom." Beavers was born on February 10, 1949, in Brookline, Massachusetts, into a family characterized by vanishing fathers and resourceful wives and daughters:

"a matriarchy . . . with no continuity of males." Beavers was four when his twenty-six-year-old father, an offset lithographer who worked at Bucks Printing near Fenway Park, died of lymphoma. The family had moved from the South End of Boston to East Weymouth, a nearby suburb, a year and a half before. They lived in a working-class enclave with a dozen small shingled homes arranged around a pond.

His Catholic maternal great-grandparents had moved to Lowell from Quebec City, and Beavers's great-grandmother supported herself and two young daughters after her husband, unhappy in America, returned home. She ran a boardinghouse and cooked for single men who had moved to the mill town for work. It was day-and-night labor, and she placed Marie Rose, Beavers's grandmother—the first of his three guides—in a convent. When Marie Rose got her first period, the terms of the convent's shelter and education ended, and with six years of schooling, she began working in the Lowell mills and later did piecework at Pritzker's textile factory in Boston. After annulling her early marriage to a Protestant Vermonter, she became an active union organizer whose provocations on the garment shop floor occasionally got her fired.

She was "the hidden strength and source in our tiny family," Beavers said. "She gave me the strength to be so wild without thinking I was." Generous without emotional condition, she supported Beavers's path, regularly sending her Social Security payments to Europe. Beavers's father's Protestant family had emigrated from Holland to New Amsterdam in the seventeenth century, eventually moving up the Hudson and settling in Rochester, New York. In the face of his father's early death, Beavers's identifications ran up the maternal, Catholic side of the divided family tree.

—

At seven, Beavers wandered into his East Weymouth neighbor's backyard. He found diminutive Bernice Hodges sitting on a bench in a rock garden she had made—granite shards arranged around begonias and pine-needle pathways—and asked her to read him a story. Mrs. Hodges chose Nathaniel Hawthorne's *A Wonder-Book for Girls and Boys* and Henry Wadsworth Longfellow's epic poem *The Song of Hiawatha*. As their friendship developed, the two always met on the porch. Mr. Hodges didn't want children inside the house; the Hodges's son Robin had died at three. "I was a reincarnation when I walked into the backyard," Beavers said.

She was the second of Beavers's guides. Her heroes were Lord Byron, Napoleon, and Sarah Bernhardt; she studied witchcraft and wore pantsuits, a cameo, and short hair. And she evinced imaginative persistence in the face of major disappointments. Following the death of her son, a loss of faith (a Protestant minister she admired had a romantic affair), and financial catastrophe (her husband's business failings led to bankruptcy and a fall in class status), she established a business for hand wood carving, producing intricate ornamentation for Boston families and institutions, including Trinity Church. Mrs. Hodges taught Beavers to carve in her basement workshop.

A year after they met, Mrs. Hodges opened a shallow box and showed Beavers a stack of loose black-and-white lithographs: Fra Filippo Lippi's *Madonna and Child*,

Raphael's *Deliverance of St. Peter*, Michelangelo's *Prophets and Sibyls* from the Sistine Chapel. She told Beavers about Renaissance artists' multiplicity: no choice had to be made between painting, architecture, music, literature, science, and engineering. Mrs. Hodges's frescoes deposited Europe into Beavers's imagination. It joined a picture of the Mediterranean that had already arrived; his mother had read him a children's version of the *Odyssey* and, after fasting on Saturdays, he listened to the Latin liturgy on Sundays at St. Albert's Cathedral in Weymouth. In eighth grade, Beavers discovered Sophocles's *Oedipus Rex* and *Antigone* in a Great Books club, and he announced to a friend that he intended to go to school in Europe. "There was an image of Greece, and of Europe, before Gregory," Beavers said.

Mrs. Hodges was a European guide, but she also exemplified a strain of "New England"—serious, independent, high-minded, strict, visionary, feminist, ethical, proud, aspirational, devoted to disseminating cultural nourishment. As a child, Beavers was impressed by Pierre Puvis de Chavannes's mural cycle *The Inspiring Muses Acclaim Genius, Messenger of Light* (ca. 1894–1896) at the Boston Public Library—allegorical renderings of the library's intellectual resources—and as a teenager he joined the Boston Athenaeum. The Boston that captured Beavers's imagination was a site of fused idealism and hardness: ordinary lives oriented toward survival and dominated by labor.

Mrs. Hodges was Protestant, like Beavers's father, an essential figure of difference. "She took me outside my family," Beavers said. "When you meet someone different as a child, it causes thoughts that you wouldn't have otherwise." She catalyzed new sequences of imaginative work that had material consequence in Beavers's life. The exclusively female universe of the Beavers family was punctured not by a man but by Mrs. Hodges; the world began to crack open along fault lines she and Beavers carved together. "She told me stories that tried to give me some clues."

From the start, their friendship unfolded via books. Mrs. Hodges had inherited the complete editions of Dickens, Thackeray, and Balzac from her father; Beavers was fascinated by the long stretches of identically sized and colored books. "With my working-class background, to see thirty volumes by one author—it was very unusual." She gave teenage Beavers a book of Roman history by Tacitus; a few years later, he lent her Virginia Woolf's *The Waves* after filmmaker Charles Boultenhouse had recommended it to him. "The writing is very beautiful; the people are awful," she reported back.

Beavers shot his first three rolls of 16mm film in 1966, all portraits: Markopoulos, his sister Gail, and Mrs. Hodges. He accidentally left the lens cap on while shooting his neighbor, but two long strips of frames were exposed: one in profile, the other a frontal pose in front of yellow forsythia blossoms.

—

Beavers recalls Weymouth as a set of buildings: house, church, school, library, and cinemas. At home, a tiny Sylvania TV delivered Buster Brown and 1930s film faces: James Cagney, Edward G. Robinson, Fay Wray, Loretta Young. *The Adventures of Prince Achmed* (1926)—Lotte Reiniger's adaptation of *One Thousand and One Nights* in silhouette animation—was dosed in short intervals, each headlined by a still frame recap from the last episode. At thirteen he began to take the subway to Cambridge, where the Brattle Theatre specialized in foreign repertory programming. He brought his mother to Federico Fellini's *8 1/2* (1963); he tried to like it but found it absurd and pretentious. (He preferred Ingmar Bergman's 1963 *Winter Light*. Ingrid Thulin "fitted more with New England"—"somber, with a depressive seriousness.")

Neither of Beavers's parents had attended college, and, at fifteen, he shocked his mother by announcing his wish to attend private school. She contributed $500 (a tenth of her yearly income working in a restaurant) when he entered Deerfield Academy, the elite all-male boarding school in western Massachusetts, as a junior. Beavers attempted to read Arthur Rimbaud in French but was more engaged by leftist periodicals like *The Catholic Worker*, *The Nation*, and *The New Republic*. The ethos of the school—oriented toward producing well-rounded young men destined for Princeton, politics, or business—was a poor match. "I felt that I wasn't going to learn what I wanted in these classes," he said.

Beavers began an avid conversation about cinema with his classmate Robert Hardman, and, intent on starting a Deerfield film club, conducted research in New York City during the summer after his junior year, in 1965. At the MoMA film library, Margareta Akermark showed Beavers catalogs filled with a curious category of films: those made by individual artists.[8] He attended his first avant-garde screening—Carl Linder's surrealist, erotic *Womancock* (1965)—at Jonas Mekas's nomadic Film-Makers' Cinematheque (then at the Astor Place Playhouse). He neither liked it nor had ever seen anything remotely like it. Afterward, Beavers bought Stan Brakhage's 1963 book *Metaphors on Vision*, and Robert Brown, the Cinematheque manager, introduced him to Markopoulos, who invited Beavers to a private screening of a new film. *The Death of Hemingway* (1965)—his semi-commissioned film of a play by George Christopoulos—showed at a tiny preview theater near Times Square. Beavers found the acting abysmal, but an elaborate montage sequence embedded in the film's center impressed him. He left without saying goodbye.

Beavers sent his inaugural program proposal to his Deerfield faculty sponsor, who reacted to mentions of nudity and homosexuality in the description of Kenneth Anger's *Scorpio Rising* (1963) by canceling the film club initiative. But Beavers left New York with a more important prospect: the idea that he could make a film. Until that summer, film had been inherently big: in budget, collaboration, narrative. But New American Cinema filmmakers like Markopoulos, Brakhage, Jack Smith, and Shirley Clarke offered another model. Film could be singular, individually made, and relatively inexpensive.

## DEPARTURE

Beavers dropped out of school in November of his senior year. Earlier in the fall, the Deerfield mismatch and the New York City stimulations produced an existential query: "Am I going to spend my life trying to make money because I don't have any, or am I going to do what I want and like?" Beavers approached his English teacher, Robert McGlynn, wondering if he should commit to deeper academic discipline and pursue philosophy—or take flight. McGlynn "gave me the Henry James answer," Beavers said. "Before you read too much, maybe you should live."[9]

In October, following a failed attempt to bring Markopoulos to Deerfield to deliver a lecture, Beavers sent a letter: "I am interested in your opinion of what a 'Filmmaker's education' should consist of. Would be grateful for any amount of thought on the subject." Three weeks later, Markopoulos replied publicly in a lecture—"Inherent Limitations"—at the New York University Christian Foundation Film Society. Quoting Greek writer Nikos Kazantzakis, he refused the role of advisor: "Responsibility. To act without guidance. . . . The creator's responsibility is a great one; he opens a road that may entice the future and force it to make up its mind." Markopoulos warned Beavers about a toxic cultural atmosphere that could easily derail him and invoked "New York's vampyrish [art] network," sullied by mediocrity, funding problems, and surface temptations of glamour. In sync with Beavers's already-swirling concerns about next life steps, Markopoulos wondered about a young artist in need of "nourishment and breath": "Should he leave the country?"[10]

Deerfield prohibited students from leaving campus without permission, but Beavers escaped for a consultation with Markopoulos at his West Eleventh Street apartment and reported on recent visits to Boston printing ateliers: he was interested in becoming a publisher of small edition books, collaborations between writers and printmakers.[11] Like Mrs. Hodges, Markopoulos told Beavers he could make both films and books. (Markopoulos's hero was Jean Cocteau: writer, filmmaker, designer, playwright.) Beavers's fascination with cinema was evolving, but an aura of passivity still hovered: "The idea of taking a camera in my hands and doing something was threatening." The hour-long meeting with Markopoulos had a decisive effect: "Film was now on the table as one of the things I could do," he recalled.

Beavers moved back to Weymouth and took a job at the *Boston Herald*, collecting ad copy and layout elements from department stores and ad agencies. Markopoulos introduced him to the filmmaker and avant-garde film connoisseur Tom Chomont, who was pursuing a master's in film studies at Boston University and worked part-time in the box office at the Park Square Cinema. Designed for the temporal limbo of travelers, the cinema offered uninterrupted projection: one could enter and exit at any time. In the form of fragments, Michelangelo Antonioni's *Red Desert* (1964) became the film Beavers has seen more than any other.

In November, Chomont invited Markopoulos to present his trilogy *Du Sang, de la volupté et de la mort* (1947–1948) at Odd Fellows Hall. Beavers attended, but he and Markopoulos left the screening early to get a drink.

—

Beavers landed on Markopoulos's doorstep in December 1965. Worried about the legal ramifications of their relationship, Markopoulos arranged for Beavers to stay in the front half of painter John Dowd's 355 Bowery loft.[12] Over the next six months, Beavers shelved books at Brentano's Bookstore, printed film at DuArt film lab, and sold tickets at the Film-Makers' Cinematheque. He also witnessed Markopoulos's determination: between January and June, Markopoulos shot *Ming Green* (1966), *Galaxie* (1966), *Himself as Herself* (1967), and *Eros, O Basileus* (1967). In *Eros*, a nine-episode forty-five-minute film, shot in Dowd's loft and edited largely in-camera,

Beavers plays the sole role. Mostly naked, he touches and holds objects (bed, desk, Bolex camera, bookshelf, egg, paintings, footstool, light bulb, motorcycle, tailor's mannequin) and strikes classical poses (including that of Eros: as if shooting arrows from a bow). Markopoulos selected all of the objects but one, a book: Beavers holds his new Bollingen Series collection of Paul Valéry essays.

Markopoulos was Beavers's first subject, for a six-minute portrait shot at his 40 West Eleventh Street apartment. He was both generic subject ("He could have been anyone") and the source of courage ("Our special connection made it the easiest thing to do"). Markopoulos offered enough guidance to load the film ("He was not the type to give instructions"). In his early use of the H-16 Bolex, Beavers focused on material logistics—exposure, lenses, tripod—and managing simultaneous awarenesses: engaging with his subject while tracking the footage counter. In his second portrait, shot in Dowd's loft, Beavers's sister Gail, her eyes closed, faces a stream of early morning light: an adolescent figure on the verge of awakening. In the summer of 1966, Beavers made his first film, *Spiracle*, another study of psychic threshold. Chomont, clothed, naked, and sometimes asleep, appears against a night sky on Dowd's fire escape and the rooftop of another Bowery building. Beavers is the photogenic object of *Eros*, but Chomont is a surrogate for the filmmaker in *Spiracle*.[13]

Beavers no longer shows *Spiracle*. "It was a modest attempt . . . the real success was simply in completing it."[14] But Markopoulos, in September 1967, was full of praise. Corresponding with the Austrian Film Museum about an upcoming New American Cinema program, he urged Peter Konlechner, the museum cofounder and codirector, to take note of the first work of an eighteen-year-old filmmaker and to buy a print of *Spiracle* for $200:

> **The extraordinary thing about Mr. Beavers is that he has had no other formal film training . . . than picking up a Bolex reflex camera and setting to work. . . . Though very young he shows a kind of perfection and nobility seldom seen in the new cinema: or in any other cinema for that matter.**
>
> **P.S. He has never been shown, to this date, by anyone!**[15]

## FILM AS FILM

Markopoulos, born in Toledo, Ohio, in 1928 to Greek immigrant parents, was raised in the Greek Orthodox Church and spoke only Greek until age six. He started making ambitious narrative films in the late 1940s—psychosexual quests and romantic meditations sprung from mythic and poetic texts (Plato, Aeschylus, Hawthorne, Cocteau, Balzac) and characterized by symbolic color, rapid montage, and improvisational work with actors. He studied film production at the University of Southern California from 1946 to 1948, where he attended Josef von Sternberg's Advanced Directing lectures and observed Jules Dassin, Fritz Lang, Alexander Korda, and Alfred Hitchcock on Hollywood sets. He returned to Toledo—completing four films—and traveled to Paris in 1950, where he met Jean-Luc Godard, pursued an adaptation of André Gide's *The Counterfeiters*, and watched Marcel Carné direct *Juliette, or the Key of Dreams* (1951). In 1953, he began an eight-year labor on *Serenity*, a 35mm adaptation of Elias Venezis's novel about the journey of Greek refugees after the Greco-Turkish War of 1919–1922.

Markopoulos arrived in New York in 1960 with an international reputation as an avant-garde filmmaker. A founding member of Jonas Mekas's New American Cinema Group and subsequent Film-makers' Cooperative, he published frequently in *Film Culture* and *Film Comment* and mentored young filmmakers including Warren Sonbert, Edward Owens, and Jerome Hiler. But soon after he screened *Serenity* as a work-in-progress at the first major international showcase of New American Cinema in Spoleto, Italy, in June 1961, the project met a disastrous end.[16] Following a protracted legal struggle, Markopoulos's investors withheld his director's fee until he returned the film negative and prints, and he never saw *Serenity* again. The *Serenity* debacle functioned as a turning point for Markopoulos, strengthening his will to greater self-sufficiency.

In 1963, as Markopoulos edited his Hippolytus myth remake *Twice a Man* (1963) (in his version, protagonist Paul is rescued from his stepmother Phaedra's incestuous advances by the healing god Asclepius, with whom he falls in love), he punctured the narrative with rapidly cut clusters of frames designed to represent characters' memories and premonitions—he called them "thought images." As he completed the film, Markopoulos wrote a statement of fresh intention: "I propose a new narrative form through the fusion of the classic montage technique with a more abstract system. This system involves the use of short film phrases which evoke thought-images. Each film phrase is composed of certain select frames that are similar to the harmonic units found in musical composition. The film phrases establish ulterior relationships among themselves; in classic montage technique there is a constant reference to the continuing shot: in my abstract system there is a complex of differing frames being repeated."[17]

He continued to pursue this hybrid classic/abstract mode, but in 1966 single-frame abstraction began to rule whole films: in-camera portraits of people and places.[18] As Markopoulos advanced and rewound a roll of film on the spot, he exposed and reexposed frames at predetermined points; no subsequent editing was required. His invention slashed money and time: "Once all the footage was sent to the lab, you had a completed film."[19] In February, Beavers watched Markopoulos make his first in-camera portrait: *Ming Green*, a farewell to his West Eleventh Street apartment made for fifty dollars. In March and April, Markopoulos shot *Galaxie*, a feature-length portrait compilation of thirty Greenwich Village art world friends and stars (including Maurice Sendak, Jasper Johns, Susan Sontag, Gregory Battcock, and Allen Ginsberg). Beavers observed nine *Galaxie* shoots—critic Parker Tyler, filmmaker Storm De Hirsch, painter Harry Koursaros and his partner Gordon Herzig, composer Ben Weber, dancer Erick Hawkins, filmmaker Charles Boultenhouse, poet W. H. Auden, critic-playwright Kenneth Kelman, and Chomont. He watched Markopoulos balance improvisation and precision. Forgoing his habitual meticulous preparatory phase, Markopoulos shot each three-minute color portrait on a one-hundred-foot roll of Kodak Ektachrome in one to two hours. "The person sat before the camera and was photographed in certain attitudes that I decided upon, and then the film was rewound back, I think in Sontag's case, perhaps ten different times, and I was able to create a wonderful psychological tension. . . . The project became a kind of revelation of the person being photographed because they gave themselves away beautifully," Markopoulos said in a May 1966 interview with Radio Free Europe. "The possibilities are tremendous."[20]

Markopoulos made twenty films between 1966 and 1970. As he freed the frame from inherent partiality—a twenty-fourth-of-a-second fragment that must meet chronological self-permutations in order for motion to accrue—and treated it with monistic reverence, the standards of cinematic legibility and motion faded. If immediate image recognition was stymied, repetition might deliver it across time, and other revelations might surface in the unpredictable aftermath of aggressive image turnover and superimposition. The abandonment of continuousness and continuity—the shot long enough to deliver movie-motion and the editing conventions designed to produce the illusion of time-space unity—drove film movement into rhythms, blinks, flashes, and blooms. "It is, perhaps, a fallacy to continue to believe that film is constant movement," he wrote in "The Intuition Space," a 1973 essay.[21] For Markopoulos, the ongoing "pulse" of micro-instants was film's essential quality. "The placement of a series of frames . . . cast towards each other; and, against one another. Therein establishing the beat to the pulse. *This is the ultimate aspect of the film as film.*"[22]

Markopoulos was counting, teaching himself to intuit the projected weight of a given number of frames in advance. The single frame became a total resource, a technical means of self-sufficient economy and the belief-emblem of an evolving philosophical position. "Who can dare to imagine what a single frame might contain? What future process could activate a single frame?" he wondered.[23] His preoccupation later reached its apotheosis in *Eniaios*: his epic film is ruled by minuscule shot duration (many only a few frames long) and universal separation (each shot is separated from the next by lengths of black or clear leader). Made of sixty-five completely new films (edited in the 1970s but not yet printed) as well as reedited footage from most of his previous films, and meant to supersede them all as an integrated epic work, *Eniaios* (ancient Greek for "unity" and "uniqueness") contains one hundred individual titles in twenty-two cycles, or orders, of three to five hours each. The frame ultimately became the crown jewel in his stripped-down Temenos ecology. One frame, one film, one screening location. He imagined "that *single Perfect spectator*"—the right one—who would complete the future vision.[24]

—

As Markopoulos's visibility spiked, Beavers was a constant spectator in the dark—at the Astor Place Playhouse, Bleecker Street Cinema, and Gramercy Arts Theatre. By the time he left New York, his intimate knowledge of Markopoulos's ongoing experiment crystallized as a dilemma: "I was seeing his work. What to do with it? What can I do with it? It was so distinct in itself." How to metabolize Markopoulos's singular model without mimicry? How to use an imprint without producing a stamp? "An impulse came to me," Beavers said. Among the films he had seen in New York—

by Fritz Lang, Carl Theodor Dreyer, Pier Paolo Pasolini, Robert Bresson, Roberto Rossellini, Abel Gance, Brakhage—Harry Smith's animated films excited him most. In *Early Abstractions* (1946–1957) and *Heaven and Earth Magic* (1957), lines and shapes (ink, paint, paper cut-out) dart, multiply, and collide. Smith's cameraless technique produced depth in a flat-on-flat landscape of mobile patterns and merging color.

Against Markopoulos's extraction of the film frame as his ever-generative constraint, Beavers imagined another abstraction: the geometric treatment of the film image with "decoration"—complex compositions constructed not across fractured time and dissembled motion but inside a single multivalent shot. The film image pulled opened, spacious enough to contain simultaneous planes, textualities, and motion types—the photographed picture and the graphic form, the reality index and the ornamental stamp. In a 1973 analysis of Beavers's films to date, Micha identified it as "the pre-montage: the montage inside the shot. The center of gravity—the 'shock' as Eisenstein preferred to call it—is not only between the images, it is in the image. The image has its own structure."[25] But in 1967, "the montage inside the shot" was, for Beavers, still a mental picture, an emergent impulse.

## POETRY BEHIND THE SCENE

When Beavers accompanied Markopoulos on his *Galaxie* shoots, Auden stood out. Beavers held a tungsten light over the poet at his 77 St. Marks Place apartment; Auden's politeness conveyed modesty, not propriety, and his capacity for recognition (he "saw the person opposite him, tried to say something")—seemed "a gift, astonishing," and somehow linked to his vocation. Beavers later encountered this mixture—a devotion to craft unaccompanied by attachment to artist-as-first-identity, an unguarded willingness to reveal one's "whole being," even with a stranger, a generosity not instrumental but soulful—in Italian writer Eugenio Montale, Polish composer Krzysztof Penderecki, and English visual artist Graham Sutherland. One didn't have to compose poems to occupy this broad-stroked "poet" category that drew Beavers into sympathetic relation. The poem—unofficial, mobile, unmarketable, temporary—was a sign of disciplined imaginative labor itself (not medium or name-tag) as primary.

But Beavers did not identify as a poet. "Such damage is done by uniting film and poetry," he wrote in a 1967 note. He refused a hyphenated identity—filmmaker-poet (like Markopoulos, Mekas, Anger, or their patron saint Cocteau) or filmmaker-painter (Brakhage, De Hirsch, Marie Menken, Andy Warhol). "I worked against this," he said. "I was in a frame of mind that film shouldn't be literary. To get to the heart of filmmaking, you had to drop the word 'poet'—whereas Gregory really believed in it." The filmmaker-diarist was no better: Markopoulos had kept a diary since he was a teenager; Mekas and Brakhage made diary films (Gide was a model). "I was against the diarist," Beavers said. His desire for the most spacious, underdetermined studio in which to work was energized by psychic necessity: differentiation.

Beavers bought a volume of Paul Klee's notebooks at Wittenborn & Company on Madison Avenue with handwritten script and graphic elements colored with gouache side by side. "For a beginner, someone just beginning to think about art, Klee was a wonderful guide. His spirit is so musical—he opened up so many things."

And Valéry's *Introduction to the Method of Leonardo da Vinci*—one of the texts in the Bollingen volume Beavers holds in *Eros*—offered an intersubjective meditation on the power of the artist's note to realize a heterogeneous mind. Beavers embraced the note as his own: an ephemeral foil to the density of Markopoulos's textual force field—the density a function of Markopoulos's multiple outputs and his prolificity (as poet, critic, diarist, self-archiving correspondent, and researcher)—and his agonistic tone of certitude.

"I created my writing structure in opposition to Gregory's," Beavers said. Discrete film-specific notebooks accumulated in time. But for now, the note itself—the prose shard produced at the fine tip of sensory experience and with unspecified aim—became the medium of development for Beavers's filmmaking, his daily method. Each of Beavers's first three surviving notes—recorded in Athens on May 1, 1967, accompanied by sketches—enacts a subtle twist away from the obvious and definitional:

> **An England of my imagination is emerging founded on Campion, William Byrd, Purcell and Under the Hill by Aubry Beardsley**
>
> **from the Roman Agora in the yard of the Byzantine church a column (part) that is strangely un-classical, reminiscent of Egyptian works**
>
> **This statue—alive, only because of its graft of moss and water pits**

Selecting a passing sensation or thought—keeping it—constitutes an experiment: notation impacts a future shape, but the scribe, who does not identify as a writer, cannot yet know how. This is highly speculative work—not because the listed subjective facts are shakily known but because the work is developing a capacity for expansive awareness as much as it is developing a future film.

—

In Greece and Italy in the spring and summer of 1967, the spacious shot took form first in words. Beavers was seeing in enlarged frames; he compressed single-location visual fields—color, space, motion, time—into notes. In Athens, irregular Syntagma Square (whose eastern side is higher than the west, and culminates in stairs) is a frame inside which he sees—and "adds"—other elements:

> **I think Syntagma Squ. is unique, the movement on the two levels and**
> **the intermediates. add the trees and birds, then idea of the buildings existing in**
> **this unsteady plan. add rain. buses in the rain moving,**
> **shining through the trees.**

In Rome, a field of green liquid is the frame: the Tiber River holds the silhouettes of dominating structures (cathedral, castle, bridge) and the sky's color combinations:

> **9/1/67: Color of the [Tevere], the green river with the green flowing**
> **reflections of Castel Sant'Angelo, the bridge and trees surrounded by pink,**
> **green and blue reflexion of the sky and St Peter's.**
> **The buildings are white, the bridge is white.**

Beavers did not identify as a poet, but as he followed the sequences of his own interest, he sometimes produced an accidental poem. At the Villa Borghese in August 1967, he wrote:

> **The velvet brown inside, under the**
> **bark of the tree—like the heart**
> **of the pansy.**
> **then the gray mole**

Beavers affirms the pleasure associated with the unexpected (rough bark lined in velvet, eyesight conjuring touch) with a comparative figure (a furry floral interior) and is rewarded with a gift: a second figure—a scampering creature, also velvety—adds speed and color to the tableau. The mole extends the found poem beyond the frame of sight.

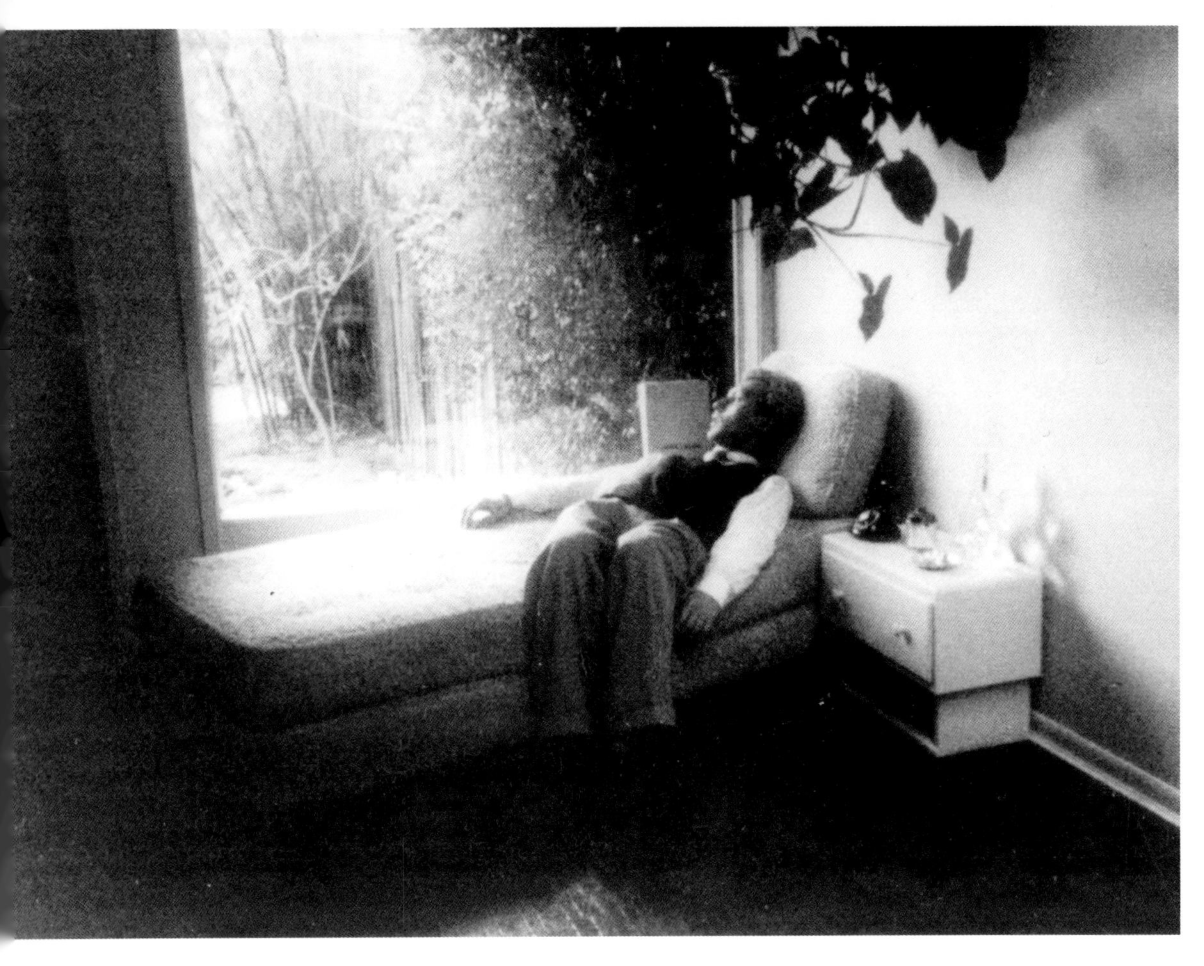

Gregory Markopoulos, *The Dead Ones* (1948)

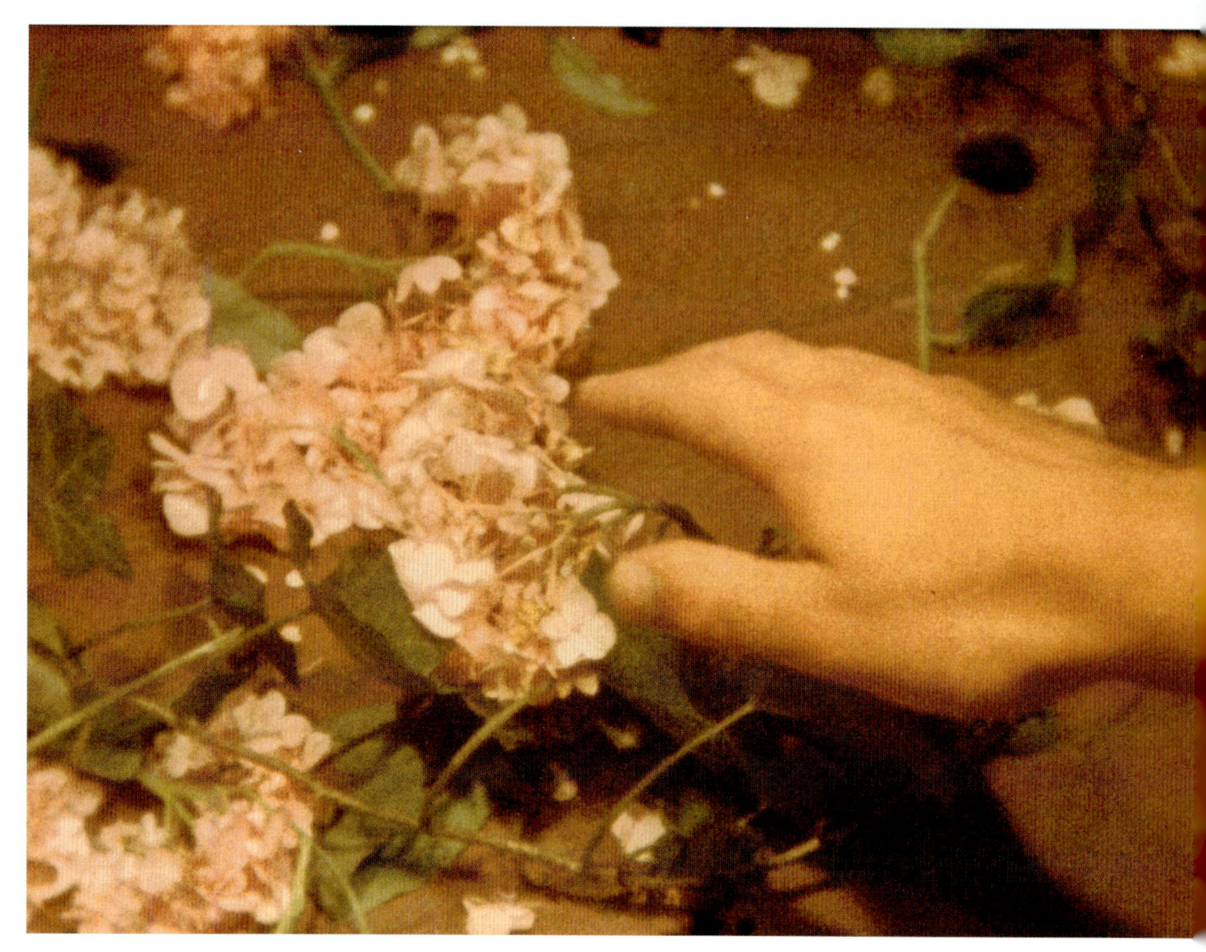

Gregory Markopoulos, *Psyche* (1947)

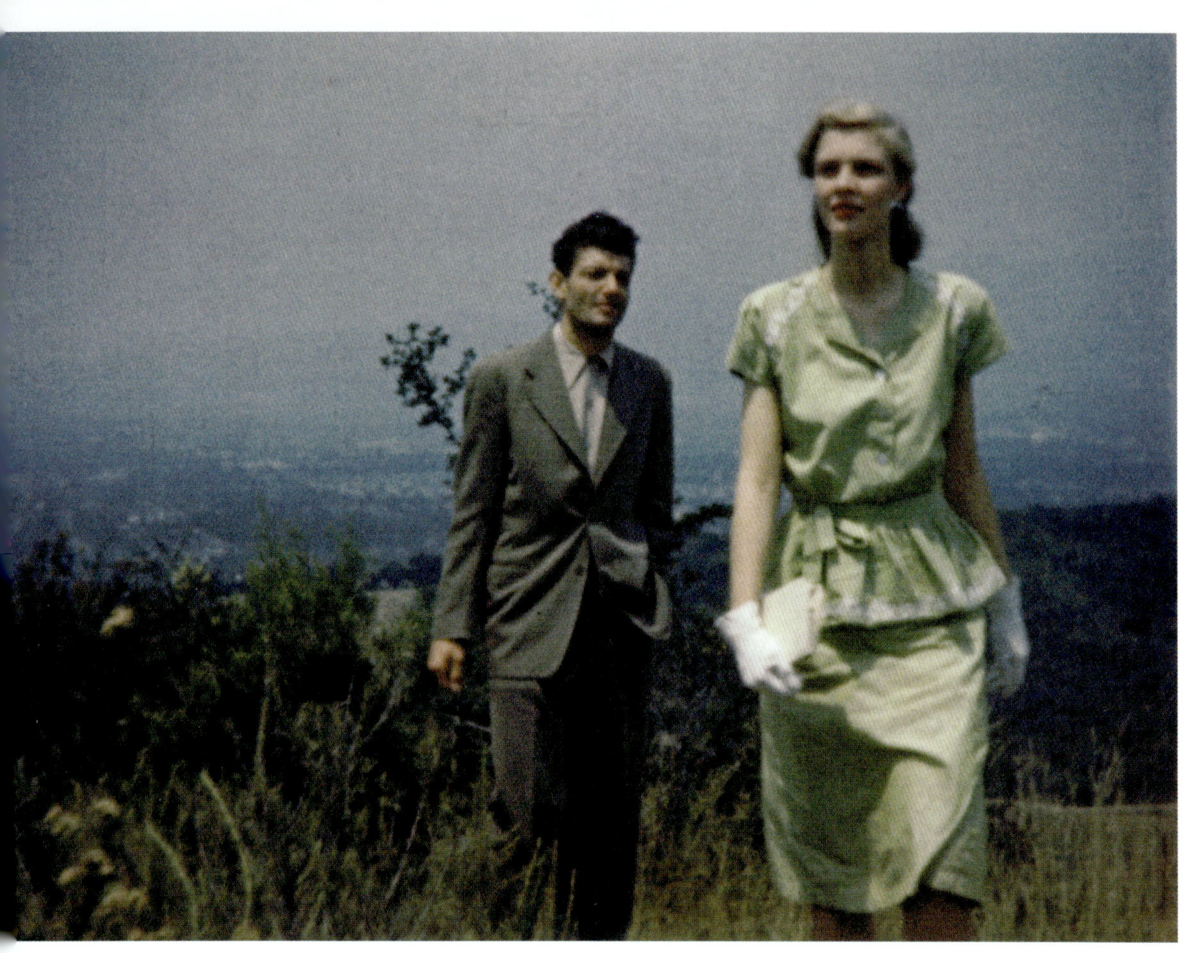

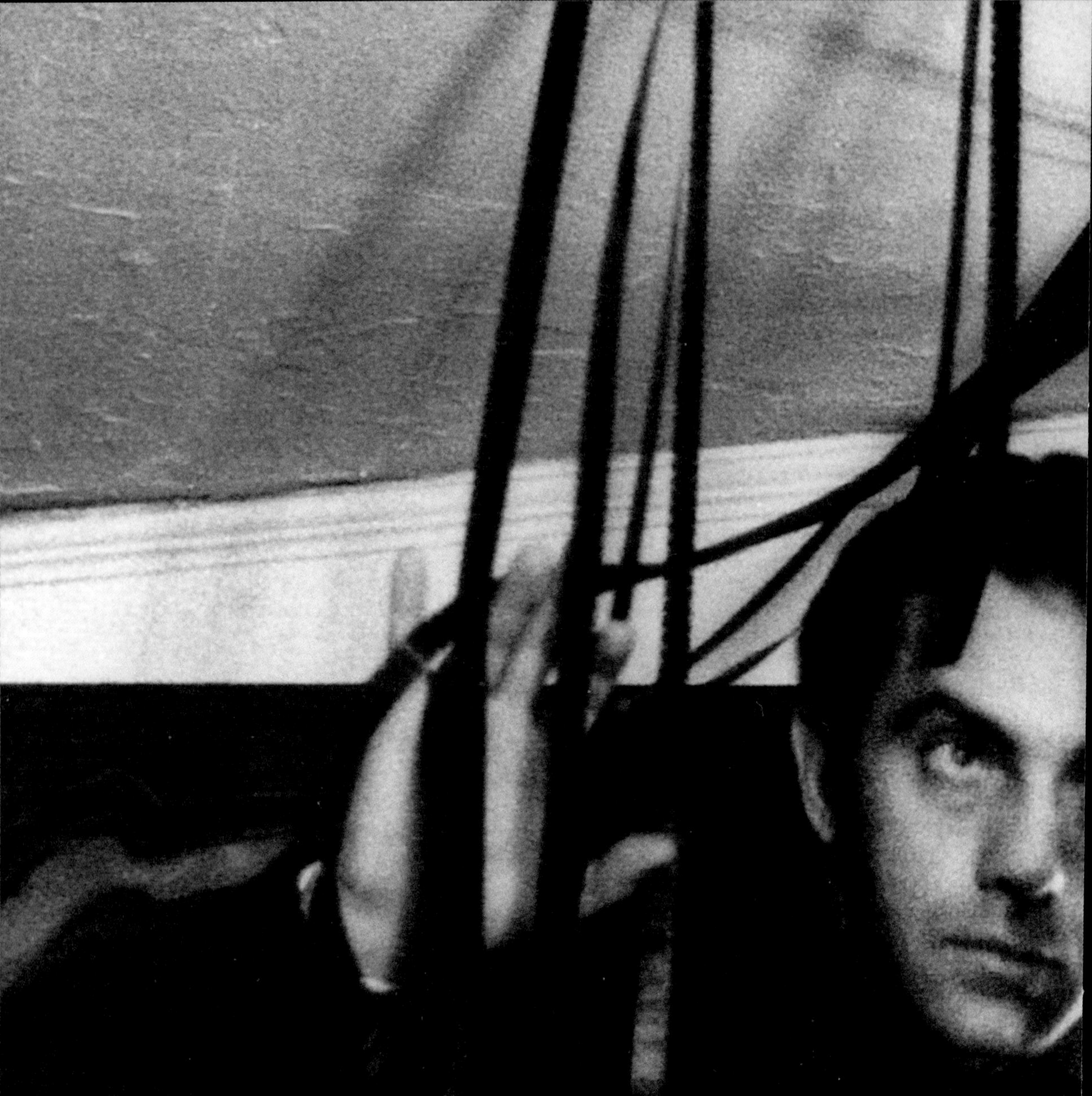

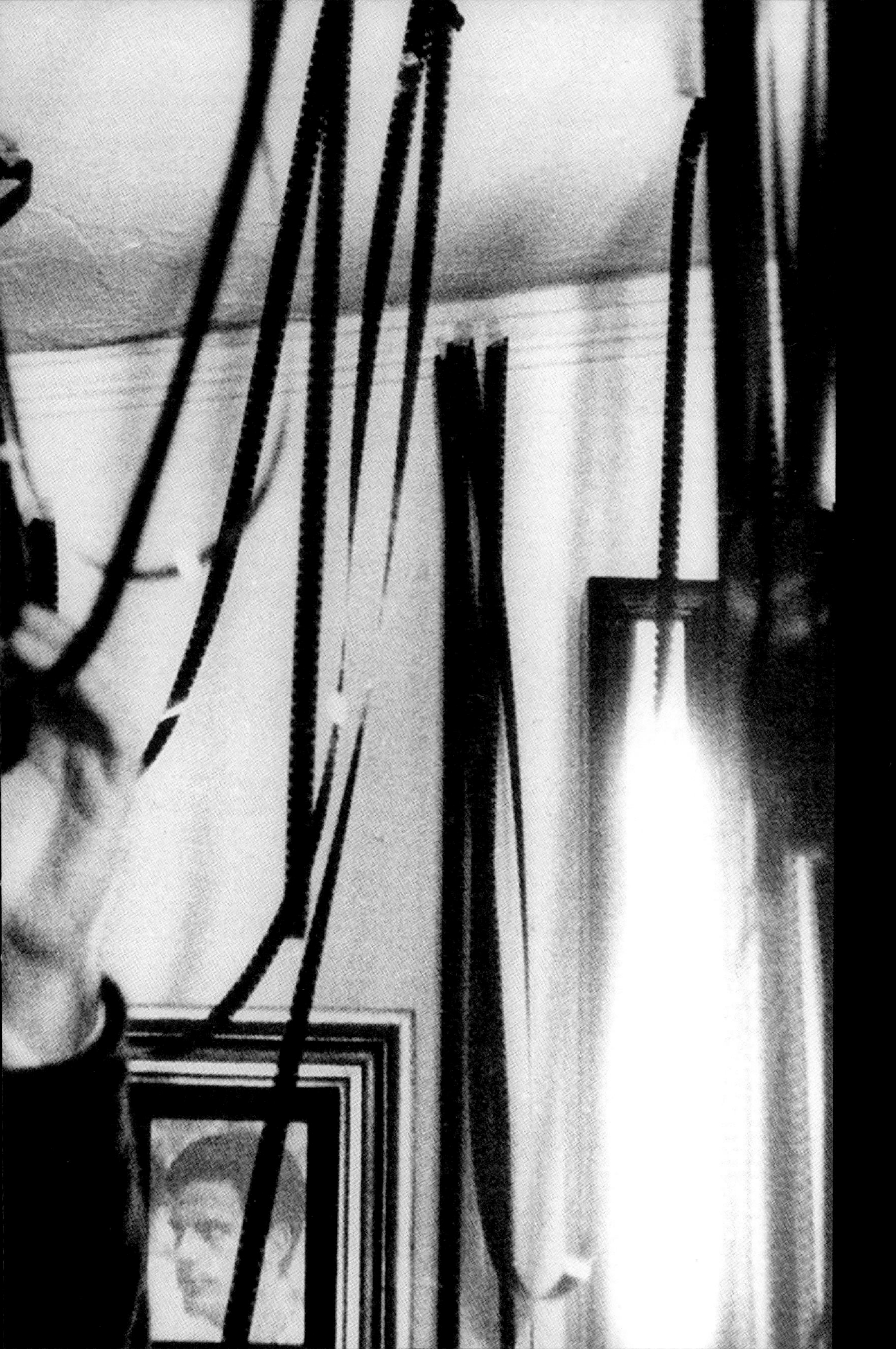

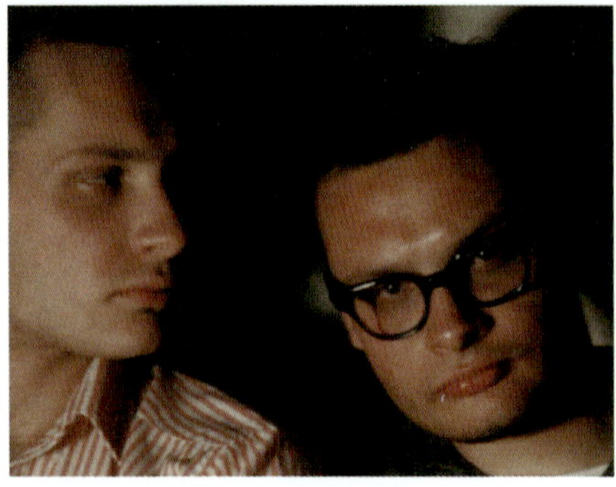

George and Mike Kuchar in Gregory Markopoulos, *Galaxie* (1966)

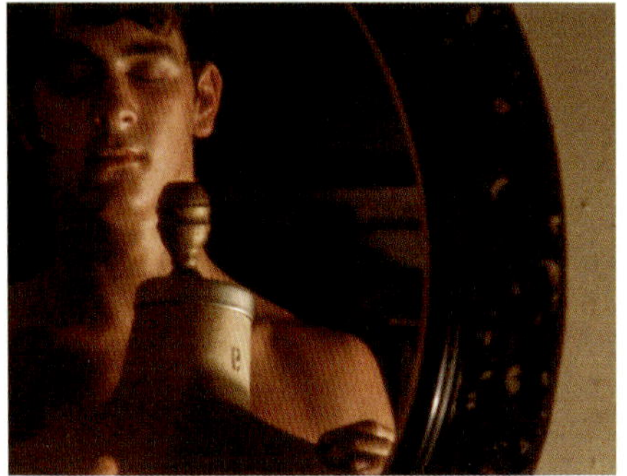

Beavers in Gregory Markopoulos, *Eros, O Basileus* (1967)

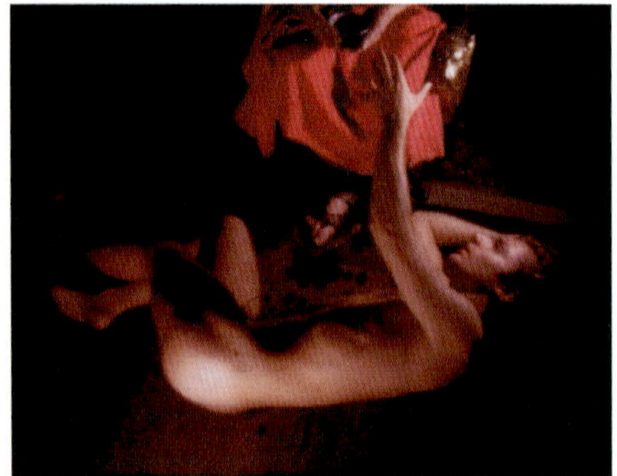

Gregory Markopoulos, *The Illiac Passion* (1964–1967)

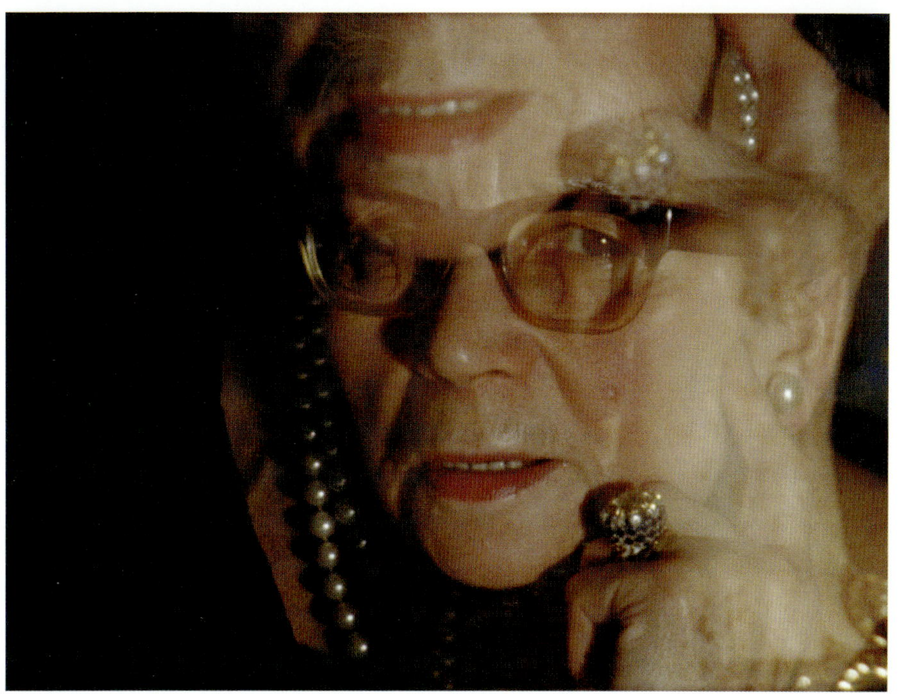

Hulda Zumsteg in Gregory Markopoulos, *Political Portraits* (1969)

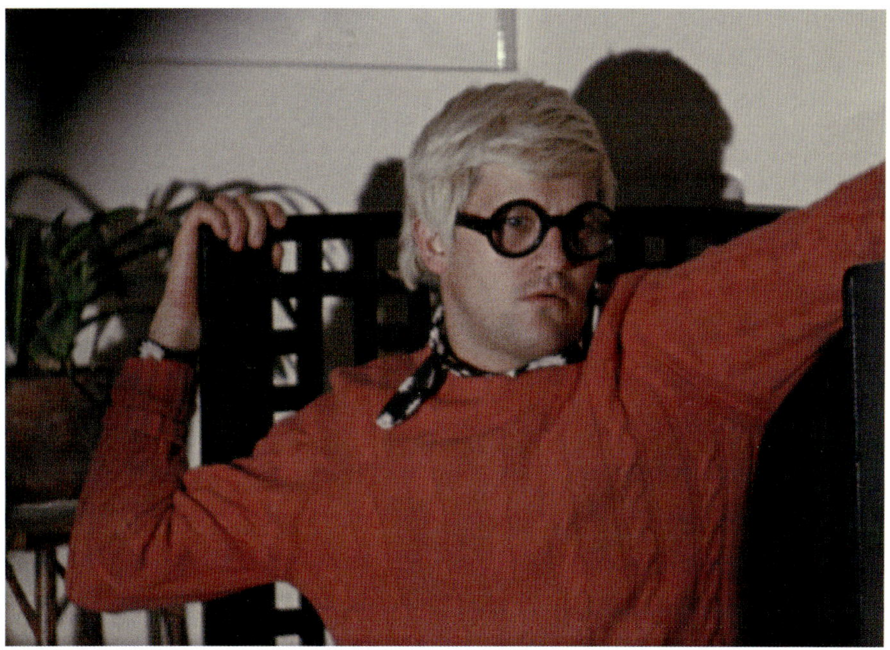

David Hockney in Gregory Markopoulos, *Genius* (1970)

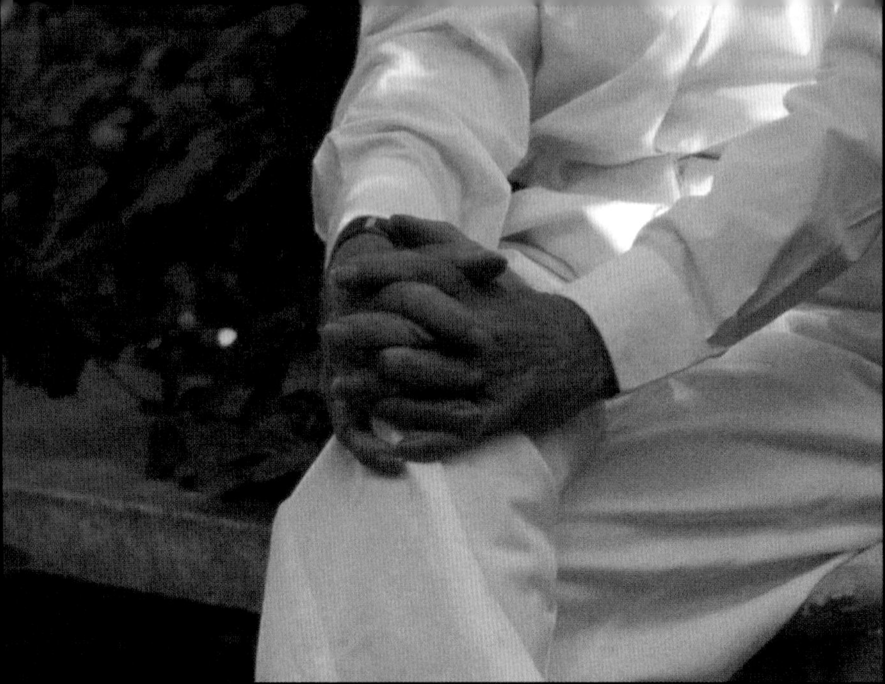

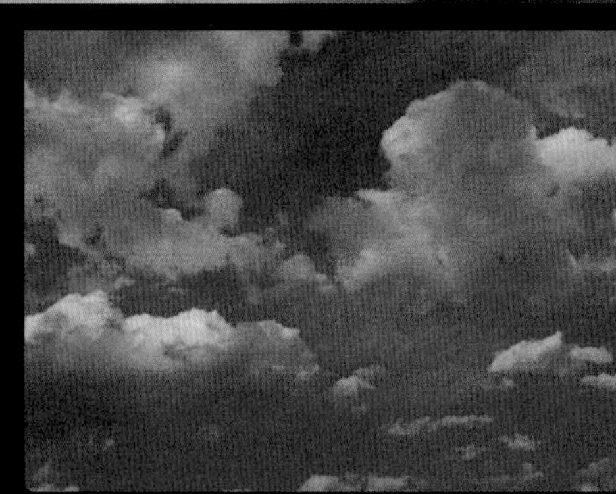

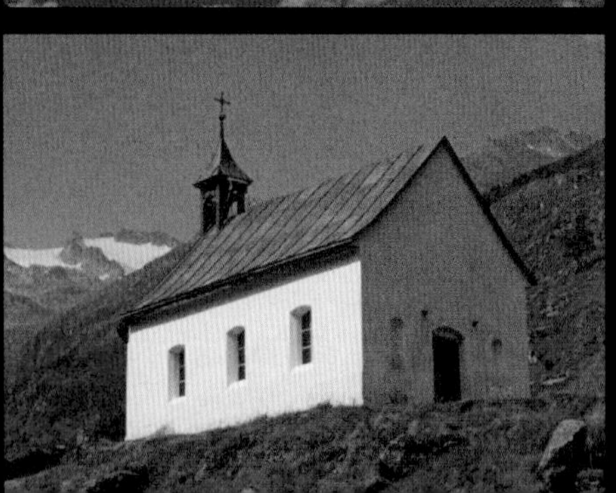

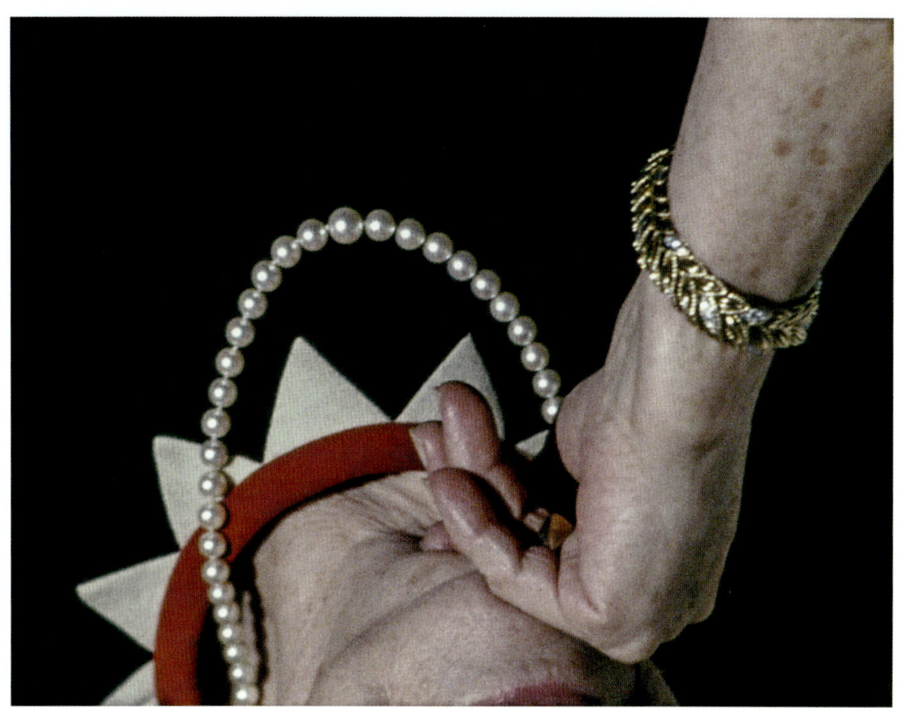

Previously unprinted portraits Markopoulos included in *Eniaios* (1948–1990): Yannis Tsarouchis, Graubünden church, Nina Kandinsky

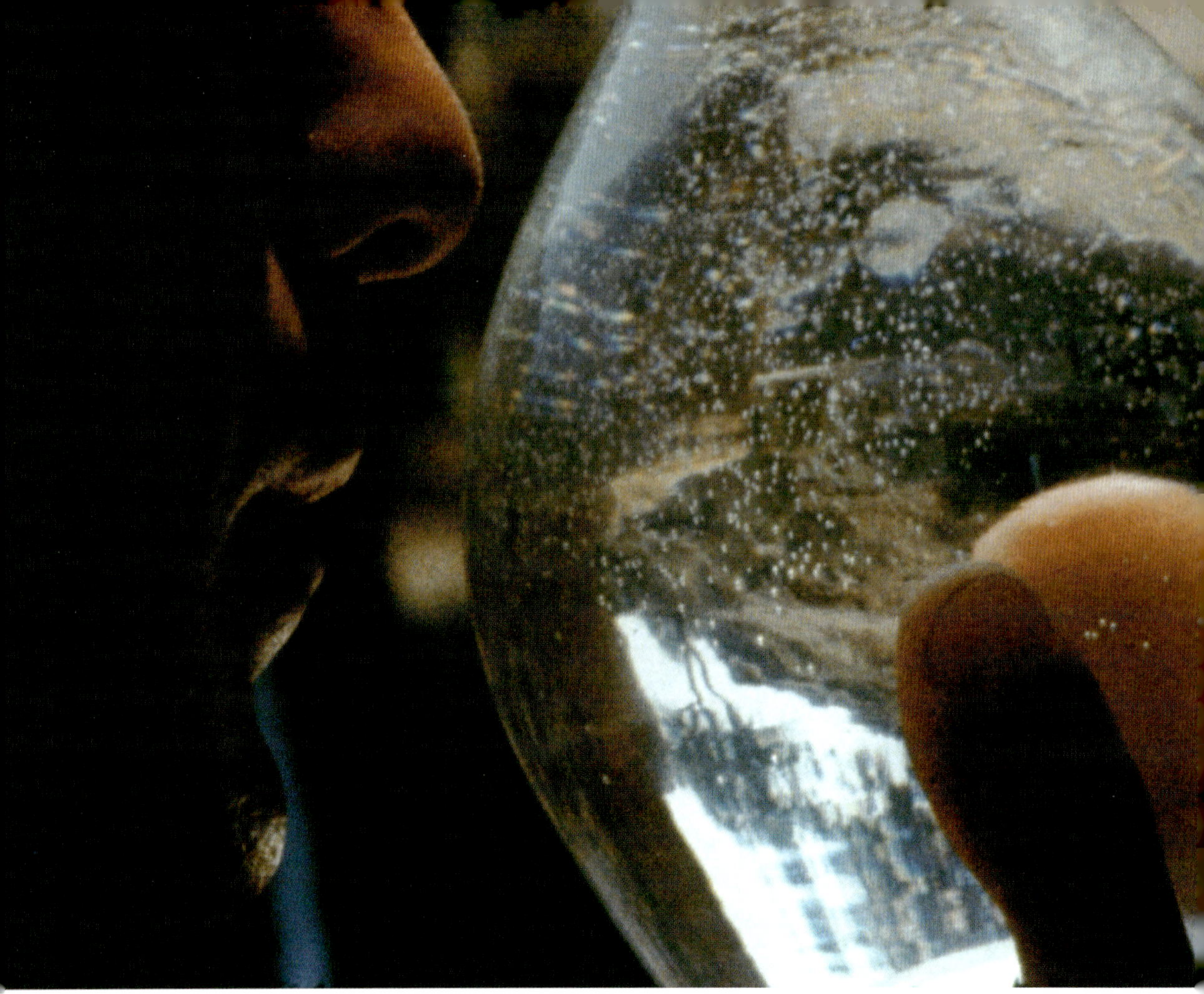

*Winged Dialogue* (1967/2000)

# LOVE STORIES

# 2

**Μικρός Ἔρως**
Τί μικρός ποὺ φαίνεται ὁ ἔρως
Μέσα στὴν γαλανή θάλασσα.
Καὶ ὅταν πέφταν
Τὰ χέρια του μέσα στὸ νερό
Ὅλλη ἡ γῆ σὰν οὐρανός
Γεμίζῃ μὲ χρυσᾶ ἄνθη
Καὶ σὰν φωνὴ ἀπὸ ῥόδα χαμογελάϊ.

**Little Eros**
How small Eros seems
In the middle of the azure sea.
And when his hands fall into the water
The whole earth like the sky
Is filled with golden flowers
And like a rose's voice she smiles.
**Gregory Markopoulos**[1]

After several days in Brussels in February 1967, Beavers traveled from Brindisi to Athens by ferry. Lilika Nakou—the leftist novelist and journalist who had become Markopoulos's friend during his 1950s *Serenity* stint in Greece—looked after Beavers. She found him a room for fifteen dollars a month in Filothei, an Athenian suburb, in a two-story building overlooking a field. When she introduced him to his landlord, Beavers asked if the price included breakfast; the two women looked at each other, paused, and said yes. He was learning to survive.

Beavers acclimated quickly to Athens and its small world ethos. "It was like walking into someone's living room," he said. Nakou insisted he learn Greek with her cook (whom she also hoped Beavers might marry), and several times a week she hosted him for lunch in her modernist house in the city center, near the Hilton Hotel. On April 20, 1967, at a gymnasium near the Temple of Zeus, a young man, the son of a colonel, instructed Beavers, "Stay at home tomorrow. There's going to be trouble." The following day, a right-wing coup d'état ushered in a seven-year military junta. Beavers was insulated from direct impact, but Nakou felt herself in great danger of being denounced. Leftist politicians were being held at the Hilton after their arrest.

When Beavers said he wanted to make a film on a Greek island, Nakou suggested nearby Hydra. By the time he arrived on the carless island in June, he spoke enough Greek to communicate. Markopoulos, who had recently resigned from his position as visiting associate professor of cinematography at the Art Institute of

Chicago, arrived later that month. Beavers shot *Winged Dialogue* (1967/2000) in the mornings and late afternoons. He used three locations: a sea captain's house where he and Markopoulos rented a room on the main harbor; Agios Nikolaos, a tiny chapel set on a reef off the island coast; and a crumbling hilltop tower.

### ΔΙΑΛΟΓΟΣ

A dialogue is a cross (*διά* "through, inter" + *λόγος* "speech, discourse"). A wordless, lyrical ode to his crossing with Markopoulos, *Winged Dialogue* transpires in the domain of Eros, the winged love god Beavers had played in *Eros, O Basileus* (1967). Eros mutated across ancient texts—a primordial divinity who helped create the cosmos, Aphrodite's son and Psyche's lover, a lyre-carrying artist, a blindfolded child. As a noun, *ἔρως* is "desire."

*Winged Dialogue* braids varieties of ecstasy—sexual, holy, creative—into three rapidly cut minutes. Segmented into seven sections separated by black, the film transpires in a pared-down Greek universe of superimposed skin, sea, sky, and shadow. Rocks and clouds, gravity and light, and two naked men in love are joined by a camera that ventriloquizes the interplay of elemental objects and forces. The film races forward via rhythmic animation, like a mobile assembly of mosaic shards, but the bed of atmospheric sound—sea, flapping wings, and bells (both in churches and on goats)—produces a simultaneous ethos of edgeless aquatic flow.[2] The film forecasts the crucial role Aegean light will play in Beavers's cinema for decades to come: turquoise, cyan, teal, and sharp black shadows establish chromatic and graphic potentials that his filters and mattes will re-create in northern climates.

In *Winged Dialogue*'s first shot, a white cross arcs into legibility. Detached from its church, the cross is both undeniable signifier and graphic fact: two intersecting lines floating on azure sky. Beavers's shadow-coated hands make circular motions that convey conducting, gratitude, and conjuring power; they part to reveal Markopoulos's naked body, lying on rocks yards below. In the first segment, Beavers's hands are intercut with details of Markopoulos's body (pans down thighs and calves) and water—a violent splash, a wide shot of the nighttime horizon line. Shot brevity erases gravitational orientation: close-ups of Markopoulos's unanchored feet, suspended over rock, intimate the end of Christ's hanging body. Beavers's fused touching/revelation of Markopoulos's distant body recurs in the film's first three segments; as its valences fluctuate (worshipful, covering/protective, desirous), we are left with the impression that Beavers is holding *Winged Dialogue*.

Markopoulos collaborates with Beavers as motion- and cross-maker in the second segment. Across a series of intercut shots, he performs a staccato body language as his arms extend out of a deep window (he stands inside, unseen) and from each side of his body as he stands against the ochre tower wall. Markopoulos's bodily position (arms crossed on his chest) and motions (right arm extending from left side, left from right) repeat as his location (indoors and out) and Beavers's camera position (facing the front and back of his subject's body) changes. When his arms unfold and fully spread, Markopoulos takes the shape of a fully articulated cross.

In the third segment, layering and semi-matched action distribute dramas of touch. Beavers's implied caress of Markopoulos's body is joined by a close-up of the filmmaker's hand blocking, via superimposition, the back of Markopoulos's head, and progressive shots of Markopoulos walking away are superimposed by images of Beavers swimming, as if his vigorously forward-moving arms are an urgent response to departure. The longing voiced by Beavers's extension toward his diminishing object is mitigated by an awareness that each man has shot the other; there are more hands present here, more kinds of contact, than those on-screen. *Winged Dialogue* runs on desire's rhythm: contact, separation, and merger in combinatory flux. Distance is trespassed by the joint work of nature (shadows touch faraway objects) and craft (in-camera superimposition and editing generate proximity, edge contact, overlap, and total fusion in material construction and image outcome). In the final shot of the third segment, Beavers's rising head shatters the sea surface and his open-mouthed expression communicates undeniable joy.

Distinct identities dissolve in the fourth segment. Beavers and Markopoulos, in the form of cast shadows, meet at camera and tripod in a series of progressively close shots that culminate in two hands reaching for each other. Midway through the sequence, a medium shot captures the shapes of Beavers (head bent over camera) and Markopoulos (an amorphous blue silhouette) rendered on brown-mottled rocks. The image resembles a cave painting, a scene of creation unleashed by the primitive forces of love. A close-up of Beavers's cupped hands, as if holding the light flooding the shot, anticipates aesthetic arrival—fruit of the generative, excessive powers of eros.

In the final segments of the film, Beavers introduces new objects into Hydra's ecosystem: a fabric swath, a round black matte, a glass pitcher of water, a set of colored filters.[3] *Winged Dialogue*'s image-making theater has shifted from revelation of Markopoulos's body to collaborative motion-orchestration to proliferation—a surge of mediating materiality, graphic intervention, and compositional division. Standing against a black background, Markopoulos is superimposed by pairs of his own walking legs (extending horizontally from both sides of his body); he is a cross-species being, a moving sunburst. Beavers and Markopoulos share split-screen space in shots of contrasting scale and posture. Water droplets on black fabric display circles of light; the hilltop tower, shot through a glass pitcher of water, appears upside down, and the fingers that grasp the container engorge. The actions of mirroring, reflecting, and opposing occur equally in love and optics.

—

*Winged Dialogue* climaxes in revelation. In the final segment, a close-up of Markopoulos's face, his gaze direct, is superimposed by a closer shot of his hands covering his eyes. Over a sequence of connected images, his hands retreat and produce a face with four open eyes: "a seer and visible soul," Beavers said. The imagery has two sources: the eyes-only framing prominent in some of Markopoulos's *Galaxie* portraits and Beavers's own experience at the National Archaeological Museum in Athens a month before. Standing before a small bronze figure, he noticed that its container, a glass box, picked up his own reflection twice—on its front and back surfaces—superimposing a pair of large eyes on the smaller recessed image of his face. "My first reflection combines with the second to create a Greek spirit, a Greco-Egyptian mummy. The eyes of the larger combined with the head of the smaller reflection. I recognized it as myself and it wasn't," he noted at the time. This double self-image dominated by expressive eyes brought to mind Fayum portraits—the encaustic and tempera portrait panels placed on the faces of Roman-Egyptian mummies. In his notes, Beavers's attentions are trained on a frame larger than the museum object. The ancient figure offers a finely profiled occasion to notice the space that surrounds it, and in the interval between self-recognition and non-identification, a third being, a mystical entity, appears. "The essence of the film is in this image," Beavers said of four-eyed Markopoulos in *Winged Dialogue*. "The development of all the images together reaches this moment of revelation."

Beavers calls *Winged Dialogue* "a happy accident"—the fruit of "beginner's luck" (an imaginative mix-up where "not being fully conscious the first time you do something" joins "not knowing how to do it" and "not being afraid") nourished by the clarity of Greek nature and a short-lived cultural zeitgeist:

> **I felt incredible freedom with Markopoulos in Europe. Greece gave me that possible life at that moment in time. And I was carrying the exploration of New American Cinema films. In the background is that extraordinary moment when New American Cinema makers [Markopoulos, Brakhage, Jack Smith] used nudity with a freedom that had never been done in film—or in gay film—open to sexualities and eroticisms and to a space between commercial film and pornography. This moment—this utopian sense of the body existed for just a short window of time. They did something that freed the body. But once they had accomplished this, [the window] very quickly closed and we were back in the world of commercial nudity—with Warhol's *I, A Man* [1967] or even Brakhage through Grove Press—he made more money with *Lovemaking* [1968] than any other work because it fulfilled that market need.[4]**

*Winged Dialogue*'s ecstatic abandon introduced Beavers to the capacity of filmmaking to enlarge reality itself: "What's possible in making a film is not totally in sync with the living person making it. Filmmaking opens up a special area which is not equivalent to the day-to-day reality of the filmmaker. The film itself is an alternate reality—I was eighteen at the time, and lots of things had happened that were very different from what you see in *Winged Dialogue*. But I can still see *Winged Dialogue* as a [part of] reality."[5]

## REUNION

In another winged dialogue, Plato's *Symposium*, as banquet attendees take turns praising Eros, Aristophanes identifies love's origins in a violent division of circles. Primeval humans were spherical in shape (as offspring of Sun, Earth, and Moon) and motion (moving in cartwheel-like fashion), two-faced, and eight-limbed, but they grew too powerful, threatening the gods' supreme rule, and Zeus split them in half.[6] Desire is the magnetic pull toward reunion; love is reparative—it "calls back the halves of our original nature together [and] tries to make one out of two and heal the wound of human nature," Aristophanes says.[7] In its construction of nearly continuous contact, *Winged Dialogue* revels in the fortune of right union. But the film is not a document of private psychic achievement.

In the *Symposium*, Plato asserts a vertical love teleology: desire attached to the beloved's physical body ascends toward other objects—virtue, altruism, wisdom, ideal forms. *Winged Dialogue*'s vertical emphasis, oriented not to divinity but to the standing human figure, is crossed by a revelatory horizontal axis. Inside the film's contracted high-speed image ecology, Beavers shuttles the spectator, as if her eyes were swiveled on his tripod's head, among spatially and temporally distant dimensions of a total image. The silhouetted scene of Beavers's tripod encounter with Markopoulos is linked, later, to the results of that event: close-up portraits of Markopoulos's face. The prismatic image is split into cause and effect; it consolidates off-screen. As the film speeds ahead, the multiplication and intermingling of limbs supersedes awareness of their individual sources, as if ultimately there is only one whole body in the film.

Toward the film's end, space opens beyond idyllic island confines toward a planetary perspective. Wide shots of Markopoulos seated under a tree are intercut with long diagonal shadows that narrate the sun's descent; in the last shot, the low orb paints an orange stripe on black sea. A series of color-soaked (violet, fuchsia, cornflower) pans across the twilight horizon simulate a 360-degree spin. Inside this rotation, which is accompanied by the sound of quickening church bells, appears not only four-eyed Markopoulos but a rainbow. When Beavers shot the landscape pans in-camera, placing a unique combination of two colored filters (horizontal or diagonal strips glued to glass) in the interior filter slot of his Bolex each time, he selected a slightly different start and stop point for each pan. This generated an out-of-alignment "registration error" look among layered shots and a zone of chromatic mutation and chance that's responsible for the brief appearance of a full prismatic spectrum down the center of the frame. "The rainbow was an accident," Beavers said.

Zeus's splitting destroyed primeval human's two-way sight: "As he cut each one, he commanded Apollo to turn its face and half its neck toward the wound, so that each person would see that he'd been cut and keep better order."[8] *Winged Dialogue* offers up its own forms of repair. As the earth turns and the sun drops, Beavers turns our heads, reversing Apollo's ancient move: a realignment with astrological origins and a restoration of sphericity.

## A RESPONSE

While on Hydra, Markopoulos made *Bliss* (1967), a six-minute in-camera portrait of the windows and frescoed interior of the Byzantine Church of St. John the Baptist. In mid-July he penned a spontaneous response to Beavers's *Winged Dialogue* filmmaking aboard a ferry headed back to Hydra from Athens. The resulting essay, "10th of July, 1967," describes the mystery of "observing Venus's latest born": "The very limited Bolex filter slot is put to such extraordinary use that another filmmaker, observing, feels certain he doesn't know what he is doing. . . . A filmmaker can never understand during the filming, especially, what another filmmaker is doing."[9]

Markopoulos claims Beavers as a particularly American artist, an identification he binds with ancient allusion: "And this filmmaker in the tradition of Aeschylus (though he is not totally aware of the similarity of both situations) has left country and home in order to brush from his myopic eyes the smog of the cities he is familiar with, and the heavy mist (now become poisonous) that drifts across the daily actions of those he calls family, friends, and acquaintances. This in order to charm the souls of the beasts who claim that his country is without Song."[10] This Whitmanesque insistence on an underheard American lyric was characteristic of Markopoulos's championing of the New American Cinema in the 1960s (Ron Rice is a "golden poet"; American filmmakers are "like the ancient priests of Egypt" and inhabit a "Garden of Eden"). But by 1970, Markopoulos's critical advocacy had shrunk dramatically to Beavers's and his own work, and he began to address his anonymous future Temenos spectator in a romantic key. In "The Redeeming of the Contrary," from 1971, he writes: "Beloved spectators of my distant Temenos, what evolved was . . . a continuous working decision not to betray you . . . not to impose a message in your laps. . . . I have always been concerned for you."[11] By the mid-1970s, nearly all of his writing was focused on the Temenos.[12]

In an early July 1967 note, Markopoulos dedicated a black-marker drawing to his partner. "Of Eros for Eros," he wrote beside a picture of hole-pocked strips (16mm film, presumably) twisted into an abstract face. Eros was one of Markopoulos's names for Beavers; *ERB* (Eros Robert Beavers) became the title of the anthologized collection of his essays on Beavers's films published under the Temenos imprint in 1975.[13] For decades, *ERB* was the most extensive critical response to Beavers's work.

### HEAVEN AND HELL

In August 1967, Beavers and Markopoulos relocated to Rome as it emptied for Ferragosto. Markopoulos had known and loved the city since 1959—he had edited *Serenity* at La Micro-Stampa laboratory when there was nowhere to do so in Greece. And now he had a reputation among Italian cinephiles who avidly embraced the New American Cinema. When they arrived, Filmstudio 70, an art cinema, and the Italian Filmmakers Cooperative had just opened. A small, teeming world of American expats and artists was also gathering. "My impression was that everyone I met was on drugs," Beavers recalled.

In search of contacts and support, Markopoulos and Beavers visited Lino Micciché, a leftist critic and Pesaro Film Festival cofounder, nearly every day. "He was very patient, though sometimes he flipped out," Beavers said. Experimental filmmaker Alfredo Leonardi led them to Peter Hartman, a well-connected American composer who lived on the estate of the Pakistani embassy. Hartman arranged for them to stay in the empty apartment of William Berger (an Austrian spaghetti western star) and his wife, near Borromini's Oratorio dei Filippini, where Beavers edited *Winged Dialogue*.

Rome was cheap—150 lire for a meal—but not cheap enough. Markopoulos convinced the downstairs trattoria to feed them on credit until payment for *Bliss* arrived. "He was sending letters to *everyone*" in search of financial aid, Beavers recalled. "It's a long walk if you're not eating very much—from the apartment to

American Express on Piazza di Spagna," where an occasional check from Beavers's grandmother or Markopoulos's Friends of the New Cinema monthly stipend arrived.

Markopoulos asked each new contact—novelist Elsa Morante, painter Mario Schifano—for money, usually in vain. "It was probably my first bout of Gregory and no money," Beavers said. "This period was absolute heaven and also hell." Using the free Agfa-Gevaert film rolls, Beavers shot *On the Everyday Use of the Eyes of Death* (1967) in the Villa Borghese Gardens—nine minutes of rapidly rhythmic pine trees and foliage, a single figure, and a policeman on horseback that he subsequently destroyed. Markopoulos shot five minutes of single-frame footage at socialite and Black Sun Press publisher Caresse Crosby's 365-room Castello di Rocca Sinibalda, in Rieti—which became, after he added more than a thousand fade-ins and fade-outs to black and clear leader (anticipating his *Eniaios* method), the sixty-minute *Gammelion* (1968).

In October they flew to Vienna, where two of Markopoulos's films were included in a New American Cinema series at the Austrian Film Museum. Revisiting the experience decades later, Beavers writes, "Markopoulos's authenticity and pretense, intelligence and arrogance make for a lively encounter with the Viennese public." He goes on to recall "[b]ackstage action: Gregory's sense of not being appreciated takes the form of threatening an ultra-right-wing statement before his screening . . . more as a prank than anything else, but this, and the question of how to insure that the Film Museum pays for our visit in Vienna and the travel to Belgium, made the interaction difficult."[14]

I asked Beavers about the origins of Markopoulos's conviction regarding entitlement to financial support. "He would often say it came from Jack Smith who after [Markopoulos's] Knokke-le-Zoute prize [for *Twice a Man* in 1963] said: 'Why do you have a job? Why are you working in a bookshop?' He was saying, 'Why don't you have the courage to do it without?'" Of their first years in Europe, Beavers recalls, Markopoulos "made this insistence [that his work merited remuneration] and his sexuality the center of his identity as a filmmaker and measured things by these criteria. Institutions such as cinematheques or film archives were seen as suspect or obstacles to his vision for Film."[15] Markopoulos immediately sensed when someone was "unaware of their own prejudice" toward homosexuality and reacted strongly, Beavers said.

In late October 1967, Beavers and Markopoulos flew to Brussels. It became their base until they returned to Greece in the summer of 1968. *Spiracle* (1966) and Markopoulos's *The Illiac Passion* (1964–1967) premiered at Knokke-le-Zoute in December. The following year, in a lecture at Kent State, Markopoulos recalled the announcement of his film's fate by the festival organizers: "[They said,] 'Although *The Illiac Passion* is considered the most accomplished film of the festival, the judges have decided to take it out of the festival because it *is* so accomplished.'"[16]

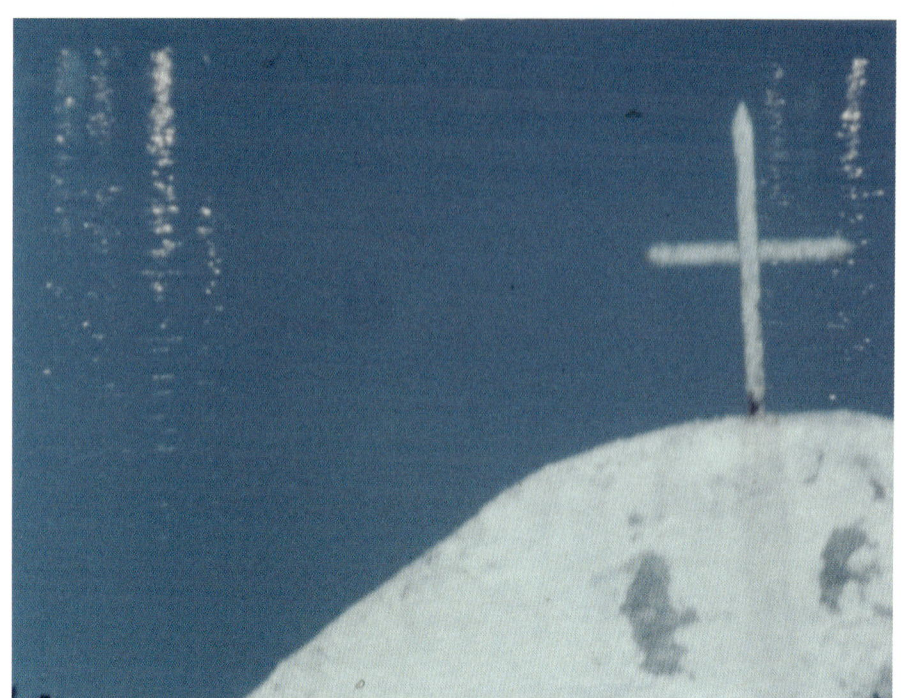

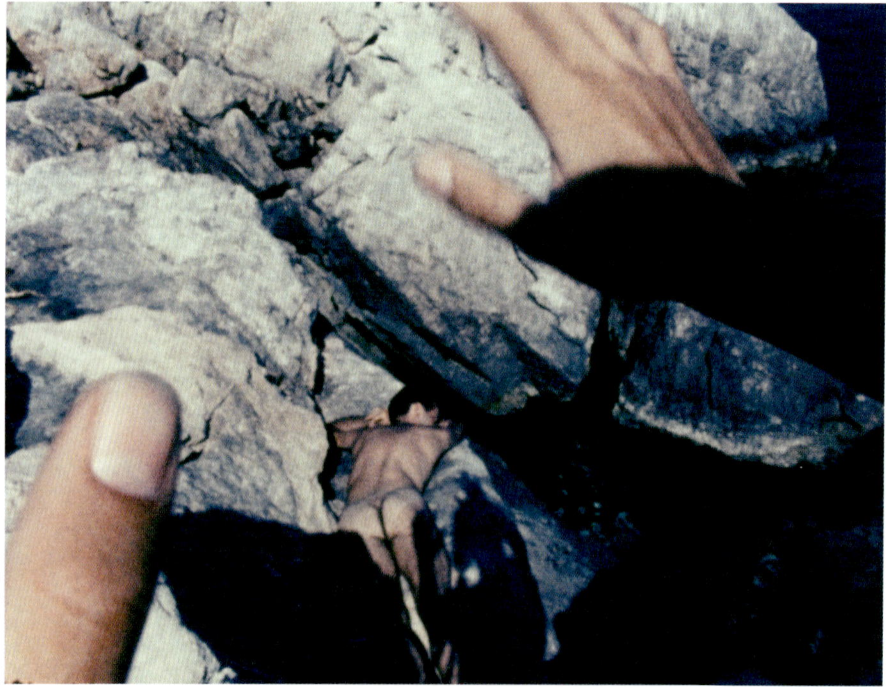

*Winged Dialogue* (1967/2000)

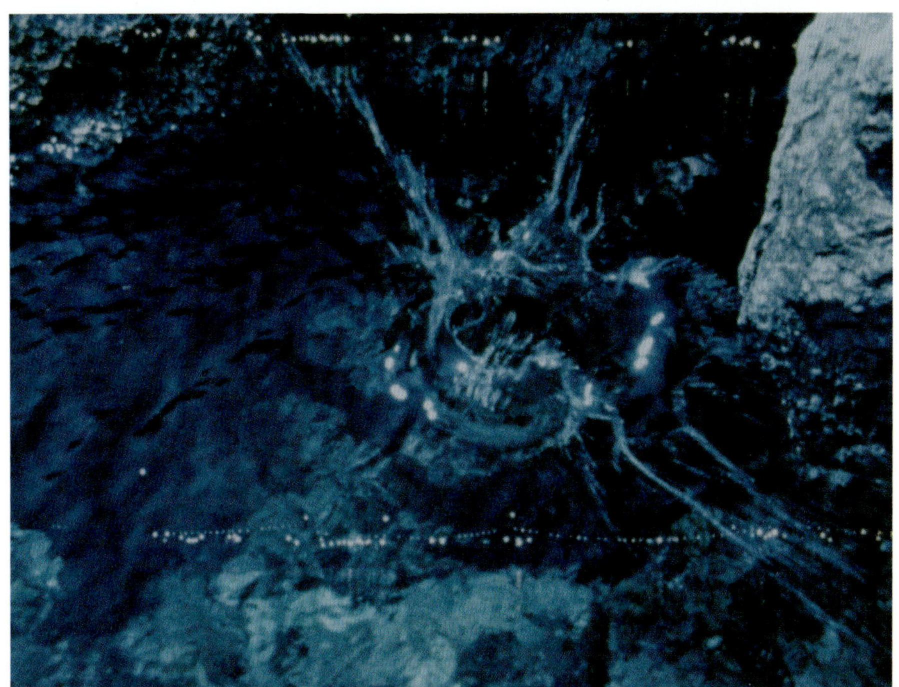

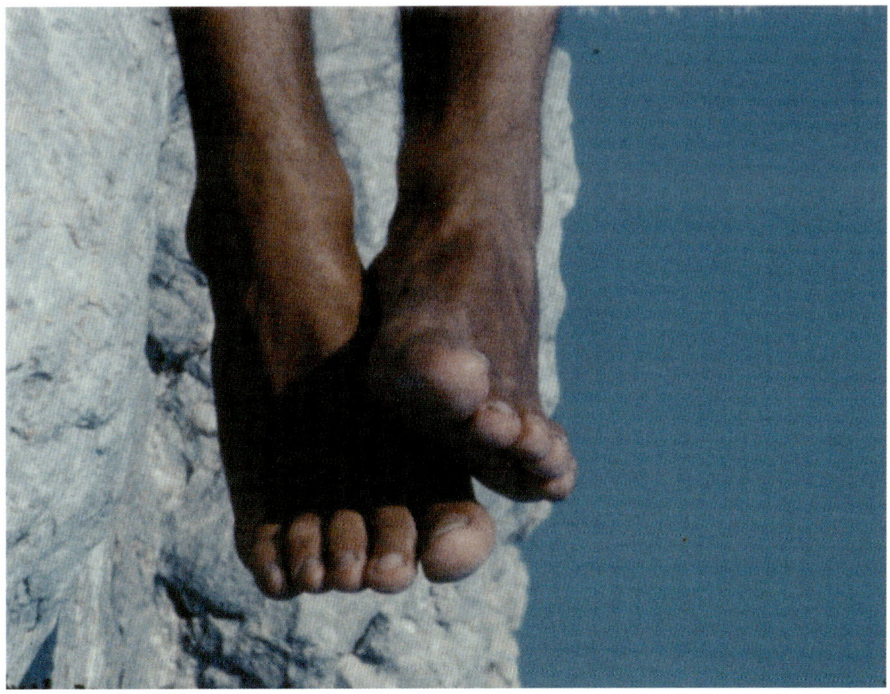

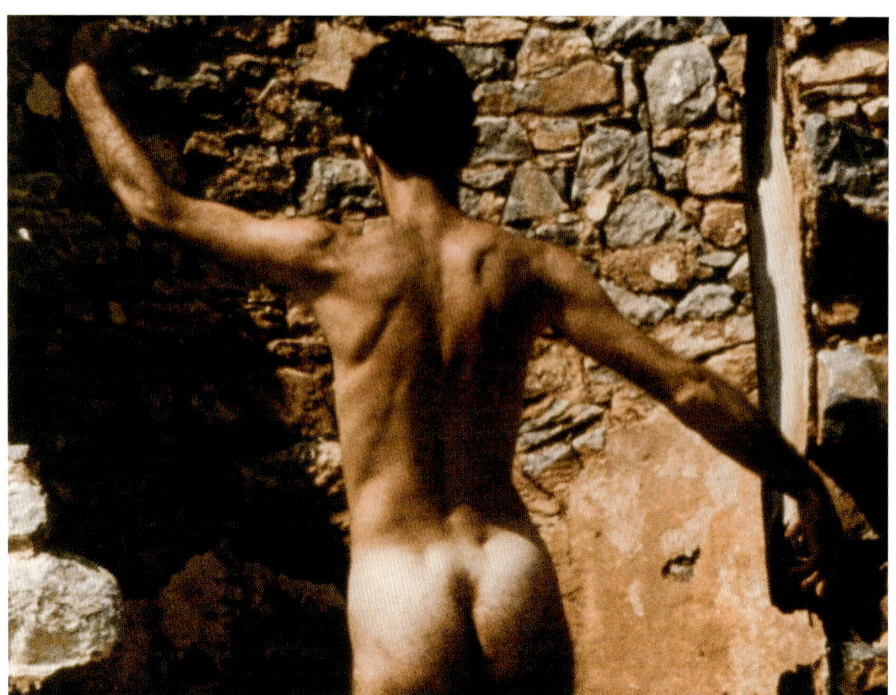

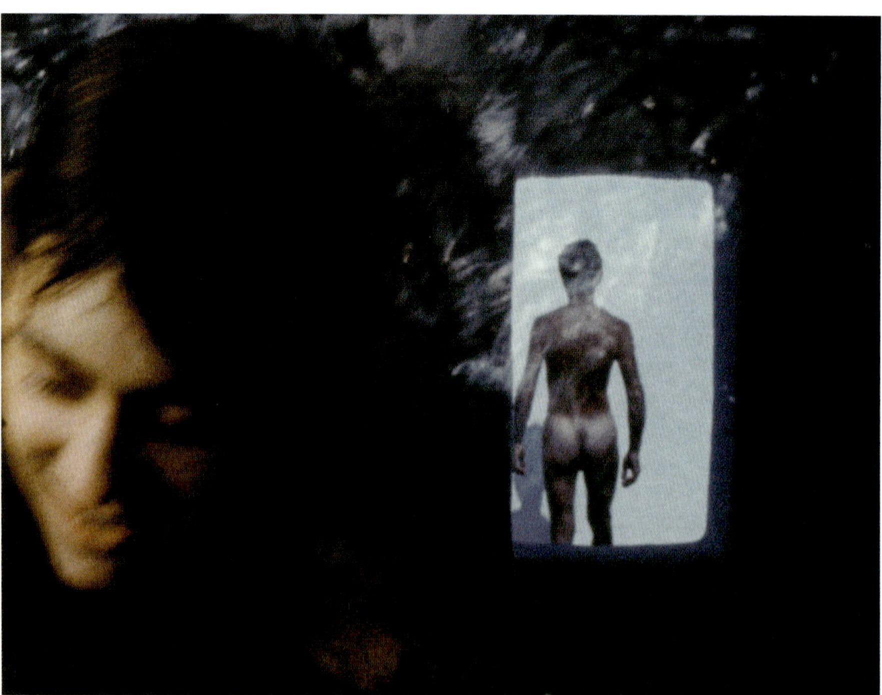

*Winged Dialogue* (1967/2000)

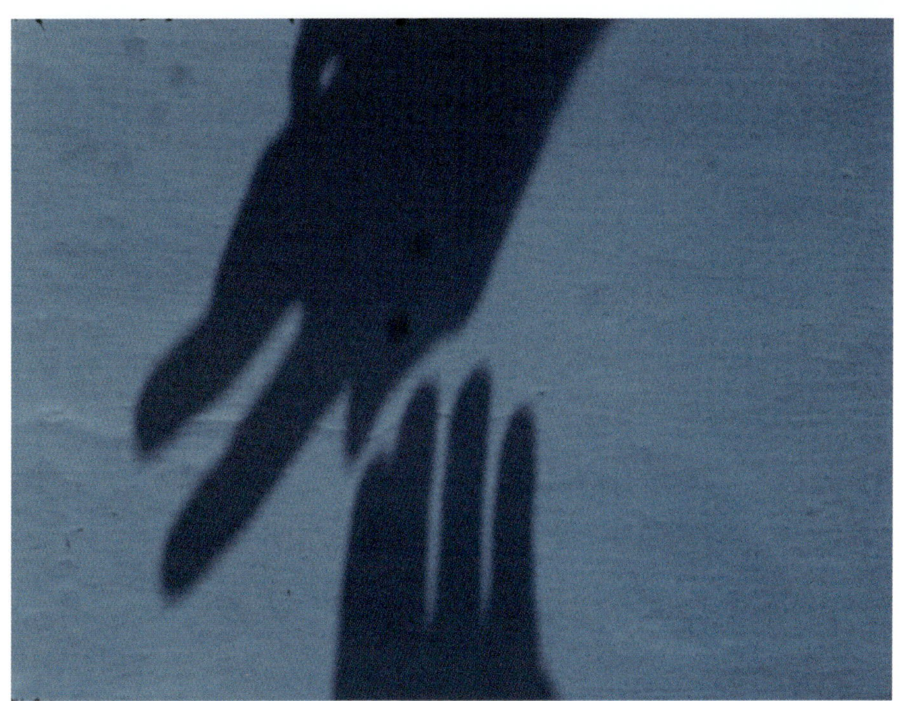

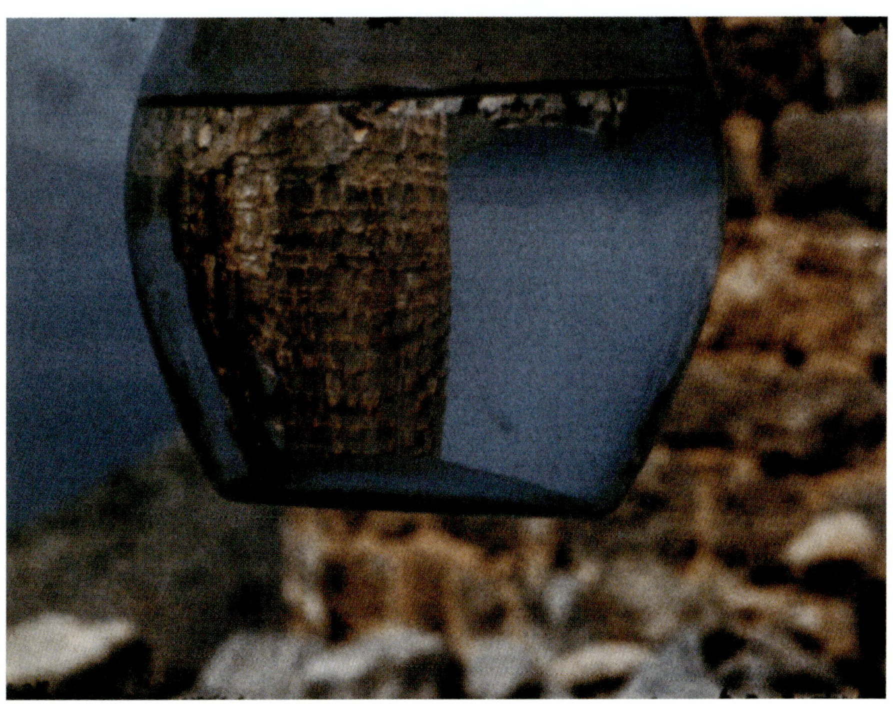

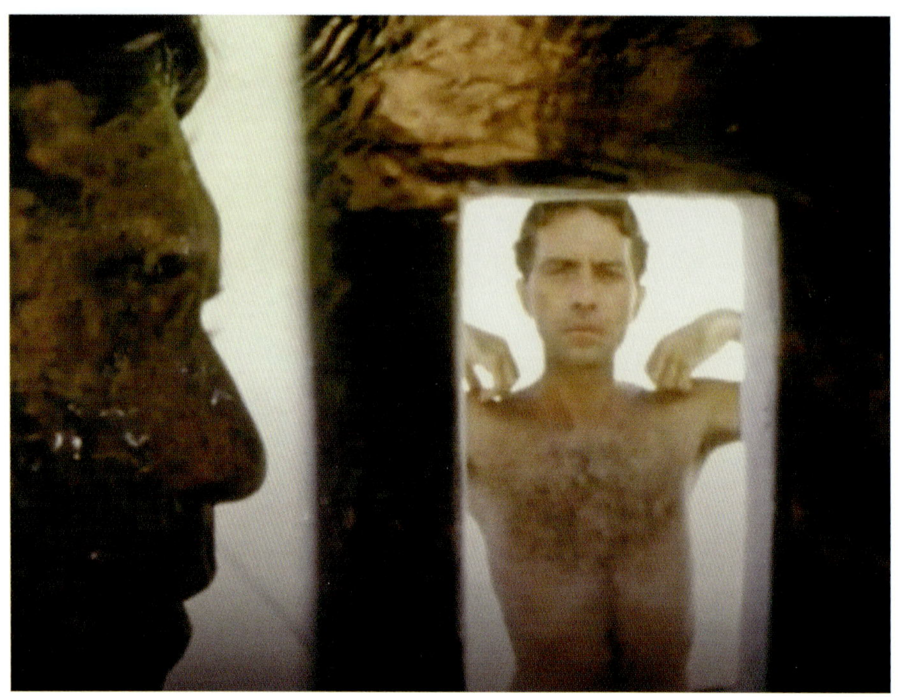

*Winged Dialogue* (1967/2000)

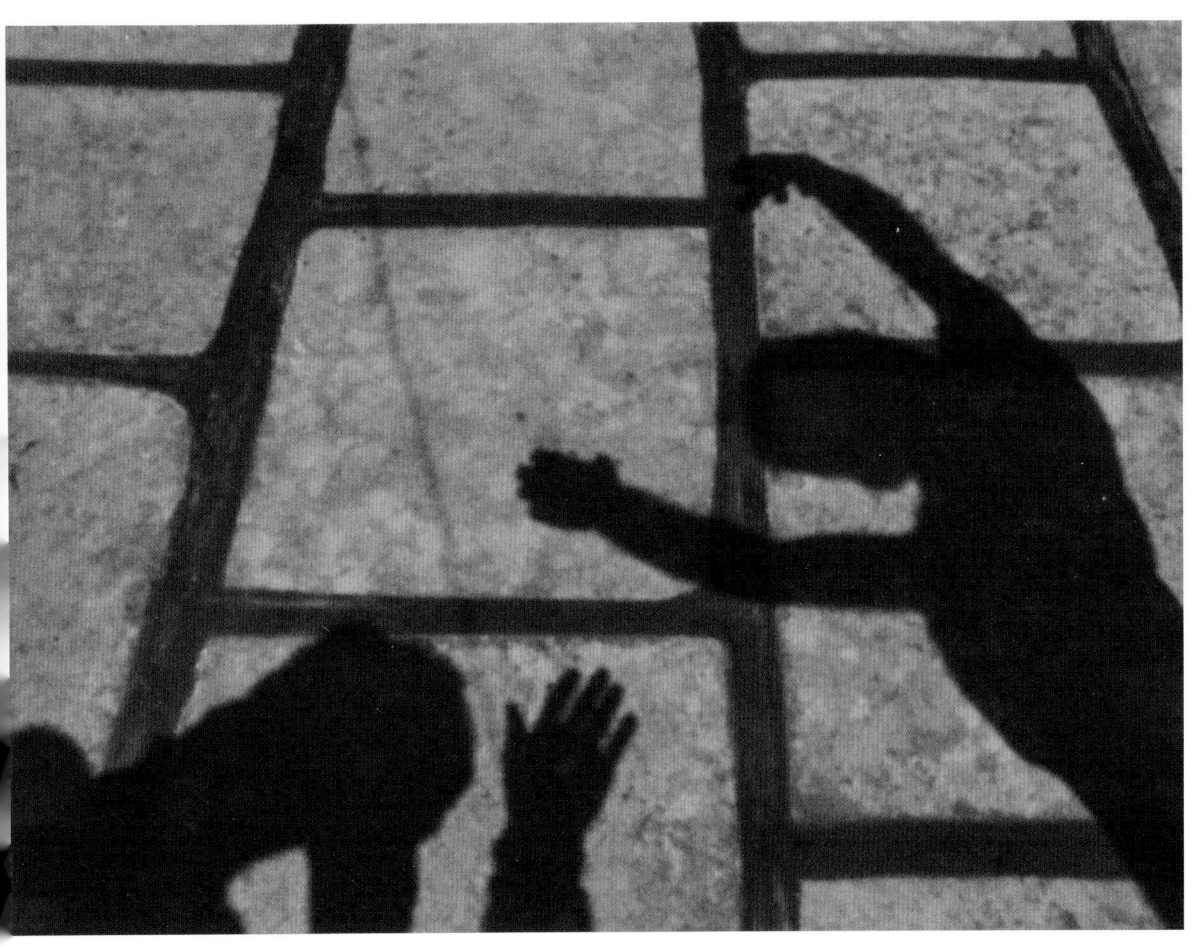

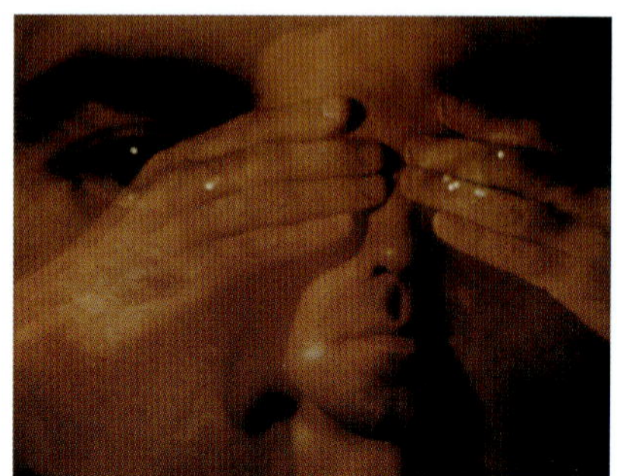

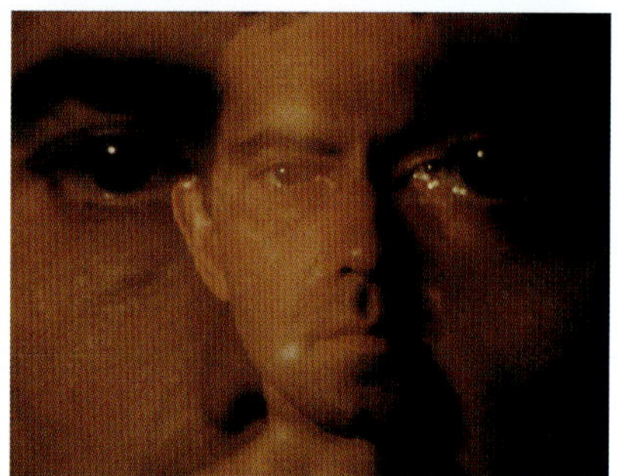

*Winged Dialogue* (1967/2000)

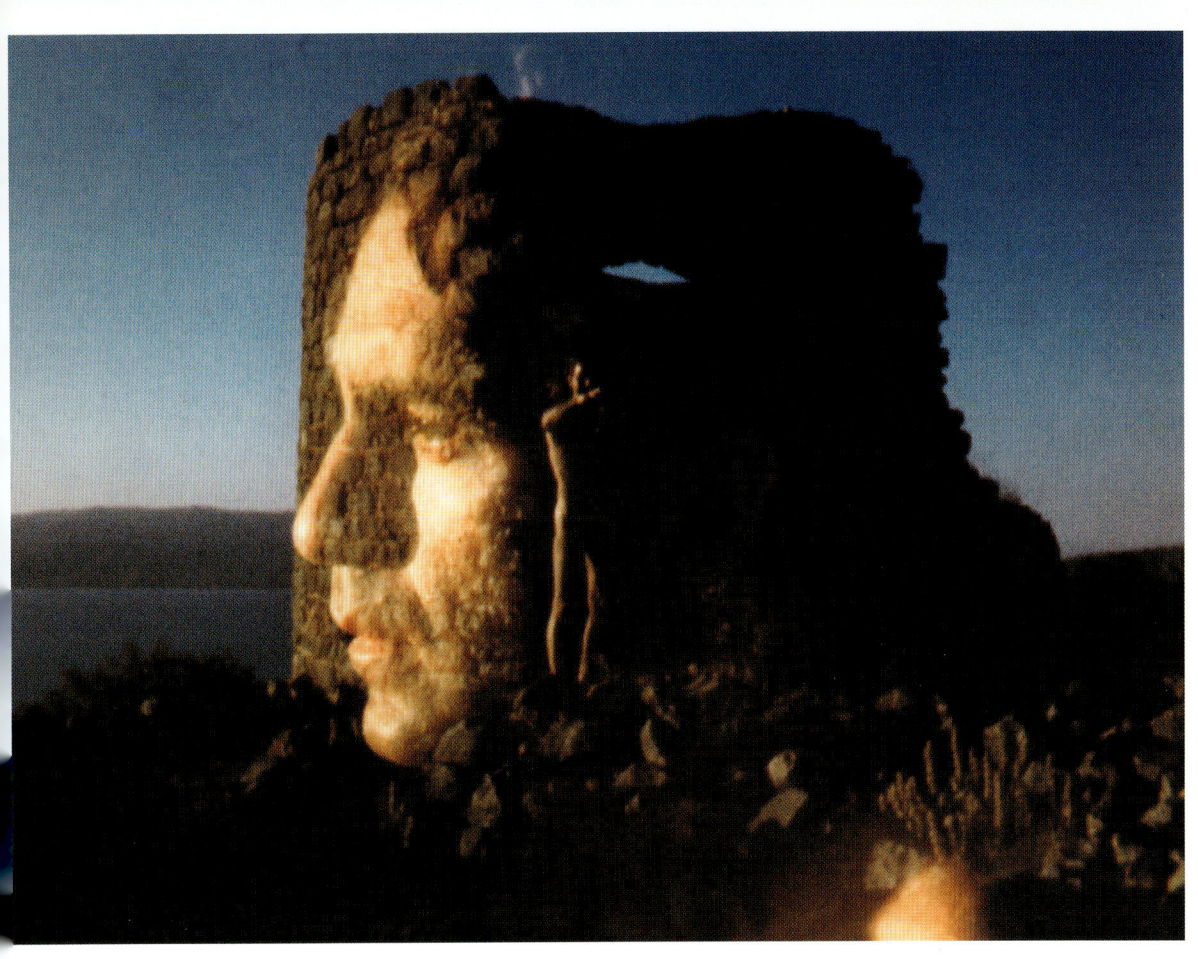

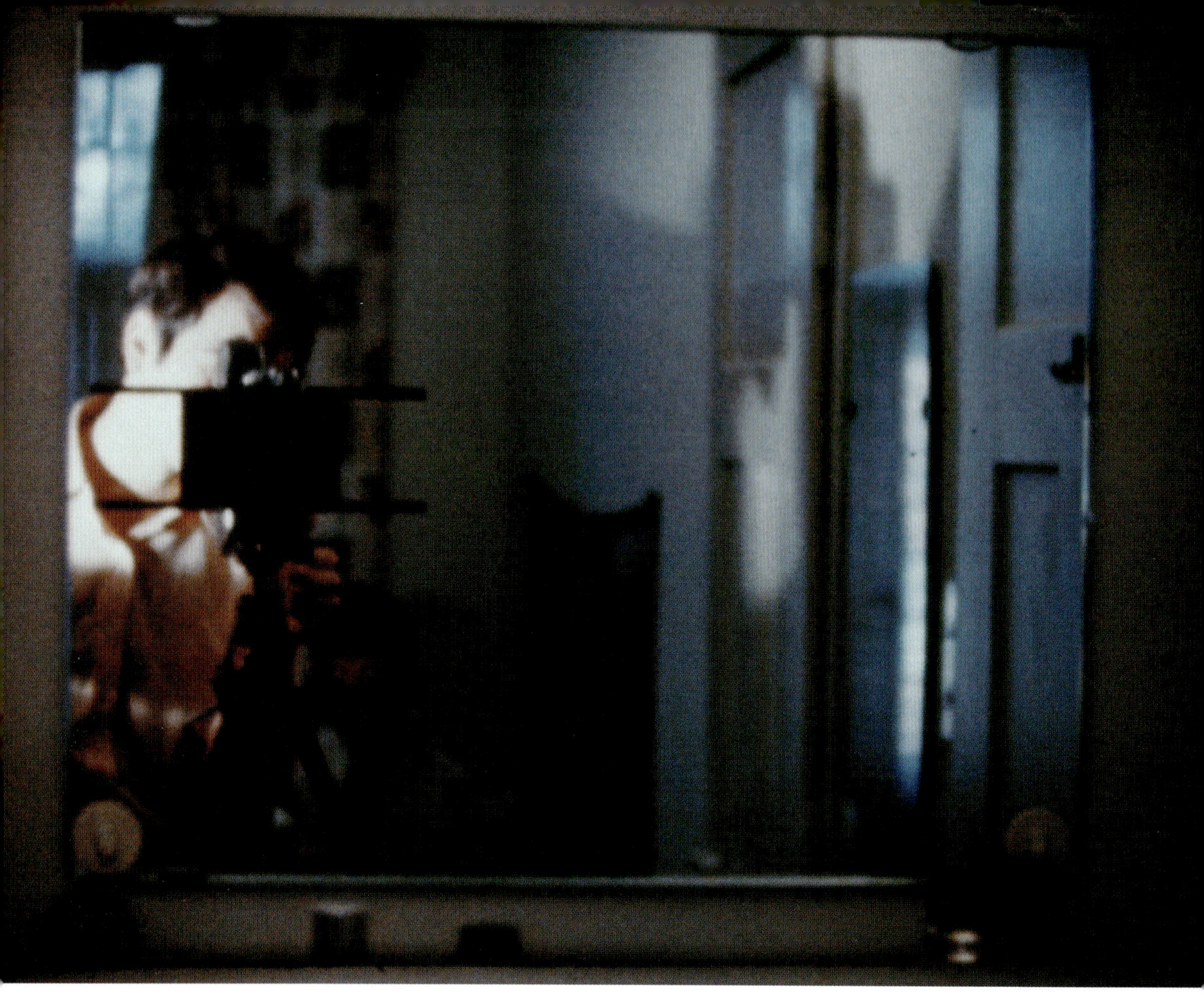

*Early Monthly Segments* (1968–1970/2002)

# ECONOMIES OF ABSTRACTION 3

## PART 1: BOY AND MAN

### INCISION

In Brussels in November 1967, Beavers reached into his dreams and extracted a recurring boy (he appeared as a prisoner, naked spirit, subway rider). He made notes about uniting this "eternal boy" with a man in a film called *The Judgment of Youth*. Cranach's allegorical *Charity* (ca. 1540)—depicting a mother caring for her five young children—in Brussels and the Balthus exhibition he had seen at the Pierre Matisse Gallery in New York offered compositional models of stirring old and young bodies together with the forces of dream and myth. The film would rely on "ideographic composition" to compress complex space and language into shapes. Beavers imagined an intricate matte structure inspired by the ceiling of Rome's Church of San Girolamo della Carità (a grid of wooden frames filled with cobalt-backed narrative scenes).

But the dilemma of psychic integration was primary. Two Bacchus figures—a boy and a man—were both violently opposed ("Thieving of another's manhood by a youth; result: death of the youth") and interdependent ("Interweave the sexual nature of child with the nonsexual nature of the man and the nonsexual nature of the child with the sexual nature of the man. All four parts are different"). As he wondered how to represent psychic splitting, twoness-in-one-body, the gilded divisions of Hans Memling's *The Last Judgment* (1467–1471) offered one solution: seated atop a full-circle rainbow in the central triptych panel, Jesus sends the saved to Heaven on the left panel; those damned to Hell go right and underground.[1]

Beavers wanted to represent not only unconscious depths but physiological interiority.[2] In the spring of 1968, he contacted doctors in Zurich about shooting a human dissection. In the fall, he consulted early anatomy books: a French translation of Italian surgeon Mondino de Luzzi's fourteenth-century *Anathomia*, the first modern dissection manual, and Johann Remmelin's *Anatomical Engravings with Superimposed Flaps* (ca. 1632), whose liftable layers reveal body parts in the process of dissection. Beavers envisioned a film structure that would assemble a split-up body: "Each segment of the dissection will create a final, perfectly geometric form," he noted. Beavers couldn't gain access to a human dissection, but he shot the dissection of an ox's eyeball at the University of Zurich. He was following René Descartes's 1637 instructions to look at the back of a freshly dead animal's eye in a dark room while its pupil-side faced outdoors: one would see an inverted version of the scene, Descartes explained, flipped by the eye's lens and imprinted on a piece of white paper that had taken the retina's place.

In August 1968, Beavers decided to dissect the film apparatus itself. He elaborated an idea for a series of short films, "each revolving around a technical device." He listed ten initial concepts, including "surface and depth movements," "two movements in one frame," "glass and mirror reflections and shadows," "filters in slot, in matte box," and "'eclipsing' with matte and filter." Between 1968 and 1970 (aged eighteen to twenty), Beavers produced short formal trials on a monthly basis. He used the film-sketches to vocalize parts and potentials of his apparatus as he was coming to know them; they foreground his early work with compendium, mattes, and colored filters, and feature Beavers himself as element-orchestrator. He conceived of the project—then called *Degeneration*—as an infinite "self-study" in addition to an apparatus one. "Make a film of myself for a lifetime, filming one hundred feet per month," he noted at the time. The title came from "the morbid idea that we fall apart as we age. I thought I was going to film for rest of my life—it would be a record. The adolescent imagining the idea of aging and degeneration over time," Beavers explained. The project title also took "a kind of rebellious stance . . . in that period, homosexuality was thought of as degenerate," he said. So was gay avant-garde film: Jean Genet's semi-pornographic *Un Chant D'Amour* (1950) was banned upon release; a decade and a half later, a New York City screening of Jack Smith's sexually graphic *Flaming Creatures* (1963) led to the arrest of Jonas Mekas (and others) and a drawn-out legal battle that eventually involved the Supreme Court. But in 1955, before he became their champion, Mekas himself had penned an attack on the films of Markopoulos and other artists, calling them "neurotic and homosexual poems . . . this art of abnormality."[3] After two and a half years, Beavers stopped the *Degeneration* project. He left the edited films unprinted and didn't look at them again for two decades.

## REVISION

Beavers never realized *The Judgment of Youth*, but he was unwittingly en route to uniting boy and man. To watch most of Beavers's films is to encounter the artist at two ages at once, and to write about them is to move backward and forward in time. The three-minute *Winged Dialogue* I wrote about earlier was made jointly by seventeen- and fifty-year-old Beavers. In its first iteration, in 1967, it was seventeen minutes long.

In 1988, Beavers reviewed his early films at the Cinematheque Suisse in Lausanne. "I thought, 'I can do better.' There were gaps between experimental ideas and their realization—and an aggressiveness in my early approach." Over the next decade, he synced old work to present-tense consciousness, radically simplifying the films he had made since 1967 and returning to original shooting locations to rerecord sound. Most of the revised films are about half the original lengths. As he altered individual films, he also unified them in the three-part, eighteen-film cycle *My Hand Outstretched to the Winged Distance and Sightless Measure* (1967–2002).[4]

Beavers had maximized layering potential in his original films by extending the 16mm A/B roll system with rolls C, D, and sometimes E, F, and G.[5] ("We were crazy about superimpositions in those days!" he said of the New American Cinema zeitgeist, citing Kenneth Anger's 1954 *Inauguration of the Pleasure Dome* and Markopoulos's portrait films.) He developed numerical editing structures based on musical counterpoint. If rolls A and B were cut to the same even-numbered frame rhythm (2/4/4/2), bands C and D might share an odd-numbered rhythm (3/6/3) of the same overall length (12 frames). His approach drew on a brief period of piano study. He said, "As a young teenager, I was lucky to have a teacher, Mrs. Richter, who used real music [Bach, Handel, Telemann, Scarlatti] as study pieces. She cultivated my awareness of musical structure, taught me about visual notation and natural harmonies between certain numbers. It was extraordinary—the idea that two voices can fit together mathematically—one rhythm can equal the other, take up the same amount of time, while being a totally distinct, second rhythm. The two hands play two different rhythms."[6] Following Markopoulos's method, Beavers projected his printed film material once, relying thereafter on the film strips in his hands and memory as he made numerical choices in editing.

In revising, Beavers reduced bands (from as many as seven to two or three) while maintaining shot lengths and phrase measures. He restored the individual image that had been crowded out by speed and layering. "I wonder if I wasn't [originally] secure enough to rely on the image as composed," he said. "When I returned to my early films, I removed most of the postproduction superimpositions and a lot of the formally driven repetition. As a result, the montage had to be made stronger in order to carry the film. I released the films from structures to a certain degree."

In the early 1970s, Beavers had assisted Markopoulos as he revisited *Psyche* (1947) and *Swain* (1950). The initial changes were technical—removing visible splices and aperture dirt—but by 1974, Markopoulos's project had become total remake. Beavers watched, alarmed, as Markopoulos cut into camera originals and discarded now-unwanted parts of past films. "I said, 'Gregory, what are you doing? This is very dangerous,'—but the irony is that it led to a great expansion of his images over time." Markopoulos was on the cusp of refiguring his cinematic past and future, transforming reedited footage from twenty (of twenty-seven) of his previous films and fifty-five completely new films (edited in the 1970s but never printed) into what would become his epic *Eniaios* (1948–1990), composed of 167 reels. Paradoxically, Markopoulos's model of resculpting earlier films and the informing Temenos structure—designed for the presentation and study of the totality of both artists' work—produced the impetus for Beavers's own revision and cycle-creation *and* actualized the differentiation of Beavers's own film language.

In 1989, early in the revision process, Beavers watched the twenty unprinted *Degeneration* film sketches for the first time. He shortened them by half, renamed them *Early Monthly Segments* (1968–1970/2002), and assigned them two roles. Headed by *Winged Dialogue* (which also doubled and became a *Segment*), they constitute a silent prelude to the entire *My Hand Outstretched* cycle; they then reappear with sound, side by side and in dialogue with the five longer films he made concurrently: *Plan of Brussels* (1968/2000), *The Count of Days* (1969/2001), *Palinode* (1970/2001), *Diminished Frame* (1970/2001), and *Still Light* (1970/2001).

–

The utopian fruits and sealed-off dyadic bliss of *Winged Dialogue* were short-lived: in the five films made alongside the *Segments*, Beavers turns to the discontents of civilization, to his own out-of-placeness in unfamiliar European cities (Brussels, Zurich, Berlin, London) and new social formations in which eros is conflicted and nakedness a problem. To watch these five films today is to encounter both the mystery of altered first works and an evolutionary trajectory across the present tense of 1968–1971. The films move from character-oriented psychodramas of self-fragmentation (*Plan of Brussels*, *The Count of Days*, *Palinode*) to apparatus theatrics starring mattes and filters (*Diminished Frame*, *Still Light*). As narrative impulses dissolve, Beavers's role-playing transitions from actor/character to performative overseer, and textual presence shifts from narrative infrastructure (excerpts from literature and opera as soundtrack) to conceptual coping with language itself.[7]

"How did you get from the lyrical unity of *Winged Dialogue* to your subsequent film, *Plan of Brussels*, a psychodrama of inner torment?" I asked.

> **It was a shift in priority. I was trying to make something that might have a place in film culture as it existed. This was a Jungian moment—if you walked by the Eighth Street Bookshop in New York at that time, you'd see the Eranos papers, [Karl] Kerényi, [Mircea] Eliade.[8] There was continuity between this "Jungian moment" and [Maya] Deren's work even if they're coming from different places and times. The postwar angst of trance psychodramas (Markopoulos, Brakhage, Deren, [Peter] Weiss) are in the background here too, the conflicts of psyche. Cocteau is also coming through—not because I was interested in him (I was more of a Dreyer and Bresson person)—but via Gregory's interests.[9] *Plan of Brussels*, *The Count of Days*, and *Palinode* were less purely lyrical than *Winged Dialogue* because I was trying to think in terms of narrative film. The figure of the alienated writer or singer in those films is a stand-in for some psychological part. And the physical contexts—the stimulations of these new cities—were so different. I was engaged with the dichotomy between the individual and society. But I don't think I was aware of the way I had moved from the united erotic psyche to the representation of a fragmented psyche. I was so unconscious of the importance of Gregory in my life. . . . I didn't have the view of a mature person. Ravel said it's a good thing to know who your parents are. It hit him over the head when he realized what an influence Debussy had had on him.**

Beavers incrementally stripped narrative convention between 1968 and 1970, but the concurrent *Segments*—constraint-driven, highly local, open-ended, and minor by virtue of Beavers's "forever" plan—were stripped from the start. "I was freer in the *Segments* than I was in the longer films," he said. As we watch Beavers reconstitute his mobile studio at each new *Segments* locale (Zurich, Berlin, Locarno, Hydra, Disentis, Orselina), the diaristic and structural marbleize: living conditions (one-room domesticity) and camera experiments are inseparable. Beavers is always at home/away from home in the *Segments*, producing an improvisational blend of intimacy and distance. Pension room spaces and objects, inherently unfamiliar (gold wallpaper, creaseless bedspread, ornate chandelier, chrome fixtures), are invitations to momentary framings and formalities, and Beavers's use of artificial lighting turns up the performative aura. He directed Markopoulos both to act ("walk outside the window, sit at the typewriter") and to shoot ("do a full take") when he (Beavers) was the subject—"but it was all based on what we already did." Formality was also native. Beavers wears collared shirts, a silk vest, cufflinks; Markopoulos wears full suits. "Did you dress up for the *Segments*?" I asked. "No, those were the only clothes we had," he said. "It came from Markopoulos." (The older filmmaker was known for his sartorial style. "Gregory has a yearning for luxury and elegances," filmmaker Curtis Harrington, who had attended the University of Southern California with Markopoulos, once said.[10]) The theatricality of the *Segments* extends from the showcasing of apparatus operations to the ethos of erotic enactment that surrounds two impeccably dressed men who collaborate with seriousness and precision.

In revising, Beavers transferred a portion of rhythmic complexity from the intra-film level to cycle scale. Cycle one presents twenty-nine film elements (including repetitions). The softened edges between individual films (created by the replacement of titles with the sound of fluttering bird wings) produces a migratory propulsion of elements down the cycle stream. Imagery shot for—and during the making of—the five longer films appears in the *Segments*; as a result, materials, techniques, and motifs repeat and morph. The relational dialogue between the *Segments* (note-like, on the side, unofficial, ongoing) and the five longer films (complete and generically formalized)—between *textuality* and *text*—is the first cycle's primary beat. And the open form of the *Segments* generates an environment in which the longer films become, en masse, a tour of Beavers's early drive to represent language in film form: as hieroglyphic (the shadow play of *Winged Dialogue*), rooted in the body (the somatic alphabet of *Plan of Brussels* and the speechless mouth of *Palinode*), via figurative stand-in (in *The Count of Days*: screen as book, scalpel as mark-maker, scratched film as paper).[11]

Twelve of the twenty *Segments* were shot in Zurich pensions. After Giorgio Frapoli, of the Zurich Filmclub, organized a Markopoulos tour in the spring of 1968 (in Bern, Basel, Lausanne, and Zurich), Zurich became an important base for the filmmakers.

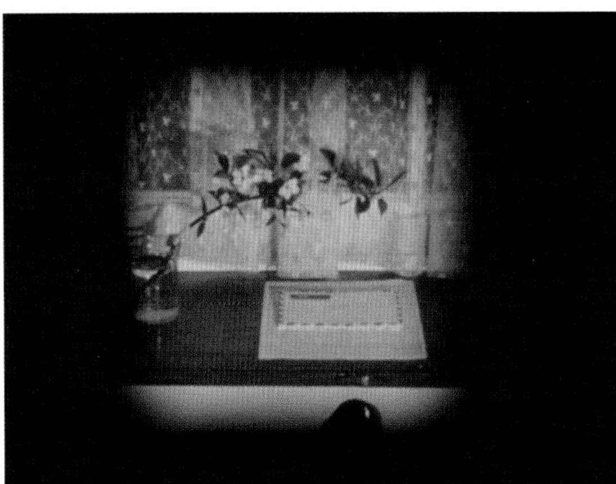

*Early Monthly Segments* (1968–1970/2002)

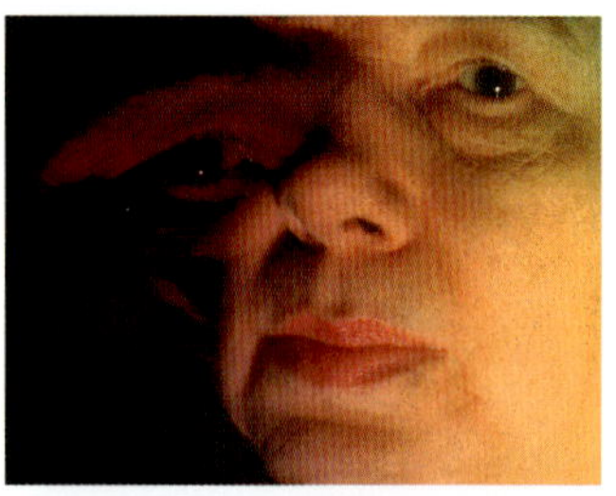

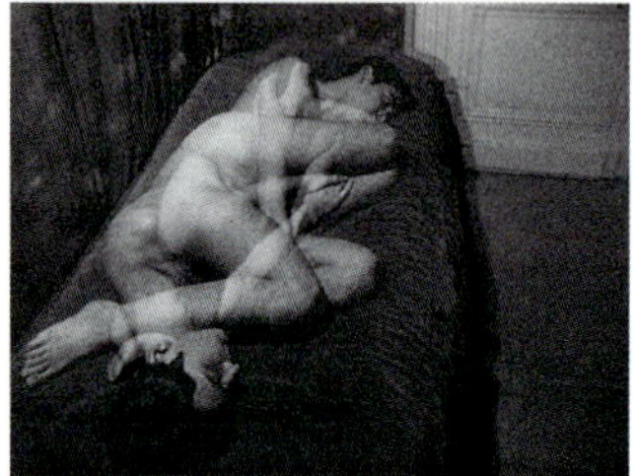

## CYCLE ONE: *MY HAND OUTSTRETCHED TO THE WINGED DISTANCE AND SIGHTLESS MEASURE*

### *Winged Dialogue* (1967/2000) and *Early Monthly Segments* (1968–1970/2002)

### *Winged Dialogue*

### *Plan of Brussels* (1968/2000)

In one of the two adjacent single rooms at the Hotel d'Egmont in Brussels, where he and Markopoulos stayed in the fall of 1968, Beavers sits at a desk and writhes in bed, naked and clothed, and is rendered as a superimposed double: a figure out of sync with itself. The plot-free drama of inner anguish, pulsing inside a kaleidoscopic array of filter colors and moving mattes, commences with door-pounding and a voice—"Lucifer!" It is the first of many fragments from a 1925 puppet play—Michel de Ghelderode's *Duvelor ou la Farce du Diable vieux* (*Duvelor, or the Farce of the Old Devil*). Though he never attended a show there, Beavers became aware of marionette drama via the Théâtre Royal de Toone in Brussels. "At the center of the film is . . . Duvelor, who is a small devil waiting to give up his human existence—with which he's bored—to return to Hell," Beavers told P. Adams Sitney.[12]

A set of adult faces encircles Beavers's solitary habitat—intrusive and threatening psychic objects, figures of authority. Beavers cast Jacques Ledoux and René Micha as well as Dimitri Balachoff, film critic and director of Meuter-Titra film laboratory in Brussels (where *Winged Dialogue* was edited and spliced), and Gisèle Frumkin, an art collector and New American Cinema supporter, in these roles—friends and figures in new social and professional worlds whose approval he might need. He incorporated brief shots of a military parade in Brussels to highlight "the place of the soldier in society as a foil to the homosexual youth."

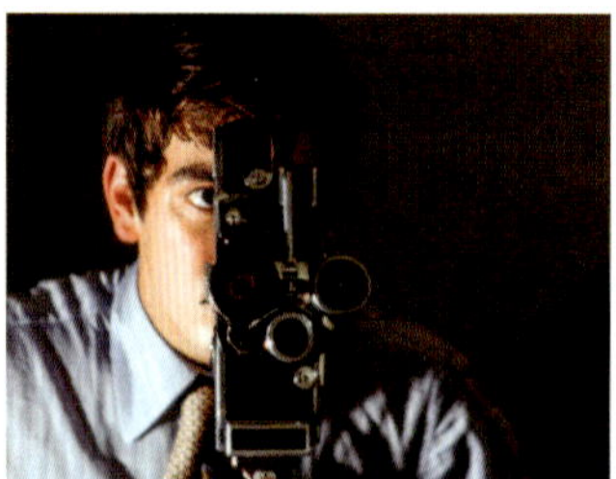

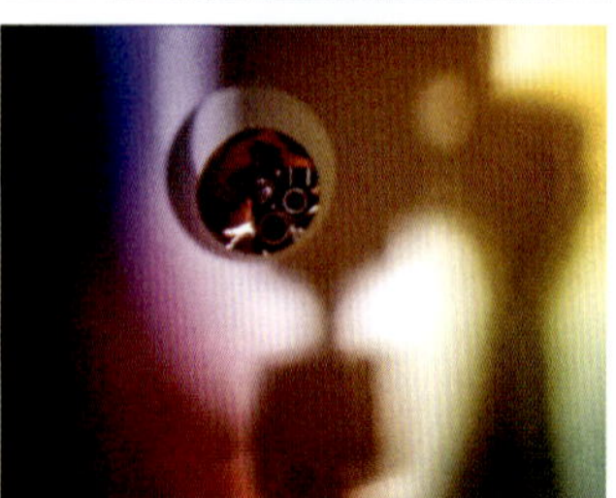

### Segment 1: "Two Relatives," Zurich[13]

A mise en abyme circle study influenced by matte use in *Plan of Brussels*. Beavers shoots himself in a mirror as he manipulates sheets of Bristol paper (they function as oversized mattes, with central circular cut-outs) in front of his camera. "It's a play on the circle of the lens and the circle of the matte as two relatives," he said. An ABAB structure cuts between Beavers at camera and the resulting dance of shapes. When a diffuse multicolor veil coats the image, it results from a four-quadrant filter (red, blue, yellow, green) having been placed in the slot between prism and lens. "When you see distinct lines between filter colors in a shot, you know I'm using the compendium. When the filter is behind the lens, the colors will inherently be out of focus. Because it's inside the camera, you get more variability in tone and other colors—that's what I liked about it," Beavers said.

**Segment 2: "On and Through," Zurich**
Pension window is image-generator: Beavers shoots trees and sky through it and gathers other images (self-portraits, room interior) on its surface; sometimes the two-paned glass produces a double image. On a round table: mattes, compendium, compass, film strip, filter container, boxes of film, lens-cleaning tissue, lens cap, light meter. Beavers used a film stock suited for the pension room, turning some of the outdoor shots blue. The blinking shot alternation was inspired by Markopoulos.

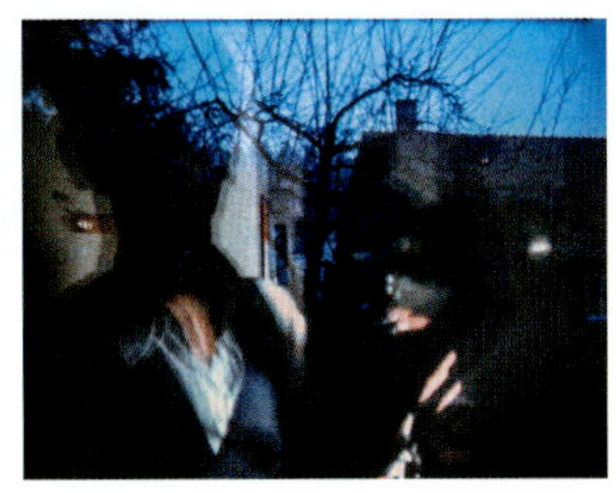

**Segment 3: "Creased Foil," Zurich**
Color (especially pink and blue), light shapes, and the filmmaker's own image move across intercut shots as Beavers explores reflective surfaces at close scale: creased foil (filter-wrapping), magenta filter, film strip. Shots of materials alternate with the tree of the last segment, now snow-covered, and freeze frames from the preceding segments appear in the compendium.

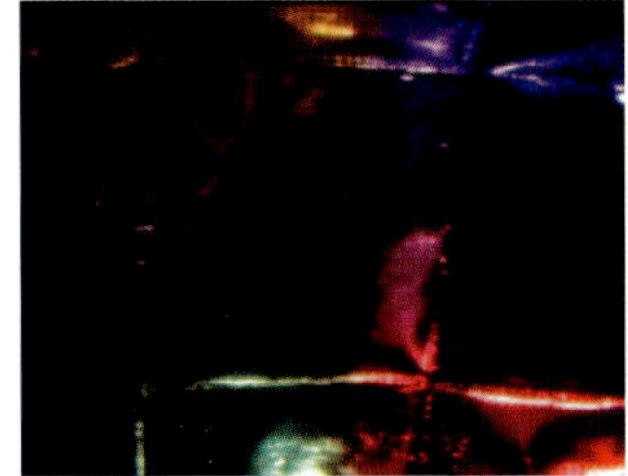

**Segment 4: "He's the source of this light," Zurich**
Shot under shifting light conditions, Markopoulos holds a small mirror; it catches alternating reflections of each man (sometimes Markopoulos's hands appear to hold Beavers's face). "I'm playing with the idea of putting one image inside another," Beavers said. "There's also the idea that he [Markopoulos] is the source of this light." Landscape pans were shot on a brief trip to Tunis.[14]

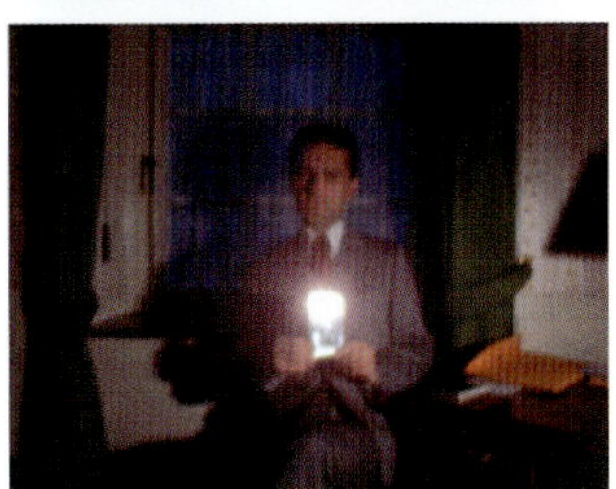

**Segment 5: "Winter Depressive," Zurich**
Intercut imagery of pension suite and a snowy Dolder hillside. Interior details—hook, doorknob—are graphic foci as Beavers dons a coat and prepares to leave; outside, he walks along a forest path, a lone figure reminiscent of a Markopoulos film character. "It's more psychological than the previous segments," Beavers said. "Somewhat surreal and winter depressive."

**Segment 6: "Pleats," Zurich**
Shots of a lampshade's interior, a light bulb at its center, alternate with images of a detached lens in Beavers's hands. He uses the lens to focus an image of the shade on a piece of paper. His face appears upside down and right side up on the lens surface (its curve produces a double image). Inside the lens, the iris—its fan form a cousin of the pleated lampshade—is visible.

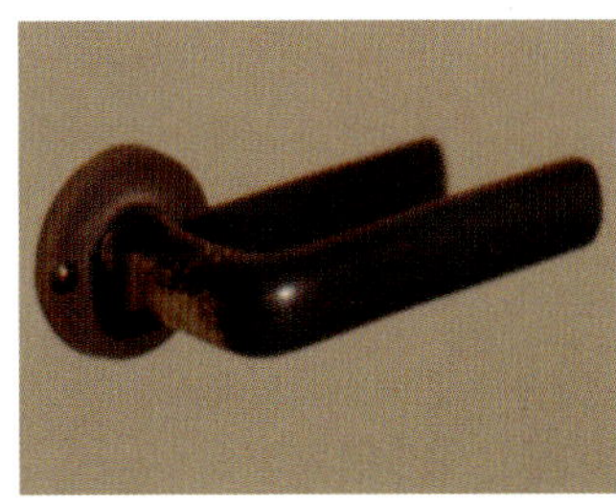

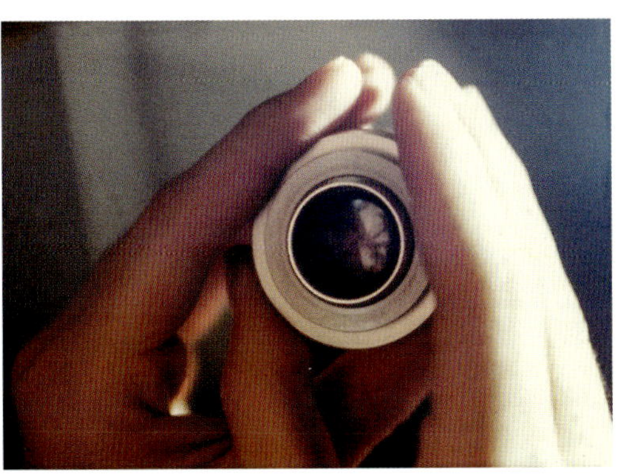

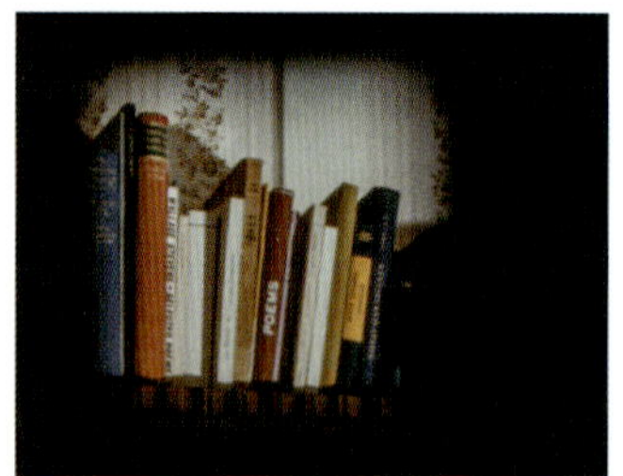

## Segment 7: "Matte-Type," Zurich

Markopoulos types in the corner of a metallic-wallpapered pension room. Fast cutting with black mattes mimics typing keys and produces various image-containing boxes and wipes. The segment reveals a carousel of domestic details: airmail envelope, wooden shoe tree, pink flowers, phone book, gold chandelier, pale blue shutters, a row of books, Markopoulos on the telephone, Beavers in a mirror.

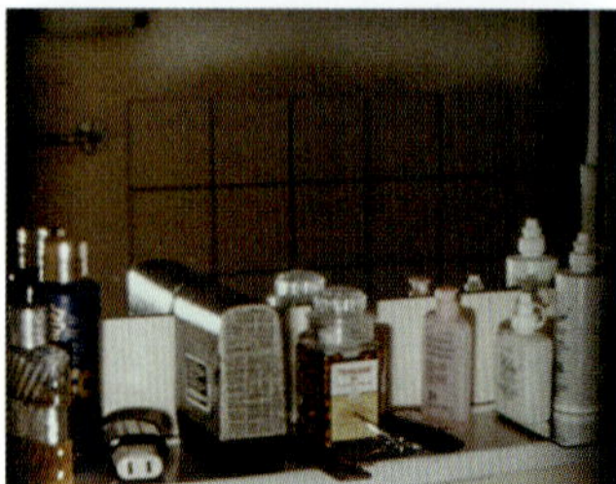

## Segment 8: "Intimate Distance," Zurich

A bathroom study. Chrome, tile, and skin alternate: Beavers intercuts environmental details (toiletries, pills, wall) with close-ups of his own penis and actions (he shaves, fills a water glass, opens his mouth). "The use of mattes is very formal but the filming of the person is quite intimate," Beavers said. "I was thinking about the matte in relation to the mouth, about the idea of ingestion as well as angst about health and sexuality."

## *The Count of Days* (1969/2001)

In Zurich, a middle-aged man (played by Stefan Sadkowski) and a young man and woman are connected by unspecified erotic conflict. Symbolic objects (shoes, rumpled underwear, a dissected rat, and surgical instruments) are divided, framed, and blocked by square mattes. Sadkowski, a Zurich-based writer, reads fragments from his own text, *Petermann verließ den Hinterhof*, which functions as a graphic element.

A psychoanalytic climate surrounds *The Count of Days*. "I came to the film via an interest in Jung," Beavers said. Beavers sought out an analyst at the Zurich Jung Institute, but she saw that his questions were aesthetically motivated and ended the dialogue. "Maybe you should have analysis," she advised. Beavers's interest in psychic, bodily, and filmic surgery produced the rat imagery—as did his struggle to read the German version of Sigmund Freud's 1909 "Rat Man" case study.[15]

Beavers discovered Sadkowski through the Swiss filmmaker HHK Schoenherr. "After *Plan of Brussels*, I grew wary of relying on young beautiful boys and turned to the middle-aged protagonists of *The Count of Days* and *Palinode*." A Polish Jew without a Swiss passport, Sadkowski was an outsider. "He and his brother, a painter, couldn't leave the canton of Zurich. He was essentially a refugee. I had sympathy for him," Beavers said.

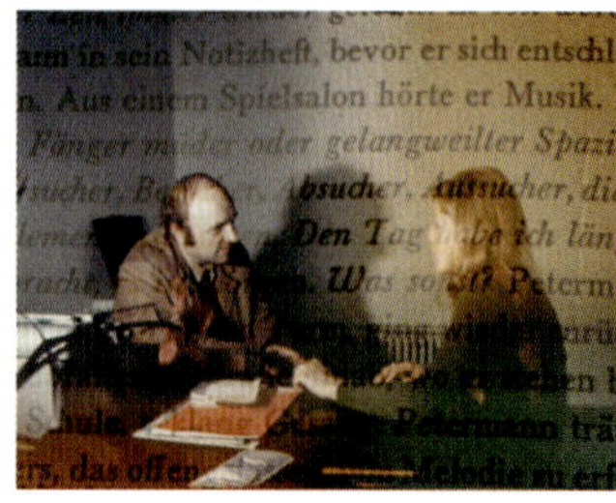

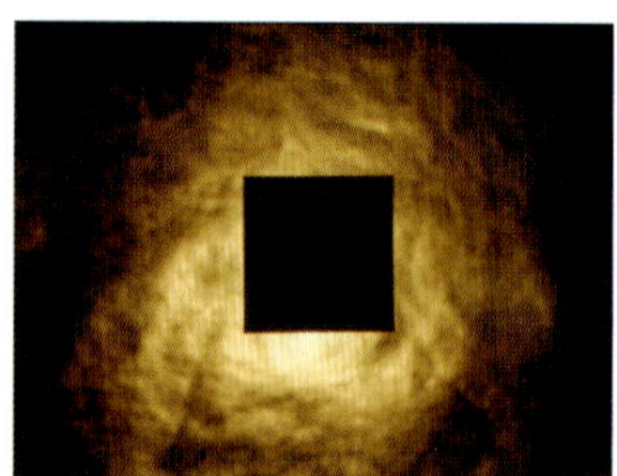

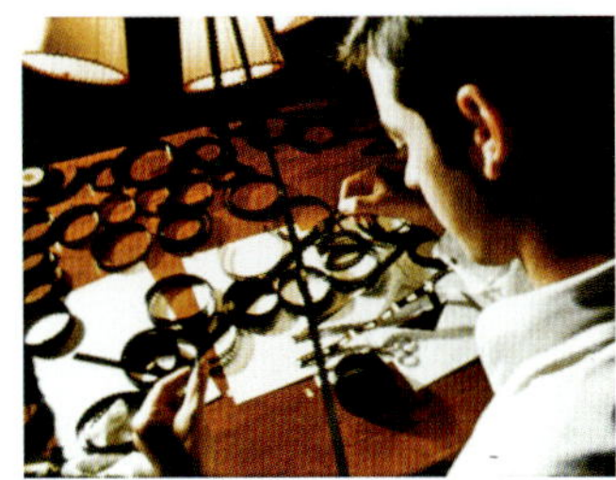

**Segment 9: "Paper Tape," Orselina, Switzerland**
Scenes of *The Count of Days* edit—shot selection, tabletop of film-strip circles—are intercut with images from the film. Beavers tapes shots together with masking tape, leaving an extra frame at each end so that a negative cutter could subsequently make a splice. "We were paying female technicians at the lab to splice [physically join the edited film] at that point," he explained. "But as we had less and less money, I realized I had to learn how to splice myself."

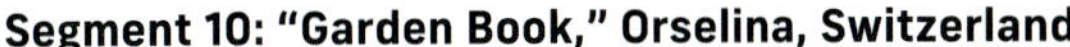

**Segment 10: "Garden Book," Orselina, Switzerland**
A vegetal study on the grounds of a rented house. Beavers constrained his filter use in accordance with the lush green surrounds. Botanical details—shaking palm fronds, undulating leaf edges—join shots of Markopoulos lying on a white sheet in white underwear, reading and framed by flowers.

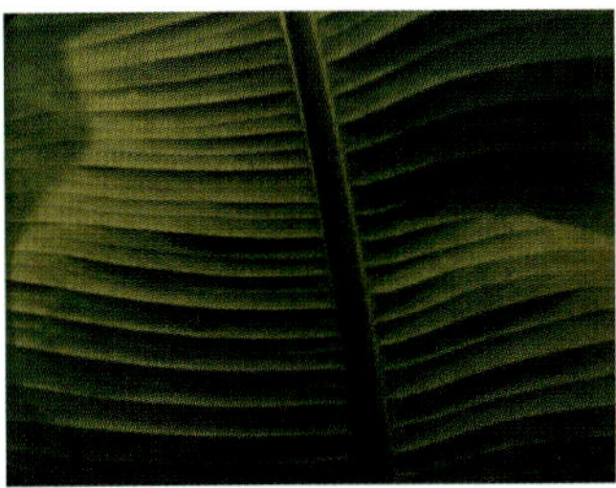

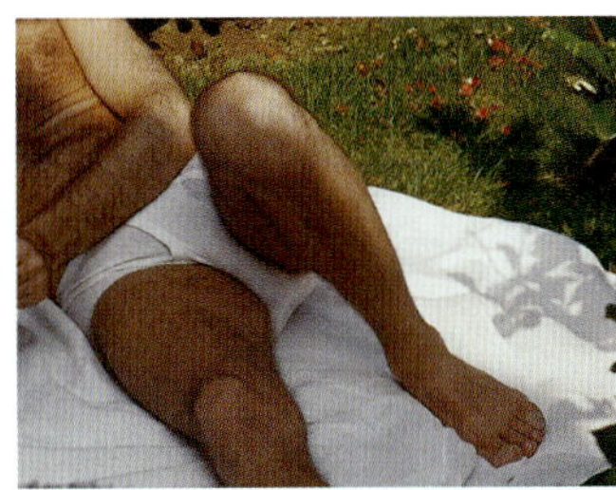

**Segment 11: "Picture Postcard," Locarno, Switzerland**
At a cafe table, Beavers and his materials: Locarno postcards, black matte (*The Count of Days* square) fixed to a glass plate. His views (port, crosswalk, tabletop) morph as he slides the plate into his compendium and changes the exposure. Another matte, hinged to one compendium side, fully blocks his view.

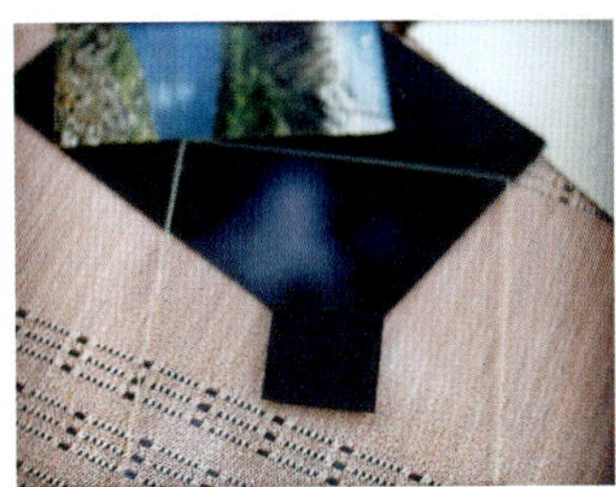

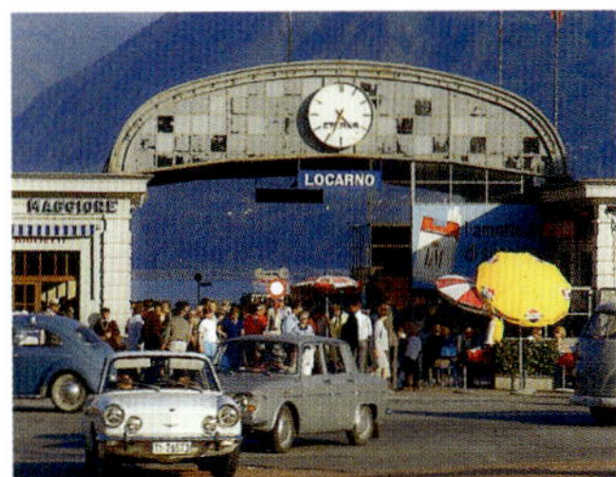


**Segment 12: "Disappearance," Zurich**
A combined pension room portrait/self-portrait structured by the same sliding-in-compendium matte strategy as the previous segment. Beavers turns the light on and off, causing his own image to disappear. In the final shot, the mirror reveals Beavers at his tripod and Markopoulos typing.

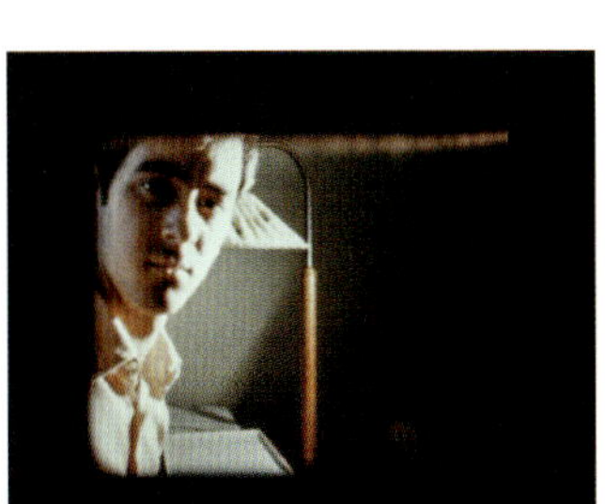

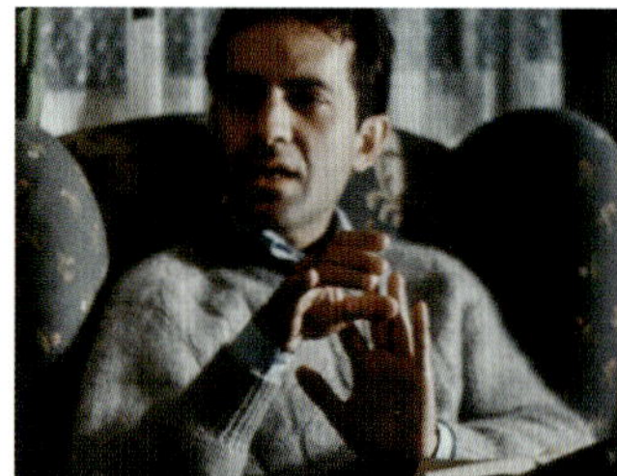

**Segment 13: "Visitors," Zurich**
Swiss train views intercut with pension room socializing scenes (Markopoulos reads and gesticulates, talks to Tom Chomont) and shots of materials connected to the making of *The Count of Days*—Beavers's notes and a sixteen-square color filter grid. When the same filter grid is placed inside the camera, images of Chomont are washed in pale color.

**Segment 14: "*Lysis* Redux," Zurich**
Shots from Markopoulos's *Lysis* (1948) (pillow, oranges, embroidered red velvet, photograph of Markopoulos as a boy), used in the order in which they appear in the original film, are intercut with Beavers's filter-drenched shots of Markopoulos sleeping. Beavers transforms *Lysis*—which he considers "an autobiography of Gregory"—into his own Markopoulos portrait.

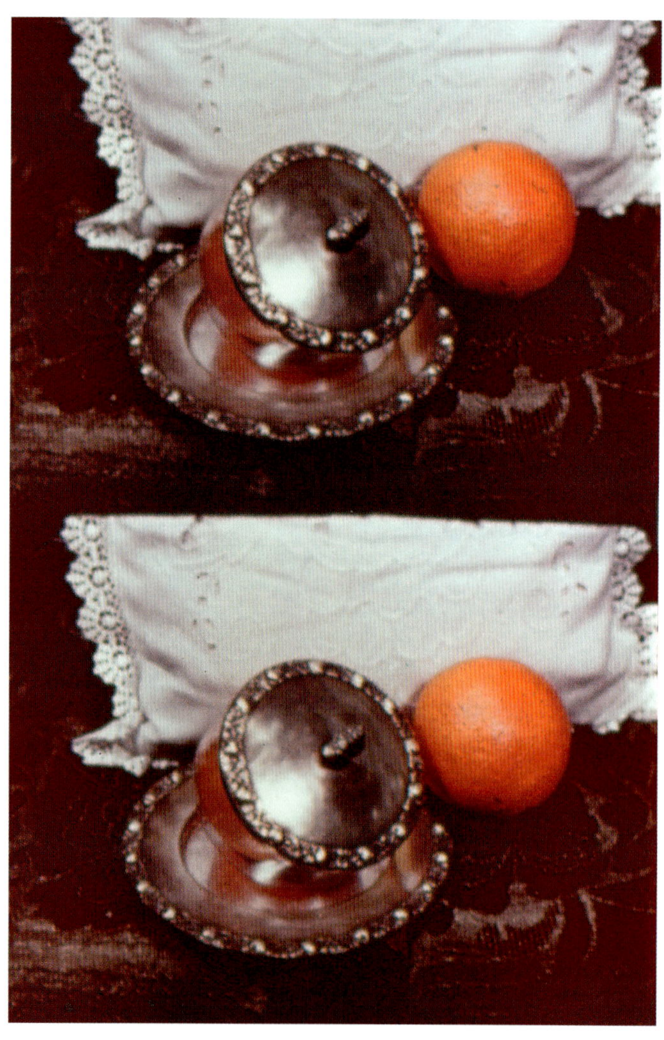

**_Palinode_ (1970/2001)**

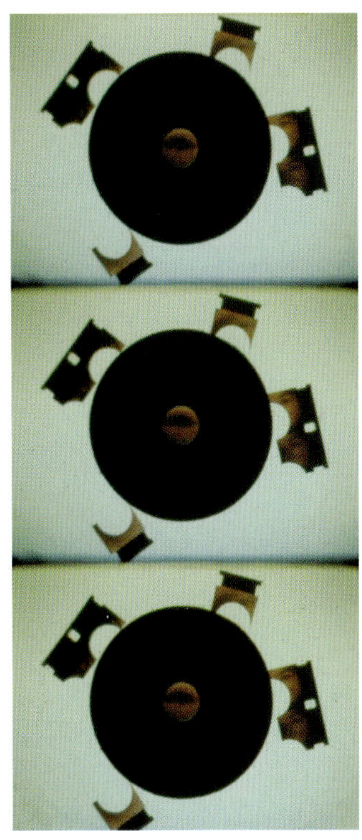

In Zurich, a male singer (Derrick Olsen, again discovered via Schoenherr) dines, shops in the Altstadt, rides in a taxi; a young girl (Patricia Walter) sometimes accompanies him. The film was inspired by Balthus's painting *Joan Miró and His Daughter Dolores* (1938)—the young girl more solid-looking than her father; the blank-stared figures glued together for life. "The singer represents a kind of unlived life," Beavers said.

Treatment by circular mattes, vertically striped filters, and focal change produces images that grow and shrink, blur and clarify. Beavers planned for a synchronized vocal sequence; instead voice manifests in fragments of Swiss composer Wladimir Vogel's 1930 *Wagadu*—one of his "drama-oratorios" that hybridize song and speech—and in close-ups of Olsen's open singing mouth (another circle). Mandala-like collages of mattes and hole-punched film frames enhance the motif.

Moscow-born Vogel had fled Germany after the Nazis deemed him a "degenerate artist"; in the 1940s his noncitizenship in Switzerland limited his ability to work. Beavers's own alienation was psychological. "I was almost lost. I had no connections to Zurich. I didn't know anything about the culture; I was just there."

**Segment 15: "_Palinode_ Host," Zurich**

Beavers hosts a *Palinode*-making portrait: production materials treated as sculpture and shots from the film rotate. Via rack focus, Beavers draws dimensions of his present-tense environment in and out of view; the blue-and-yellow vertically striped *Palinode* filter gives way to the space of the pension room.

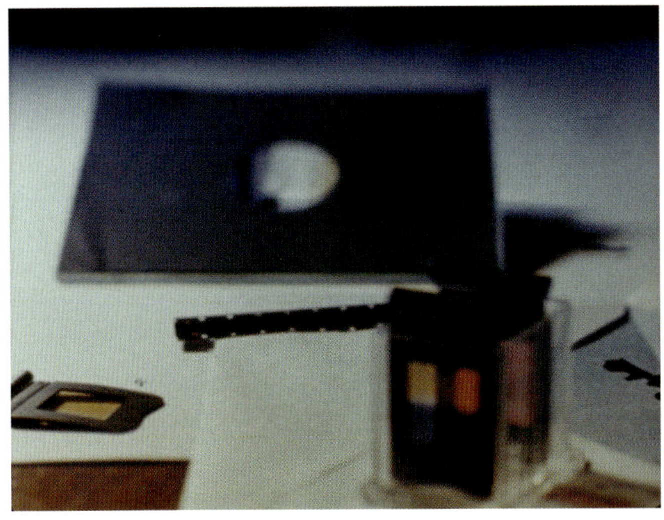

**Segment 16: "Turret Turn," Berlin**
Beavers's first experiment with what will become a signature move: he turns his lens turret (changing from one of three lenses to the next) *while* shooting Markopoulos. "I've chosen the composition for one of the lenses, but the other compositions are by chance," he said. By shooting into two mirrors (an angled three-way and a single pane), Beavers also reveals images of himself at work.

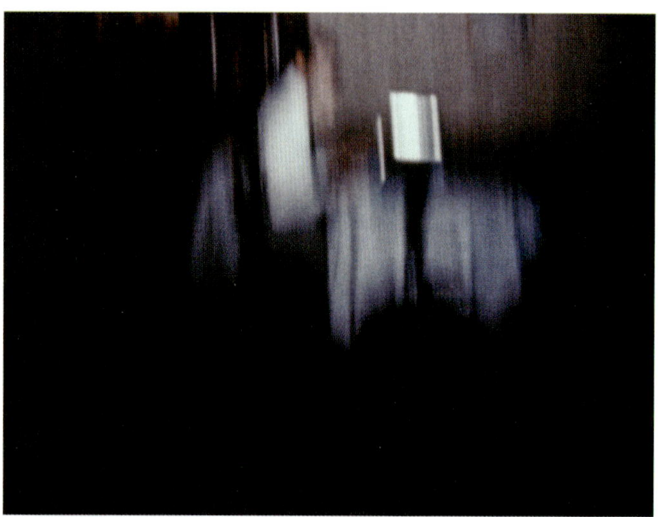

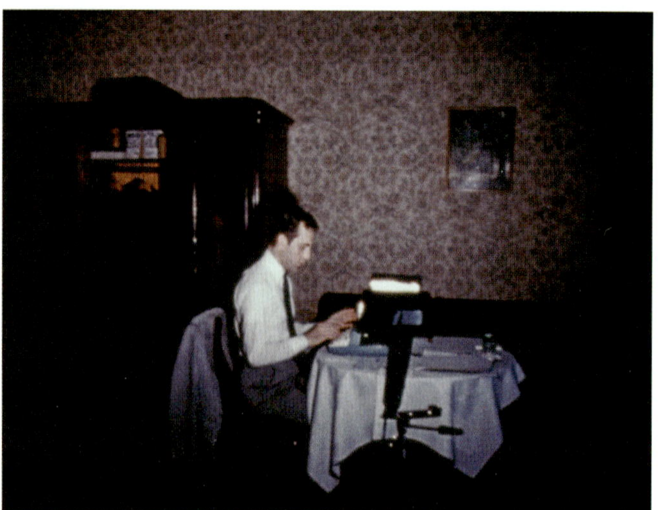

### ***Diminished Frame* (1970/2001)**

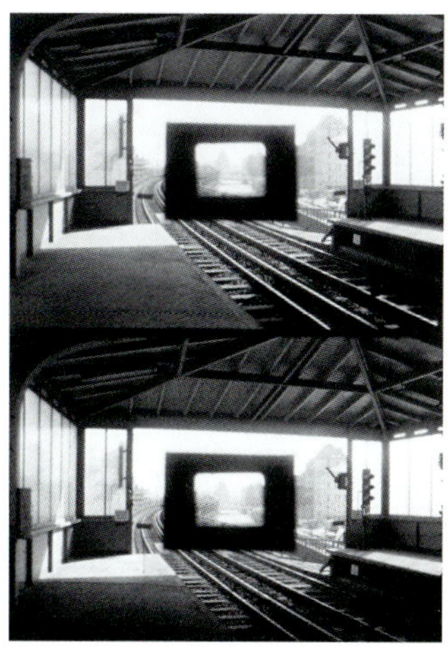

Beavers spent the winter of 1969–1970 in Berlin through a German Academic Exchange Service (DAAD) grant. "I didn't speak the language, it was winter, and Gregory was very unhappy there. We stayed only three of the six fellowship months. But I was determined: 'I will make a film there.'"

The title references both apparatus work and the postwar city: "Berlin was in a diminished frame when I first encountered it," Beavers said. The film transits between color and black-and-white and between the compendium space and spaces of the city's past. "Each location is intercut with a different filter combination I decided was appropriate for it. Some locations were chosen knowingly as I searched for the war's aftermath [Reichstag, former Gestapo headquarters], others [U-Bahn stations, Kaffe Schiller, Kurfürstendamm] were connected to my everyday life. But my attitude is that history is always there." The shape of a Maltese cross on an exposed building firewall signifies its former connection to other structures, now destroyed.

Sound elements conjure the Nazi past—crackling fire, archival "Sieg Heil" cries, swarming bees—and vocalize the filmmaker's actions: dragging a glass plate through the compendium, changing focus.

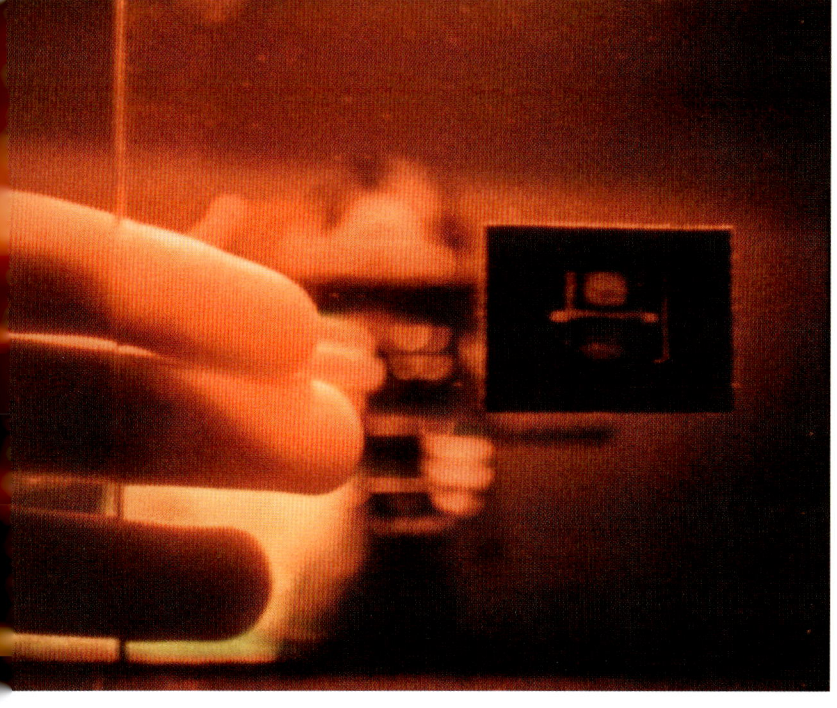

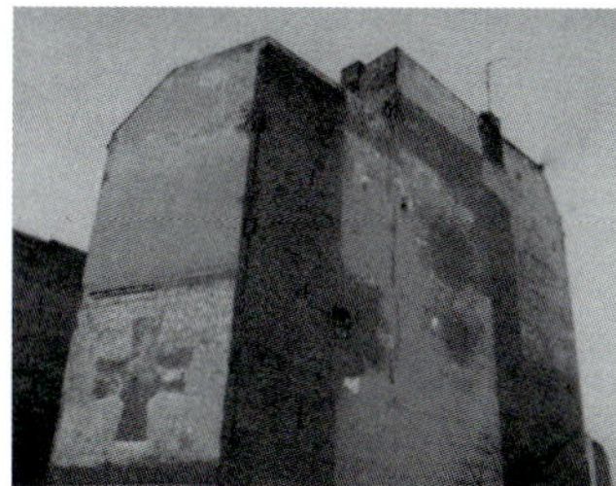

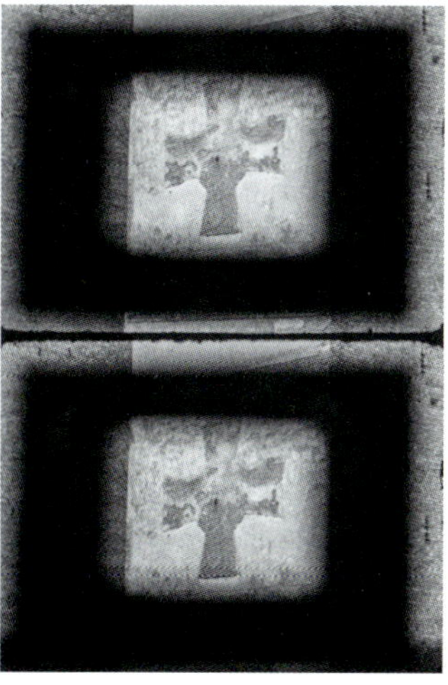

**Segment 17: "Climate Contrast," Swiss Alps and Kos, Greece**
Contrasting climates and colors are unified by the rectangular *Diminished Frame* matte as it moves in and out of focus. Snowy black-and-white Alpine landscapes accompany Beavers and Markopoulos on a moving train. On the island of Kos, views of a donkey, a mosque, and an old woman are enhanced by a yellow/blue filter combination.

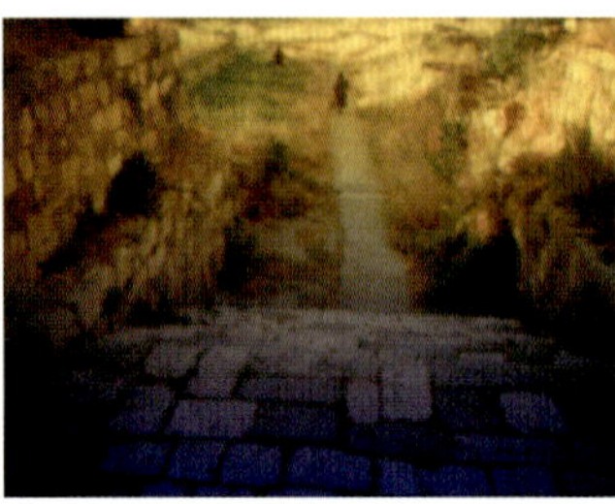

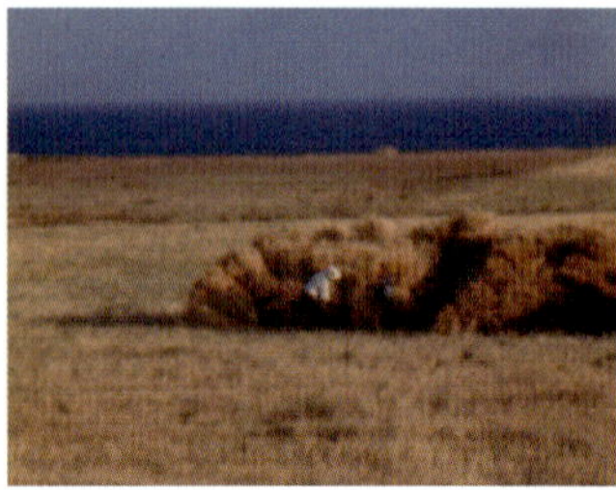

**Segment 18: "16-Grid," Kos, Greece**
Brief glimpses of Kos life organized around a window and the square matte and sixteen-color filter grid of *Still Light* (Beavers had already shot the first part of the film). Outside, Markopoulos talks to the landlady, rides a bicycle; inside, a Beavers self-portrait.

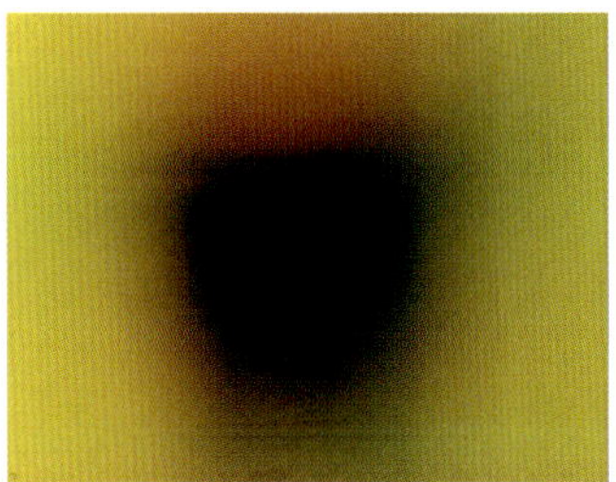

**Segment 19: "Kafka + Cup," Orselina, Switzerland**
Sun-dappled, nearly naked Beavers drinks tea and reads *The Diaries of Franz Kafka, 1910–23* on a yellow chaise lounge. The teacup is graphic center in increasingly close shots of concentric circles (liquid/cup/saucer) as the tea (its yellow matches the chair) disappears. "It's definitely someone looking at me and not the way I look at myself," Beavers said.

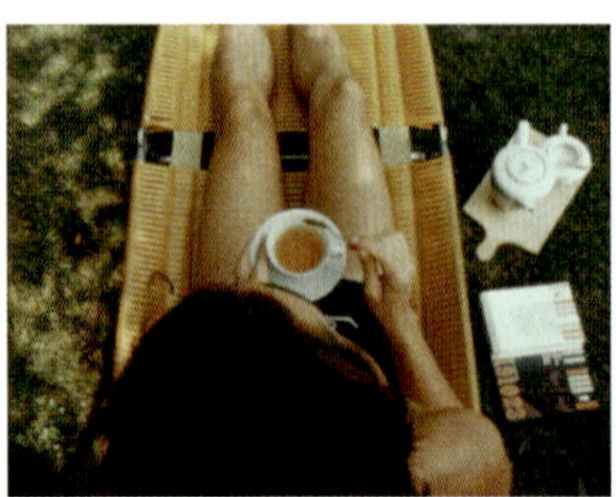

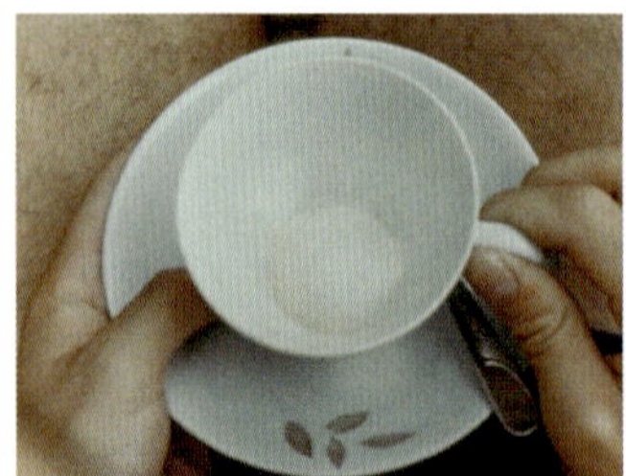

**_Still Light_, part 1 (1970/2001)**
Close-ups of Ron Krueck (a young architect, the partner of curator A. James Speyer, whom Markopoulos knew from Chicago) against the rocky Hydra landscape. Beavers explores Krueck's face as a constellation of light points in shifting focal dialogue with background elements and saturated, jewel-toned scrims of filter color. The sounds of water, cicadas, and church bells overlap. "I was aware of the Color Field painters but I wasn't consciously thinking about Rothko or Newman," Beavers said.

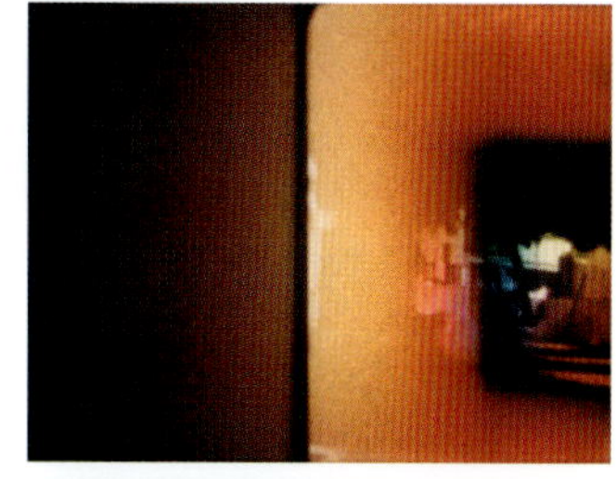

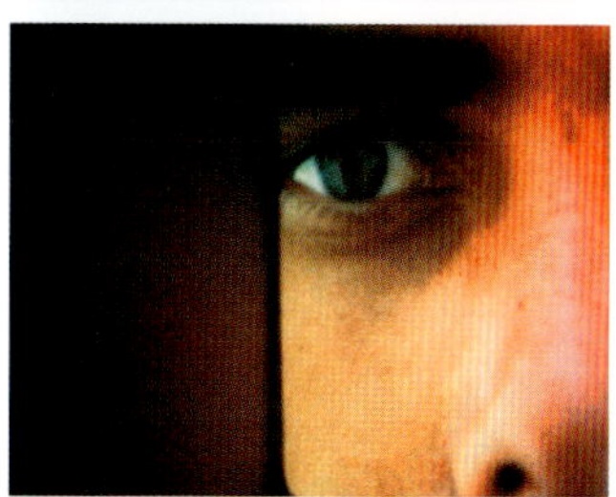

**Segment 20: "Circles of Hydra," Disentis, Switzerland**
Hydra *Still Light* imagery intercut with details of Beavers editing and splicing the film in Disentis. The final image of the *Segments*: Krueck's extended hand (palm open, seen through the *Still Light* filter grid) comes into focus: "my hand outstretched."[16]

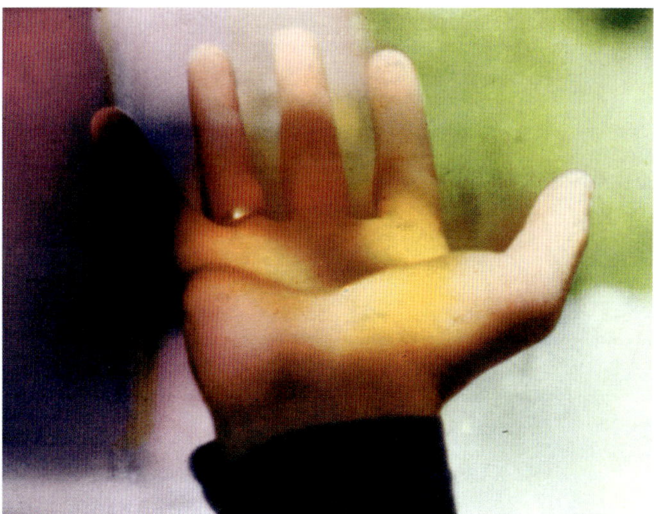

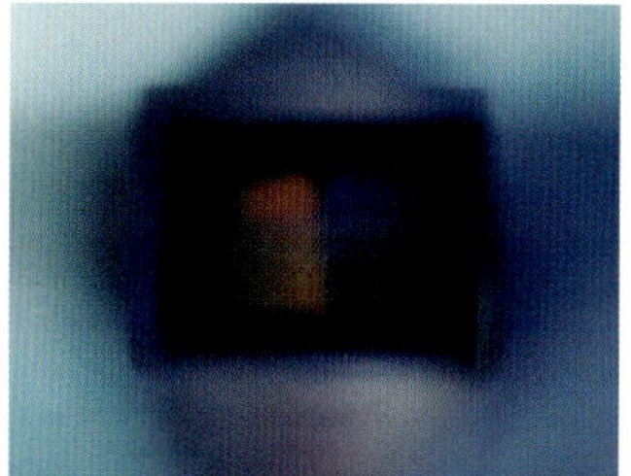

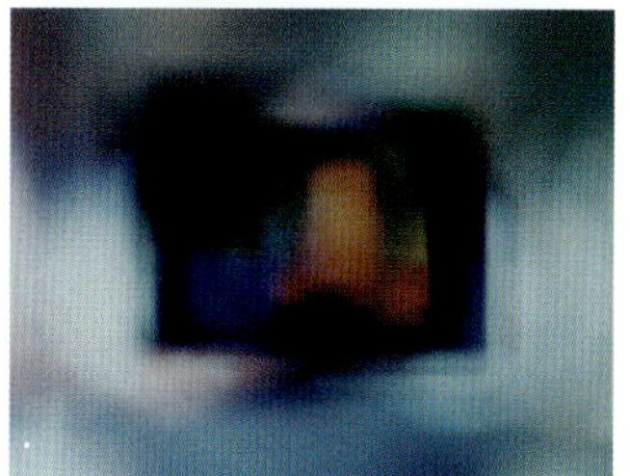

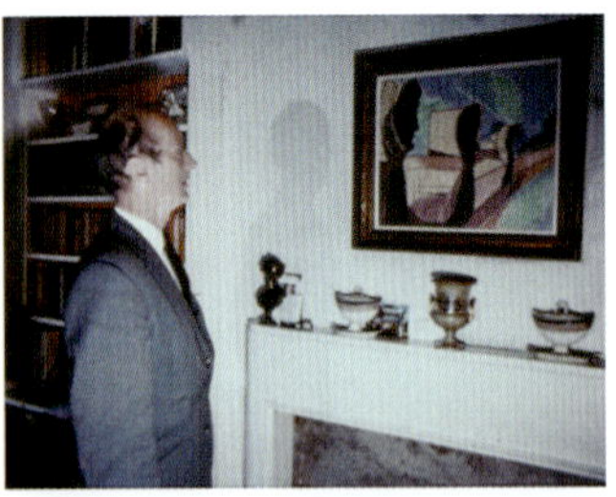
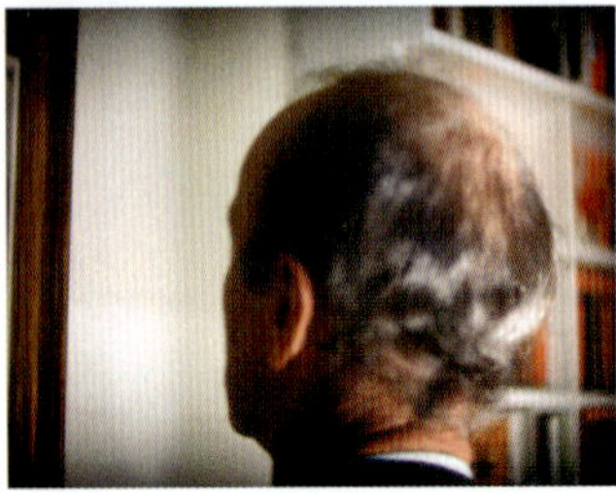
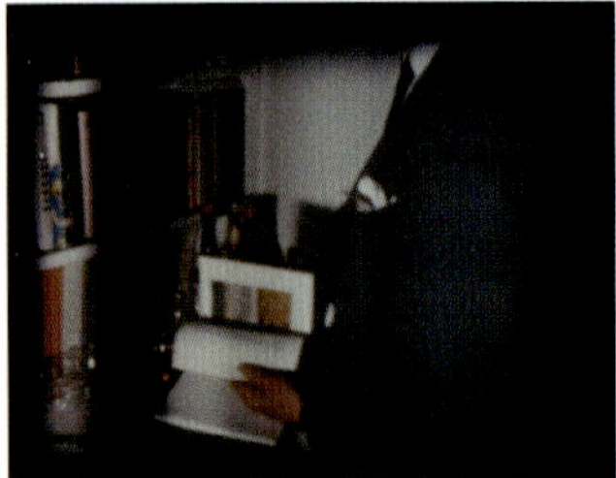
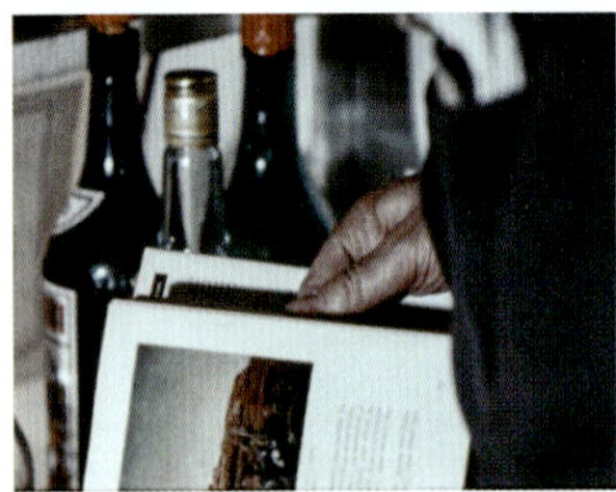

***Still Light*, part 2 (1970/2001)**

Following the first part of *Still Light*—a speech-free encounter between actor and filmmaker, a fluctuating space of male beauty and color abstraction fused by Greek light—its foil: part two features *Observer* art critic Nigel Gosling in his London apartment as he pontificates (via voiceover) on filmic medium specificity.[17] Gosling was a new contact: after his son's enthusiastic report on seeing *The Illiac Passion* (1964–1967) at Knokke-le-Zoute in 1967, Gosling invited Markopoulos to screen the film in London for Greek stage designer Nicholas Georgiadis, German composer Hans Werner Henze, and Russian ballet dancer and choreographer Rudolf Nureyev (with whom Gosling hoped Markopoulos might make a film).

Beavers comes close to satirizing Gosling in *Still Light*—professional writer in a legible bourgeois space (objects on fireplace mantle, rows of books, framed paintings, leather chair, television set) who sets imaginative limits on film. In a particularly Marshall McLuhan-esque moment, Gosling explains the problem with film—what it is *not*—by invoking ideals of painting and literature. "[There's] a very comfortable relaxed feeling . . . when you're reading a book beside your own fireside, if you have a fireside . . . and then the telephone rings and you answer it and you go on reading and you pull the curtain and then you go on reading. Somehow you're not cut off from your ordinary life." In contrast, he says, the film image is "a very artificial and pre-prepared thing" that curtails freedom: "It's an image which I am presented, which I am fixed by." As he speaks, Gosling gazes at an abstract painting and flips through a heavy art book with color plates. Shots from part one, projected on a corner wall of his living room, recur: film is "in the corner" according to the media hierarchy Gosling (a cinephile) unfurls in his remarks.[18]

Beavers's film defies Gosling's opposition: it doesn't "fix." *Still Light* is made of Hydra and London, chromatic ecstasy, and art world criticism. Lyricism trumps the dyad by incorporating the discursive as one of its elements. Hydra sounds (cicadas, bells) and the intermittent sound of fluttering pages recur as Gosling speaks; the elements of part one freely move across the border into part two—just as Gosling's reading "goes on" even when the phone rings and the scene changes.

In 1970, in Florence, two-sided *Still Light* gave way to a many-paged film. That year, Beavers stopped making his monthly sketches, but the mental and material theater of the artist's studio—a readymade atmosphere in the *Segments*—bloomed into his most ambitious film to date.

## PART 2: A NOTE

### DRAWING AWAY

Modernist storytelling presents abstraction as an inevitable formal choice, but the development of Markopoulos's creative economy was consistently advanced by material problems—and by a refusal to let others (people/timetables/institutions) thwart progress. When he was no longer able to materialize his film *Serenity*, Markopoulos converted the lost project into text, publishing *Quest for Serenity*, excerpted from his notebooks about the film's making, through the Film-Makers' Cinematheque in 1965. When Paul Kilb didn't show up to a *Twice a Man* recording session in 1963, Markopoulos directed his costar, Olympia Dukakis, to read all the dialogue parts herself as a monologue, and later instructed the lab to remove certain syllables, thus producing the film's soundscape of linguistic abstraction. Ever-increasing economy—the continuous shot broken up, the in-camera dialect of single frames, the ultimate disavowal of printing, distribution, and screening as well as titles, sound, and dialogue—nurtured an esoteric approach to art-making and a speculative philosophy of film.

Abstraction is a drawing-away (Latin *abs-* [away] + *trahō* [to pull, draw]), and the effort of ongoing removal leaves lines—language forms—behind. Markopoulos had been writing all along, but the chronically futuristic nature of the Temenos vision, combined with the complete cessation of participation in film culture, put fresh pressures on writing. The word became paramount; Markopoulos's writing functioned as primary materialization of idea. He hated the modern, but he conducted himself like a conceptual artist. His Temenos rhetoric was frequently over the top, a mix of certainty and fantasy. "Past the gates of the Temenos, and upon the twin hills, the film spectator of the future will encounter the immeasurable works of Beavers and Markopoulos. On one hill will be *the space of Beavers*. On another hill there will be *the space of Markopoulos*. The spectres of distribution will have been vanquished," he wrote in 1972.[19] He envisioned built structures at the Temenos site—a screening space (later called the Amor, after Beavers's 1980 film) for his and Beavers's films, and an archive and library for the study of their work.[20] Film and writing were inseparable.

But before his Temenos conception had concretized, Markopoulos was already preparing his textual objects. In the fall of 1968, he brought all of his writings and films from Toledo to Zurich, and "binding mania" (Beavers's term) commenced. For the next two and a half decades, Markopoulos and Beavers sent their writings and most prized books to bookbinders (including Flügel in Basel and Duval in Paris) and deposited them in a walk-in bank vault (first in Bern, then in Basel): an archive-in-waiting. Today, at the Temenos Archive near Zurich, hundreds of color-coded volumes and handmade boxes—embossed with gold letters, covered in hand-painted paper, organized by distinct categories of thought and activity—line the shelves. Markopoulos's materials include *Ein Eidelweiss* (52 volumes of his journals from 1954 to 1992), *Cerberus* (30 volumes of correspondence from 1965 to 1992, including mimeographed copies of his outgoing letters), as well as film notes, scripts,

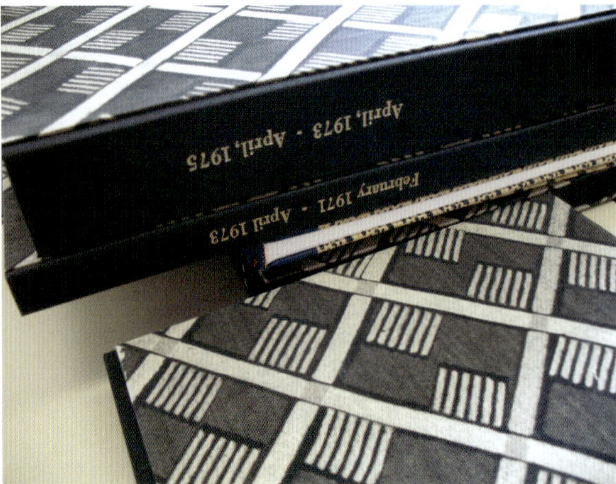


Boxed volumes of Beavers's film notes

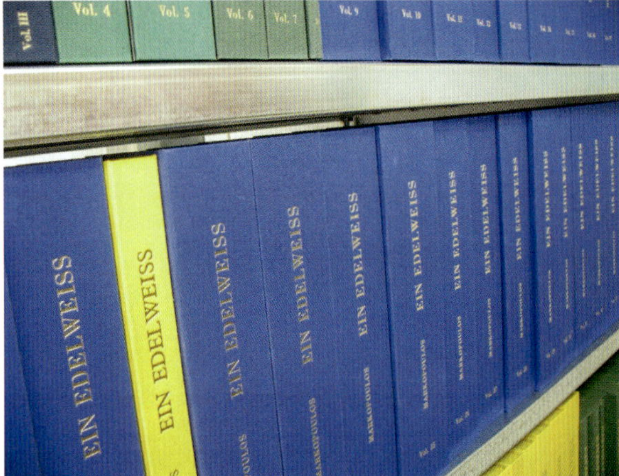


*Ein Eidelweiss*, Markopoulos's fifty-two-volume collection of journals, correspondence, and other materials

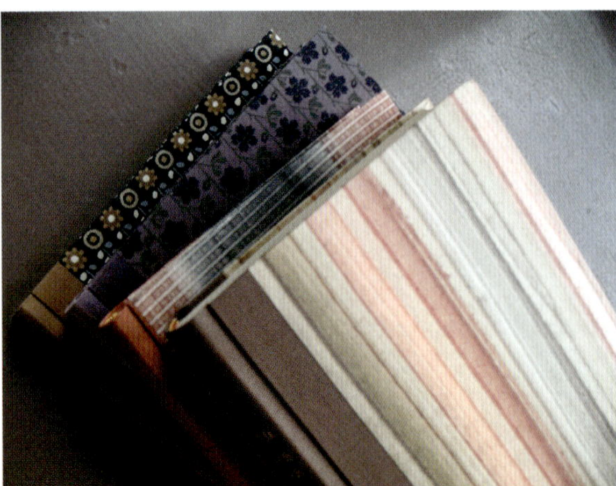

Hand-bound books of literature and philosophy

library research notes, and patron-seeking efforts. Even misunderstandings are archived; the booklet *Heracles* is subtitled *A Bibliography Containing the Marvelous Distortions of My Films as Reviewed in Books, Programs, Periodicals, and Newspapers During Thirty-Three Years: 1945–1978*. Notes for projects never realized are bound, as are invoices and debt collection notices. The scrupulous preservation impulse also left behind a transcript of non-economy: bills for customized Swiss galoshes, haircuts from Visconti's barber in Milan, bespoke Italian suits—and the bookbinding itself.

In the *Segments*, the central role of reading and writing economies in the Temenos household is evident: images of a mobile library (Kafka, Wallace Stevens, Stefan George, Max Beckmann); Markopoulos at his typewriter with airmail envelopes ("He was constantly looking for funds," Beavers said). For both filmmakers, writing was a stabilizing, portable site of home amid nonstop movement (Beavers's log of 1986 train travel: 111 trips). The Temenos Archive speaks both to the jointness of the Temenos project and to the distinctness of Beavers's textual economy. On his sparer side of the archive, five decades of his filming notes fit on one shelf.[21] As a teenager, Beavers had conceived of both his note-making method and his vision of the multivalent frame "against" Markopoulos's word/image economies. Beavers's notebooks are a log—not as personal narrative but as fact/act—of his own means of abstraction.

The note—method more than object, *writing* with fluidity intact—is emblematic of a heterogeneous textuality that marks Beavers's cinema: the embrace of textual encounter as film source (not "a film about *The Stones of Venice*" but a film that rewrites a reading of Ruskin), the essential attraction to book-as-image ("To bring a book into the film frame is to open possibilities," Beavers said, recalling his 1967 viewing of Carl Dreyer's 1932 *Vampyr*),[22] the refusal of textual stability via revision,[23] the performative enactment of language-making work. Moving lines—tailor's thread, bookbinder's string, candlewick, graffiti stroke, plant stem, leaf vein, split screen, scaffold seam, stonemason's mark, decorative Gothic incision, his own limbs shaped into spontaneous gesture—dart in and out of Beavers's films. They are traces of labor balanced between rigor and surrender, connective associative binding, drawing and painting by proxy, site of resonance among work done by film subject, maker, and spectator. Protolinguistic forms that materialize and transit the distances and discrepancies of analog film space, Beavers's lines—like his films—embody and provoke thought not opposed to, but *held in*, awareness.[24]

Soon after Beavers arrived in Athens in 1967, he noticed that his own "continuous line games"—the unconscious doodles he made during an evening phone call (chains, tendrils, spirals) matched the very patterns he saw on Mycenaean objects the next day at the National Archaeological Museum. "Geometric decoration—a sensation in the movement of the hand. The object when completed is transformed," he wrote. Beavers's notes are an extension of his "continuous line games," a form of mark-making that will indirectly "transform" his own artwork.

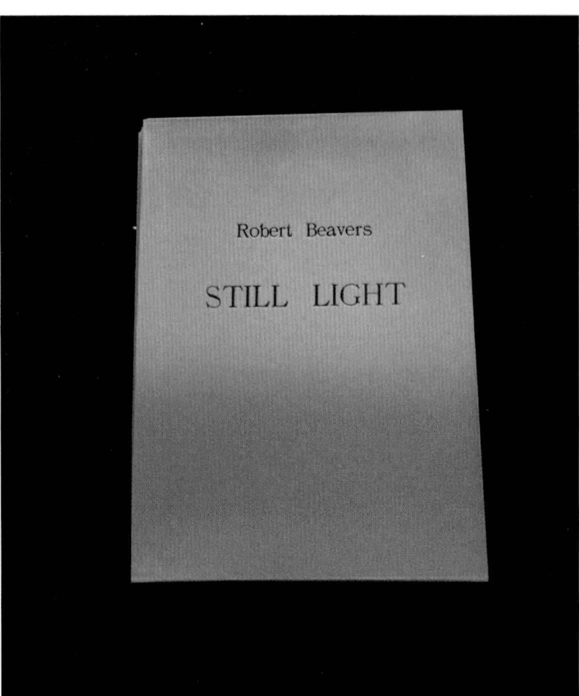


Beavers's 1971 Temenos imprint publication *Still Light: Film Notes & Plates*

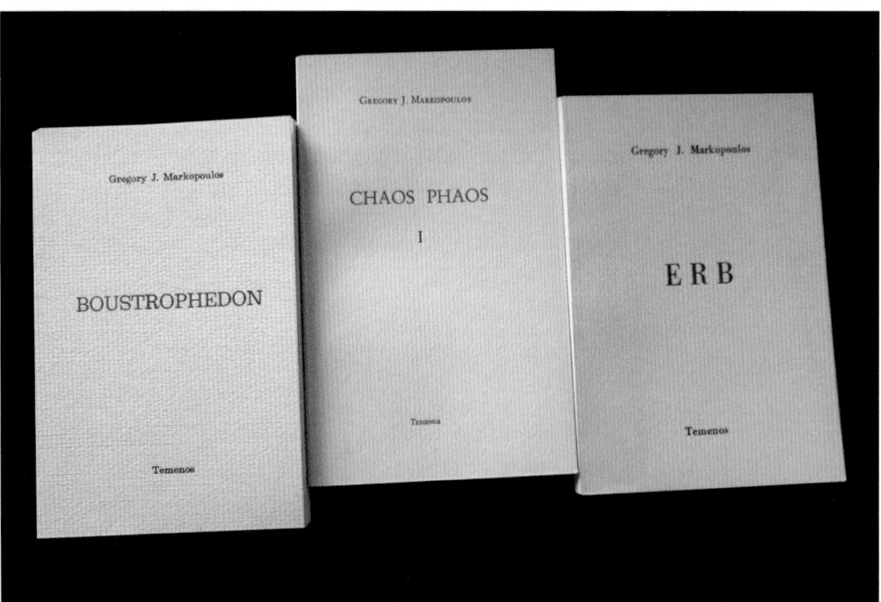


Temenos imprint publications by Markopoulos: *Boustrophedon* (1977), *Chaos Phaos*, Vol. I (1971), *ERB* (1975)

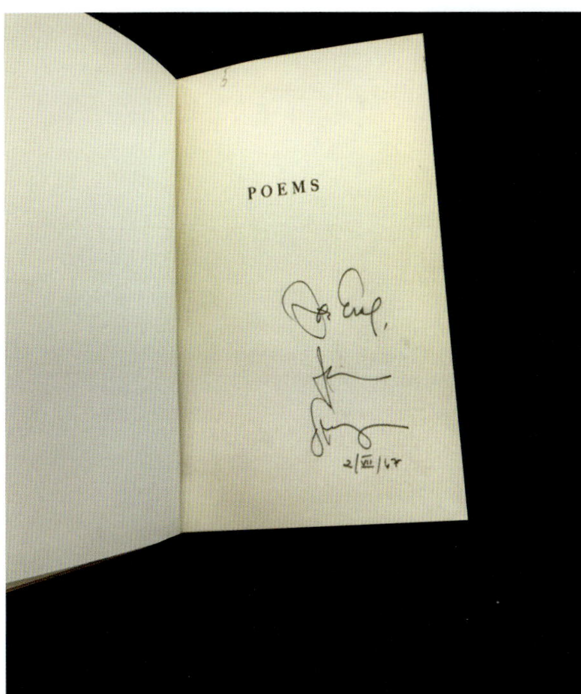


Markopoulos's *Poems*, published by Film Culture in 1964, inscribed to Beavers

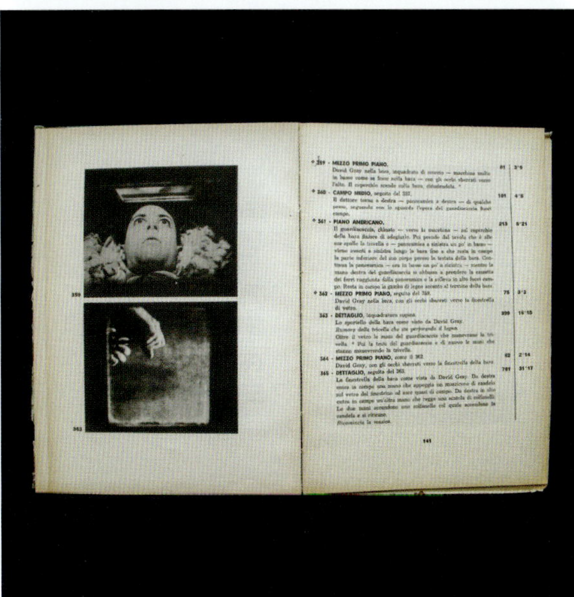

Pages from Beavers's copy of *Carl Theodor Dreyer / Vampyr, L'Étrange Aventure De David Gray*, ed. Aldo Buzzi and Bianca Lattuada (Milan: Poligono Società Editrice, 1948), purchased in 1967

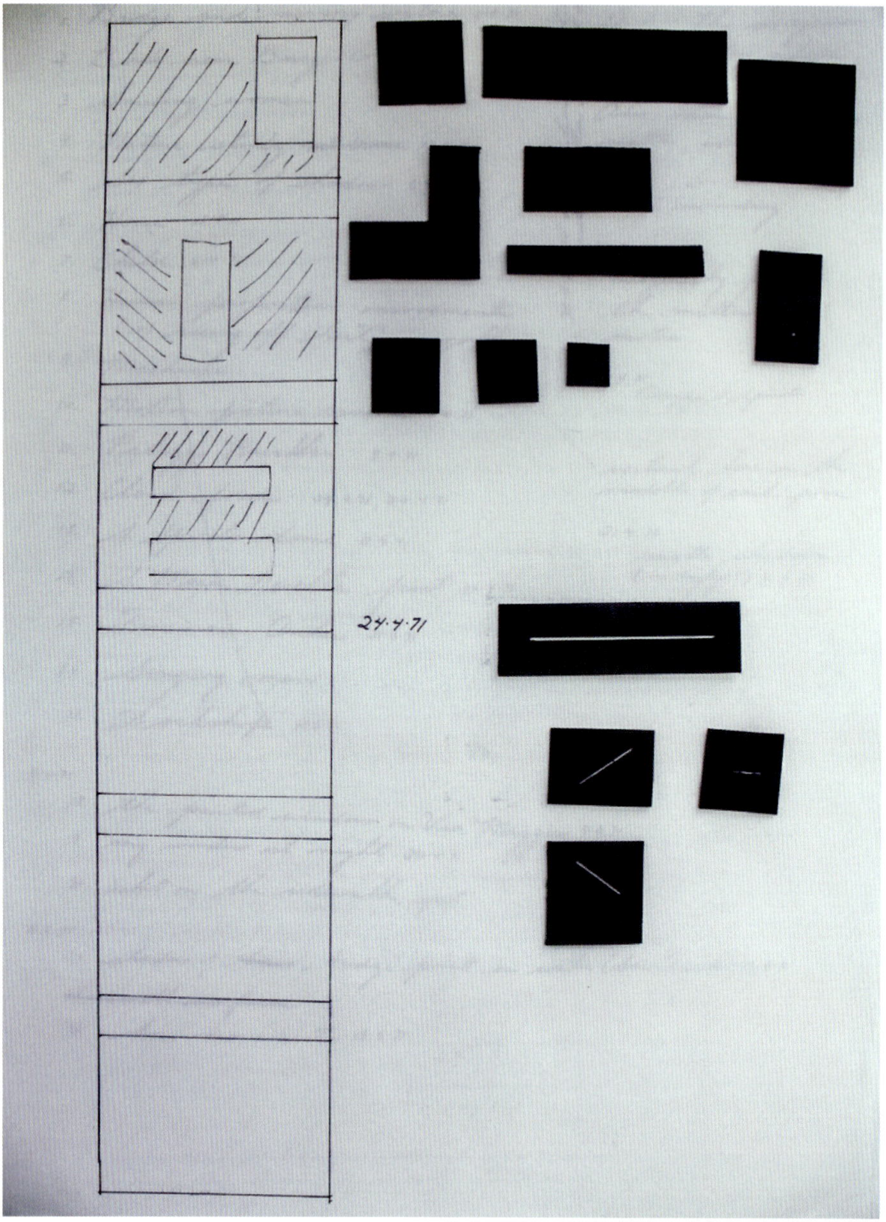

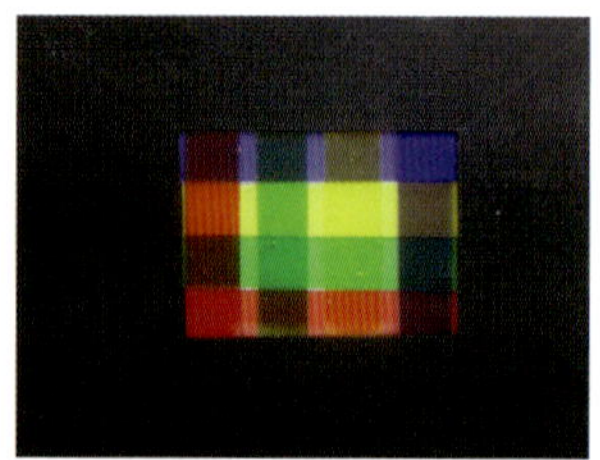

*From the Notebook of . . .* notebook page with mattes used in the film

*Still Light* filter grid

*Work Done* notebook page with filters used in the film

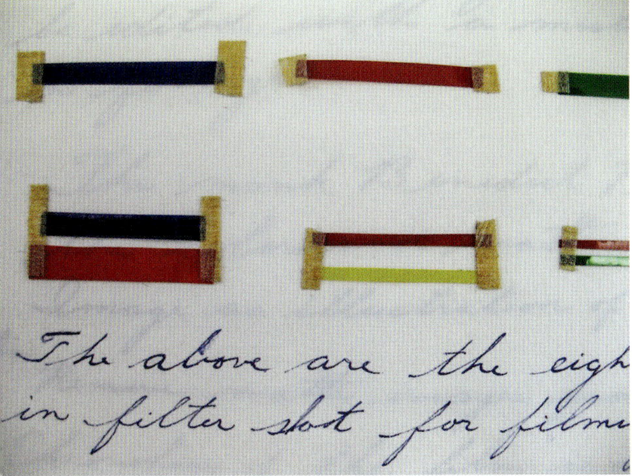


*From the Notebook of . . .* notebook page with filters used in the film

*The Painting* notebook page detail

Divine arrows:

Each thought is like an arrow—that in the dark illuminates an object by forcing it.

Undated note

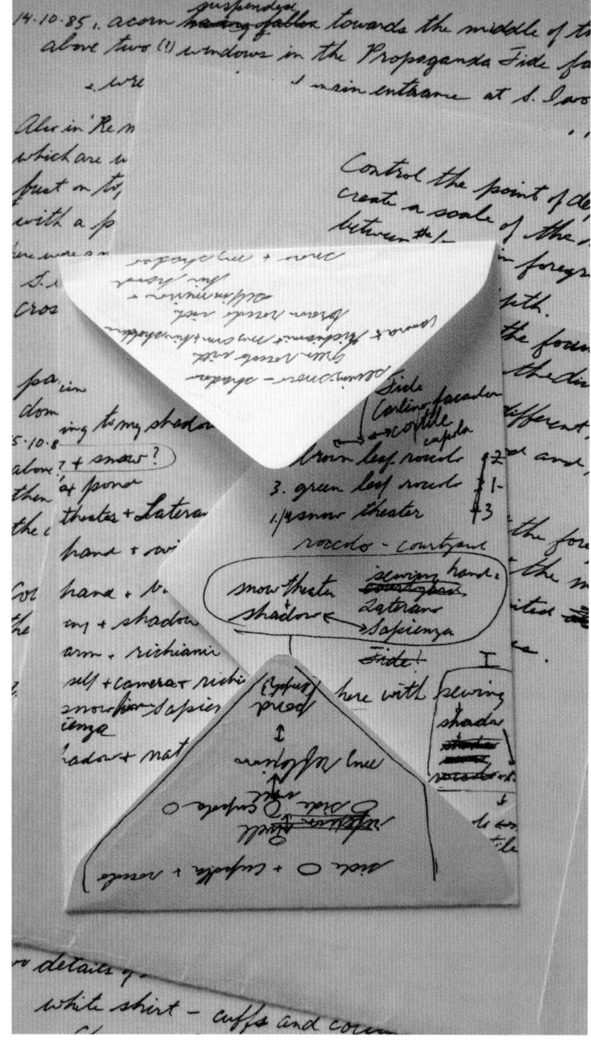


Notes for *The Hedge Theater*

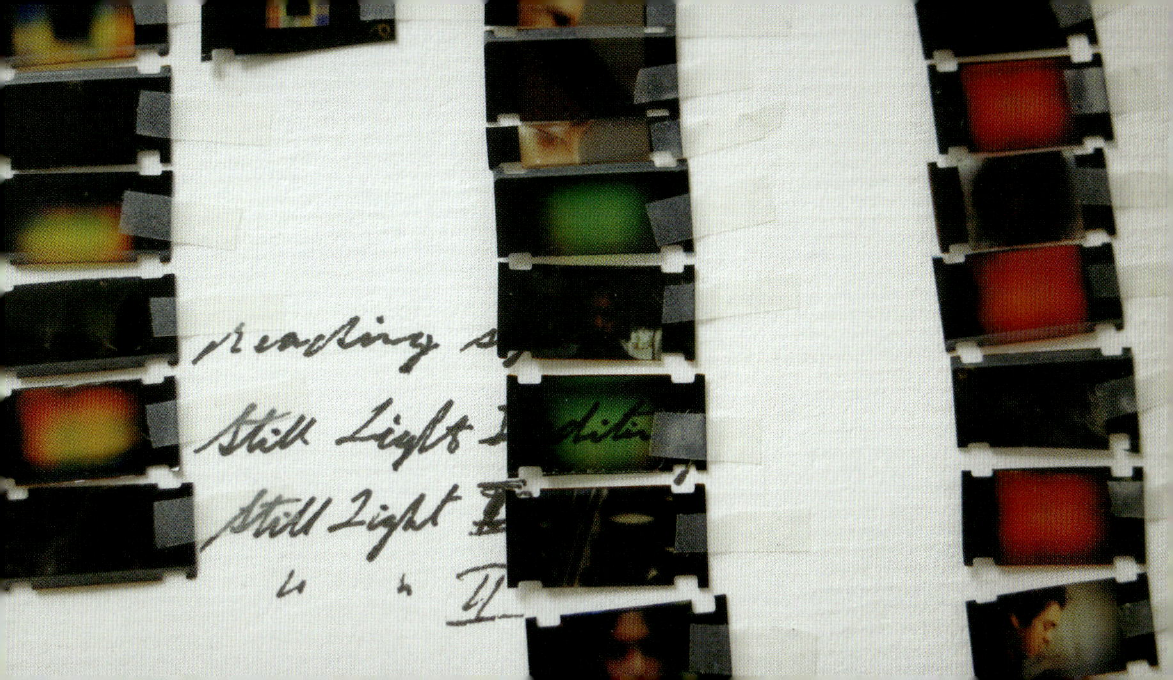

reading
Still Light
Still Light

15.8.72 The objects are made from elements.

| | |
|---|---|
| ice | object |
| river/hill | 2 elements |
| trees, cut | act-object |
| (book) | |

next: simple act (indoors)
then first spoken statement(?)

Each part of the film being object, element, or act; or a mixture of these.

20.8.72 The tree is cut: the film is cut
the ice is frozen: the frame is frozen
Each object has its film essence

4.9.72 Filmed 200 ft. of grass location above Bad Ragaz

11.9.72 Each spoken statement starting during the indoor objects and related to the order of Element, Act, Object. Two or three sentences with each having the same word order.

Statements beginning over image(s) of an unopened book

17.9.72 Object: not of value or age. — The book interrupted this intension. (a Latin text)

30.9.72 Vertical pans with camera on the same level as the book, very close. (To be filmed at Bruscoli's)
(23.10.72 Filmed five hundred feet at Bruscoli's)

9.10.72 The chest, side and arm of a man while he is speaking; the sound will be his words. (see 15.8.72, last part)

25.10.72 Filmed three hundred feet of the blood pancakes.

29.10.72 ~~Reorder~~ Re-order the footage to form the object on the screen

element (act) object (statement)

to equal the form of film making (20.9.72)

filming editing printing projection
recording

*Work Done* notebook pages

2·1·72 Twenty objects/scenes - Europe
each ten minutes

The parts controlled by the color
of each object/scene, removed and
modulated by the filters (which
will not be self-apparent as
when used earlier.)
Remember the filming of the
wheat(?) field on Cos. Yellow-blue.

1·6·72 10 objects, 10 scenes

List
Ice , river
Blood
Trees, grass
Book, blue flame
Arm
Stones mountain

15·3·72 Ice / outre-tombe / the frozen frame
different images in the mirror
as the camera moves closer

16·3·72 Filmed six hundred feet. Fifty shots.

21·3·72 The object and surrounding space;
the relations are infinite and
in a film one may ~~progress~~ change
for another in the manner that
a single piece of music may be
in more than one key.

1·12·72

| | | | |
|---|---|---|---|
| 200 | F | ice | |
| 200 | S | | river |
| 500 | F | book | |
| 200 | S | | tree |
| 300 | F | arm | |
| | S | | mountain |
| 300 | F | stones | |
| 300 | F | | blood (all) |

Eleven
Sixty.

8·4·72 Via dei Serragli - the blood crêpes
in October (25·10·72)

12·4·72 Alternate indoor with outdoor

27·4·72 No main title, just the word of
each object before it. Or is this
necessary?

28·5·72 Freeze the last
frame surrounded
by black.
Superimpose the
beginning of next
object/scene?

1·5·72 Tentative title: Work Done

1·6·72 Scene/view from Scuol
Add and subtract quantities of blue,
white, and green: sky, snow, trees
Use wratten no. 85 to naturalize the
unfiltered part of frame

To reveal the
sense of time in
the making of
the object; and
the sense of when
in the time of the
film, it was made.

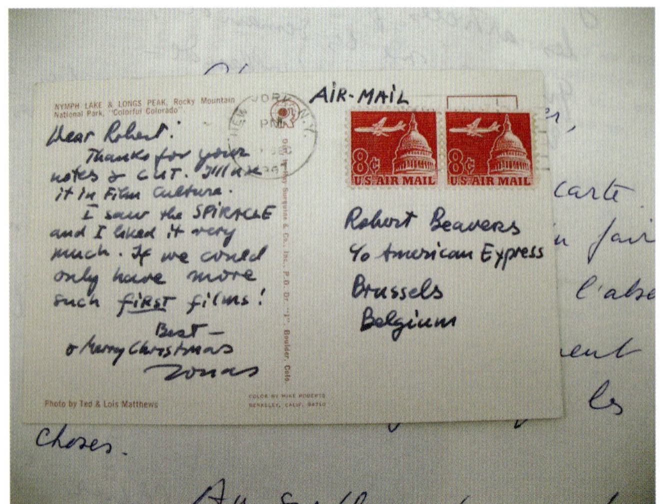
NYMPH LAKE & LONGS PEAK, Rocky Mountain National Park, "Colorful Colorado"

AIR-MAIL

Dear Robert:
Thanks for your notes & CUT. I'll use it in Film Culture.
I saw the SPIRACLE and I liked it very much. If we could only have more such FIRST films!
Best —
& Merry Christmas
Jonas

Robert Beavers
c/o American Express
Brussels
Belgium

Photo by Ted & Lois Matthews

1967 postcard from Jonas Mekas to Beavers

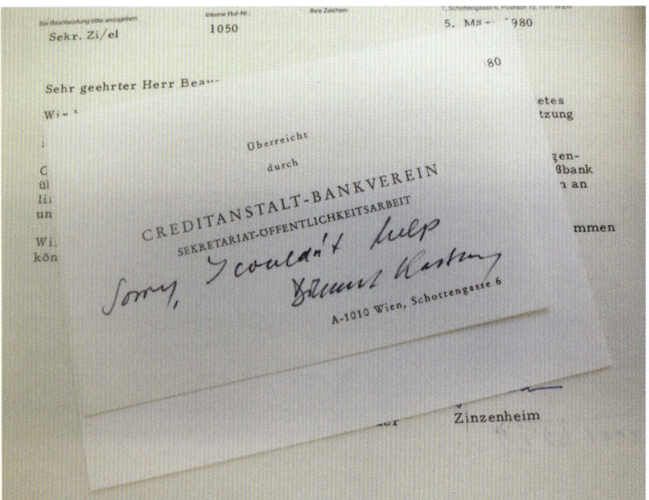
Sekr. Zi/el 1050 5. Mä... 1980

Sehr geehrter Herr Bea...

Zinzenheim

Überreicht
durch
CREDITANSTALT-BANKVEREIN
SEKRETARIAT-ÖFFENTLICHKEITSARBEIT
Sorry, I couldn't help
A-1010 Wien, Schottengasse 6

Rejection of financial assistance from a Vienna bank

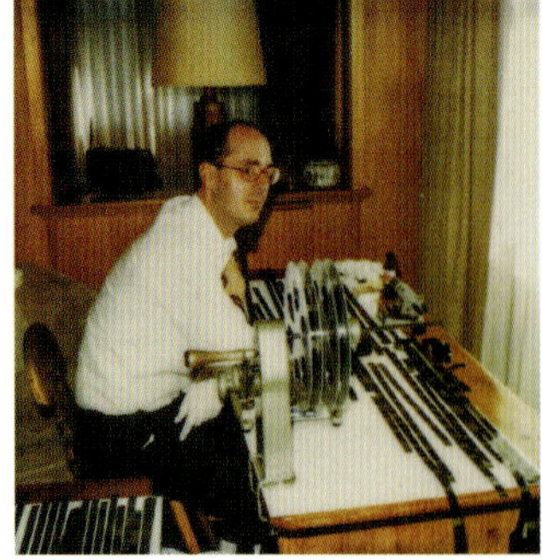
Beavers editing in Gstaad, ca. 1980. Photo by Gregory Markopoulos

### *FROM THE NOTEBOOK OF . . .*

In September 1970, several of Markopoulos's films screened at the International Underground Film Festival in London, organized by Simon Field, David Curtis, and Albie Thoms. There, Beavers and Markopoulos met Neapolitan filmmaker and painter Silvio Loffredo, who encouraged Beavers and Markopoulos to visit Florence, his current home. They relocated from Zurich months later. Each move was a risk: "You go somewhere and hope you find means," Beavers said. In Florence, Loffredo generated consistent support for the filmmakers in small doses. He solicited modest donations from friends and bartered his own watercolors for restaurant meals.

Soon after their arrival, Beavers and Markopoulos met wealthy art book publisher Ferruccio Marchi at a Florentine print shop where the first Temenos imprint books—Markopoulos's *Chaos Phaos* and Beavers's *Still Light* (both 1971)—were later produced. Marchi recognized the men from a recent Sicily screening of their films and invited them to a dinner party for Louis Kahn. There, Markopoulos addressed the architect directly: "How does one continue?" "You beg," Kahn replied. "The seed landed on fertile ground," Beavers recalled. "Gregory kept that advice. Or—it confirmed something Gregory already had. But often people [from whom financial support was solicited] wanted something in return too—they wanted the new but not at the expense of the existing social structures. They don't want to see you eating at their restaurants."

Beavers and Markopoulos stayed at Pensione Sorrelle Bandini, in the Palazzo Guadagni. "We let our bill go on and on for weeks and weeks. Bills kept coming to the pension, including from the printers." (Marchi ultimately funded the printing of *Chaos Phaos* and *Still Light*.) Six months later, they left Florence as abruptly as they had arrived. "You're leaving like fire," one of the Bandini sisters said. "Fast as can be." In the meantime, Beavers had made his longest and most complex film to date, *From the Notebook of . . . .* It was his last film to centralize apparatus demonstration and to use superimpositions, moving mattes, and a numerical editing approach.

A new city, Renaissance art, financial anxiety, the warmth of Loffredo's support, and Markopoulos's certainty about their lifestyle ("put the work first and the rest will sort itself out") drew *Introduction to the Method of Leonardo da Vinci*, the essay that had spurred his own note-making, out of Beavers's Valéry collection. He also read Jean Paul Richter's 1888 translation of da Vinci's notebooks and Giorgio Vasari on da Vinci in *Lives of the Artists*.[25] In March 1971, Beavers wrote: "These notes will be the form of the film on L. da V.'s method" and "The notes are the device of the life, an outgrowth of it, not independent like a 'work of art.'"[26]

*From the Notebook of . . .* (1971/1998) is structured as a notebook; inside its simulated turning pages, image and text elements (fragments of Beavers's own notes) alternate rapidly. "Writing is thinking; so is filmmaking and film watching," Manohla Dargis writes of the film.[27] *From the Notebook of . . .* interlocks three sites—city, pension room, notebook—in a repeating rhythm of look/think/write. Dynamic Florentine views shot on a tripod (an elderly woodcarver, the Ponte Vecchio, the Arno River) are followed by pension room scenes (under a window whose shutters Beavers opens and closes, the filmmaker composes notes at his desk) and then the matte-animated notebook pages. "I'm first looking at the location and then bringing back my thoughts [into the room] and finally placing my thoughts into the notebook—I move from location into room onto page," Beavers said. "It was a very different method of making for me. The way I filmed with the mattes and squares [thus producing multiple openings and subdivisions within the shot] gave me a lot of freedom during the editing process. . . . [I was able to] place notes and images and colors into the composition, to place anything with anything, as if I were assembling pages." The persistent and ecstatic event of creative assembly is underwritten by sharp, recognizable sounds: window opening and closing, hurried writing, ringing church bells, camera operations (single-frame clicks, rewinding, running). Along with Beavers's notes and Florentine architectural details, the insets are populated by images inspired by da Vinci's drawings (children [the Marchi siblings], vegetation, nude anatomical details, birds) and Vasari's writing on the artist (doves both caged and released, a reference to Vasari's description of da Vinci's penchant for buying and then freeing birds).

A fourth space, the camera—*camera* is Latin for "room"—joins the in-out transit. In shots of a second running Bolex (cover removed), we see the shutter opening and closing, making a fast-flickering striped filter visible. "I wanted to show you the movement of the shutter in the aperture and for you to see the camera from the film's point of view—from behind the shutter," Beavers said. One of Beavers's full-screen notes reads, "Shutter in camera is like wings on insect—both create movement, one in space the other in the eye." In the first version of his film Beavers enacted the "shutter like wings" comparison by "placing" the sound of fluttering bird wings with the camera interior imagery. In the second, he expanded the associations, syncing other sounds—writing, rushing river, wood carving—with the shutter/aperture shots. The film brings the spectator into the camera—but with its editing-centric approach to composition, "it is the opposite of an in-camera film," Beavers said.[28]

"Shutter : wings" began as "a spontaneous thought," Beavers said, but the comparison became the film's analogy-spreading germ. Bird wing: page; room: camera interior; camera shutter: window shutter; pension window: Renaissance painting. As opening and closing movements mutate, analogical parts touch. The dome of the Basilica of San Spirito is like a round wood object in the carver's hands; a trompe l'oeil window on a Via Maggio building facade matches the geometry of a filter and matte composition; blue and red links the diffuse stripes generated by in-camera filters to parked cars on Florentine streets. Analogy-making as native action of imaginative mind is at the center of both Valéry's contemplation on da Vinci and Beavers's film.

Beavers's note fragments do not sync with the looking acts that precede them, cannot be folded back into the film in a lock-and-key way. The phenomenology of coexistent looking/reading is a more primary facet of spectatorship; one encounters reading, wanting in vain to read, not trying to read, refusing to read. Particular eye and mind postures are activated by the sheer presence of text; the prospect of reading surprises the eyes out of the expectation of continuous seeing. Beavers told Michael Guillén, "I sometimes use the word 'locomotion': it's a movement in place. The movement is a dual movement of reading and seeing. The spectator is constantly being guided from one to the other and back. It's a constant flux between these two different ways of using the eyes."[29]

Beavers's conception of the duality of reading itself—"What is reading? Half discovering someone else thoughts and half confirmation of what you're already thinking," he mused—is a near repetition of Valéry in his da Vinci essay. "Remembering that he was a thinker, we are able to discover in his works ideas which really originate in ourselves: we can re-create his thought in the image of our own," Valéry writes. "It would be necessary to invent him if he did not exist. . . . A Leonardo may, as a notion, exist in our minds without our being too bewildered."[30] Valéry's essay is not a portrait of an individual artist's method; it is a meditation on creative consciousness, on a supreme balance between analytical intelligence and hyper-awareness that renders all thoughts, feelings, and objects as "phenomena"—equalized "mental images" available for limitless forms of "construction" and innovation. In *From the Notebook of . . .*, da Vinci and Valéry are "devices" (like the note), fellow autodidacts rather than artist-objects. "The overall thought that's holding it all together is the notebook—not biography or something else," Beavers said.

The notes in *From the Notebook of . . .* cover a motley spectrum. There is logistical documentation ("Ordered Kodak filters nos. 29, 22, 12, 61, 48, 36"), future film conceptualization ("A film of mistakes to show the possibility of creating by factual error"; "Film all actions having nothing to do with making films"), self-instruction ("Film at close range to remove color of object"; "Make the composition equal the editing"), and hypothesis ("Will the movement of the matte stop the light?"). There are technical reminders ("Note the first frame of a shot sometimes receives more exposure"), aphorisms ("Film is not an illusion of movement—it is movement"), quotes (da Vinci: "If you look at the sun or other luminous body and then shut your eyes you will retain it inside your eye for a long time").[31] But register leaping is not simply a function of the editing of *Notebook*; it characterizes Beavers's chronological writing in his film notebooks. Such a tendency to jump confounded da Vinci's translator Jean Paul Richter in 1888: "On one and the same page, observations on the most dissimilar subjects follow each other without any connection. A page, for instance, will begin with some principles of astronomy, or the motion of the earth; then come the laws of sound, and finally some precepts as to colour. Another page will begin with his investigations on the structure of the intestines, and end with philosophical remarks as to the relations of poetry to painting."[32]

—

The third entry in Beavers's *From the Notebook of . . .* notes, from February 1971—"A matte bisecting the lens, moving from right to left and back, disappearing when perpendicular"—captures the moving matte strategy responsible for the illusion of turning pages in the film. Beavers taped one of three mattes (black, white, or two-sided black/white) to the center of his compendium outer frame. While shooting, he flicked the matte, causing it to swing left or right, thus blocking half the frame. A matte mid-swing produced the diagonal motion of a page moving through space. And a fully perpendicular matte, per his note, was visible on-screen only as a vertical line (like a notebook seam). The "disappearing" matte became an important analogical figure for Beavers: it suggested the invisible discrepancy between two distinct images in depth perception and binocular vision. As the matte generates a divided screen and then disappears from view, the *Notebook* spectator is witness to an enactment of stereopsis.

A dialogue between cinematic and Renaissance representations of depth is encoded into the film's making. Some of the deep space compositions in *Notebook*—the receding Arno, Basilica of Santa Maria Novella seen at an angle—are not only decentered, but Beavers's own eye is decoupled from his camera: his profile is visible at the edge of the frame. The unhinging of vanishing point from composition is not ideological (à la apparatus theoretician Jean-Louis Baudry) nor is it the consistent conceptual center of the film's structure. The destabilization transpires inside a film dominated not by a horizontal line (the horizon) but by a vertical one (a notebook), and not by enduring insight but by fleeting analogy. Ahead of making a painting, da Vinci maintained linear perspective by sketching a compositional outline on a "window" or glass pane placed between his eye and the selected scene. When Beavers opens the shutters in his pension room, he reveals his own window; his action brings his body and illuminated workspace into the analogical language games of the film.[33]

In Florentine art, twenty-two-year-old Beavers encountered "the most serious investigation of space" he knew. "But *disegno* was, for me, the most important discovery. The word has a very different meaning than if we translate it as simply 'drawing' or 'design,' as something only decorative. It places the hand in relation to the mind and thought—the two are together. This is *disegno*. You think through drawing," he said. The Renaissance practice of continuous drawing (studies, sketches, cartoons) was not simply apprenticeship for fresco finality but a means of enacting intellect, of realizing a totality of conception and composition via moving strokes on paper. *Disegno* represented unification—of idea and execution, of creation (Vasari called *disegno* "the father of" painting, sculpture and architecture)—and invention itself.

Near the end of *From the Notebook of . . .* , a close-up follows Beavers's hand as he neatly composes a note—a sequence of capital letters representing color filter combinations. The note complete, he inscribes an accompanying date that precedes the making of the film: 27.6.69. Nearly all of the notes that appear in the film were originally composed before Beavers came to Florence, during the period when he was pursuing *Degeneration*. "There is a distance between my handwritten notes, which are remnants of earlier intentions for filming, and the actual filming as it develops its own direction," Beavers writes.[34] This note-distance joins other ones—between the two sides of the divided screen and the two images of binocular vision, between fourteenth-century Florence and 1971 and 2000, between the "independent artwork" and the "device"—to produce the prismatic space of the filmic notebook. In a 1976 note, composed five years after completing the film, Beavers wrote, "A note and the same note written after some years. Where is the meaning if the same words were intended differently?"

—

In the fall of 1971, Beavers and Markopoulos paid their pension bill in Florence and went to Disentis, a village in the Swiss canton of Graubünden, for the first of many months-long periods in the decade to come. "We literally starved," Beavers said. There, Beavers edited *From the Notebook of . . .* and Markopoulos edited *Cimabue! Cimabue!* (1971), a portrait compilation of friends and acquaintances he'd shot in Florence (including Loffredo and art restorer Umberto Baldini as he repairs Cimabue's *Crucifix* [ca. 1268–1271], damaged by the 1966 flood in Florence). Markopoulos also shot an in-camera portrait of a baroque church in Graubünden; like *Cimabue! Cimabue!* and other 1970s portrait films, it was left unprinted and later incorporated into *Eniaios*.

12.1.70
Projection of the ima
onto glass or a mir
with a second foc
change to return
to the original.

9.9.70
The sound should
start at a very high
or low speed and
graduate to norma
/cut/ second sound

*From the Notebook of . . .*
(1971/1998)

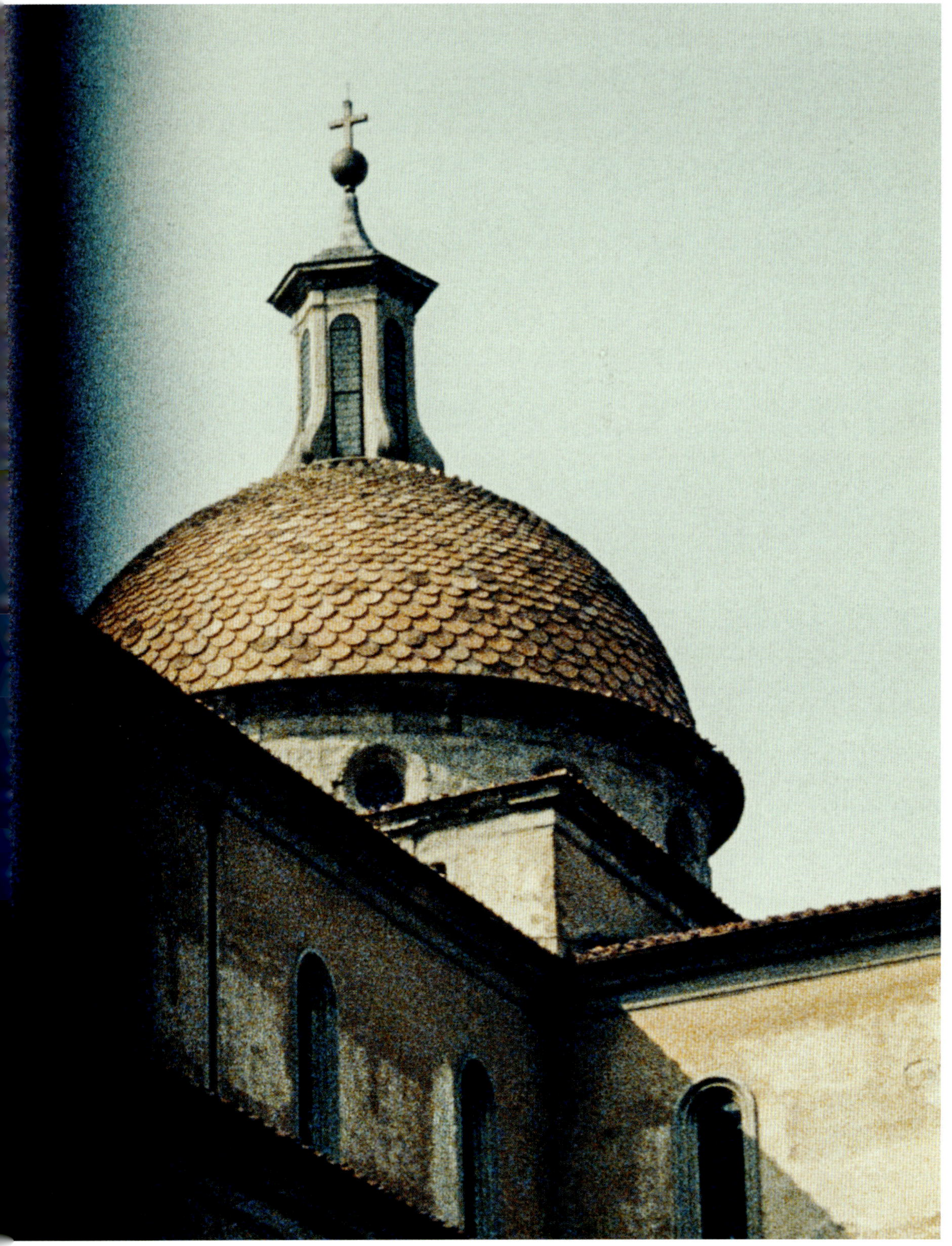

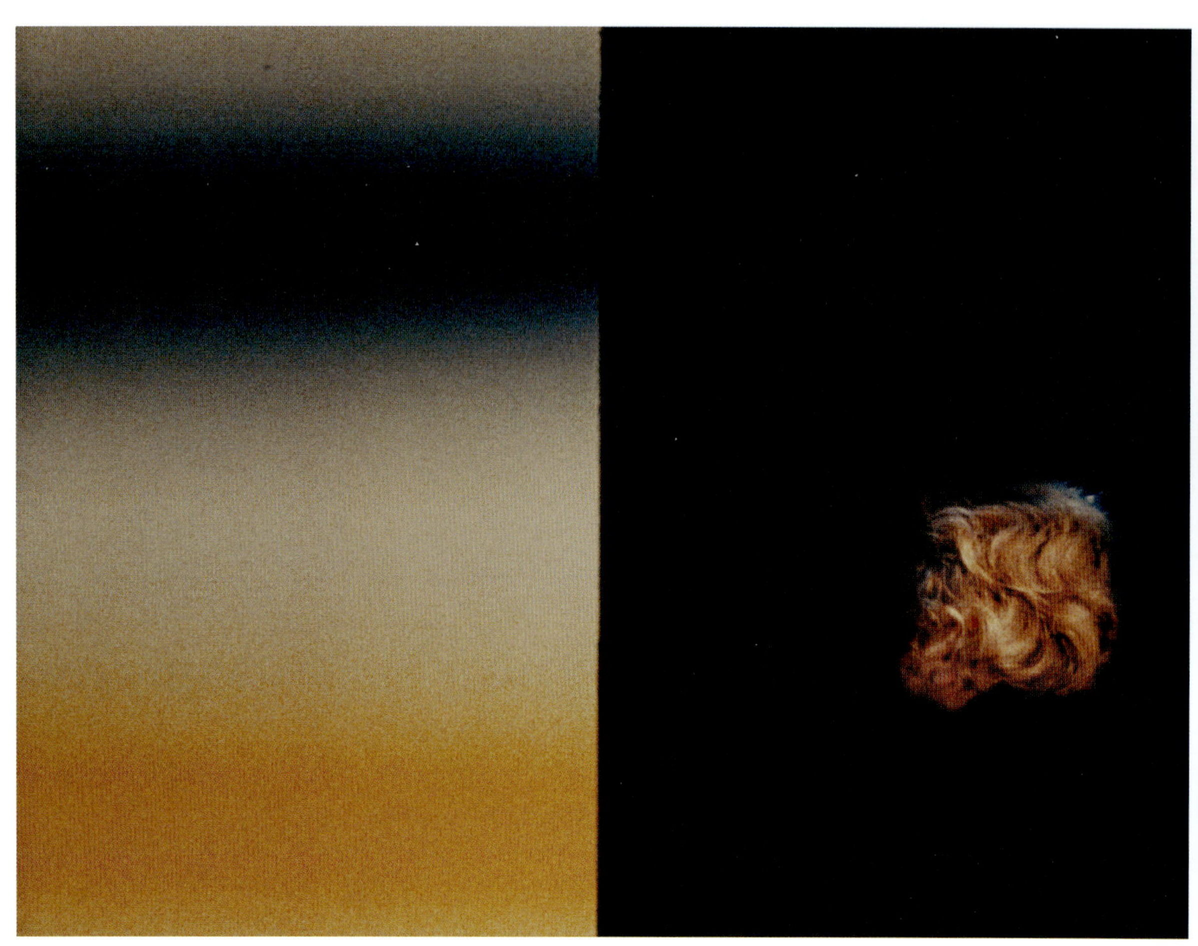

*From the Notebook of . . .* (1971/1998)

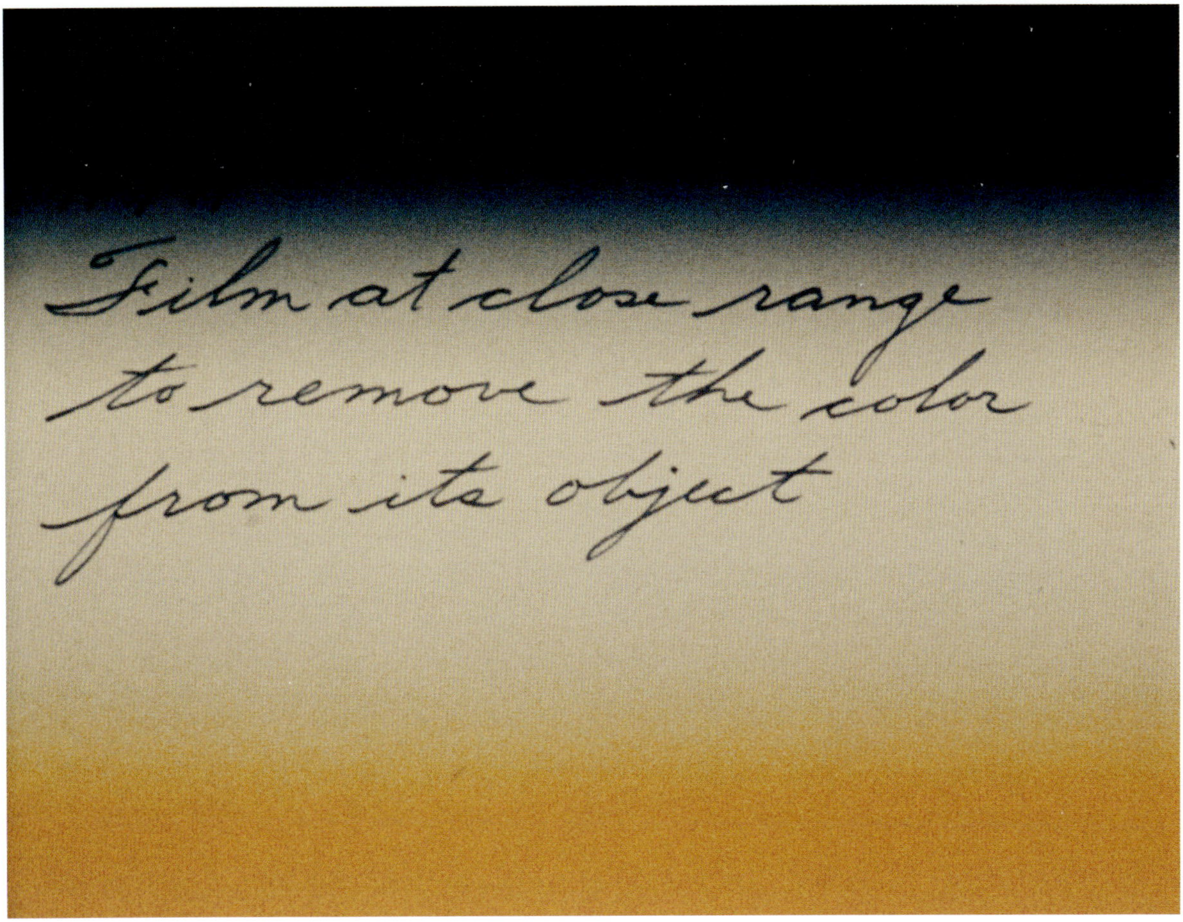

Film at close range
to remove the color
from its object

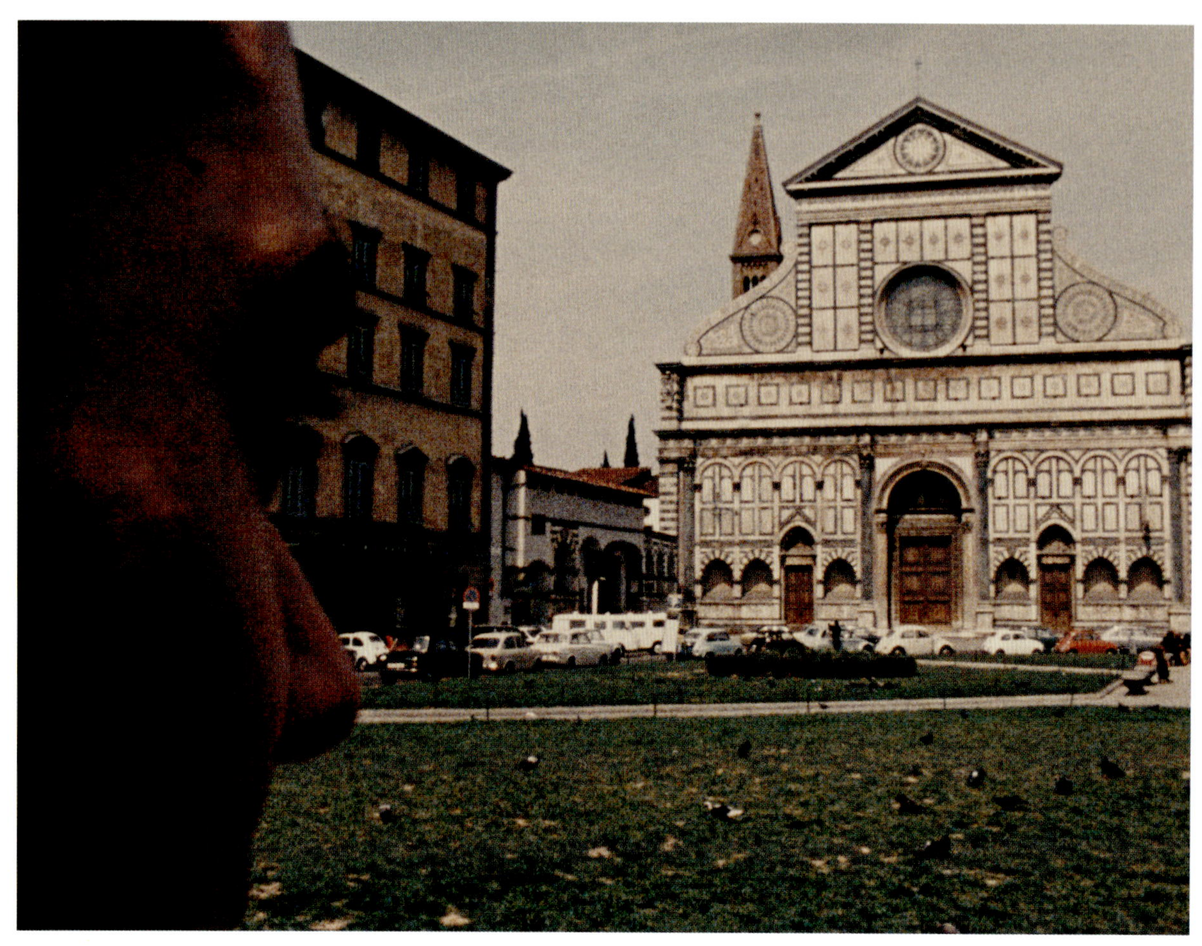

*From the Notebook of . . .* (1971/1998)

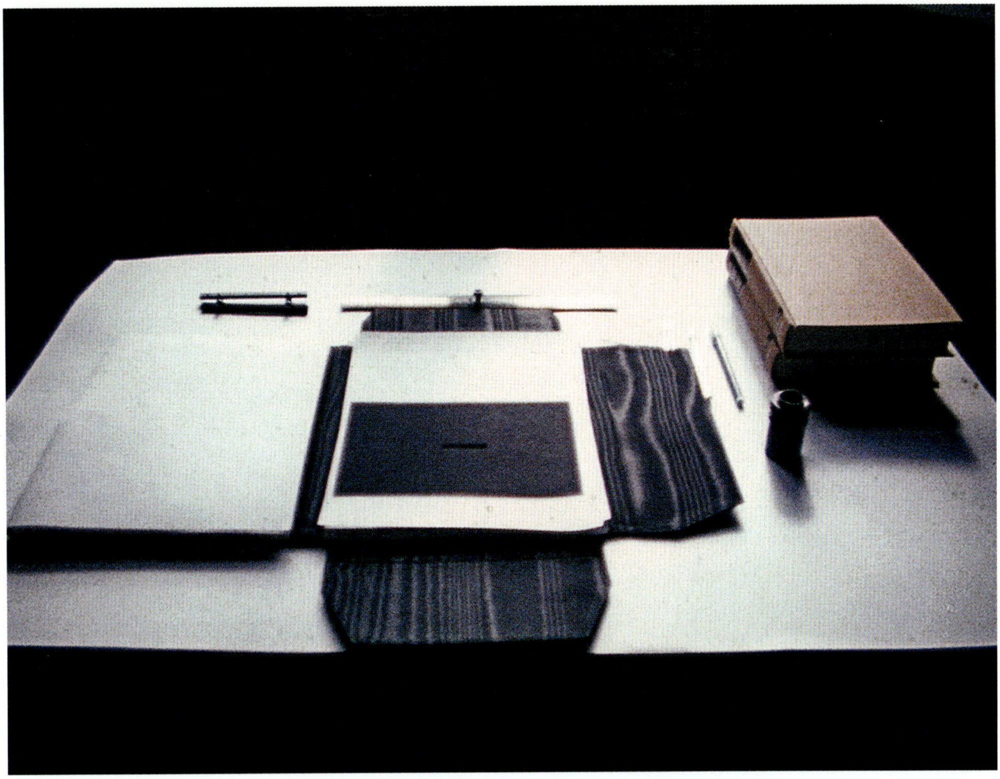

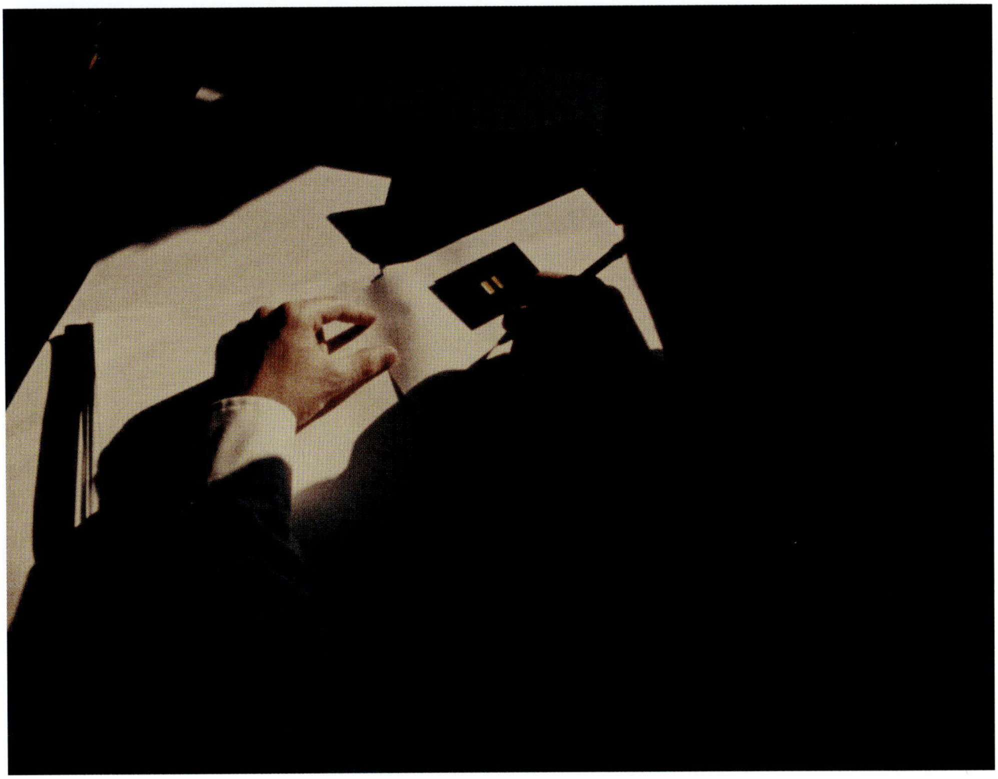

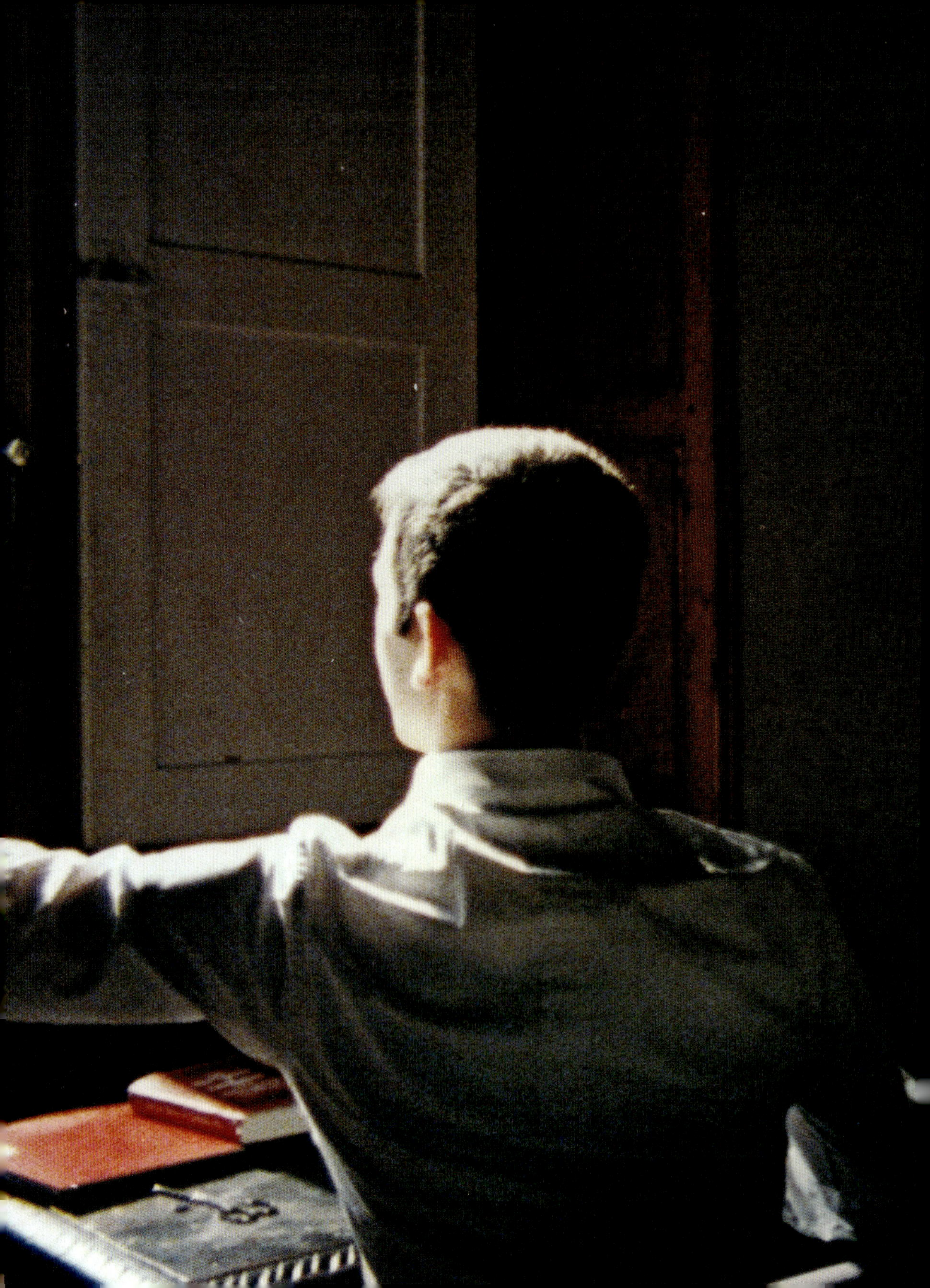

*From the Notebook of . . .* (1971/1998)

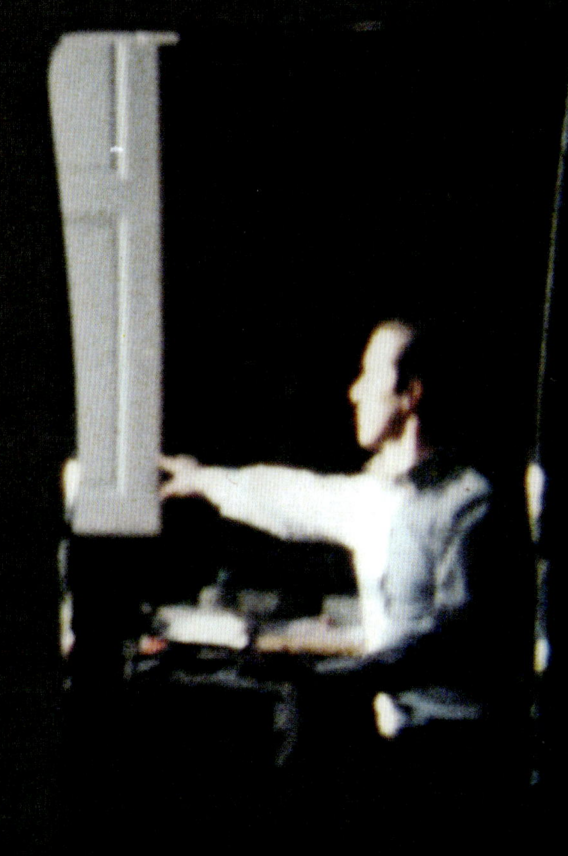

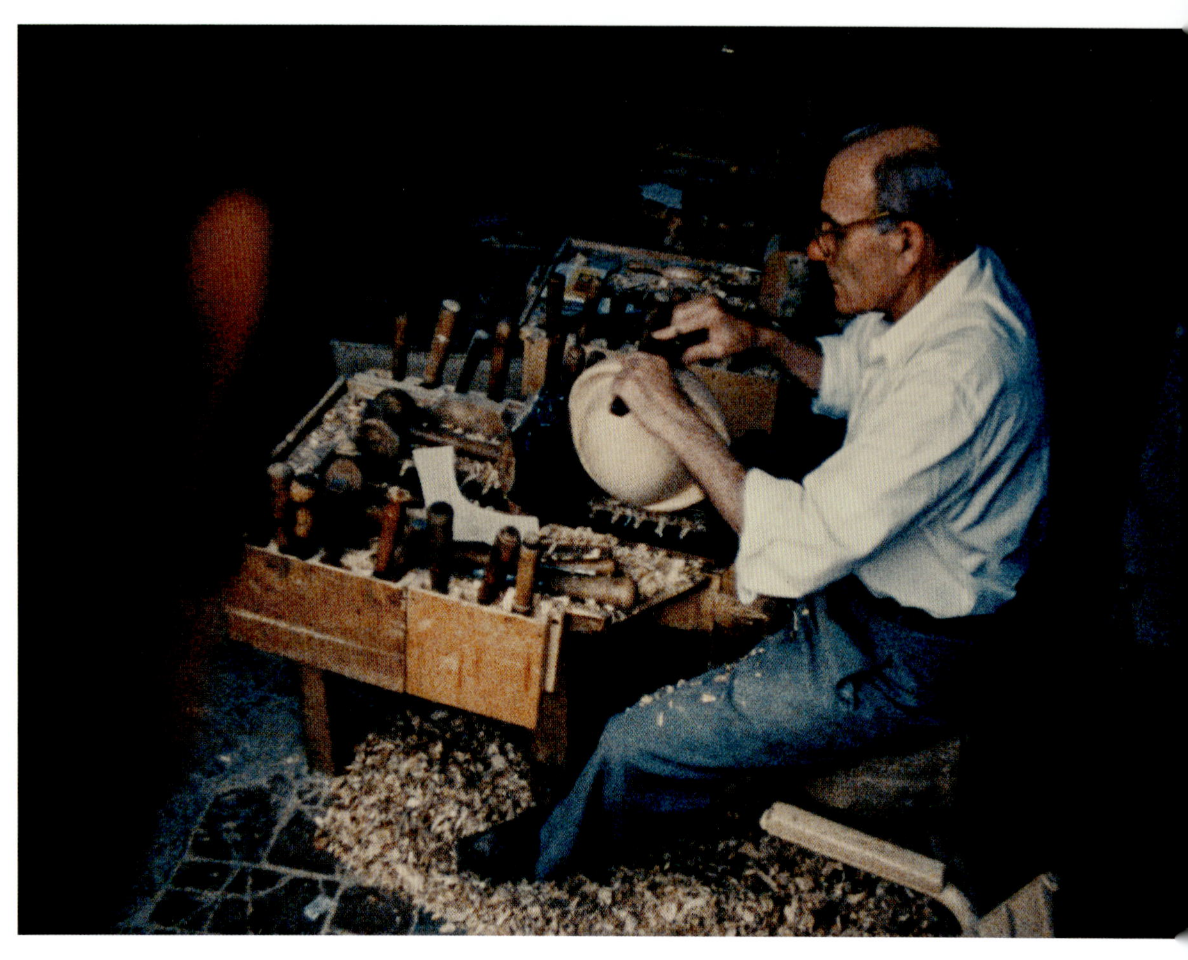

*From the Notebook of . . .* (1971/1998)

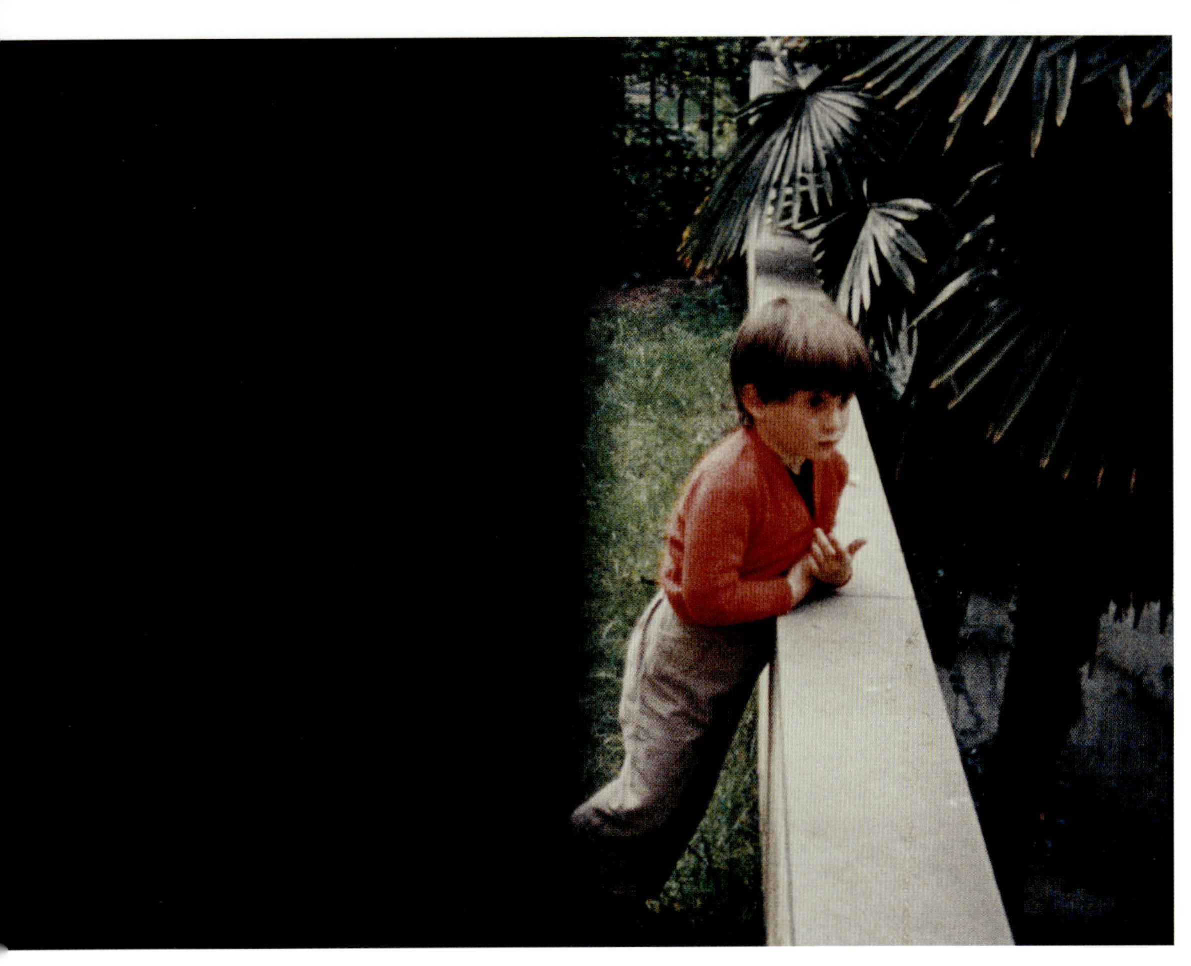

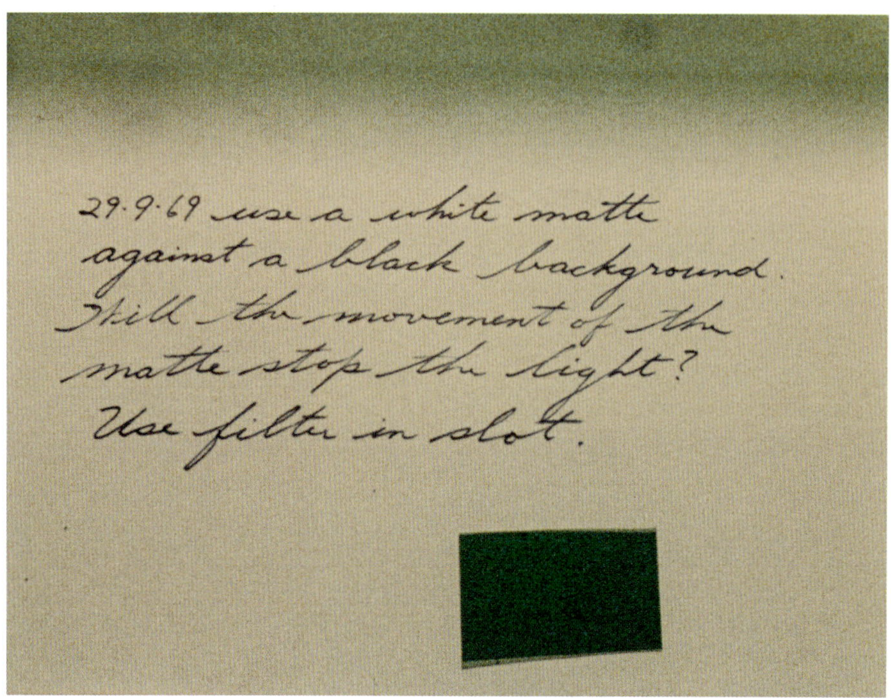


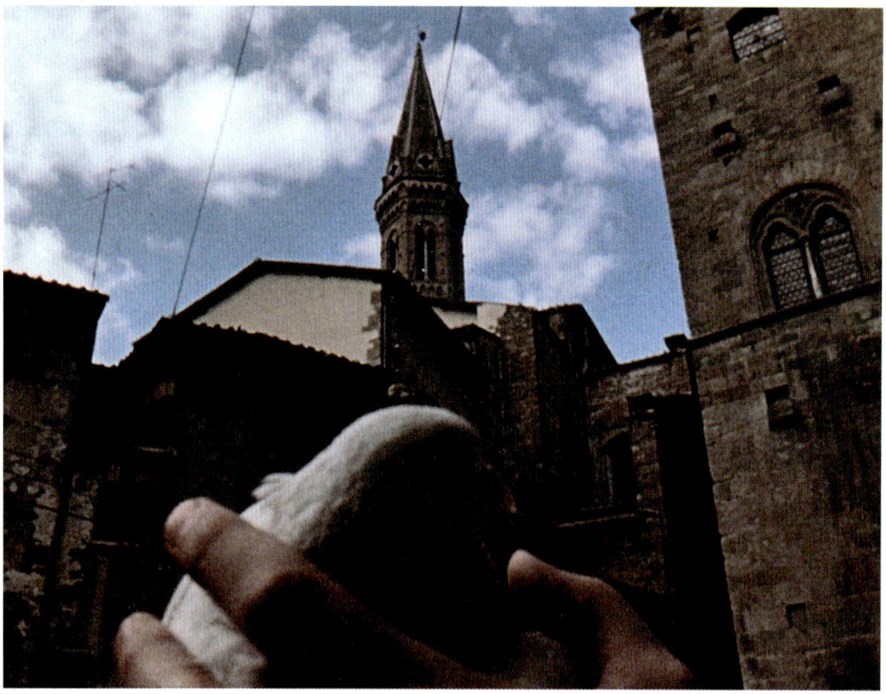

*From the Notebook of . . .* (1971/1998)

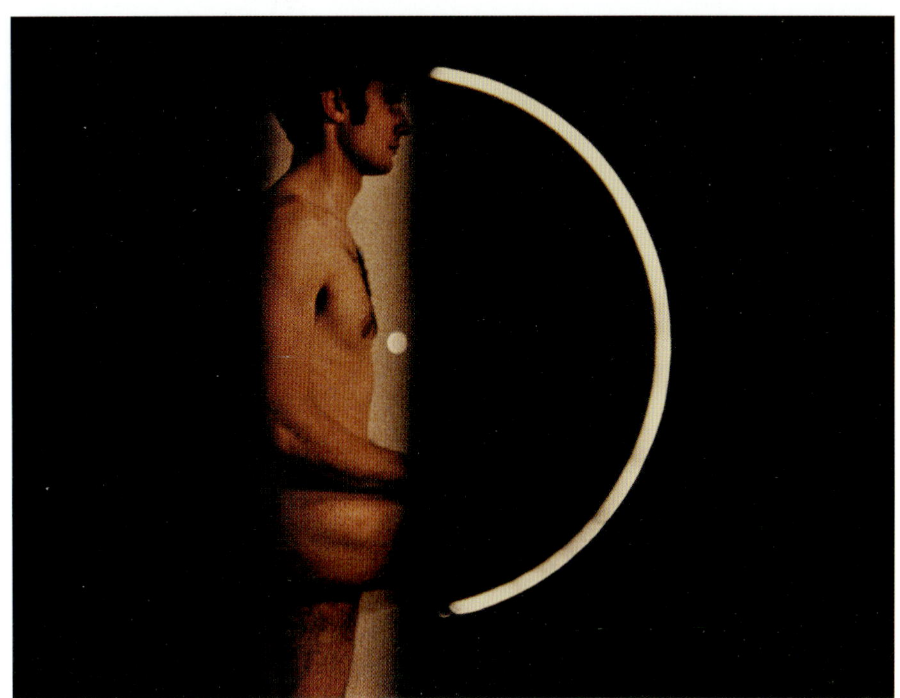

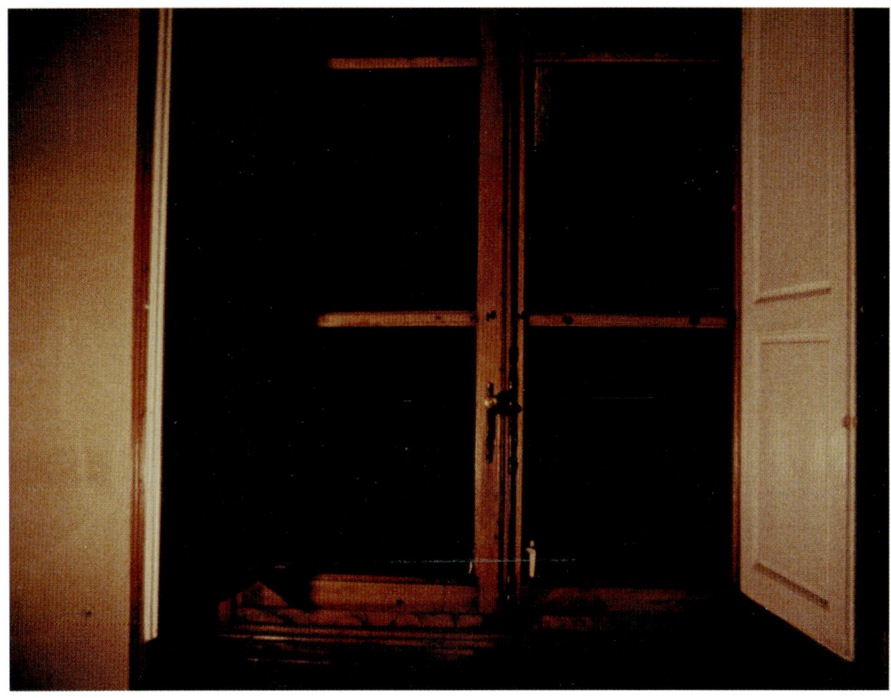

*From the Notebook of . . .* (1971/1998)

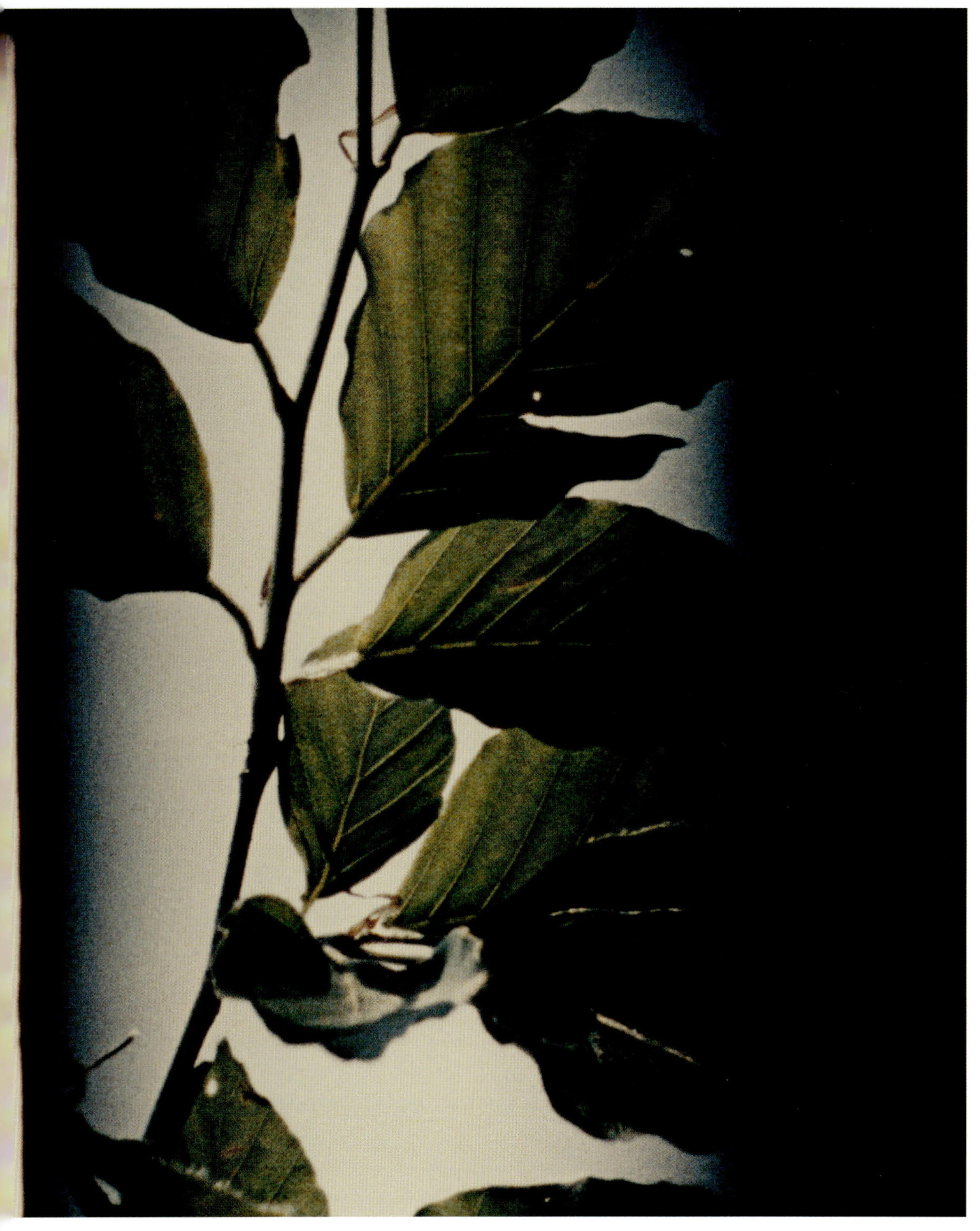

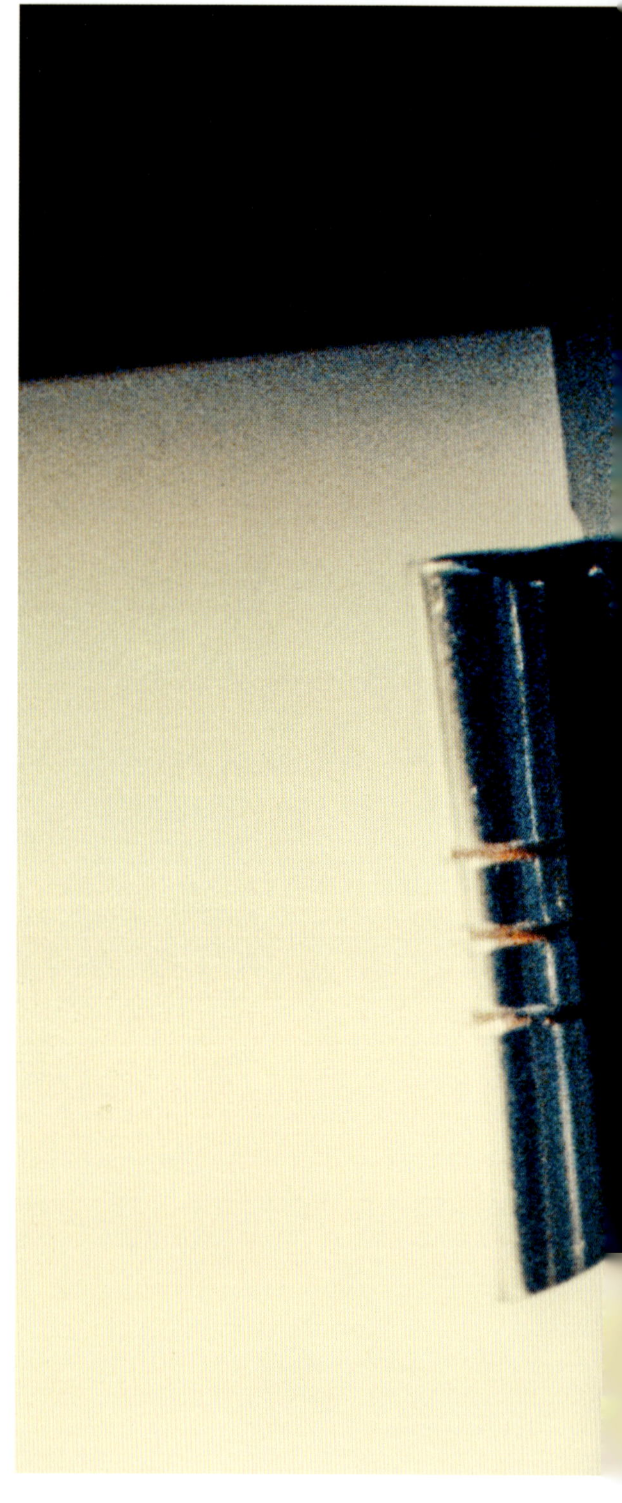

*From the Notebook of . . .* (1971/1998)

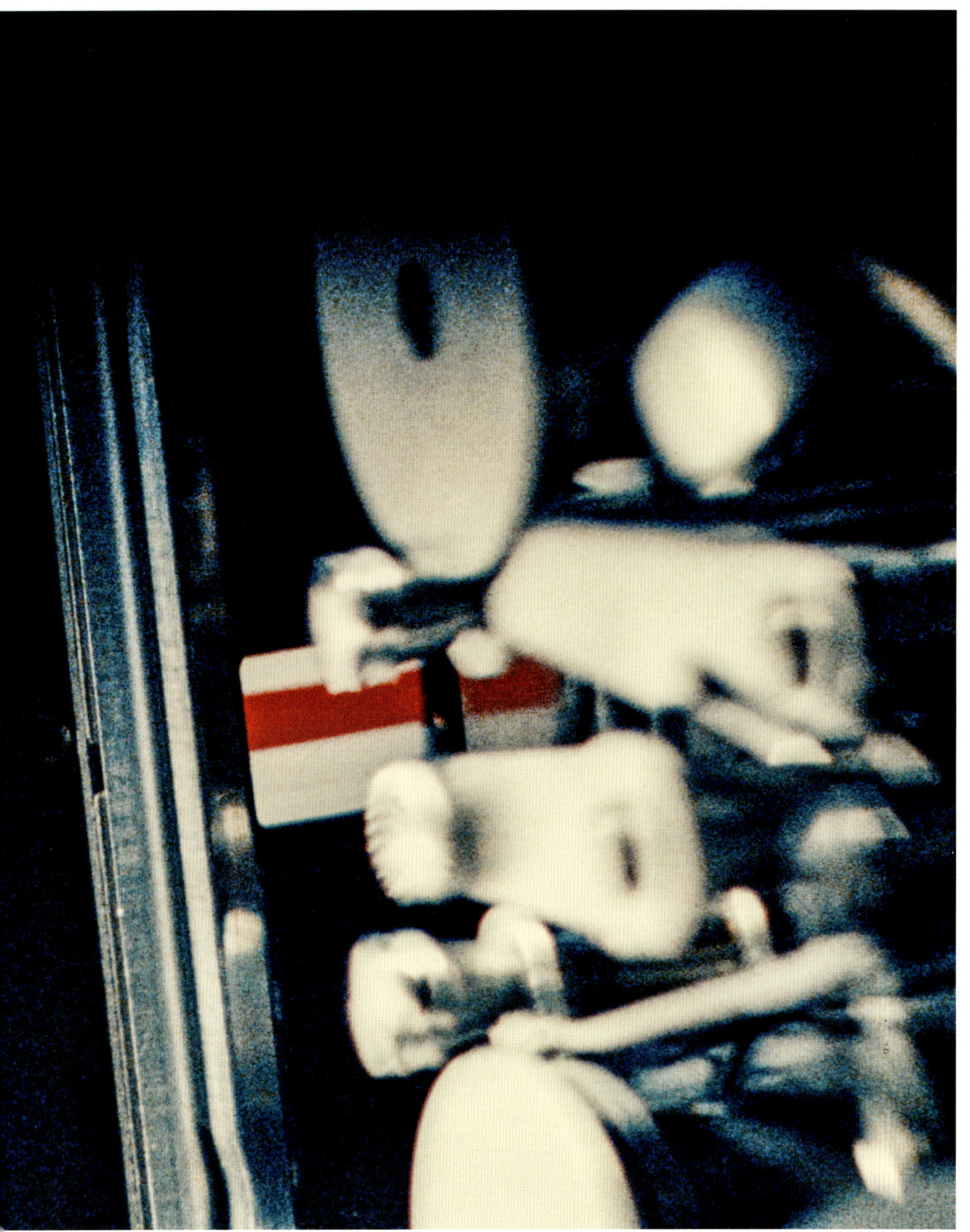

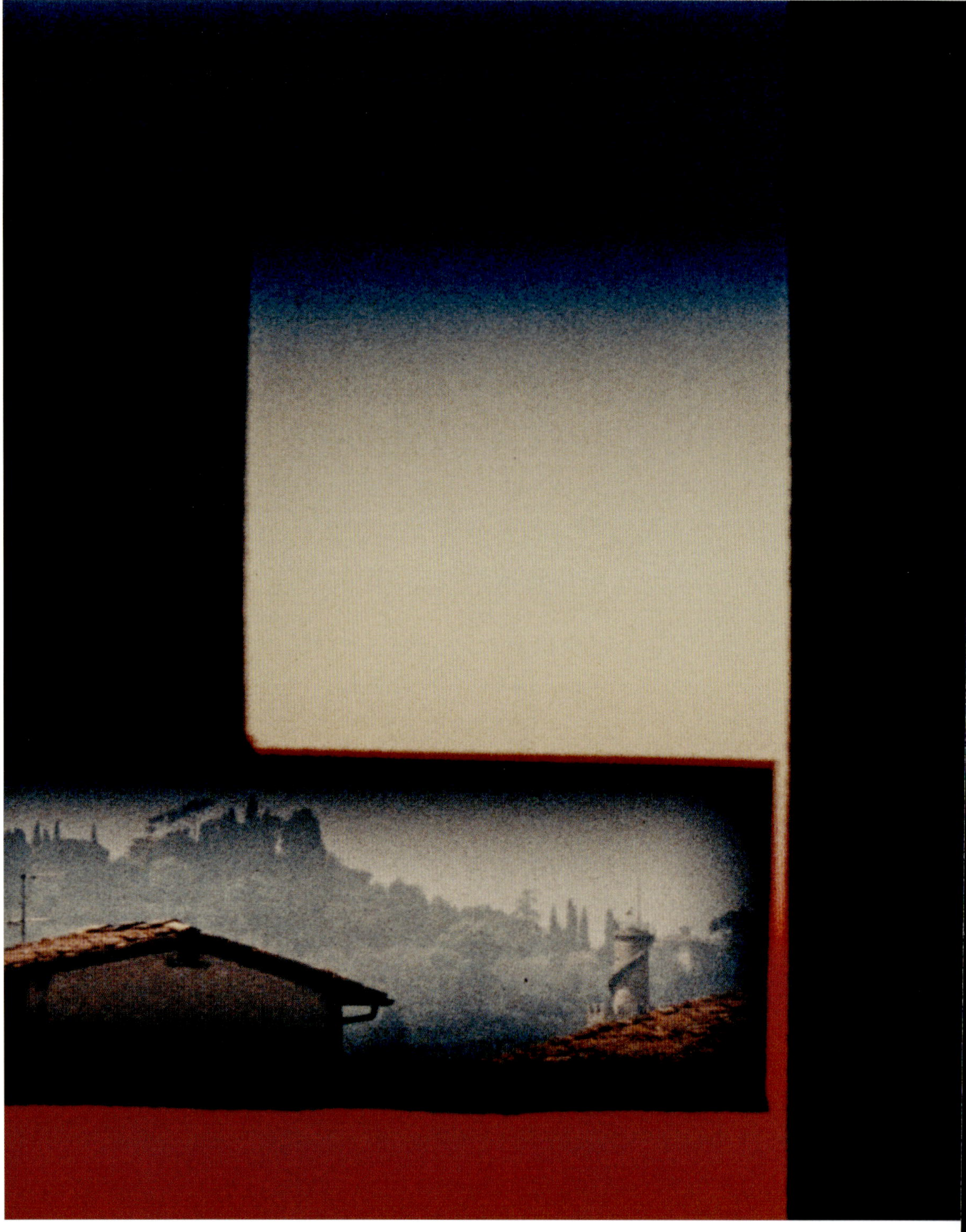

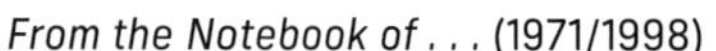

*From the Notebook of . . .* (1971/1998)

*From the Notebook of . . .* (1971/1998)

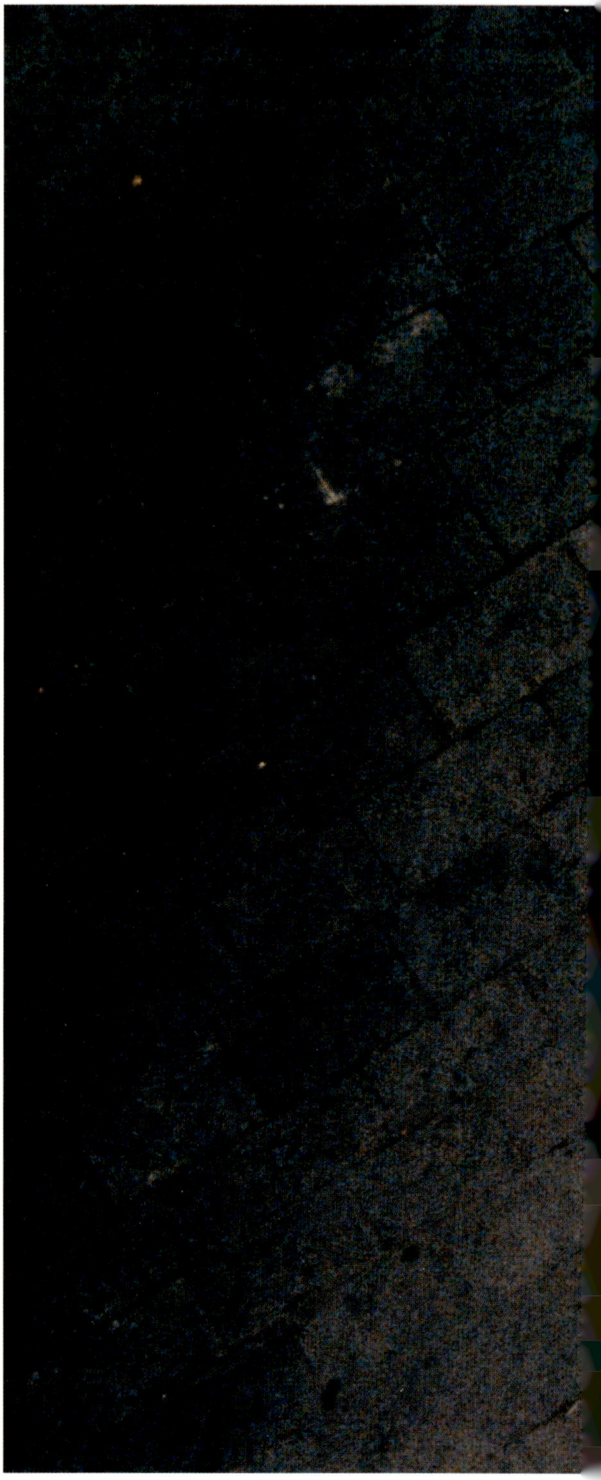

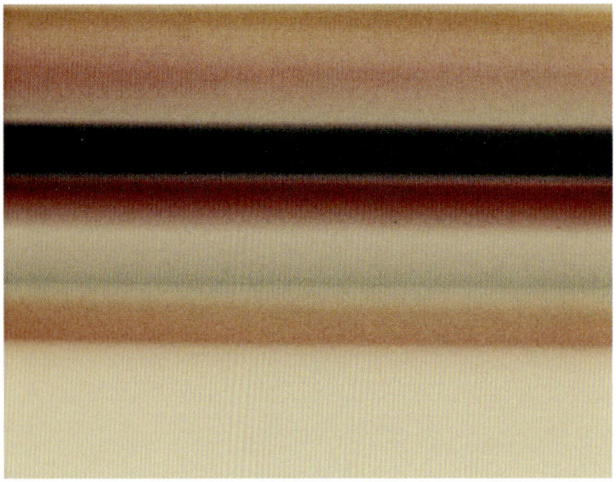

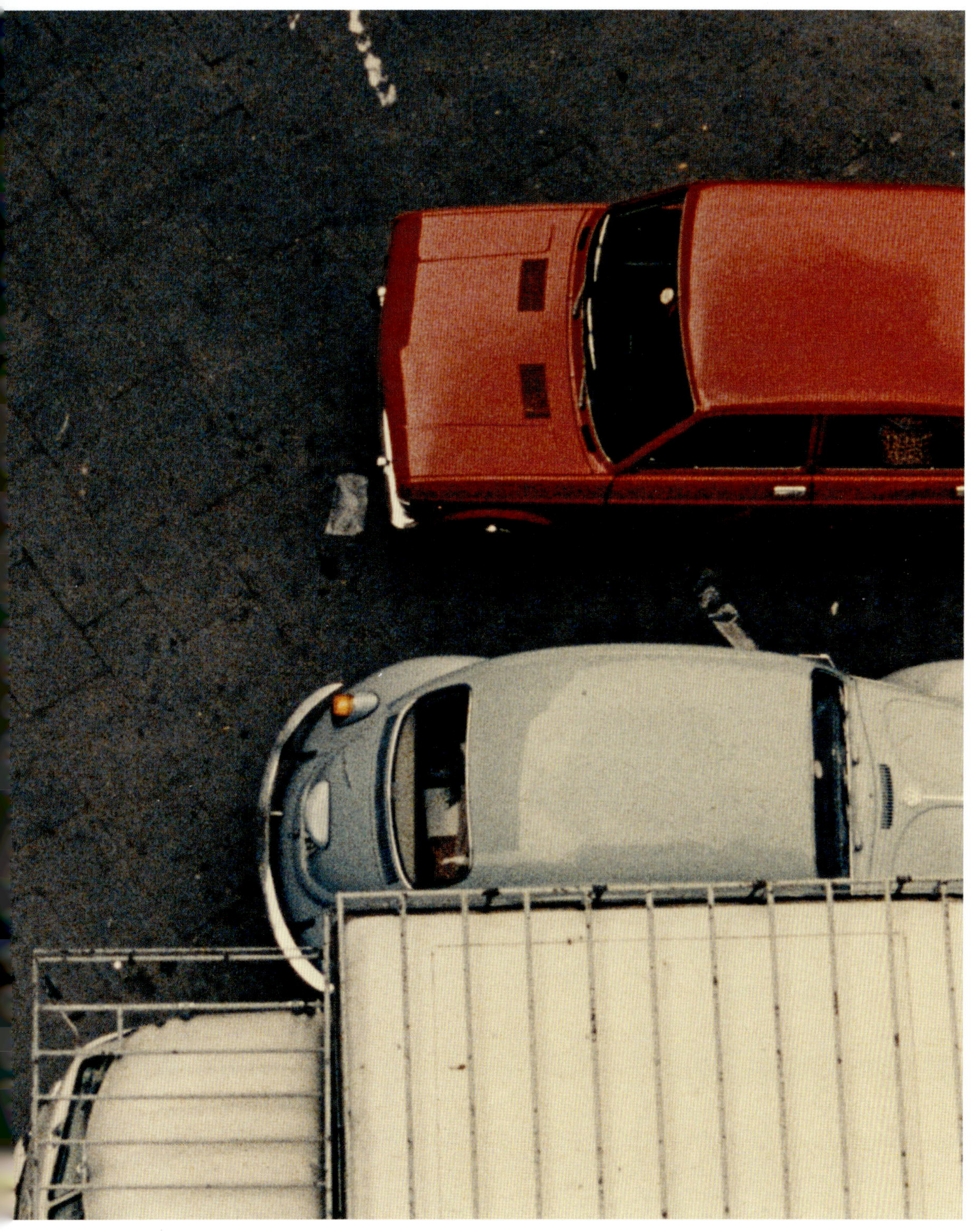

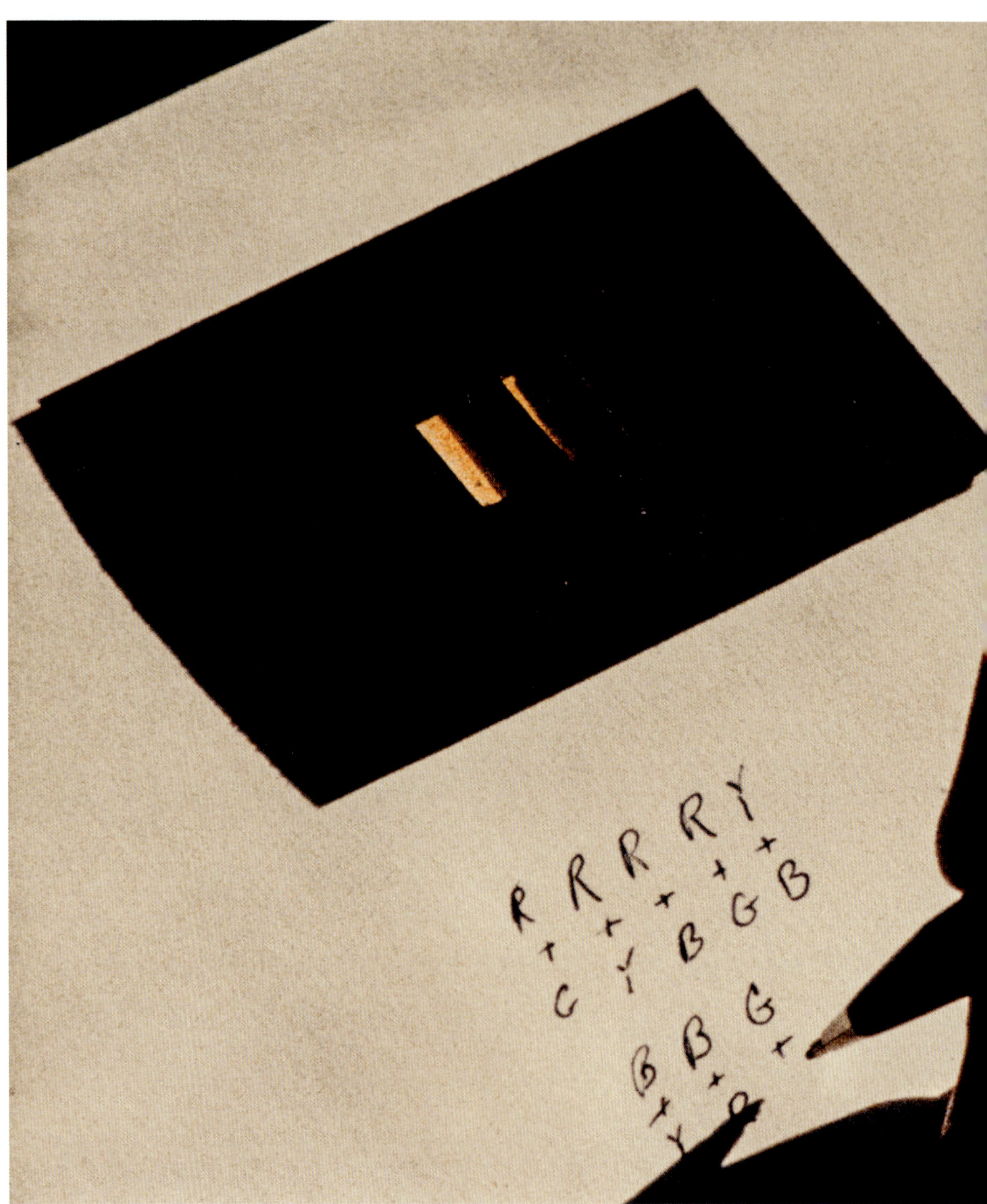
R R R R Y
C Y B G B
B B G

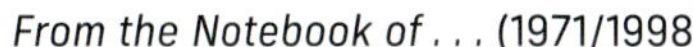

*From the Notebook of . . .* (1971/1998)

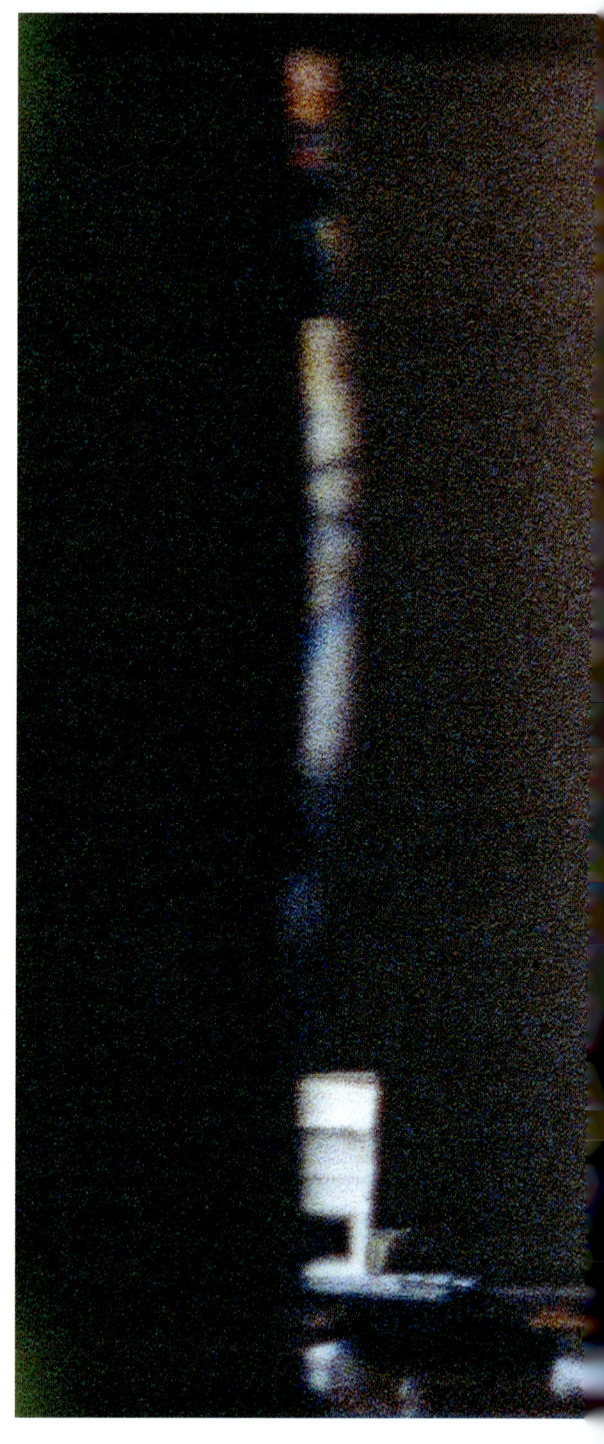

*From the Notebook of . . .* (1971/1998)

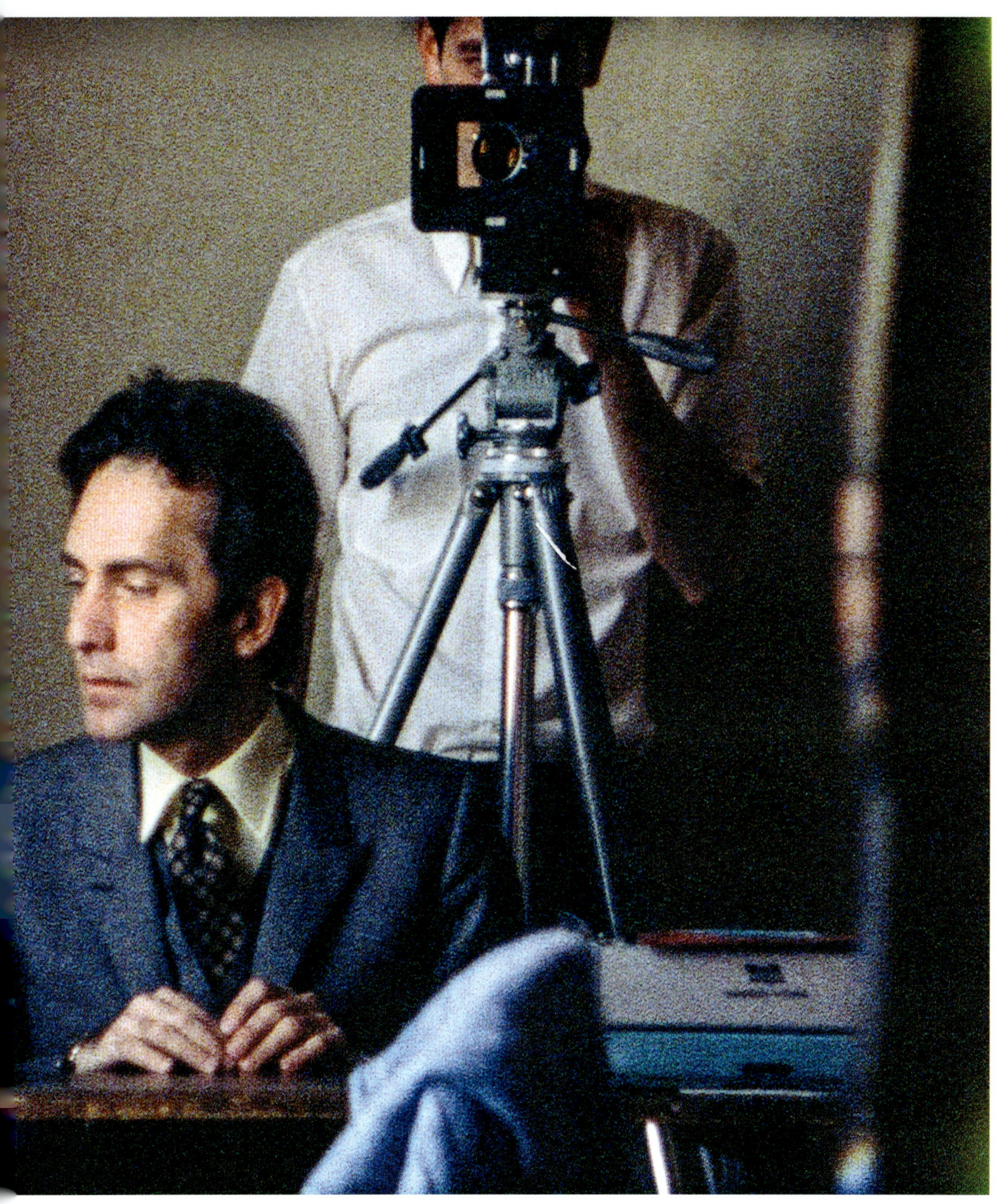

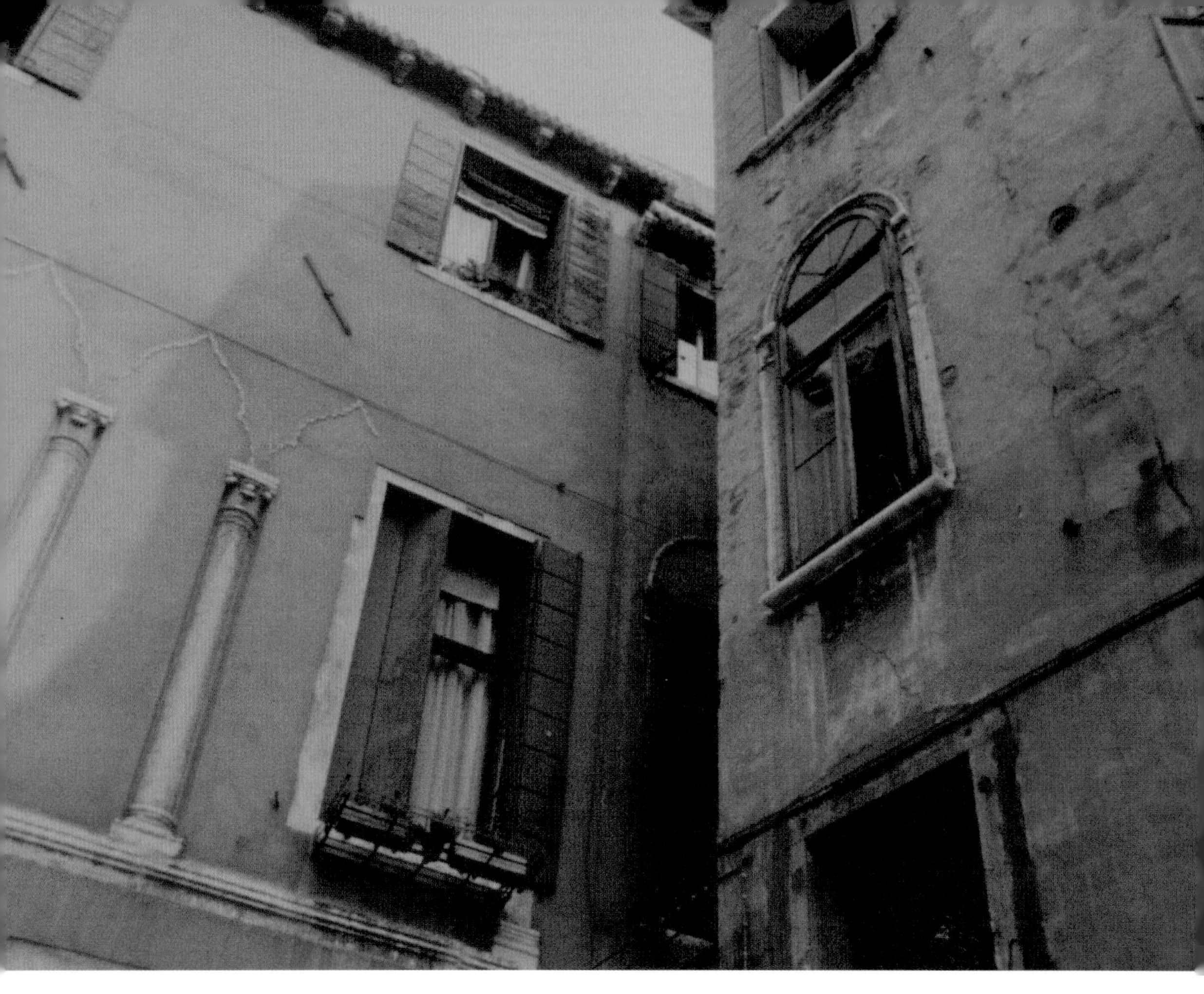

*Ruskin* (1975/1997)

# 4

# RUSKIN, A READING

When the (beautiful) object is a book, what exists
and what no longer exists?
**Jacques Derrida**[1]

Actor's incident: separate act from word.
**Robert Beavers, notes for *Ruskin***

## CHRISTMAS GIFT

On December 25, 1973, Beavers made notes while looking at a Christmas card standing on a table in Venice. From his observational position, it became an architectural curiosity. The front and back leaves appeared to merge into one plane; their top edges formed one continuous line. And while the angle of the card rendered the image on its front a trapezoid, the internal pictorial perspective of that image remained in place. Beavers was by then several months into making notes for *Ruskin* (1975/1997), the last of a series of four films shot in Italy and Switzerland (after *From the Notebook of . . .* , *The Painting*, and *Work Done*).

Three years earlier, in 1972, on a trip back to Weymouth from Europe, Beavers discovered an old gift from Mrs. Hodges: the Victorian artist/critic/naturalist/social reformer John Ruskin's *The Stones of Venice* (1851–1853)—three volumes with colored plates, a treatise on the history of Venetian architecture across the Byzantine, Gothic, and Renaissance eras. Reading it produced the certainty of desire—"I want to go to Venice and make a film." He relocated to Venice with Markopoulos the following year and completed the fugal *Ruskin* in 1975.

Ruskin was thirteen when he received an important gift: Samuel Rogers's *Italy* (1830) with watercolor vignettes by J. M. W. Turner. A year later Ruskin saw three of Turner's oil paintings at the Royal Academy and, at twenty-four, he began to write a defense of Turner's atmospheric landscapes—a simultaneous assault on the one-noted art establishment taste for Old Master mimeticism—that became the five-volume *Modern Painters* (1843–1860). Beavers was also twenty-four when he began to make *Ruskin*. Images of a small book recur in the film; it is raised and lowered against a table edge under Beavers's palm: vertical, horizontal. Shot in black-and-white, without a visible title, the book remains closed.

—

*Ruskin* opens amid the marshes of Torcello—the island that preceded Venice in its rise and fall as an economic and trading center—before arriving in central Venice. The buildings (Palazzo Ducale, Santa Maria Mater Domini, Basilico San Marco, San Giovanni Evangelista) and architectural details (windows, arches, columns, gargoyles) that Ruskin drew, painted, and wrote about in *The Stones of Venice* join material shot in the Alps and London (also sites of Ruskin's writing). These exterior locations—all shot in both color and black-and-white—engage in both compositional (intra-image) and rhythmic (across the film) play with the book and other signifiers of interiority and process: shaped mattes that block, expand, and shrink; glimpses of apparatus (compendium, matte holder, lens); graphic wipes. The visual exchange is propelled by discrete sound events (moving water, turning pages, flapping bird wings), grounded by ambient multiplicity (traffic, church bells, footsteps, voices, rattling metal, birdsong), and punctuated by two sounds associated with the book—a thud of contact and a held organ note.

Beavers shot the color material at three different times—early morning, midday, late afternoon—to catch the sun's turn, but used only one stock.[2] "I left it to chance; I selected a film stock meant for light between 10:00 a.m. and 3:00 p.m. but shot before and after that period." The early shots are tinged with orange; late-day footage has a silvery tone. As in *Diminished Frame* (1970/2001), alternation between black-and-white and color signifies transit between past and present.

Ruskin's own line drawings in *The Stones of Venice* prompted Beavers's use of black-and-white film; nineteenth-century image-making was also on his mind: "Ruskin was an early photographer . . . so I thought I would try to relate the quality of the filming to the period in which he was in Venice and to that period of photography," he said.[3] A stereoscopic beat is engrained in the film's rhythm: Some *Ruskin* images briskly drop into and exit the frame from above or below—Beavers shot them *while* turning his lens turret (changing from one lens to another). "It creates a rotating, like slides being changed," Beavers said.[4] As this vertical shot transit meets the graphic horizontal emphasis in the film, *Ruskin*'s spatial articulations fluctuate and surprise. Horizontal-vertical dynamism, acted out between the filmmaker's hand and Ruskin's book, is part of the film's architectural metabolism.[5]

—

In his second *Ruskin* note, from April 1973, Beavers copied lines from Gustave Flaubert's 1849 notebook—a recollection of coping with pending separations before his departure for Egypt: "The next two days I lived lavishly—huge dinners, quantities of wine, whores. <u>The senses are not far removed from the emotions</u>, and my poor tortured nerves needed a little relaxation."[6] Identifying not with Flaubert's method but with his dilemma, Beavers added, "The artist—keeping alive sense and emotion—his means: extravagance." In reading da Vinci and Ruskin, Beavers found his own means of keeping alive. "Somehow my connection to these figures allowed me to make the films. I wanted to show my enthusiasm for them. This is the point." As with *From the Notebook of . . .* , Beavers's aim was neither biography nor emulation. "How to do this without using these wonderful inspiring figures as a crutch or imposing upon their own work? You could say they're, in a way, 'homages.'"

To run on *enthusiasm* is to allow a divine impulse to catalyze action (*enthous*—"possessed by a god [*theos*], inspired"). Beavers asked Jonas Mekas to purchase a copy of *Still Light*; he used the $1,400 payment (the first of two) from Anthology Film Archives to rent a room at the Albergo San Marco in Venice for several months. Keeping alive outside the energizing machinations of capital was one of Ruskin's primary concerns; *The Stones of Venice*, ostensibly an architectural encyclopedia, is a warning about the losses of life endemic to modernization. The imperfections, variations, and handmade "savagery" of the Gothic style Ruskin champions are signs of a craftsperson free to bring mind to hand in the creation of communal art forms and the spiritual health of his medieval society. Ruskin bundles the regularizing aesthetic ruin wrought by the Renaissance with spiritual collapse and the decline of the Venetian Empire—and delivers the trifecta back to his own industrializing British Empire: a warning about damages to hand, heart, and mind in a mercantile economy where men are "divided . . . into small fragments and crumbs of life."[7] *The Stones of Venice* is iconoclastic, a literary reading of forms of truth inscribed on architectural surfaces.

—

I asked Beavers what struck him so forcefully about Ruskin. "His sentences," he said. Informed by deep ensconcement in romantic poetry and the Bible, Ruskin's *The Stones of Venice* prose is succinct in aphoristic certainty—"To banish imperfection is to destroy expression, to check exertion, to paralyze vitality"[8]—and circuitous in hyper-descriptive direct address as he seeks to make certain his reader is also *seeing*:

> **And now come with me, for I have kept you too long from your gondola: come with me, on an autumnal morning, through the dark gates of Padua, and let us take the broad road leading towards the East. . . . We have but walked some two hundred yards when we come to a low wharf or quay at the extremity of a canal, with long steps on each side down to the water, which latter we fancy for an instant has become black with stagnation; another glance undeceives us,—it is covered with the black boats of Venice. We enter one of them, rather to try if they be real boats or not, than with any definite purpose, and glide away; at first feeling as if the water were yielding continually beneath the boat and letting her sink into soft vacancy.[9]**

Beavers selected eighteen "key fragments [from *The Stones of Venice*] that [he] wanted the spectator to be aware of."[10] After the Shakespearean actor John Gielgud turned him down (Beavers knocked on his London door), a young English writer recorded the excerpts as voiceover.[11] Beavers shot in Venice, London, and Soglio, Switzerland, between October 1973 and March 1974. "Editing of 'Ruskin' completed," he wrote in April. The film won the Maeght Foundation Prize at the Asolo Film Festival, in Venice, in May 1974.

But Beavers "wasn't satisfied" with Ruskin's voice as a legible, word-by-word element: "I thought [it] made less of the film," he told Tony Pipolo.[12] In July he began to work on a second iteration, producing an "appendix" or "coda" that approached voice indirectly: he shot his own hand flipping through the pages of an open book. "I still wanted Ruskin's voice to be in the film, and the only way that I could do it was to go to the pages—the way that they move, the way that certain words stand out, and the way that they stopped moving always at certain points—and in the editing this gains the meaning of 'seeing into reading'; it is both more direct and retains a clearer distance."[13]

Beavers saw the coda as a "replacement" for the extracted *Stones of Venice* voiceover, but the pages belong to Ruskin's *Unto This Last*, his 1860 diatribe against free-market capitalism. In 1997, when Beavers revised *Ruskin* into its third and final forty-five-minute form (the coda comprises the final fifth), he reconceptualized the organ note he had added to the second version as another "stand-in for Ruskin's voice." The organ volume increases gradually across the film. "Each time the organ sound is heard . . . it takes on a different meaning," he said.[14]

## GRIDS AND INCRUSTATIONS

In October 1973, Beavers found a wall near Saint Mark's Basilica studded with broken pieces of sculpture. "Encrusted with at least 100 fragments," he noted. He shot a portion of the wall where two different figurative fragments touched, framing it to look as if one figure is guiding the other with a gripped hand. *Incrustation* is Ruskin's word for an essential fact of Venetian construction: "The whole early architecture of Venice is architecture of incrustation. . . . The Venetian habitually incrusted his work with nacre; he built his houses, even the meanest, as if he had been a shell-fish,—roughly inside, mother-of-pearl on the surface: he was content, perforce, to gather the clay of the Brenta banks, and bake it into brick for his substance of wall; but he overlaid it with the wealth of ocean, with the most precious foreign marbles."[15] Ruskin's *incrustation* straddles documentation and poetic perception; it is a descriptive term for decorative overlay (precious topcoat over sturdy foundation) and an abstract vision of temporal and geographical superimposition. He reads Gothic building surfaces chronologically ("Renaissance engrafted on Byzantine") and in reverse (ancient leftovers embedded in brick), and Venetian architecture as jointly textured by the historical influence of cultural extremes: "the glacier stream of the Lombards" and "the lava stream of the Arab."[16] Ruskin uses *incrustation* to historicize, to prove coexistence, to vocalize his aesthetic.[17]

Beavers inserts his encrusted wall fragments into the black-and-white heart of a sequence bracketed by wide color views (an enclosed Venetian courtyard [Corte Seconda del Milion] at the beginning, an autumn Soglio hillside at the end). Inside the sequence, as framing tightens and color disappears, forms of likeness jump into relief. The black branch lines of a Soglio tree pick up the incisions of petals and peacock wings on a carved courtyard arch. A close-up of the "guiding" stone hand—dust visible in its crevices—is followed by a Soglio detail in which a leaf falls from a tree: both wall and tree are subject to decay. A shot composed by intention (selective framing produces the "guidance" narrative in the wall) is joined to one made by chance (the falling leaf).

In my own viewing, a silent phrase erupts as the sequence ends: "Surface has/is a structure." In close-up, the rough wall surface is layered by scales; at a distance, so is the grassy hill. Both appear pebbly and undulating, crossed with creases. "My discovery" is, of course, a version of a basic Ruskin idea (a passionate surface advocate, he refused to subjugate the lives of color, texture, and "variegation" to overdetermined structure), and yet it feels as if Beavers has organized revelatory contagion so that seeing is distinct for writer, filmmaker, and spectator. The psychic/aesthetic/ethical orientation that informs Beavers's wish "not to impose" on Ruskin or da Vinci, nor "disturb" their creations, also extends to the spectator. Discovery cannot be illustrated.

—

Like Beavers, Ruskin is enthusiastic. His prose is excited by the tension between the motions of water and his own ink; he imagines Venice as a dying rhythmic creature, "outwearied" and "aged" with spots of "lingering pulsation" that he must transcribe before time runs out. The eroding power of water and the forces of cultural decline conflate in Ruskin's "Sea City" of time-based forms: "I would endeavor to trace the lines of this image before it be for ever lost, and to record, as far as I may, the warning which seems to me to be uttered by every one of the fast-gaining waves, that beat, like passing bells, against the Stones of Venice."[18]

"If filming in Venice, the water must be given its own character," Beavers noted in August 1973. In the encrusted wall sequence, the sharp sounds of lapping water register, as they do elsewhere, as the source of lines, grooves, and channels. Reflected light casts unstable linear designs up canal facades and across water surfaces. The two artists share inscription-making drives (lines in the world invite tracing; writing picks up the impulse to draw), but *Ruskin* doesn't replicate Ruskin's affect and urgency. Ruskin was a high-level sublimator—the forces of repression, obsession, curiosity, and talent produced highly particular imaginative authority ("genius"). My interest is not in psychoanalyzing Ruskin, but (with Leo Bersani on the sexual shape of textual output in mind) in considering the totality of *Ruskin* as an erotic literary creature.[19] The final *Ruskin* realizes greater rhythmic complexity than the 1974 version; the pacing of the earlier film is dominated by the thinking rhythm of Ruskin's words, which sonically press images into a background position. In the revised *Ruskin*, stillness continually touches open-eyed speed. Spacious, corporeal, grounded qualities (breathing ovals, up-and-down motions—the suggestion of images bouncing on water, seductive locational presence via atmospheric sound and color portraiture) meet planar-oriented structural impulses (monochromatic frame divisions, graphic shapes and motions, architectural corners, compendium tours). The choice between cinematic absorption and distanciation doesn't apply. Looking at the two *Ruskin* versions side by side, my impulse to attribute all to image reveals its limitations: with Ruskin's voice excised from the revised film, the sounds of moving pages, wings, and water actively produce and mold shapes, stamping and structuring *Ruskin*'s architectural space. They are the sounds of reading and writing in progress.

—

Beavers shot the Alps material for *Ruskin* within walking distance of Soglio, the Swiss terrace village above the Bregaglia Valley where he had edited *Work Done* in 1972. He and Markopoulos returned there for working retreats over the next decade. "It was an important winter base for us," he said. "We were there under the protection of Rilke." The poet recovered and wrote there after World War I.[20]

The Bregaglia Valley is home to the largest chestnut forest in Europe. In *Ruskin*, shots of an elderly man foraging with a metal basket on his back join a sequence centered around the door of a thirteenth-century house in Campo Santa Margherita that Ruskin wrote about (and drew) in *The Stones of Venice* and *Examples of the Architecture of Venice*. Ruskin "reads" the grid of "small squares of cast brick" on the door tympanum: "Whichever way the courses of them are read, laterally or upwards . . . two similar patterns shall never be in juxtaposition . . . no regular recurrence of pattern . . . shall be traceable."[21] Underneath the grosser presentation of sameness, seven cast patterns—petals, crosses—generate total internal variety. Beavers follows Ruskin's reading motions—long sweeps across Campo Santa Margherita and up the Gothic door—and assembles his own grid of squares around them: city shots framed by a square matte; the black book (shot in close-up, it is a square; seen inside the compendium frame, it is like the decorative imprint *on* the cast square); matte and Bristol paper combinations in his workspace. In this context, a shingled cottage roof reads as a grid; so does the chestnut collector's metal basket. Grid-making also exceeds the pictorial: that some shots in the sequence are brought into the frame by moving swaths of black (as Beavers changes lenses while shooting) draws attention to the fact that other images arrive on-screen in the usual way—"inside" their rectangles.

—

When I asked Beavers a second time what had struck him so forcefully about *The Stones of Venice*, he replied, "the arrangements on the page." In addition to full-page color plates, dozens of black-and-white insets break up Ruskin's text. Often jutting out from the page margin, they hold example series: a group of molding forms are represented as opaque shapes (they look like a set of Beavers's mattes); globular-beaded chamfer edges have native appeal as forms. In attuning to "arrangements"—text and picture relations on the page—Beavers was reading *The Stones of Venice* from a distance. But out-of-context reading is pressed into the fabric of Ruskin's own pages. His illustrations sometimes mislead in their evidentiary appearance: a grid of thirty-seven arches—a chronological catalog of changing shapes spanning three centuries—belies not only Ruskin's assertions of temporal coexistence but his figurative infusion of arches with religious and psychic powers. Ruskin's drives toward taxonomy, poetic vision, and moral judgment play out irregularly across image and text as he redefines the elements of architecture, arguing for a new alphabet of forms away from received taste and convention. "Mostly, matters of any consequence are three-sided, four-sided, polygonal, and the trotting round a polygon is severe work for anyone stiff in their opinions," Ruskin said in the inaugural address to the Cambridge School of Art in 1858.[22]

## ACTOR'S INCIDENT

Beavers wanted "to show his enthusiasm" for Ruskin's book—and "this is the point." "To show" is to display, to make visible (as a noun, *show* tips toward theater, spectacle). Beavers favors the word when recalling his intentions. (Ruskin is a frequent user too: *show* holds his wish to divine a craftsperson's exact mind-state. Spacing between marble inlays "would have looked awkward, if there had been the least appearance of its being an accidental error; so that, in order to . . . show that it is done on purpose, the upper triangles are made about two inches higher than the lower ones.")[23] About *Ruskin* in relation to *From the Notebook of . . .*, Beavers said, "I'm showing much more of the text that I'm actually following and reading, of the book that I'm not showing. In *From the Notebook of . . .* I'm involved much more with my own notes."

Beavers distinguishes between "showing/reading" *the text* and "not showing" *the book* (which is closed, unidentified, unquoted). He is showing the text he is reading in the present tense of making the film: performative means produce the fruits of ongoing exchange (between Beavers and Ruskin and between Beavers's original reading of *The Stones of Venice* and its imaginative aftermath). The film does not report back on the definitive impact of bound words. "Reading" *The Stones of Venice* spanned twenty-five years as Beavers made the film (and this orientation was there from the start: in December 1973, Beavers noted, "*Ruskin* is a 'reading.'"). But the open field of "reading" is not homogenous. The beat of direct visual citation—what Beavers calls "following"—is crucial to the rhythm of *Ruskin*. "I followed very carefully locations that he mentions in the book. I even followed drawings that he did." We see not only Ruskin's buildings and details (Church of San Donato in Murano, arch in Corte Seconda del Milion, sculpted relief on the Palazzo Ducale) but also his long-preoccupying natural forms: stone, mountain, cloud, fog, snow.

In writing about the 1997 film, I sometimes integrate notes Beavers made while working on the first and second versions. A "first" or "final" version is an inherently retroactive notion, and each iteration does not sync up with a pure and consistent intention. While working on the original voiceover version, for example, Beavers already wondered, in his notes, about representing Ruskin's voice abstractly: "Can the voice become the movement in the film? A line in more than the usual sense." And his coda notes reveal a plan to generate a voiceover from *Unto This Last*.[24] Beavers's memories sometimes conflict with the evidence of his notes—perhaps due not as much to "forgetting" as the way that the consolidation of intention, a form of belief, overrides the book-keeping memorization of ideas in time.

—

The closed book under the filmmaker's palm is an actor in a show. Beavers's performative deliberateness (he slowly lifts and lowers the volume with the movement of his wrist) and the unfamiliarity of the gesture exude intimate formality and, amalgamated with the organ note, solemnity. It is a *necessary* gesture. Graphic contrast heightens theatricality: Beavers covered table and wall with black and white pieces of Bristol paper ("Film the Ruskin volume against black and white and in black/white," he instructed himself in October 1973). As planes separate by visual contrast, semiotic links also get pulled apart. "Actor's incident—separate the act from the word, use the one as a double for the other," he wrote in a July 1973 note. The image of the book hitting the table (act) is rarely in sync with the recurring thud (word). Instead, the sound frequently accompanies a shot change.

The persistent sound of fluttering pages in the first part of the film won't meet its image (Beavers manipulating the open book) until the coda. Separations and diegetic zigzag make the total contact between Beavers's palm and the book bracing: an image of feeling amid so much deregistration.[25]

Even untouched, the book performs. Subject to angles of encounter, it changes shape: centrally recessed slab, edgeless field, dimensional shadow-caster. And it ascends and drops (via pan) inside a round-edged metal frame: by pushing the far face of his adjustable compendium forward—away from the camera—Beavers brings this extension of his camera into the shot. "Filmed 600 feet of mattes and book. Continue to show the matte box with matte and the dimensions of the book—the sides, corners, etc.," he noted in December 1973. The book is associated with the family of apparatus elements in the film, and Beavers's table (site of both reading and filmmaking elements) functions as a kind of architecture studio where other imagery in the film gets metabolized and re-presented. A three-dimensional triangular structure built from black mattes on the artist's table, for instance, follows a sequence of shots dominated by triangles (decorative Murano inlays, Swiss mountains "encrusted" by matte). Beavers has pulled triangles off the brick wall and out of his compendium and placed them on his table.

### DECORATION BY DISKS

A silver handle allows a Bolex user to select, with a turn, one of three available lenses mounted on a flat, semicircular turret. Conventionally, one switches lenses *between* recordings ("I record shot A with lens #1 and then shot B with lens #2"). In the sixteenth of his *Early Monthly Segments* (1968–1970/2002), Beavers first experimented with incorporating the motion of a lens change *into* a shot. The turret turn "became a strong feature" in *Ruskin*, Beavers said to Pipolo.[26] Beavers kept shooting as he moved between 10mm wide-angle and 25mm and 50mm telephoto lenses. As a result, images arrive and depart in motion—vertically deposited into or pulled out of the frame, via black. The moving lens "opens the shot . . . it creates possibilities in editing," said Beavers. Unlike the dissolve (the consistently gradated sign of "joinedness"), the irregular black trace of the turret turn obscures the border between shots; it links the kinetics of two shots—as if transferring motion. The move also externalizes the always-there facts of projection: individual frames separated by black (frame lines) reach the shutter gate in motion.

A lens that is *not* moving while askew from a centered position over the aperture leaves a curve on the top or bottom of an image. In *Ruskin*, a black arc hangs over a shot of the shadow cast by Andrea del Verrocchio's equestrian statue of Bartolomeo Colleoni, in Campo Santi Giovanni e Paolo. The downward camera angle fits the shadow snugly under the curve. The spectator is situated, by identification, as if she is looking at the ground, but she is looking straight ahead: at the image on a screen hung vertically. "You're seeing the image as if it's horizontal, but you're seeing it vertically," said Beavers. "Its possibilities seemed to expand because of the locations used," he said to Pipolo about the use of the moving turret in *Ruskin*. "As you choose your angle to film in relation to the placement of the lens, it is possible to create a new perspective. . . . There is a special concern in *Ruskin* with what is horizontal and what is vertical, and by placing the lens in these unusual ways, one can reach other elements of the horizontal and vertical you could not normally get to. And for a film on architectural themes, this was useful."[27]

*Ruskin*'s primary curve source is not the lens but an oval matte. In the first minute of the film, it has multiple representational outcomes: a floating, hazy-edged, expanding/shrinking shape, a frame for a Torcello landscape (like a nineteenth-century photograph), a documented object (a rectangular piece of white board with a hole punched out of its center). "I had been looking at the ceilings in the Scuola San Rocco and in the Palazzo Ducale, and the framing of the images in these ceilings when you look up at them have something of a dual dimension. It was probably from these ceilings that I developed the use of the oval matte," Beavers said. Tintoretto's Old Testament scenes on the Scuola Grande di San Rocco ceilings are recessed behind ornate, geometrically shaped frames. Looking up, Beavers could read the round painted scenes in two ways. Seeing according to the totality of the space produced a field of flat ovals and circles. But by narrowing his attention to a single shape, dissociating from the contextual logic of the larger space and submitting to the angle of his perspective, Beavers could read the far edge of a circular painting (the portion farthest away from him) as dropping down: it looked as if a circle were hanging down perpendicularly from the ceiling. He was reading top to bottom rather than front to back.

Beavers wanted to convert this cameraless observation into experiential potential for the spectator. With an abrupt exposure change, a plump oval shape (produced by the matte) appears to "turn over" and occupy recessive space. "I'm creating a rhyme between that observation in space [looking at the Venice ceilings] and the matte and the lens—the three are interacting," Beavers said. An off-screen "moment of seeing"—for the filmmaker in the palace or the viewer in the cinema—is one of the elements involved in the rhyme scheme.

In November 1973, Beavers made notes on the compression of seeing-in-time-and-space into a film image that holds the filmmaker's "decisions" as well as "unseen" elements: "The moment in seeing has as much to do with the image created as the space which is seen. In film, the space is transposed to a moment, and the maker's decision is of how it will be done. This is shown one way by the film frames which catch the unseen image of natural action or camera movement." In *Ruskin*, a female pedestrian walks into one of the carefully composed shots of the equestrian statue shadow, emphasizing the line painted on the ground. "We are never seeing space alone; we are always in the moment—we can't experience one without the other," Beavers said. Because the lens itself is generally out of mind in spectatorship and because the roundness of the lens is designed not to be seen or used (a central rectangular portion correlates to the film frame and the screen), its full circumference and surface area become zones of transfer for excess seeing and awareness. "Everything I have filmed has been with the entire frame of the lens," Beavers told Markopoulos while making *Ruskin*.[28]

The lens turret turn's movement through black establishes a communicative ligature with the blacks of black-and-white images and the mattes (rectangle, oval, triangle) that frame, block, emphasize, and reverse. A triangular matte follows a diagonal London roofline; vertical mattes cordon off the outer thirds of a shot and mimic the light poles on a London sidewalk.[29] At the same time, formal/figurative dialogue links buildings and book (shadow, angle, window, column, surface) and crosses locations and senses (Beavers's knuckles on the book, in close-up, look like a mountain range; accompanied by water sounds, they are a series of waves). The A and B of figurative comparison lose their roles: neither source nor imaginative double are stable. Such varieties of formal equanimity limber up the film image and facilitate space-sculpting as the true enthusiasm and full-bodied vocal independence of the film.

## TIME PUNS

When, in the black-and-white coda, Beavers manipulates the pages of *Unto This Last*, picture and sound finally meet. We discover that the now familiar sound of pages fluttering accompanies an arc: the falling pages of a fully open book produce a semicircle in space. "The rectangle of the book has become a circle by its movement—a rotation, ascending and descending," Beavers wrote while making the coda in 1975.

The horizon line is also a site of latent roundness. "The viewpoint in *Ruskin* is suspended above the horizon," Beavers wrote in his coda notes in late 1974. When I asked if the horizon note was important, Beavers replied, "I think that the answer is 'yes and no.'" A mobile lens takes the horizon line with it (vertical pans, the turning turret). Unfixed, the horizon line becomes an active element in the film, performing "up and down" as both an architectural and a divine concern: the organ note reaches maximum volume over a sharp-angled pan to the crest of Santa Maria della Salute near the end of the first section. In the coda, a thin white line descends on a black screen, the pages *fall*, as did Venice (and with it art and spirit), according to Ruskin. Beavers has organized ascension and decline between structural organizing principle and figurative motif: he has *used* Ruskin's voice.

Reading unfolds unevenly in the coda: some of the *Unto This Last* pages stop moving "on their own" mid-fall; Beavers willfully points to a certain phrase with his finger ("ascertain the nature of PRICE" or "this PLACE, observe"); the spectator catches single words and assembles her own sequences. The controversial *Unto This Last* marked a focal transition for Ruskin from art to social reform. It gathered the undercurrent of capitalist diatribe in *The Stones of Venice* into a working-class manifesto: for a living wage, against the free market. "There is no wealth but life," he writes. "The art of making yourself rich, in the ordinary mercantile economist's sense, is therefore equally and necessarily the art of keeping your neighbour poor."[30]

Once Beavers used the Maeght Prize for *Ruskin* to pay off lab debts, he and Markopoulos were on the precipice of starvation. He asked the Maeght Foundation—the dealer Aimé Maeght's private collection of modern art in Saint-Paul-de-Vence, in southeast France—for a place to stay. The resulting residency "was a disaster—we were eating grapefruits off the trees on the property in this jet-set village." Beavers's mother sent money and Markopoulos called James Baldwin, who lived in the village. "I'm sorry—I don't have any money to give you," Baldwin said.

—

While making the coda, Beavers inserted Ruskin's date of death—"20 January 1900"—between the two film parts. "[My intention was] first that it was 1900 and the beginning of a century [and] then . . . the simple transcendent fact of death as release into another world. With this date Ruskin becomes his work," he said. He removed the date in 1992, but the wish to conjure the nineteenth century remained: "How we perceive space and sound is directly related to the period in which we are living. How a musical note is heard in the eighteenth century is different from how it is heard now. I am using a nineteenth-century way of seeing as a filter or mirror, and I wanted to show this." Beavers removed his lens while shooting near Champéry, Switzerland, giving the shots of falling snow in the coda the look of cosmic debris. He got closer to the primitive structure of a camera obscura, a box with a hole that functions as an eye.

Beavers rarely invokes photography. "It's still a mystery to me how much connection there is between filmmaking and photography; I have a feeling there is not too much. The whole [notion] of develop[ing] photos—one moment printed onto paper, [whereas] in film, projected light is the essence. There is a fundamental difference." He limits his authority—"I'm saying this as a filmmaker who doesn't know"—and identifies his origins not in the technical but in text. "From the beginning, as a boy, I was not interested in the [mechanical side] of cameras and projectors—I was more of a reader, a big reader."

Following Ruskin's writing to the sculpted corners of the Palazzo Ducale, Beavers shows us Noah's "profusion of flowing hair and beard" and the grapes that inebriated him.[31] Four decades after Beavers shot Noah, photography historians discovered daguerreotypes that Ruskin made in preparation for *The Stones of Venus*; among them is a black-and-white image of Noah and his grapes. Beavers unwittingly replicated Ruskin's daguerreotype as he looked through a nineteenth-century filter.[32]

Early in his *Ruskin* notes, Beavers wrote: "A time-pun: 2 different moments in the same image (sign)." *Ruskin* compounds multiple moments of seeing and reading into its encrusted images: 1900 + 1969 + 1973 + 1974 + 1992. Beavers called the film *Ruskin, A Reading* before he changed the title to *FAULT* (a play on geology and ethics) and then, after seeing *TENNYSON*, Jasper Johns's 1958 encaustic-and-canvas collage work, selected *Ruskin*. "Johns was another visual artist responding to a nineteenth-century writer," Beavers said. Alfred Tennyson's last name appears in stenciled Roman letters along the bottom edge of the painting; Johns painted and folded a portion of the canvas down onto itself, like a page.

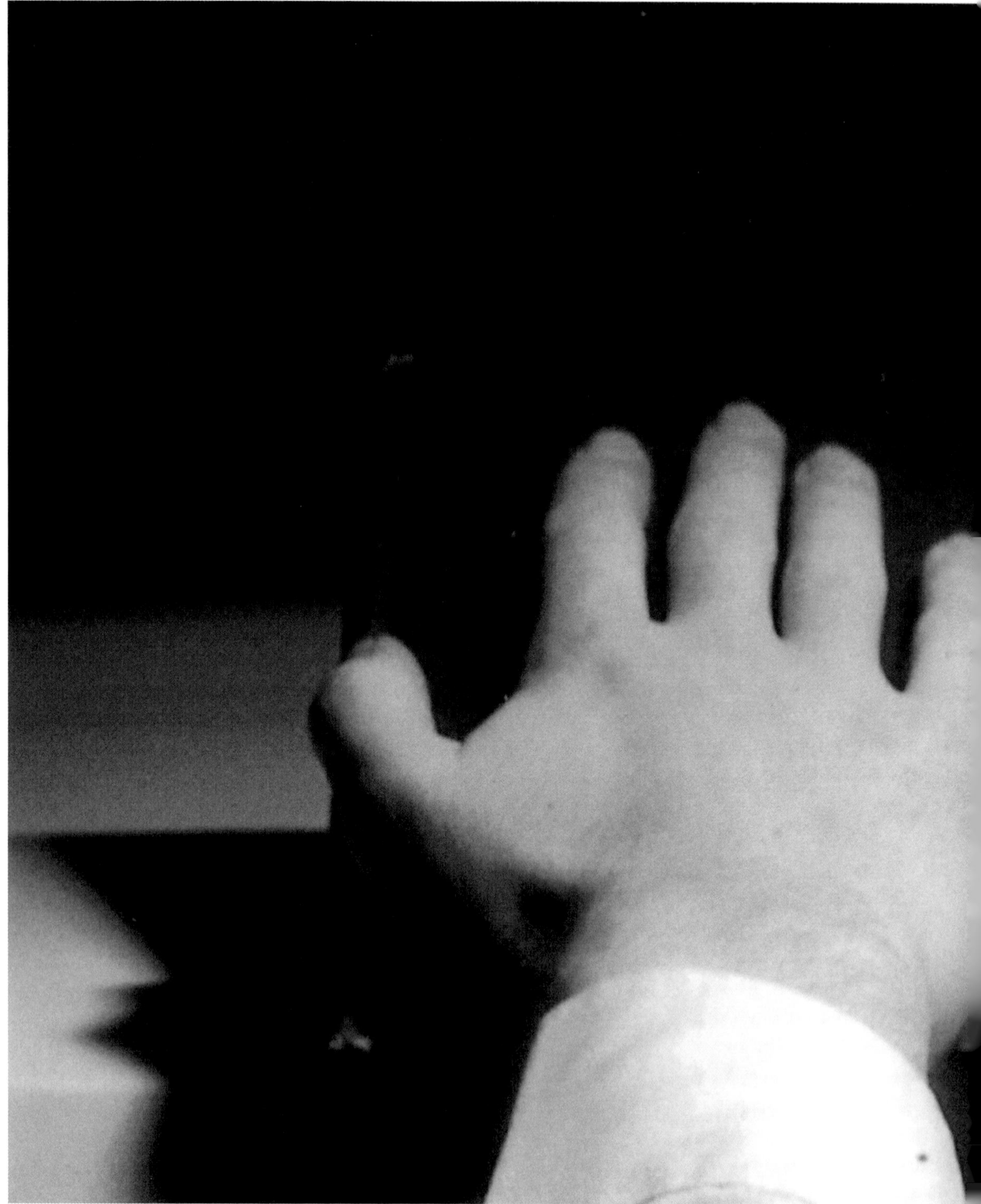

*Ruskin* (1975/1997)

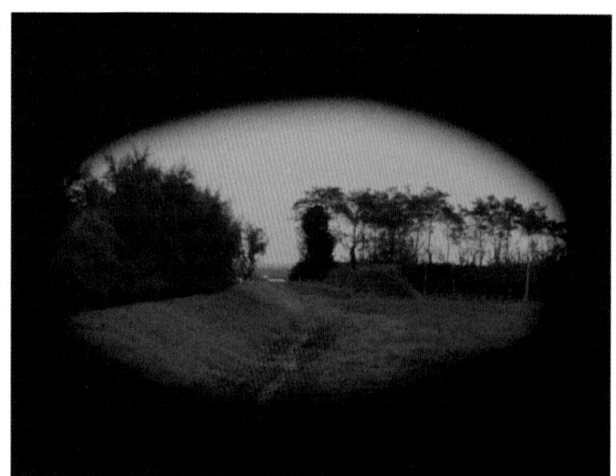

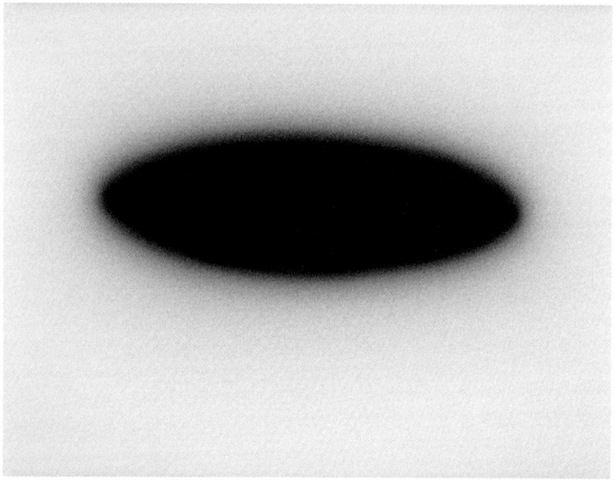

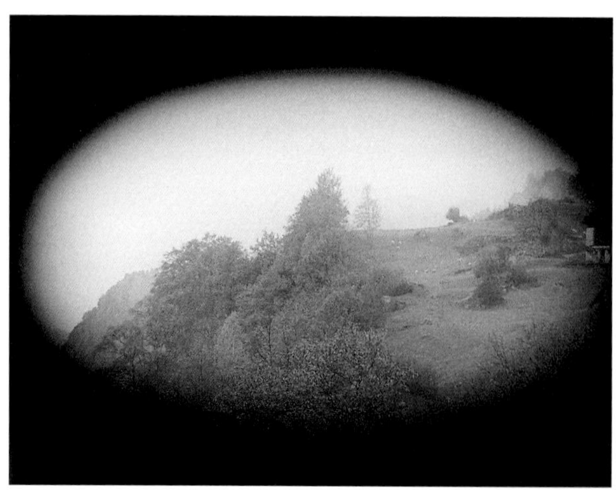

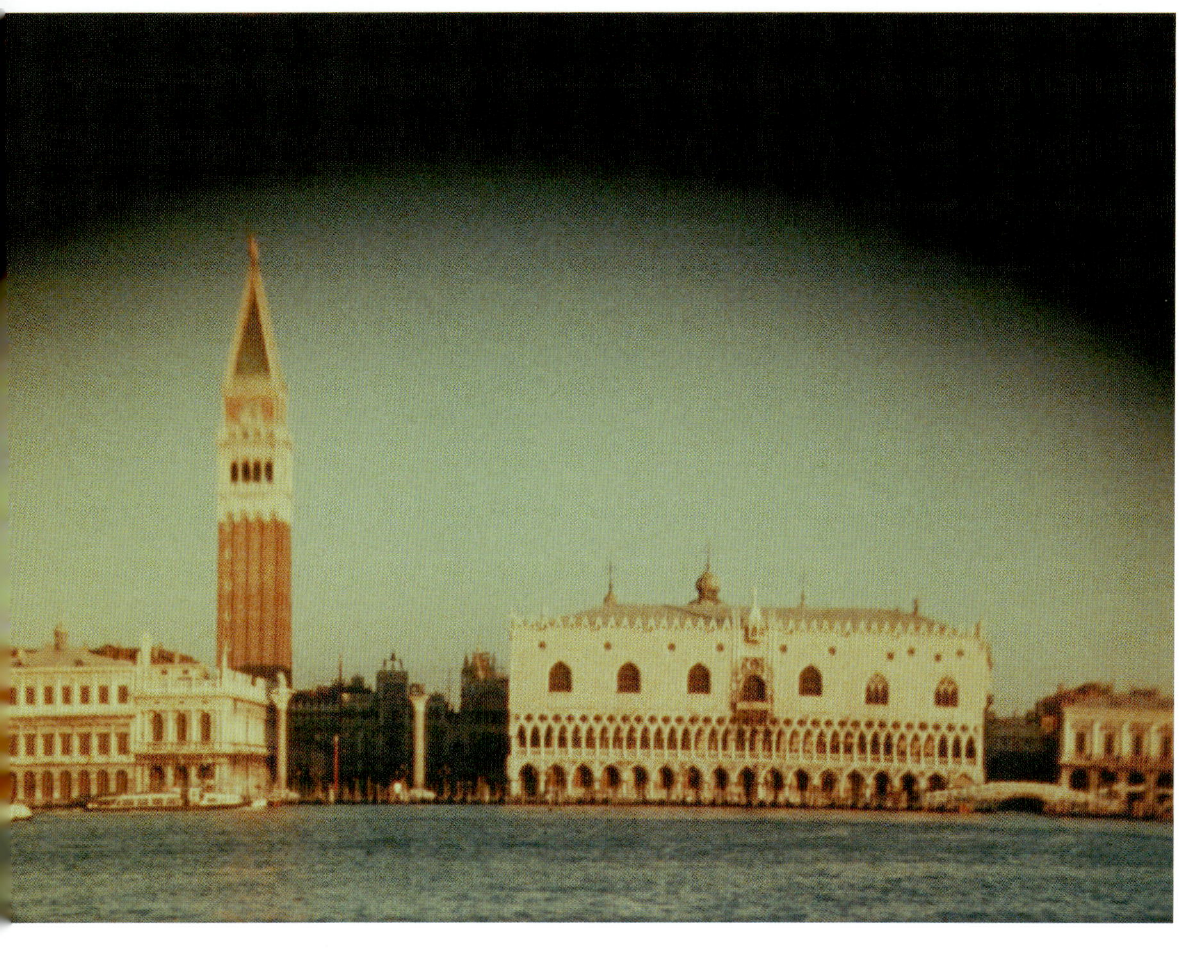

*Ruskin* (1975/1997)

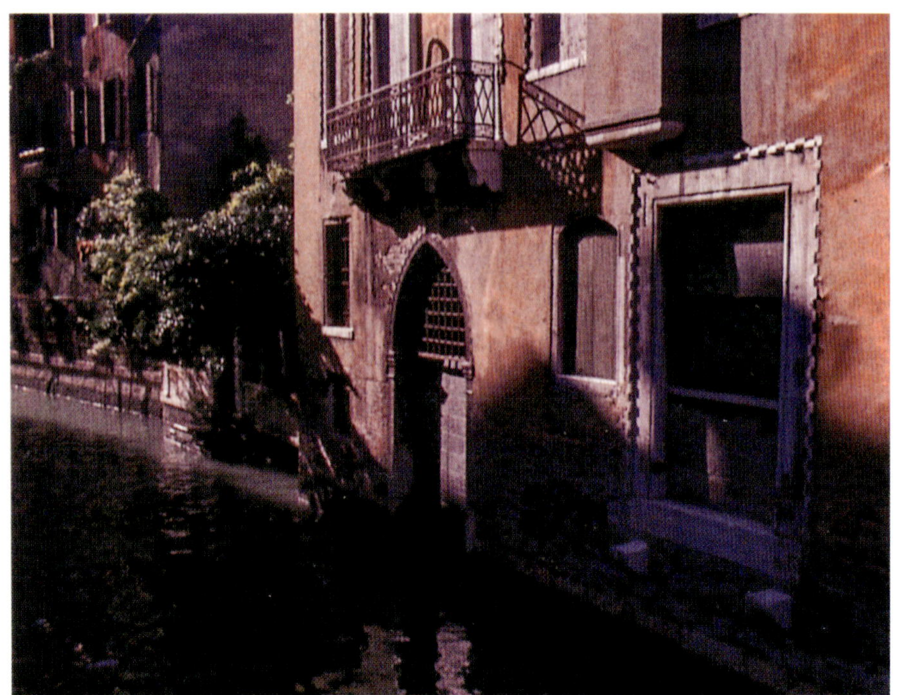

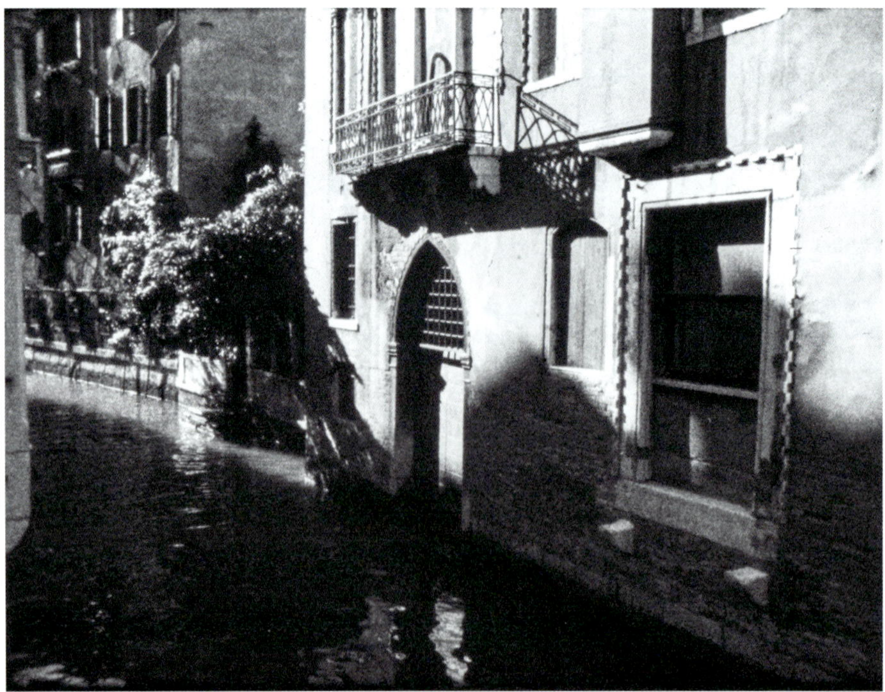

*Ruskin* (1975/1997)

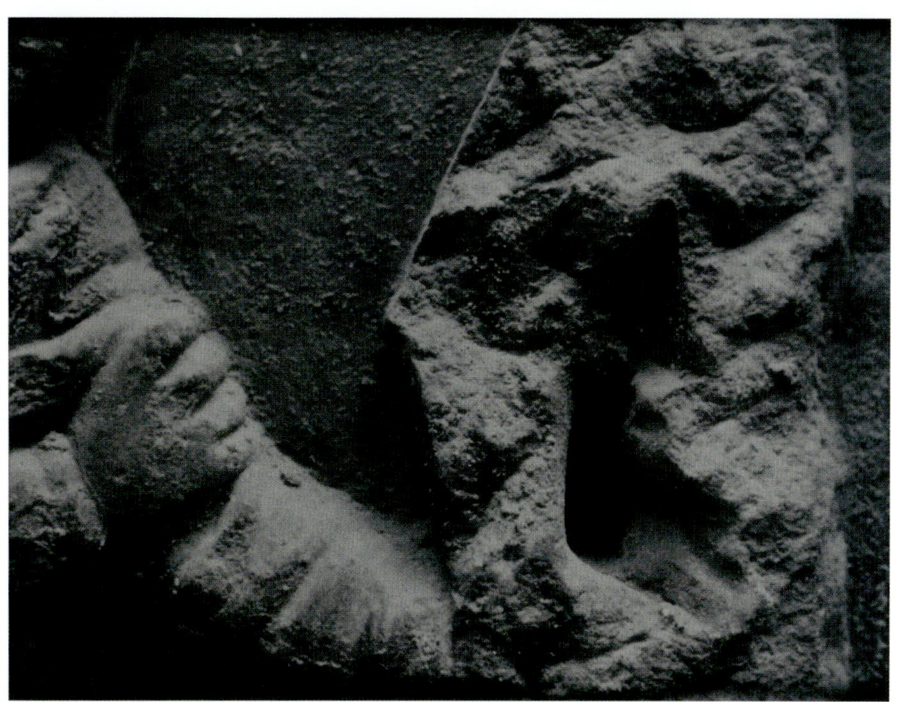

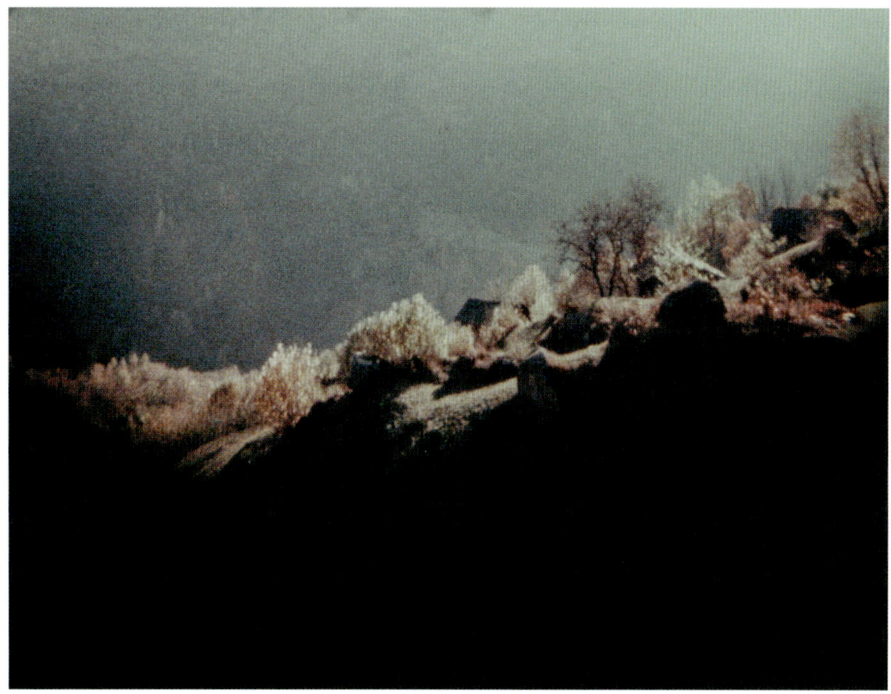

*Ruskin* (1975/1997)

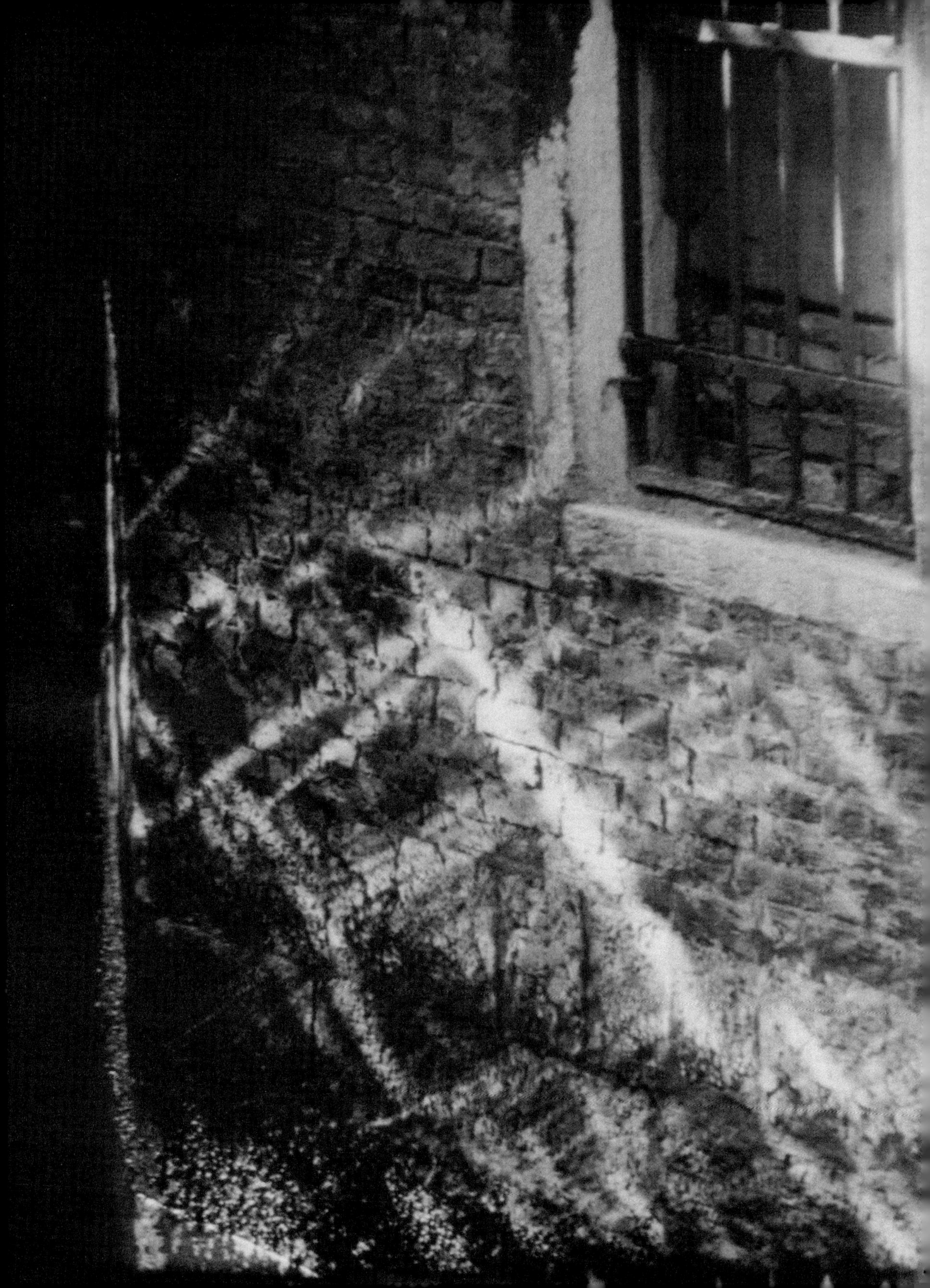

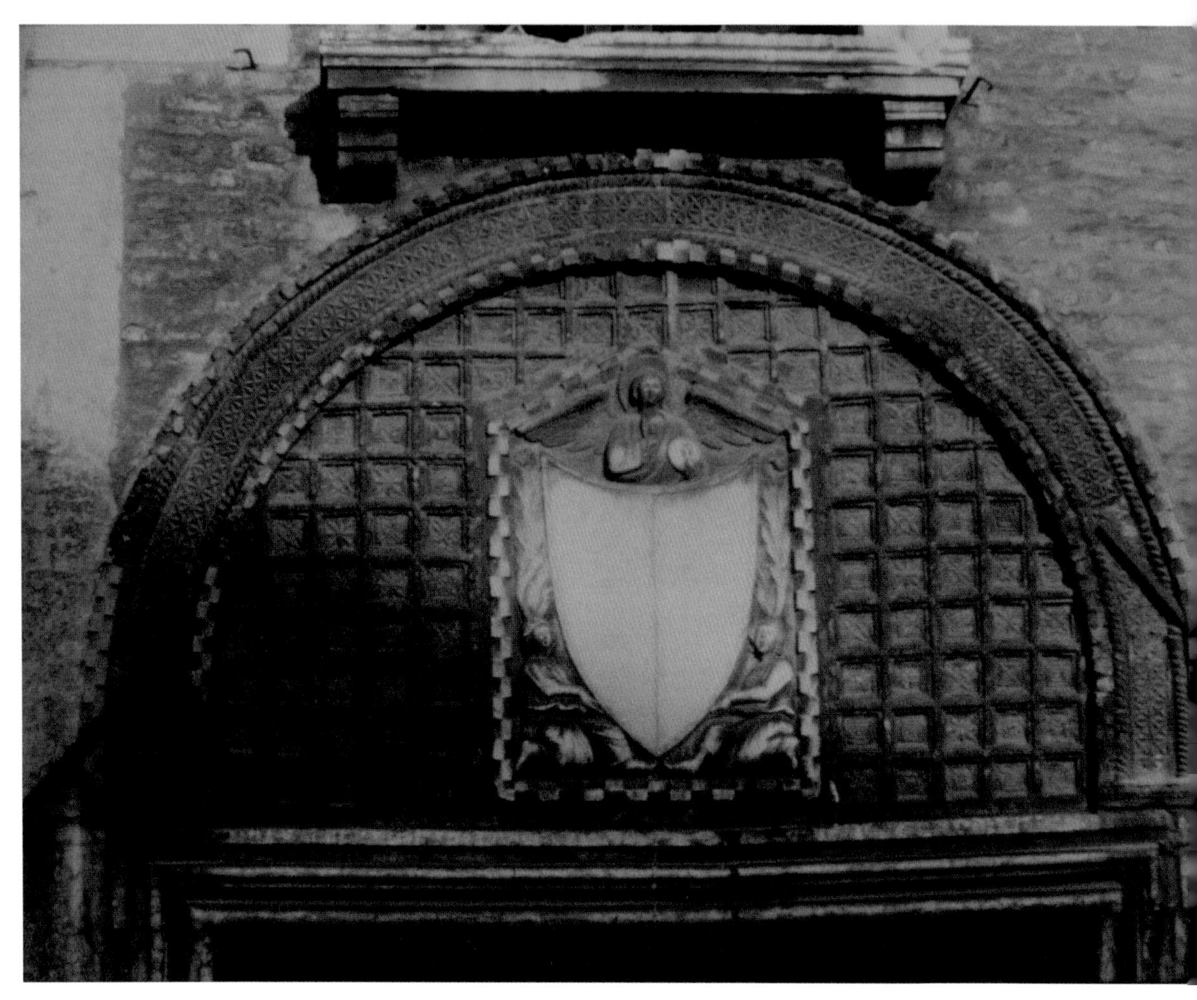

*Ruskin* (1975/1997)

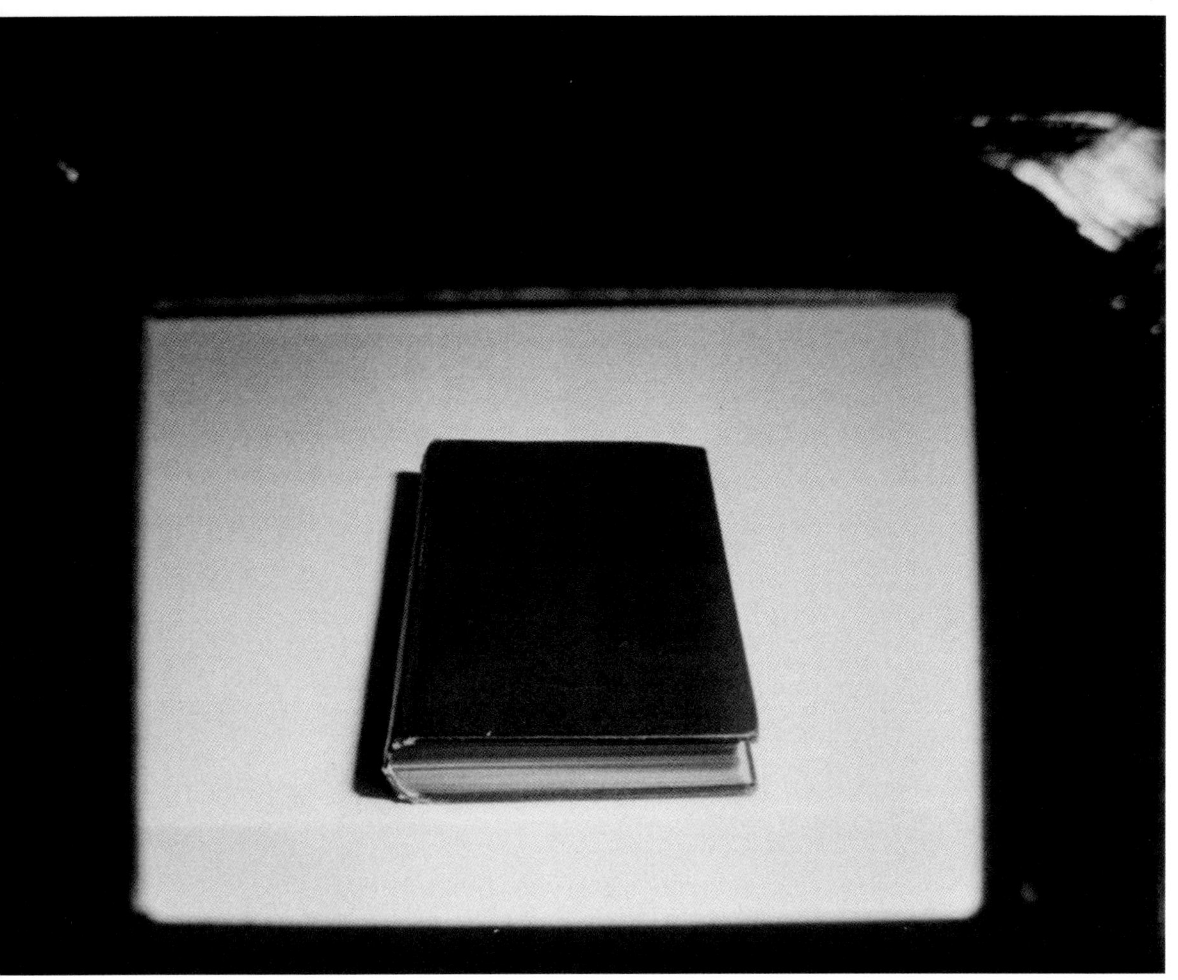

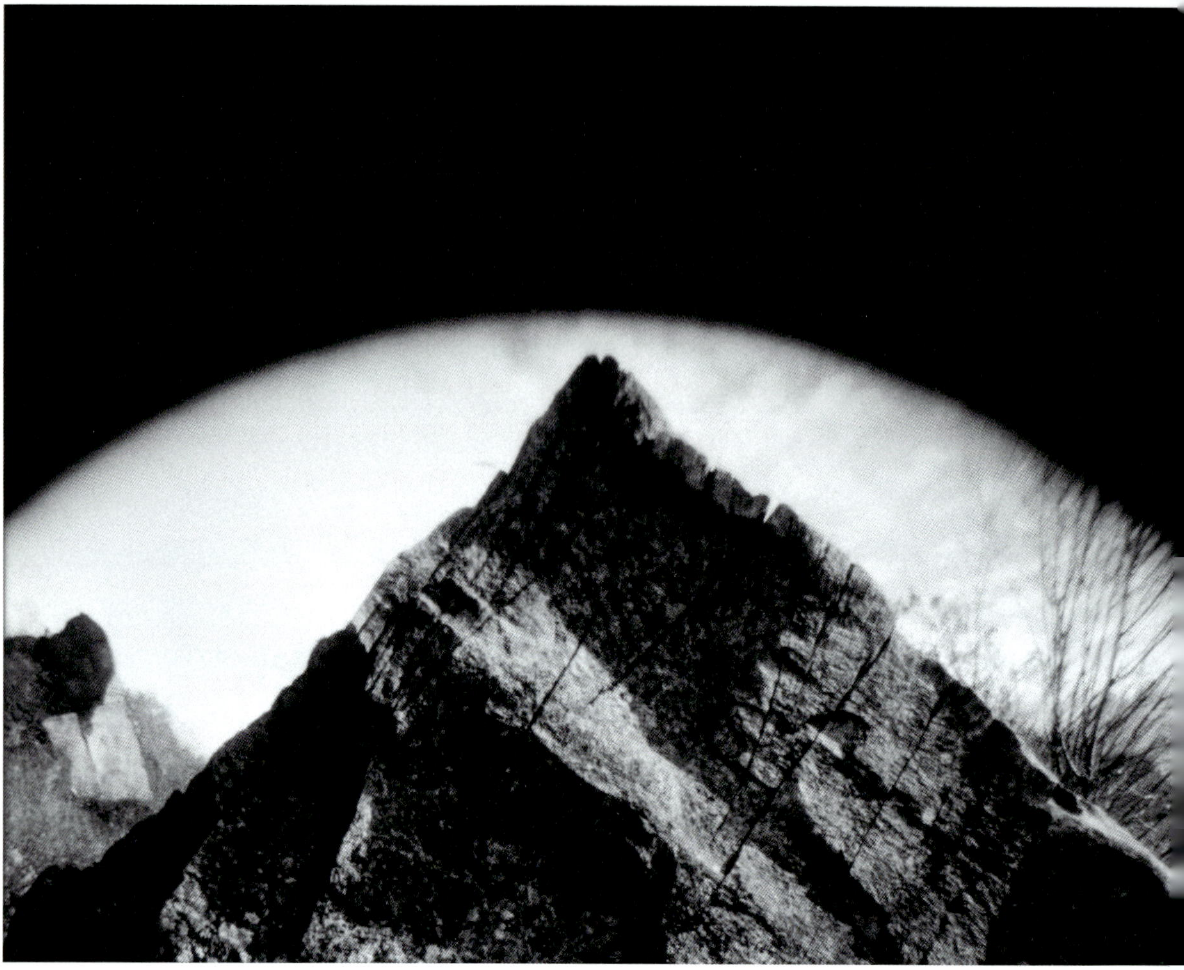

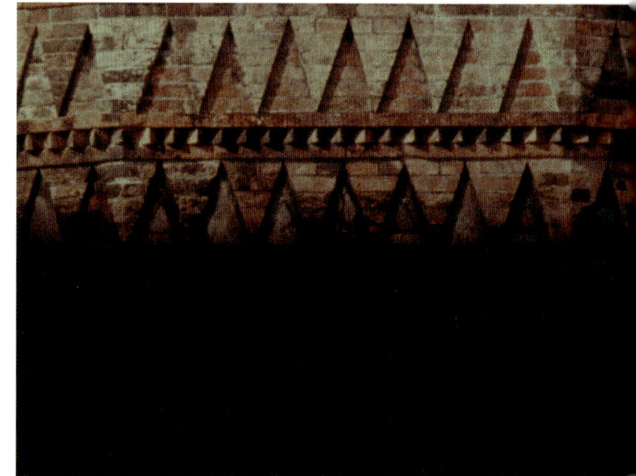

*Ruskin* (1975/1997)

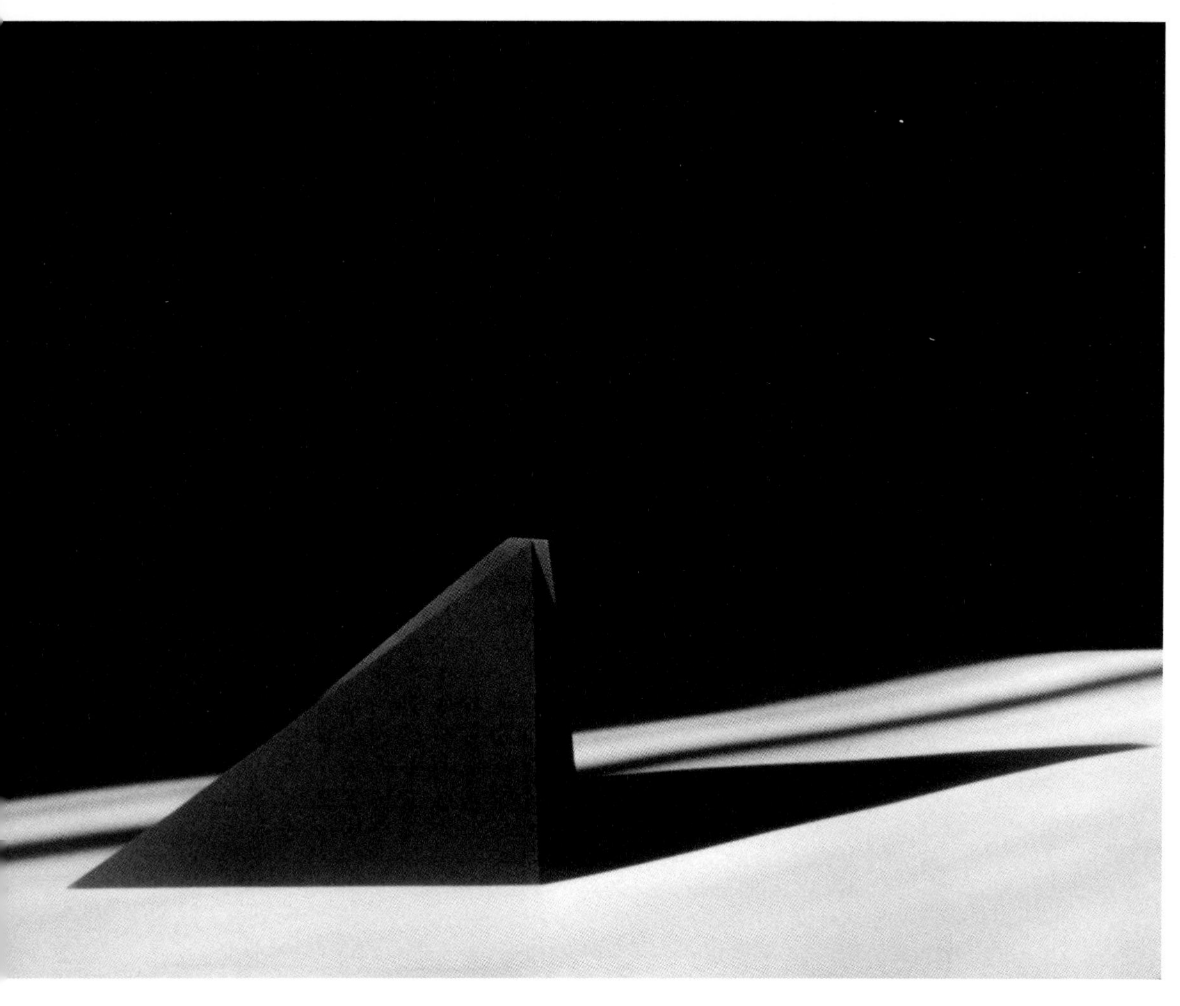

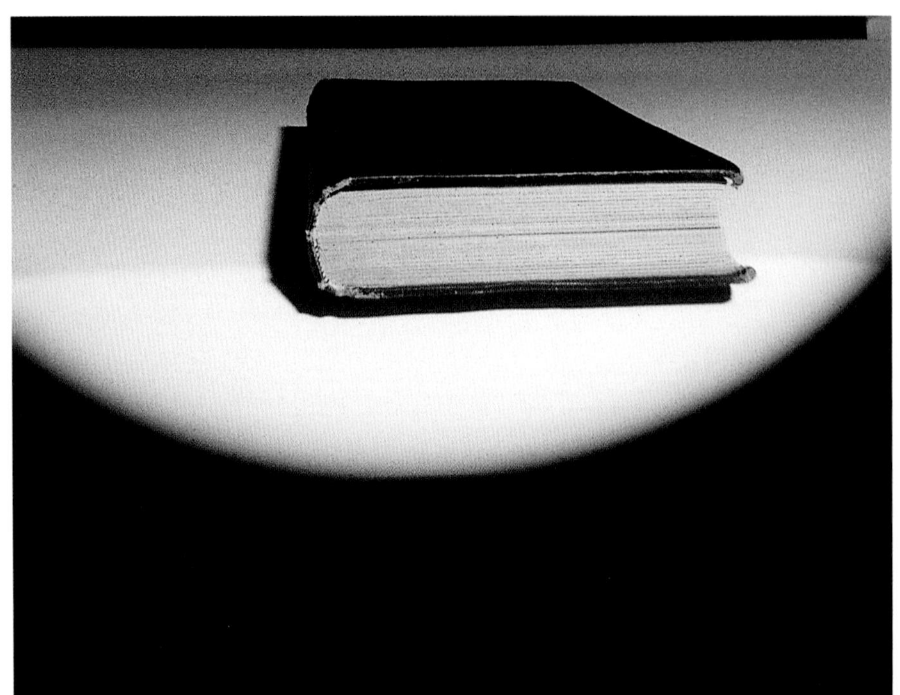

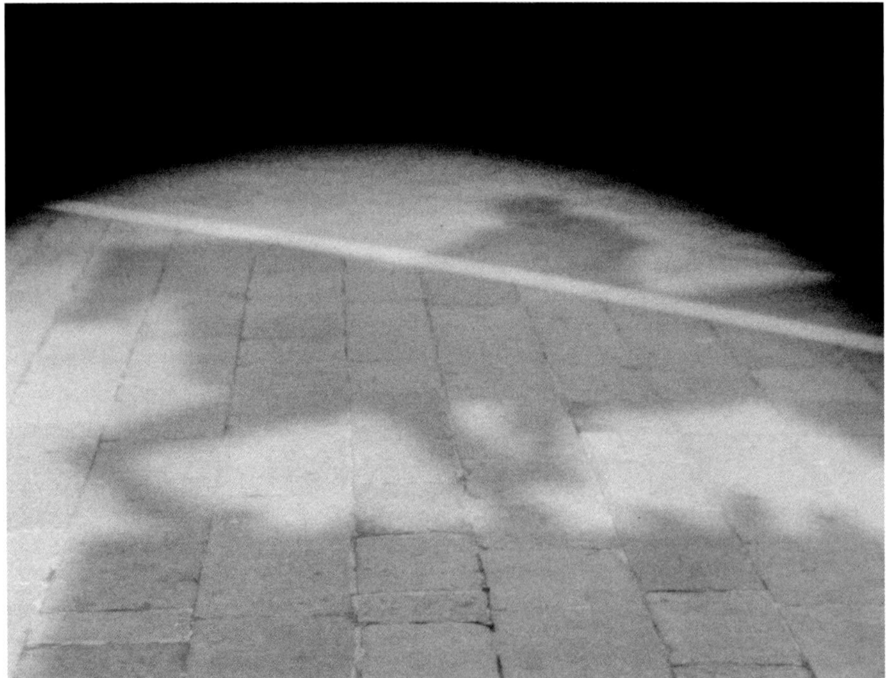

*Ruskin* (1975/1997)

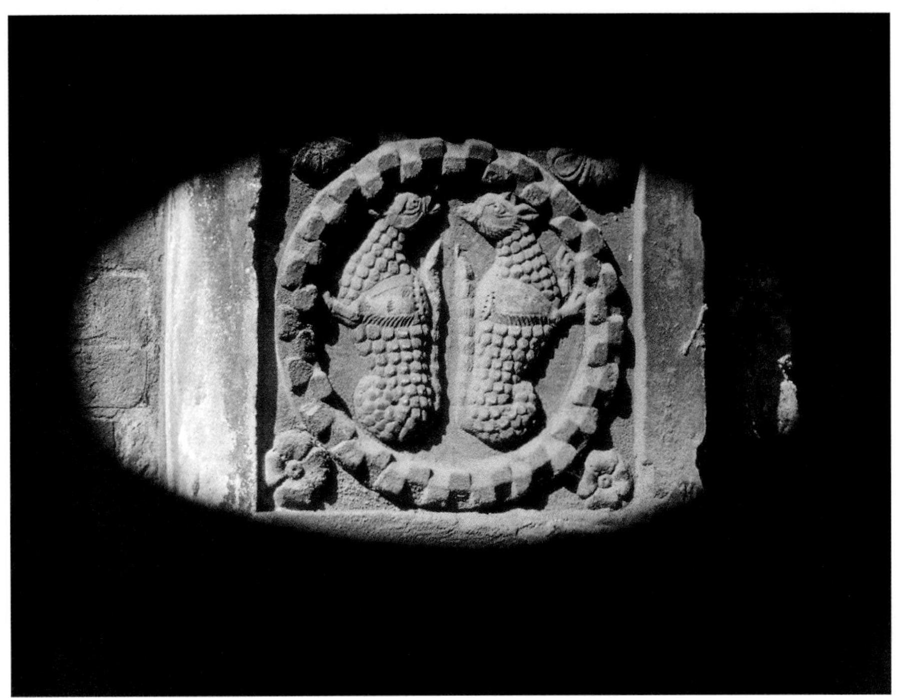

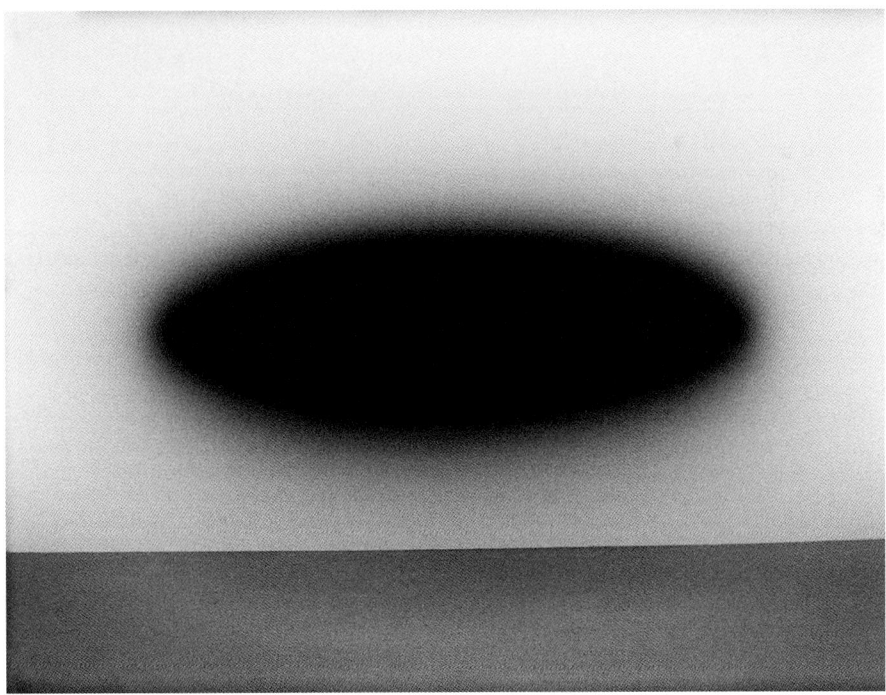

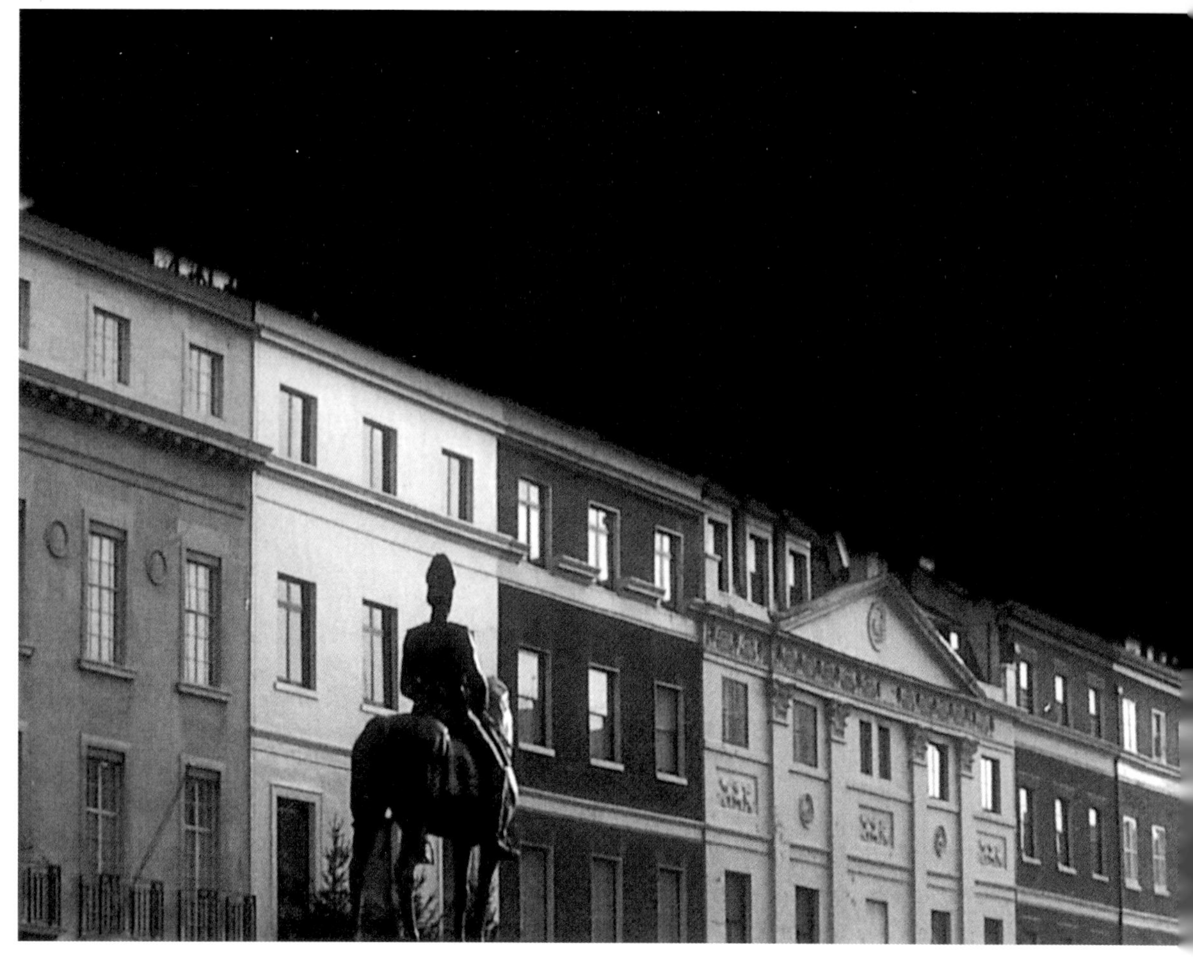

*Ruskin* (1975/1997)

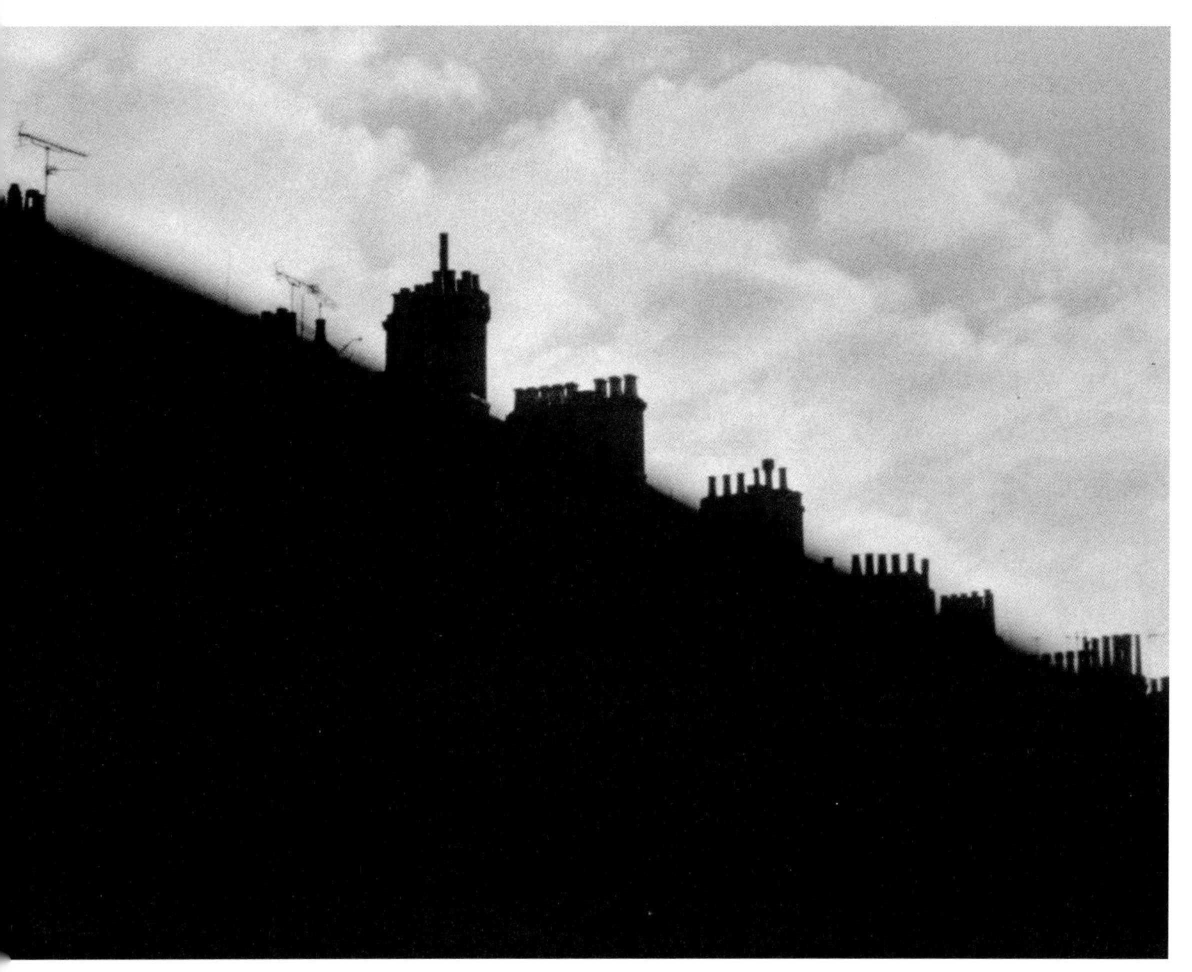

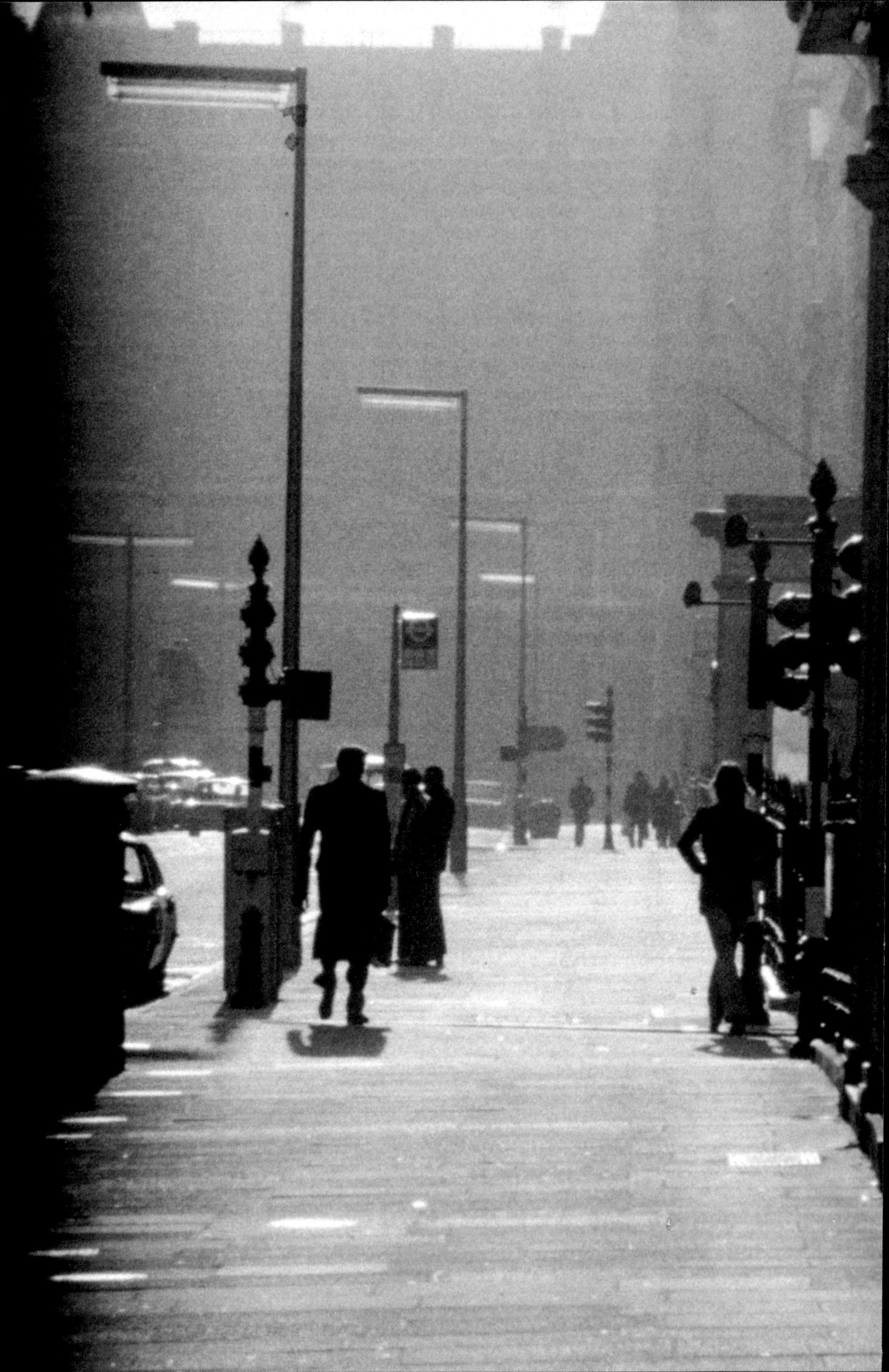

*Ruskin* (1975/1997)

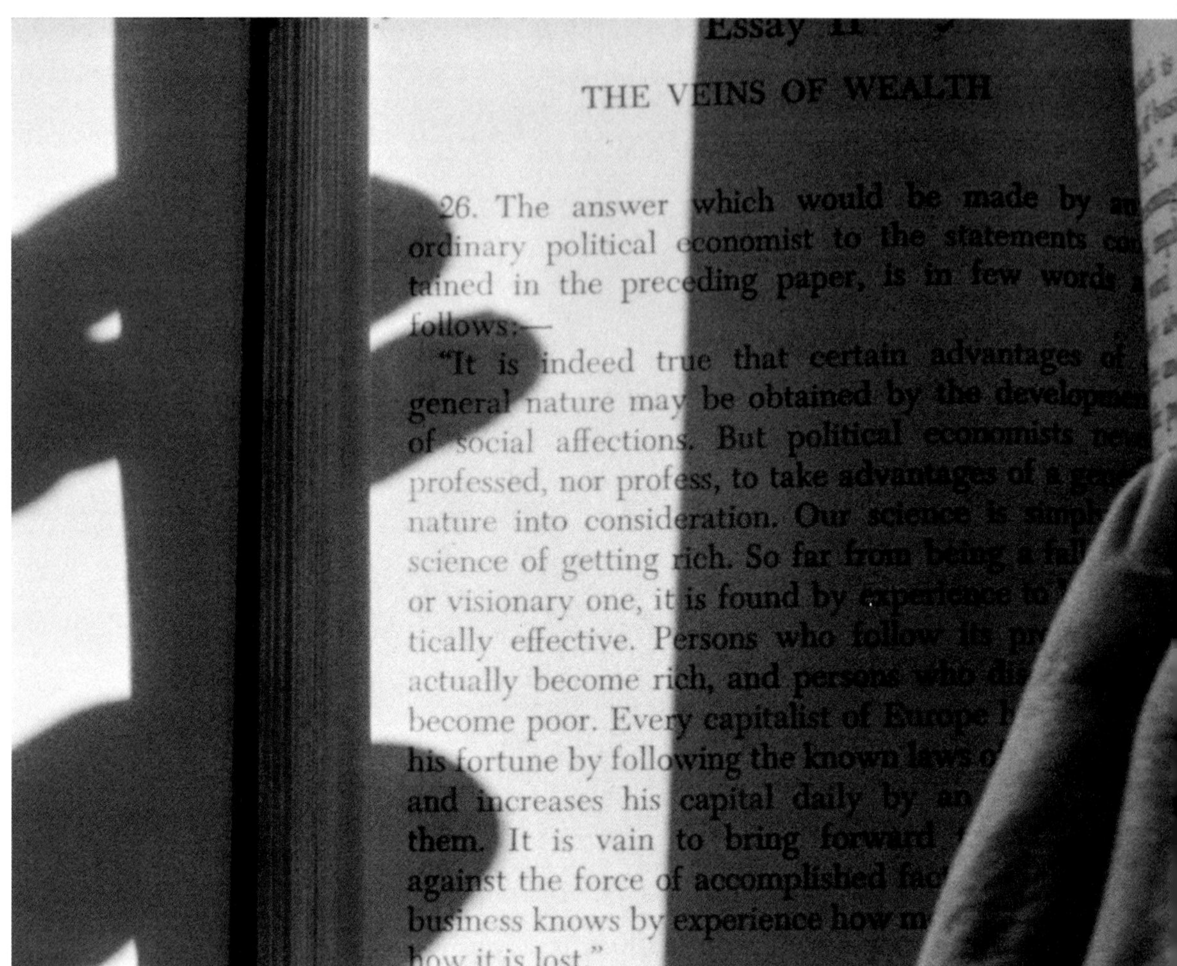


*Ruskin* (1975/1997)

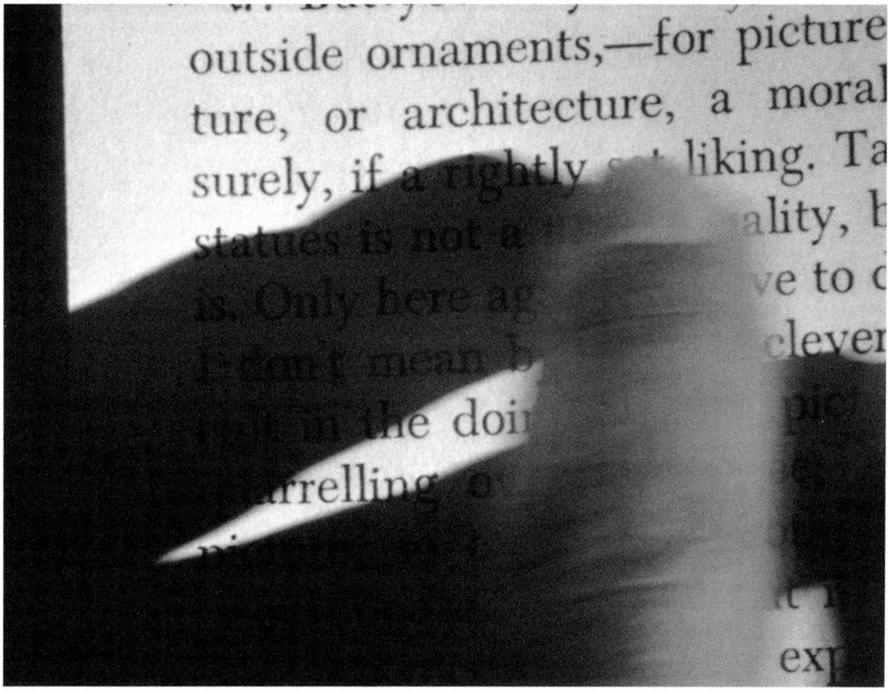
outside ornaments,—for picture
ture, or architecture, a moral
surely, if a rightly
liking.

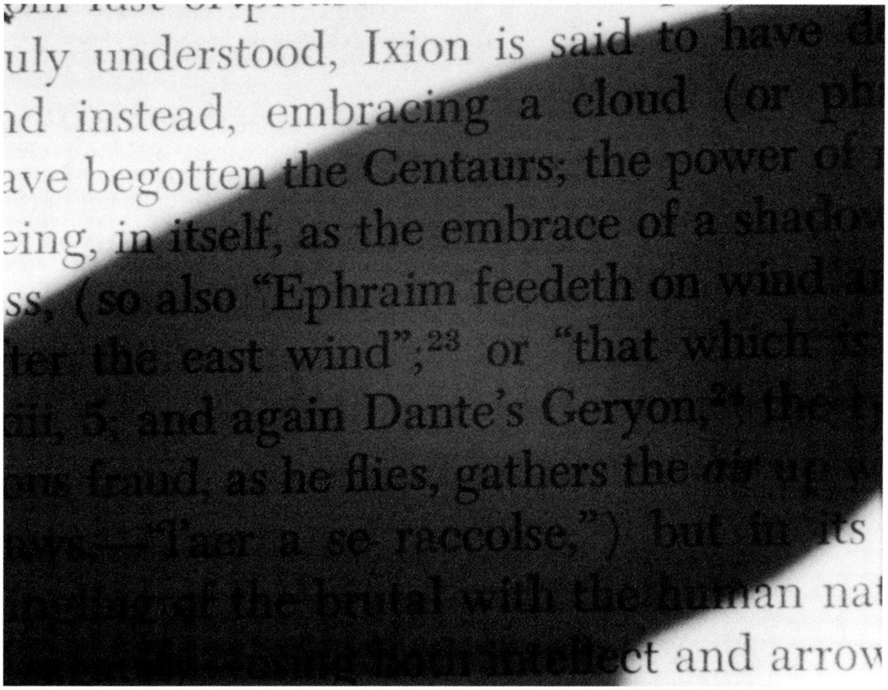
uly understood, Ixion is said to have
nd instead, embracing a cloud (or
ave begotten the Centaurs; the power of
eing, in itself, as the embrace of a shadow
ss, (so also "Ephraim feedeth on wind
ter the east wind";23 or "that which
and again Dante's Geryon,
fraud, as he flies, gathers the air
"l'aer a se raccolse,") but in its
of the brutal with the human nat
ct and arrow

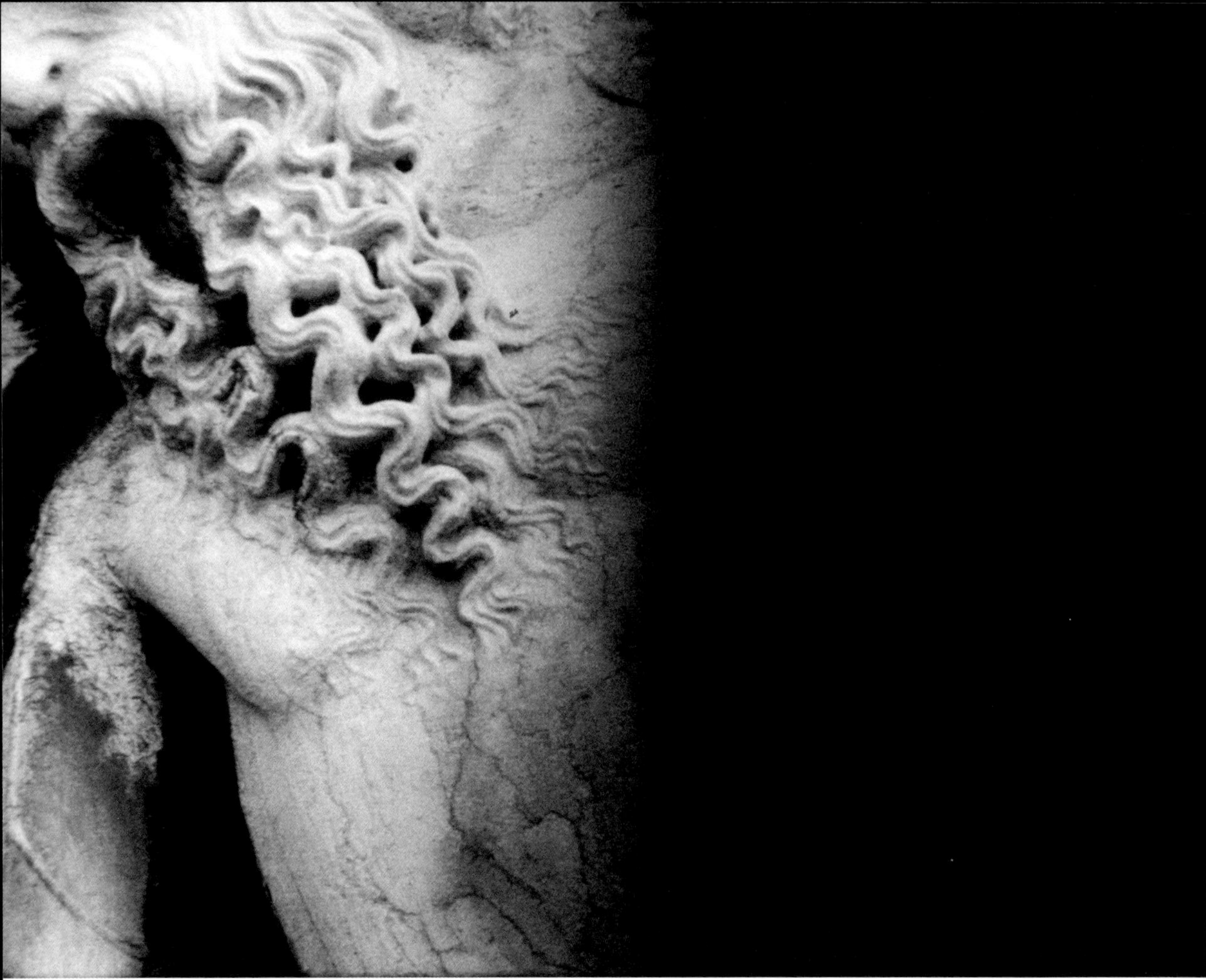

*Ruskin* (1975/1997)

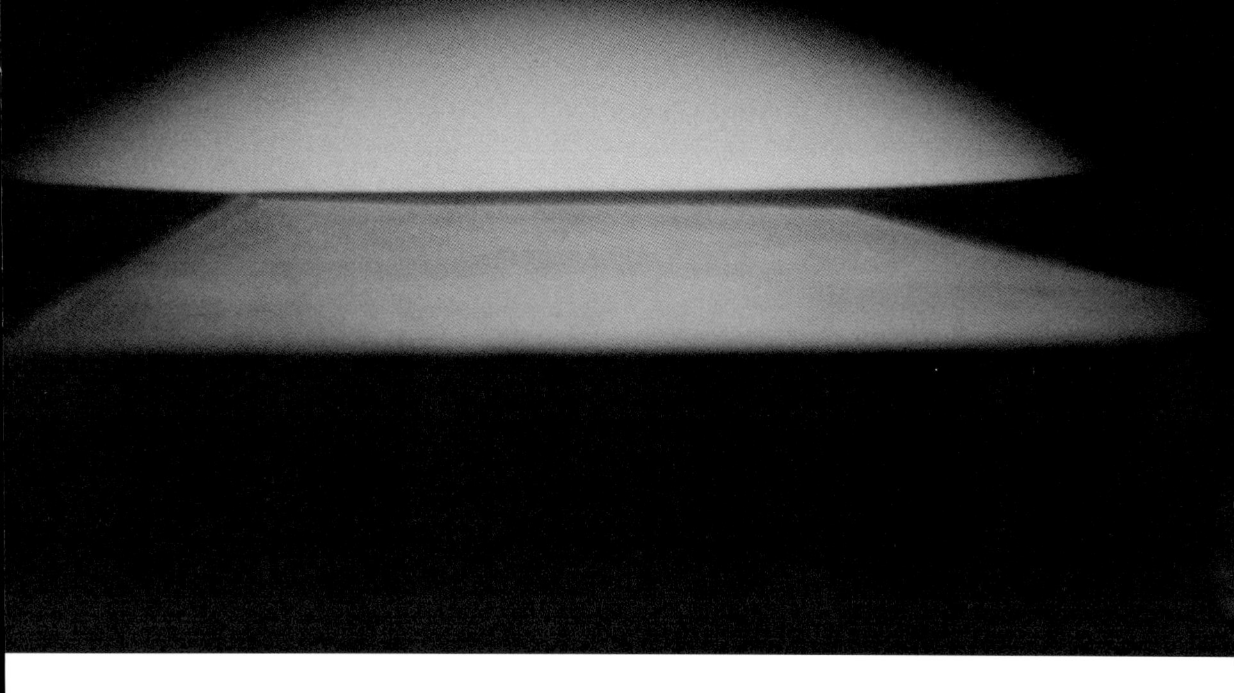

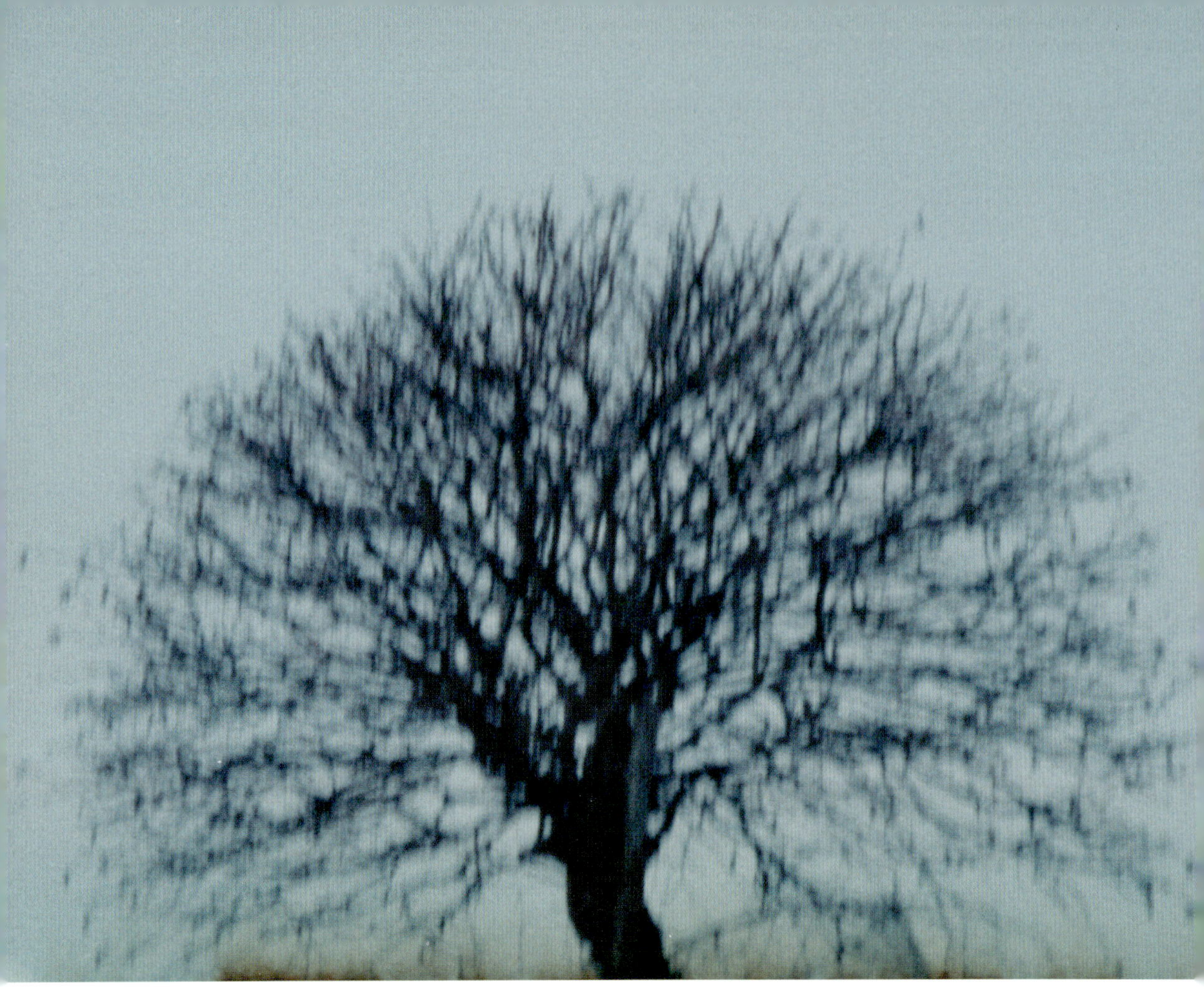

*The Hedge Theater* (1986–1990/2002)

# OBJECT RELATIONS AND SOLID FORMS

# 5

## PART 1: TRIPTYCH / ICE BLOCK

> The creation of a 'perspective' is as subjective as that of a 'theory of color.' In each case the investigator is evident.
> **Robert Beavers, notes for *The Painting***

### ART BEHIND GLASS

In 1972, Beavers received permission from Perry Rathbone, director of the Museum of Fine Arts in Boston, to remove the Plexiglas box covering a late fifteenth-century Flemish triptych, *The Martyrdom of St. Hippolytus*, so that he could shoot it for a new film. The body of Hippolytus, a Roman legionary who refused to relinquish his new Christian faith, is stretched in four directions, his limbs connected to horses: a frozen moment just before gruesome disassembly. The unknown artist used the central panel of a triptych by Hugo van der Goes in the Saint Sauveur Cathedral, in Bruges, as his model, but he pulled the scene apart, spreading it across all three panels, and breaking the northern European convention of depicting a separate scene on each. Ties encircling Hippolytus's wrist and ankle cross the gold frame into the side panels, attaching to horses whose riders prepare to draw and quarter the soldier.

In the spring of 1971, Beavers had made notes on the amalgamating powers of Renaissance paintings, at the Uffizi Gallery, in preparation for a new work—"the painting film." He noticed "two types of combining color and noncolor"—the Italian merger of monochromatic and colored figures on a single surface (Luca Signorelli's *Madonna with Child*, ca. 1490) and the Flemish application of monochromatic grisaille to the backs of triptych side panels (Van der Goes's *Portinari Altarpiece*, 1475–1478). "In both types noncolor is a reference to sculpture," he added.[1] The structural plurality of the triptych—a single object designed to unfurl and contract in shape and image range—attracted him: "[When folded forward, the] two noncolor panels form the two halves of one image." The closed *Portinari Altarpiece* rewinds time and replaces a colorful Nativity scene with a grayscale Annunciation: Gabriel's announcement to Mary that she will conceive.

Beavers included *The Martyrdom* in his triptych notes.[2] When the artwork is folded, an image of devotion replaces the scene of violence: grisaille portraits of the triptych's commissioners—Hippolyte de Berthoz, financial advisor to the Duke of Burgundy, and his wife, Elisabeth Hugheins—identified by their coats-of-arms and shown side by side with their patron saints, Hippolytus and Elizabeth of Hungary.[3] It's an object of self-commemoration and a double portrait of patronage and fidelity sealed by money and paint.[4]

Beavers decided that *The Martyrdom* in Boston would anchor his new film, and in the spring of 1972, he relocated to his grandparents' home in Mount Vernon, New York. Like the artworks in his notes, *The Painting* (1972/1999) "combines color and noncolor." Matted portions of the triptych alternate with static shots of a Bern, Switzerland, intersection (Theaterplatz), images of swirling dust orbs in undefined black space, and details of planar play among matte, glass, and light inside Beavers's compendium. The folds and scalar exchanges of *The Painting* are articulated by the sharp sounds of opening/closing (squeaks and creaks, a metallic slam) and division (a whip cutting through air, the tearing of paper).

When Beavers reedited *The Painting* in 1992, he pulled in personal material. A Florentine pension scene (shot for a never-realized *Early Monthly Segment)* teases and denies biographical gratification: a swift panning glimpse of Markopoulos in bed; images of Beavers severing his own image (he stands under the thick band of sunlight slicing the room and cuts to a black-and-white photograph of himself, torn in half).[5] A wide shot locates the ripped picture—it lies on a table between the two men—but the autobiographical material will neither resolve beyond fraught ambiguity nor become the vanishing point of the film. The personal imagery is a charged psychic thread inside the narrative weave of sacrifice, violence, and desire that extends from painting into film. Violent imminence migrates from details of Hippolytus's body to sounds of an orchestra's preparatory tuning, and aftermath shows up in shots of the cracked compendium glass—damaged but not destroyed: an internal shatter contained inside a rectangle.

Glass cracked, triptych fragmented, portraits refused, interpersonal narrative unspecified: as *The Painting* moves in and out of artwork, apparatus, and pension, Beavers fragments a host of subjects and objects. He prioritizes oneness across them instead. "Progress of the Hippolytus through the locales . . . yet in one continuous movement," he noted in early 1972, before shooting the painting. "Always in film it is the space between the elements that is important." But the roles of "element" and "space between" cannot be determined by name (the represented thing) or location (the in and out points of a shot). A matte races by like a flat graphic wipe (an official transition) and is also a photographed object with dimensionality. Markopoulos's image appears in charged relief, bound with an important proper name—but in the context of the whole film he also recedes as one element in a scene that delivers the film's crucial "window." The cracked-open pension aperture highlights the interior-exterior rhythm of the film and allows us to attach "open/close" to a repeating creaking sound. That sound migrates—it accompanies, for example, the loss and gain of detail in the Flemish painting details as Beavers turns his lens. He turns the painting—*The Painting*—from a narrative of Hippolytus's martyrdom into a source of allusion *and* abstraction. *The Painting* is a second artist's search for a complex frame.

—

Glass is a sign and seal of art-value; it works in tandem with the proper name of the artist on the museum wall to finalize an object. "Critic's comment about 'Art behind glass,'" Beavers wrote in his January 1972 notes, a reference to Nigel Gosling in

*Still Light*. "My plan [is] to use glass plates in film with the 'St. H.'" Beavers wanted glass to admit itself in *The Painting*, to receive marks as a canvas might. In March he noted:

> **Scratches on glass**
> **a coat of dust on glass**
> **Paint stroked onto glass**

The same compendium glass that is cracked is elsewhere imprinted with the circular reflection of the camera lens. The glass rectangle is an externalization of the lens: one of the violences of the film is the artist's refusal to comply with ready-made structures for seeing and showing. (Beavers recruits the force of the erotic into the work of rearrangement.)

Plexiglas removed, Beavers orchestrates a direct encounter with the fifteenth-century painting. He isolates portions of the painting with shaped mattes; he enlarges fine Flemish detail full-frame (rose thorns, horseshoes, clothing folds, socked foot); he retracts focus so that a matted selection becomes a cloud, akin to the dust orbs we see in other shots. Beavers unfixes the paint surface with the addition of colored filters: "plus dark red"—"plus light green"—"plus dark B[lue]," he recorded in his shooting log. And he condenses the painting's perspective (that totalizing organizing principle, per Erwin Panofsky, that must color the whole picture plane if it is to function as a window) to detail scale: a shot of receding mountains fading to white.[6]

Beavers reserves the total view for the Bern intersection, presenting it as undisturbed perspectival shot. "Alternate the shots of the painting which range from close-up to long shot with the filming of the location [Bern] which should remain in the same framing throughout," Beavers instructed himself in his notes, contrasting "the fixed frame" around Theaterplatz—static wide shots containing the transit of traffic and pedestrians—with his varied treatment of "the fixed object": the painting. "In the first, the view is fixed with movement within it, in the second the (point of) view is moved on a fixed object," he noted. The intersection is rendered by a conventional camera (deep space revealed along diagonal lines, proportions maintained, historical specificity registered); it is the film's indexical ground. But this "fixed" document becomes the film's ultimate "space between." Images of the intersection catch and carry color from the painting shots—a blue car, red coat, and green bus stand out as if they've been given filter treatment (they have not). Powered by traffic sounds, the dotted street lines that direct cars around a central curve draw the latent roundness out of the film—connecting the circles of horseman's waist sash (a painting detail), lens reflections, and matte openings into a collective spin: "one continuous movement." Under the conditions of this motion climate, it becomes possible to watch how an "element" is made.

—

Beavers's films stage complex sets of object relations. In psychoanalysis, *object relations* refers to internal representations of self and other (and their parts) in relation—a constellation whose imprint informs "selfness" and generates a template for love. I use the term more loosely here—imagining the way Beavers's films braid identification with and difference from the art forms and works that have inspired them, balancing idealization, internalization, and rejection in the process of their own self-substantiation as *films*. Identification might be with category (book, sculpture, painting, architecture), part (page, perspective, dome), or singular artwork (*The Martyrdom of St. Hippolytus*). Some objects are officially valuable and parental, and others are nameless peers (ordinary objects or anonymous craft).

In the hundreds of detailed notes Beavers has kept on encounters with art, film plays a scant role. But while his primary interlocutors are works of painting and sculpture, a Beavers film doesn't seek to become an object. Beavers embraces the fragilities of projection, poetry, and perception and eschews the hardening conferred by official knowledge systems and art historical discourses. His film notes articulate other kinds of solid-seeking: for aesthetic resolution ("to create the 'film object'"), for language-free embodiment of mental process ("[a] solid form for the strength of a thought"), for representation beyond index ("form the object on-screen"). Solidity signifies distinctly at every site between form and content, poetic speculation and screening logistics. All impermanences—the come-and-go of matter, mind states, projected images—are not created equal. Celluloid degrades—and does so even faster in the absence of preservation structures and stewards. Beavers's films often engage rhymes that occur among these variously scaled object dilemmas.

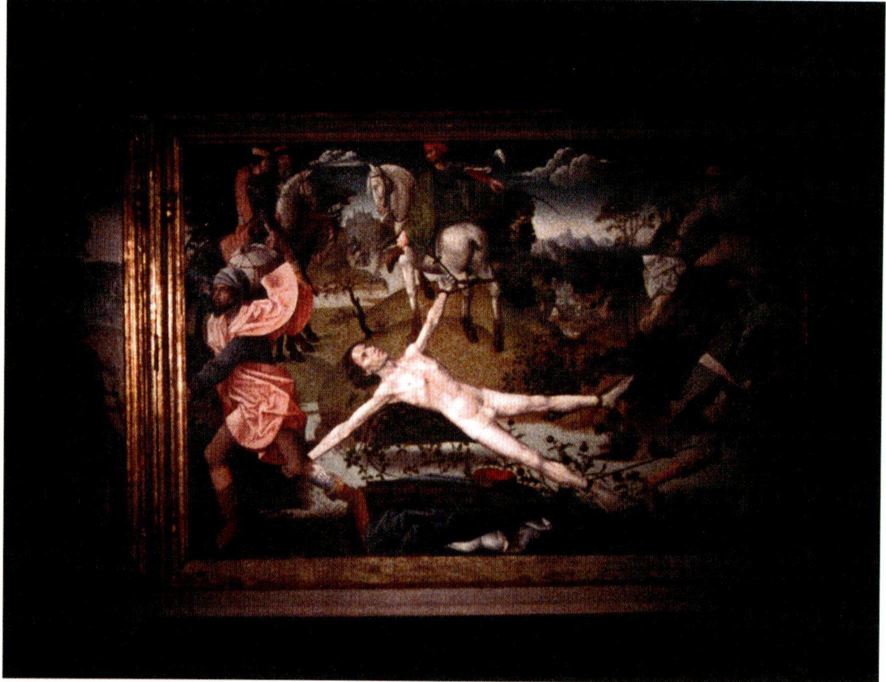

*The Painting* (1972/1999)

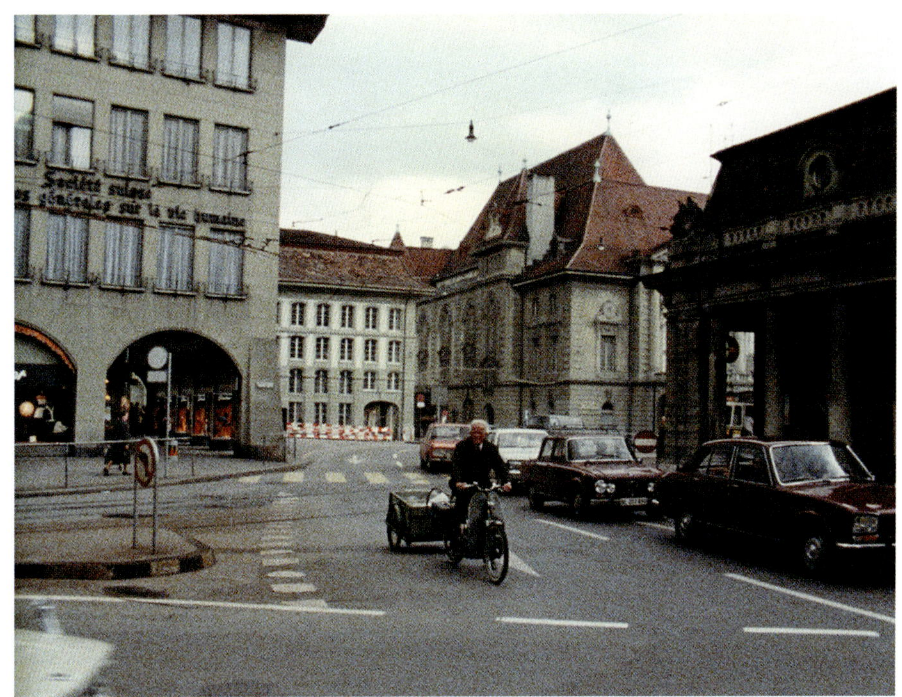

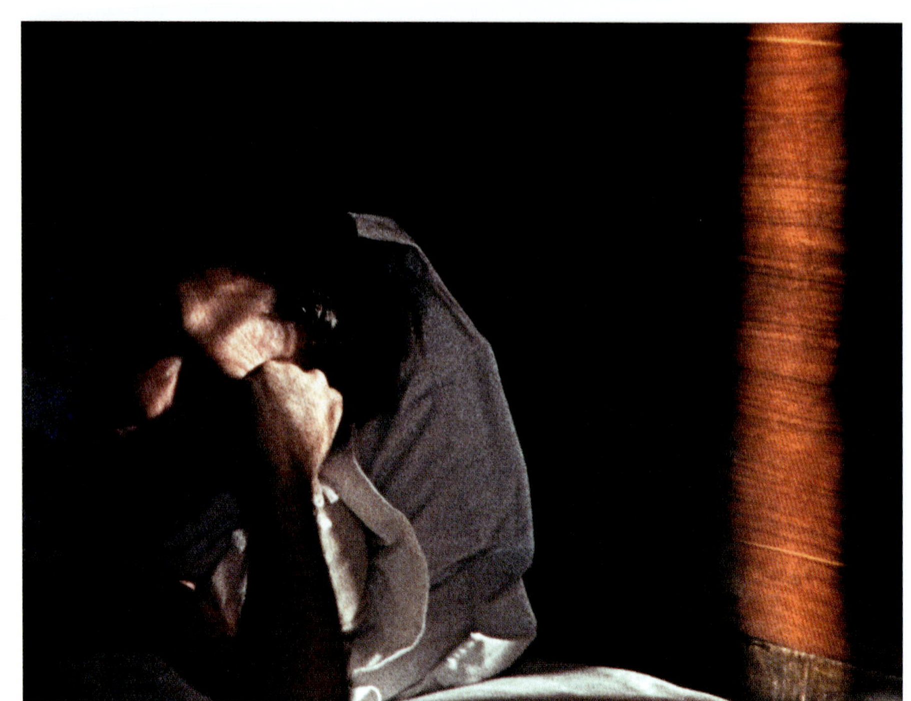

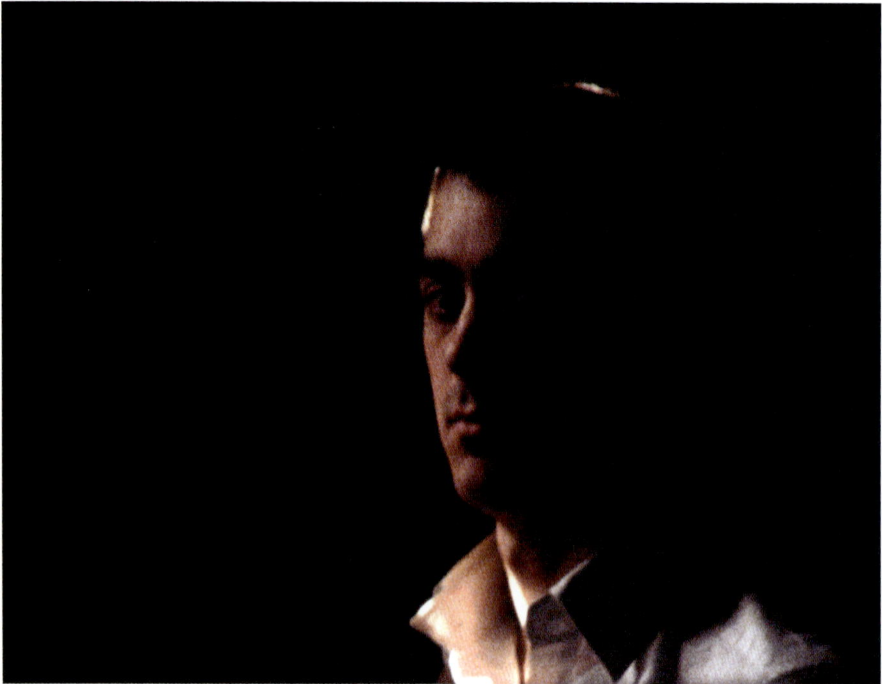

*The Painting* (1972/1999)

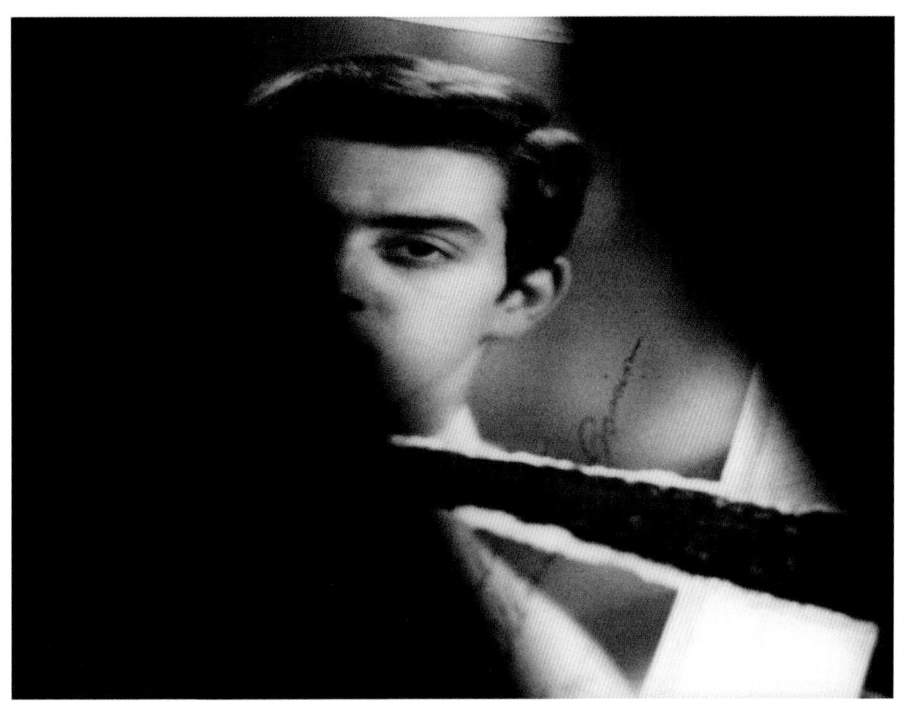

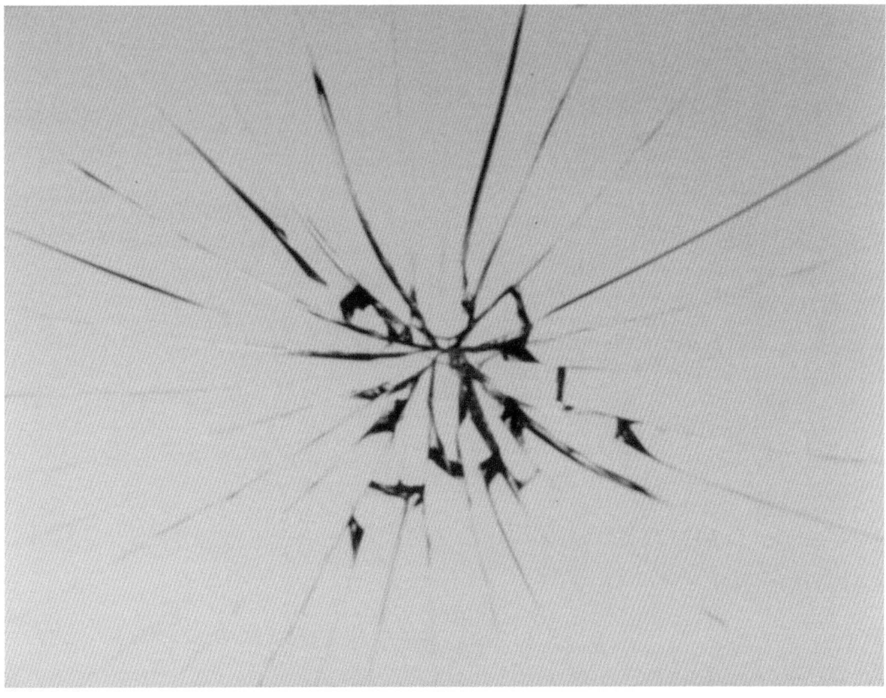

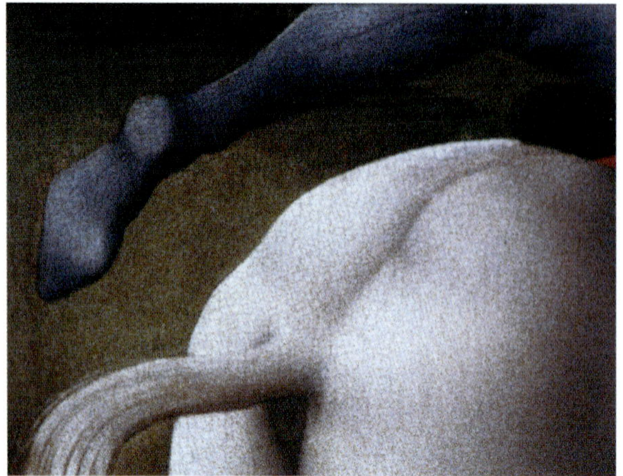

*The Painting* (1972/1999)

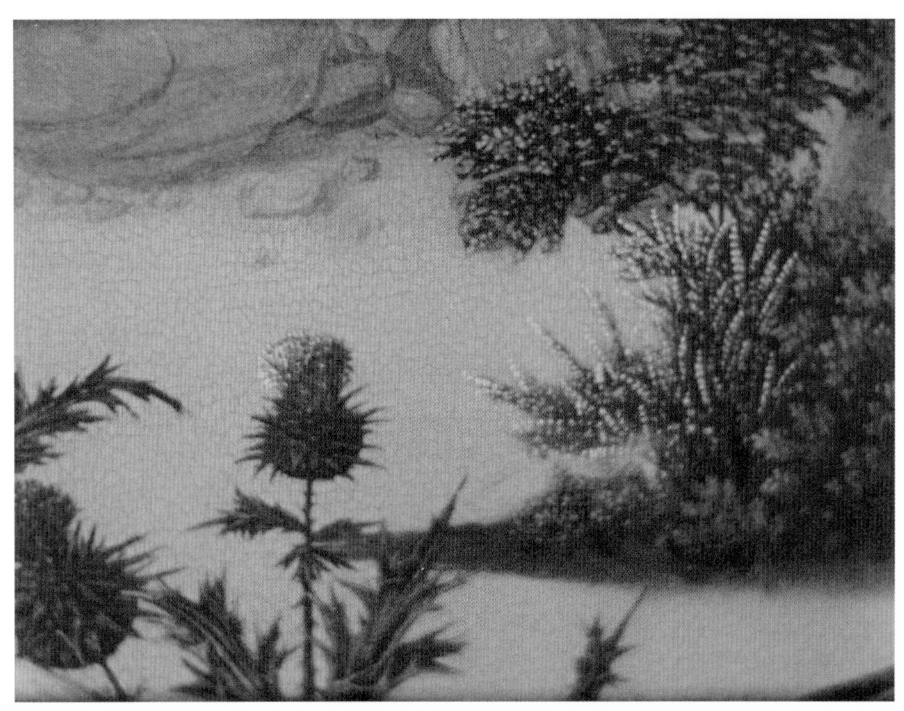

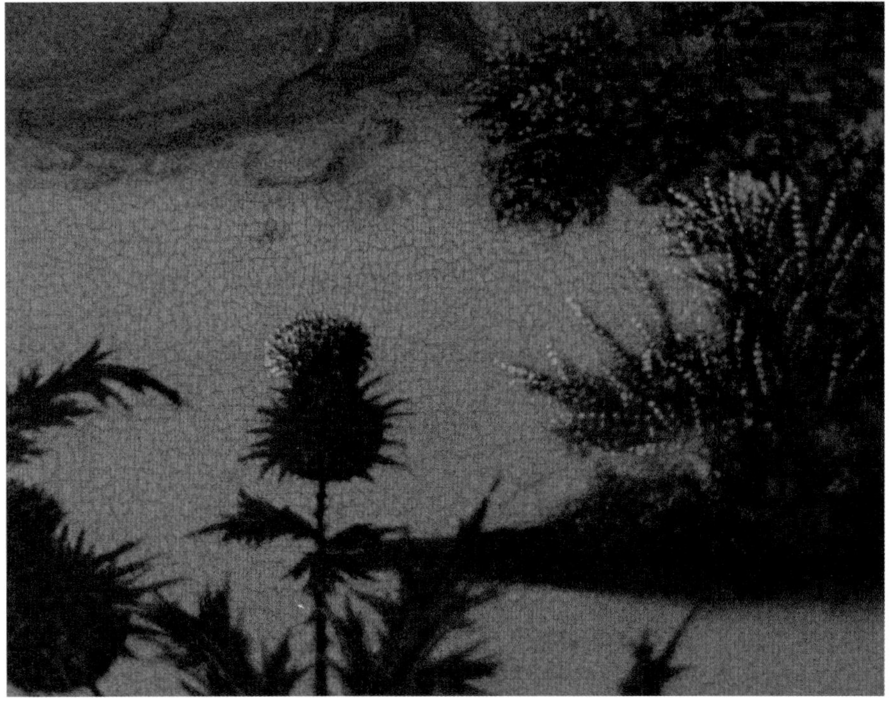

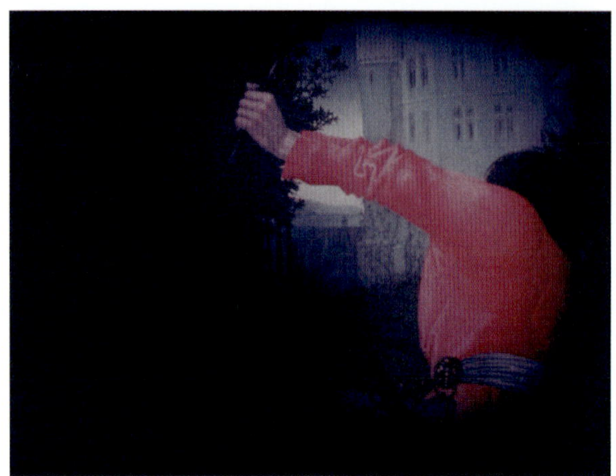

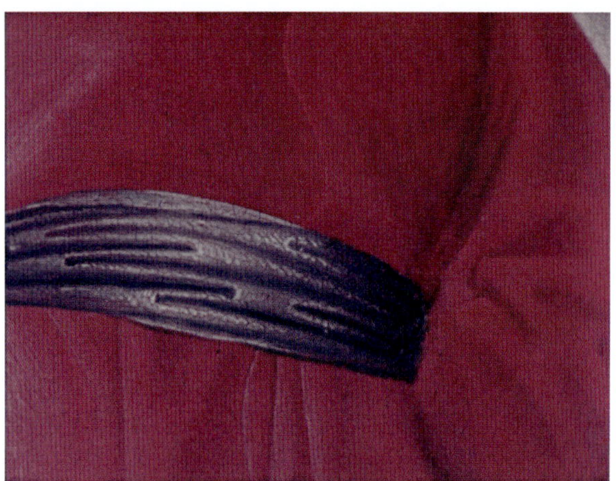

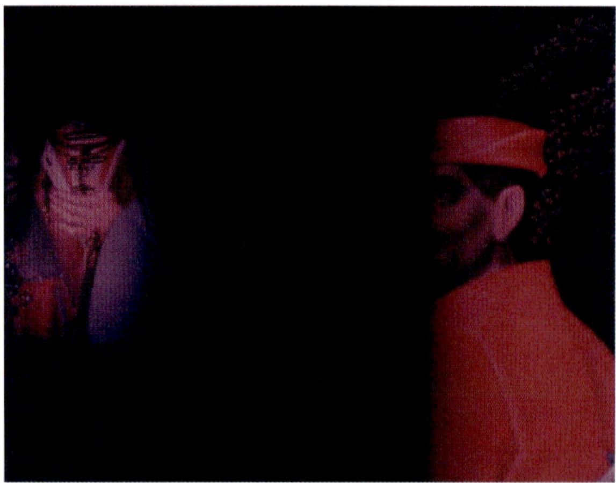

*The Painting* (1972/1999)

## ICE BLOCKS AND INTENTIONAL OBJECTS

> We must go back to the "things themselves."
> **Edmund Husserl**[7]

In 1971, Beavers and Markopoulos returned to Florence. It was a transitional moment: Beavers wanted to keep shifting away from the psychic interiority that had anchored *Winged Dialogue*, *The Count of Days*, and *Plan of Brussels* ("I couldn't go forward in the direction of the isolated figure," he said) and toward a developing awareness of "qualities which are common and shared and can be presented directly."[8] To realize this "basic change in . . . intention," he turned to objects.[9] His initial structural constraint for a new film—"twenty objects/scenes—Europe—each ten minutes"—gave way to a group of nine:

> ice: ice-making workshop off Via de' Tornabuoni, Florence
> river: River Inn, Scuol, Grisons
> grass: field, Bad Ragaz
> book: repair of flood-damaged Latin manuscript, Il Torchio, Florence
> tree: tree-felling, Scuol, Grisons
> arm: actor's torso, Florence
> stones: street demolition, Piazza San Pancrazio, Florence
> mountain: Falknis mountain, between Liechtenstein and Switzerland
> blood: blood pancake-making, restaurant, Via dei Serragli, Florence

Beavers established a new discipline—a "way of concentrating on an object" and becoming aware of his attraction to an object or scene in the filming moment.[10] He aimed for the precision of in-camera filmmaking—making choices on the spot about shot composition (including matte and filter use), order, and length. "I tried to have every (filmmaking) action realized in relation to the object during the filming," he told Tony Pipolo.[11] In his filming notes, Beavers sometimes granted his objects decision-making agency: "The object decides the editing ratio which will be constant and integral," he wrote in July 1972.

Early Renaissance art also directed Beavers as he searched for the "clearest composition and length" for his images.[12] "I was attached to a simplifying view of objects—nourished by the clarity of Florentine painting. When I saw the Orsanmichele with its altar and exterior sculptures or the Old Sacristy doors by Donatello in San Lorenzo or the Masaccio frescoes in the Carmine or the early paintings from Siena, there was a refreshing clarity and seriousness of thought. More than specific paintings, it was the sum of the entire experience," he recalled.

But in confronting a block of ice or a blood pancake in the moment of shooting, there was no predetermined model of aesthetic clarity to call up. Beavers had to identify his point of view in a limitless field. "The object and surrounding space; the relations are infinite," he noted in March 1972. Like a true phenomenologist, he knew intentionality produced a limit on boundless perceptual potential (consciousness *needs* an object) and he turned to time—and work—to help him see his objects clearly.

In May, he noted his intention "to reveal the sense of time in the making of the object." Beavers was thinking doubly about the coming into being of an object: the work in time to bind a flood-damaged manuscript or to make a pancake from a vat of boiling blood—and to make a film. "The sense of time to make" shows up in shots that register the methodical care of labor: the bookbinder applies pressure to ensure glue bonds between pages. But "the sense of time" also arrives as a camera movement: curved pans across the bookbinder's objects and tools—wooden binding apparatus, a bundle of thread, an ivory paper knife—convey processual time. We also see *behind* the table—a disarrayed scene of labor (heap of rags and tape) that has, as do other images in the film, a more classically documentary feel, as if a wider frame or longer shot is needed in order to see a work scene clearly and to balance the impulses of abstraction that dominate elsewhere. "Compositional clarity" shifts in relation to its objects.

Beavers decided to call the film *Work Done*. When labor appears as an *event* in the film, it is as a single representative action: a sliced-into tree trunk falls; a loop of thread closes around a spindle; a ladle fills a black skillet with liquid. As Beavers applied his object-orientation to work, he noted his aim for "actions as objects—simple, useful actions, ones that complete themselves" and his wish to limit his investigations inside a field of nonspecific *ordinariness*—"Object: not of value or age."[13] In August 1972, he figuratively aligned his own film work with these values:

> **The tree is cut: the film is cut**
> **the ice is frozen: the frame is frozen**
> **Each object has its film essence**

At a structural level, *Work Done* (1972/1999) approaches making on a longer timeline, where object formation is not visible in discrete acts. In his notes, Beavers broadly organized the 1972 version of *Work Done* in pairs—"objects" followed by their originating "elements" ("ice to river—book to tree—stones to mountain")—in a rhythm of recession followed by change: "from the object back to its element then onto another next object." Each object or scene exists in self-contained sequence; the rule of separation breaks when Beavers intercuts the final scene—blood pancake-making—with shots from all previous sequences except that of the ice. "It was as if I were saying that it needed all of these images to represent the ice in the film. This is one way of seeing it," he said to Pipolo.[14]

The solid-to-liquid event that catalyzes *Work Done*—"I began with an image of a block of ice, then went to the transformation of the solid element in the next image, which was a river"—is recapitulated structurally: the film starts with ice and ends with blood.[15] But the blood itself begins as liquid—a pot of thick, bubbling, cherry-red substance—and, in the course of cooking work, becomes a solid: a round pancake, nearly black ("liquid to solid," he noted). Singular in its absence from the final sequence, the inaugural ice has melted, been dispersed across the film, and is reconstituted by the final solid object (pancake)—and by the film itself, which has taken solid-enough form to end.

Beavers's limited filter use in *Work Done* is distinct from that in his other films: colors enhance, rather than wholly alter, what is already there. He placed strips of horizontal color between the lens and aperture of his Bolex, producing a bleeding or gradated chiaroscuro effect. The red blood in *Work Done* is not enhanced by a filter.

### DISEGNO

The ice block is the master element of both versions of *Work Done*. When he revised the film in 1999, Beavers maintained the original order (ice, river, etc.) but subjected the sequences to dosed intercutting. An alternating A-B rhythm across the elements (book + tree-felling followed by tree-felling + torso) is punctuated by A-B-C threesomes—book-tree-torso—at the juncture of change. The ice remains self-contained as the first sequence, (though the sequence has been recut) and absent from the final sequence, in which all the other scenes are intercut.

The ice block is intention itself—substantial, formally definitive, the initiating object of Beavers's new seeing program. Its surface sheen acknowledges that all is subject to change. The pan that opens the revised *Work Done* moves to and from the ice in its wall cavity; it delivers functional context (a dark basement workspace with surfaces marked by use—rust, dirty paint) and spatial singularity (curved ceilings, a Gothic-shaped door). We know where we are, then, when Beavers limits and centralizes his view to a glistening form—the face of the ice block topped by the receding plane of its upper surface. Appearances morph: the entire image is subject to a frosty coating caused by reflected light; focal change extracts dimensionality; a framing matte pushes the ice back in space. The exchange between line and form inherent in Beavers's cubic ice-play extends to other views of the space; when we see images of a large rusty hook hanging from a vaulted ceiling whose gray-blue planes are lined by seams, it feels as if we are witnessing Beavers as he follows the object's lead and perceives a fresco on a workshop ceiling.

—

"It was one of the reedits where I really hesitated, not knowing if it was right—I was carried along," Beavers said of the risk of revising *Work Done*. "Sometimes when you get carried along . . . it can lead you somewhere you don't want to go." When he revised the film, his 1972 intentions produced new clarities. The original conceit—per his notes, a "quality in one object transformed but continuing in the next"—had applied, in 1972, to the shared matter in object/element pairs (ice/water), but as filming progressed, it also generated an interobject lens—a way to see one object *through* another. ("Angle of green grass follows the subjectivity of the falling tree," Beavers wrote after shooting a Bad Ragaz field on a sharp tilt at ground level.)

In revising, he ushered some of these connections out of latency. In the later *Work Done*, both image and sound are intercut—first in diegetic sync and then independently—and relational potential propagates.[16] In the intercutting between tree-felling and shots of the actor's body, we see the distinct profile of ivy between the man's arm and torso—as if the two environments (body/woods) have been superimposed. A new zone of spectatorial freedom also opens—a space for tracing interseeing effects that might exceed the maker's plans. The sound of a gas flame under a red ellipse (the pot of blood) pulls the blue flame of the bookbinding sequence back to mind; when the intensely blue-filtered sky and snowy mountain imagery follows, it feels as if I've placed it there.

—

Beavers's "way of concentrating on an object" coincided with his reading of Rainer Maria Rilke's 1907–1908 *New Poems* (*Neue Gedichte*). Rilke had been Auguste Rodin's secretary from 1905 to 1906, and the sculptor gave the poet models for method and concentration: one might generate art from observation rather than inspiration. The poems search the concrete and condense as objects themselves (mostly sonnets)—Rilke called them *Dinggedichte*, or "thing poems." In "Archaic Torso of Apollo," Rilke accounts for the power of a headless god—a statue—in the transport of liquid light.

> We cannot know his legendary head
> with eyes like ripening fruit. And yet his torso
> is still suffused with brilliance from inside,
> like a lamp, in which his gaze, now turned to low,
>
> gleams in all its power. Otherwise
> the curved breast could not dazzle you so, nor could
> a smile run through the placid hips and thighs
> to that dark center where procreation flared.
>
> Otherwise this stone would seem defaced
> beneath the translucent cascade of the shoulders
> and would not glisten like a wild beast's fur:
>
> would not, from all the borders of itself,
> burst like a star: for here there is no place
> that does not see you. You must change your life.[17]

Perhaps the gleaming fluidity of Rilke's Apollo was in the air as Beavers wrote about shooting his actor's body for *Work Done*. He reached for the Anavysos Kouros, a life-size marble statue of a young warrior at the National Archaeological Museum in Athens: "The solid movement in the body of the [kouros] . . . the space between the arms and the torso sides which extends down to hands and is like a liquid to its surrounding form." In *Work Done*, the actor's arm and torso are separated like those of a kouros. Each iteration of the torso imagery is distinct in motion and color—sometimes the arm moves slightly, or the breath blooms, but movement results primarily from the work done by lens, light, sound, and a blue filter. Body and negative space alternate as solids.

After a 2009 screening of his films at Yale, Beavers returned to Rilke—this time as a provocation to the students gathered. "I made some of these films at about the same age as my audience. While I was watching the films, I thought of Rilke, describing an Apollo sculpture. His poem ends: 'You must change your life.'"[18]

—

In a March 30, 1975, letter, Robert McGlynn, Beavers's former Deerfield teacher who had affirmed his instinct to leave school (and change his life), told Beavers that he could no longer send money: "Clearly what you require is a patron who can send you a monthly allowance for the next half dozen years. And just as clearly such patrons are somewhere out there. . . . My pittance might buy a meal or three, but it's like plugging a keyhole while a hurricane is blowing down the door. . . . Presently I've no more money. . . . I'm genuinely and deeply distressed. . . . I am convinced that you have some sort of genius that should be served."

Two years earlier, Markopoulos had met Athanase Ghertsos, the Greek Honorary Consul in Zurich, who became his most consistent patron for the next two decades. The older filmmaker's pursuit of private patronage was long-standing. In Toledo in the 1940s, Mariam Canady (wife of the producer of the military Jeep) had supported his work; Clara Hoover, publisher of *Film Comment*, contributed to the making of *Twice a Man* (1963). In his essay "Stoa Palikari," originally published in 1968, as he rails against the "mediocre professionals" of foundations and academia who hurt the very filmmakers they purport to support, Markopoulos calls for patrons to take the place of film producers and cooperatives (and also presciently wonders why galleries "lack the imagination to sell films through a limited print sales plan").[19]

On June 5, 1974, Markopoulos severed ties with the infrastructures of New York experimental film culture by publishing a letter in *Variety*: "I wish it to be known publicly that I dissociate myself from the New American Cinema, and, from Anthology Film Archives."[20] His declaration—the climax of an extended three-way contractual dispute among the filmmaker, his then distributor Dieter Meier, and Anthology Film Archives—marked the end of his participation in film-rental distribution circuits.[21] His institutional dissociation dovetailed with another event. In August 1974, Markopoulos wrote: "Day to day the Intention has become clearer . . . the startling Decision has been made. It was made one hour, some weeks ago, after breakfast, after feeding the birds, in the sight of the wondrous waterfall. Action was taken. Dedications were discarded and left to the mystery of their creditors. And, the prints that now exist have become but work prints, a fitting jest to the speculators of my work, known and unknown."[22] Markopoulos's total "Decision" to reedit his films into what would become the superseding *Eniaios* brought the Temenos, in mental development since the 1960s, into sharper form.

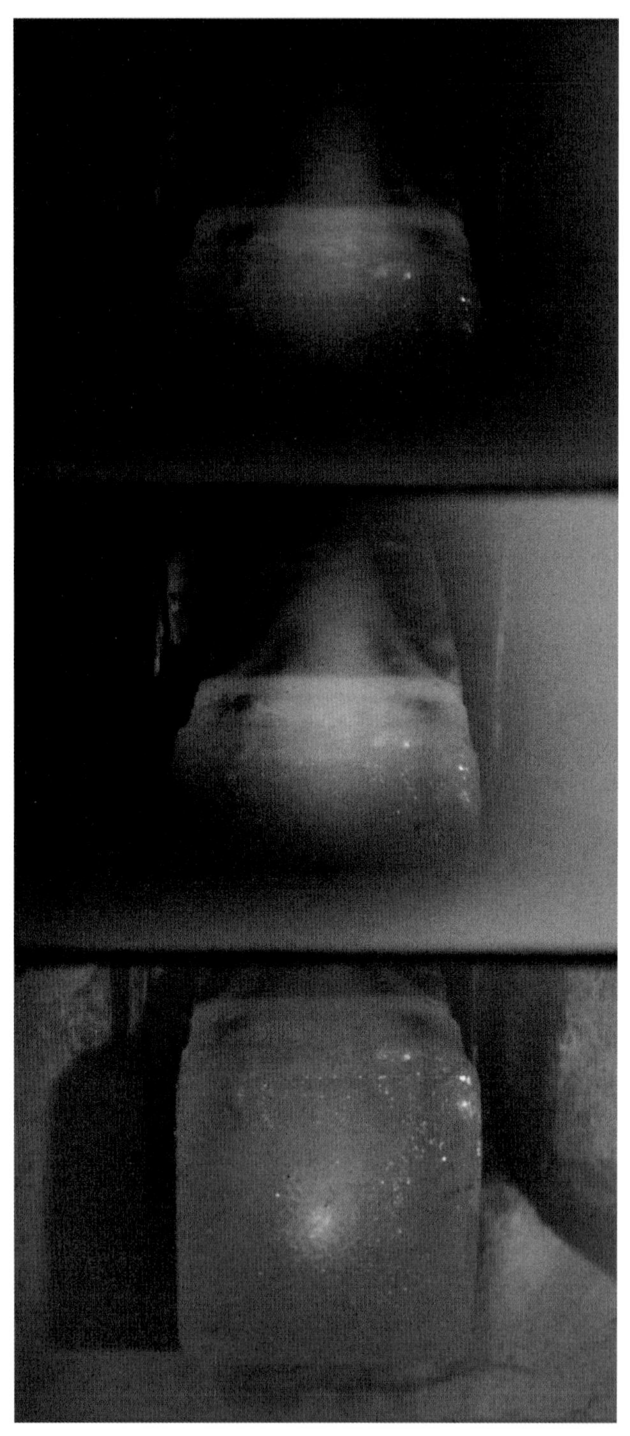

*Work Done* (1972/1999)

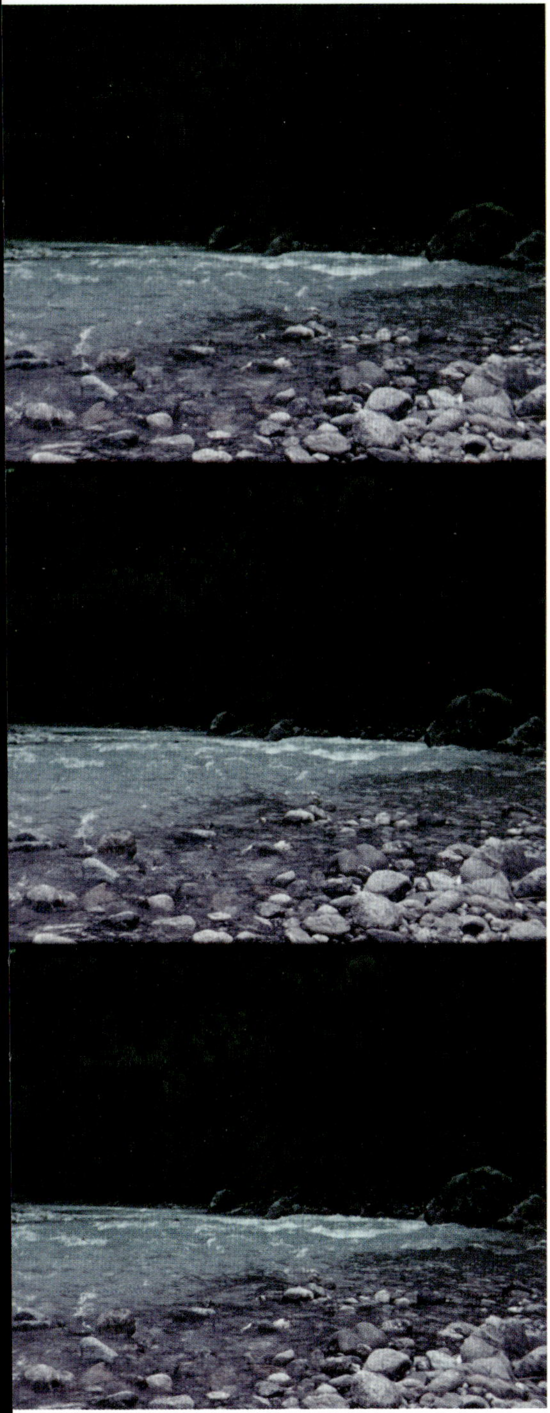

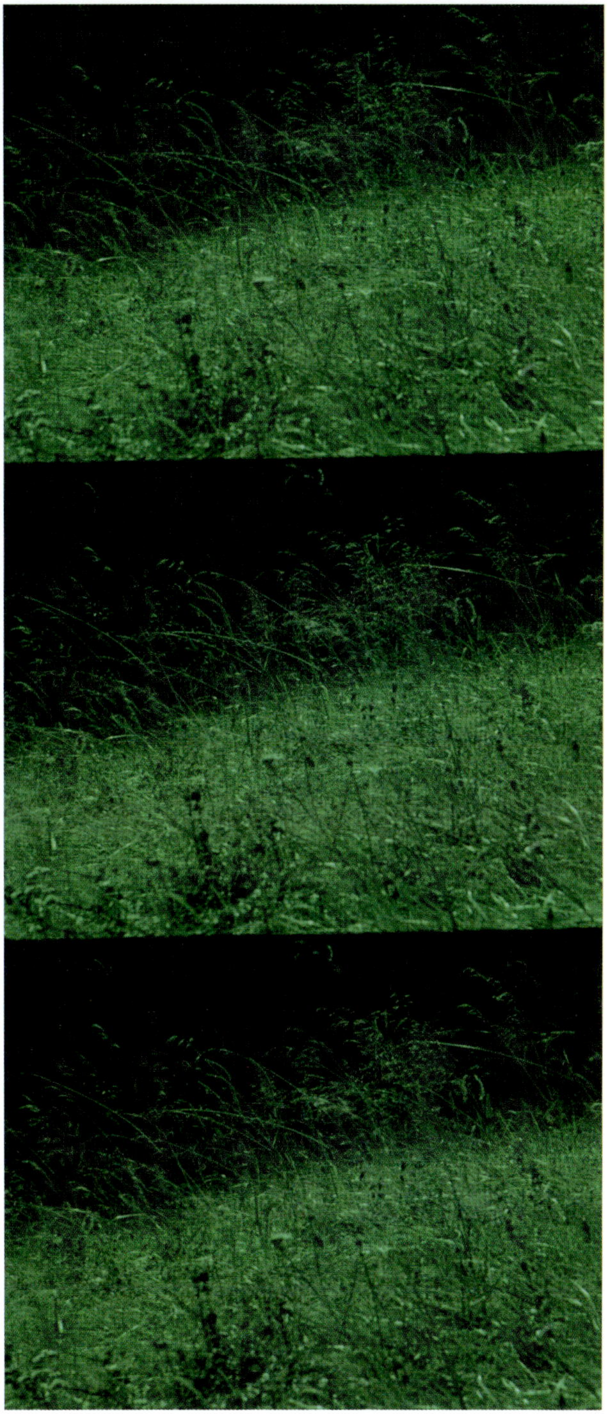

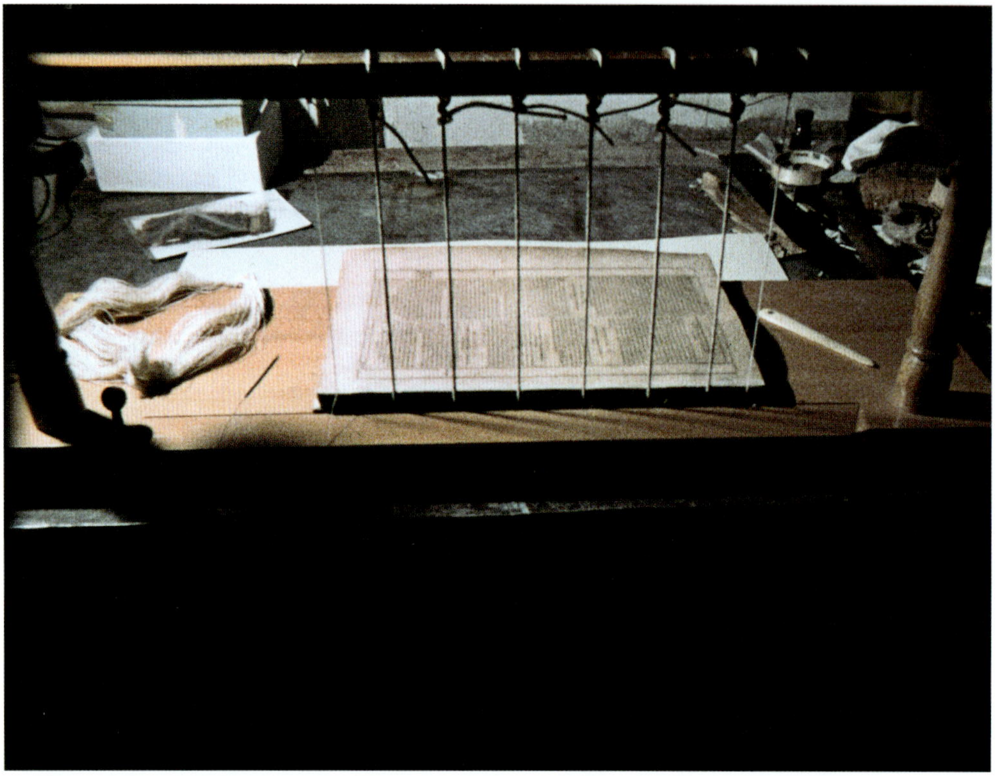

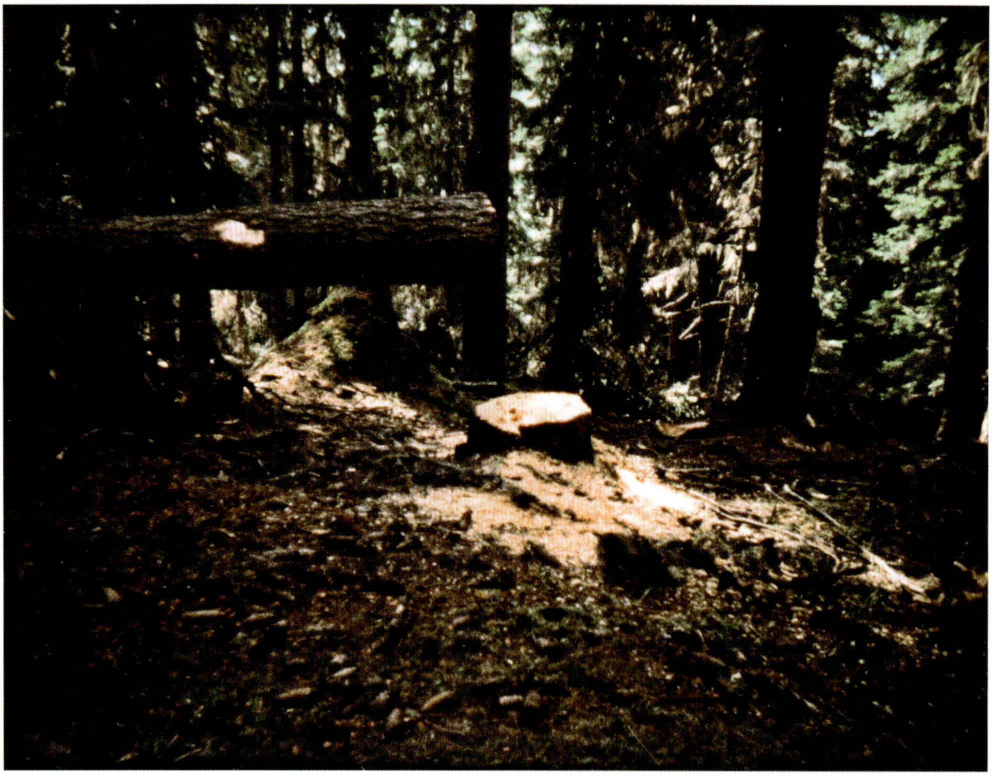

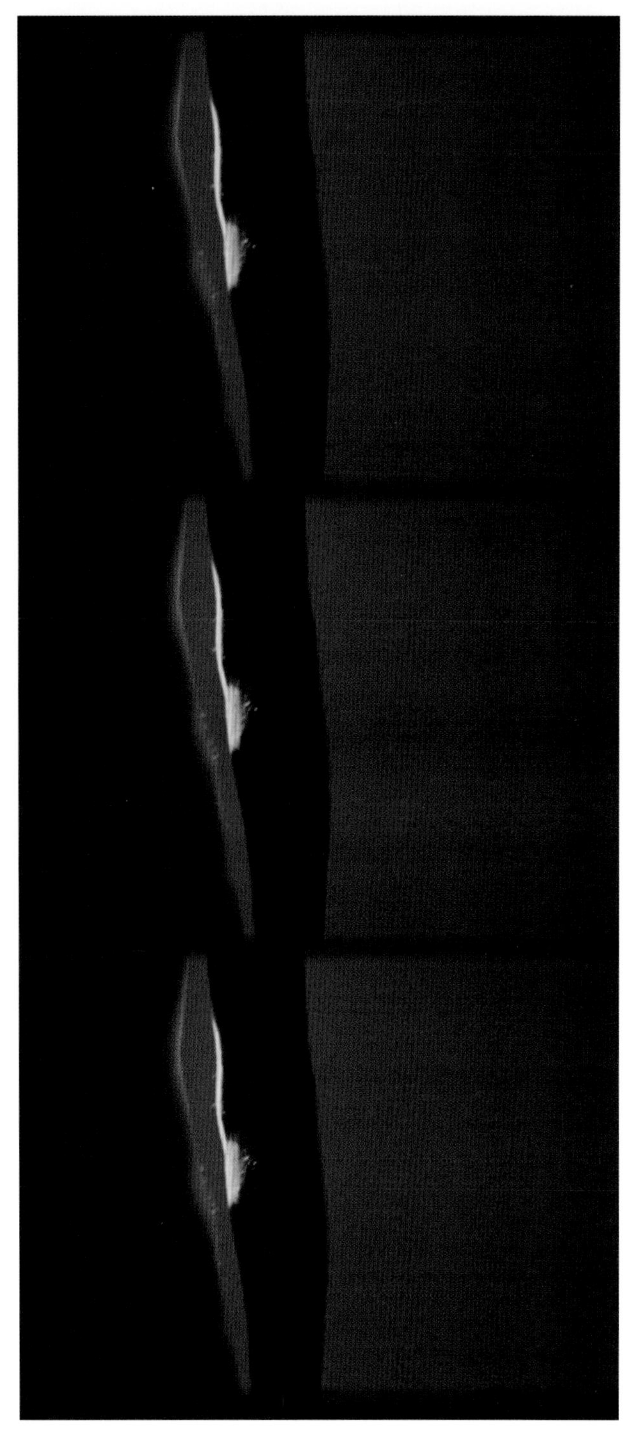

*Work Done* (1972/1999)

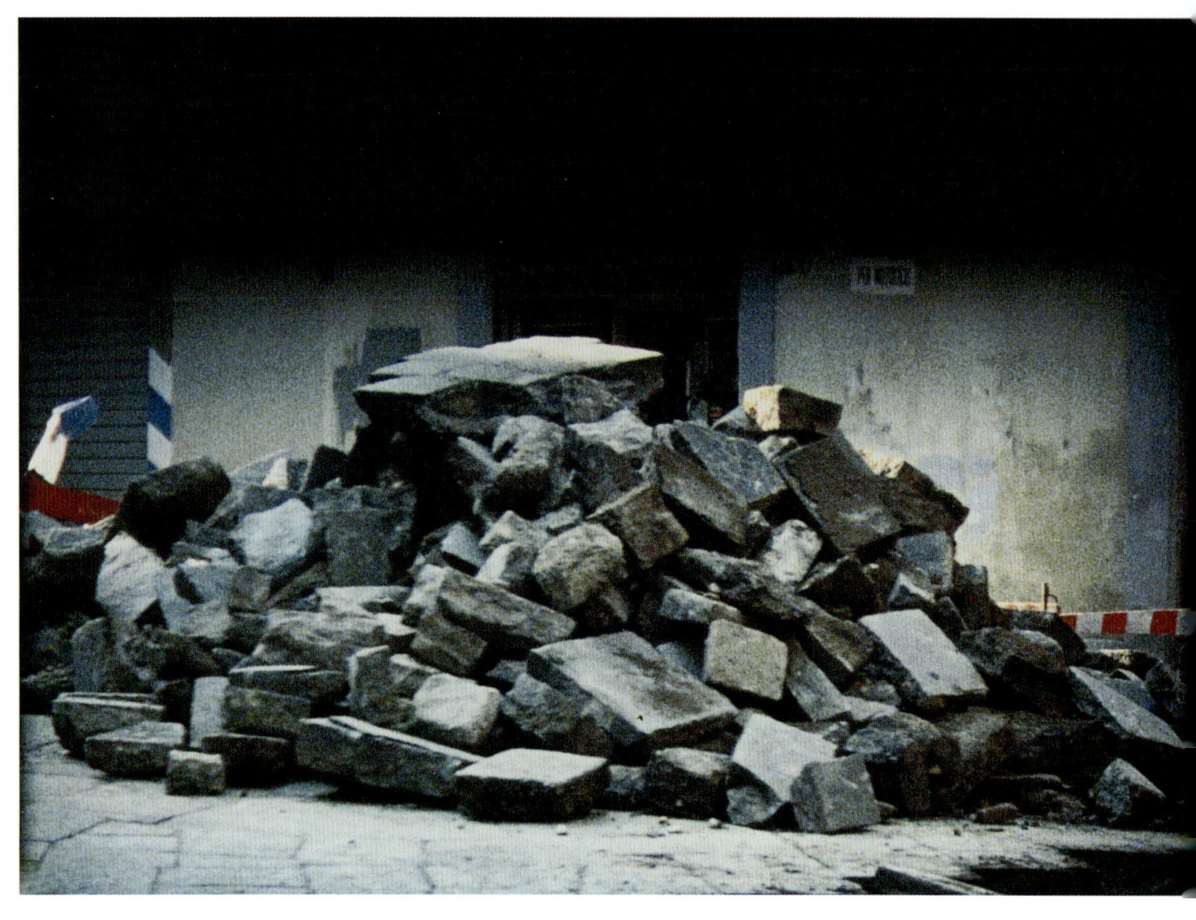

*Work Done* (1972/1999)

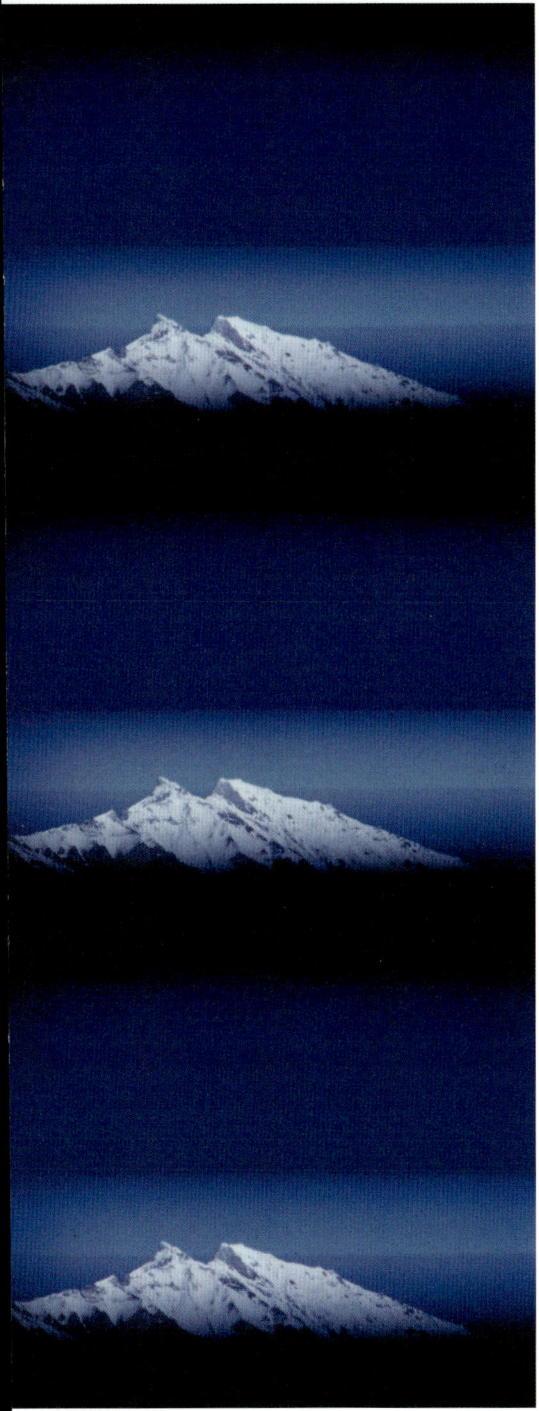

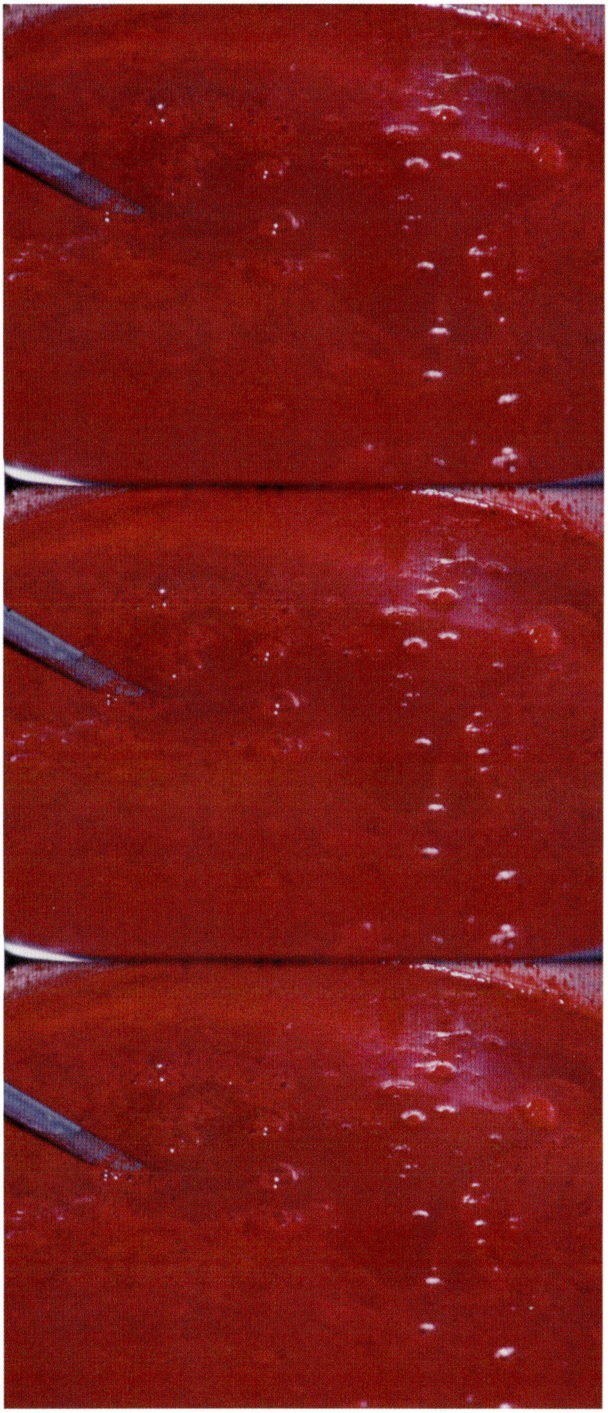

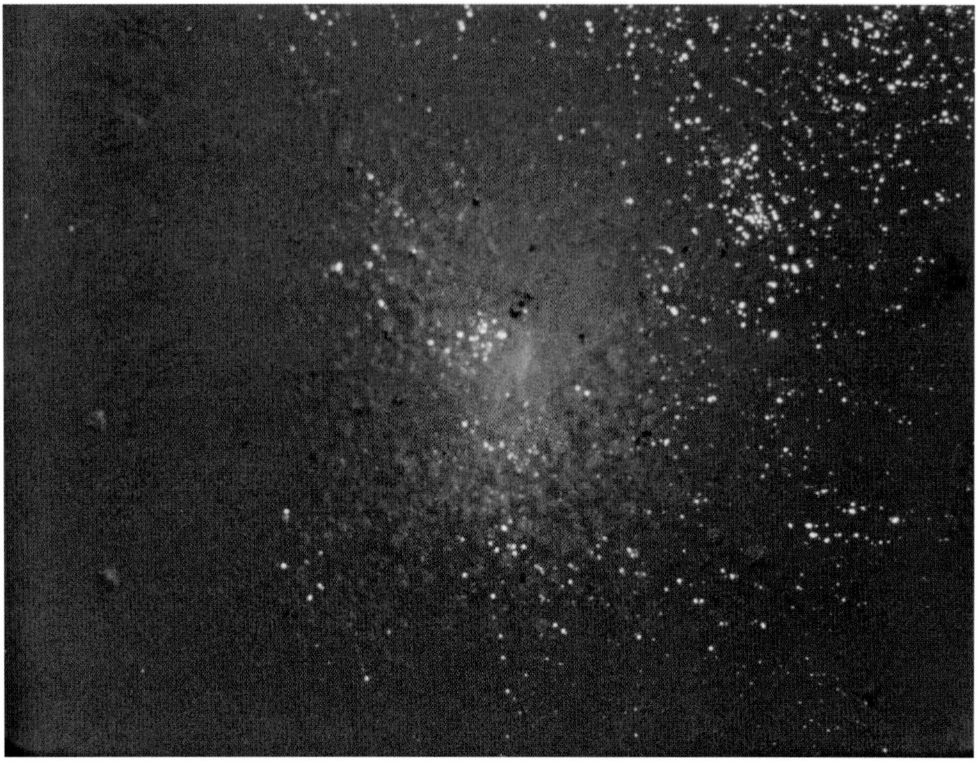

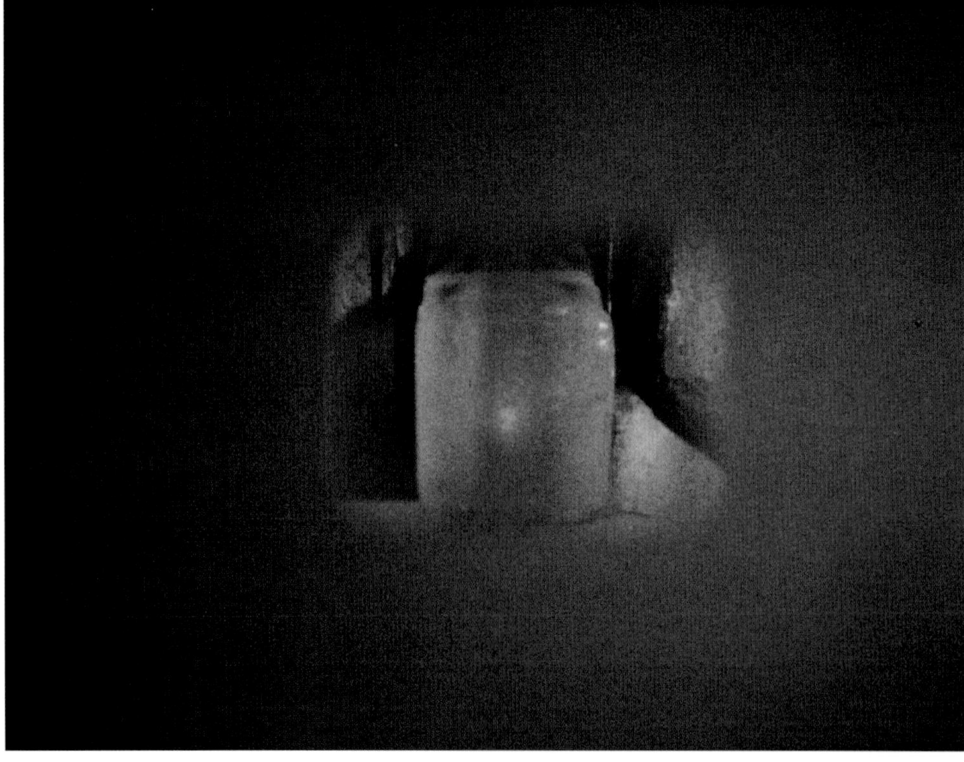

## WINDOW EJECTIONS

Beavers completed *The Painting* and *Work Done* in 1972. Next to his ice block and Plexiglas box encounters, the early 1970s cubic confrontations of other American artists line up in my peripheral vision, a set of minimalist solids. Pausing on the centrally framed pile of road rocks in *Work Done*, Robert Smithson's 1971 pile-on-a-box—*Rocks and Mirror Square II*—comes to mind: pre-fused in a name/noun pair (Smithson/rocks), intention stable and value straightforward, an art historical fact, a mental image whose durability is independent of experiential encounter.

Works of art cannot be stripped of their potential to generate fresh experience, but nor can the summarizing and fetishizing forces of storytelling be denied: a concept on top of a Plexiglas box. When the canvas-as-window began to feel suffocating, the modernist story goes, the frame had to be destroyed. Sometimes the window got ejected directly from the canvas, and perspective turned into a minimalist box. Minimalist work can invite and reward delicate phenomenological presence—but when cubic delicacy gets a chapter name in a long story, it is hemmed in by a priori discourse from every side ("Go into that white room if you want to experience some presence!") and becomes a figure of identity: a "Judd."

One of the ancillary pleasures of Beavers's work is the opportunity for fresh encounters with necessary images and modernist impulses that are not totalizing, and cannot be extracted from lyrical play or unfamiliar contexts—that cannot be objectified, even in a film still. Paint had always exceeded its objects (see the splattered paint on the reverse side of Michelangelo's hyper-illusionistic portrait of Ginevra de' Benci, ca. 1474–1478), but the discursive forcefield of modernism can obscure frame-deconstructions of other kinds, and the habit of limiting poetic potential to preformulated categories and proper names is hard to break. Alongside the intended interfaces with Ruskin, da Vinci, and Borromini, unsolicited contact with versions of images by Mark Rothko, Barnett Newman, Ad Reinhardt, Ellsworth Kelly, John Baldessari, and James Turrell sometimes occurs while one is watching Beavers's films. In this context, such images are as subject to phenomenological melt as an ice block. They appear neither as allusions nor replicas but rather as engrained habits of naming particular visual forms and stimulations.

*Work Done* (1972/1999)

## PART 2: LOVE FORMS / BANKNOTES

### THE PERSPECTIVAL STAGE

In 1979, Beavers performed in front of his camera on the triangular stage of the Naturtheater (also called the Heckentheater) in Salzburg's Mirabell Gardens, an outdoor theater sculpted from two receding rows of clipped shrubs. In *AMOR* (1980), Beavers thrusts his hand into its serrated leaves. His arm whips down the spatial recess of one of its wings, as if cutting depth. In close-up shots, his wrist rotates: palm, back of hand. The film's first image, a wide view of the Naturtheater, is accompanied by birdsong and the sound of many scissors snipping: this space has been actively *created*—"nature cut into a special shape," he said.

We see Beavers's full body too (he wears a tailored gray suit)—but his head is always out of shot. His clapping hands momentarily meet as one: they are surrogates for his absent eyes and the two distinct images that merge in the perception of depth. The slapping sound speaks the sharp singularity of the theater space. As Beavers performs perspectival space-making, he draws a curve into the Naturtheater—a black arc tops or cups the image. His lens is askew on the turret, as in *Ruskin* (1975/1997), blocking the aperture, noncompliant with the viewfinder. The curve rewinds depth perception to its origin in eye orbs. "The way I use the lens in relationship to the aperture changes the perspective because the lens is not in the expected position," Beavers said. The Naturtheater begs for a camera; a lens is designed to maintain the appearance of deep space while converting three dimensions into two. In *AMOR*, the centers of lens and shot are unsynced. This not only reshapes the cinematic image but exaggerates depth and blurs the image edge. Beavers heeds the cubic impulse and undermines it.

The curve arrived by way of a dome. Beavers wanted to use his fascination with the domed ceilings of baroque cathedrals in Salzburg to make a new film. "How can the idea of the dome extend (evolve) from arch, and the curve of the lens?" he asked in his 1979 notes. The lens, doubly curved (round and convex), arcs in and out of *AMOR*, one of three cycle films that Beavers didn't reedit.[23] A fifteen-minute poem-puzzle shot in Rome, Verona, and Salzburg, *AMOR* unfolds around two stages—the Naturtheater and the rococo Piazza Sant'Ignazio, designed by Filippo Raguzzini in 1727 to resemble a theatrical set with wings and exits. Beavers cuts curves and corners into brisk dialogue, connecting official architectures (Roman and Veronese facades and arches, surfaces under restoration) with softer space-constructions (stationery- and suit-making, filmmaking) along the dotted lines of a tailor's thread and the black sweep of his flying lens.

### AWAY FROM THE WINDOW

The two-ness of "perspective"—a point of view in an infinite spectrum (mine or yours), and the fixed link between point of view and infinity on a picture plane—shows up in Beavers's 1978 note of admiration for Paul Cézanne's downward-cast gaze: "The perspective in a Cézanne still life contains the sense of the eyes turned downward. It's an exact representation of this particular viewpoint, which is so different from the other perspectives (centered and distant). The Cézanne perspective is also away from the scenic, window quality because of this downward angle."

Downward-cast eyes, capped by lids, were part of the imaginary pigment Beavers placed inside *AMOR*'s black lens arcs. In his essay "La Terra Nuova," he links the film's arcs to his encounter with Michelangelo's round painting of the Holy Family (*Doni Tondo*, ca. 1507), at the Uffizi. In 1978, the panel painting hung inside a set of receding wall rings.

> Taking an example from Michelangelo's *Sacra Famiglia*, I would suggest that the circular form of the painting is completed by the curved wall and figures in the background that draw the viewer into a "totally rounded orb." Imagine how a film can extend such a perspective in time, bringing it closer to the subjective sense of how we see. It was with such an impulse that I used the full circle of the camera lens in *AMOR*, turning it in front of the aperture to create a movement like the eye turned upwards or cast downwards. I allowed the lens to suggest a rounded field of vision amplified in the form of the film: a "totally rounded orb, in its rotundity joying" (Empedocles).[24]

As his *AMOR* vision took shape, Beavers extended the idea of the dome in writing. In his notes, he cataloged curves as sense organs ("the eye, itself, and the ear, itself"), sense capacities and their objects ("four different things"—seeing, the image, hearing, sound), and speculative shapes ("curve: of the psyche placed between the self, as a point, and nature, as a circumference"). He transcribed awareness of his own eyes, observing that an object traveling on a horizontal line appeared to approach him as it passed by his eyes, as if moving along a curve, and that focal change catalyzed blinking ("I was interested in the fact that when the head moves, the eye is still, but when you glance"—the head still and the eyes moving—"the eye automatically closes," he explained). These observations about optical curves and closures weren't destined for film symbology; rather, they energized Beavers's hand as he turned the lens. The value of his phenomenological noticing does not concretize in an assertion of universality ("Is it true?" I asked about his eye insights. "I never looked it up," he said. "We're in the realm of the half-educated and I think it can stay there—a scientist might have a different explanation") but in the reanimation of seeing *as* subjectively spacious. "A rounded field of vision" includes the Michelangelo painting as object and the surrounding awareness of environment/time/space rooted in the spectator's body.

On the *AMOR* stage, Beavers's hand replaced a first intention to use a mirror in the film. "Turn of hand: change in viewpoint as in mirror," he noted in August 1979. The hand enacts sonic perspectival mobility too: the palm—interior, vulnerable—is associated with acoustical layering (birdsong, sewing, construction); the protective back with the sharp, identifiable sounds of cuts and claps. The hand's two-sidedness—*recto/verso*—makes it a representative *emblem* for Beavers. He associates the word—a recurring figure in his writing—with Dürer's *Portrait of a Young Man* (1507), which he saw in Vienna in 1968. On its reverse, *Avarice*: an allegorical image of a half-naked old woman. "I thought it was a way of telling a story," he recalled.[25]

*Emblem* commonly signifies symbolic singularity ("the national emblem")—but in early modern print culture, *emblem* equals multiplicity. Renaissance "emblem books" collect three-part compositions made from image and text: a colloquial motto (*inscriptio*), picture (*pictura*), and epigram (*subscriptio*). When I tried to historically locate Beavers's particular two-sided conception of *emblem*, however, I encountered resistance from Renaissance experts—"Beavers has misunderstood the meaning of an emblem!"—until I asked the art historian Marisa Bass, who replied:

> I would say that Beavers is not misusing the word "emblem" but actually getting at something crucial about the way that they work. The history of emblems as a genre traces back to the medieval and early Renaissance practice of individuals adopting mottoes, devices, or what are called *imprese* in Italian: written phrases and/or encoded images that were meant to express their referents' character and identity. One of the first visual uses of these devices came in the form of portrait medals, on which the portrait of the individual appeared on the front and the individual's device on the back. As the genre of the emblem book developed in the sixteenth century, the standard visual structure of an emblem instead came to comprise placing motto and image together on a single page, but the larger history of emblematics does encompass two-sided images and is all about the notion that images are themselves double-sided or even multi-sided in meaning.[26]

On the Naturtheater stage, Beavers stands on the reverse side of his image-making device. Object of his camera's gaze, he refuses the usual distribution of filmmaking roles. Casting himself as a headless character, he shuns the fantasy of the fully intentional image, dreamt up in advance by director, executed by cameraman: "I am opposed to the film director's conception of theatrical mise-en-scène *in front of the camera* and to the cameraman being asked to create a *style* for the image. By dividing the act of filming between director and cameraman, the image is reduced to illustrating a preconception; whereas, in the hands of a filmmaker, the camera functions to create an image that is newly seen, one that projects into the past and future," he writes in "La Terra Nuova."[27] While Beavers is onstage, the black arc is static—his hands are out of range and can't turn the lens. The filmmaker is balancing the limits of a single perspective with a drive toward totality (his awareness is both held in place by the running camera and, across the line, rooted in front of it). From the dome—the perfectly round climax of religious space, portal to the sun—Beavers constructs his own architecture of expansion. "Curve—the entire field of awareness," he wrote in his 1978 *AMOR* notes.

The filmmaker also steps definitively *behind* the camera and out of his onstage suit in *AMOR*. Classically observational close-ups frame the objects and labor of suit construction and tailoring: cloth-cutting, spools of thread, scissors, the long stitches that bind a rough assembly. For *AMOR*, Beavers shot at the Milanese atelier of the tailor, Guiseppe Pallino, who made his and Markopoulos's bespoke suits (including the one Beavers wears in the film).[28] "I learned very interesting things about southern Italian craftsmanship from him," Beavers recalled. "Tailoring is very much like sculpture." Seamsters at Pallino's workshop bathed fabric—softened cloth is easier to cut and sew—and assembled a suit with a single strand of thread, waxed to protect the fabric. They traced chalk lines around cut-out patterns onto fabric—it reminded Beavers of an architectural blueprint.

At the Milanese stationer Pettinaroli, Beavers selected a white envelope. "[Use as] an intermediary between the suit and building [to] make similarities clear," he directed himself in a note. Shot in extreme close-up, the envelope evokes touch (it is lined by gray paper) and acquires complex structure: a hybrid of angles and rounded edges, a square assembled from triangles in precisely folded flaps. The envelope repeats the shapes of Beavers's lapels and vest and the unexpected curves of Piazza Sant'Ignazio facades. With kinship of structure and built-ness foregrounded, object names recede and stitching continues: a billowing scaffold has seams; the Roman building underneath is touched by cloth. As Beavers stands in the leafy crease of the Naturtheater, the fold—envelope, cloth, scaffold, eyes, emblem—is a site of touch between architecture and craft, the cubic and the curved.

—

In *AMOR*, we see recurring close-ups of a 10,000 lire banknote featuring a portrait of Niccolò Machiavelli on its front. When backlit, the note becomes transparent and a second portrait of Machiavelli—a watermark—appears, producing the phrase "two men" in my mind and reminding me that *AMOR*, per its title, is a love film.[29] (Another reveal of "two men"—a medallion portrait relief on a Verona facade is, in a wider shot, one of two such portraits of men side by side.) The film's darting erotic energy—insistent cutting, Beavers's own angular motions, and the mobile lens—creates an atmosphere of hide-and-seek, or a puzzle.[30]

"I noticed how the words in the sentences that I was translating fitted together like cut stones," Beavers writes of his attraction to Latin as a boy.[31] In *AMOR*, a string of Latin letters on a Verona facade belong to a connected spectrum of language elements in the film: the palindrome of its title (*AMOR*/ROMA); letters embossed on the envelope (the stationer's address: MILANO, VIA MARINO), printed on the banknote (BANCA D'ITALIA), and abstracted via the tailor's stitches. And a caption—"*Mezza luna.*"—accompanies one of the film's recurring curves: the drawn image of a semicircular wooden tool printed on a *sartoria* (tailoring) book page. From the start, the dome represented a feeling structure for Beavers; it held the potential for undivided love: "the concept of religious love that doesn't exclude the erotic," he said.[32] In the pursuit of a most capacious awareness ("Empedocles's rotundity joying") that doesn't exclude the sharp edges of cut stones and alphabetic shapes, *AMOR* is a dome in formation.

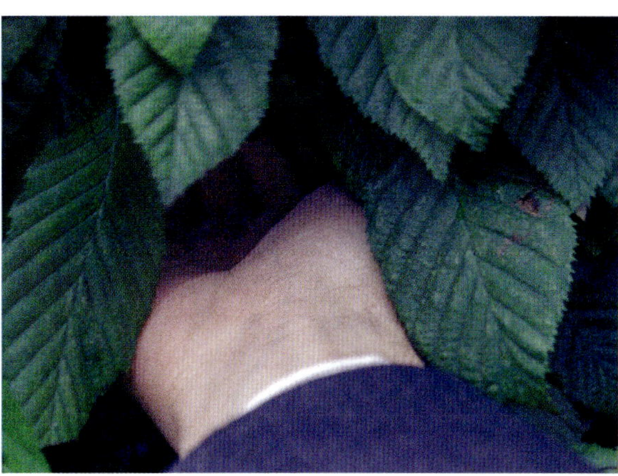

*AMOR* (1980)

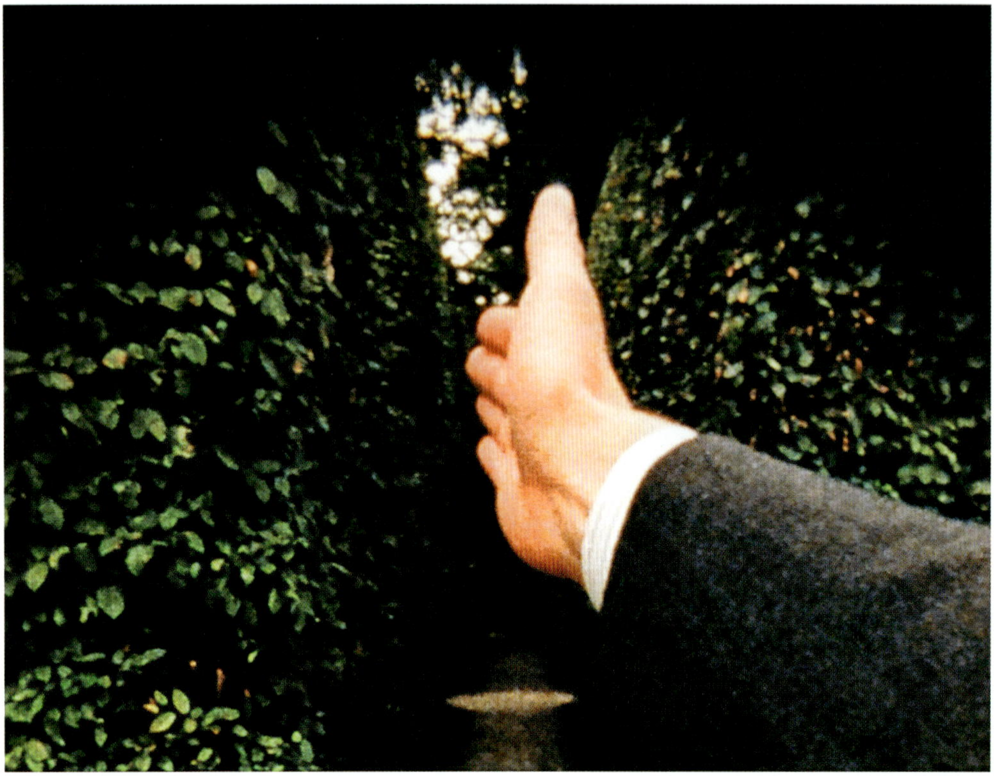

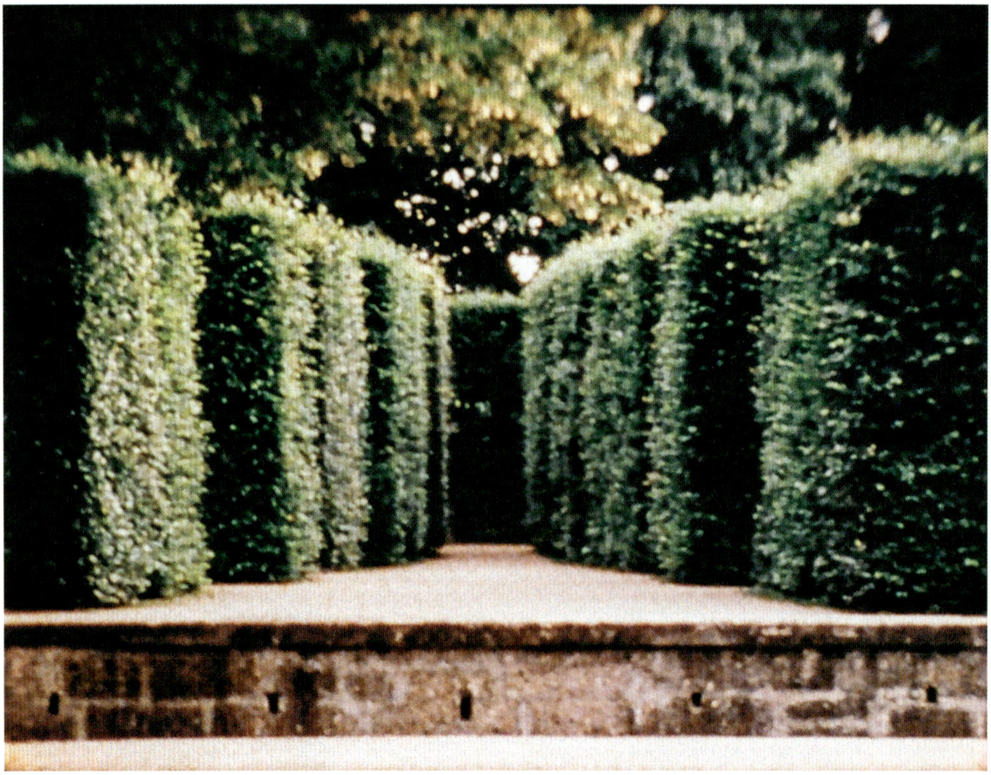

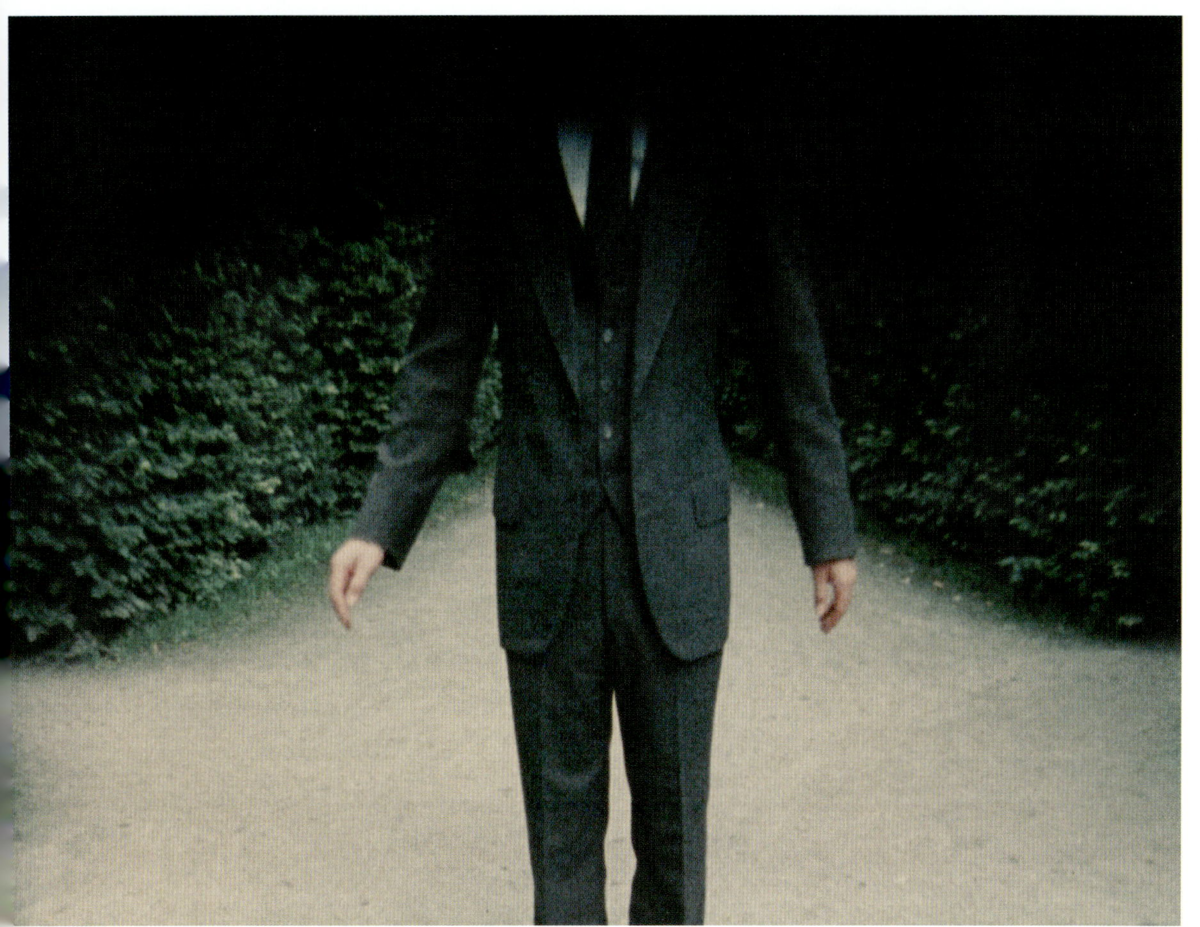

*AMOR* (1980)

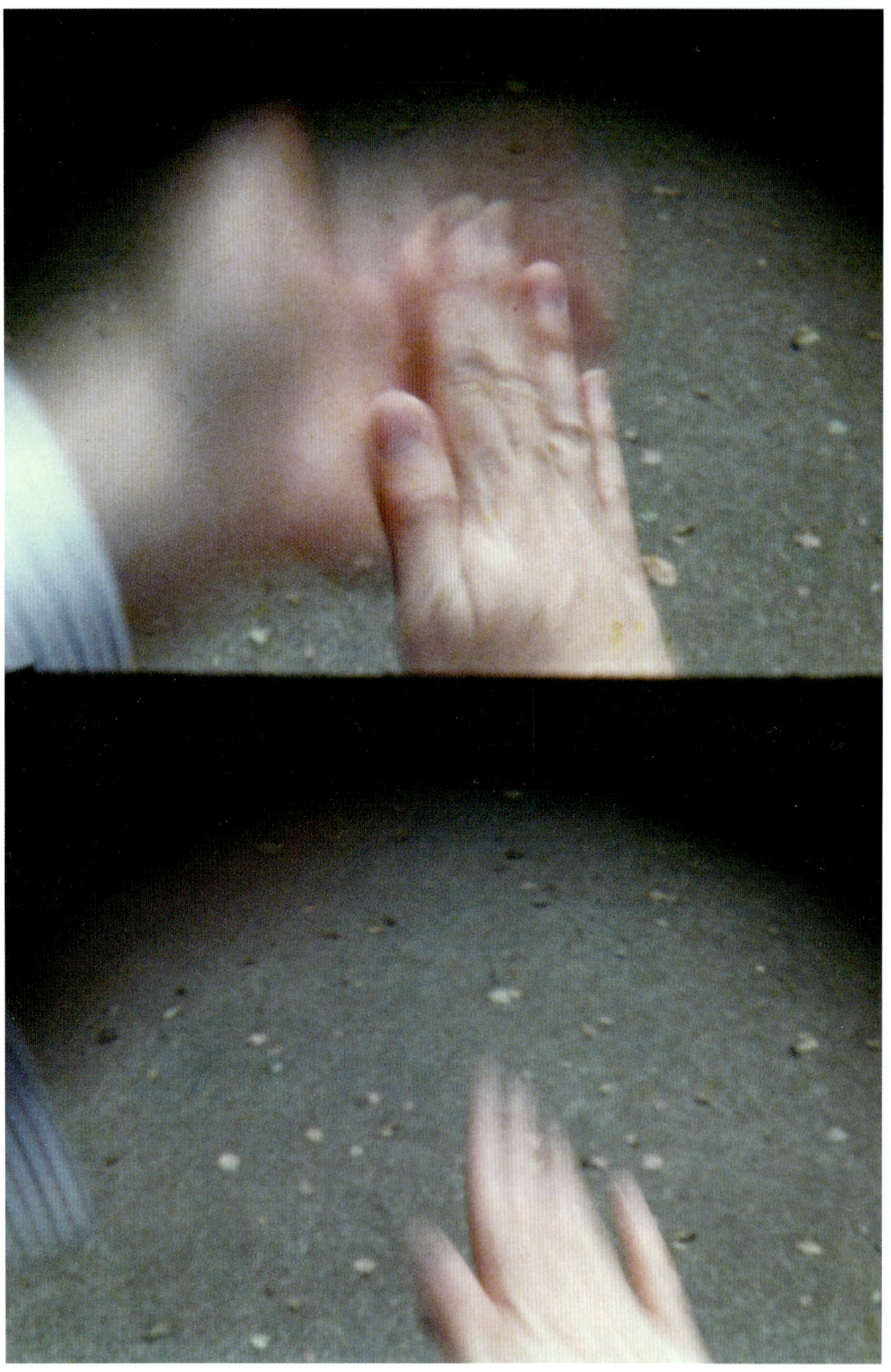

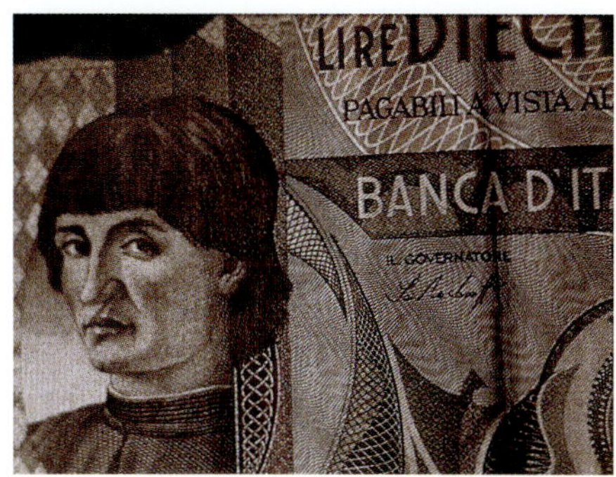


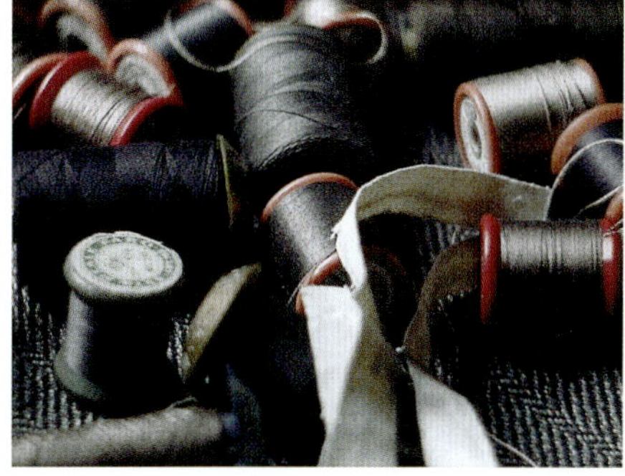

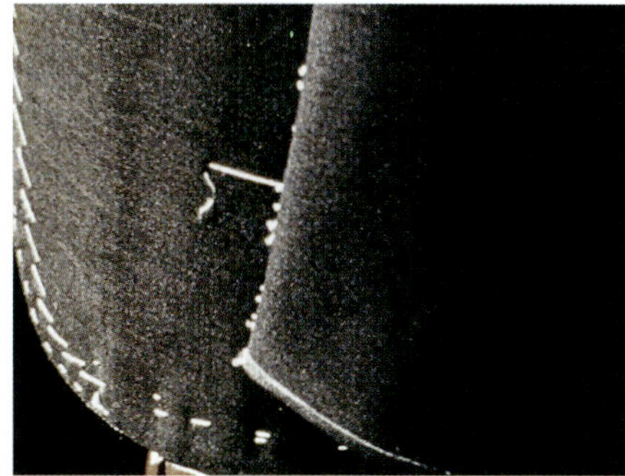

*AMOR* (1980)

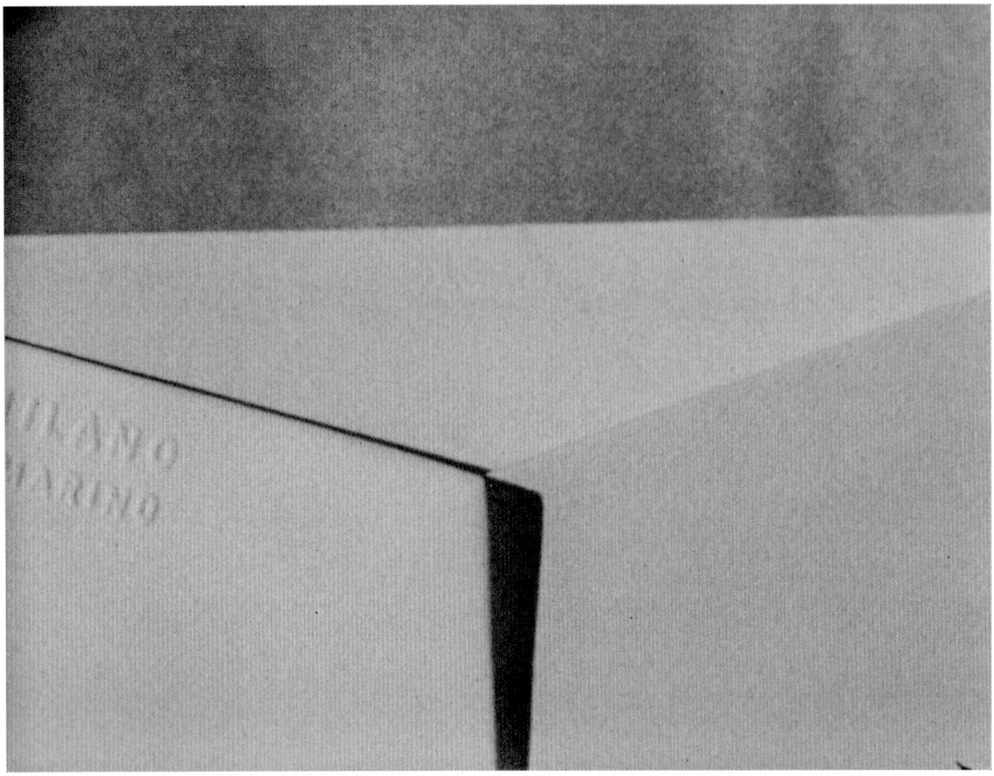

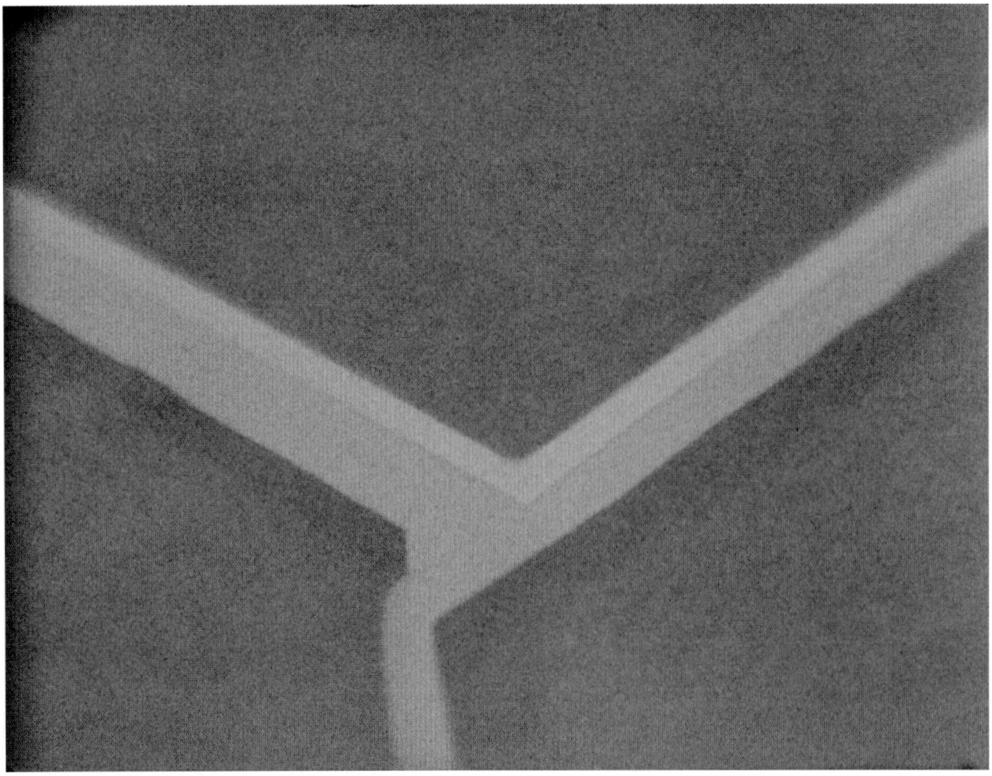

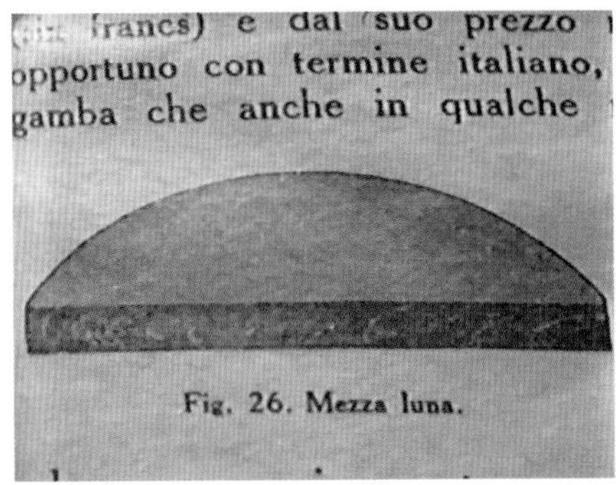

(six francs) e dal (suo prezzo
opportuno con termine italiano,
gamba che anche in qualche

Fig. 26. Mezza luna.

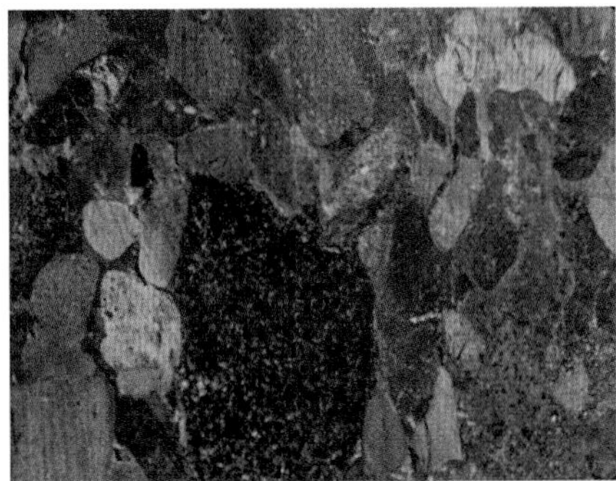

*AMOR* (1980)

## CONSTRUCTING AN INVISIBLE DOME

"With the turning of the lens—I couldn't reach the cupola [in *AMOR*]," Beavers said. He couldn't fully realize his film-as-dome intention. But six years later—inside the seventeenth-century architect Francesco Borromini's churches in Rome—he retrieved it. *The Hedge Theater* (1986–1990/2002) and *AMOR* constitute "a rare case in which the starting point of one film was the letting-off point of another," Beavers said. We see the elliptical dome of Borromini's San Carlo alle Quattro Fontane and the round cupola of his Sant'Ivo alla Sapienza (as well as the Palazzo di Propaganda Fide exterior) in *The Hedge Theater*, but Beavers was wary of direct representation, of wishfully using the camera to "pick up" the feeling-scapes of Borromini's Counter-Reformation symbolic forms. "Not images of architecture without meaning built in (between them) . . . . For each architectural detail that I film, a meaning equal to it in the film," he noted in the fall of 1985. The two-part film combines two originally distinct works: *Borromini* (1986) and the shorter *San Martino / Il Sassetta* (1987–1990), an exchange between a fifteenth-century painting—il Sassetta's *Saint Martin Sharing His Cloak with a Beggar* (1433)—and the Salzburg Naturtheater.[33]

Borromini was a choreographer of visible and hidden geometries, a high baroque fuser of sharp edges and curves. In *The Hedge Theater* we see the folded facade of San Carlo alle Quattro Fontane—undulating convex and concave curves. Indoors, light forms transmitted through a lantern overlap with the interlocking ovals, circles, hexagons, and crosses permanently stamped on the elliptical cupola. We come close to the climax of Borromini's upward sweep of alternating scallops and edges in Sant'Ivo: a circle of unmediated natural light. Beavers was moved by "the extraordinarily special meanings [Borromini] connected to forms," he said. The architect built San Carlo for free in 1641, a gift to the Trinitarians. The dome grows out of a floor plan that merges an oval and a cross.

The first shot of *The Hedge Theater* frames an ellipsis superimposed by a cross: a pool of water beneath the intersection of a horizontal branch and a slender tree. Beavers collected shadows of Borromini's geometry in a hilltop Brescia *roccolo*, a circular grove of trees designed for bird-hunting (like the Naturtheater, a structure built from nature). Borromini's repeating sunburst (the crowning gold shape inside Sant'Ivo's dome, the cut-out rays on the San Carlo ground-floor facade) reappears in the *roccolo* as a circular array of spiny branches. As in *AMOR*, cloth work joins the film's building studies; in close-ups of a seamstress's fast-moving hands, a buttonhole is a sunburst too: a stretched ellipsis fringed by vertical stitch lines.

The vegetation and birds of the *roccolo* and its *richiami* (a metal cage with decoys to attract other birds) generate sonic and visual siblings for Borromini's sculpted angels and leaves. But the film is not a catalog of coinciding image-facts; Beavers builds a foundation from these shared motifs and uses it as a stage: a nature-theater for his filmmaking. Sliver shots of Beavers at his camera in a pension appear between the architectures of marble, nature, and cloth. At first his head, and the apparatus, are off-screen; instead, his torso and arm fill the frame in intuitive gestures of extension into the space and shot (when he bends his arm, he produces one of the film's many wings). He buttons and unbuttons his white shirt; with his collar up, his own shape is like that of the church columns and tree trunks. Beavers's white shirt escapes the observational register of the sewing shots and draws the filmmaker into skin contact with Borromini's interiors (always white).

Beavers's literal presence in these shots draws the theater of his filmmaking—the trace of point of view—out of other imagery. An elliptical relief under the San Carlo portico is visible only because Beavers's camera is angled upward (the relief is perpendicular to the ground). The feltness of the *roccolo*'s subtle structure comes from the way its canopy of intertwined branches appears like a dome as it is reinforced by Beavers's lens arc. Neither shapes nor rhymes are given—and both often depend on the less obvious work of sound. The assertive whir of Beavers's running Bolex pushes shots ahead and highlights sonic architecture. As it coincides with an image of the *richiami*, a rhythmic metallic clang produces a mental image of a bird climbing rungs—as if I've *seen* this action—and makes the wrought-iron window grating on the San Carlo facade as vivid as Borromini's cut-out sunburst.

## WHITEOUT

A tone of imminence brightens the conclusion of the first section of *The Hedge Theater*: a fast move up Sant'Ivo's corkscrew spire; a new symbol from Borromini's canon—a crown (also Sant'Ivo); church organ music that steps boldly into the acoustic foreground. Locations and seasons change—a winter Naturtheater replaces the *roccolo*; snow coats its lions and stage. A new hand appears in the shots with Beavers; an arm—another white shirt—is draped over his shoulder. We later see it is Markopoulos; he is seated behind the camera, his hand over his eyes, while Beavers, head out of shot, grasps the camera. Their two hands coincide as one in the shot-space. Echoes of Beavers's first weave of erotic and holy love, *Winged Dialogue* (Beavers's hand moving in shadow; Markopoulos's covered eyes), add to the spirit of ascension and arrival.

In his notes for *The Hedge Theater*, Beavers transcribed lines from the Greek pastoral poet Bion's "The Boy and Love," in which a novice bird catcher receives counsel from an experienced elder who implores him not to chase the love-bird but to allow it to arrive: "Thou wilt be happy, so long as thou dost not catch him, but if thou comest to the measure of manhood, this bird that flees thee now, and hops away, will come uncalled, and of a sudden, and settle on thy head."[34]

—

In the last shot of the film's first section, Beavers primes the screen in preparation for the arrival of a Renaissance painting. His low camera pulls away from the triangular end of the Naturtheater stage until the entire shot is snow—indistinguishable from a "white screen" in a cinema on which no image is projected. In his notes, Beavers imagined a boundary breakdown among whites—light/snow/marble/screen: "The white surface and the film screen. The white of the image returning to the screen—is the screen, the shadow, then a reflection." This alchemy-by-color is a means of space-making, of reaching into the spectator's space of reception. Beavers aspired for a filmic version of the negative space sculpted by Borromini's curves—immaterial shapes rendered by concrete ones. In October 1996, he had written: "The arc of the entrance to Propaganda Tide suggests an invisible dome; this is one of Borromini's powers—one element can create the (hidden?) presence of another. The secret is perhaps in the complex curves and diagonals which project beyond the basic surface of the building and suggest that the space in front of the building has been given shape. It would be wonderful to continue this in the film: the image, the screen, and the space in front of the screen. And to create my presence, the arm movement, etc., and Gregory's hand, there in that space." As the upward-moving image trajectory at the conclusion of the film's first section meets Beavers's gestures of extension into the field of film projection and reception, *The Hedge Theater* sculpts a dome. Love is fully dimensional—its objects and aspirations specific (Markopoulos), anonymous (the spectator), and divine. The resolution of the dome is the resolution of love.

### THE DIVIDED CLOAK

A ripping sound and shots of the painting—*Saint Martin Sharing His Cloak with a Beggar* by il Sassetta (Stefano di Giovanni)—open the second part of *The Hedge Theater*. In Sassetta's image, a red cloak is held jointly by St. Martin, on horseback, and a naked beggar. As in *The Martyrdom of St. Hippolytus*, the painting precedes total disassembly: we see St. Martin slicing his military cloak with his sword in order to share it with the beggar. Beavers intercuts details of the painting—its surface cracked and gold leaf still iridescent—with images of a newborn Naturtheater, green in the spring rain. "The simplicity of early Renaissance painting—it's so different from someone like Michelangelo—the grace, and there's a joyous quality because of the colors. It's like early music—there is a clarity and lightness because it's closer to the subject and the technique," he said. Convention hasn't yet produced an instructional, intention-directing scrim; real choices can still be made.

St. Martin's gift, like love, is proximate to violence (the cut, the sword). Freshly cut branches are visible in the springtime Naturtheater. In 1667, Borromini killed himself by deliberately falling on a sword in the Roman Oratory, whose facade—a concave curve partitioned by pilasters—he had designed as a gesture of expanse: "I created the figure of the human body with open arms as if it embraces everyone who enters."[35] Borromini, the depressive foil to his charismatic rival Gian Lorenzo Bernini, knew the risks of following his highest aims. "If your work involves inventing something new, you do not see the fruit of your labours until much later, if indeed at all," he wrote.[36] In 1977, the publication of Leo Steinberg's dissertation on San Carlo—*Borromini's San Carlo alle Quattro Fontane: A Study in Multiple Form and Architectural Symbolism*—stirred a revival of interest in the long-forgotten architect.[37]

Like Sassetta, Borromini was born with a different name. Francesco Castelli might have changed his name in 1633 (as he set up his architecture office in Rome) with Saint Charles Borromeo, a key figure in the Counter-Reformation, in mind. In *The Hedge Theater*, we see BORROMEO inscribed around the oval oculus of San Carlo. The church is dedicated to the Catholic saint. Names are elements of both inscription and inconstancy in Beavers's films: martyrdom transfigures both souls and names (Saints Martin and Hippolytus), proper names disappear in favor of more oblique ones: *Borromini* and *San Martino / Il Sassetta* became *The Hedge Theater*. Beavers elevates a structure sculpted from nature—not art object but mediating aesthetic space—with his definite article.

In late 1985, early in his work on what would become *The Hedge Theater*, Beavers noted:

> **To add to the meaning (of the life). A film not repeating its meaning + not limited to the earlier bounds:**
> **To give. Only a real choice can do this.**

In *The Hedge Theater*, Beavers returned to the implied "solitary figure" that he had set aside with *Work Done*—a structuring psychic subjectivity unifies its symbolic cosmos. By the time he completed the film, he was also finishing the decade-long process of reediting his earlier work, and decided to extract his name from films as he assembled his *Hand Outstretched* cycle. He had stopped printing individual film titles in the 1980s.[38]

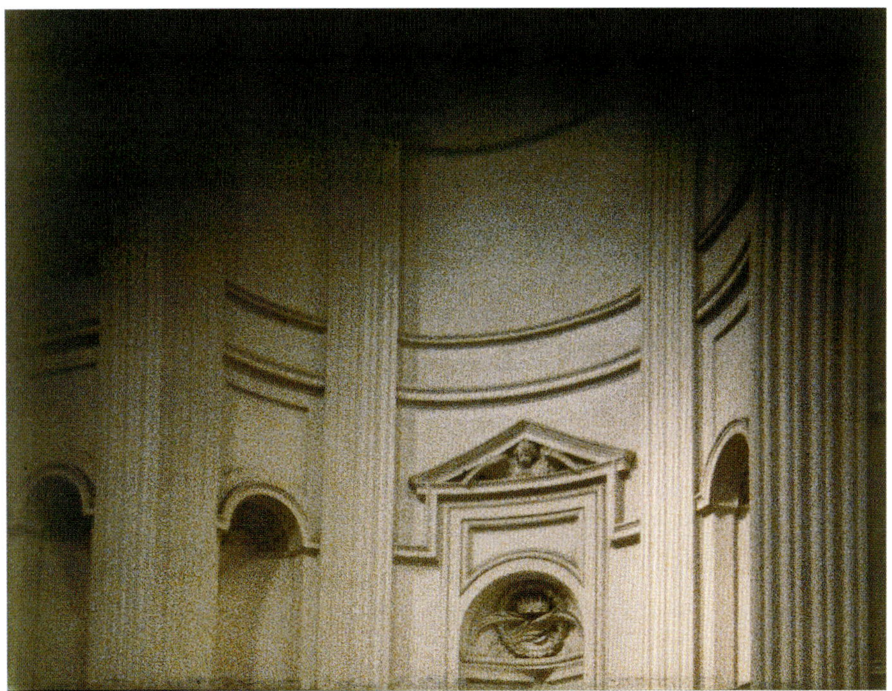

*The Hedge Theater* (1986–1990/2002)

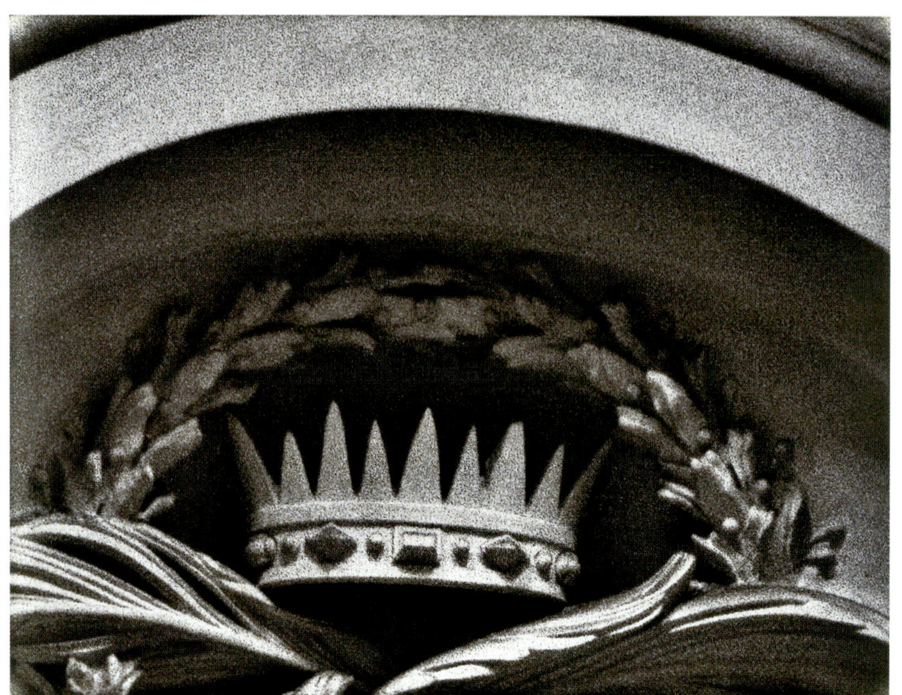

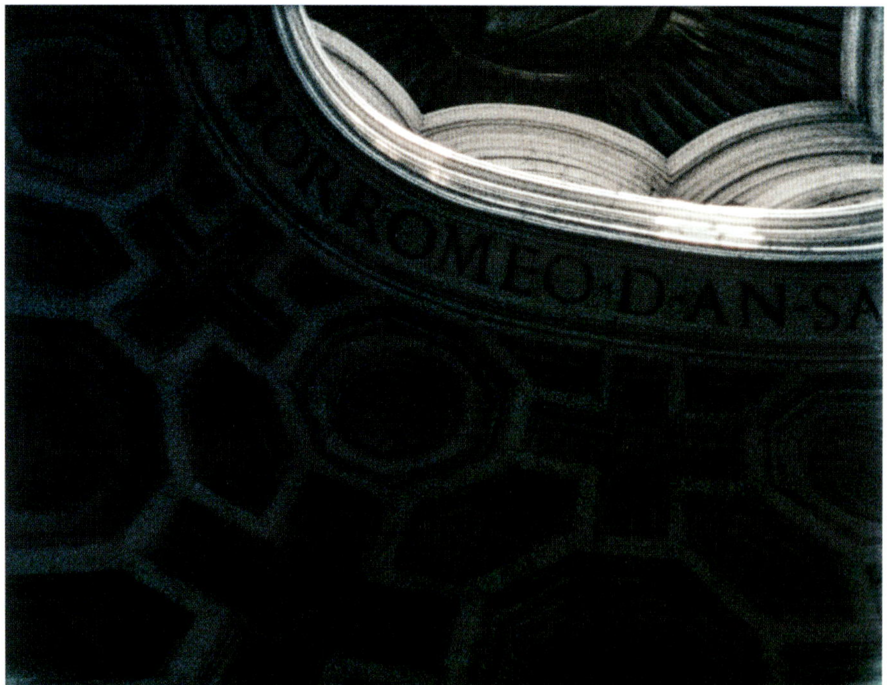


*The Hedge Theater* (1986–1990/2002)

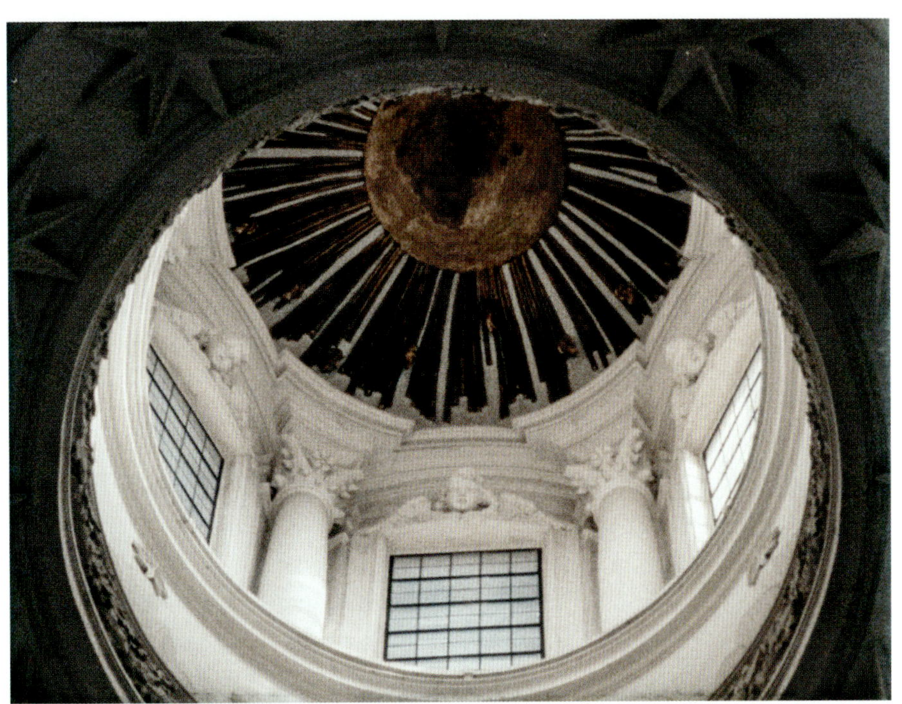

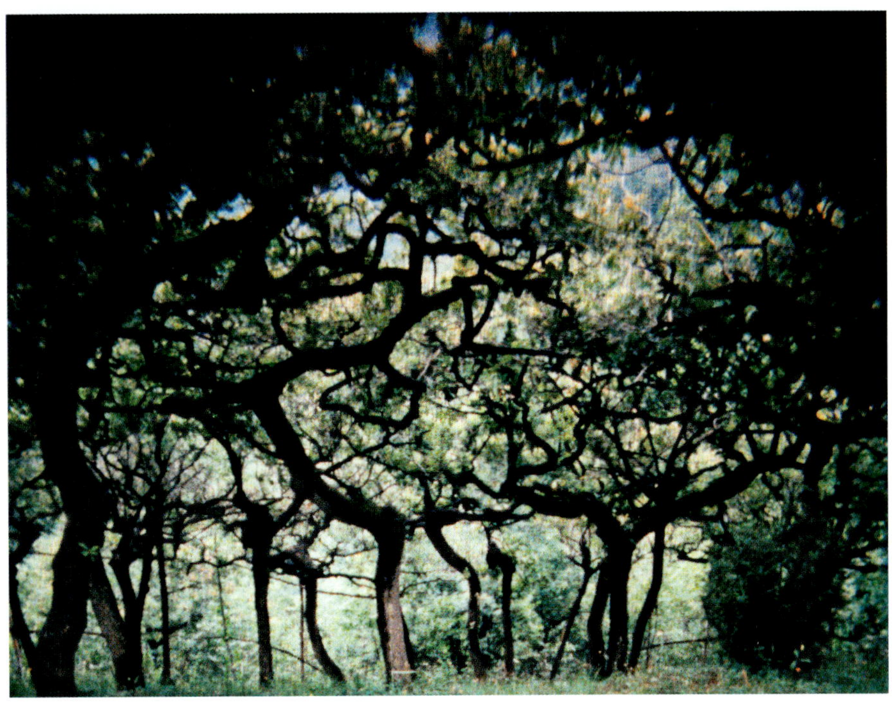

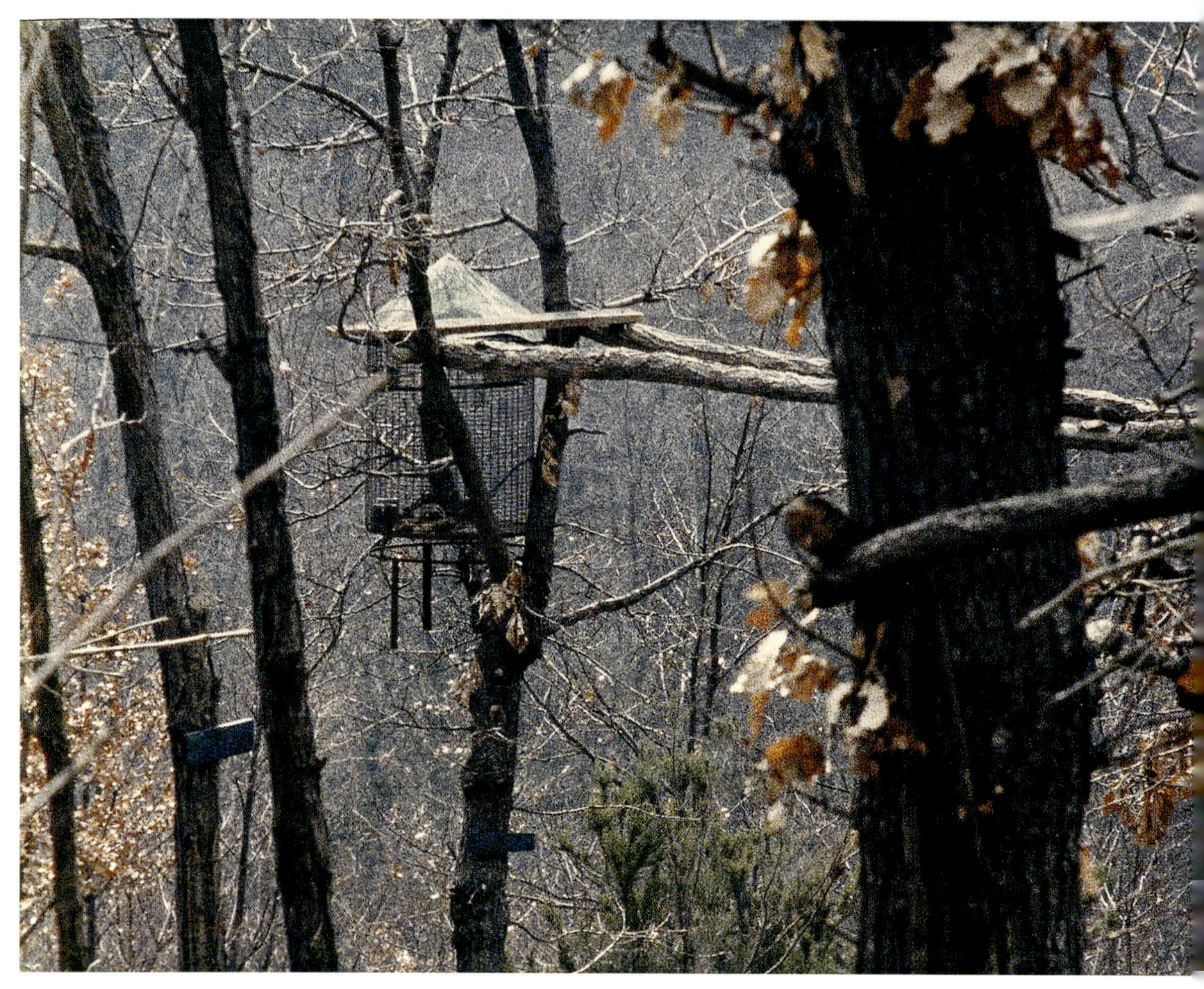

*The Hedge Theater* (1986–1990/2002)

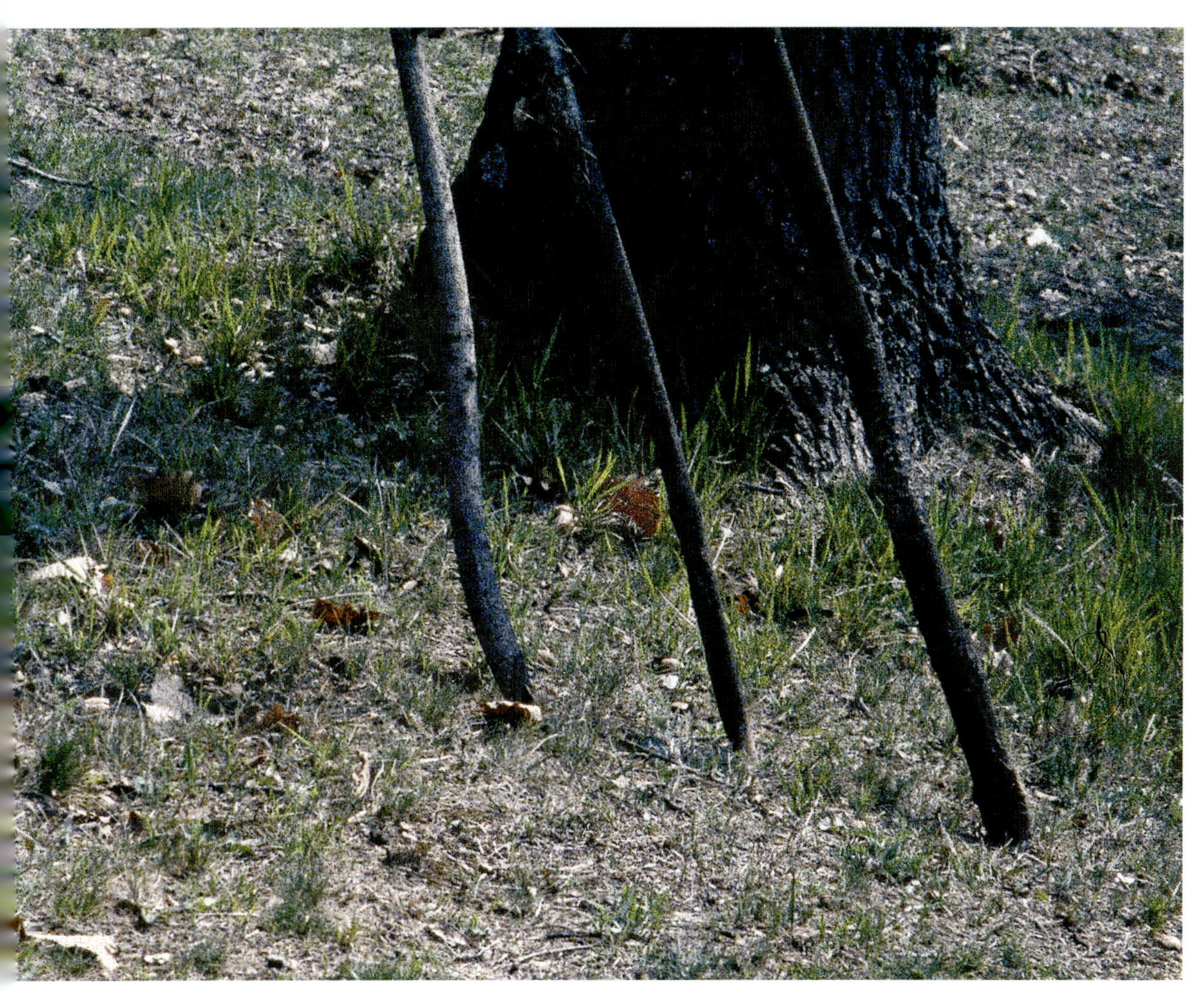

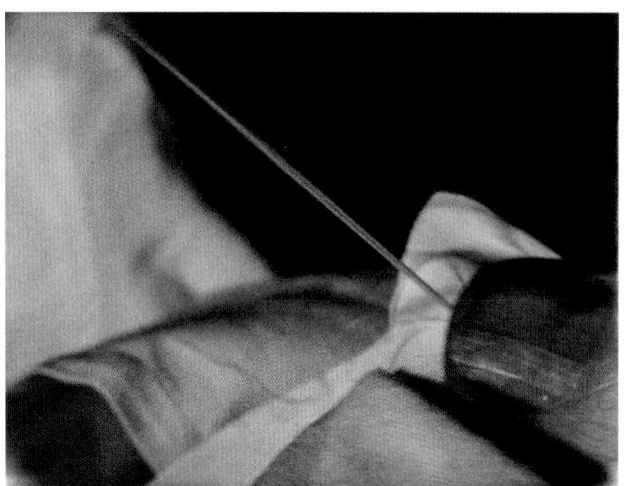

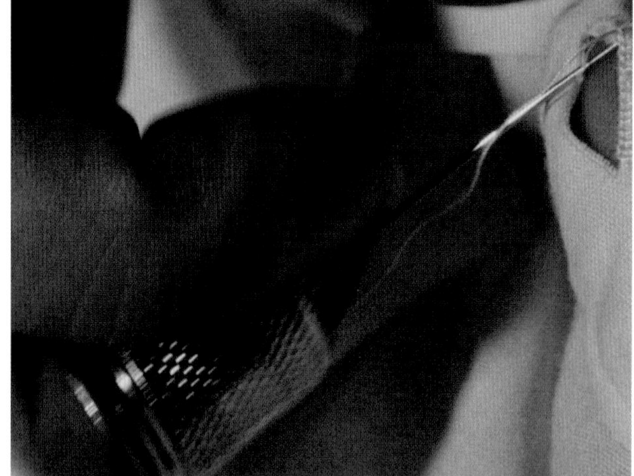

*The Hedge Theater* (1986–1990/2002)

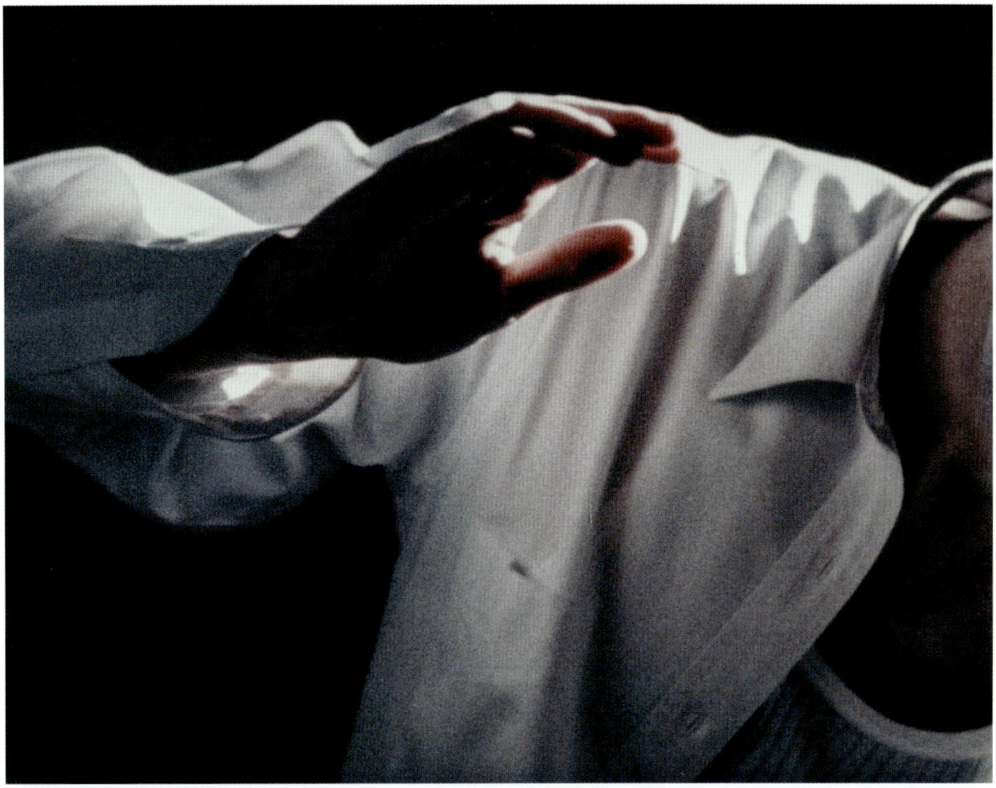

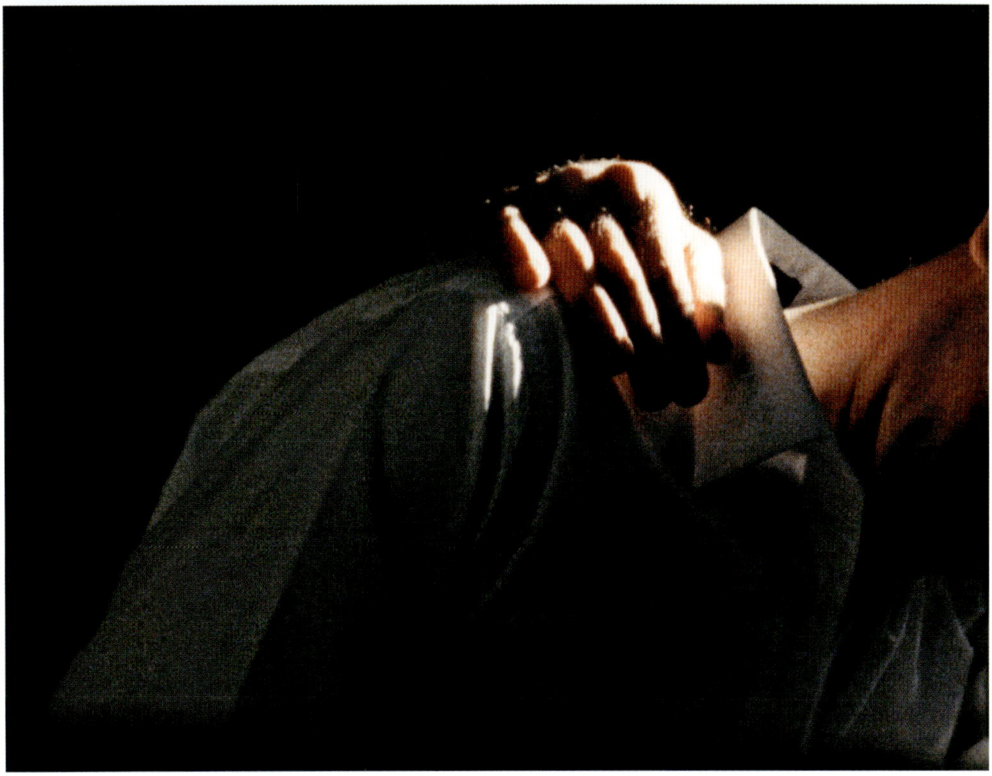

## BANKNOTES AND REAL DIAMOND WALLS

As Beavers and Markopoulos prioritized filmmaking impulses above all, pictures and words often catalyzed first choices. The discovery of Anthony Blunt's book *Borromini* led to the architect's churches.[39] In March 1986, after Beavers found *Architettura Contadina in Valtrompia* and read about the *roccoli* of Lombardy—"*la cosi detta 'pancia' del roccolo*," he copied into his notes—he and Markopoulos took a taxi into the Brescia hills, where Beavers found a single hanging *richiami* and the circular grove.[40] "The location proved to be all that I could hope for," he wrote. At a Roman bookstore, Beavers opened Count Raniero Gnoli's *Marmora Romana* and found grids of colored stone types and accounts of their sources.[41] His visit to Gnoli and his marble collection in a seventeenth-century castle north of Rome generated the full-frame shots of marble that appear in *AMOR*. And at a shop near the Louvre, Beavers saw the Sassetta painting on an old postcard. "It gave the occasion [to visit the painting]. We had no resources, but we made a decision." In Siena, Beavers procured a letter of permission from the Banca Monte dei Paschi di Siena to shoot the painting at the Chigi Saracini collection.

But freely following creative instincts produced a constant need for other kinds of banknotes. In 1987, Beavers and Markopoulos visited a Munich bank with historical ties to the Kingdom of Bavaria and requested a meeting. "Gregory gave off an air of intransigence," Beavers said. "But he also had a special dignity—people didn't know who he was, this person in a tailored suit—and sometimes he got a response. Suddenly we were meeting with four bank officials." Markopoulos didn't hedge: "Is there not someone like Ludwig?" Composer Richard Wagner was his hero, and so was Wagner's patron—King Ludwig II of Bavaria.[42] The bankers declined to play Ludwig and suggested the men contact a foundation created when the monarchy was absolved. When the foundation provided the name of the Duke of Bavaria, Beavers located him in the Munich phone book and they spoke directly. Franz von Bayern became Beavers's longest-term financial supporter.

—

Real choices and real gifts arrive on a spectrum. Backlit, the Italian banknote in *AMOR* is "see-through": a sign of value now also insubstantial. The note is engraved with an image of the diamond-pointed facade of the Church of Gesù Nuovo in Naples, and the same design—called "diamond rustication"—appears off the bill; we see a painted trompe l'oeil rendition and then a three-dimensional version (both are on Verona walls). Beavers distinguished the three in his notes, poetically reorganizing value and reality: "Money, diamonds, real diamond wall." The two-dimensional illusion represented on the banknote is not the same as "a real diamond wall." But money hardens objects into art, reorders strivings, clarifies careers, finalizes names. And Beavers and Markopoulos always needed it.

Beavers's *The Hedge Theater* notes record the day-to-day material challenges of willing the film into existence. Between October 1985 and February 1988, he and Markopoulos moved (at least) among Basel, Bologna, Verona, Milan, Athens, Rome, Florence, Salzburg, Munich, Brescia, Zurich, Gengenbach, Gstaad, and Turin. At every step (acquiring film stock, developing film, viewing rush prints, recording and producing magnetic sound elements), it is a narrative of relocation, conflicting currencies—and debt. Motion caused debt ("4.11.86: We had to make many debts to make the return") and debt determined motion—both starts (the pursuit of a new patron, access to equipment) and stops ("13.5.86: All of my footage will be put back in storage, also the new splicing instruments from Hammann").[43] Goals were supremely present tense. "It was never really about cash flow," Beavers said.

Beavers's notes transcribe a trail of short-term fixes. Business owners granted extensions: "14.11.85: Paid 100,000 lire on the hotel bill, leaving 65,000 owed"; "20.3.86: Four rolls obtained on credit from Kodak-Munchen." Patrons sent infusions: "30.4.86: Doris [Epstein][44] gave a check for the continuation of filming. 800SF"; "20.11.87: Gregory . . . reached Dr. Ghertsos at 8:20. He asked for 3,000SF and was told at 11:30 that 2000 would be telexed. . . . It should allow us to leave Munich." Radio and television stations loaned equipment: "15.10.86: I viewed two rolls of rush print on a Prevost moviola in the RAI building [in Turin]"; "24.3.87: Note sent to Paolo Bachmann at Televisione Svizzera Italiana about arranging the loan of a tape recorder."[45]

Beavers logged expenses: "14.7.86: I have obtained the cores, clear leader, 7 boxes and 300 meters black leader from Arnold + Richter, at a cost of 10,00DM"; "20.5.87: First sound recorded: a single bird fluttering in a cage (*richiami*). I had to give 15,000 lire for the use of the bird then returned it." He also noted the pains of unanticipated costs. In 1989, Beavers shot with negative film for the first time. With reversal film, he had edited the camera original; in editing *The Hedge Theater* (then *Borromini*), he realized that negative film was too fragile for direct handling and the eye strain (from looking at a negative image) was unsustainable—he'd have to produce a new copy for editing. "7.6.90: Having to make this [work] copy creates an impasse," he wrote.

"Debt became a catalyst," Beavers said. "It forced others to act." In July 1987, Beavers arranged a screening of *Borromini* at Schweizerische Nationalbank, in Zurich, and proposed that the bank acquire a copy for 10,000SF. After the screening, an executive "asked . . . what the meaning of the *roccolo* was in the film," Beavers noted. Nine days later, the bank press officer wrote to Beavers: "We have come to the conclusion that it is nothing but impossible. . . . Your film would not be of any direct use to the National Bank. . . . This is in no way a judgment on the quality of the film . . . [the decision] does not represent any doubt that you, in your very special field, are an outstanding artist."

Sometimes chance intervened: in the mid-1980s, Beavers thought he recognized art collector Dominique de Menil at an Athens cafe. It was her sister—Anne Gruner Schlumberger. "We look just alike," she explained. She wrote Beavers a check to support his Borromini film before she left Greece the next day.

## OTHER WORK DONE

Patron-seeking was labor intensive: phone calls and letters, express packages (press clippings, Temenos publications, photographs), private screenings, cancellations, no-shows, and persistent follow-up that sometimes produced a request for fund-seeking correspondence to cease. Beavers sought aid from foundations, corporations, individuals and royalty. In early 1988, he requested a meeting with Italian princess Marie Gabrielle de Savoie. "I have had the privilege for the past two decades of making films free from the usual constraints of the industrial or commercial uses of Film," he wrote. He asked for 25,000DM to print *Borromini* and to reestablish good standing at his film lab—"I am indebted to the film laboratory which has repeatedly extended my credit for the work done." At their meeting in her Gstaad chalet, Beavers projected *AMOR* and *Work Done*. In June, he responded to her decision not to help: "I do understand the well-intentioned comment about my part of the art world being different from Your Royal Highness's. To be more exact, it is a matter of the private continuation of my work apart from the art world. Today, it is more urgent than ever to be free of these bodies and the quantity of work which they gather."

As the 1980s progressed, the nature of Beavers's requests shifted to the completion of his cycle and the realization of the Temenos. In a 1987 letter of introduction to the Prince of Wales, Beavers describes the "unique collection of film works which is the nucleus of what is known as the Temenos Archive. . . . This most crucial moment . . . must lead to the presentation of this work in the structures we intend to build [at the Temenos]." In 1988, a single meeting and screening with Jan Philipp Reemtsma, son of entrepreneur Philipp Fürchtegott Reemtsma and the founder and director of the Hamburg Institute for Social Research, resulted in a 50,000DM fellowship. Beavers projected his *Borromini* film-in-progress; the two men never met again. Reemtsma also paid two years of lab fees. The gift enabled Beavers to print his film cycle; Markopoulos now had the freedom to complete the final *Eniaios* edit. Their patron streams were generally distinct, but "I subsidized that because Gregory had so often subsidized my work through Ghertsos," Beavers said. "It brought our mode of activity to a higher level, and it took some fear out."

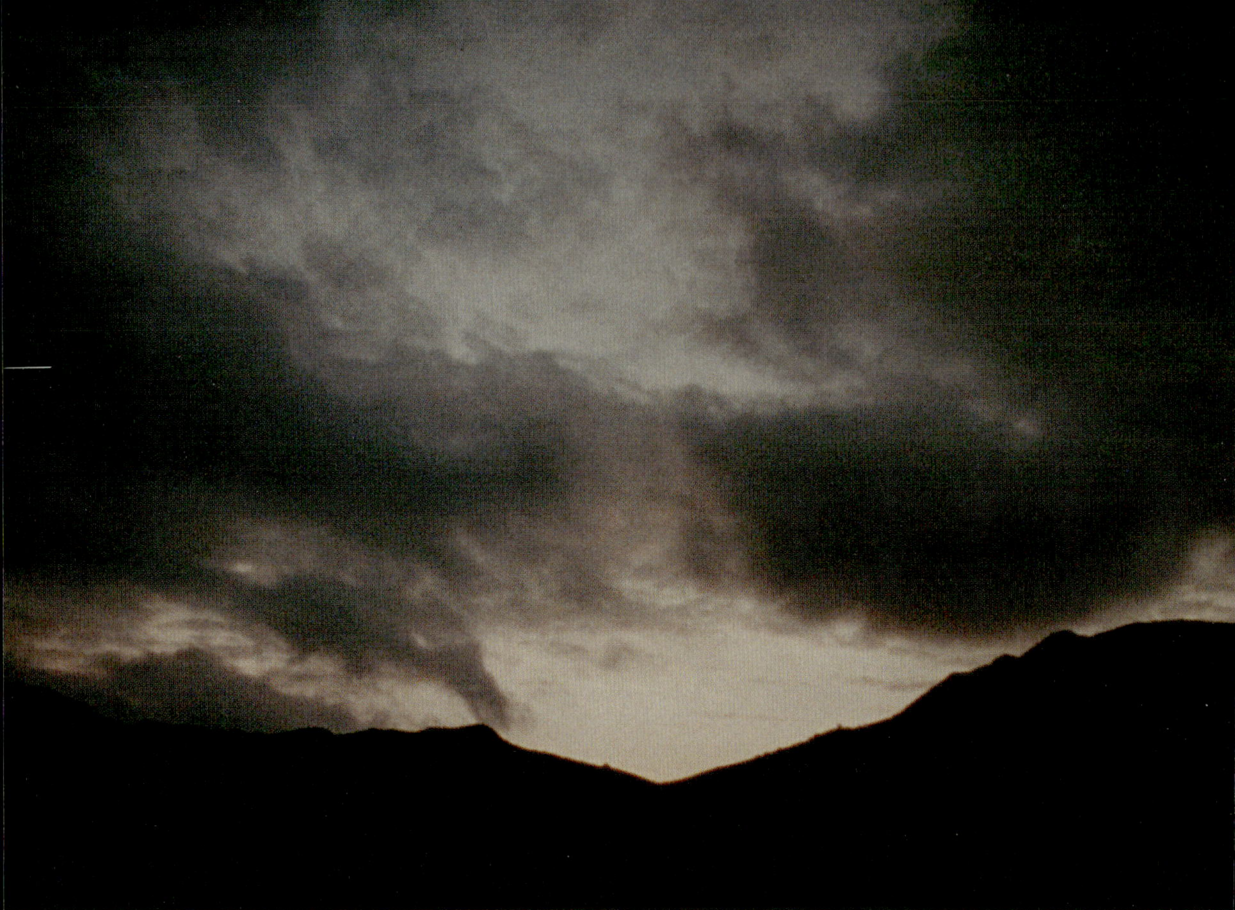

*The Ground* (1993–2001)

# STOAS AND VASES

# 6

Greece: the degeneration of all its meanings.
**Robert Beavers, notes for *Sotiros***

Ὁ ἄναξ, οὗ τὸ μαντεῖόν ἐστι τὸ ἐν Δελφοῖς, οὔτε λέγει οὔτε κρύπτει ἀλλὰ σημαίνει.

The lord whose oracle is at Delphi neither speaks nor conceals, but gives a sign.
**Heraclitus**[1]

"[I was] greeted by a red sun and sky and blue-purple mountains when I first saw Greece . . . tonight, looking out from YΔPA [Hydra], the sight is the same threatening combination, with the green-red of the heliotrope or blood-stone in the sea," Beavers wrote in June 1967. Heliotrope, used by ancient Greeks as a health-protecting talisman, is a dark green jasper spiked with red dots. It appears completely red when placed in water under direct sunlight. Weeks later, as Beavers left Hydra for Patmos with Markopoulos and 1,700 feet of *Winged Dialogue* film, he saw Greece as a set of synchronous blue and white bands:

**Greece—Blue and White, blue and white glazing each other. The light reflects a blue (from something painted—it's a favorite color) onto the white (white ships, most houses etc.) the light which is white is part of the sea.**
**sky blue white**
**water blue white**
**land white blue.**

In order to energize his efforts of "reaching"—filmmaking as objectless spiritual pursuit—Beavers relies on forms of what he calls "nourishment," and Greece has perhaps been the most primary. His first ideas about the use of mattes and colored filters developed during his early months in Athens and Hydra. And Greece offered training in sensory disciplines soon after he dropped out of Deerfield. The same sun was responsible for an operatic sunset and the transparent color of Delphi pine nuts ("like the giant amber of Edith Sitwell . . . lets the light through . . . a spiral green," he noted in 1967). Modern Greece narrates elemental relations in material form, producing a landscape of partial symbols that resist translation.

For Markopoulos, analog film and Greece were explicitly fused. He blended multiple griefs—personal disappointment ("wounded by the critics"), cinematic sickness ("Film [is] suffering from every malignant growth possible"), and a neglected ancient past ("These thoughts are born as the Parthenon disappears, betrayed")—into one devotional stance.[2] As he remade his early films into *Eniaios* (1948–1990), Greek signifiers remained intact. Portions of *The Illiac Passion* (his 1964–1967 retelling of Aeschylus's *Prometheus Bound*) appear in every *Eniaios* cycle; portraits of both ancient sites (the Pyre of Heracles, Delphi, Eleusis, Kos, Epidaurus,

Bassae, Phigalia, the Theatre of Dionysus) and modern Greek artists and writers (Nikos Hadjikyriakos-Ghikas, Diamantis Diamantopoulos, Yannis Tsarouchis, Pandelis Prevelakis, Lilika Nakou, Odysseus Elytis) are strewn throughout. His textual soil was Hellenic—both directly (Plato, Pindar, Homer, Euripides, Aeschylus) and via modern reception (Jung, Nietzsche, Heidegger, Wagner, Karl Kerényi, Stefan George).[3] "Film as film" was a Greek project.

In contrast, Beavers's absorption of antiquity manifests in poetic aftereffects and vascular impact. His Hellenism is redistributed inside modern Greek landscapes, both urban spaces of commerce and craft and remote sites where "the atmospheric clarity, the nearness of distant objects seen in Greece, shares the same quality for its sound."[4] His Greek films are forms of self-psychagogy—intuitive soul-balancing projects constructed at the crossroads of multiple sign systems. "Greece is a loaded place," he said.

—

In 1960, Markopoulos began to refer to himself as "filmmaker-physician" (and later used the term for Beavers as well), an allusion to Asclepius, son of Apollo and the preeminent ancient god of healing.[5] Ailing pilgrims slept inside the god's sanctuaries—most famously at Epidaurus in the Peloponnese—in a state of "incubation," hoping to precipitate dreams with curative keys.[6] Asclepius, who had first appeared as the "artist physician" in *Twice a Man* (1963), was a touchstone for Markopoulos as he conceived of the Temenos. The extremity of *Eniaios*—its eighty hours, the rhythmic operations of its separated images—was meant to function as filmic therapy, to intervene in the spectator's unconscious, stimulate psychic depths, and refresh habits of seeing in a remote location.[7] "In the Temenos the visual incubation shall be the metaphysical journey," he wrote, bringing ancient medicine and site-specific cinema into contact.[8] Markopoulos framed the Temenos—and the therapeutic possibilities of film—as antidote not only to medium-specific problems but to "the poisoned courses of conditioned thinking."[9] The agents of "false culture" were widespread: pop art, modern art, curators, "the PhD set," "Art World Families," "the commerce man."

Indeed, Markopoulos freely imported illness and cure rhetoric into nearly every domain of thought and provocation. In "Unification of the Frame," composed in 1990, he wrapped his tirade against the "collapse" of film form with ideologies of purity, jointly lamenting the "diabolical introduction of sound" and German reunification and offering up the possibility of gender exclusivity at the Temenos as salve: "The works of the Filmmaker Physicians will be shown to a pure audience of men."[10] He dated his essay "282nd Day of Herakles, 1990"—a personal calendrical system that treated December 25 as the first day of "the homosexual year."[11] Markopoulos's pride as a gay man and his critique of "creativity in the common, heterosexual sense" drew directly on Platonic ideals and fed off German romantic aestheticism.[12]

In 1980, his long-evolving Temenos vision took event-form for the first time. On September 6 and 7, Markopoulos and Beavers projected their films (*Twice a Man* and the 1980 version of *Sotiros*) in the chosen Temenos field, Rayi Spartias, near Lyssarea. The event, called "Film as Film," was a gesture toward the ultimate

Temenos ideal. The screenings were attended by local families and priests as well as a handful of guests from Athens and abroad who had braved the journey on unpaved roads (the region was not yet connected to Athens by highway). As Erika Balsom describes, the September event was to have followed—and drawn on the public attention generated by—an April screening of Markopoulos's and Beavers's films at the National Gallery in Athens, but organizers canceled the screening upon learning about the presence of nudity in *The Illiac Passion*. "The [National Gallery] episode worked to shore up the filmmaker's conviction about the inhospitable conditions encountered within the institutional context," Balsom writes.[13] The 1980 screenings in Arcadia became the first of seven annual "Film as Film" gatherings held every August or September until 1986. Over the course of the decade, Greece became a more regular base of return for Beavers and Markopoulos.

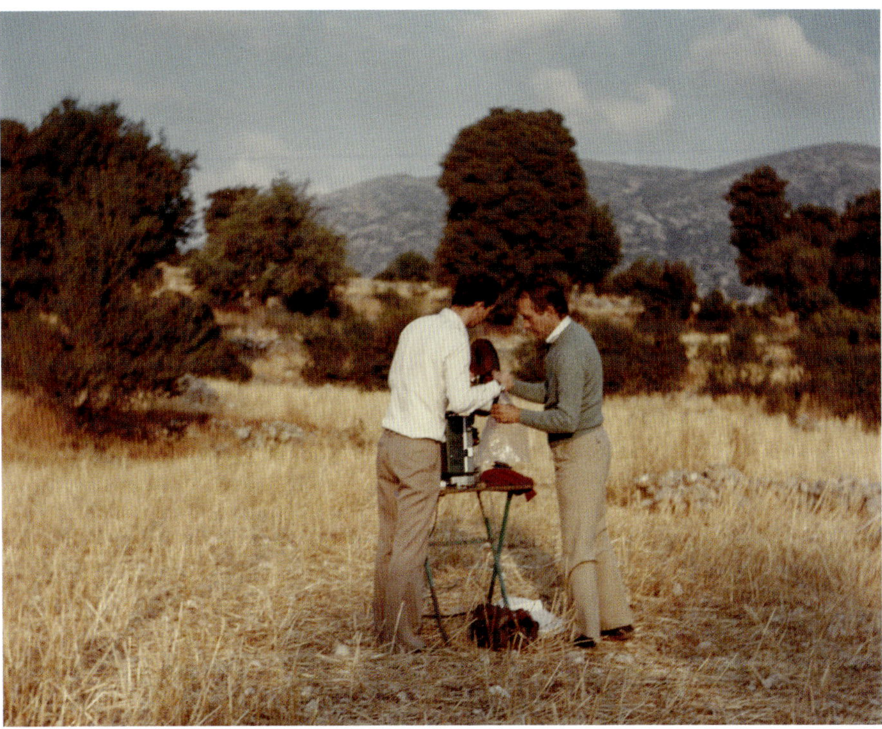

Beavers and Markopoulos at the Temenos site, 1980. Photo by Tassos Dambergis

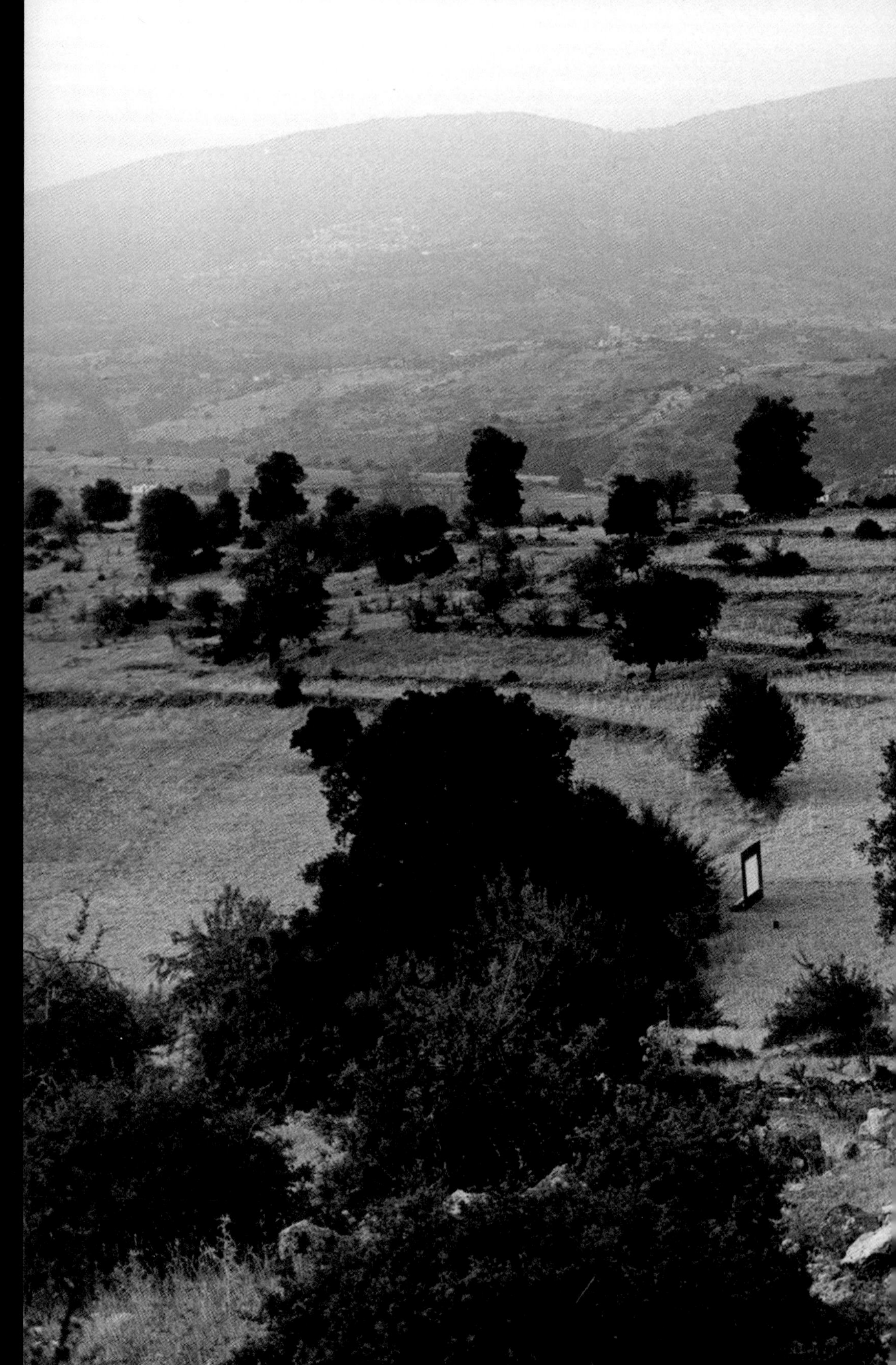

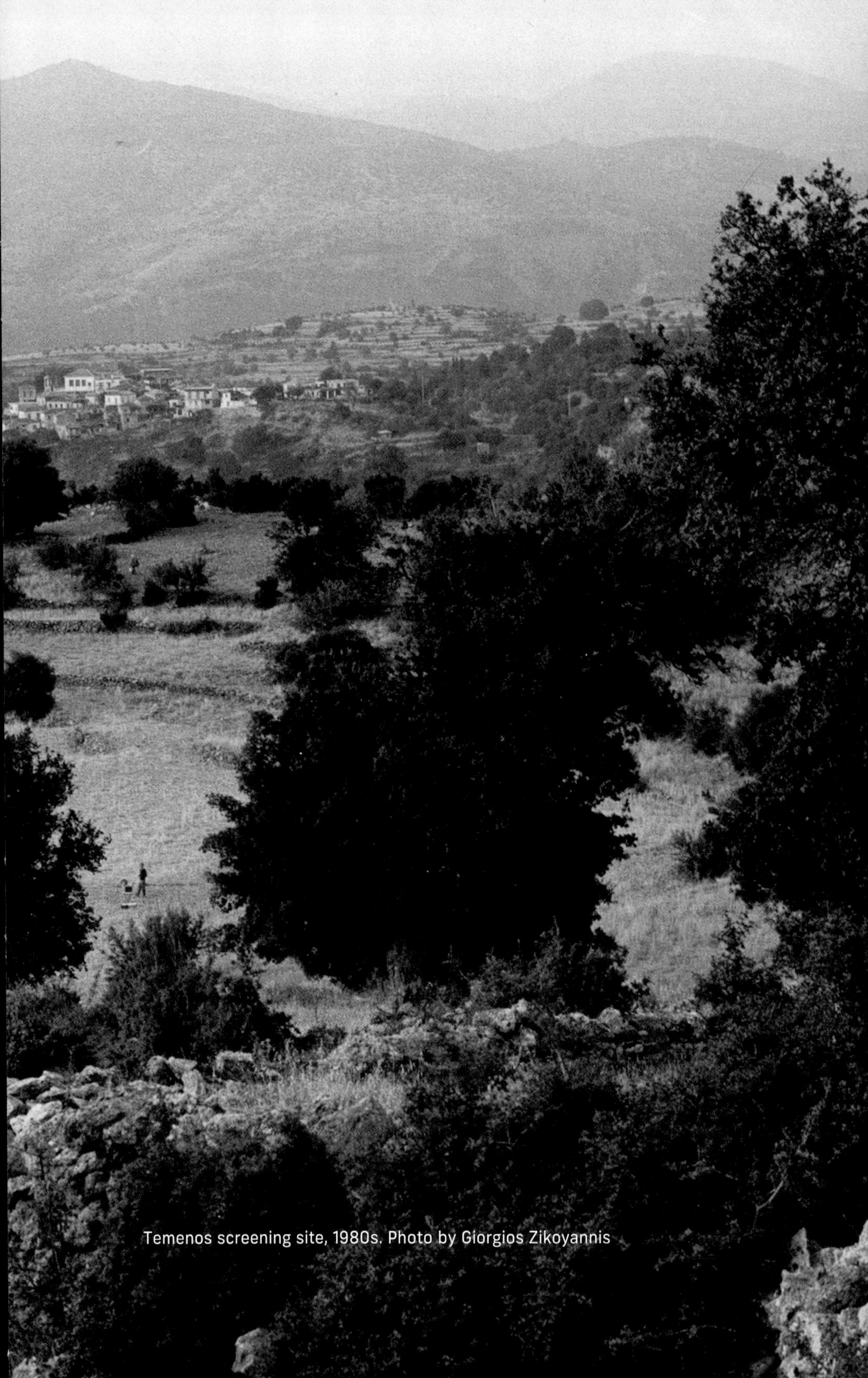

Temenos screening site, 1980s. Photo by Giorgios Zikoyannis

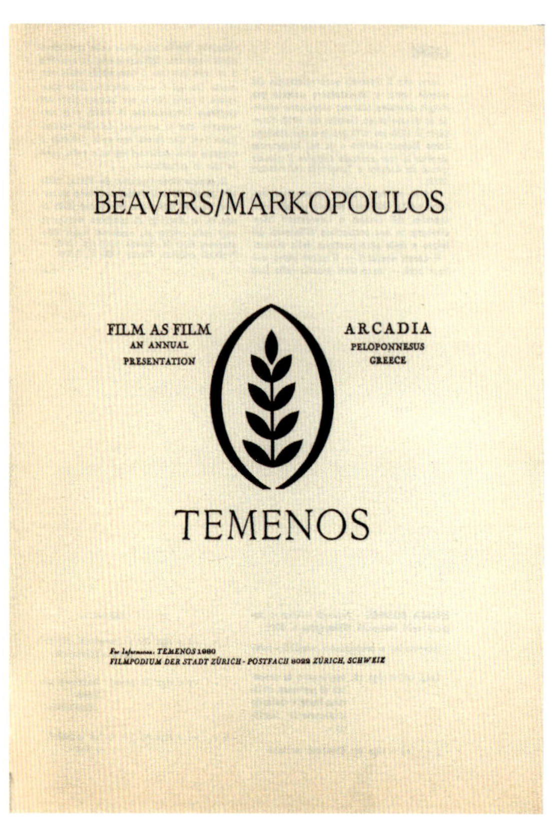


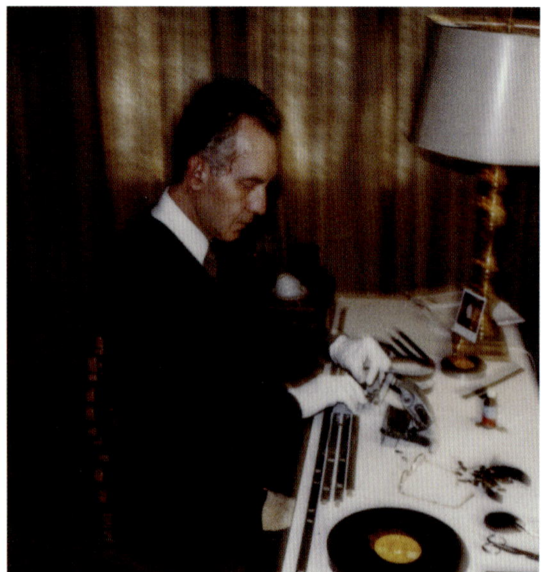

Advertisement for the first Temenos event in 1980

Markopoulos splicing *Eniaios*, ca. 1989/1990. Photo by Robert Beavers

## HELLENIC UNCANNY

> One sees the body most concretely by means of the soul.
> **Robert Beavers, notes for *Sotiros***

> Why do we not move in circles? Our souls, our real selves,
> which are "private wholes," do so move.
> **Plotinus**[14]

Multiple Apollo—god of sun, prophecy, poetry, music, healing—stands at the center of "uncanny" (Beavers's word) forces that surround *Sotiros* (1976–1978/1996), a two-part film recut from an original trio of films: *Sotiros Responds* (1975–1976), *Sotiros (Alone)* (1976–1977), *Sotiros in the Elements* (1978). After a visit to the Temple of Apollo Epicurius (Apollo as healer) in Bassae in 1975, Beavers made notes for a new film concerning a wound:

> **The military-masculine love wound:**
> **emotion-destruction, Greece-Germany.**
> **Meeting of one part of the body and another**
> **is a healing of the wound.**
> . . .
> **Sweat, part of the image-wound.**

The resulting *Sotiros Responds* organizes material shot in the Peloponnese (Bassae, Leonidio, Sparta, and Evrotas), Athens, Aegina, and a hotel room in Bern, Switzerland, with Beavers's one-time use of intertitles.[15] The phrase "he said" (white text on black) appears alternately on the left and right sides of the screen and introduces/closes image sequences, as if representing a dialogue. No literal wound appears in *Sotiros Responds*, but there are two vulnerable figures (an elderly blind beggar on Charilaou Trikoupi Street, in Athens, and a man with a wild gait, who Beavers said "moved about like a village fool," in Leonidio) and a gap produced by the uncoupling of dialogic structure from signs of speaker or vocal content.[16]

The name Sotiros is linked to one of Apollo's healing epithets—Apollo Soter. Both mean "savior." The man with the unanchored step was named Sotiros, and coincidence intensified as Beavers finished the film. He told Tony Pipolo:

> **While I was still in Switzerland, completing the editing of *Sotiros Responds*, I heard on the radio an extraordinary fragment from Alban Berg's *Wozzeck*, conducted by the great conductor Dimitri Mitropoulos at La Scala. This was nearly impossible to find because it was only a fragment on tape. I sent a letter to the Archivio di Stato in Rome, which had a copy of the tape, and we stopped in Rome on our way to Greece so that I could listen to it. When I came out of the session, I saw a dead bird before me and felt that it was a bad omen. Then we went to Greece and almost immediately afterwards, on Pentecost, we had this accident.**[17]

Beavers and Markopoulos were hit by a bus in Ekali, an Athenian suburb, in July 1976. Beavers's left hip was fractured, and his right eye dislocated by two centimeters. A visit to the temple of a god of prophecy and healing, and the completion of a film concerned with woundedness, preceded Beavers's experience of portension, injury, and recuperation. Beavers himself replaced the blind man and the fool: his own eye and leg were now injured.

Markopoulos arranged an artist residency in Epirus following Beavers's hip surgery and recovery at an Athens hospital. But Beavers couldn't navigate the residency house staircase, so they relocated to Ioannina for a month, and then to Graz, where Beavers recuperated in a monastery outside the city. As a result of his injury, the filmmaker who had long been preoccupied with the joining of two images into one via binocular stereopsis now had a literal case of double vision.[18] A Basel doctor proposed complex plastic surgery to repair his eye, but a professor of ophthalmology in Bern told Beavers to do nothing: the eye would heal on its own. Beavers heeded the advice, and his double vision resolved.

Recovering near Graz, Beavers read Berg's *Wozzeck* libretto (further uncanny: Berg had written it outside of Graz) and two of his essays. He selected six phrases from the three-act melodrama (tormented Wozzeck murders the mother of his child after learning of her romance with another man) for the soundtrack of his second film, *Sotiros (Alone)*. He returned to the same Bern hotel room and shot details of his healing body. As in the first film, a hotel/exterior location rhythm structures *Sotiros (Alone)*, but shots of Beavers's tripod (and his hand manipulating it) replace the intertitles. Once mobile, Beavers returned to Austria and shot locations outside of Graz loosely associated with *Wozzeck*.

A year later, Beavers made *Sotiros in the Elements* in Athens. He superimposed words (references to film imagery) over certain shots, rendered in conventional and reverse order (*red* and *der*, *still* and *llits*). In 1980, Beavers published a booklet of prose, *Sotiros: A Sequence of Notes*, under the Temenos imprint, which corresponds, in numbered shot order, to the fifty-minute *Sotiros* trilogy.[19] And in 1996, he produced the integrated twenty-five-minute film. The final *Sotiros* is structured in two parts, condensed versions of *Sotiros Responds* and *Sotiros (Alone)*, and marks his final use of mattes.[20]

Sigmund Freud famously ran into the uncanny in Greece. Revisiting a trip to the Acropolis at forty-eight, he analyzed his "I can't believe it's really here!" thought and identified two consciousnesses: the disbeliever and the one who hadn't been aware that such skepticism existed. He understood this "derealization" as Oedipal; he had exceeded his father.[21] Perhaps modern Greece invites the de-registered uncanny. The matrix of illegibility and inscription lends itself to testing out modern inhabitation of a pantheistic world. Every ancient fact is followed by mystery: the Bassae temple likely stands on an older structure, and theories conflict about its interior—it was so dark that many fires burned at once, or a central column reflected light in honor of Apollo. Its origins are uncertain: did the Phigaleians dedicate the temple to Apollo Epicurius believing the god had spared them destruction by plague—or from Spartan invasion?[22] Regardless, it was a structure built around an image of wounded bodies. Beavers originally titled the first film *Sotiros Responds: The Battle*.

## VOCAL PATTERNS (PART 1, *SOTIROS*)

> Speech and sound have only a limited meaning in the conventional film because [they] do not unite with the image beyond the usual dialogue synchronization. The relation of word and image must combine in all senses; then the film is raised above performance.
> **Robert Beavers, notes for *Sotiros***

At the heart of continuity editing in classical narrative filmmaking is shot-reverse-shot: the structuring of dialogue in over-the-shoulder shots that produces the illusion of time and space consistency. It is an exchange of looks, with voice and identity assigned to opposite sides of an alternating screen. Spectator and off-screen character coincide.

In *Sotiros: A Sequence of Notes*, Beavers calls the unarticulated voice between intertitles "the silent statement": "The silent statement does not express but presents an image or series of images."[23] The *Sotiros* dialogue, produced collaboratively by light, camera movement, sound, and editing, enacts form-making itself, actively filling out the film-body via patterns that originate in the Bern hotel room. "The room becomes a silent conductor through which a multitude of particulars move into relation," Beavers writes.[24] The nearly empty space (Markopoulos appears in one shot) is a mold for vocal exchange: two made beds, two chrome-framed circular mirrors above side-by-side sinks. "He said," (screen left) and "he said." (right) bracket sequences that alternate between hotel room and exterior imagery (Arcadian sky, mountains, and animals; Athenian street, rooftop construction, and kafeneion scenes) and between fixed shots and fast (mostly horizontal) pans.[25]

Beavers used the movements of low winter sunlight around the hotel room to link the three films. "Where the highlight has ended on the wall above the beds in the first two films, it begins in the third. From this point, the light completes its circle," he writes.[26] This "completed" circle of light is not visible in the final *Sotiros*, but the hotel room's vertical windows, highlight orbs, and sun stripes still drive the film. Light and shadow glaze across the film: on Markopoulos's cheeks, Beavers's body, goat's fur, Styria pond waves, kafeneion walls. Inside the film's rhythmic pulsation between compositional completion and speed, the white intertitles appear to belong to the same body of light that's dispersed across city and country.

Unlike shot-reverse-shot, Beavers's two-sided exchange produces not communicative content but pattern. Some shots begin in clarity (a Giorgio Morandi–looking tabletop composition of marble, glass, cup, and shadow) and end with a rush (the camera pans off-table into a smear of unintelligible space). "A pattern of camera movements away from fixed points becomes a measure of the interval," Beavers explains this subset of shots. The pattern is not printed representationally; it "becomes," in repetition, a temporal element—an undulating "interval" of stillness-to-movement contained in a single shot. "The pattern *rests* upon the screen as the film is projected," he continues, extending the interval into the time-space of projection.[27]

In his *Sotiros* revision, Beavers redrew intertitle/camera movement/sound relations to emphasize left- and right-sidedness: a pan right to a black coat hanging on a white door leads to a right-side white-on-black "he said"; a pan left ends with the sound of a water drop. Resonant with insideness and close-up reverberation, ambient sound—shaving, metal hangers, closet doors—supports the hotel room as "central conductor." "The sense of each sound—its direction, volume, echo—speaks of its own space and is reflected in the image and its movement," Beavers writes.[28] The sound of running water moves a pan across a glass bathroom shelf; a shaking metal twang drives a pan over hotel beds and lands in a shot of Arcadian weeds, disturbing their apparent stillness. Vocal shape is elaborated a step above the hosting images—at the crossing of sound, camera movement, and editing.

—

In *Sotiros: A Sequence of Notes*, Beavers writes of an energetic transfer between camera motion and cut:

> **The energy released by the moving camera changes meaning of the film cut. It changes both the function of the spectator's sight and the projected light.**
>
> **If the camera movement is into the film cut, an opening is made into darkness or light; it negates, in part, the closure of the film cut or at least carries it differently.[29]**

He treats the cut—and film more broadly—as constituent of more openings and potentialities than usually granted. "While something is being made, boundaries and viewpoints are in flux; possibility includes the presence of opposites," Beavers writes.[30] Events of turning extend from camera pan to screen along a chain of substitution; image is not end but passageway to "becoming":

> **Near Bassae and the temple of Apollo Sotiros, the highlight moves along the horns of a goat as it turns: an almost circular camera movement within the room.[31]**
>
> **The shifting pattern of camera movements becomes a pendulum turning in the solidness of projection. The pattern, its curve, passes through the image.[32]**
>
> **The camera moves across an object; in projection this becomes a turning of the object towards the spectator.[33]**

*Sotiros* is a mysterious film. But it doesn't insist on stay-put transcendence above the mediating image. The film's in-out flux includes rebound back into moments of diegetic satisfaction and consolidated visual beauty.

## VOTIVE (PART 2, *SOTIROS*)

> ἥ τε τοῦ ἔτους ὥρα καὶ χώρα καὶ φύσις τοῦ θεραπενομένου σώματος
> **Galen[34]**

The tripod, stable structure for uneven ground, is Apollonian. Priestess Pythia sat on a tripod at Delphi as she relayed the god's prophecies. Early in the second part of *Sotiros*, Beavers unscrews his tripod knob and guides the panning handle left.

A right-moving pan ends on his own parted lips; a shot of his turning head follows, exposing his ear. The accompanying *Wozzeck* excerpt—"Langsam—! Eins nach dem Andern!" (Slowly—! One by one!)—also travels from lips to ear, announcing, in a dramatic register, the artist's construction of shot-by-shot meaning.

Shots *of* the tripod (Beavers's hand steers left and right) replace the intertitles of part one. They are followed by pans *made with* the tripod in the opposite direction: "The tripod holds the center as a pivot of the plot; it turns between what is said and is heard. The context moves from the Greek to the German, yet like the tripod itself, a point of balance is formed from these different directions."[35] Part two abandons Arcadia for dim Graz views: field, alley, forest and pond, smokehouse. Hotel room light has contracted into highlights. Darkness grows: in part one, a hazy black stripe, the result of a matte attached perpendicularly to the compendium, bisects shots of the blind beggar and Sotiros (the man in Leonidio); in part two, the matte moves with pans, surrounds square insets, blocks all but a central image channel.[36] Interior sounds play more performative roles (in a close-up, Beavers's eyelashes shake as we hear the ring of metal vibrations) and intermingle with the opera fragments, inviting a faster-paced metabolic investment. "Plot" is available not as standard storytelling but as one of the elements Beavers is turning. "[The] quotes from . . . *Wozzeck* become a single Voiced highlight moving in the room," he writes.[37]

Signs of drama in part two—both the music and images of a literal wound—render a more graphic film-body and voice. The body-*in*-the-image prevails: shots of Markopoulos (writing at a table, opening closet doors, his face) but especially of Beavers's body in fragments—hand, eye, ear, mouth, chest, abdomen, foot, knee, scarred leg. "The tripod is juxtaposed to the leg and the scar" in an alternation between steady structure and Beavers's wounded appendage. "I was still not walking much," Beavers told Pipolo: his handicapped state determined his shooting positions.[38]

In *Sotiros: A Sequence of Notes*, Beavers frames the shots of his body parts as ritual offering: "These images of the leg are like the small Greek votive offerings which show the part of the body that has been healed—usually an ear, a leg, genitals or eyes. In ancient times, they were made of marble, now they are metal foil, but the shape and size have remained nearly unchanged for more than a millennium."[39] Ancient pilgrims left sculpted objects of supplication and thanks at Epidaurus; embossed tin votives hang on the corners of Orthodox icons today. In January 1977, soon after shooting his own body parts in close-up for the film, Beavers noticed fourth-century BCE votive reliefs, some from the temple of Amynos, a healer/hero, at the Archaeological Museum in Athens. "These small marble images are very similar to frames from the filming, even similar in color," he noted.

—

In repeated shots of Beavers's two pointer fingers approaching each other, the moment of contact is occluded by a bisecting matte. "On close observation the dialogue of any two figures is like a meeting of fingertips; the reflexion extends and intermingles before the hands actually touch," Beavers writes.[40] His fingertips enact relationality within single-body bounds: approach, extension, mutual influence, contact. In several shots, Beavers's hand touches his own body: rubbing, scratching, resting.

On ancient dedicatory stelae left at Epidaurus in gratitude for healing, Asclepius rests his hand on the supplicant's head. In *Sotiros*, the responsive, therapeutic hand does not belong to the cure-dispensing doctor or artist. Instead, subtle awareness of embodied dialogue (the sensations of touching hand and touched wound are felt by the same body) produces fresh openings for contact through which otherness can be reached. A tapping sound accompanies the first image of Beavers's long scar; it calls back the cane held by the elderly blind man in Athens. A dotted line—the stitched wound, the Morse-code tapping—links the two men, filmmaker and anonymous beggar, across the two *Sotiros* sections. In *Sotiros: A Sequence of Notes*, Beavers writes: "One understands that Film is not the image-sound but what is reached in (and through) the image-sound. Awareness becomes silently transparent; a separate life is projected: *χώρα* means 'the place' and, in ancient music, the limit of each interval; *ὥρα καὶ χώρα* the final precision in time is Space."[41]

*Sotiros* ends in resolution: plot (Wozzeck drowns), body (Beavers's whole body visible), media (the film and opera conclude together). "The action resolves in the final quaver rhythm of Berg's opera," Beavers writes.

> **"Ich wasche mich mit Blut!—das Wasser ist Blut . . . Blut . . ." The camera pans down from the pines to their reflection in the pond, and the sound continues downwards into a drowning.[42]**

The descent imagery is intercut with shots of the filmmaker's hands tearing up paper and casting it away. The brief performance strikes a unique key—*acting*—as if the film itself has crossed into another register as the opera ends. A flurry of transmutation follows: the discarded white paper reconstitutes as a "second screen"—the hotel wall—on which a shadow play unfolds.[43]

Sitting up in bed, Beavers adds to a light mural on the wall by casting a hand shadow that moves in three directions at once: "The hand leaves the tripod and reappears as a triple shadow."[44] His face and body seen together for the first time, the filmmaker is in full command and play. A match-on-motion between Beavers's closing C-shaped hand and merging blocks of shadow makes the filmmaker appear to be moving the wall shapes and closing the film's curtain. A surge of melodic music accompanies the final shots—it affectively drenches the wall theatrics and generates a rare burst of integrated "cinematic magic." The filmmaker, and *Sotiros*, are cured.[45]

*Sotiros* (1976–1978/1996)

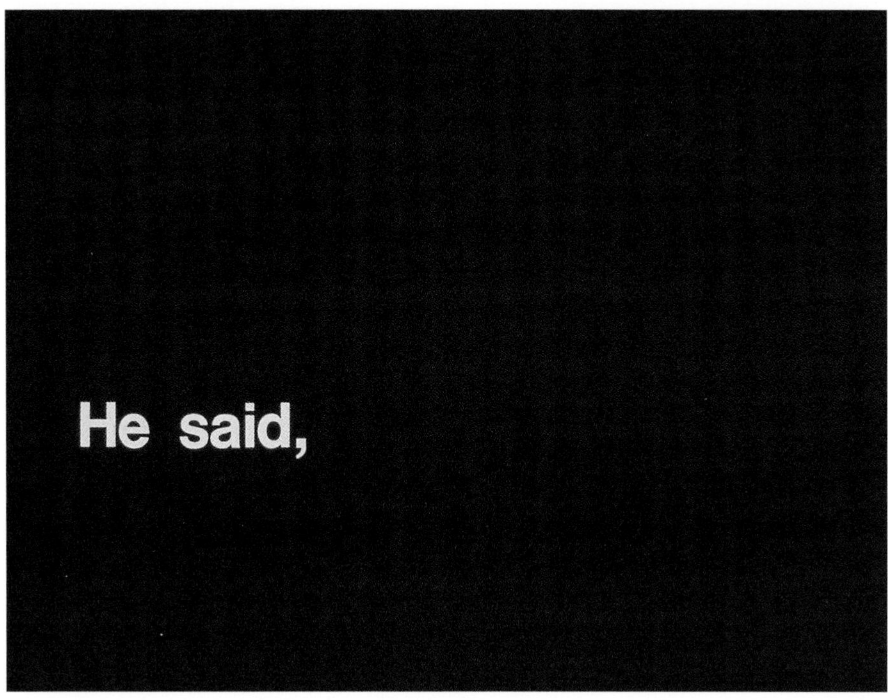
He said,

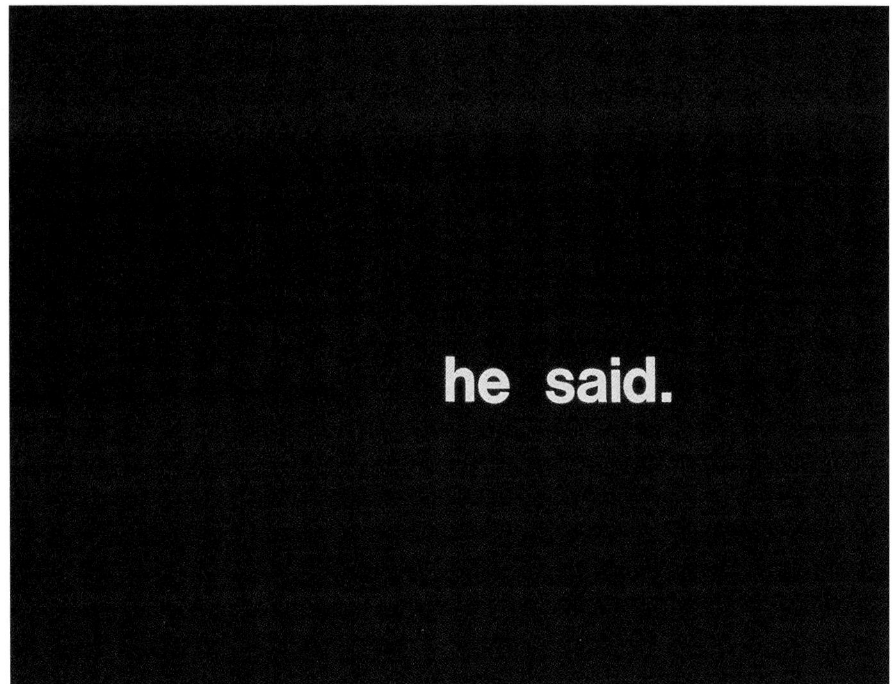
he said.

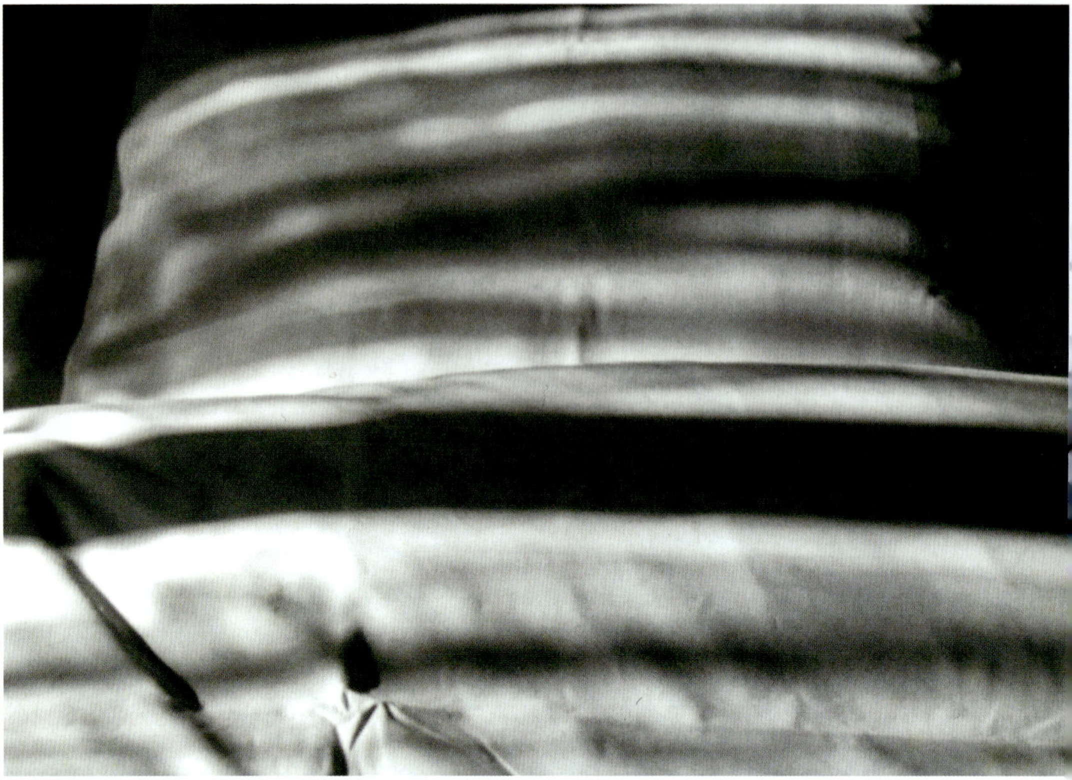

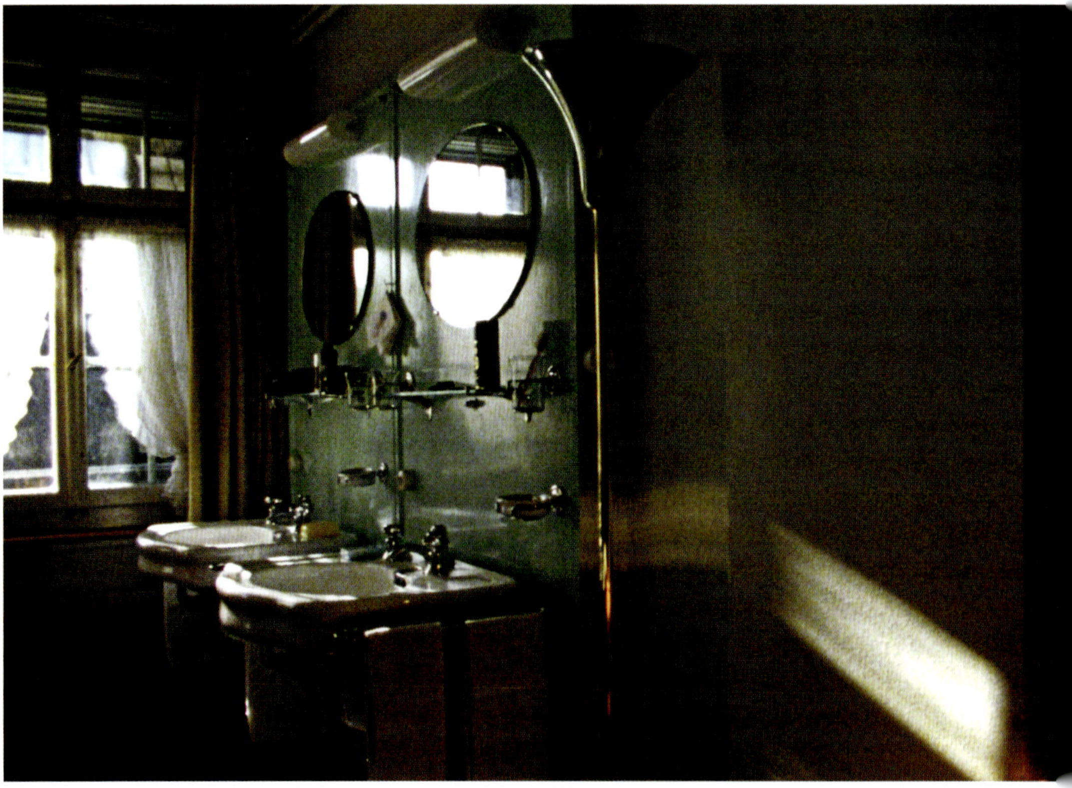

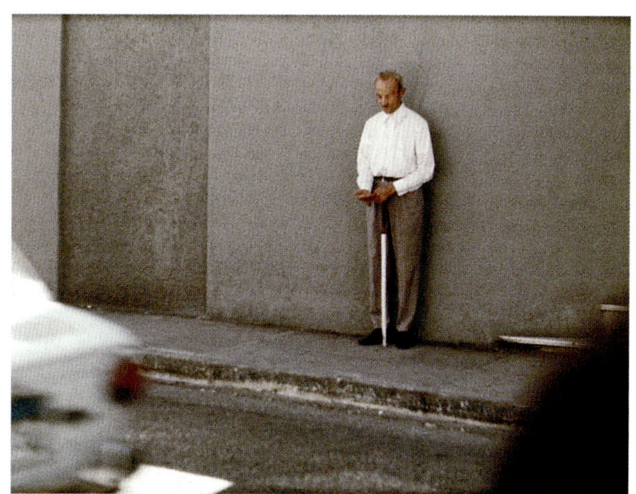

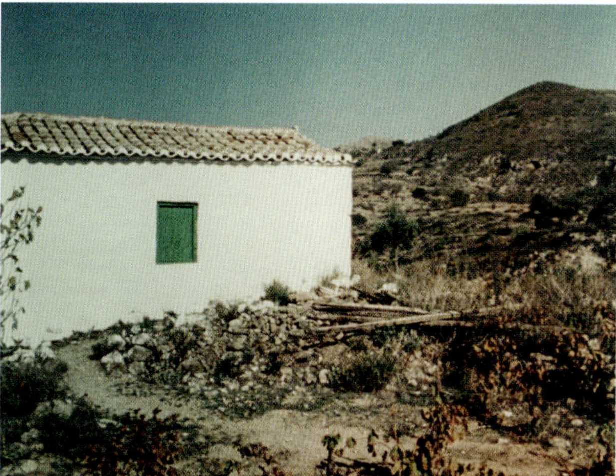

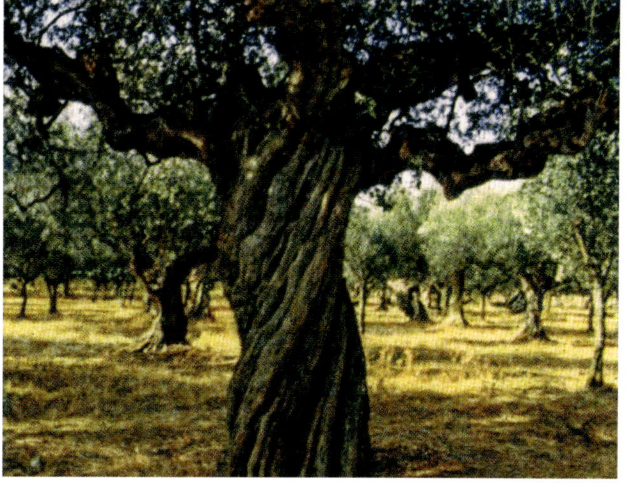

*Sotiros* (1976–1978/1996)

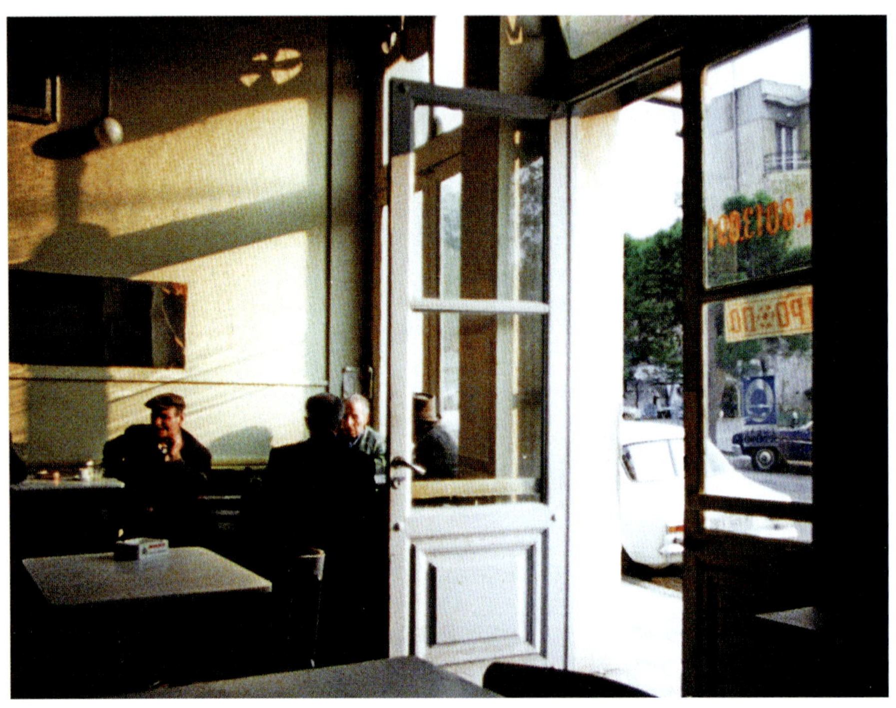

*Sotiros* (1976–1978/1996)

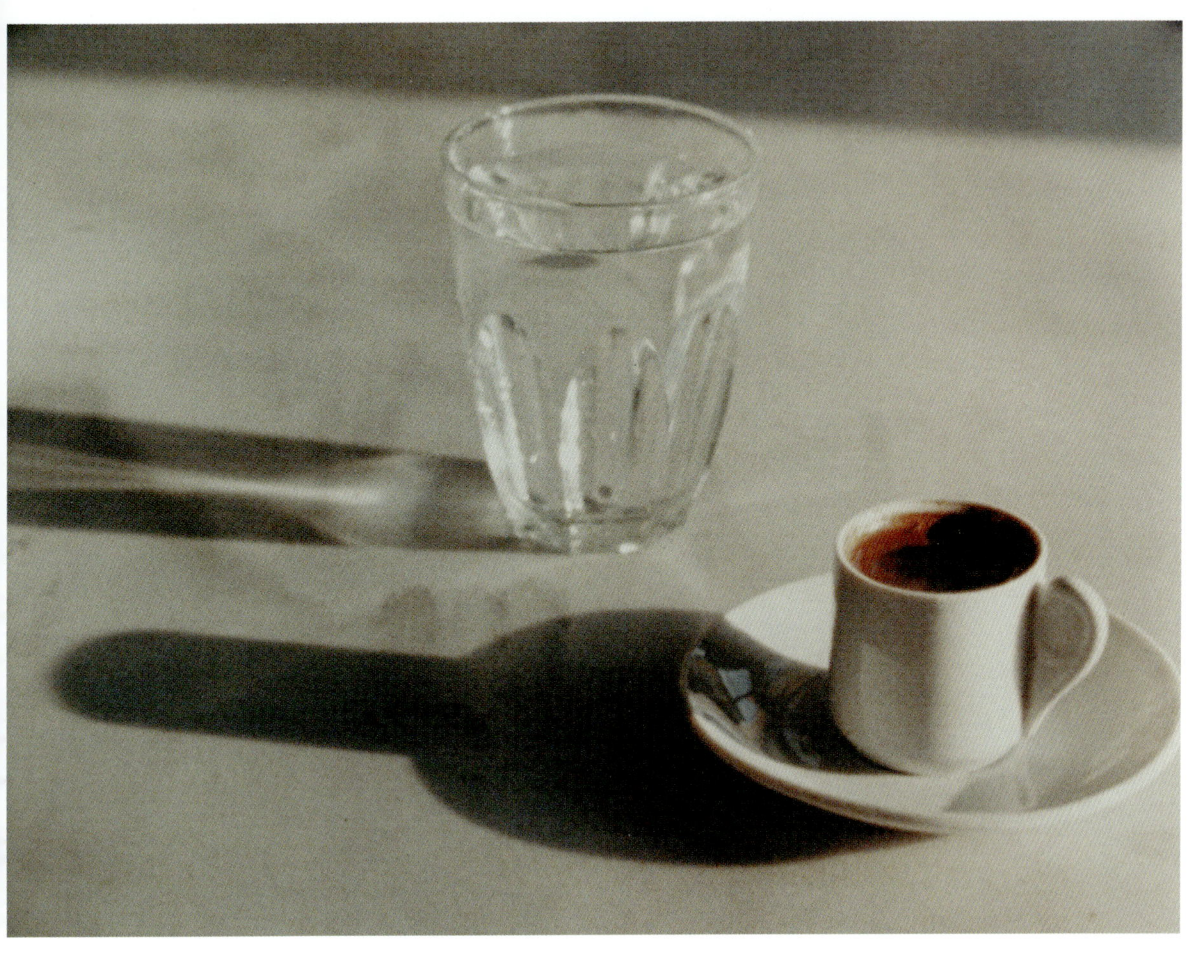

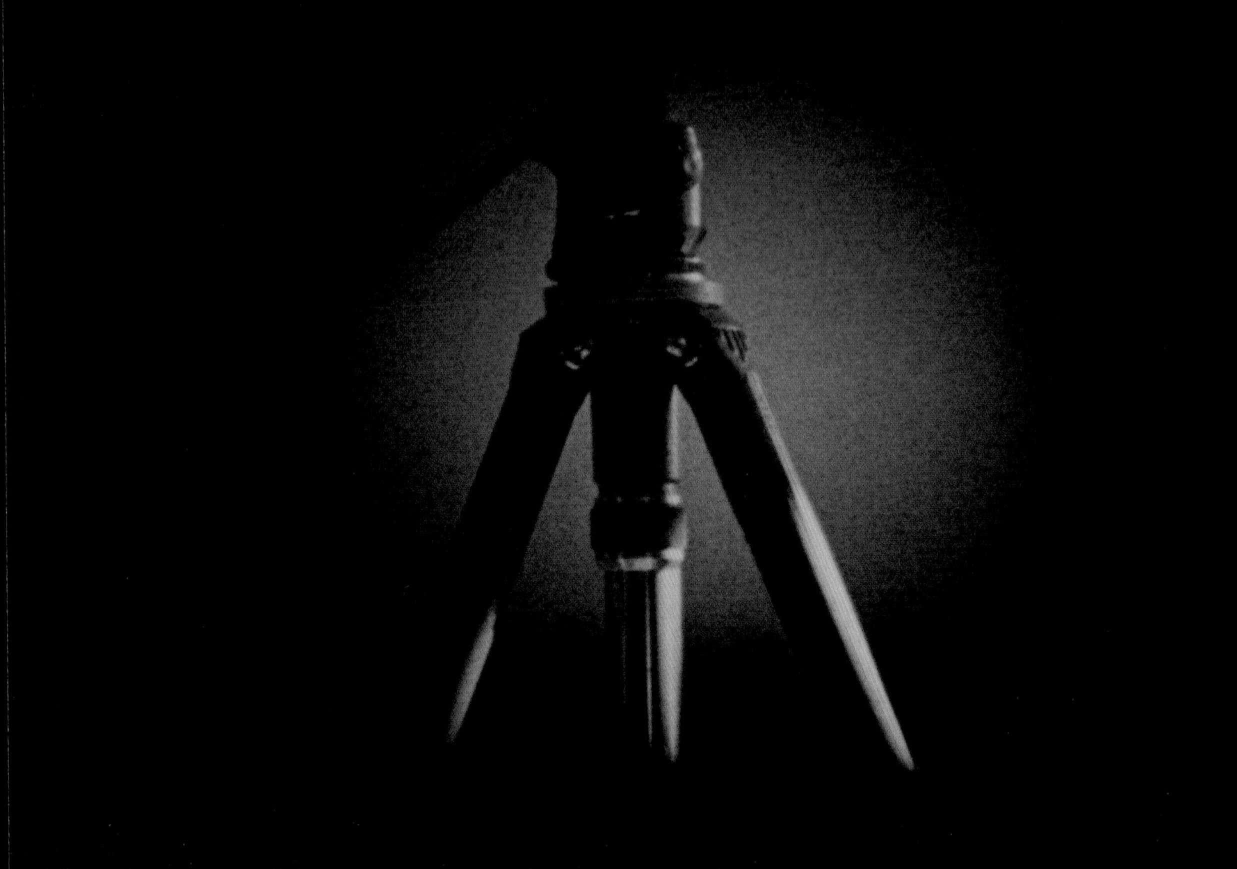

*Sotiros* (1976–1978/1996)

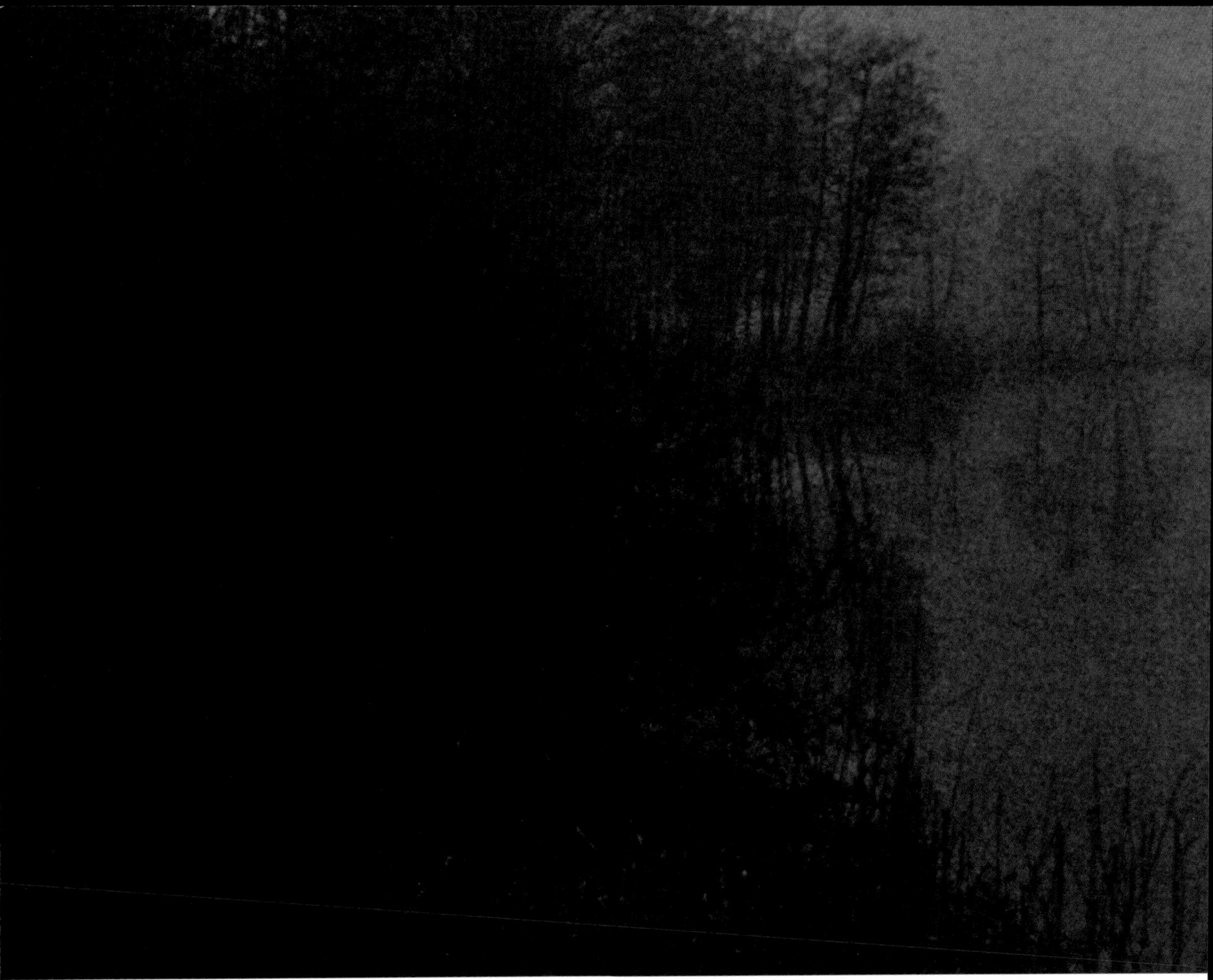

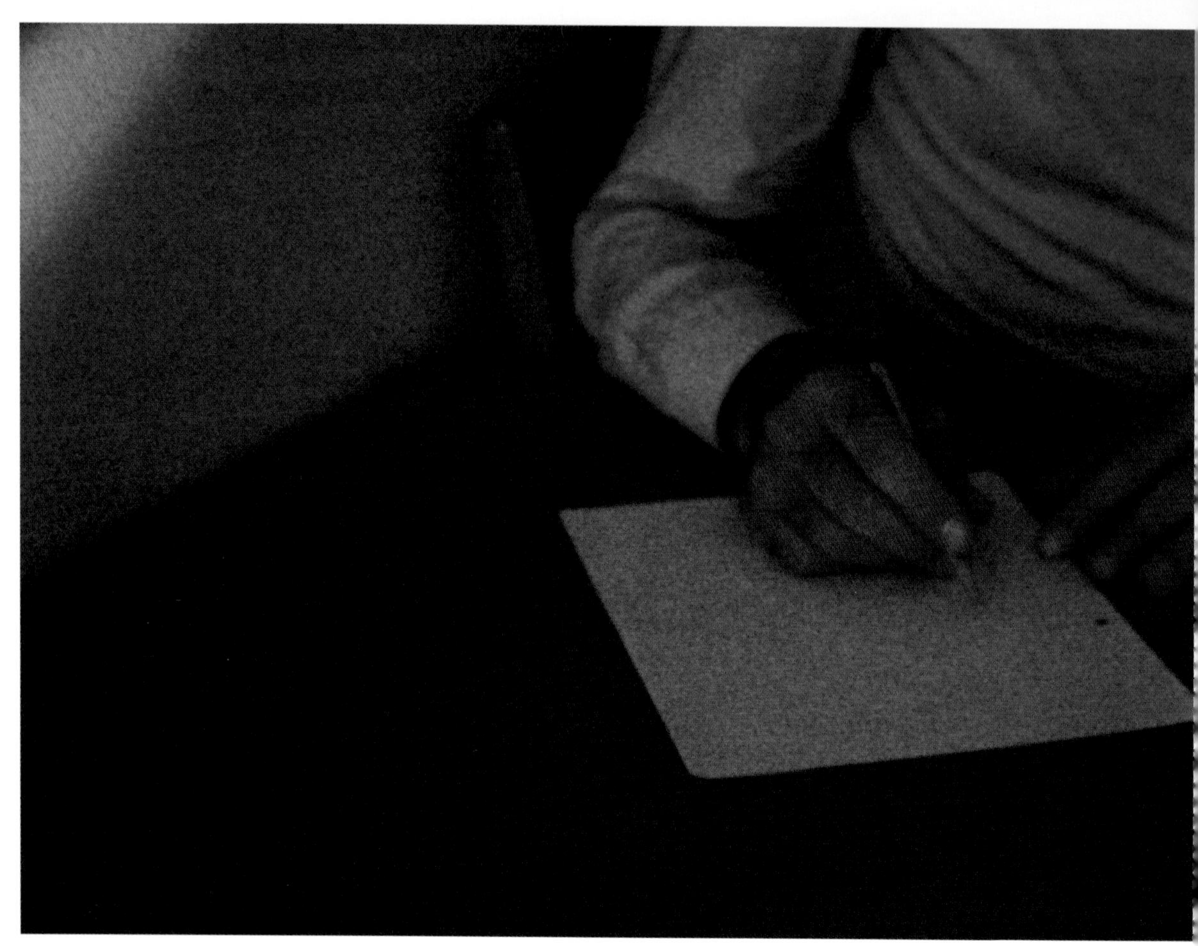

*Sotiros* (1976–1978/1996)

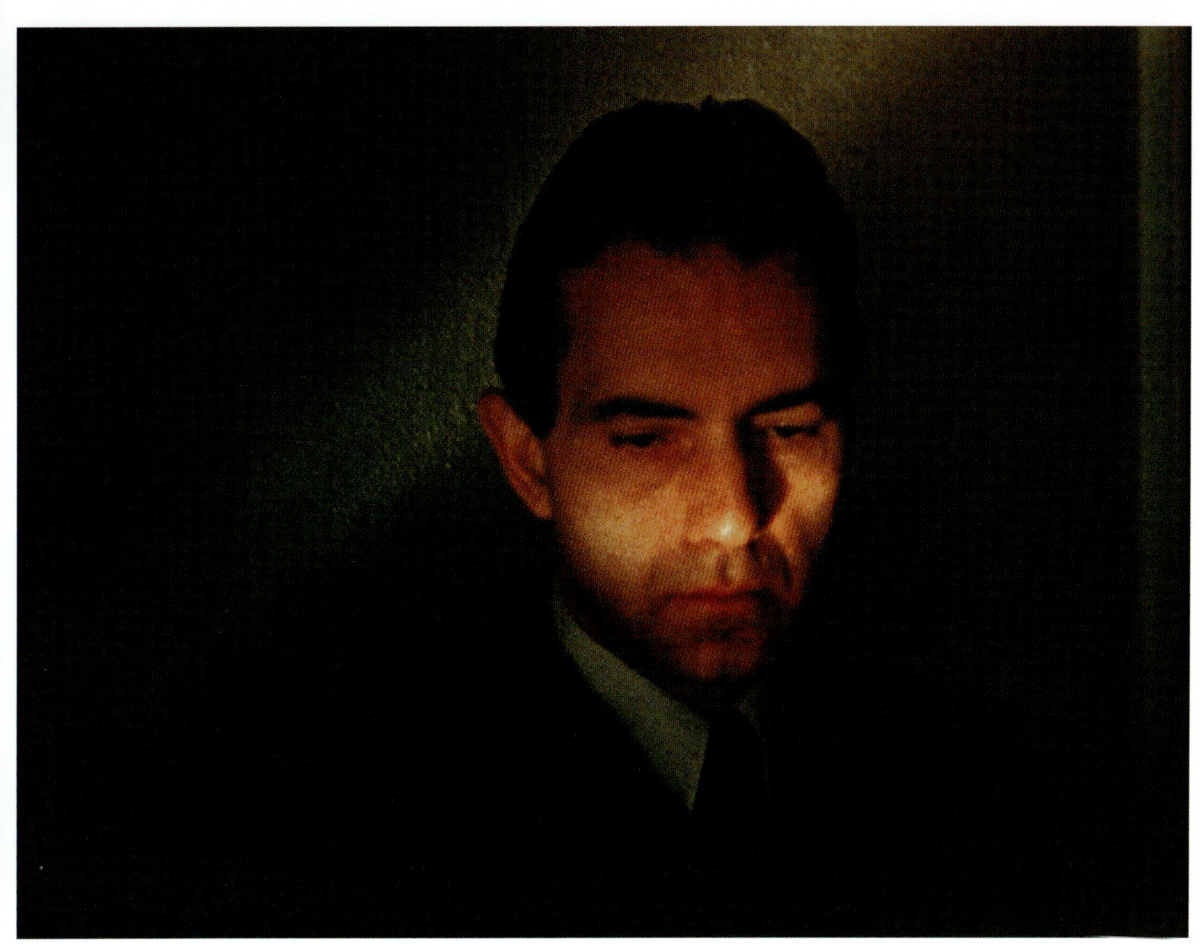

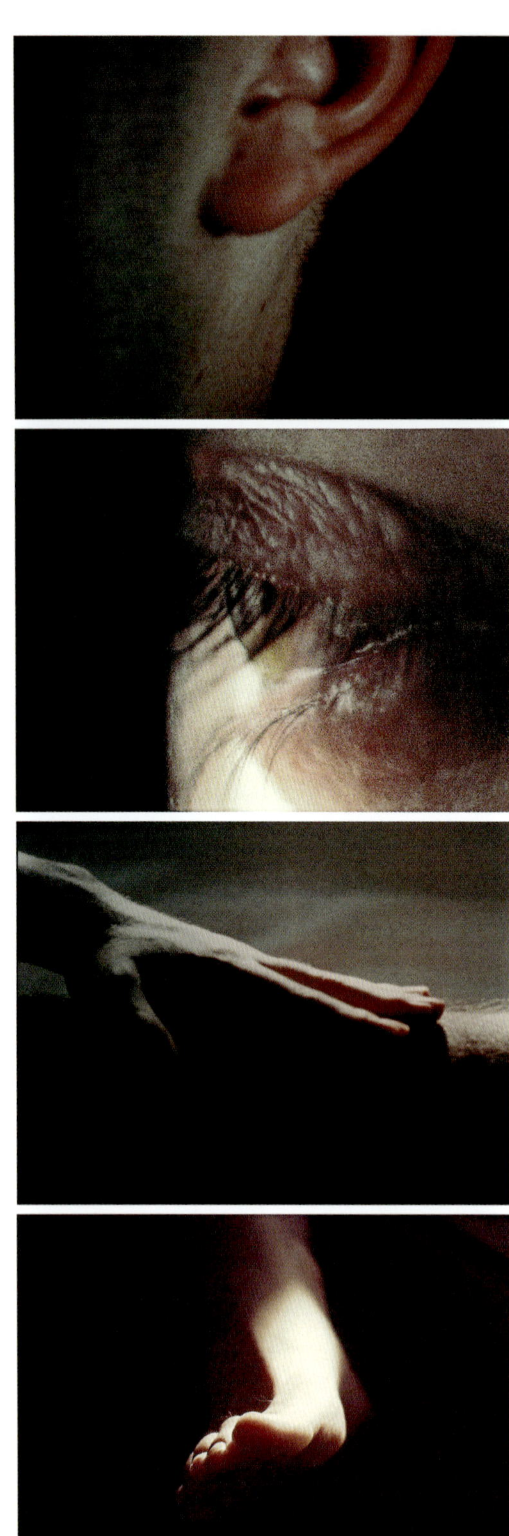

*Sotiros* (1976–1978/1996)

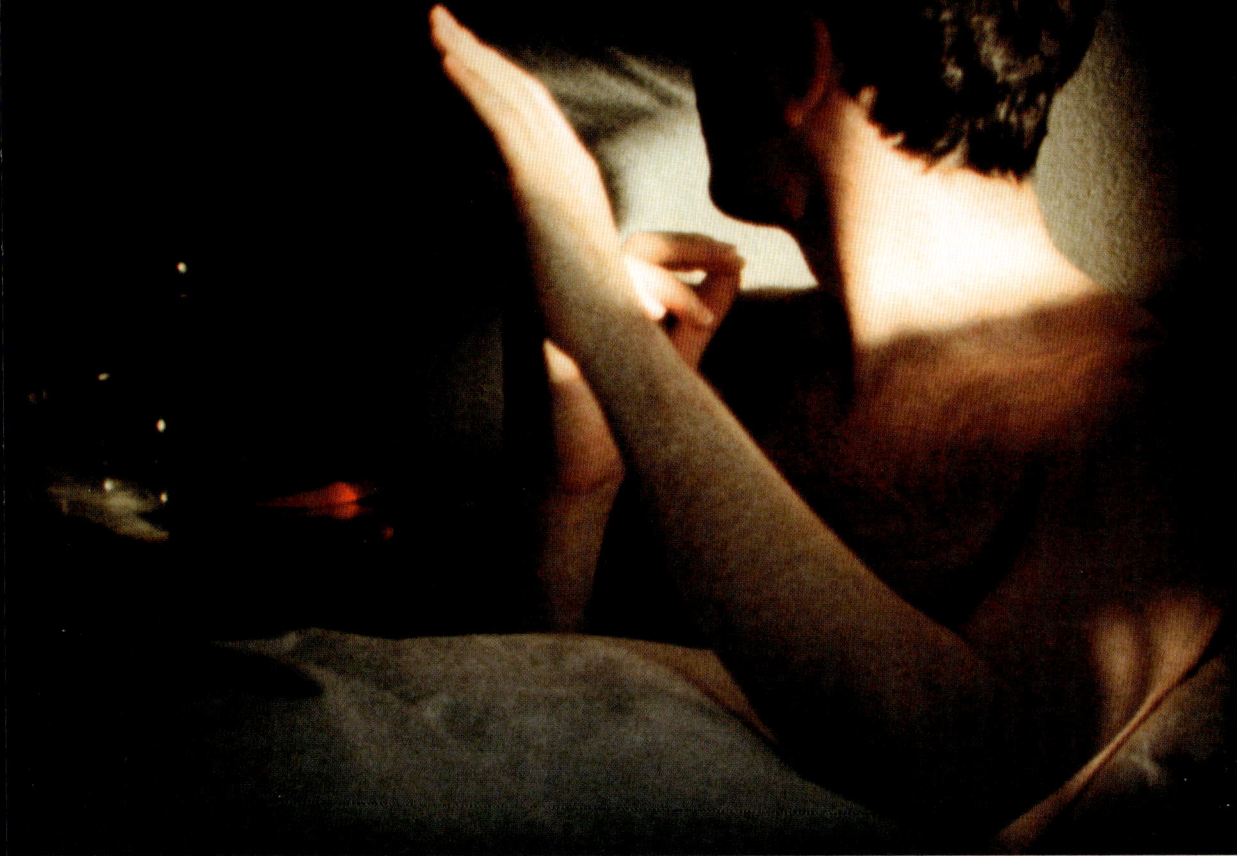

## LIPS : EYEBROWS

> Dream of two broken classical columns,
> seen both from the side and from above.
> **Robert Beavers, notes for *Efpsychi***

> I got bored looking at the stage
> and raised my eyes to the box circle.
> **Constantine P. Cavafy, "At the Theatre"[46]**

In the winter of 1979, when he and Markopoulos stayed at a Plateia Theatrou hotel as they awaited resolution on the accident insurance claim, Beavers got to know Psyri, the area immediately surrounding the Athenian Central Market. Lined by postwar industrial architecture and deteriorating neoclassical buildings, the neighborhood was dominated by wholesale commerce (shoes, cheese, meat, herbs) and hand-labor (leatherwork, broom- and candle-making). Beavers shot *ΕΥΨΥΧΙ* (*Efpsychi*) (1983/1996) in Psyri between 1980 and 1982.

*Efpsychi* opens with a receding view down empty Evripidou Street and the sounds of work (clanging metal, men shouting). When I first saw the film, I couldn't catch hold of its implied intimacy (its contracted chromatic universe and dusty atmosphere, after Beavers's earlier saturated lushness, felt like an obstruction), but over time, the film's languid erotic charge, conducted along a set of correspondences between urban space and a young man's face, revealed itself.

Beavers spotted Vangelis Tsindoukidis weaving garlic buds in his parents' basement broom-making workshop and engaged him as an actor. Shot in extreme close-up, his face is a sensual surface of mediation that pulls dormant energies out of this unassuming commercial district. The shapes and movements of his abstracted eyes, eyebrows, mouth, earlobes, and chin become analogic links to the Psyri surrounds: rotating head / left and right sides of the street; vertical rise between neck and brow / stairs between rooftop and basement; open red mouth / graffiti-painted omicron (O) on a building exterior. His repetition of the word *τελευταία* / *teleftea*, a vendor's term meaning "the last one," anchors a soundscape that pulses between ambient labor and transaction (shouted prices, metal carts in transit, mechanical rattles) and silence.

*Efpsychi* is sculpted from spatial and cultural distance between high and low. Many of the small streets surrounding Plateia Theatrou are named for classical playwrights (Aristophanous, Evripidou, Aeschylou, Sophocleous), signifiers of Western cultural origins, while artisanal labor transpires below street level in cooler workspaces. In low-angle shots of feet striding on sidewalks, the filmmaker is literally standing in basement space, tying his work to craft. Beavers's camera treats handwork with identificatory attention: brooms assembled from wire, wood, and straw; candles wrapped in paper tubes, taped shut, and hung in rows like edited film strips.

By the time Beavers and Markopoulos stayed in Plateia Theatrou in 1979, its origins were apparent only in name. In the nineteenth century, it was home to the first Athenian indoor theater, whose audiences included Greece's first king and queen, Otto and Amelia. The creation of Plateia Theatrou (and the playwright-named streets) grew directly from the nation-making effort that linked the new modern Greek state, established in 1832, to ancient glory (and, by extension, evacuated signs of the Ottoman past that didn't serve the Western civilization story). Occasional images of ornate blue walls with gold embellishment—shot at the monarch's first Athenian residence—are folded into *Efpsychi*.[47] The curled decorative lines echo the shapes of wrought-iron designs visible in shots of Psyri doorframes and balconies.

In this theatrical zone, Beavers perceived multiple masks. "The pedestrian level (business of street) and above it the classical authors . . . the mask," he noted in October 1981. In a short essay about *Efpsychi*, composed after the film's completion, Beavers calls the Greek letters on street signs—ΟΔΟΣ (*odos* means "street")—a "mask" for Vangelis: omicron-delta-omicron are like two eyes and a nose. In the essay, he also imagines Vangelis's face as a mask—a provocation for the filmmaker to convey the human underneath: "The face carries a double sense as direct element within the film frame and as a performance. It is both meaning and mask. When these qualities are present in the image, the face itself will possess a voice and its own lyric." Finding the subject's "nature" and "essence" beyond his "physical image . . . happens at that moment when the habits of seeing open toward a sudden awareness, when the filmmaker can see the other opposite him," he writes.[48]

—

In his *Efpsychi* notes, Beavers sifted his Psyri images into binary pairs—up-down (street sign/pedestrian foot), inside-outside (wick/candle), odd-even (building numbers), man-woman (muscle-man gymnasium ad/newspaper photograph of Anita Eckberg in *La Dolce Vita*). But he also wondered how to torque difference away from polarity: "What is the form in the film for the pedestrian's crossing? How can one establish the two different directions—more than just left to right and right to left?" In the summer of 1981, as he shot Psyri street signs, Beavers returned to "emblem," his ongoing two-sided figure, in his notes, this time seeing it as a motion-based ideogram. "The word itself contains a symbolic structure of having two sides [em blem] as if the movement were in the '-bl,' a movement of something being turned around to its other side. The meaning is in the turning between the two unconnected elements . . . it is not a placement side-by-side in space or vis-à-vis but . . . the movement from front to back which is a movement beyond the appearance of the first image."[49]

In *Efpsychi*, straight lines become diagonals. Beavers shot street and shop signs at angles, as if mid-rotation, half-freeing them from conventional sense. Now a rhombus, white-on-blue ΑΙΣΧΥΛΟΥ (Aeschylou) is more (and less) than a sign. It becomes part of the film's dense diachronic world of linguistic materiality: newsprint, graffiti, posters, advertisements; letters painted, glued, stenciled, printed; syllables distributed between Vangelis's moving mouth and voice. Legibility is maintained while word-images simultaneously signify "beyond appearance." Textual superfluity includes the numerical: close-ups of building numbers (28, 44B, 66, 82) suggest a search for underlying order (or an effort to "get the right numbers," evoked by images of ΠΡΟ-ΠΟ sports betting tickets and the sounds of their vendor's calls). In his short *Efpsychi* essay, Beavers writes that numbers represent "the illusion of more" but also "point toward the unseen and unknown."[50] Ancient oracle supplicants in pursuit of Apollo's counsel cast stones inscribed with numbers; the results pointed them to answers engraved on sanctuary walls. As Beavers unhinges signs, linguistic deconstruction and pantheistic potential spin together.

## THE SCALES OF EROS

*The Hospitality of Abraham*, a late-fourteenth-century icon at the Benaki Museum—black and golden bowls, vases, and cups arranged on a tablecloth between angels' hands—moved Beavers while making the film. "Look at some of the common objects as if they were 3,000 years old," he noted in July 1981. In *Efpsychi*, handcart, wooden pallet, bale of mountain tea, garlic strings, and bundles of dried herbs receive the compositional attention of painted space.

"I see how an object, resting its weight and pressing down on the ground, possesses a movement; this invisible gravity is equivalent to quiet desire," Beavers writes in his essay about the film.[51] "Quiet desire" alternates with signs of sexual transaction and commerce in *Efpsychi*: shots of men exiting and entering Evripidou Street brothels, a woman in a red dress, fast-striding sailors in tandem. Desire moves between excess (lottery tickets, stacks of red mullet, shouted prices) and the sanctity of singularity: *teleftea*, the last one—one word that animates one face. Vangelis's eyebrows rise, his lips contract, his nostrils flare.

The etymology for the ancient Greek word *efpsychi* is "good soul" (*ef* + *psyche*). In the final sequence of the film, Vangelis, now seen in a wider frame, his torso bare, holds a small wax figure shaped like a baby. This ritual object, discovered in the candle shop where Beavers filmed, reminded the filmmaker of El Greco's *The Burial of the Count of Orgaz* (1586). "In the center of the painting an angel holds a small figure representing the soul of the dead person, and its shape reminded me of the wax figure," Beavers said. In this final sequence, Vangelis is bathed in gold light, as if lit by the preceding images—the "quiet desire" of objects, the fire-to-come of the hanging wicks. Balance has been struck between eros and soul.

In a 1981 *Efpsychi* note, Beavers associated a scene carved on a Mycenaean knife with the violence of sexuality:

> **Image of the lion pouncing upon an antelope as metaphor for**
> **the part of sex which equals a stain (victor—victim)**
> **Image of the chase = the blood sport element in sex**

When I asked about the note, Beavers said: "I was interested not only in how much violence there is in sexuality—but also the connection between the mystical and uncanny and sexuality. I allowed myself such a theme through Cavafy. His main early source of inspiration is Baudelaire—he transferred the extreme truthfulness of Baudelaire to the homoerotic, opening up a whole new subject area. But Cavafy leaves all that out—he's very sovereign. He leaves an awful lot out."[52]

## DEATH MASKS

In an essay about *Efpsychi*, Paul Arthur contrasts Beavers's maintenance of real-place specificity and context with structural films of the 1970s (such as those by Ernie Gehr and Paul Sharits) in which "images which spark metaphoric associations to properties of cinema are stripped of any local or historical significance in order to secure the equation of process/representation."[53] The unfamiliar abstraction/context fusion in Beavers's work can sometimes promote engagement with a film long after it was made or seen. A spectator—and a new moment in time—might extend a local sequence set in motion by a film.[54]

In 2022, the candle workshop at 28 Aristophanous that Beavers shot for *Efpsychi* was still operating. Founded by Yiorgos Trakas in the mid-1930s, it is now run by his grandsons, who supply candles to churches in Athens, Paros, Naxos, Rhodes, Aegina, and other islands. They no longer produce baby-shaped figures (offerings for pregnancy or newborn health) like the one Tsindoukidis holds in *Efpsychi*, but other votives—rows of newly made three-foot-tall candles—hang in rows to dry. The shop had been producing 400 tons of candles per year less than a decade ago, but since "the catastrophe" (the height of the economic crisis in 2015), business has been precarious. The church pays 25 percent less for candles, and paraffin prices are dependent on petrol. Candle demand is dwindling; growing agnosticism means fewer people go to church. "In my grandfather's day, people were ashamed of being gay and proud of being Christian. Now it's the opposite," Yiorgos Trakas Jr. said observationally, wondering how long the business would survive. He had already opened—and then closed—a restaurant and was considering new options.

Most of the businesses in this quarter have disappeared since the film's making. Brooms and shoes are mass-produced; there are fewer artisanal laborers and more plastics emporiums and Chinese import/export outlets. The Hotel Athinaikon in *Efpsychi* is gone; new hotels (whose names include "Manor," "Luxury," "Suites") have cropped up around Psyri's quickly gentrifying edges. The calls of lottery ticket salesmen are still audible—but the currency has changed from drachma to euro. Many of Psyri's small businesses collapsed in the face of Greece's calamitous interfaces with the world economy—its 2001 Eurozone entry and Troika interventions in 2010 and 2015.[55] The increasingly deserted area became a site of inexpensive space where migrant workers from Bangladesh, India, and Pakistan could set up new businesses—restaurants, markets, barbershops, money transfer services.

Two blocks down from the candle shop on Aristophanous, Saeed Hassan runs a spice shop he opened after migrating from Bangladesh in 2002. "A tourist might say, 'Wow, Greeks are so friendly.' But it's different on the inside. They once found some pieces of ancient stone," he said, pointing just outside his shop, "while they were fixing the streets. They closed the street for six months so the archaeologists could work; no one came to the shop [during that time]. I don't understand why they pay so much attention to the dead. They should be asking, 'Who is alive?'" He asked why I'd been talking to the candle shop owners, and I told him about their grandfather and the making of *Efpsychi*. "Every single life is a film," he said in response.

*Efpsychi* (1983/1996)

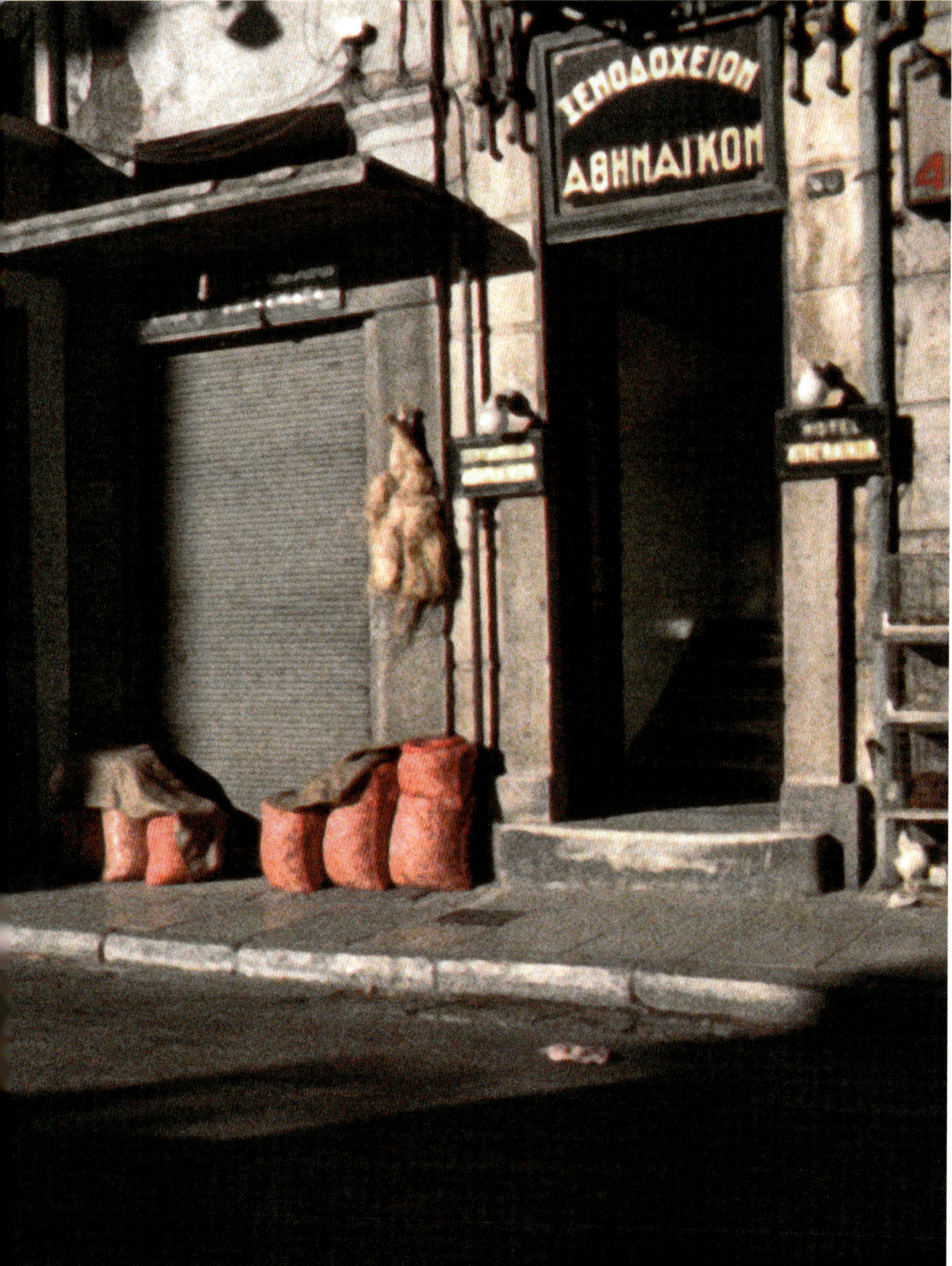
ΞΕΝΟΔΟΧΕΙΟΝ
ΑΘΗΝΑΙΚΟΝ

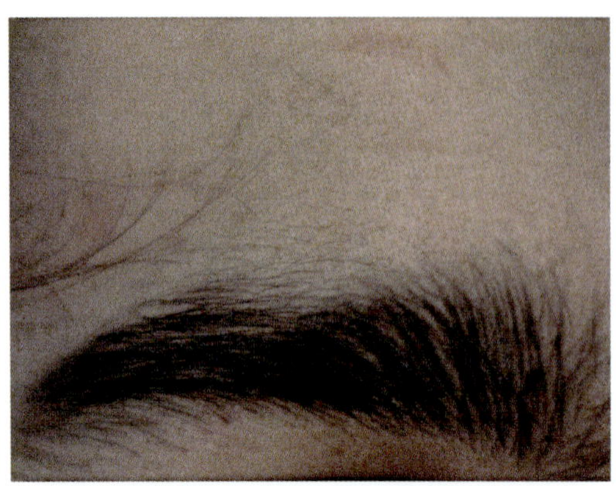

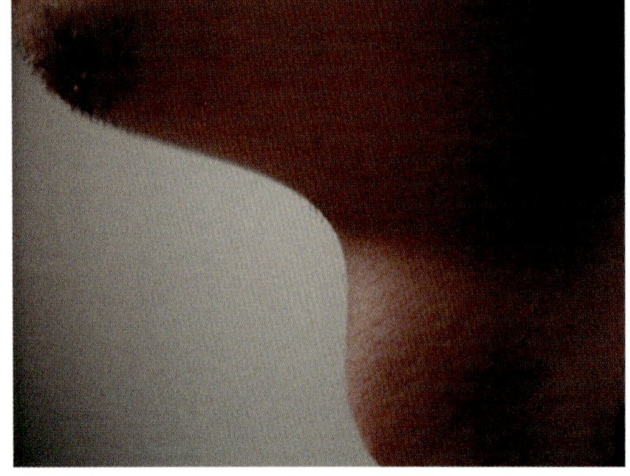

*Efpsychi* (1983/1996)

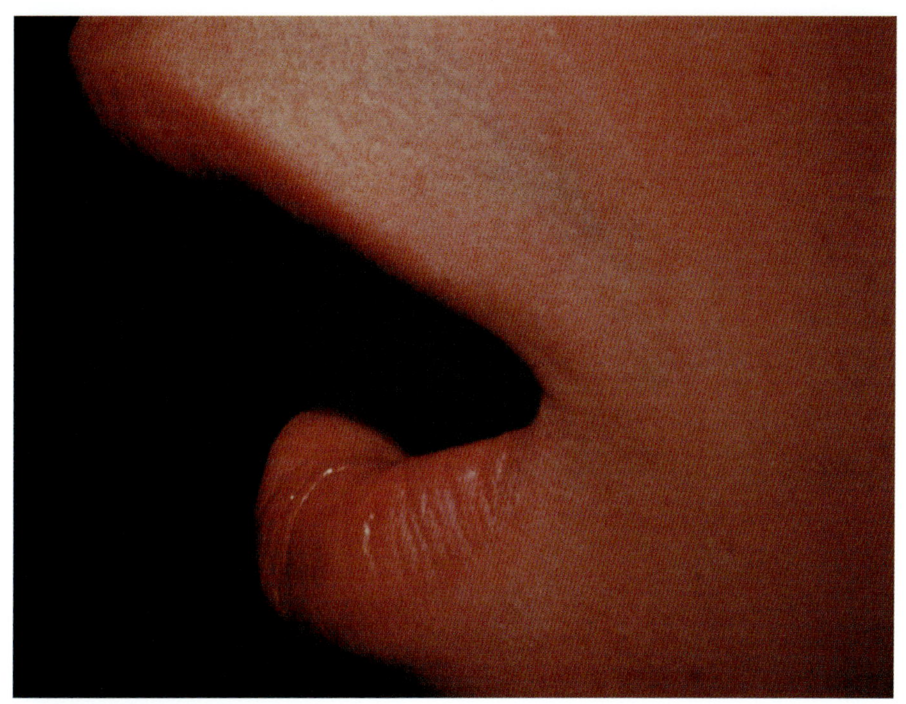

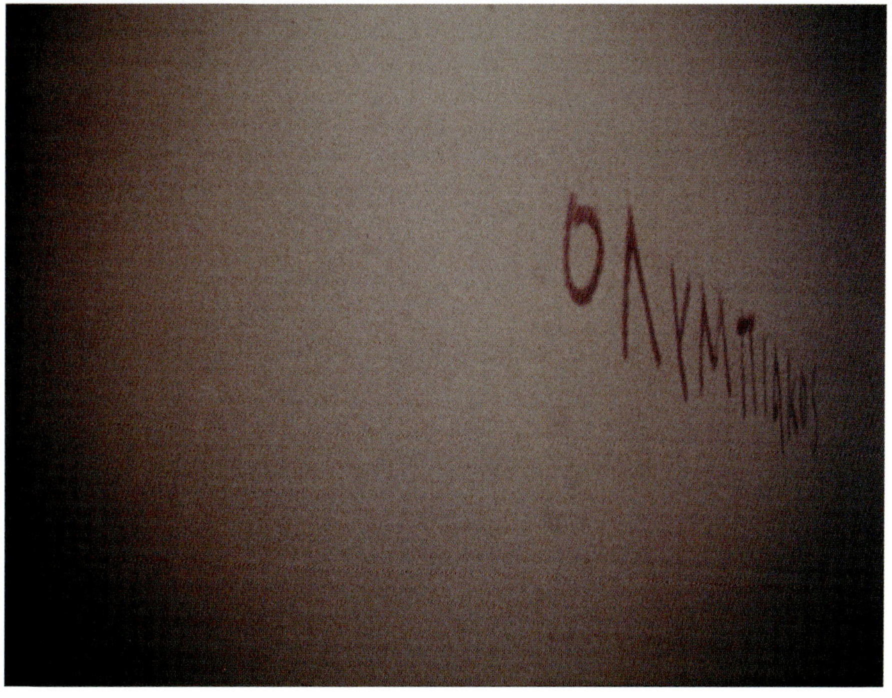

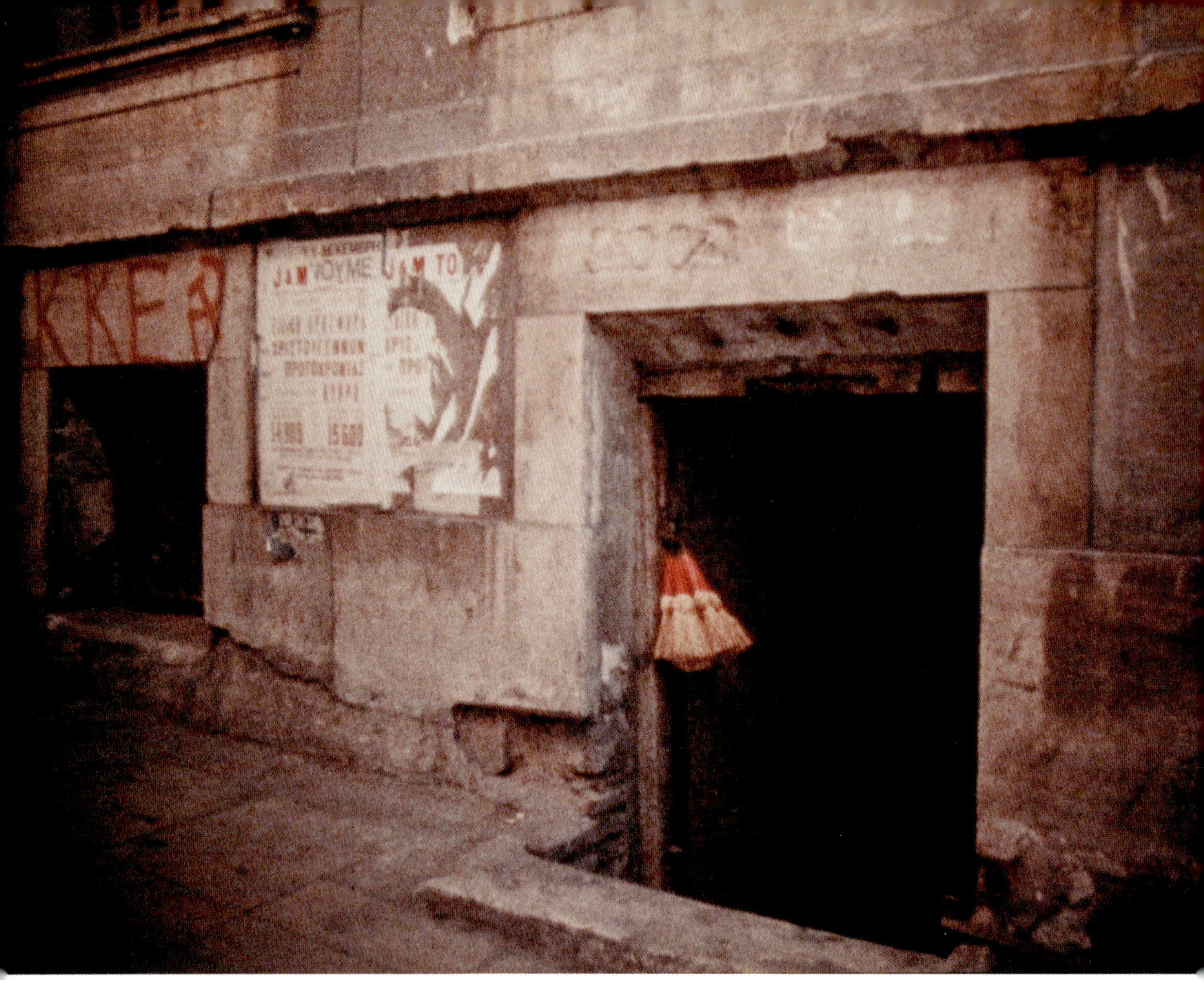


*Efpsychi* (1983/1996)

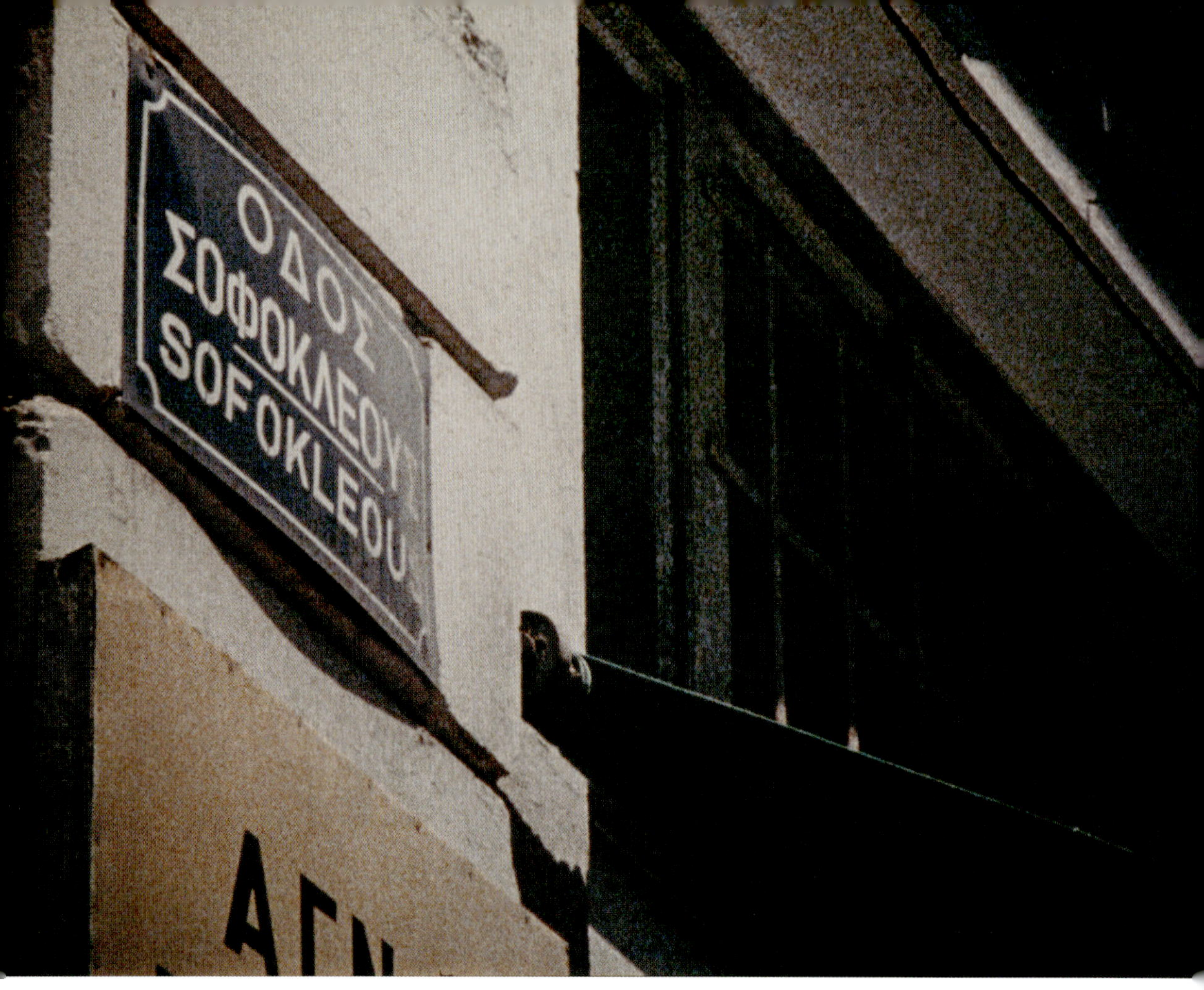


*Efpsychi* (1983/1996)

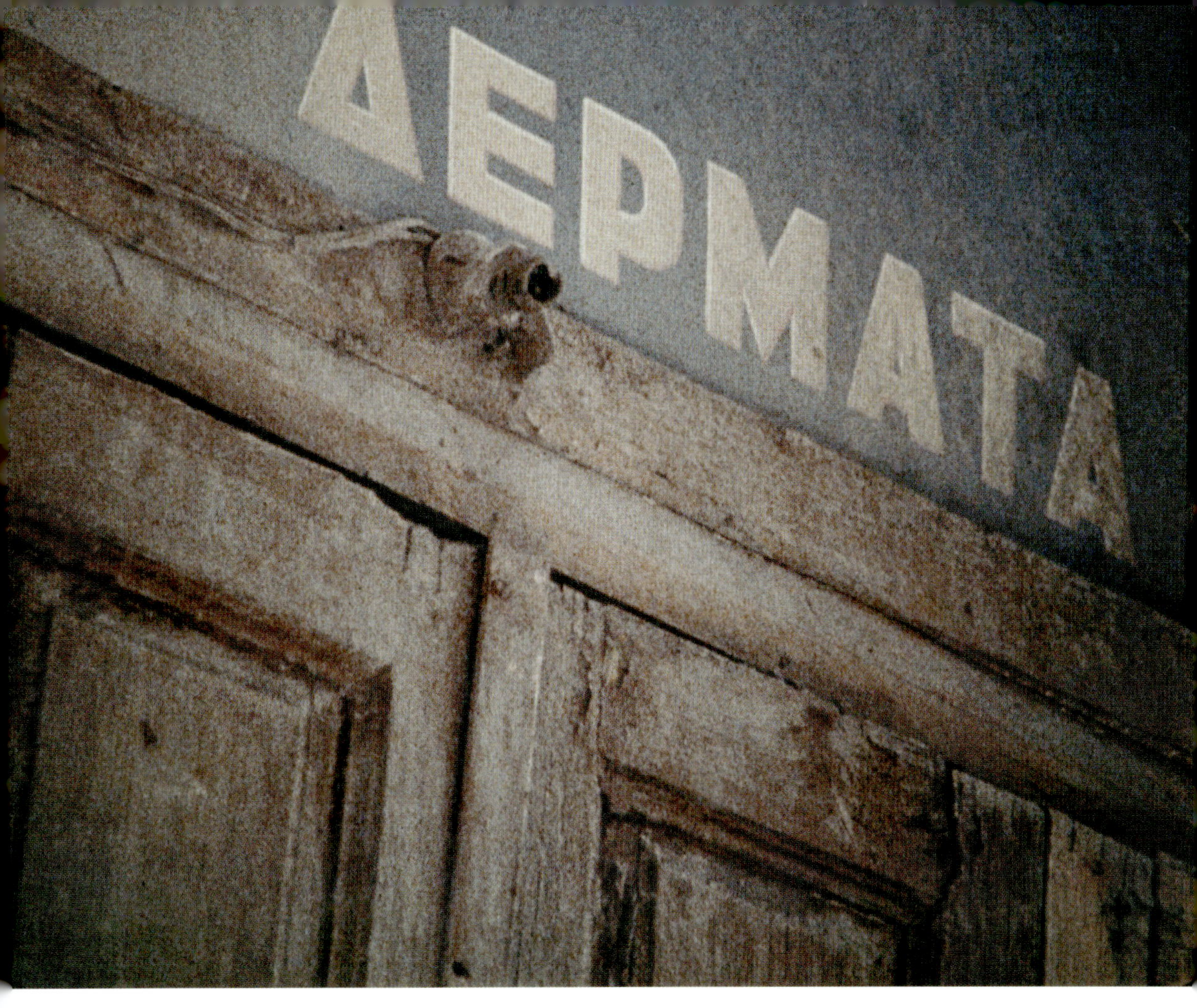
ΔΕΡΜΑΤΑ

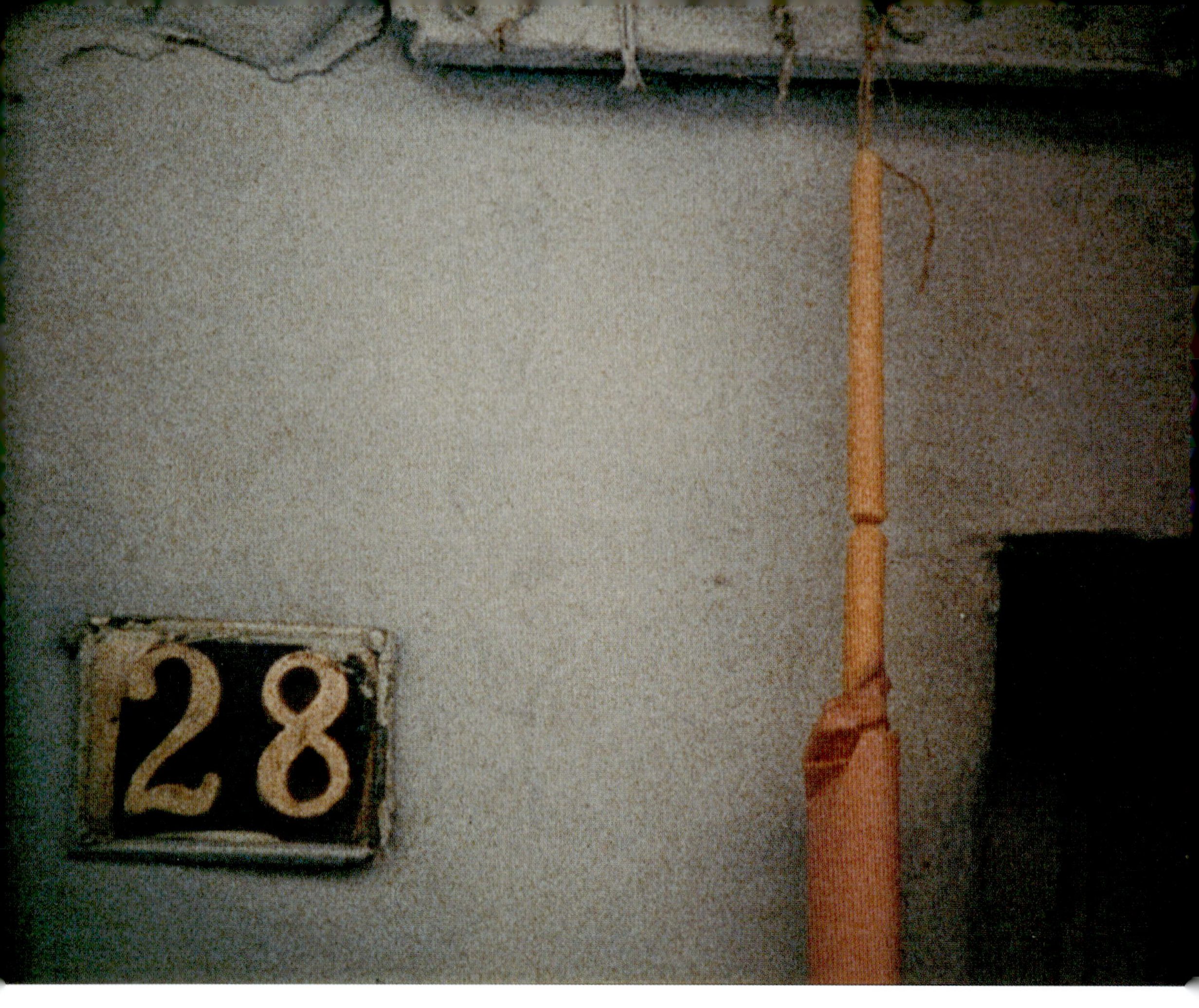


*Efpsychi* (1983/1996)

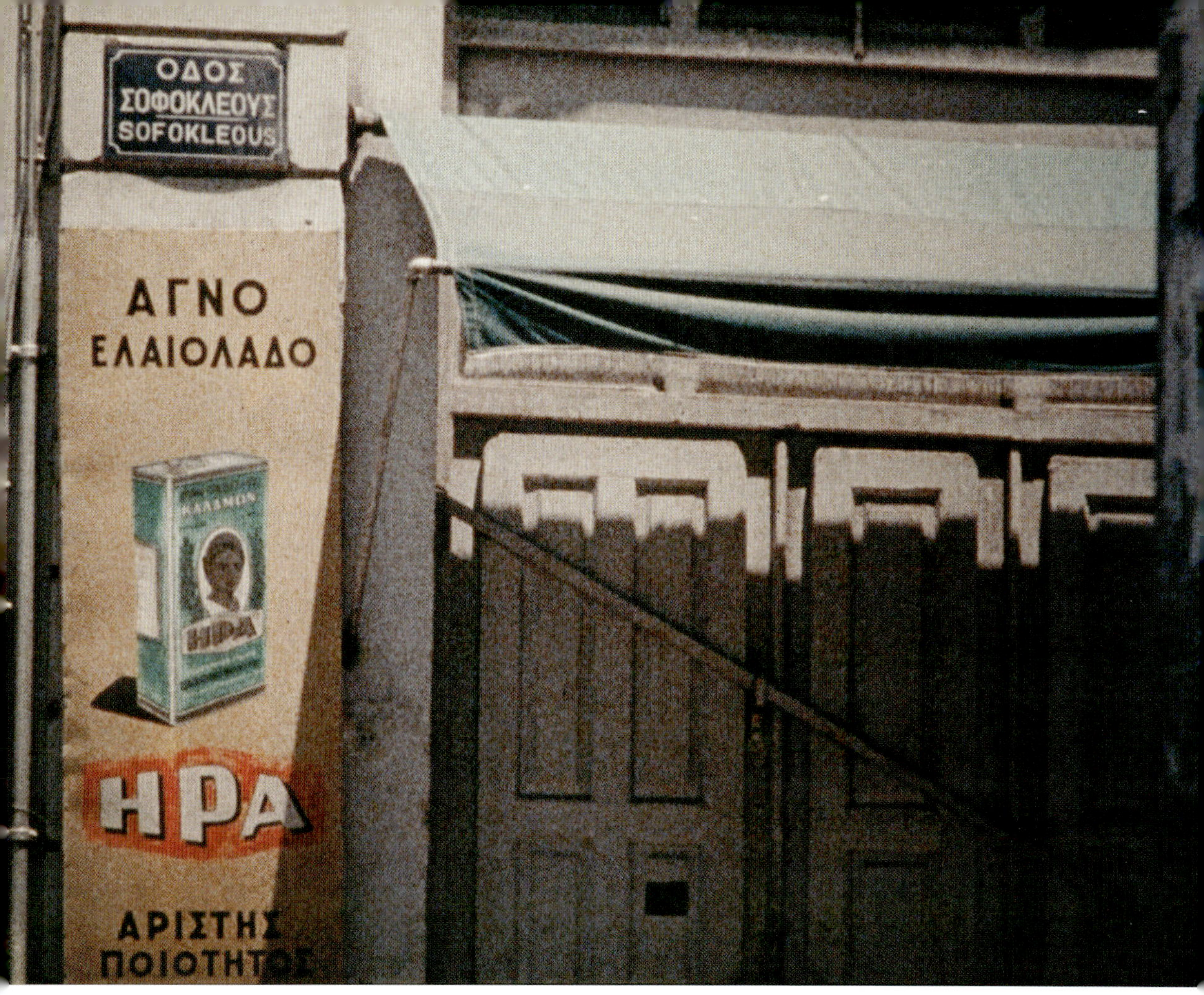
ΟΔΟΣ
ΣΟΦΟΚΛΕΟΥΣ
SOFOKLEOUS
ΑΓΝΟ
ΕΛΑΙΟΛΑΔΟ
ΗΡΑ
ΗΡΑ
ΑΡΙΣΤΗΣ
ΠΟΙΟΤΗΤΟΣ

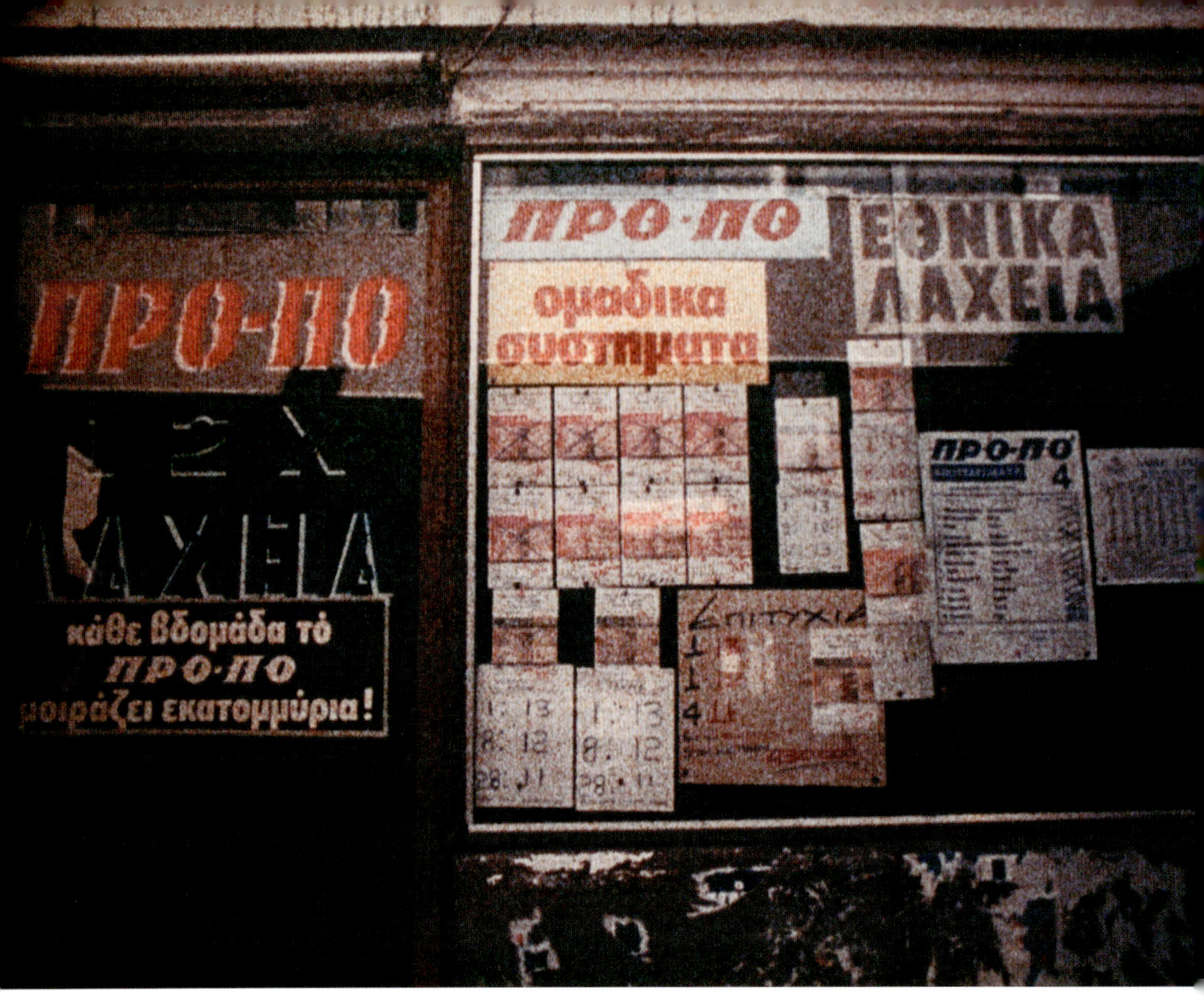


*Efpsychi* (1983/1996)

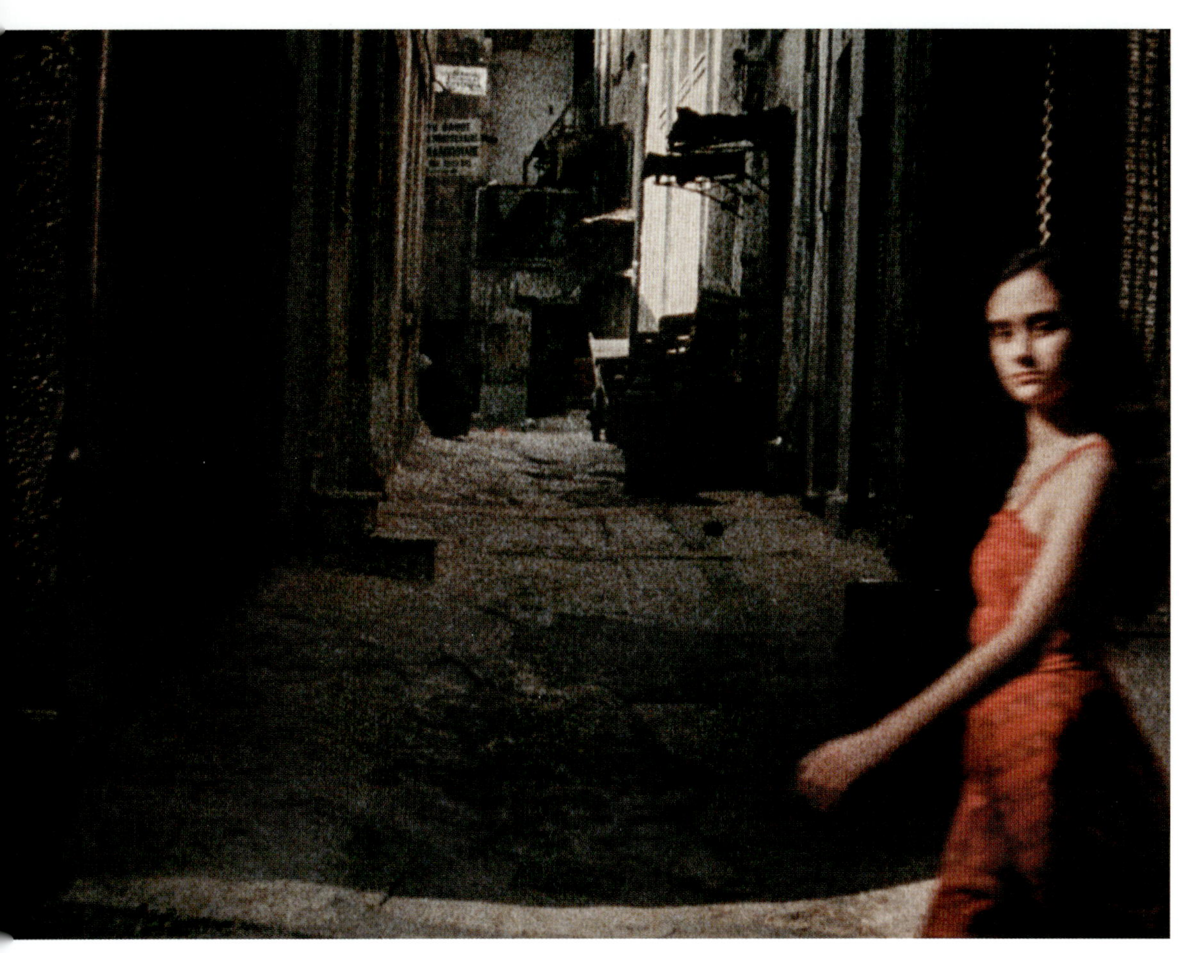

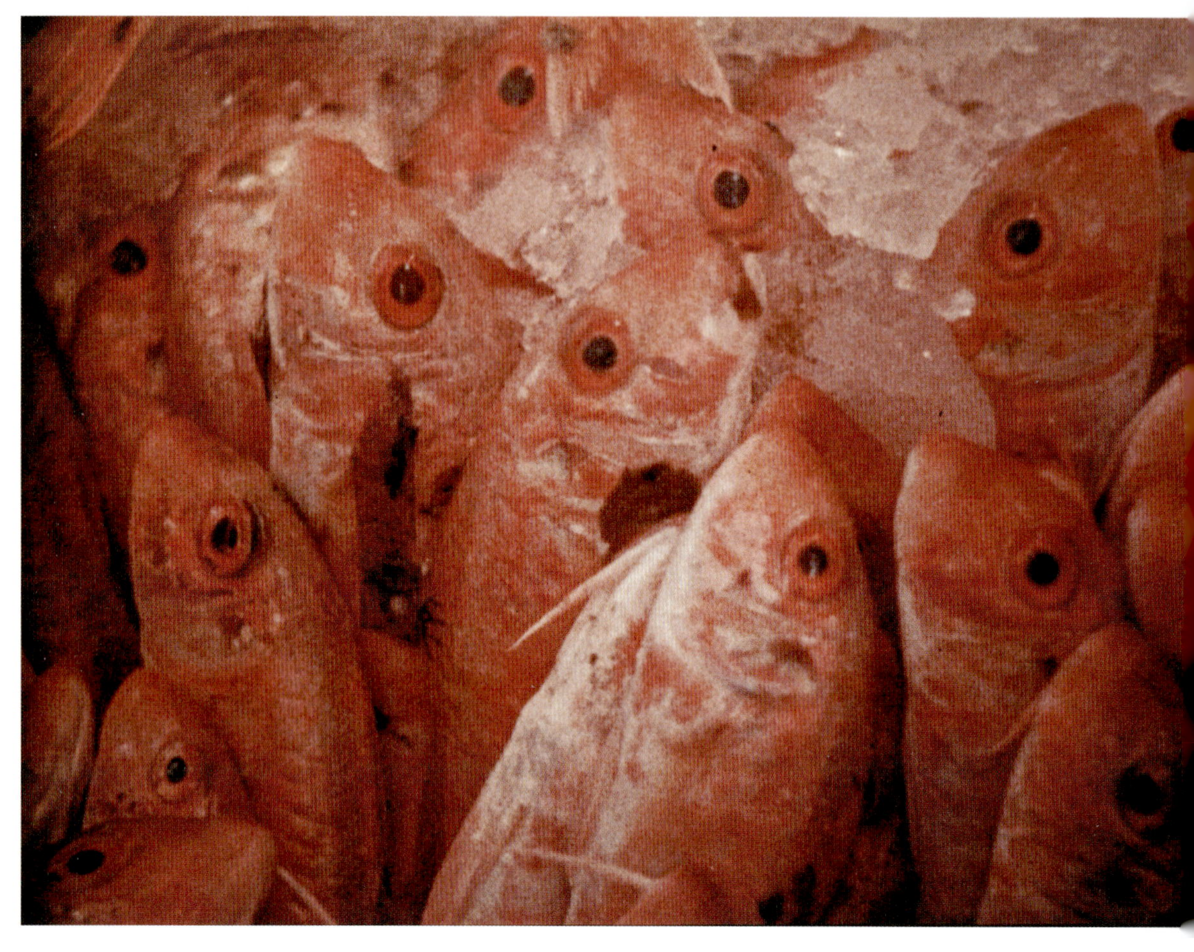

*Efpsychi* (1983/1996)

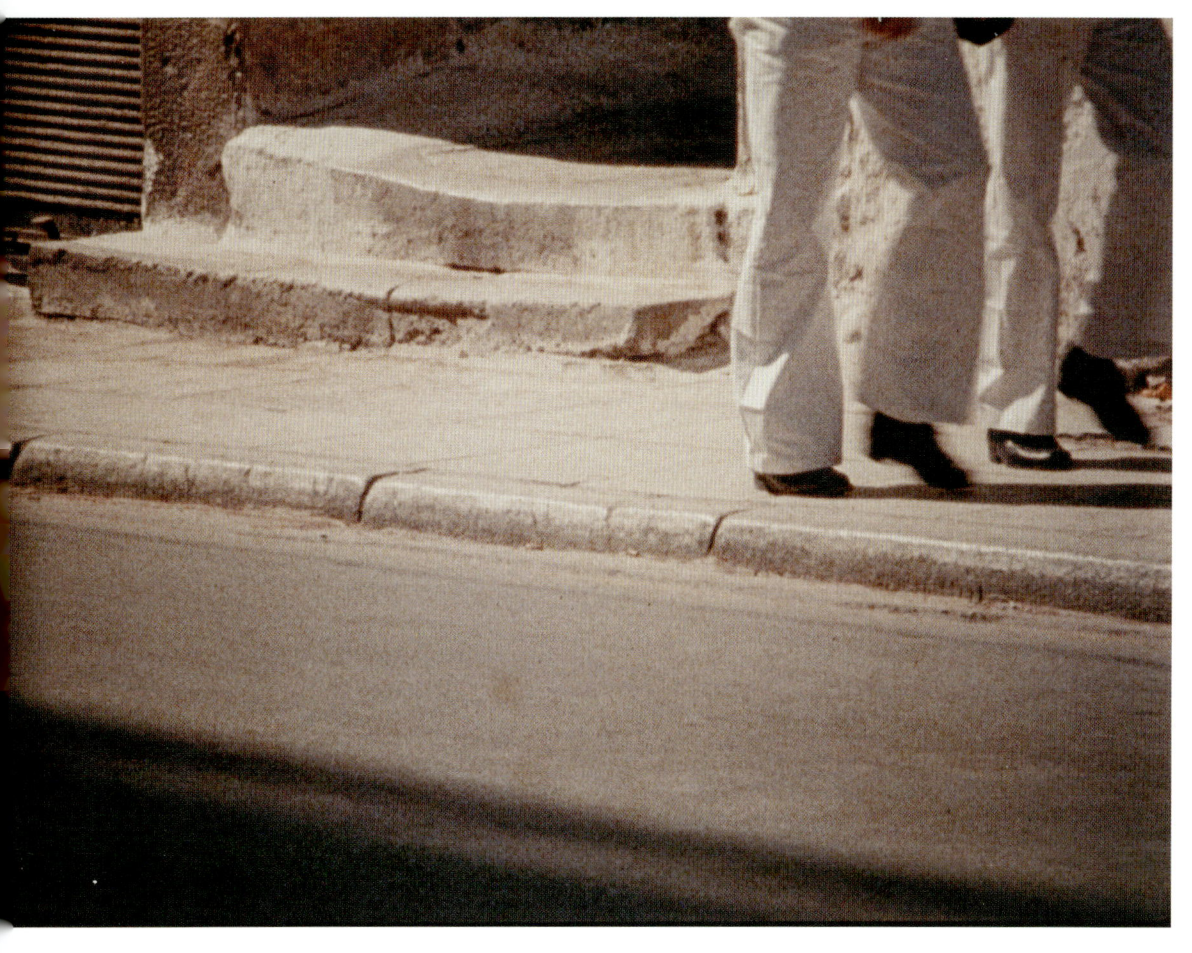

## APOLLO'S BODY

Beavers returned to Psyri in March 1989 as he pursued a new film inspired by ancient vases. He made notes on vessel form ("The shape contains") and unseen dimensions ("the voluptuous inside of the vase"). The film, *Stoas and Vases*, would set vases alongside an Athenian architectural structure—the arcade or stoa—that also blends interior and exterior space. Like the playwright-branded streets in *Efpsychi*, modern Greek stoas, named for the covered walkways that functioned as public gathering and commerce spaces, reference the ancient past.[56]

Modern stoas—built in the nineteenth and twentieth centuries—are diverse in style and use: luxury shopping spaces, storage sites, zones of shade, transit, and intra-building connection. They can be portals between parallel streets (a single-line passageway) or intersecting ones (L-shaped or angled). Stoa entrances belie what's beyond them: some stoas conclude in a dead-end back wall; others lead to hybrid space where ceiling has become sky; internal stoa doorways open onto staircases, elevators, levels to come. In their irregularity—the entrance on one stoa end might be square, the other a trapezoid—they produce somatic awareness of the slanted planes and oblique angles of urban space. The Psyri and central Athens stoas Beavers shot in 1989—including Stoas Ikaros, Levi, Sophokleos, Aristophanous—are industrial spaces, empty of people. The clarity of documentary detail (metal scale, burlap tea bundle, bag of animal feed, sonic ambience of gates and cars) rests inside phenomenological visual space. The stoas appear as volumetric containers whose interiors are alternately illuminated (by sun or the pulse of fluorescent lights) and sites of darkness. Beavers holds the stoas still (allowing their gates, windows, skylights, and staircases to articulate permeability) and moves with them (by shooting some stoas from both ends, Beavers reveals new views, frames through which the surrounding urban space is visible).

*Stoas and Vases* became *The Stoas* (1991–1997). "I had a sense that [the vase] would not work as a film image," Beavers told Ute Aurand.[57] Instead, recurring shots of Beavers's hands joined in a cupped shape, as if *holding* a vase, are interspersed with the stoa studies. And halfway through the film, the containment of hands and stoa structures gives way to liquid. In the second of the film's three parts, Beavers follows the course of the Lousios River in Arcadia from its springs near Kaloneri to Karytaina, where it empties into the Alpheios River. Shot from multiple sites and angles along its route, the river is seen from above (through the lacy scrim of oak and plane tree leaves) and in close-up, lined by red grass at the shore. It is as diverse in appearance and depth as the stoas—a gliding thin skin, a black foam rush, an aqua field bending around rocks. Sometimes it moves in two directions at once. I have the sense of watching the Lousios imagery *through* the preceding stoa material: every substance and object connected to the river—water, rock, tree, leaf—has the potential to transition to black.

Like the vase, the image of the human body disappeared from the film. Beavers originally shot an actor, directing him in the water and out (swimming, drying himself, lying down) but was unhappy with the result. "The figure was of a lesser beauty than the river, on a much lower level," he noted in August 1991. He destroyed the resulting work print and negative and instead drew on an earlier experience he'd had while visiting the river. "There is in Greek culture—through the powers of Apollo, the god of appearances, an experience of the visible world. I saw in the river the divinity of appearance. That was very important. It gave me strength to film the river in the way I did," he recalled.[58] Once he had rejected the figure, Beavers understood that "the river itself is a body."[59]

—

Shots of purple Corinthian grape clusters embedded in thick leaves arrive in the final minutes of the film. The distant rhythmic sound of a *talando*—a percussive wooden instrument—that has accompanied the Lousios material (along with sounds of water and a shepherd's whistling) intensifies. The grapes, like earlier shots of baskets of bread in an Athenian stoa, spur my own impulse to reach out by hand. "You're always trying to reach something and not always grasping it," Beavers said of his work as a filmmaker. In July 1991, as he was editing the film, Beavers discovered a dictionary etymology for "grape" that included "to gather grapes with a vine hook," "art of seizing," and "hollow of the hand." He noted, "The meaning 'hollow of the hand' fits exactly my use of the grapes at the end of The Stoas, and coincides with the meaning of *δῶρον*, 'gift,' as 'hollow of the hand.'"[60] Such a "fit" is a confirming fruit amid intuitive work.

Beavers completed *The Stoas* in December 1991. While they were in Fulda, Germany, in February, Markopoulos became ill. In Freiburg, Markopoulos's new patron, German manufacturer Franz Morat, referred him to his own doctor. Weeks later, Markopoulos was diagnosed with Waldenström macroglobulinemia, a rare form of lymphoma, at the Freiburg University hospital. Over the next eight months, he underwent chemotherapy and physical rehabilitation in Triberg, a Black Forest village (while Beavers rented a room in a nearby forester's house) and restabilized. "How to go back into the life we had led while he was in the condition he was in, recovering? We both thought, 'Can we go to Greece?'" Beavers said. Markopoulos took short trips to the Basel bank vault and Zurich, but in the early fall his doctor ordered him back to the hospital. "This is such a beautiful room," Markopoulos said on arrival. "It must mean I'm going to die." He died on November 12, 1992.

"We were very lucky that Gregory's medical expenses were completely carried by the welfare system of the German state," Beavers said (Markopoulos did not have health insurance). But he faced sizable debts after Markopoulos's death. "Even though Mr. Reemtsma's aid had stopped in 1991, I still had the bank account that his money had gone through, and I was able to use that to draw on a line of credit. And then, in 1994, 3sat [the German-language public television channel] bought the rights to two of Markopoulos's early films, and within a few months I was able to pay off all our debt. I was suddenly in a very different kind of life."

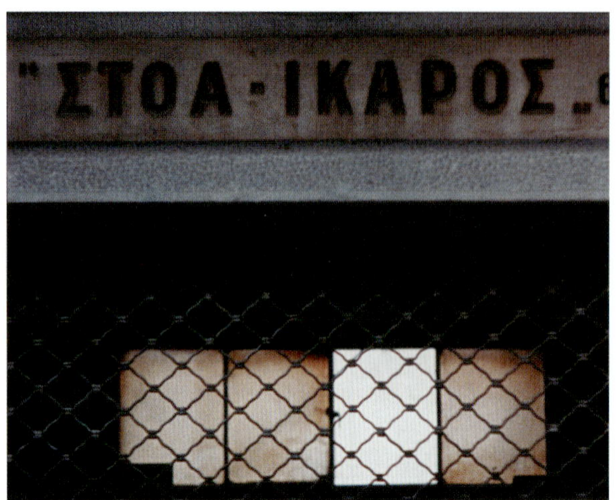


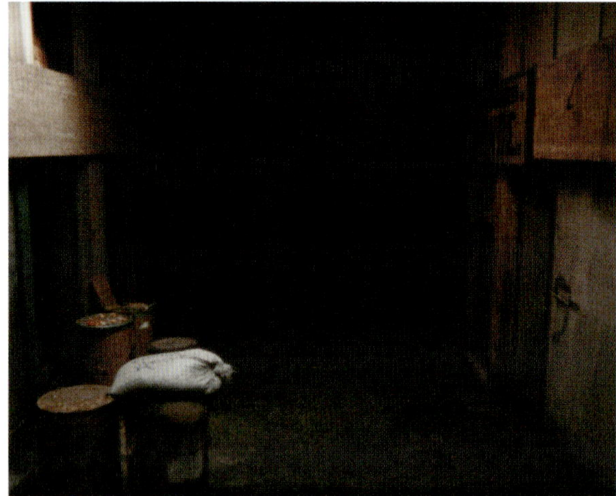

*The Stoas* (1991–1997)

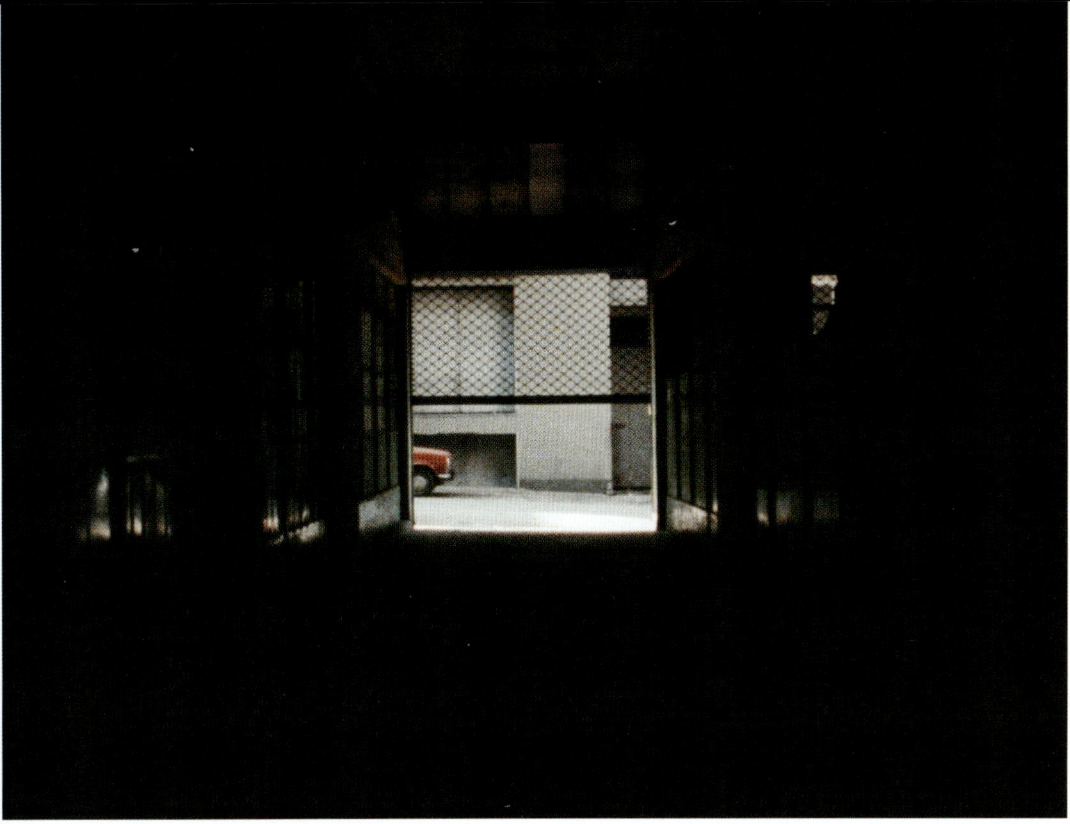

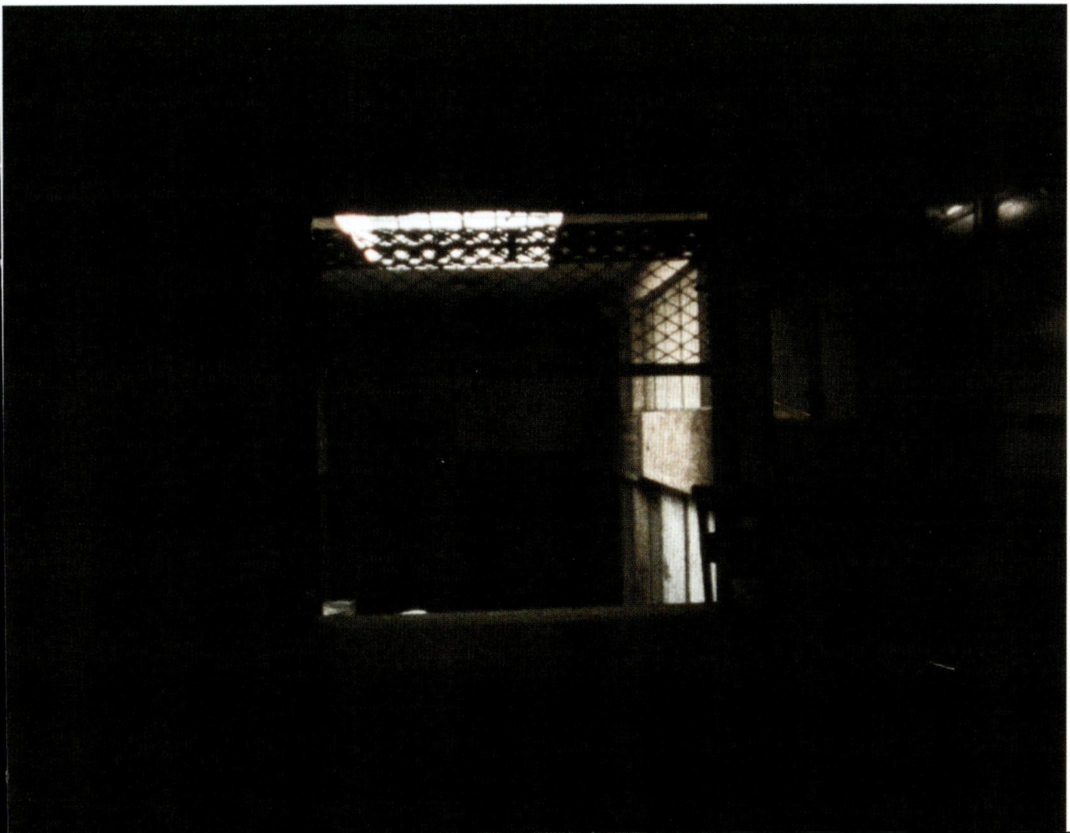

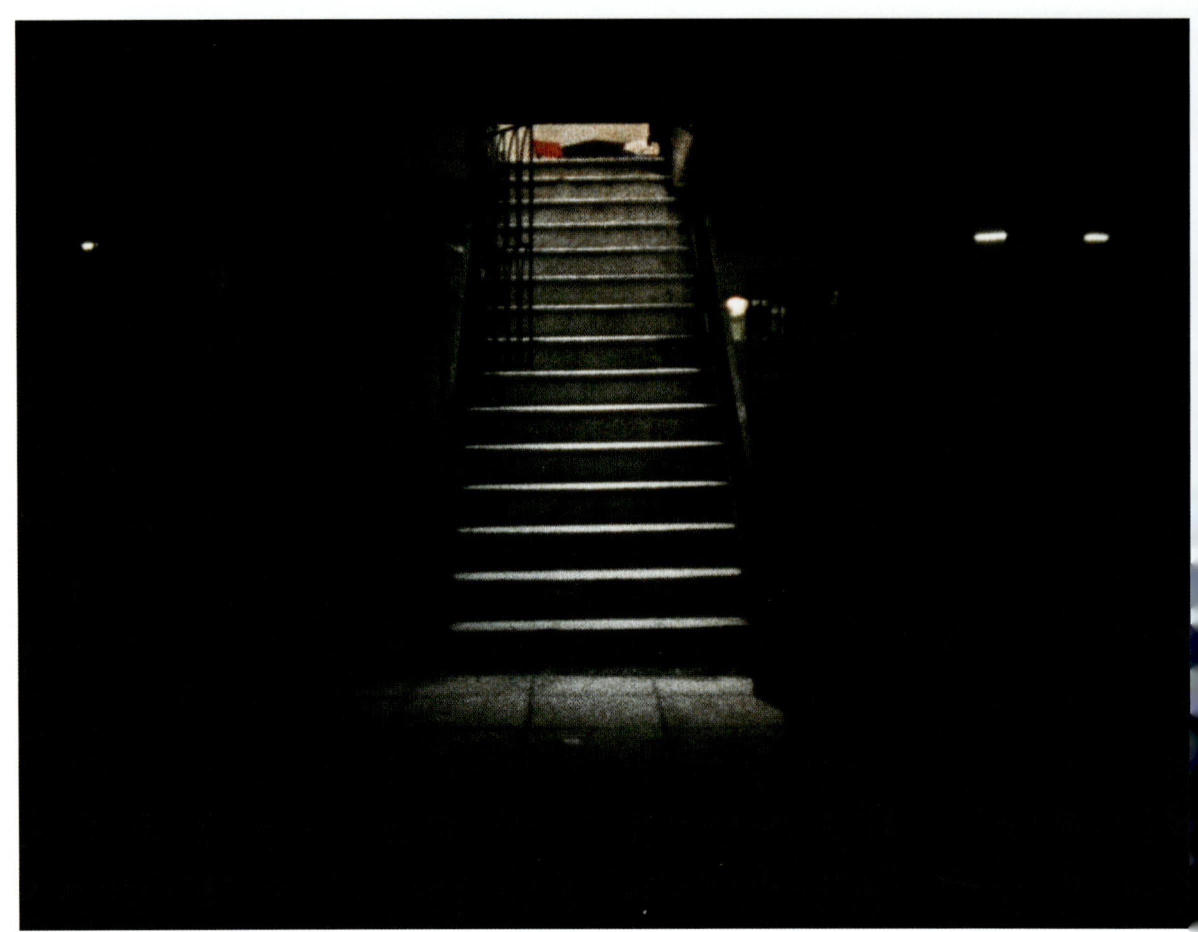

*The Stoas* (1991–1997)

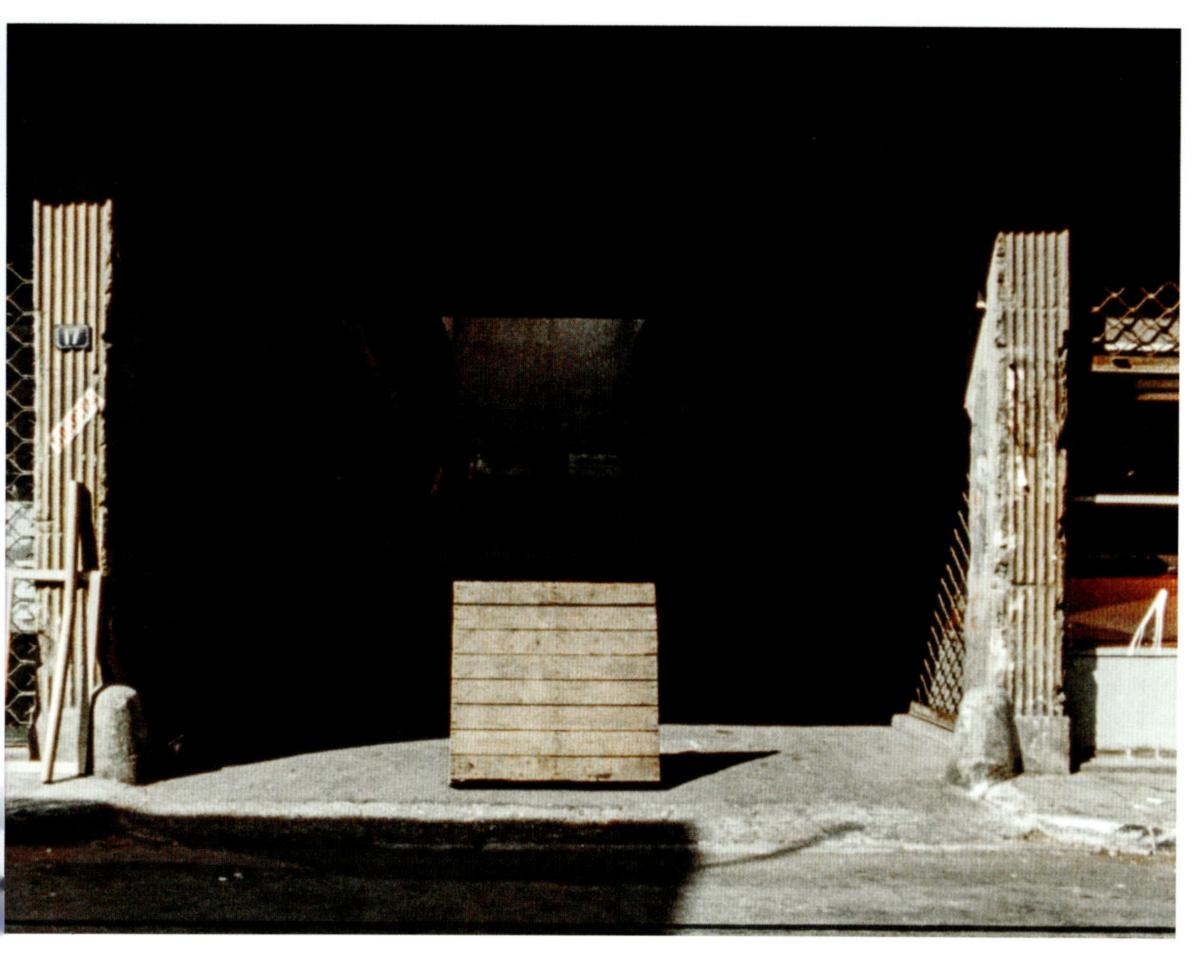

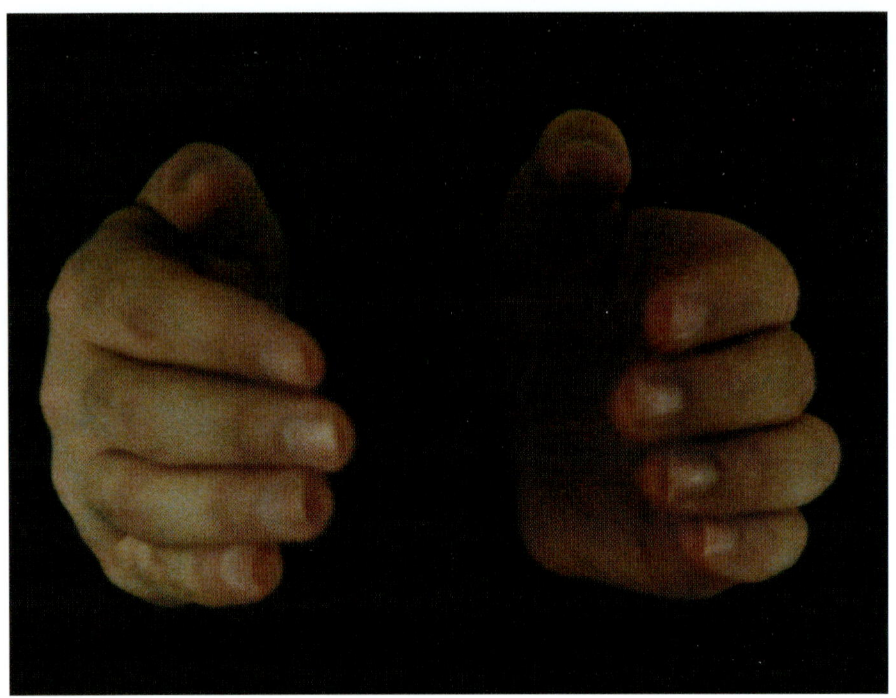

*The Stoas* (1991–1997)

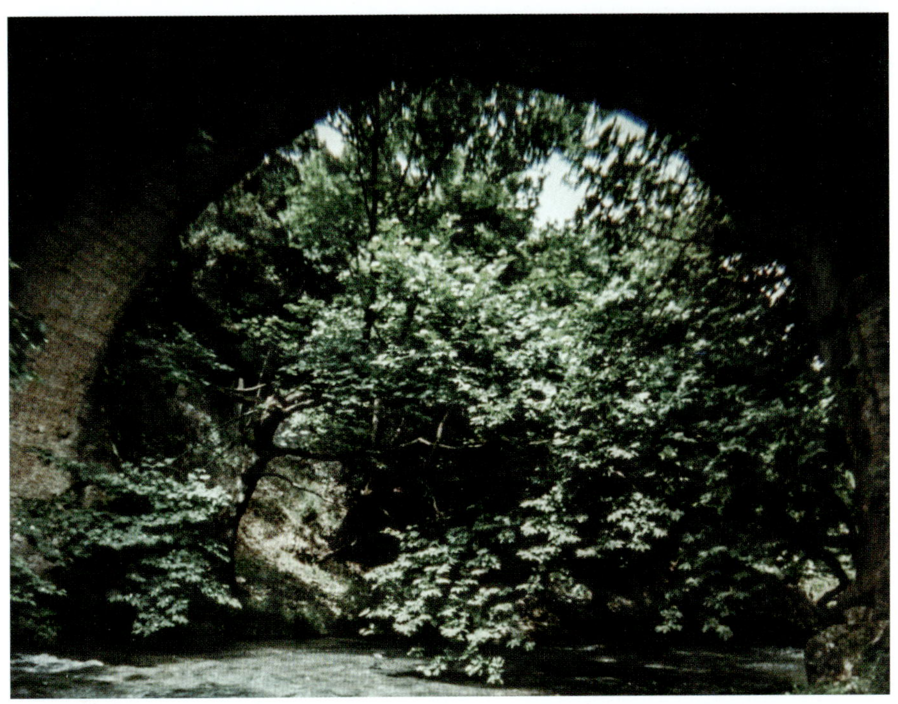

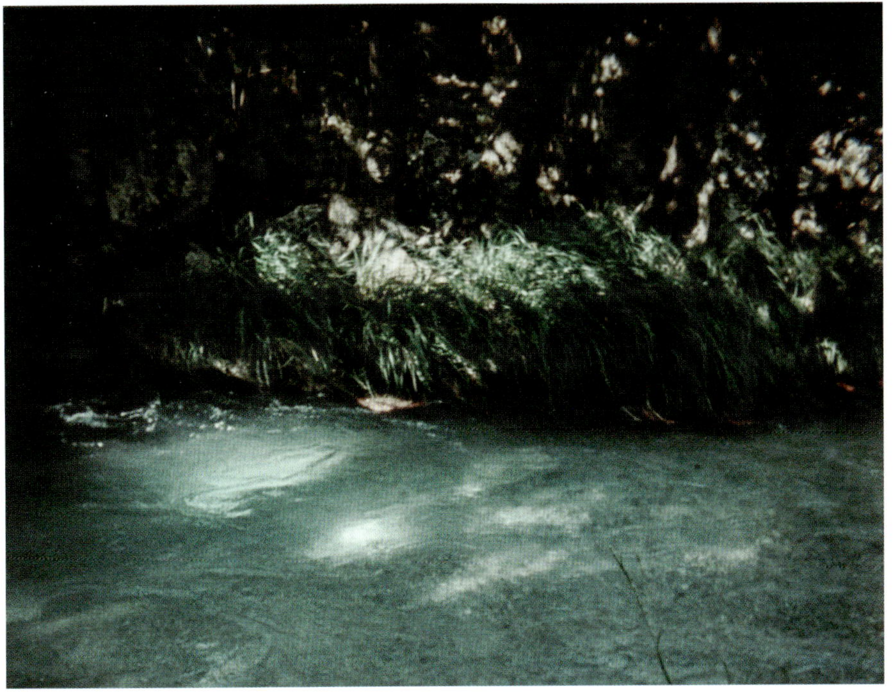

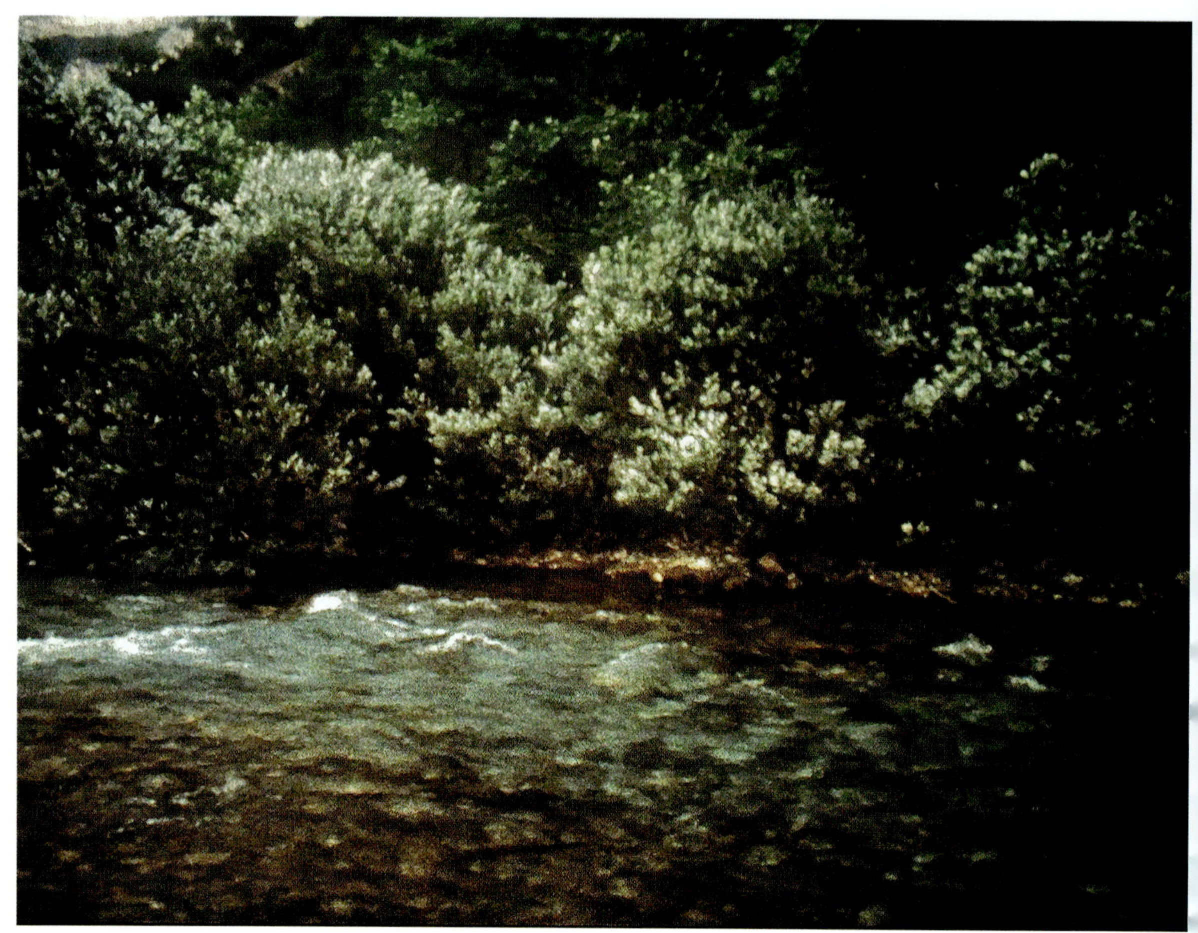

*The Stoas* (1991–1997)

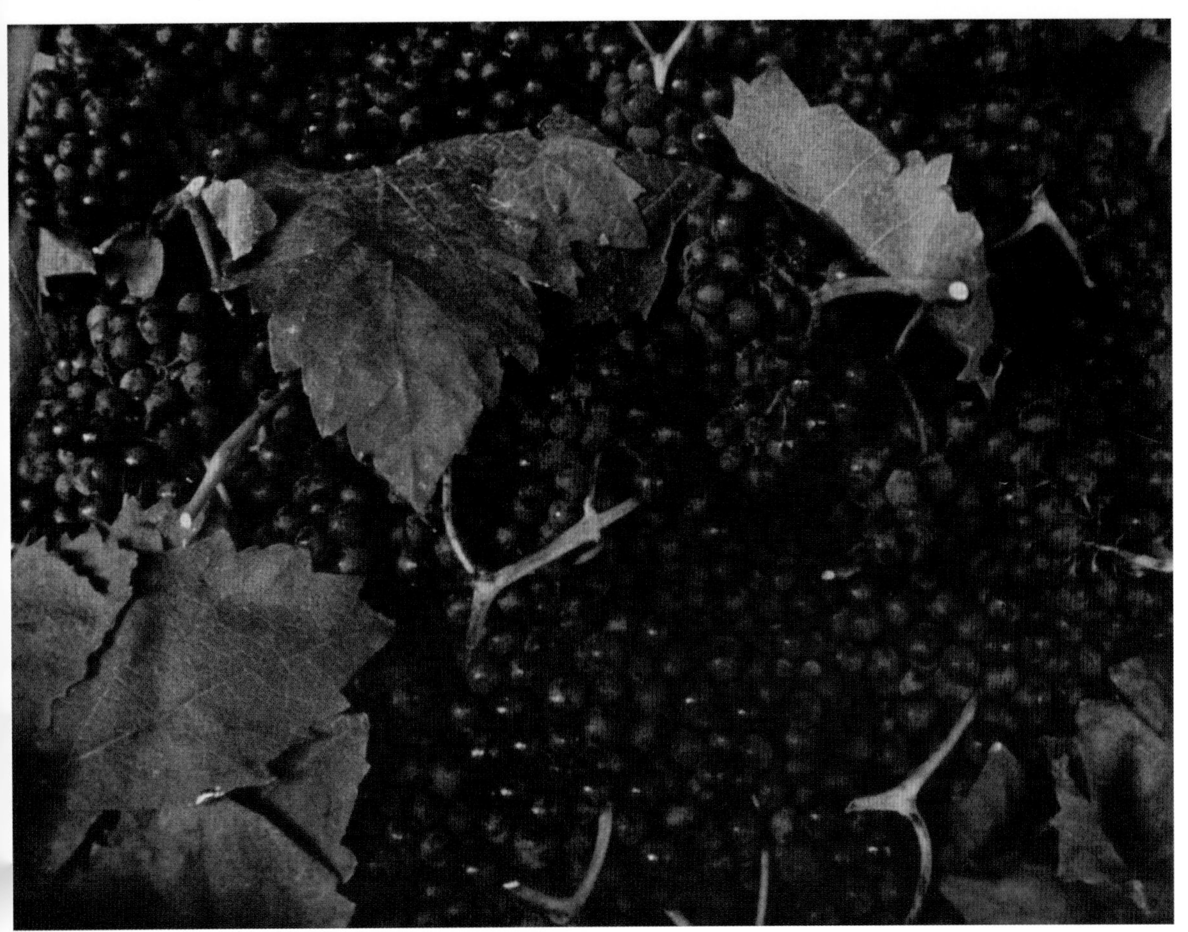

## CONTEMPLATING A CLOUD

In the fall of 1993, Beavers returned to Hydra. Created over the eight years following Markopoulos's death, *The Ground* (1993–2001) features the crumbling hilltop tower of *Winged Dialogue* (1967/2000), his first Hydra film. Agios Nikolaos, where he had shot Markopoulos in 1967, is visible in the distance. *The Ground* became the concluding film in his eighteen-work cycle and *Winged Dialogue* became the first.

A dialogue between two male figures structures both films; in *The Ground* it transpires between the filmmaker and a stonemason. The film immediately links their hands by motion: initially cupped, holding a shard of light and sea-sound, Beavers's hand draws up his bare chest and out of frame; vertical motion continues up the tower and stops in a close-up of the mason at work. One hand grips a red chisel, the other a mallet. His strokes incise white lines into a gray stone mass (its surface looks as if covered by a primitive writing form). The chiseling sound joins imagery of Beavers forcefully striking his chest and its guttural sound. "<u>The ground</u> and each effort, each struggle—a rock," Beavers wrote in an early film note. The work of grief, like the mason's labor, is solitary and slow.

We never see Beavers's face—only his gestures: holding, striking, releasing. Sometimes his hands are isolated against black: making a fist (preparation for a strike), or fingers tautly extended. Inside a layered island soundscape (crowing rooster, buzzing insects, barking dog, ringing bells of both monastery and goats), pounding and water sounds alternate as Beavers's hands speak both effort and surrender. "Beating the chest + waves," Beavers wrote in December 1993. In one iteration of the chest/hand imagery, Beavers's fist uncurls irregularly, as a ball of paper might reexpand, without provocation, after being crumpled. The hand is rock and flower: synced to intention and driven by an unconscious intelligence of its own.

"I began with a relation to death and asceticism," Beavers said. An 1863 drawing by Odilon Redon—*Centaur Contemplating a Cloud*—generated his first impulse. Beavers saw it in an exhibition on the ascetic tradition at the Kunstmuseum Basel. "The centaur is lying against some rocks looking at a cloud. It was so extraordinary to see this very large horse-man looking at a cloud. That's why I included the close-up of the cloud in my film and, perhaps also, the hooves," he said. Within touching distance of the weary centaur's face, Redon's cloud is composed mostly of blank paper—compositional relief next to the crosshatched creature and sharp rocks. In *The Ground*, shots of angled hooves poised above a donkey's long shadow, and a close-up of its quivering leg, inject an animal's lower body into a film anchored by Beavers's torso. In working through grief, the filmmaker is drawing animal and human parts together.

—

Ascetic impulse carried Beavers only so far. In October 1994, he noted how "unconcentrated" and "unclear, not to say polluted, my state is." A fuller understanding of his filmmaking object remained out of sight. "At the moment I am repeating endlessly the same two gestures without thinking of how they should develop further," he wrote. But months later (Beavers returned to Hydra multiple times to make the film), while shooting the irregular ring of pines around the stone tower, Beavers's own feeling state turned over. "It was an astonishing experience for me. I realized the film itself was turning me back towards life. When I think of the central question of pattern, repetition, and so forth, I think of Scarlatti and Handel or Mozart and how diametrically opposite results can be created. This is also true of film. It's such a subtle thing but film can very suddenly slide into its opposite," Beavers said. "The strength of life against the ascetic and the negative. I hadn't known this combination before I made the film."

Midway through the film, images of yellow blossoms below the tower signal a tonal shift. A gold orb—a loaf of bread—appears, placed in an opening of the tower like a missing stone. And the sound of water accompanies Beavers's cupped hand as it rests against his chest; later, the sound of birds' wings is synced to his opening hand (as if released by it) and continues as pigeons fly into the black chasm of a cave. Today Beavers sees "an unconscious [movement] toward the cathartic" in the film.[61] *Catharsis* (from *καθαίρειν*, "to purify, purge") was Aristotle's term for the affective release felt by dramatic tragedy spectators.[62]

Unnecessary images also had to be purged. Beavers intended to include shots of Markopoulos—sleeping during his illness, or by the tower or under a tree in *Winged Dialogue*—but eventually the image of a sunlit rectangle on his Hydra hotel room wall took Markopoulos's place. The morphology took two years.

**13.9.93:** **Is there a weakness in reintroducing images from W.D.?**
**3.10.94:** **The rectangle of sunlight may be equal to the rectangle(s) in which I filmed Gregory in Winged Dialogue.**
**19.7.95:** **It will be a delicate matter to remove even a single image.**
**10.9.95:** **The true image of Gregory in the film is not the ones taken from Winged Dialogue but the image of the morning light on the wall as it entered my room.**
**17.11.95:** **I consider removing the images of Gregory? It is "inexplicable" in the way that they appear, now.**
**9.12.95:** **The images from Winged Dialogue have been removed: why didn't I do this earlier**

In October 2000, back in Hydra, Beavers noted, "I met Stamati, the stone cutter (mason), whom I had filmed (perhaps in 1994!). . . . It is fine that I could find him after such a length of time." Beavers rerecorded the mason's chiseling sounds. Days later, after a visit to an Athens bakery, Beavers wrote: "I heard the word . . . to designate a special bread which is used in the church liturgy for the dead. When I filmed the bread placed in the wall of the tower I had some thought about this without a more specific knowledge." A *prosphoron* is a loaf of Orthodox holy bread used as an offering.

As in *Winged Dialogue*, the day concludes with the film: the sky has enlarged, holding charcoal-edged clouds at dusk. The final sounds in *The Ground* come from the percussive *talando*, used to call monks back to the monastery, and then the sea.

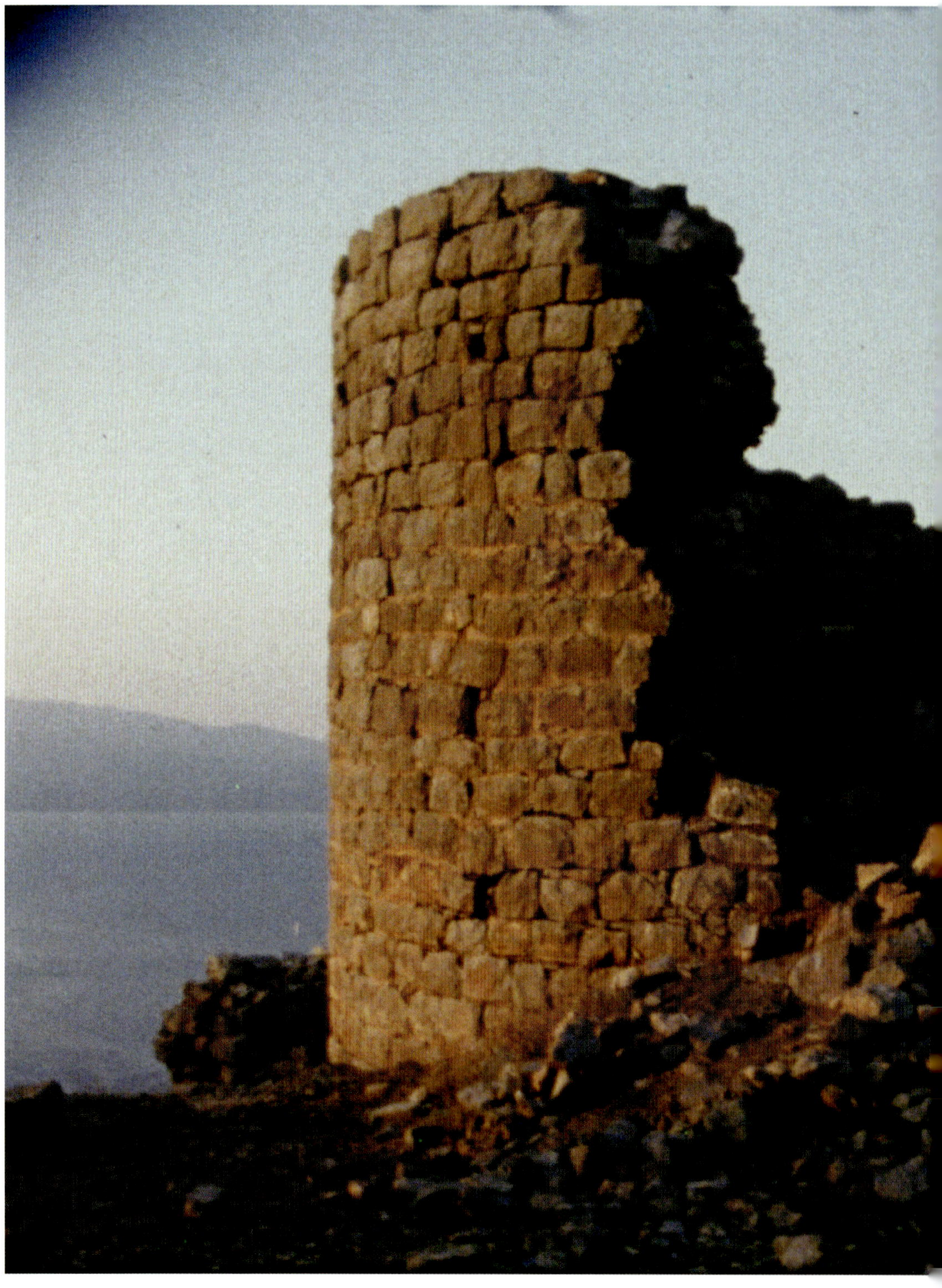

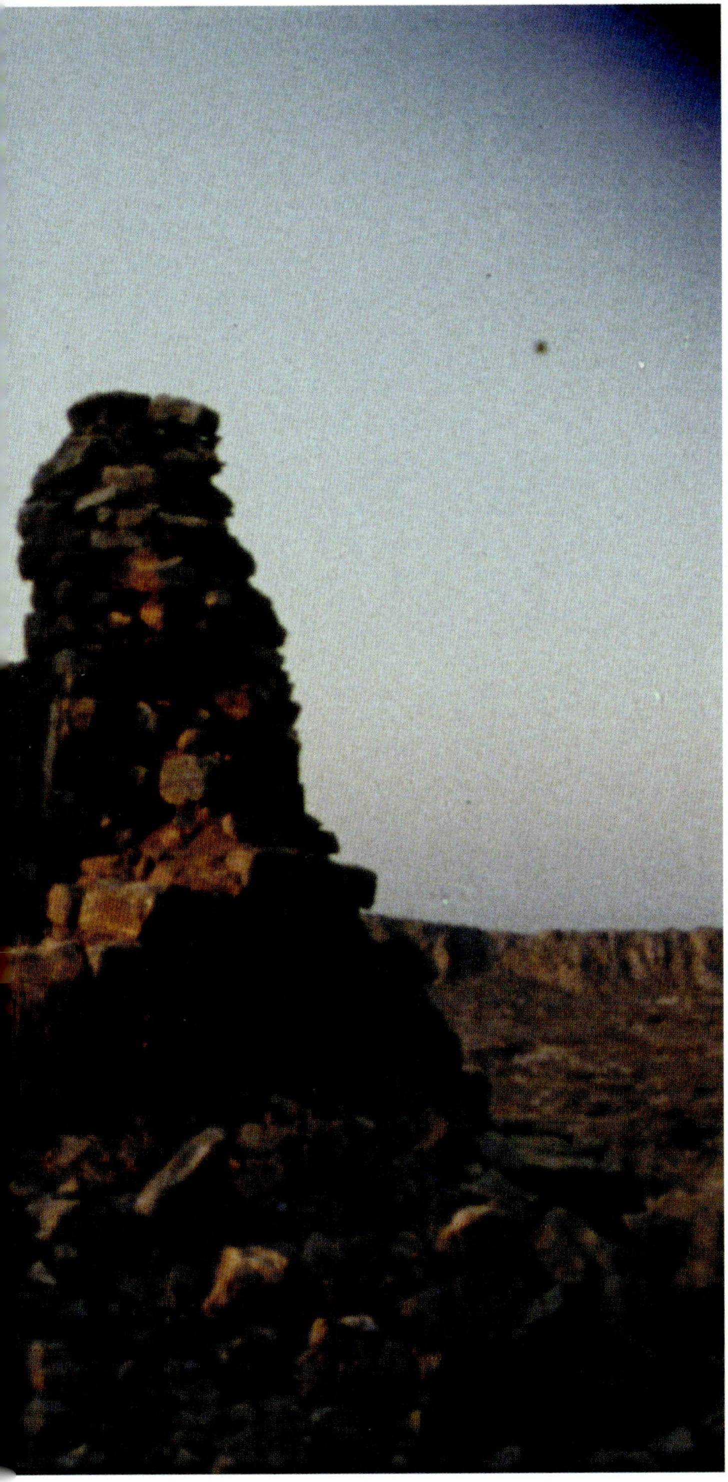

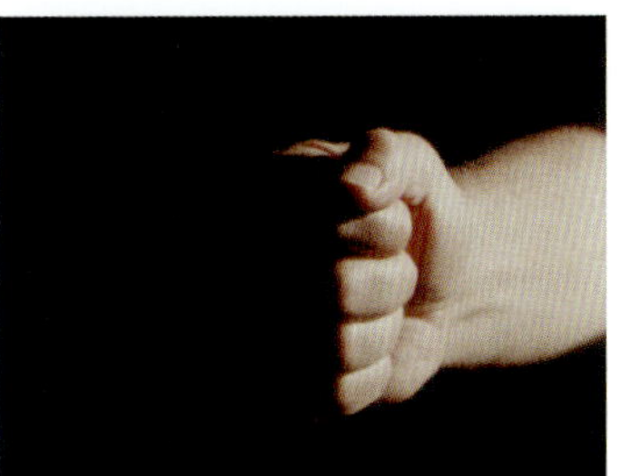

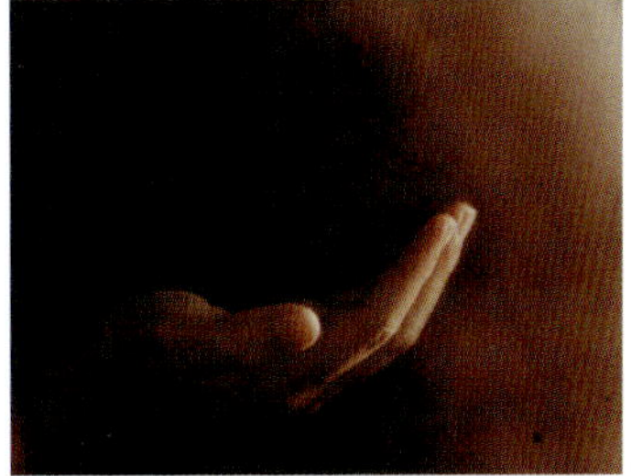

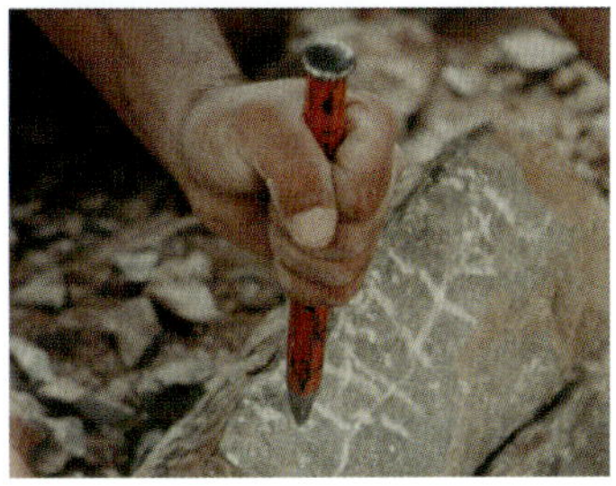

*The Ground* (1993–2001)

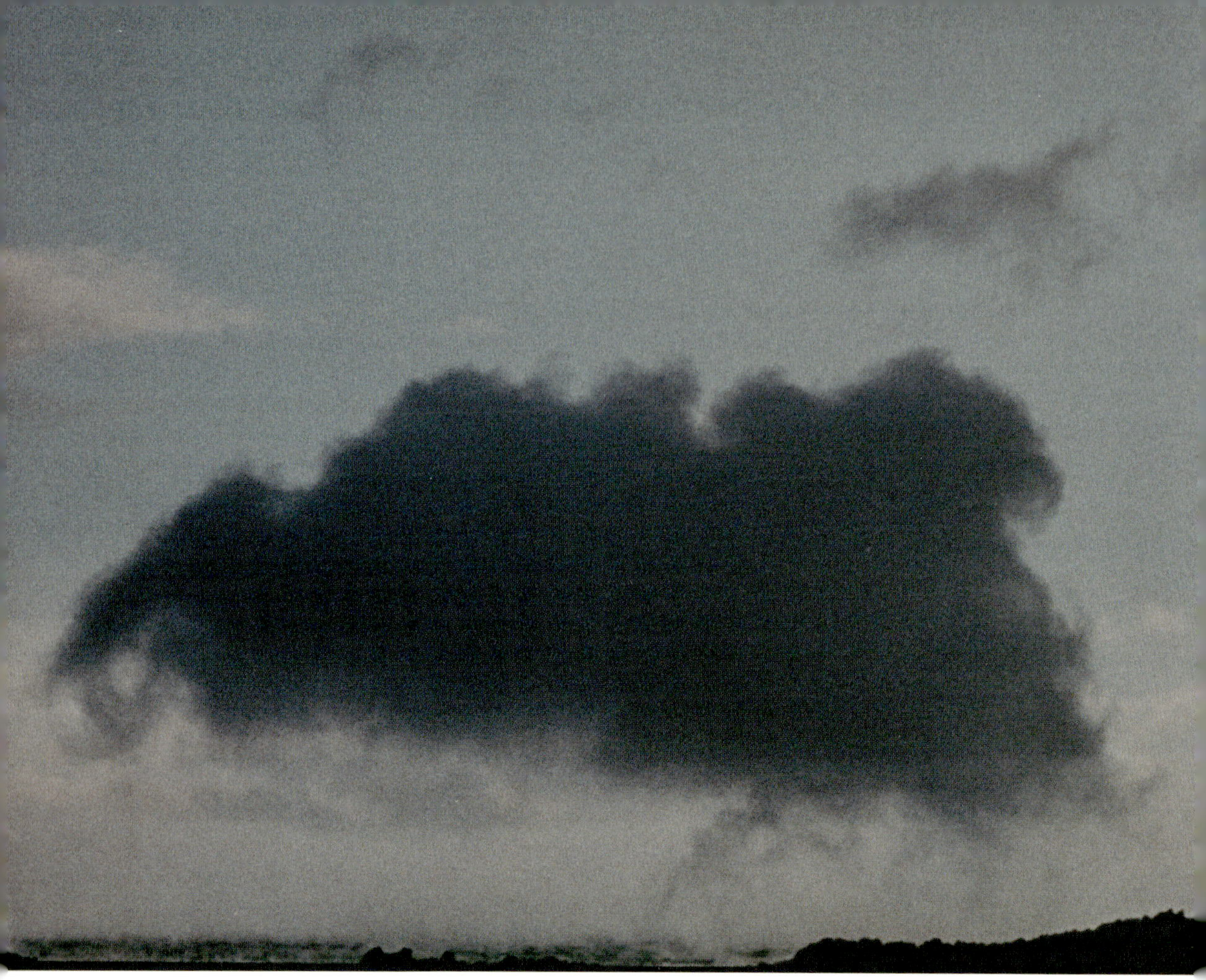

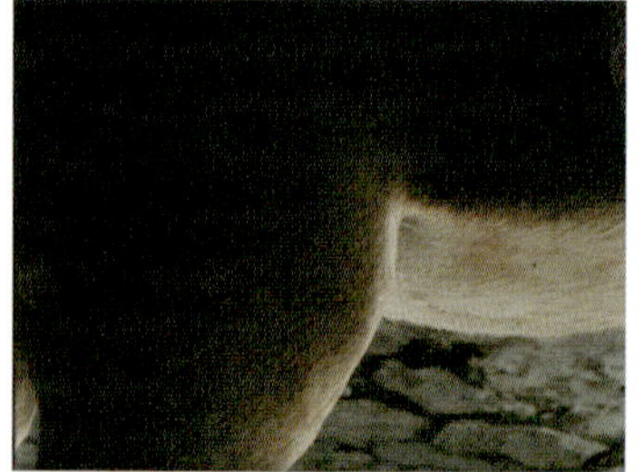

*The Ground* (1993–2001)

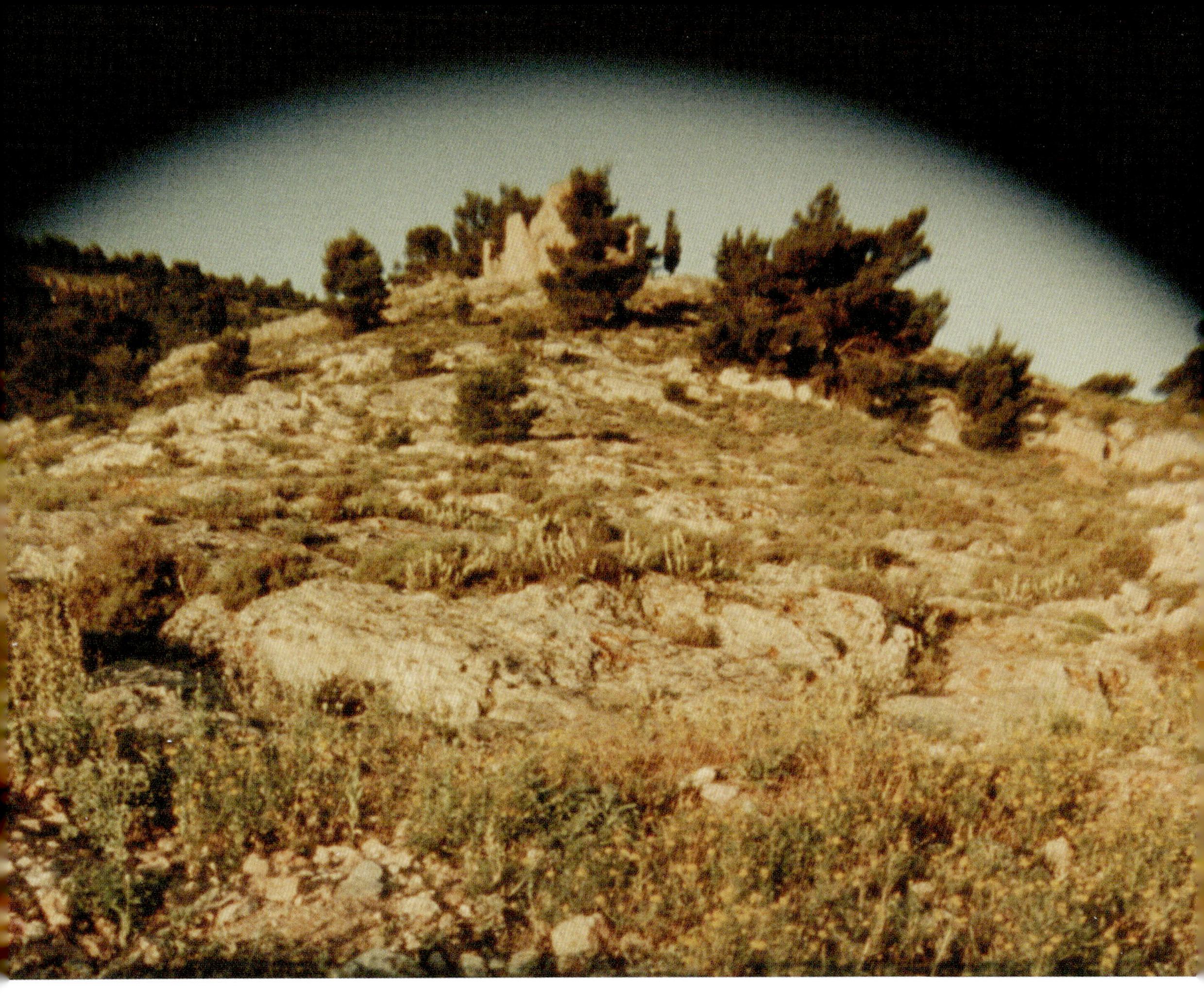

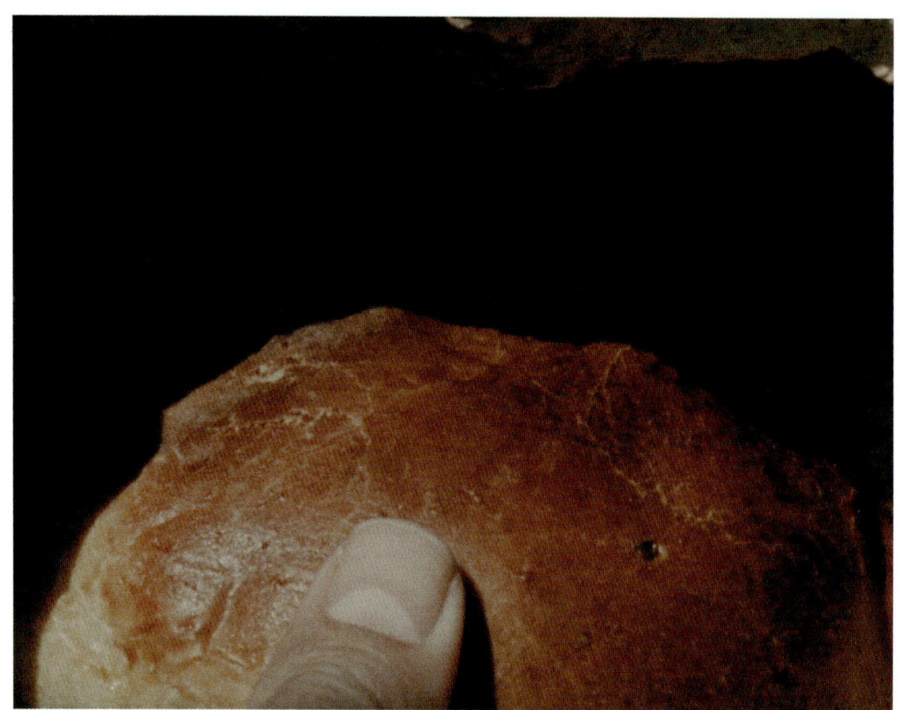

*The Ground* (1993–2001)

## MAGIC WHEEL

Since 2004, Beavers has hosted five Temenos events in Arcadia, bringing newly restored cycles of Markopoulos's *Eniaios* to its first audiences. During the most recent event—in June 2022—I read *Vegetation* by Francis Ponge, the French "poet of things" whose work Beavers has long admired. Ponge's language of vegetal explosion—"foliage fades, leaving fruit, globular seeds, suspended in the air—like the heavens, stars, celestial bodies—those provisions of life (cut off from the previous life that spawned them), those bombs that will go off and disseminate in good time and if need be"—seemed an exact description of Arcadian vegetation in June.[63] One sees blossoms, berries, and leaves in every life phase on a single plant: darts, fruits, husks. Ponge's words also called to mind Beavers's *Wingseed* (1985), a film that dramatizes and eroticizes poetic heat in Greek botanical form.[64] Creased and crinkled weeds and wildflowers shot in Anavyssos—spiral stems and white and ecru pinwheels and lace-stars—shake and vibrate in bursts of rapid back-and-forth motion, mimicking the film's "vibrant ostinato": a crescendoing mélange of goats' bells, shepherd's calls, and the sounds of a flute.[65] The filmmaker is releasing their seeds. "The power of Greek nature, the heat, can produce particular kinds of forms and movements. Coiled forms pop open—if the climate were wetter, they wouldn't—and seeds fly out, carried by the wind. I was playing with the idea of fructification, the strength to produce fruit," Beavers said.

In 1983, in his first *Wingseed* notes, Beavers listed "three heroes" bound by fire—Borromini, Heraclitus, and Gerard Manley Hopkins. The exterior lantern of Borromini's Sant'Ivo alla Sapienza culminates in a flame-shaped iron structure, and in "That Nature Is a Heraclitean Fire and of the comfort of the Resurrection," Hopkins copes with the pre-Socratic philosopher's vision of damning fire at the world's origin and end, and finds solace in the compound identity of resurrected Jesus, mortal and eternal. A "diamond" delivered at the poem's conclusion figures this "comfort": carbon atoms redeemed from ash, pressured and heated into form. The heat of creation takes another form in Beavers's *Wingseed* notes a year later: excerpts from *A Glossary of Greek Birds* (given to him by Markopoulos) about the *iynx*, an ancient love charm. Composed of disks with punched-out holes for string, the magic wheel spins and emits sound when the string is wound and released. Eros used the charm to draw out passion or unite lovers. Like botanical dissemination and generation, the *iynx* theatricalizes erotic extension and delivery across heated space.

Struck by the overlap in these images of creative birth (diamond, fruit, Eros), I asked Beavers if the visible drama of Greek nature—trajectories of becoming, explosion, and disappearance—was fundamental to his poetic perspective. "I know nothing about botany," he replied. Instead, he pointed away from forms and toward another "poet of things"—Russian writer Osip Mandelstam. "I wouldn't say nature as much as light. The famous light in Greece opens processes of thinking differently—thought comes differently because of the light. That has been a constant thought ever since I was eighteen." "So you've been able to hold on to that potential outside of Greek light? It introduced your mind to something?" I asked.

**Yes, definitely. *Hellenism* is a rarefied word, but I still think it exists. [Earlier this year], soon after I finished my newest film, *The Sparrow Dream*, I was reading Osip Mandelstam's essays. He makes a very interesting statement. He says Hellenism changes very neutral objects into utensils, and gives the utensil a soul that the object doesn't have. He says that any person who sits near an oven and feels the warmth of it knows the warmth of Hellenism. It's an astonishing paragraph.**

In his 1922 essay "On the Nature of the Word," Mandelstam writes:

**Hellenism is an earthenware pot, oven tongs, a milk jug, kitchen utensils, dishes; it is anything which surrounds the body. Hellenism is the warmth of the hearth experienced as something sacred; it is anything which imparts some of the external world to man. . . . Hellenism is the conscious surrounding of man with domestic utensils instead of impersonal objects; the transformation of impersonal objects into domestic utensils, and the humanizing and warming of the surrounding world with the most delicate teleological warmth. Hellenism is any kind of stove near which a man sits, treasuring its heat as something akin to his own internal body heat. . . . Hellenism is a system, in the Bergsonian sense of the term, which man unfolds around himself, like a fan of phenomena freed of their temporal dependence, phenomena subjected through the human 'I' to an inner connection.**[66]

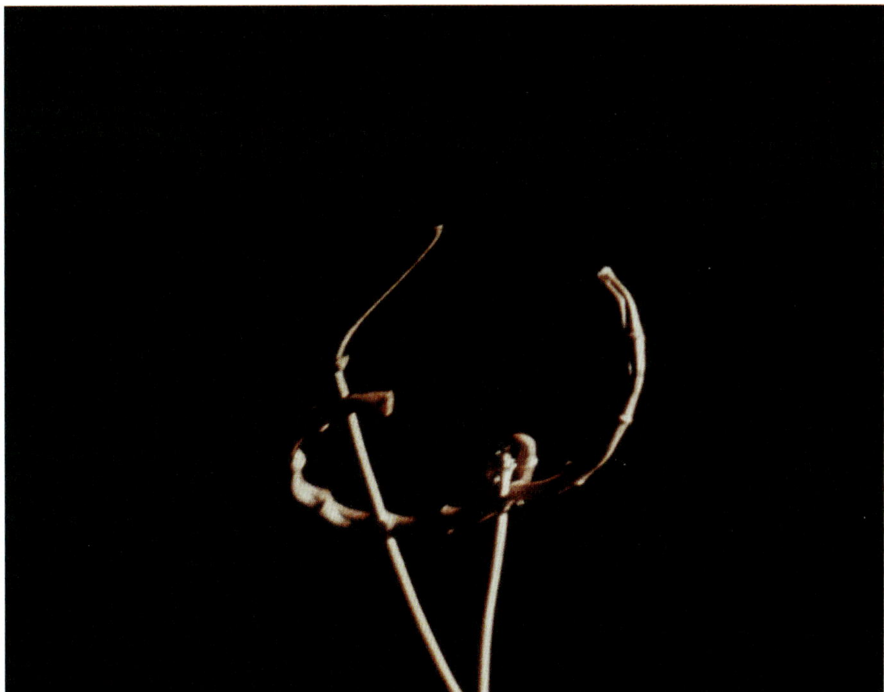

*Wingseed* (1985)

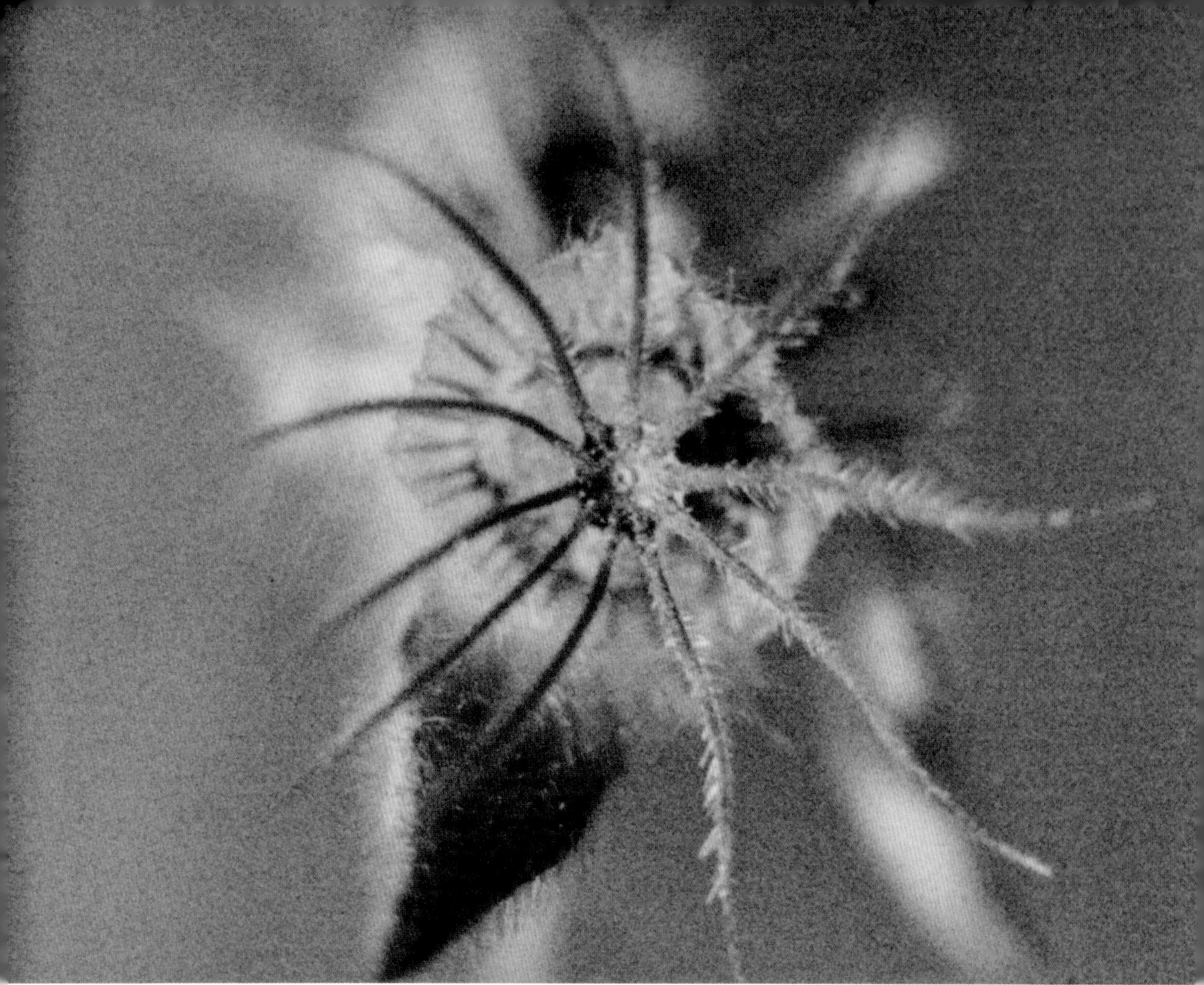

*Wingseed* (1985)

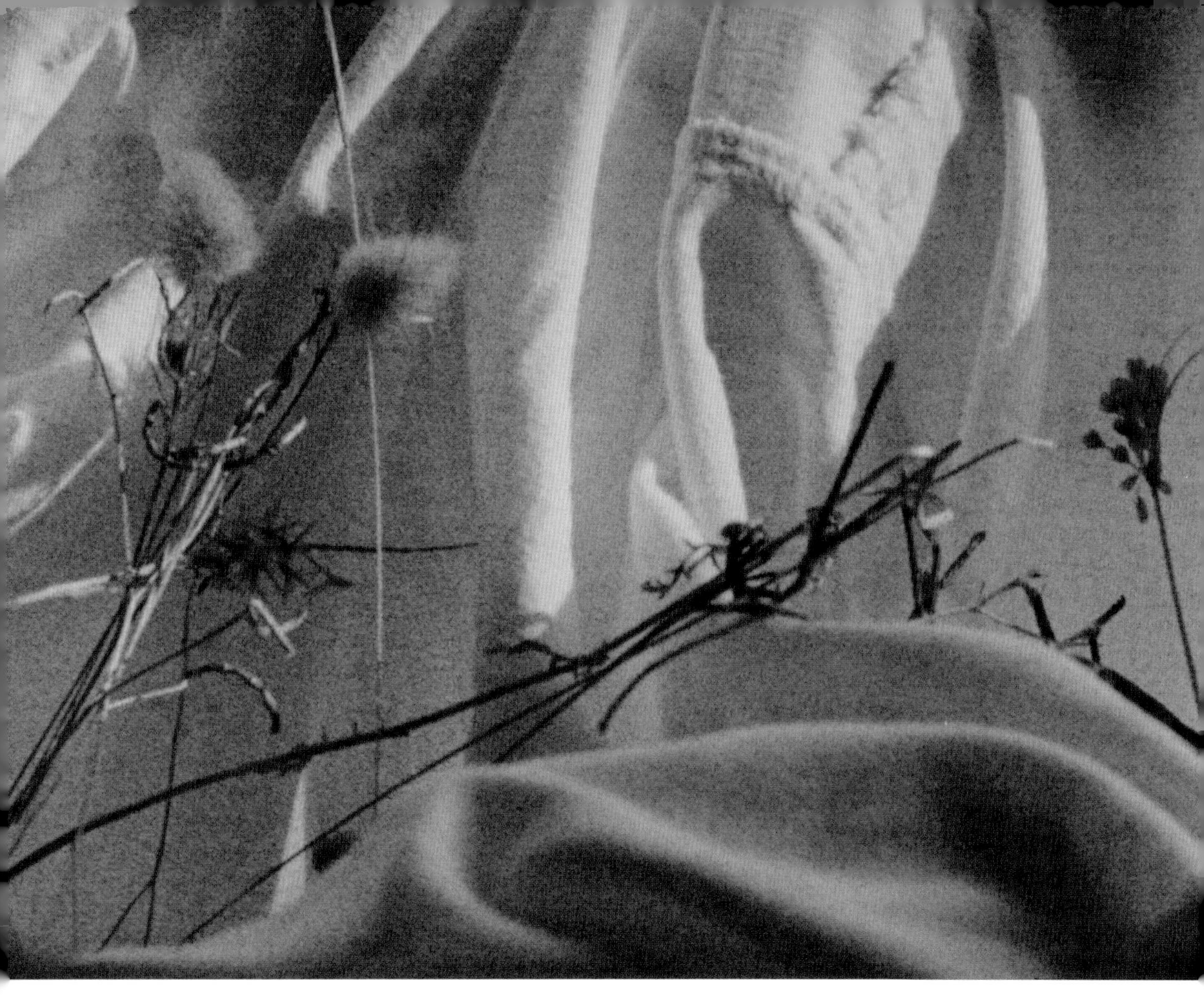

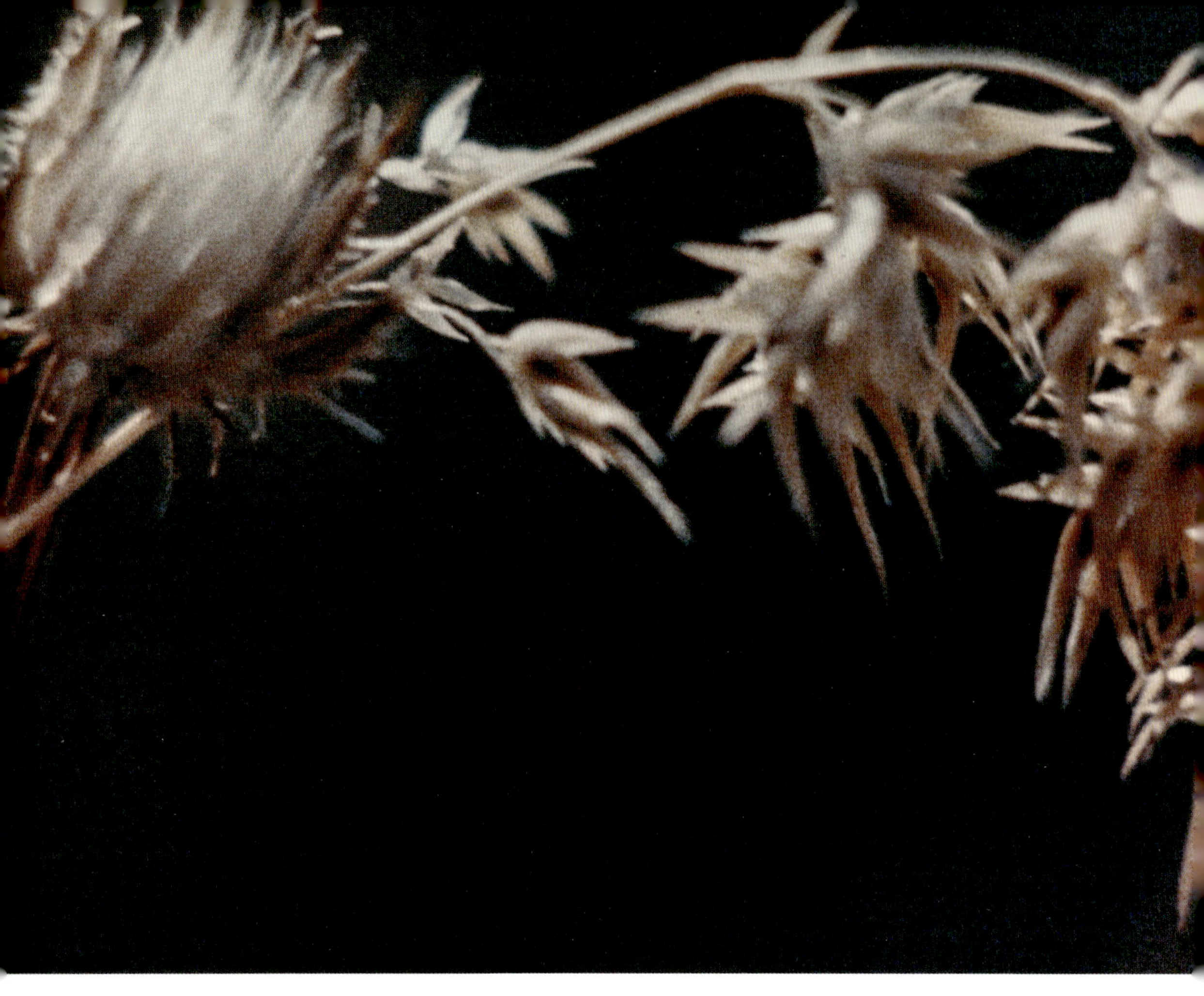

*Wingseed* (1985)

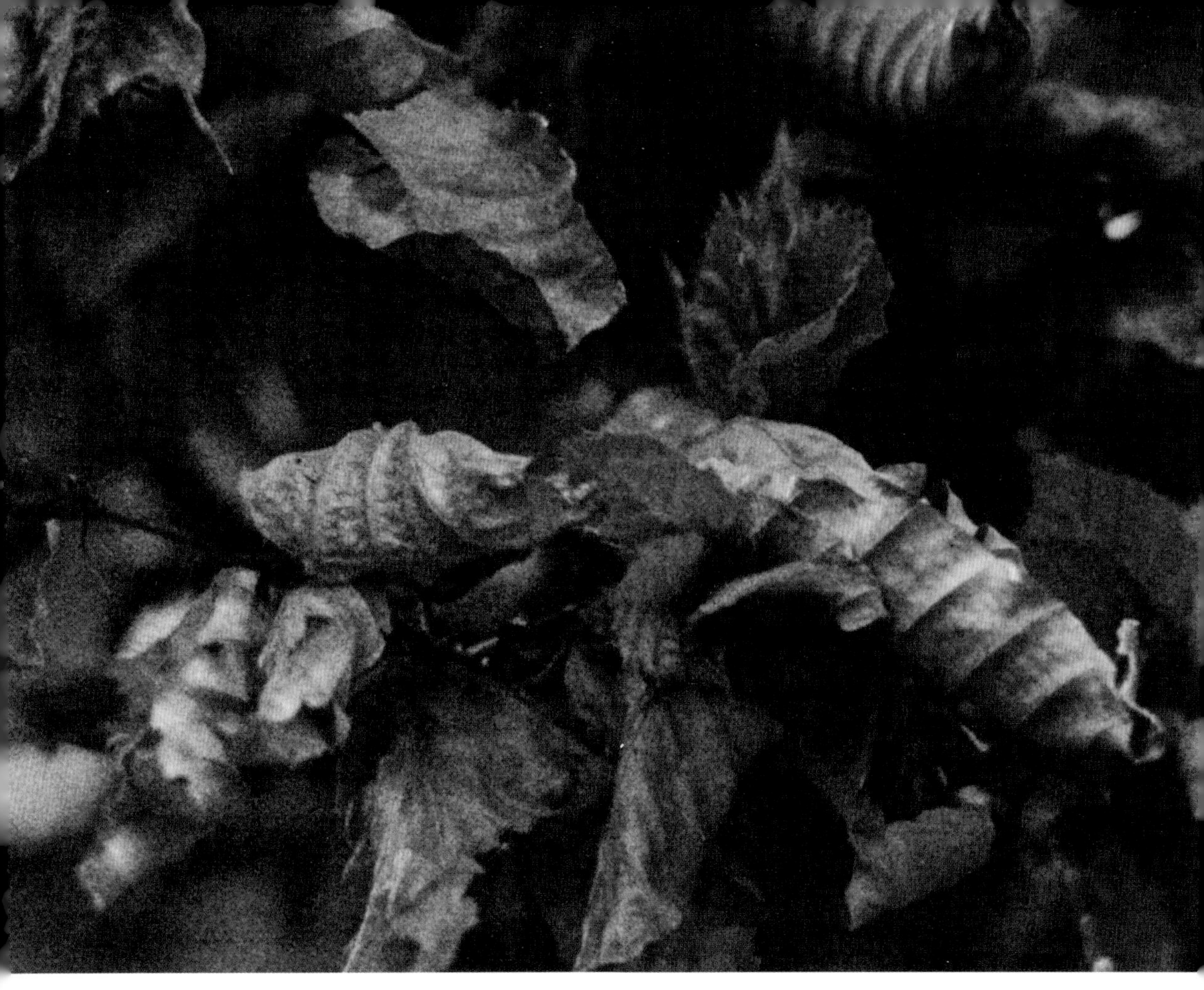

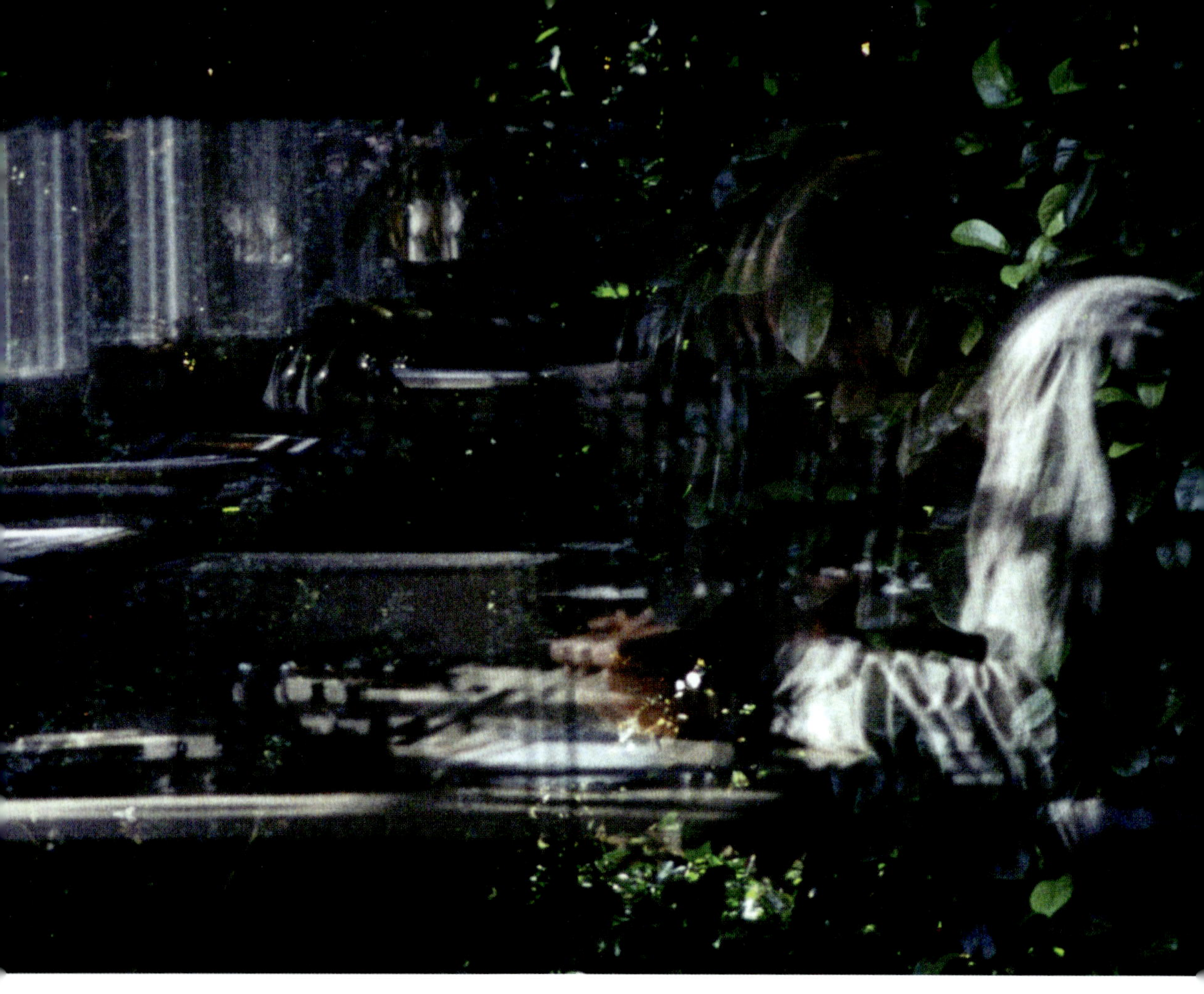

*Listening to the Space in My Room* (2013)

# NEW LEAF

# 7

A filmography presents a singular progressive sequence. Since completing *My Hand Outstretched to the Winged Distance and Sightless Measure* in 2002, Beavers has made six new films: *Pitcher of Colored Light* (2007), *The Suppliant* (2010), *Listening to the Space in My Room* (2013), *Among the Eucalyptuses* (2017), *"Der Klang, die Welt . . ."* (2018), and *The Sparrow Dream* (2022). But when I met with Beavers in July 2022 to discuss his post-cycle filmmaking, he emphasized overlap, simultaneity, and the inseparability of the work of this period from seismic shifts in his own life circumstances (see full interview on page 259).

"Gregory's later years were incredibly stressful, very difficult—and expensive," he said. Between 1992 and 2002, Beavers set a new course for the future of his and his late partner's work: he removed their materials from Basel bank vault storage, established the Temenos Archive in Zurich (first on Badenerstrasse and then in Uster, in industrial spaces donated by Swiss art collectors Thomas and Ruedi Bechtler), and began to show their films again. In 1994, Swiss entrepreneur Ulrich Straub offered Beavers a place to live in Zug for five years.[1] "Living on one floor of a very old farmhouse for free was the opposite of living in hotels and pensions. Between no rent and creating the archive space and not-for-profits [Beavers established the Temenos, Inc. in New York City in 1995 and the Temenos Association in Zurich in 1999], it was a big shift. All of that happened in the first ten years after Gregory's death. I also came back into contact with friends from my youth, some of whom were extremely helpful during this period. Life opened up."

In 2000, as he completed his *Hand Outstretched* soundtracks at sound designer Christian Beusch's studio in Egg, Switzerland, Beavers also began filming at his mother's house in Falmouth, Massachusetts, his friend Jacques Dehornois's Brooklyn, New York, apartment and in Piraeus and Nafplion, Greece, generating material for what would become *Pitcher of Colored Light*, *The Suppliant*, and *Among the Eucalyptuses*. "For a long time, I lived without a permanent residence—and these films are situated in the places where I frequently stayed as I moved between Europe and the United States, setting up new structures for the archive and our films."

In 2001, Beavers moved to a house in the village of Zumikon, Switzerland, in order to be closer to the sound studio in Egg. For a decade, he lived below his elderly landlords, Cécile and Dieter Staehelin, a retired physician and cellist/composer. Between 2008 and 2011, he shot the linked *Listening to the Space in My Room* and *"Der Klang, die Welt . . ."* with the Staehelins in the Zumikon house. And his most recent film, *The Sparrow Dream*, shot from 2015 to 2020, moves between Berlin (where Beavers has lived with his partner, German filmmaker Ute Aurand, since 2011) and Massachusetts (at his mother's empty Falmouth house and South Shore nursing home)—a realization, perhaps, of an intention he expressed in a 1970 note: "When in the U.S. I hope to begin a project that will gather the American and European parts together."

The films of this period are lyrical offerings of gratitude, studies of shifting residence (of place and psyche), and portraits of relationality.[2] At the 2019 Punto de Vista Film Festival, in Pamplona, Spain, Beavers titled a program of his post-cycle films "A Guest in the World." In his screening notes, he included a poem composed by Hadrian on his deathbed in 138 CE:

animula vagula blandula
hospes comesque corporis
quae nunc abibis? In loca
pallidula rigida nudula
nec ut soles dabis iocos

Little soul, you charming little wanderer,
my body's guest and partner.
where are you off to now?
Somewhere without color, savage and bare;
you'll crack no more of your jokes once you're there.[3]

**Pitcher of Colored Light, 2007, 23 min.**

I have filmed my mother's house and her garden in East Falmouth, Massachusetts. The shadows play an essential part in the mixture of loneliness and peace that exists here. The seasons move from the garden into the house, projecting rich diagonals in the early morning or late afternoon. Each shadow is a subtle balance of stillness and movement; it shows the vital instability of space. Its special quality opens a passage to the subjective; a voice within the film speaks to memory. The walls are screens through which I pass to the inhabited privacy. We experience a place through the perspective of where we come from and hear another's voice through our own acoustic. The sense of place is never separate from the moment.

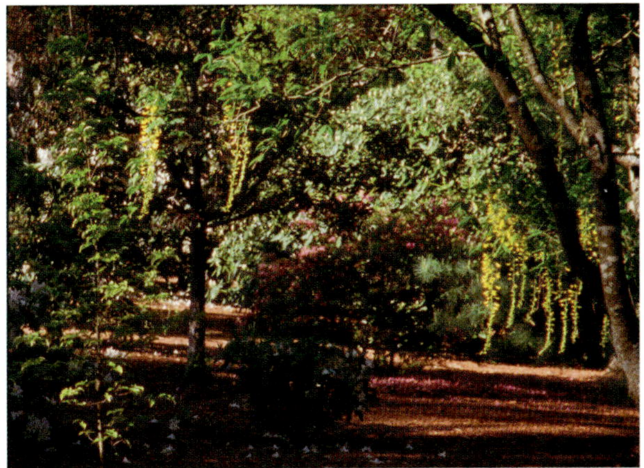

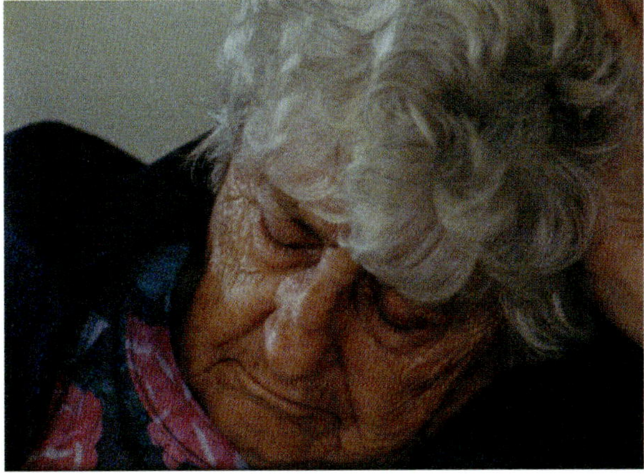

*Pitcher of Colored Light* (2007)

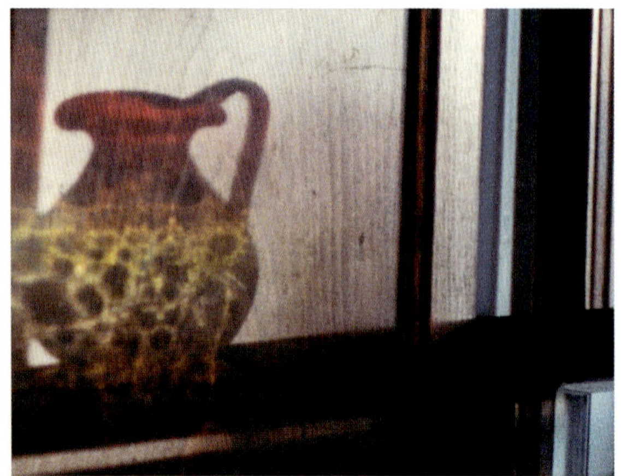

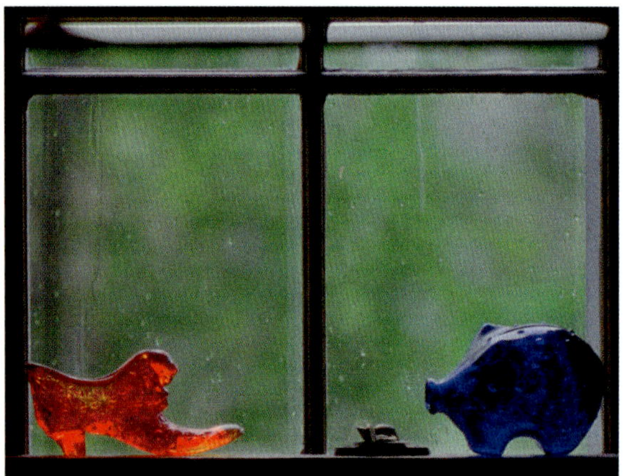

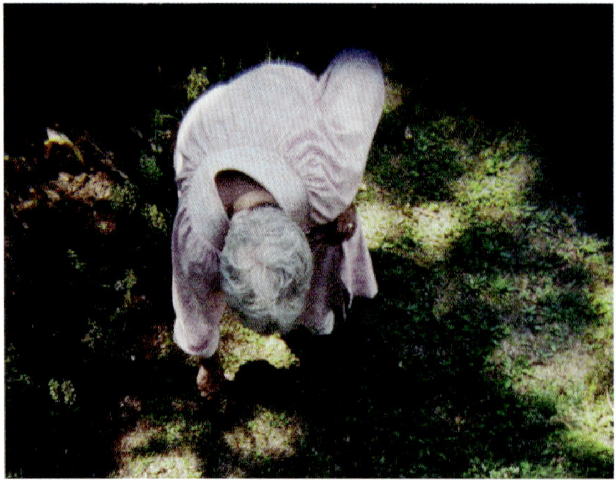

*Pitcher of Colored Light* (2007)

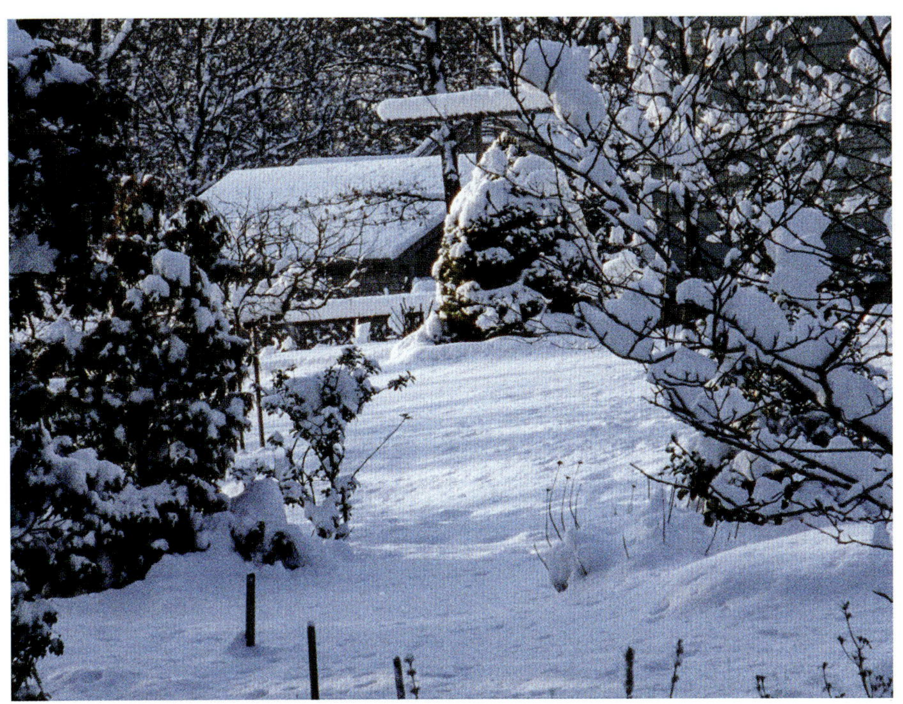

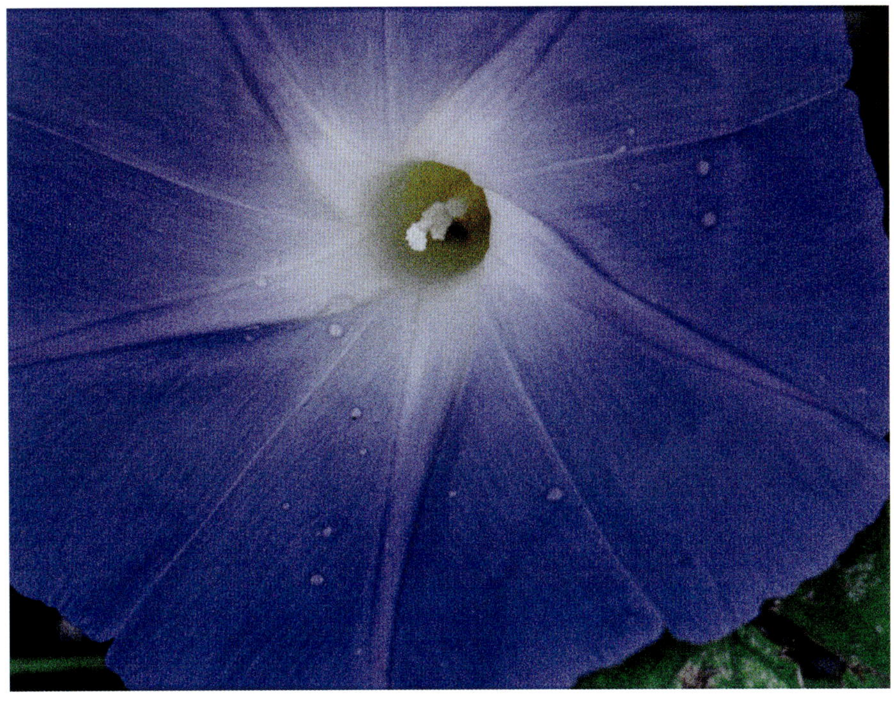

### The Suppliant, 2010, 5 min.

My filming for *The Suppliant* was done in February 2003, while a guest in the Brooklyn Heights apartment of Jacques Dehornois. When I recollect the impulse for this filming, I remember my desire to show a spiritual quality united to the sensual in my view of this small Greek statue. I chose to reveal the figure solely through its blue early morning highlights and in the orange sunlight of late afternoon. After filming the statue, I walked down to the East River and continued to film near the Manhattan Bridge and the electrical works; then I returned to the apartment and filmed a few other details. I set this film material aside, while continuing to film and edit *Pitcher of Colored Light*; later I took it up twice to edit but could not find my way. Most of the editing was finally done in 2009; then I waited to see whether it was finished and found that it was not. The last image, of a bird in the trees, was filmed from the window of my apartment in Berlin. In May 2010, I made several editing changes and created the soundtrack with thoughts of this friend's recent death.

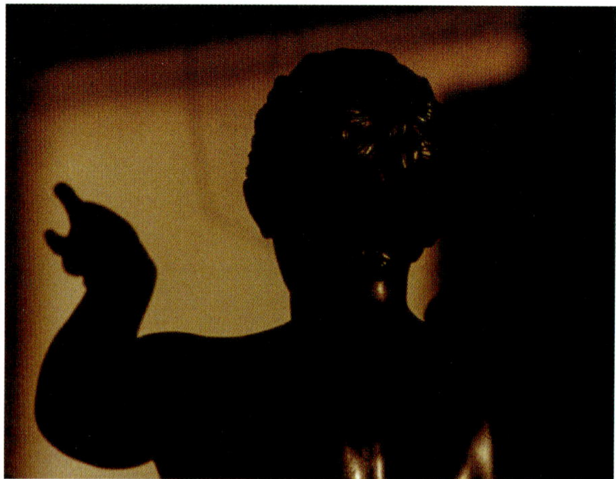

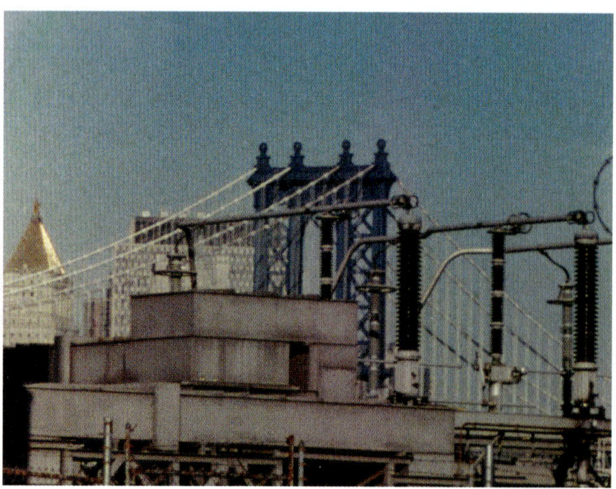

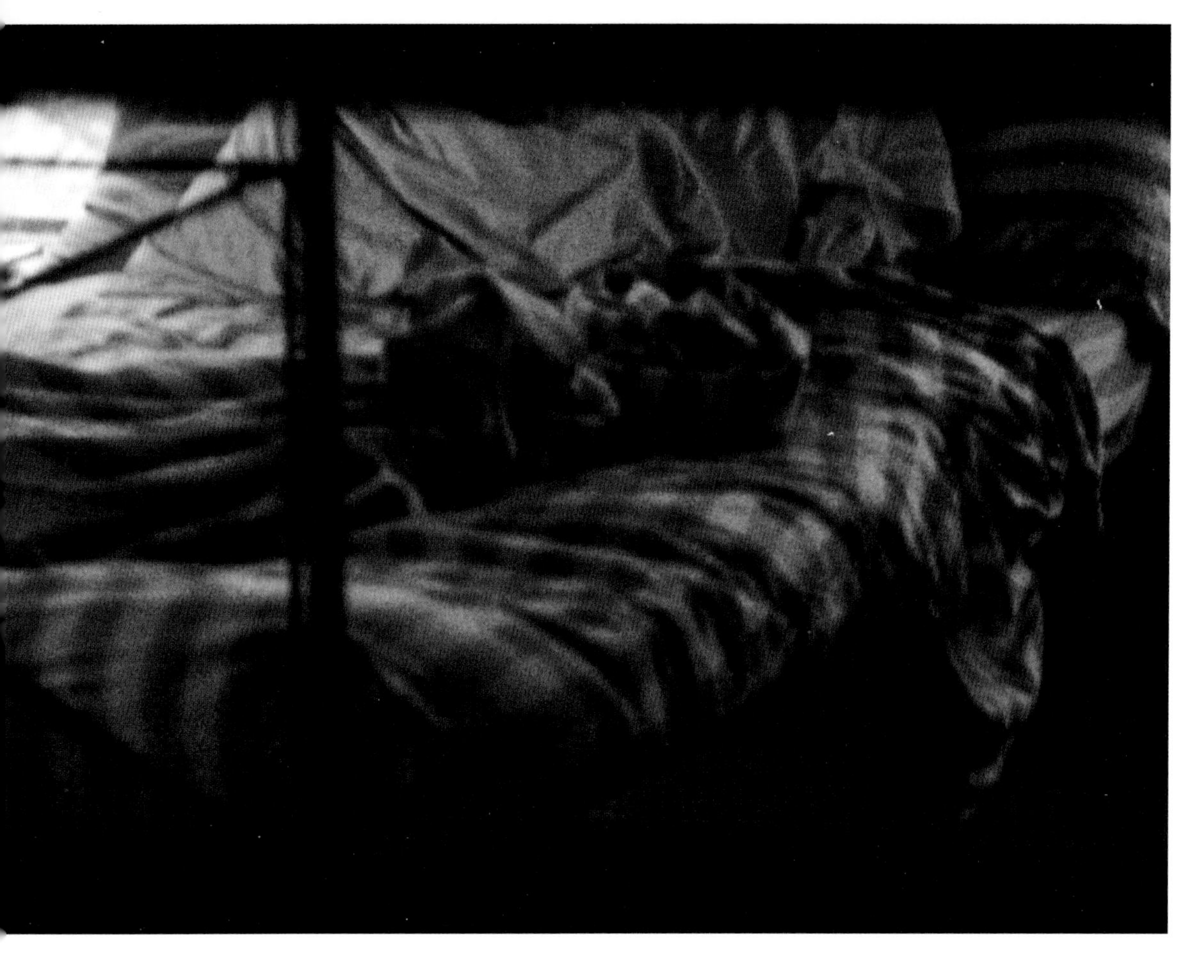

*The Suppliant* (2010)

**Listening to the Space in My Room, 2013, 19 min.**

Cécile and Dieter Staehelin's house in Zumikon, Switzerland, resonates with the daily rhythms of his cello practice and her housekeeping. Cécile's extreme reduction of the housekeeping to essentials is the ethical counterpart to the nature in her garden. Dieter's music practice in the morning or later in the day was my example of an artist in conversation with death, what he called "waiting in the antechamber." My own movements in the ground-floor apartment below them—the shifts in perspective, the sudden turns in a different direction, or passing a threshold to the outdoors—are a constant questioning.

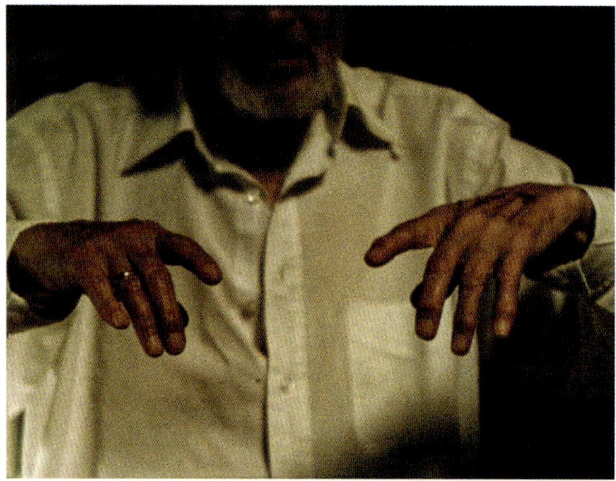

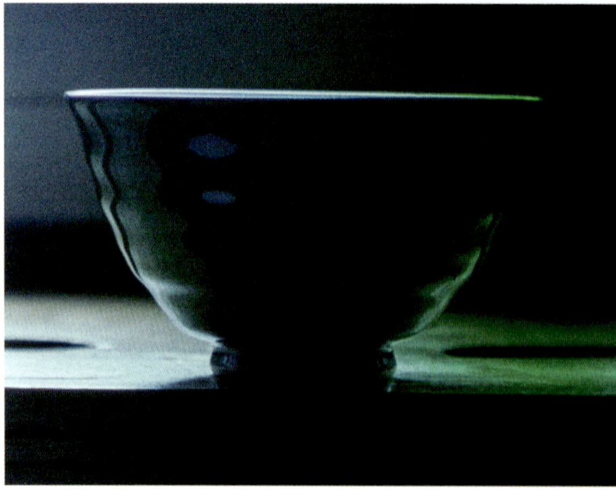

*Listening to the Space in My Room* (2013)

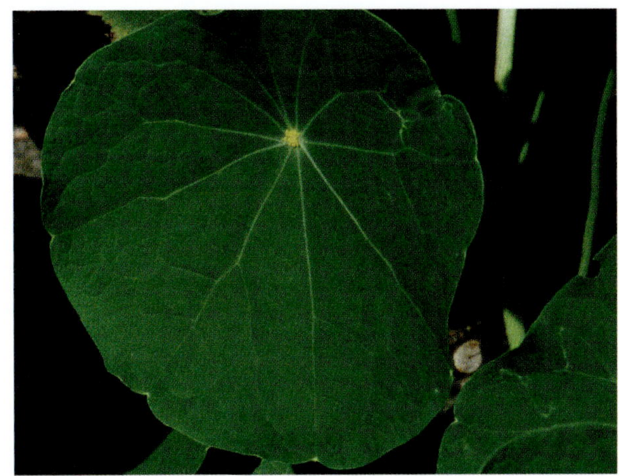

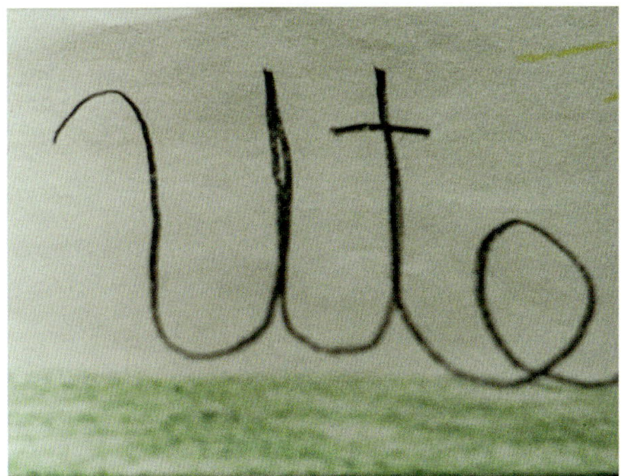
Ute

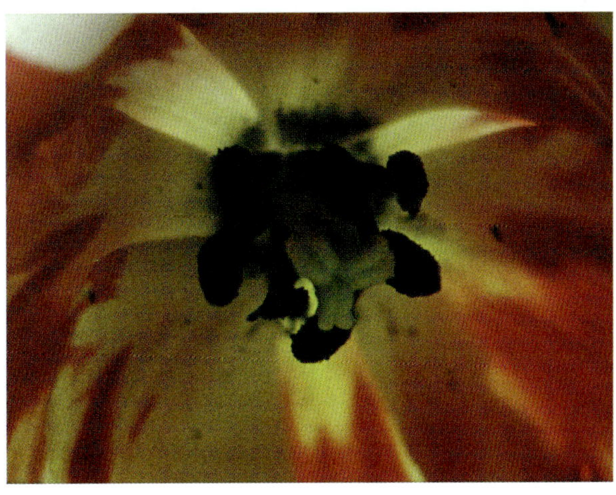

**Among the Eucalyptuses, 2017, 4 min. (filmed ca. 2002, edited 2017)**

Late afternoon quiet and a silent figure seated on a bench; the old factories and machinery, warehouses, and train lines are part of a Greece now disappearing.

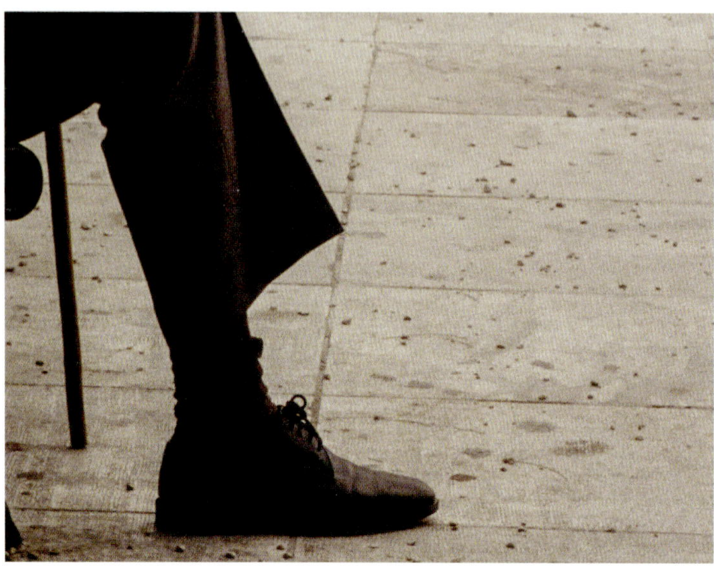

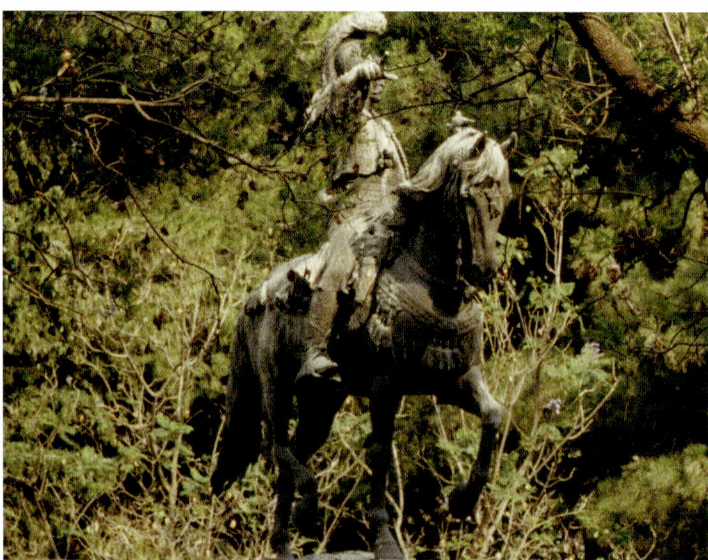

*Among the Eucalyptuses* (2017)

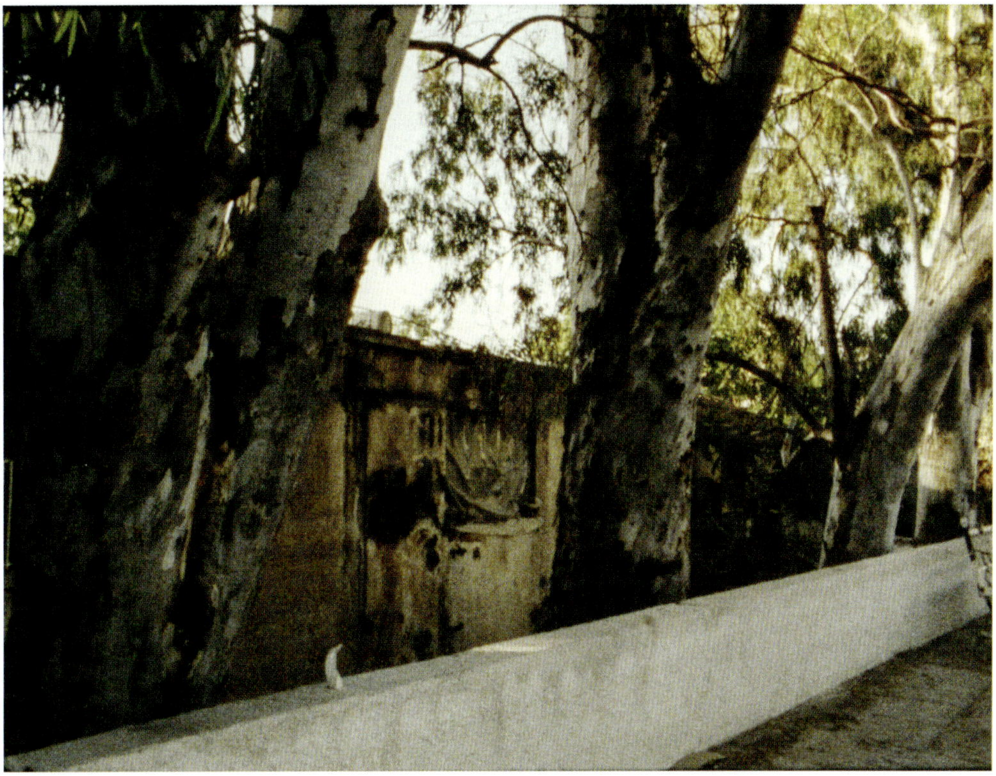

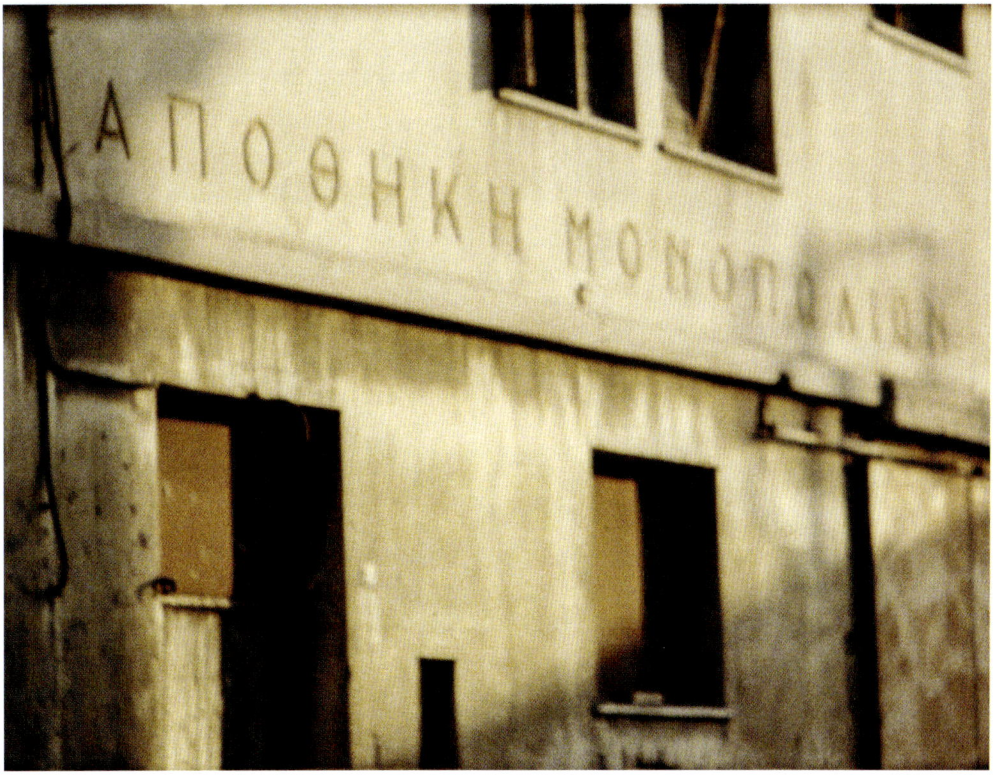

ΑΠΟΘΗΚΗ ΜΟΝΟΠΩΛΙΟΥ

### *"Der Klang, die Welt . . ."*, 2018, 4.5 min.

Filmed in the same site as *Listening to the Space in My Room*, *"Der Klang, die Welt . . ."* was intended as a gift to Cécile Staehelin, who lived alone in the house following the death of her husband, Dieter. I shot the material before Dieter died—he speaks about the place of music in his life, and we see him and Cécile playing an *Arabesque* by Bohuslav Martinů. Cécile had once told me of her wish that her life end like the last notes in this piece of music.

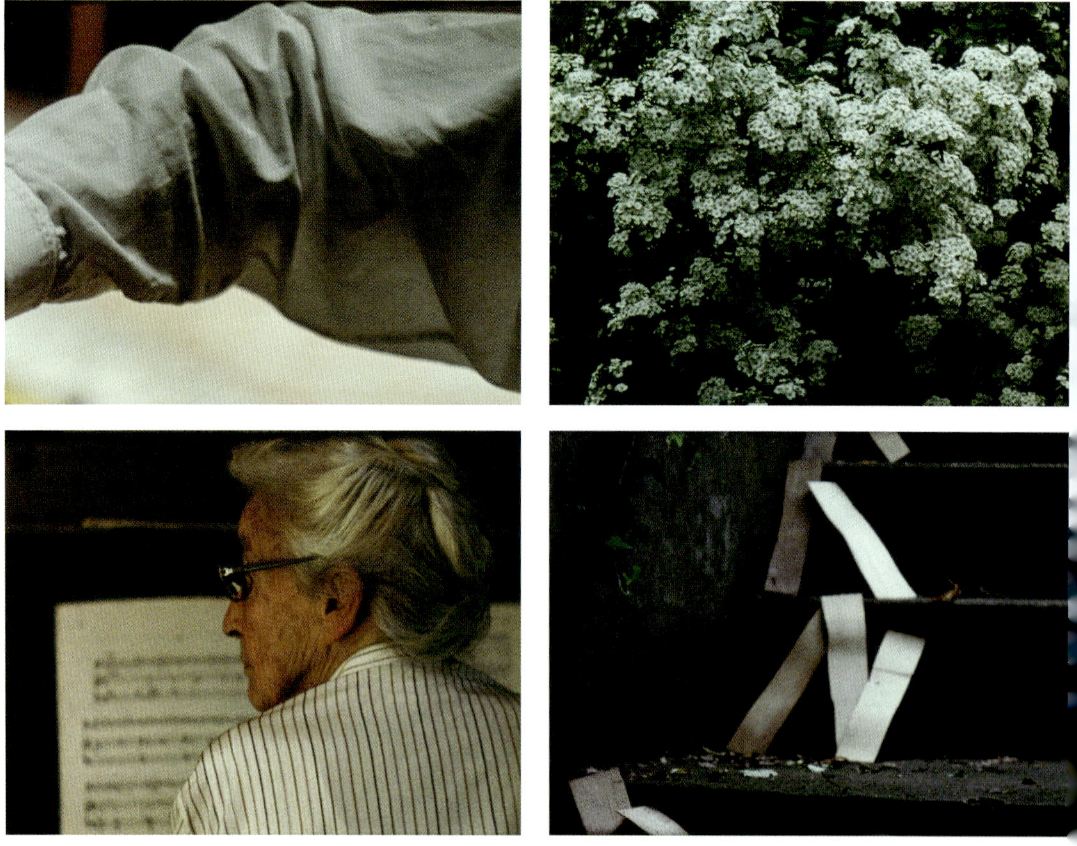

*"Der Klang, die Welt . . ."* (2018)

**The Sparrow Dream, 2022, 29 min.**

My starting point was a question about how the places where I have lived have influenced how I see.

I returned to one or two locations in Berlin that I had filmed for *Diminished Frame* in 1970. One was the milestone opposite Schloss Charlottenburg. In 1970, the milestone stood as a somber sphere topped by a Prussian spike, filmed in black-and-white; now I see it as a golden globe surrounded by regenerate leaves with a view to Fortuna. I also found a version of the statue that I had filmed in Brooklyn in 2002 for *The Suppliant* standing in Leopoldplatz.

Filming in Berlin and Massachusetts: The turning pages of a child's version of the *Odyssey* and the site of a Korean War monument in my hometown, Weymouth, suggest different sides of the same subject: *nostos* or homecoming. The vision of Greece, first awakened in my childhood, remains a source. Despite different histories, one culture reflects another.

"Why have I returned to film these places, which I left so many years ago?"

"For the deep view it gives now."

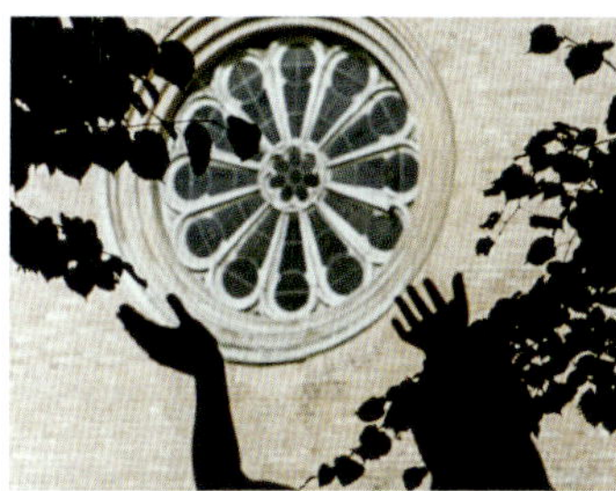

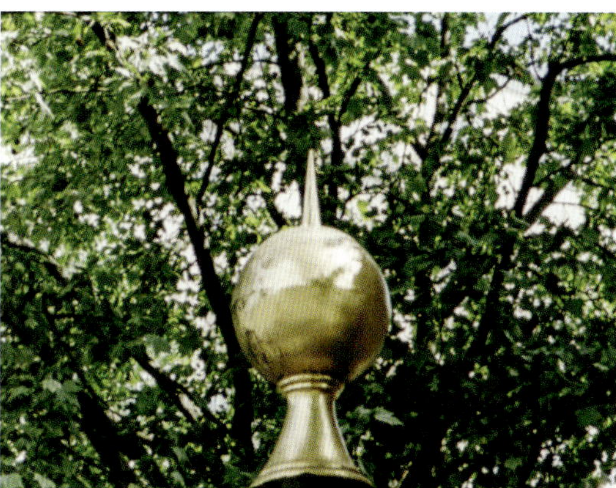

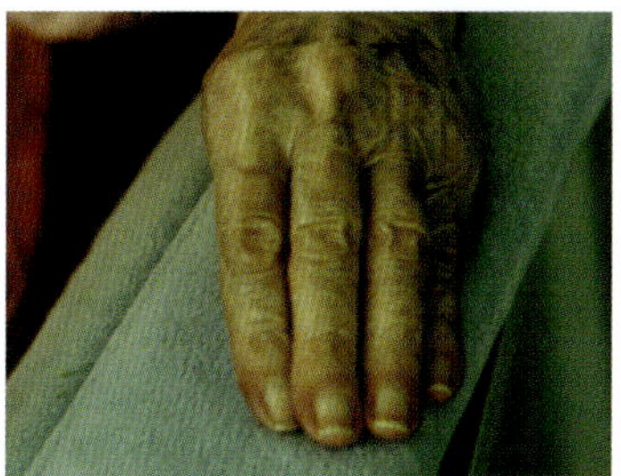

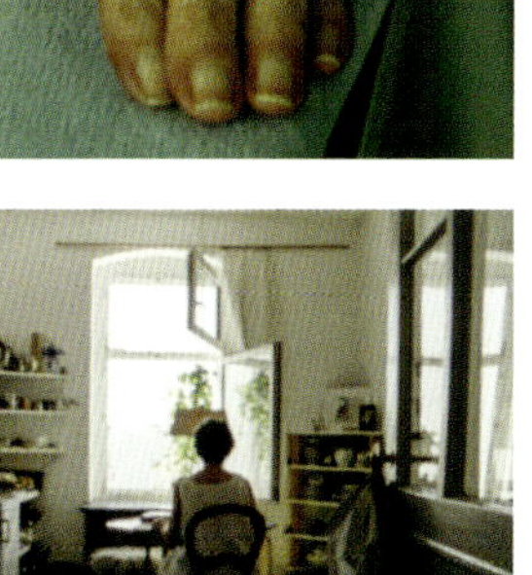

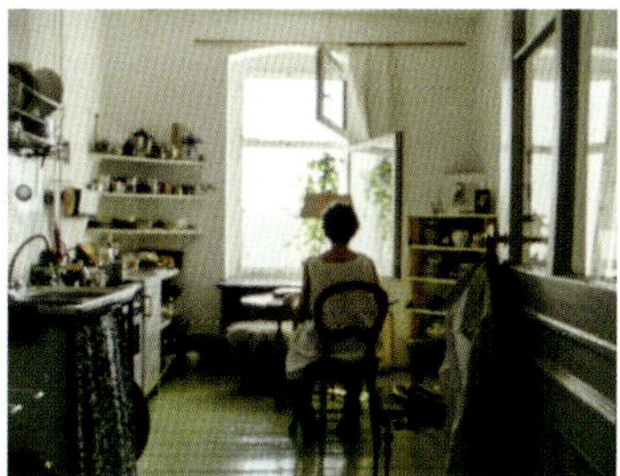

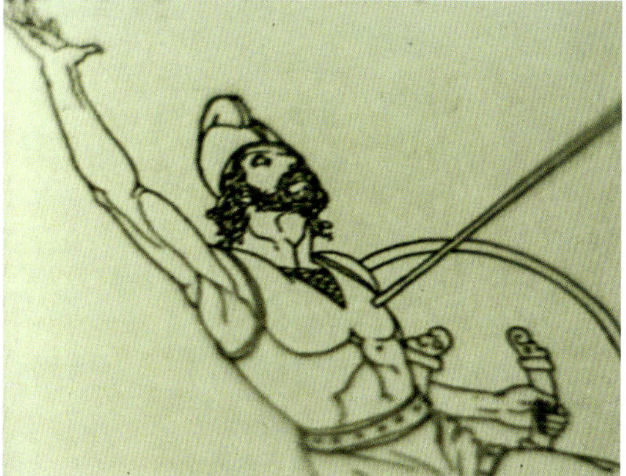

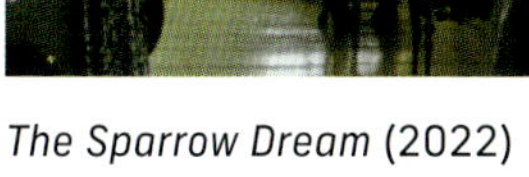

*The Sparrow Dream* (2022)

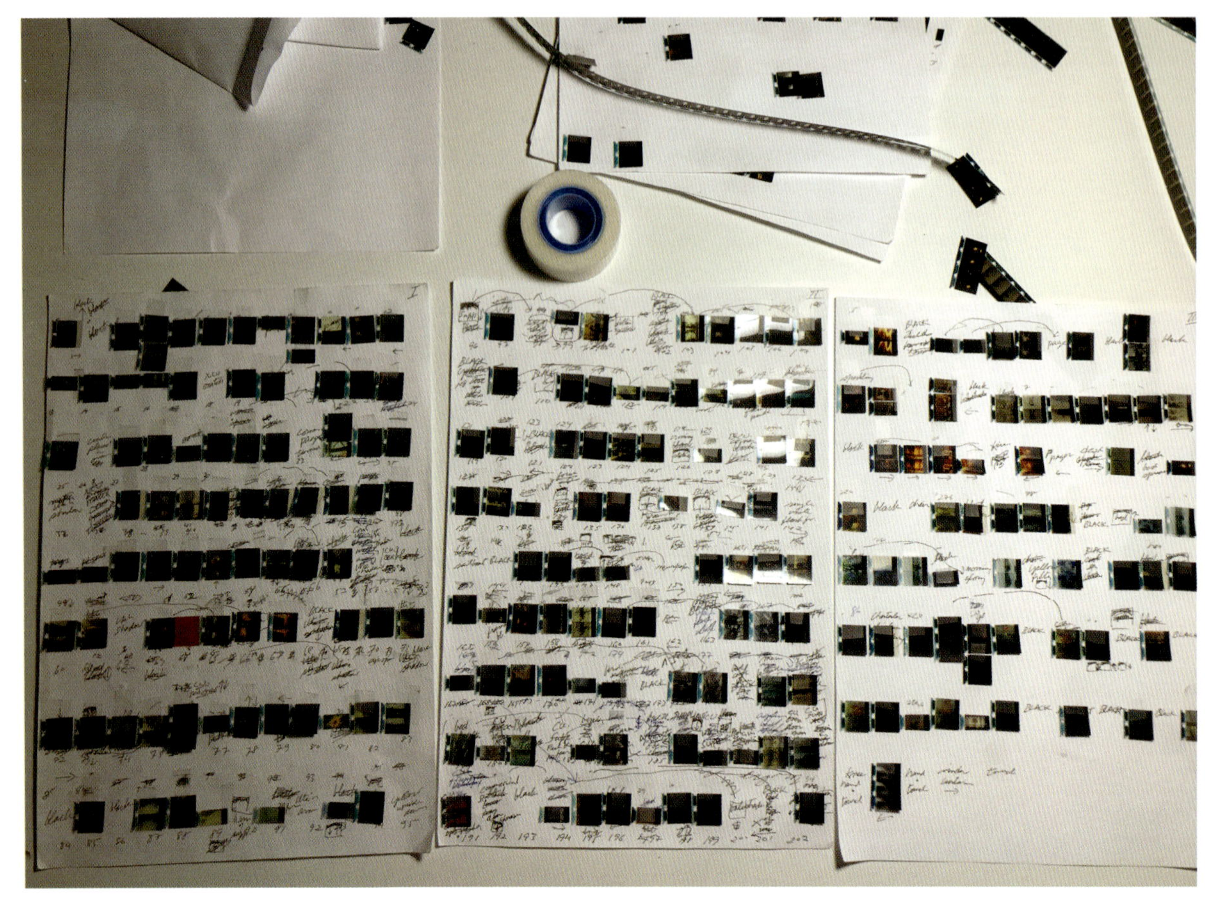

Editing pages for *The Sparrow Dream*

## Embrace of Color

**Q:** Following the restricted palette of *The Ground*, associative color regains a primary role in *Pitcher of Colored Light* and *Listening to the Space in My Room*—much of it carried by the plants and flowers in your mother and Cécile's gardens: azalea, hibiscus, hydrangea, and dogwood in East Falmouth, and sunflower, aster, kosmea, and nasturtium in Zumikon. Colored filter use returns in *Listening* as well. You used the phrase "greeting mortality" to describe the films of the last two decades, and wrote, "The ascetic direction is matched by a force drawing me back into life."[4] Does color play a role in this life-death dialectic?

**A:** Beginning with *Winged Dialogue* through *The Ground*, the source of my filmmaking was a particular way of living, my life with Gregory. The completion of the cycle was the end of an entire way of life. I knew it would be impossible to repeat what I had been doing—it would be bad for my filmmaking. At that moment, I could choose to stop making films or to change.

I became freer in my filmmaking—I used the camera differently; I was less reliant on the tripod or the centrally composed shot. And yes, I felt that I needed to return to color to express emotion and the psyche. In *Pitcher* I was interested in an unfolding of color across the whole film through the flowers; I wanted to bring this exterior color into the darker interior spaces of the house. Color also resonated with my mother's loss of sight and the intensity of both her solitude in the house and my relation to her. In both films, I establish a continuity between colored fabric or glass, the garden, and a particular sound or phrase of music. In *Listening*, the floating camera movements and the sound of Dieter's cello or details of Cécile working in the house are juxtaposed directly to a color. And the addition of the color filter to certain images—my handwritten notes or a flower stem—intensifies their value.

**Q:** As phrases, "pitcher of colored light" and "the space in my room" have identifiable references: the glass object that casts red and orange light on a wall in your mother's house in *Pitcher* and, in *Listening*, the downstairs apartment in the Staehelins' house, where you lived. Do these phrases have other references as well?

**A:** A film is itself "a pitcher of colored light." In the case of *Listening*, I would say that "the space in my room" is like the resonant interior space of a musical instrument. The Staehelins' wooden house also resonated—I could hear my ninety-year-old neighbor practicing upstairs every morning. This was at a moment in my life when I was thinking, "How does one renew onself as an artist?" Dieter gave me an answer without knowing it.[5]

**Q:** In *Listening* we hear sounds muffled by walls and floors—footsteps, cello practice, baroque music (Brahms, Bach, Vitali), conversation. There is movement up and down the house (Dieter practices on the upper floor, Cécile sweeps the kitchen floor, you edit film below) and in and out to the garden. In your voiceover—your first since 1966—you invoke sites of spatial transition in the house, "the mirror/the windows/the thresholds." A "threshold" is a hybrid opening/limit. It's a pause between connected spaces in a house, but it's also part of the architecture of love. The film seems as much a portrait of intimacy as it is of spatial commingling. In a shot of your filming notes, we see reference to Roland Barthes's *A Lovers' Discourse*, and a passage you read from A. W. Price's *Love and Friendship in Plato and Aristotle* frames romantic love vis-à-vis separateness and permeability:

> **Two souls of a dissimilar nature come together in a partnership which, giving each a role complementary to that of the other, achieves a mutual interplay, without conflict or hiatus, that makes for differentiation not assimilation, harmony not unison. Each responds to the other immediately and intuitively as if there were no obstacles of egoism or ignorance. Their lives become not the same, but at one.**[6]

There is the shadow of family organization in *Listening*—the elderly couple, the owners, above; you and your partner, Ute, below. But more than that, we see many forms of love overlapping and coexisting inside one structure. How do you work with space as both architecture and psyche?

**A:** For me, the essential challenge in filmmaking is to articulate space; I use this articulation of space to express my inner relation to a theme. This is not necessarily something I'm conscious of as I begin making a film, but it develops and becomes clear as I continue. Later I may read something that confirms or gives words to what I have discovered. In the case of *Listening* it was a statement by Octavio Paz about the intersubjectivity of an embrace that I found in his book *The Double Flame*. He writes that in the completion of the embrace is also the question "Who are you?"[7] His statement confirmed the words I used in my *Listening* voiceover.

**Q:** "Who are you?" acknowledges the otherness of the beloved. In *Listening*, you repeat that question in a sequence that cuts from an image of Ute's name written in a child's script to her face in profile to a single nasturtium leaf.

**A:** Her signature was a keepsake, her first name written as a child. The nasturtium leaf adds a deeper mystery.

## Two Languages

**Q:** At the center of *The Suppliant* is a small bronze figure, a replica of a Greek statue in the Altes Museum in Berlin, in your friend Jacques Dehornois's Brooklyn apartment. Its form is revealed indirectly—in the dark, via lines of light—and is accompanied by the sound of mark-making.

**A:** In the harmony of the young male figure, there is a quality that's not directly erotic but subtly so—and not in conflict with the idea of a soul. I wanted to film it in such a way to engage these qualities. When I think about my admiration for this kind of balance in the Renaissance art I had seen in Florence as a young person, Donatello comes to mind. The drawing sound was directly connected to Jacques. He was a successful interior designer and art director, but at that moment in life, he wanted to go back to the beginning of his training as an art student—he wanted to draw again.

**Q:** *The Suppliant* moves outside of Dehornois's apartment to the surrounding landscape along the East River—skyline, barbed wire, sirens. One exterior shot startles me as it's so plainly referential: a frame-filling section of the American flag, shot symmetrically, seen through the diamonds of a chain-link fence. The American flag can't simply be "an image."

**A:** Years ago, I had read *The American Scene* by Henry James, and there is a passage about his seeing Aphrodite's head at the Boston Art Museum—seeing this Greek object in the North American light. This passage stayed with me for decades. You know I'm an autodidact so it's all bric-a-brac—and I'm just retracing my thoughts as I remember them now. But I think the flag in *The Suppliant*—in connection with this Greek figure of idealized youth—represents the possibility of a different America, and a different masculinity. Some of the social problems in the U.S. are connected to its warped view of masculinity.

**Q:** *Among the Eucalyptuses* shares certain imagery with The Suppliant—statues of men, mechanical landscapes, male solitude. It has a palpable sadness and softness about it, as if carried by the eucalyptus leaves that frame many shots. Much of the film is shot in Piraeus, Greece, a port city where people get boats en route to islands—not an obvious destination. And we're on its desolate backstreets—trains, abandoned warehouse. This material is intercut with images of two statues—Ioannis Kapodistrias, the first governor of modern Greece, and Theodoros Kolokotronis, a general in the Greek War of Independence. How are you setting these figures of Greek statehood—both shot in Nafplion, a city with ancient origins and the first capital of modern Greece—alongside the Piraeus imagery?

**A:** Much of that Piraeus footage was shot in 2002, at the same time that I shot *The Suppliant*, and for a time I thought it might all become one film—a combination of New York and Greece. Since *Still Light*, I have often combined two locations in one film. Goethe said that you can know one language only by knowing two—I can extend this to say you know one country only by knowing two. So *Among the Eucalyptuses* is salvaged from that early intention. In the long period between shooting and editing, I wanted to bring my other experiences of Greece into a film—different from the very personal approaches of my earlier Greek films. The film intends a loving sympathy, with a melancholy about it, for the Greeks and their society.

**Q:** There is a close-up of a monk's face in *Among the Eucalyptuses*—the whites of his eyes are cut by the frameline. Was he in Piraeus as well?

**A:** The monk was up in the Taygetos mountains, in the Peloponnese—a very beautiful location I don't know if I could ever find again. I went with a friend who had a car, and we slept outdoors on cots outside a monastery. There was a full moon and the mountain was absolutely lit up, and there was a service that went all through the night. Only women seemed to attend. The next day there were just two or three monks at the monastery—and I asked one if I could film him.

**Q:** I am struck by the presence of women in these films—your mother, Cécile, Ute—and their roles as creators: films, gardens, homes, bread, children, wisdom (your mother shares thoughts about prayer and facing mortality in *Pitcher*). Your filming notes include details of dialogues with Ute about your works-in-progress and the crucial role of her responses. What is the nature of your respective roles in the evolution of each other's filmmaking? The energetic speed of bright color in *The Sparrow Dream* reminds me of Ute's work.

**A:** There may be a transfer in both directions with respect to our impact on each other's films. In my life with Gregory, we worked more by osmosis than through conscious comment. It was not verbal—we didn't show each other films and expect a response, though sometimes Gregory responded to my films by writing something later. I knew Ute and her work—both her own films and her programming—before my personal life with her began.[8] And in the 1990s, I was very attached to the writing of Marianne Moore and Elizabeth Bishop. So that enters into the same nexus. I also returned to the States, and to my family, which happens to be all women. I tie all of this to a more general sense of finding my own balance and being able to see how my own personality relates to women—directly—without Gregory's anxieties about women and his relationships to women, without the filter of the society of two male homosexuals.

**Q:** *The Sparrow Dream* is a collage of return. You return to the pages of a first childhood book (Padraic Colum's *The Adventures of Odysseus and The Tale of Troy*), to memory ("I have been calling to the next world ever since I was a child," you say via voiceover), and to sites and elements of earlier films. But we also see less directly personal imagery—a statue representing a Korean War veteran in East Weymouth, Massachusetts, and many American flags—real ones and images *of* them: on a bedsheet and a firetruck. The memorial statue and flags seem to engage a different register of return.

**A:** The presence of the U.S. flag in *The Sparrow Dream* has expanded beyond the view behind chain-link in *The Suppliant*. During the years that I was commuting to Massachusetts to look after my mother, I was often moved by seeing the economic and social decline on the South Shore, and I reflected often about the flag in that context. The flag represented something so different for my mother's generation. Over the course of my own lifetime, I have seen the militarization of American society as the domestic side to the empire abroad. In the background of *The Sparrow Dream*, there is *nostos*, the homecoming of soldiers, whether Odysseus or the Korean veteran whose likeness we see in statue form.[9] There is, of course, my own very different homecoming. In one way the flag tells me that I am a visitor in my own country.

**Q:** Like *Listening, The Sparrow Dream* incorporates a dream fragment. In *Listening*, you say, "I was awakened by a dream in which I spoke to myself in German: 'Ich bin ein andere Person geworden'" (I have become a new person). And in *The Sparrow Dream*, "I dreamt after my first night back [to Berlin from the United States] that I was speaking to a sparrow and that she told me her name."

**A:** Just last night I picked up an academic collection of essays about Zeami [the fourteenth-century Japanese Noh playwright, actor, and theorist] and read about the connection between his Buddhist background and his way of seeing dreams and the place of dreams in his work. It reminded me of what I say [in my voiceover] in *The Sparrow Dream*—"sleep, thought, memory," not "sleep, *dream*, memory."[10]

## Archive of the Future

**Q:** Several books with torn-off covers sit on a shelf at the Temenos Archive—books that Markopoulos had been preparing to send to the bindery before he died. How did archiving and preservation priorities shift after his death?

**A:** The most important change was the creation of a space for the archive. I focused less on the paper part of the archive and more on the film. I began to make internegatives of the films Gregory made between 1948 and 1972 and to distribute them—as well as my own films—through the Temenos Archive.

In the creative context that he produced for himself, Gregory made some very important intuitive decisions, but bringing his work into the world was difficult. He was so isolated, and he couldn't endure the compromises involved in working with other people or institutions. How an artist can make work but cannot complete it by bringing it into the world is a fascinating question. I think of Dickinson and Cavafy—they let the work find its public after their death. Gregory was like a composer writing a score that he doesn't live to hear, or who has gone deaf, like Beethoven or Fauré or Bruckner.

There's also a historical dimension to his conceptual orientation. When he began to make work, filmmaking was almost totally in the hands of the film industry. The period after World War II was a new beginning—16mm film technology had developed during the war and there was leftover equipment—but it was still very risky to pursue filmmaking as an individual artist. It was in this context that someone like [the Scottish experimental filmmaker] Margaret Tait went to Centro Sperimentale in Rome to learn filmmaking. Or Gregory . . . to USC. For *Psyche*, his first 16mm film, he had only a borrowed camera and no editing equipment, and it was made without permission from the school. They [Tait and Markopoulos] both drew on their relationships to other arts in order to conceptualize a step in filmmaking that is outside the "photoplay" of narrative cinema—both were poets and had very strong relationships to literature.

**Q:** What was it like to start showing your and Markopoulos's films again after such a long period of refusal?

**A:** Larry Kardish at MoMA let me do private screenings. This was an opportunity to try to introduce the work to new curators in the U.S. At one point I invited Richard Peña, director of the New York Film Festival, and he was very enthusiastic about *AMOR*. At the [1996] festival, he paired it with a feature film by John Greyson [*Lilies* (1996)]. It was a disaster. The screening was in Alice Tully Hall and the New York gay public had come because of Greyson's film, and they absolutely hated *AMOR*. When I got up to speak afterward, I was booed. Someone yelled, "Black-tie fascist!"[11]

Gregory's work screened first at the Ontario Cinematheque and Pacific Film Archive—Susan Oxtoby, Kathy Geritz, and John Mhiripiri were important early supporters. With Peter Pappas I organized a Markopoulos exhibition at the Foundation for Hellenic Culture in New York after the Whitney Museum retrospective of his work in 1996, which was curated by John Hanhardt and Matthew Yablonsky. My Whitney Museum retrospective, organized by Chrissie Isles, was in 2005, followed by a Tate retrospective, curated by Mark Webber, in 2007.

**Q:** In 2000, you made the decision to bring *Eniaios*, Markopoulos's eighty-hour film left unprinted when he died, to the public. You've organized five Temenos screenings in Arcadia, presenting newly restored portions of the film (in 2004, 2008, 2012, 2016, and 2022) to audiences of about 150 people each time. The labor-intensive repair of the film original—refixing thousands of splices before printing can proceed—is the heart of this work.[12] How did the restoration develop?

**A:** In the beginning I did the repair on my own, at Cinema Arts, a photochemical lab in Pennsylvania, sometimes living there. But I would not have been able to continue without the support of young filmmakers who have joined me. The British filmmaker Lucy Parker was the first—she approached me after my 2007 screenings at the Tate, and she came to Switzerland and we worked together. Since 2015, the repair has taken place in Berlin, in the small studio space Ute and I share in Wilmersdorf, with a roving group of young filmmakers and artists from Europe, the U.S., and South America. We all share a certain enthusiasm for the future of 16mm filmmaking. They are at different points in their own development as artists, but we come together in a way that's not so connected to career.

**Q:** At what point did you decide that you would not show your own work at the Temenos? Perhaps this is an "Arcadian rumor," but I was told that Gregory, as he was dying, advised you not to show your own films in that context.

**A:** That's not the case. When he was very ill, I asked him, "What should I do with all this?" And he said: "Do whatever you want." This was very liberating. Regarding my own films, there was no single moment, but it became clear ahead of the 2004 Temenos event. The decision grew from an inner dialogue about my own work and my reflections about Gregory.

**Q:** What is the future of the Temenos Archive—a repository founded on independence from institutional affiliation?

**A:** I don't know. I am filming and editing and sound recording on one side and on the other side I think about restoration and the final home for this work and about who can act as a partner in the future—these two sides are important to keep in balance. I have values and perspectives that inform what I'm doing, ones that are not necessarily the same as what is represented by the name "Gregory Markopoulos" or the Temenos. Gregory's special Asclepian speculation has its own values. I'm not suggesting the two are in conflict—but they are distinct. The life that produced *Eniaios* ended in 1992. But the life of *Eniaios* goes on, and maybe in better ways. I can sit there in Lyssarea, at the Temenos screenings, and feel it is a great gift. And there is the joy of saving his work no matter how the future may judge it. Problems present their own dynamic gifts if you're willing to take them on.

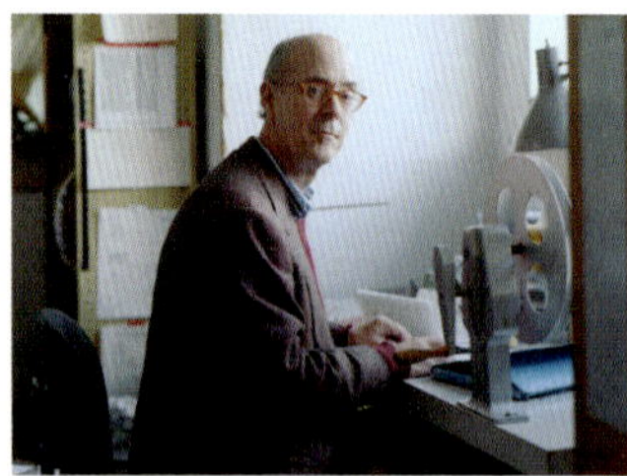

Robert Beavers in 2016. Photograph by Petra Graf

**Q:** Films go on beyond the lives of their subjects: your mother, Dieter, and Cécile are no longer alive; you no longer live in the Zumikon house. Turning "greeting mortality" toward film itself: celluloid requires infrastructures of caretaking and preservation to survive. At this year's [2022] Temenos, you announced that Cinema Arts, the photochemical lab you've worked with since the 1980s—and that has printed the restored *Eniaios* reels—was on the verge of collapse.

**A:** Yes. When a major U.S. art museum—Cinema Arts' biggest client—decides to preserve film mostly in digital format, it has a big impact on the survival of a small artisanal lab.

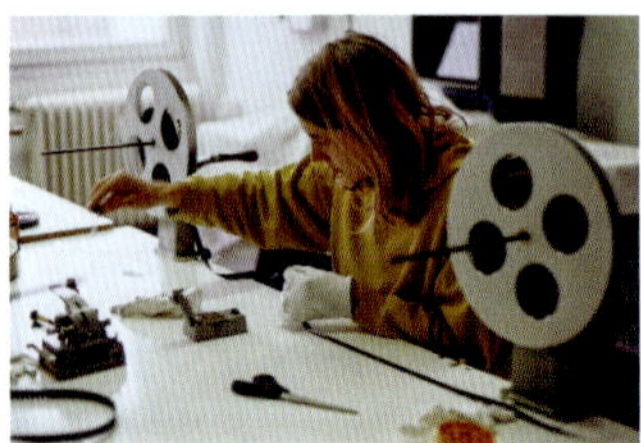

Eva Claus, *Eniaios* restoration, Berlin. Photograph by Petra Graf

**Q:** What would it cost today to complete the job—to repair and print the rest of the film and to pay those doing that work?

**A:** About $250,000.

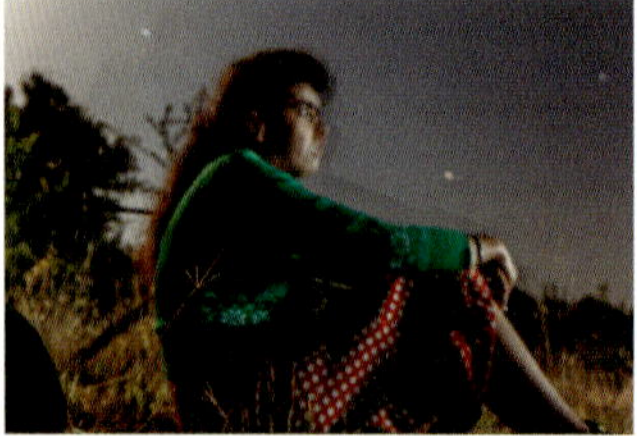

The Temenos, 2012. Photograph by Linda Levinson

**Q:** Where do you stand on digitizing your own and Markopoulos's work? In 2016, *From the Notebook of . . .* screened as DCP as part of Projections at the New York Film Festival. And in the spring of 2022, you presented a digitally transferred portion of *Eniaios* via Zoom for an event hosted by the Stavros Niarchos Foundation Public Humanities Initiative—a double digital mediation of a work known to be religiously medium- and site-specific.

**A:** It's both an economic and aesthetic dilemma. It's not something I could do on my own. For someone with unlimited resources, there is the ability to preserve in multiple formats. With the resources I have, I have chosen to pursue definitive analog copies on 16mm or 35mm. Digitizing is a kind of translation—it will never have the exact qualities of the photochemical original: the body or weight or richness of color that analog film emulsion has. But I also see the value of reaching out to a public that does not have access to analog film projection. I was recently able to watch a Vittorio De Seta documentary online, via the Criterion Collection. It's wonderful that work like this can reach new audiences. I'm not 100 percent opposed to the possibility of digitization—but if it's to be done, it should happen while I'm alive and can participate in the color grading, etc.

—

In the course of our conversation, Beavers projected a silent edit of a new short film in his Wilmersdorf studio. At its center was the 1967 footage he had shot of his childhood neighbor and friend Bernice Hodges. "One has no idea the meaning something will have later," Beavers said, regretting having discarded all but a handful of frames after discovering that he had left the lens cap on while shooting.

Surrounded by forsythia blossoms, Mrs. Hodges's face fills the screen. The flash of her image—her high collar and cameo pin and subtly knowing smile—telegraphs a human from another century. Her portrait is intercut with shots of a workshop with rows of metal tools—a call-back to her woodworking vocation and to Beavers's early training in her craft—and images of a wooden tray shaped like a veined leaf.[13] Mrs. Hodges made it and gave it to Beavers as a gift. A close-up of a rotating crystal joins the spare montage. Mrs. Hodges kept cut-crystal bowls filled with colored water on her windowsills, Beavers explained. New England rooms can be dark, and the chiseled glass cast prisms of colored light on her walls. "The new film might be part of a series," he said. "Perhaps 'late monthly segments.' I am still searching for the form that will hold several films. I sense that is still in process."

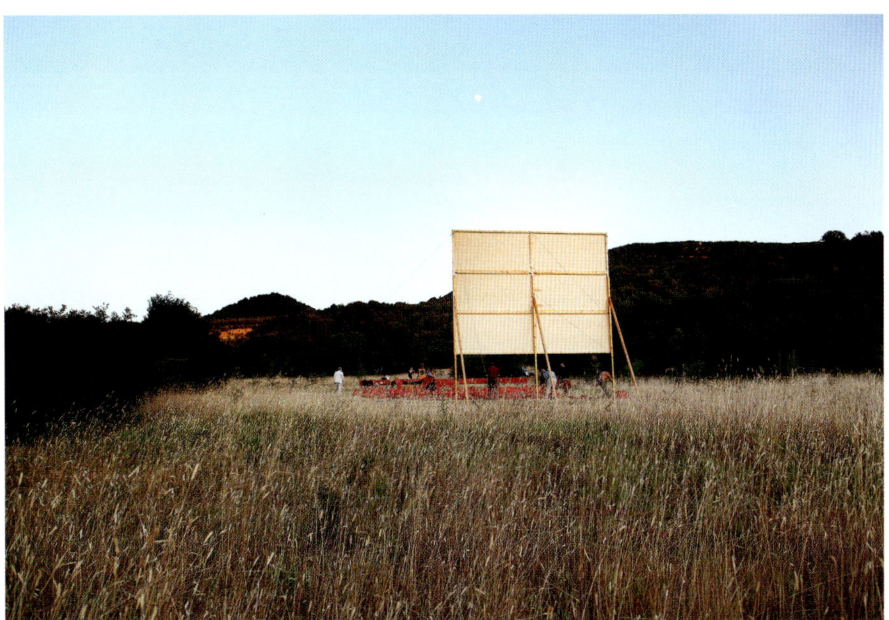

The Temenos, 2012. Photograph by Linda Levinson

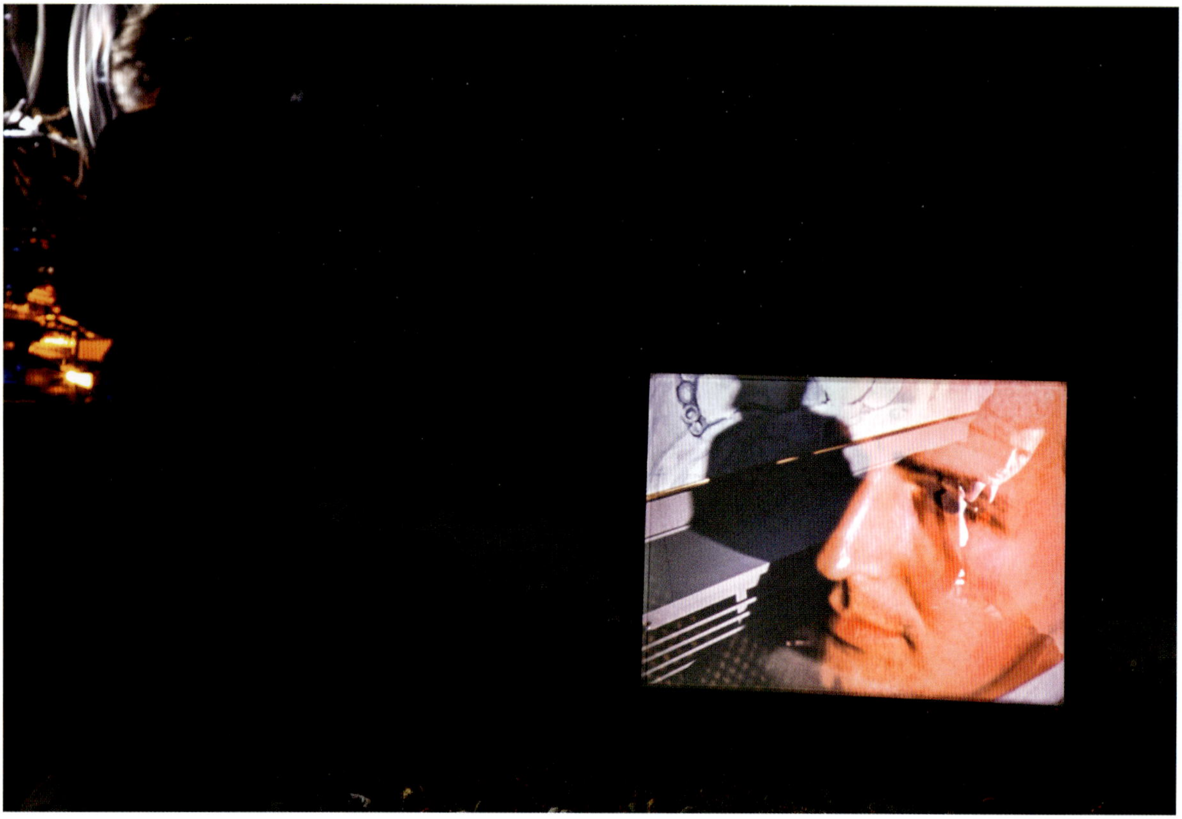

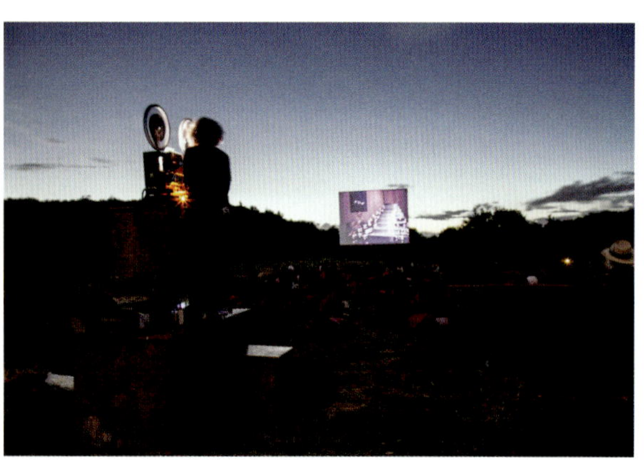

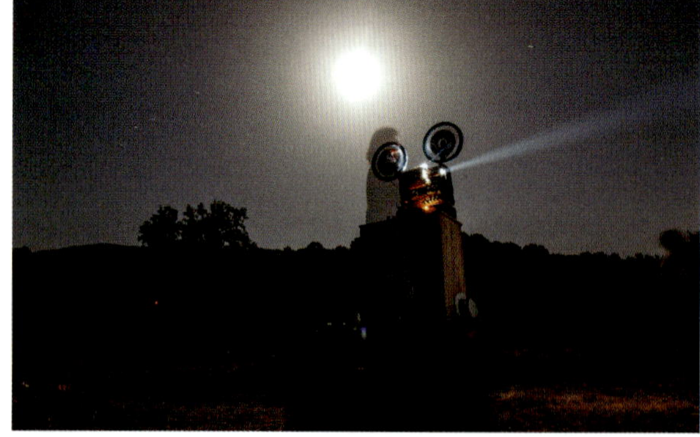

The Temenos, 2022 (top, bottom left) and 2012 (right). Photographs by Linda Levinson

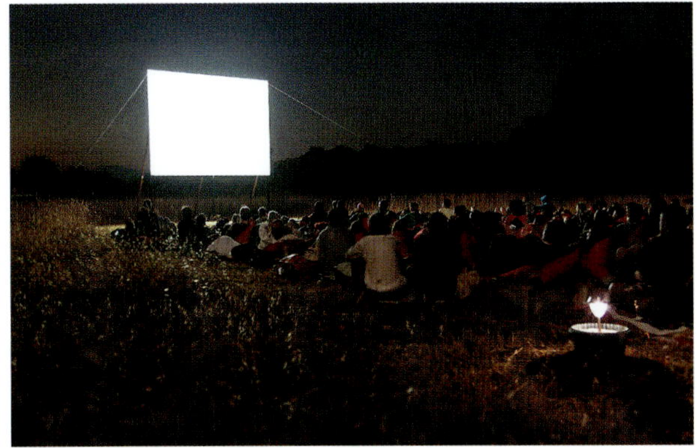

The Temenos, 2012. Photograph by Linda Levinson

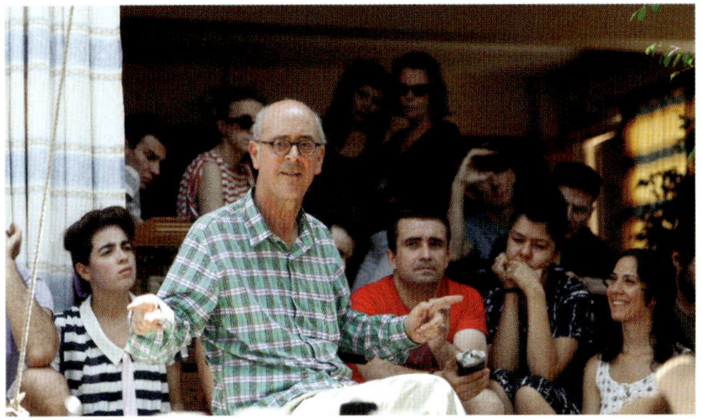

Robert Beavers hosts a discussion with Temenos attendees, 2012. Photograph by Linda Levinson

## Acknowledgments

My thanks go first to Robert Beavers. I have learned more from his films than can be compressed into this book. In conjunction with making materials at the Temenos Archive available, his patience with my endless questions and his willingness to revisit decades-old dimensions of his life and filmmaking have made this project possible.

The Austrian Film Museum in Vienna provided access to the first versions of Beavers's films and offered counsel and support at every level. Thank you to Alexander Horwath, Regina Schlagnitweit, Georg Wasner, Michael Loebenstein, Gabriele Adebisi-Schuster, Eszter Kondor, and Janneke Van Dalen. At the Harvard Film Archive, Amy Sloper and Mark Johnson—and most especially Haden Guest—have consistently gone out of their way to facilitate screenings and, in collaboration with Perry Paolantonio at Gamma Ray Digital, generate film stills. I am also grateful to Susan Oxtoby, at Berkeley Art Museum and Pacific Film Archive; Josh Siegel, at the Museum of Modern Art; and Enrico Camporesi, at the Pompidou Museum. Mark Webber, at the Visible Press, helped me wade through Markopoulos's vast writings.

Crucial research support came from the Center for Hellenic Studies at Princeton University, the Onassis Foundation in Athens, and the Institute for Advanced Study, Princeton. Karen Bassi's "Facing Death in Ancient Greece" NEH Summer Seminar and a Patrick Leigh Fermor House writing residency, sponsored by Princeton University and the Benaki Museum, arrived at exactly the right moments. Thank you to Dimitri Gondicas, Kathleen Crown, Yve-Alain Bois, Heinrich von Staden, Angelos Chaniotis, Marcia Tucker, Polina Kosmadaki, and George Manginis. In seeking to understand the ancient and modern Greek dimensions of Beavers's work, I relied on the expertise of friends and colleagues including Nicolas Nicolaides, Soo-Young Kim, Dimitris Antoniou, Katerina Zografou, Dimitris Christofor, Brooke Holmes, Joshua Billings, and Sean Coughlin.

I thank P. Adams Sitney, Joan Richardson, Wayne Koestenbaum, Ivone Margulies, Jeffrey Stout, Susan Howe, Harry Tomicek, and the late Tony Pipolo for essential early encouragement and inspiration. This project developed in part via opportunities to publish and present on Beavers's work along the way; thank you to Drake Stutesman, Dennis Lim, Don McMahon, David LaRocca, James Cahill, Meghan Sutherland, Brian Price, John David Rhodes, and María Palacios Cruz. Don Daniels provided critical feedback on the manuscript, and David James was unstinting in his attention and editorial aid.

My engagement with the somatic and contemplative dimensions of Beavers's work has been deepened by work with teachers and practitioners including Sara Weber, Bill Auerbach, Joan Halifax, Eve Holbrooke, Thea Daley, Anne Hammel, Koshin Paley Ellison, and Robert Chodo Campbell.

At the New Jersey Institute for Technology, I am lucky to have colleagues who have so consistently supported me through the many iterations of this project. Thank you to Calista McRae, Burt Kimmelman, David Rothenberg, Christopher Funkhouser, Nancy Steffen-Fleur, and Gabrielle Esperdy.

This project has benefited from too many forms of assistance to catalog—among them love, levity, a place to stay during a research trip, disciplinary expertise, and professional counsel—and I thank those who provided it generously: Moshe and Dante Amores Rutkoff, Josh Rutkoff, Lynn Amores, Jane Brailove Rutkoff, Peter Rutkoff, Michael Brailove, Peter Israel, Laska Jimsen, Paige Sarlin, Jason Livingston, Tamara Faith Berger, Cathy Lee Crane, Irina Leimbacher, Jim Supanick, Kelly Sears, Rebecca Meyers, Ken Eisenstein, Miciah Hussey, Imani Wilson, Gabrielle Zadra, Aoibheann Sweeney, Mark Cohen, Lynne Tillman, Sarah Christman, Rebecca Ward, Cathérine Hug, Judith Rodenbeck, Christina Gomez Barrio, Wolfgang Mayer, Thomas Beard, Stefanie Schlüter, Volker Pantenburg, Gary Dauphin, Ben Tiven, Henriette Huldisch, Pablo de Ocampo, Glenn Philips, Bill Brand, Mark Toscano, Peggy Parsons, Bronwen Wickkiser, Marisa Bass, Wen-shing Chou, Julie Johnson, Eliza Jackson, Margo Halverson, Gavin Smith, Mark McElhatten, Gregory Nagy, and Natasha Bershadsky. Temenos-forged friendships and conversations—with Mitsos Triantopoulos, Matthew Lyons, F.P. Boué, Lizzie Calligas, Luke Fowler, Francisco Algarín, François Bovier, Aaron Scott, Joel Newberger, Ron Martin Wilson, Sam Kerbel, Sam Engel, Stravros Petsopoulos, Adeena Mey, Sílvia das Fadas, James Edmonds, Stephan Hauser, Daniel Heller-Roazen, Oleg Tcherny, Nicolas Niarchos, Christina Phoebe, and Erika Balsom—have enriched this project, as have Linda Levinson's indelible Temenos photographs and Petra Graf's documentation of the restoration of *Eniaios*. Support from David Streiff and an anonymous donor has made the production of this image-intensive project possible.

It has been a joy to work with Victoria Hindley, Gabriela Bueno-Gibbs, Kathleen Caruso, and Margarita Encomienda at the MIT Press. Victoria's artist mind, belief in this project, and steady guidance have made all the difference. This book is dedicated to the memory of Jonathan Schwartz and Maja Naef. They both loved Robert Beavers's films.

## Filmography

Robert Beavers is responsible for concept and realization (including camera, sound recording, and editing) for all of the following films. All works were originally shot on 16mm film. All camera originals or negatives, internegatives, interpositives, magnetic soundtracks, optical soundtracks, and projection copies of the works are preserved in the Temenos Archive.

A star (*) marks those early works that Robert Beavers no longer shows publicly.

**Spiracle***
1966, 16mm, color, sound, 12 minutes
Filmed in the United States (New York)

**On the Everyday Use of the Eyes of Death***
1967, 16mm, color, silent, 9 minutes
Filmed in Italy (Rome)
Note: The camera original was destroyed by the filmmaker.

**Winged Dialogue**
1967/2000, 16mm, color, sound, 3 minutes
Filmed in Greece (Hydra)

**Plan of Brussels**
1968/2000, 16mm, color, sound, 18 minutes
Filmed in Belgium (Brussels)

**Early Monthly Segments**
1968–1970/2002, 35mm, color, silent, 33 minutes

**The Count of Days**
1969/2001, 16mm, color, sound, 21 minutes
Filmed in Switzerland (Zurich)

**View***
1969, 16mm, color, sound, 8 minutes
Filmed in Switzerland (Zurich)
Note: The camera original was destroyed by the filmmaker.

**Palinode**
1970/2001, 16mm, color, sound, 21 minutes
Filmed in Switzerland (Zurich)

**Diminished Frame**
1970/2001, 16mm, black-and-white and color, sound, 24 minutes
Filmed in Germany (West Berlin)

**Still Light**
1970/2001, 16mm, color, sound, 25 minutes
Filmed in Greece (Hydra) and England (London)

**From the Notebook of . . .**
1971/1998, 35mm, color, sound, 48 minutes
Filmed in Italy (Florence)

**The Painting**
1972/1999, 16mm, color, sound, 13 minutes
Filmed in Switzerland (Bern) and the United States (Boston)

**Work Done**
1972/1999, 35mm, color, sound, 22 minutes
Filmed in Italy (Florence) and Switzerland (the Grisons)

**Ruskin**
1975/1997, 35mm, black-and-white and color, sound, 45 minutes
Filmed in Italy (Venice), Switzerland (the Grisons), and England (London)

**Sotiros**
1976–1978/1996, 35mm, color, sound, 25 minutes
Filmed in Greece (Athens, Sparta, Leonidio), Austria (Graz, Rein), and Switzerland (Bern)
Note: Three films were combined into a single work.
Original versions: *Sotiros Responds*, 1975–1976, 16mm, color, sound, 25 minutes
*Sotiros (Alone)*, 1976–1977, 16mm, color, sound, 12 minutes
*Sotiros in the Elements*, 1978, 16mm, color, sound, 6 minutes

**AMOR**
1980, 35mm, color, sound, 15 minutes
Filmed in Italy (Rome, Verona) and Austria (Salzburg)

**ΕΥΨΥΧΙ (Efpsychi)**
1983/1996, 35mm, color, sound, 20 minutes
Filmed in Greece (Athens)

**Wingseed**
1985, 35mm, color, sound, 15 minutes
Filmed in Greece (Anavyssos, Lyssarea)

**The Hedge Theater**
1986–1990/2002, 35mm, color, sound, 19 minutes
Filmed in Italy (Rome, Brescia)

**The Stoas**
1991–1997, 35mm, color, sound, 22 minutes
Filmed in Greece (Athens, Gortynia)

**The Ground**
1993–2001, 35mm, color, sound, 20 minutes
Filmed in Greece (Hydra)

**Pitcher of Colored Light**
2007, 16mm, color, sound, 23 minutes
Filmed in the United States (Falmouth, Massachusetts)

**The Suppliant**
2010, 16mm, color, sound, 5 minutes
Filmed in the United States (New York)

**Listening to the Space in My Room**
2013, 16mm, color, sound, 19 minutes
Filmed in Switzerland (Zumikon)

**Among the Eucalyptuses**
2017, 16mm, color, silent, 4 minutes
Filmed in Greece (Piraeus and Nafplion)

***"Der Klang, die Welt . . ."***
2018, 16mm, color, sound, 4.5 minutes
Filmed in Switzerland (Zumikon)

**The Sparrow Dream**
2022, 16mm, color, sound, 29 minutes
Filmed in Germany (Berlin) and the United States (Massachusetts)

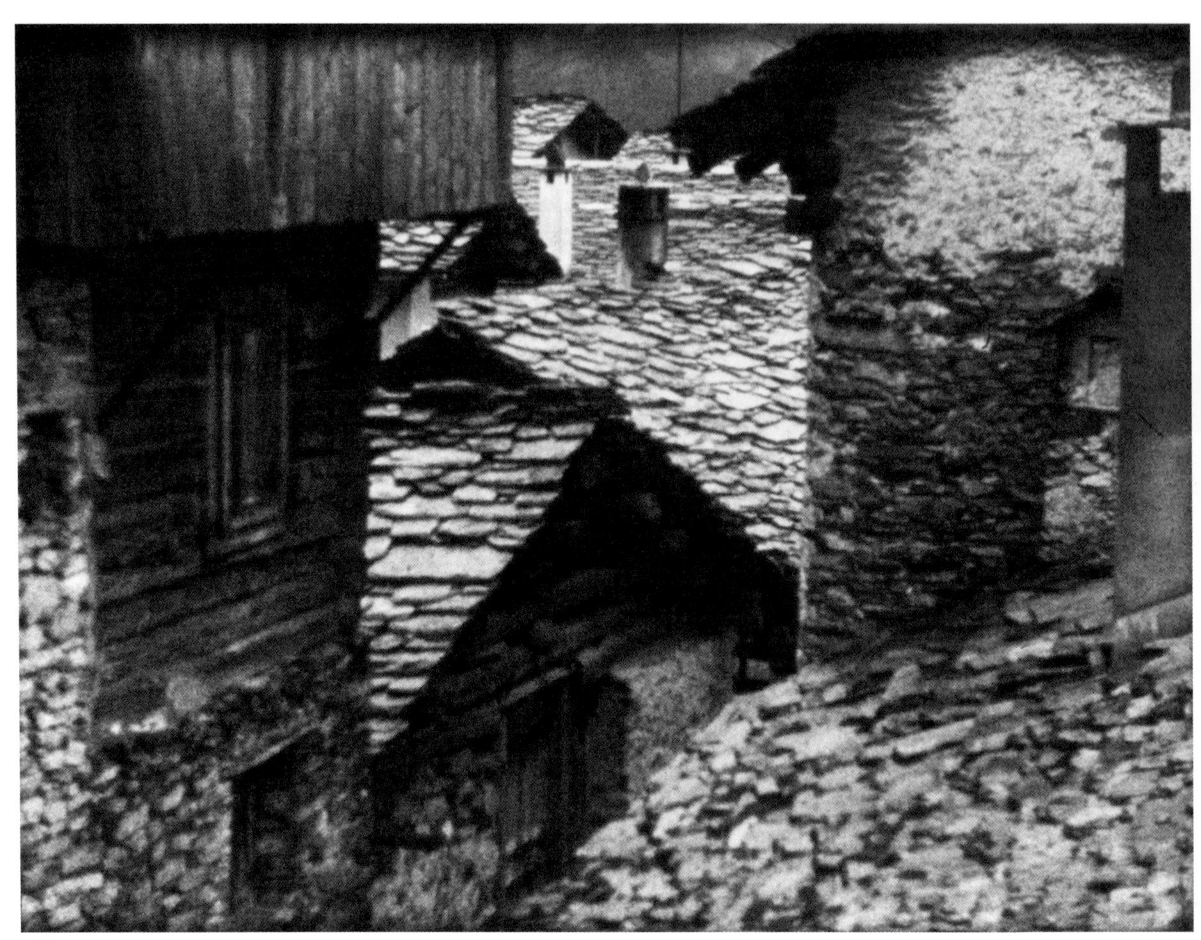

*Ruskin* (1975/1997)

## Appendix: Robert Beavers on Films in *My Hand Outstretched to the Winged Distance and Sightless Measure*

### Diminished Frame (1970/2001)

There is a balance between a sense of the past seen in the views of West Berlin, filmed in black-and-white, and a sense of the present in which I filmed myself showing how the color is being created by placing filters in the camera's aperture. It is the space of the city and of the filmmaker. I search for signs of war's aftermath and a few moments of daily life.

### From the Notebook of . . . (1971/1998)

When *From the Notebook of . . .* was filmed in Florence in 1971, I had already made several films with colored filters and moving mattes. Each film was formed by the place in which I then lived—either Greece, Brussels, Zurich, Berlin, or London. The initial choice of filming locations in Florence was more complex because they were selected by drawing upon certain details from Leonardo da Vinci's life related to the city—the little that is known—and from other comments in his notebooks. The first scene, of doves being set free from a shop near the Bargello, is inspired by the mention of such a scene in Giorgio Vasari's biography of Leonardo. It is then suddenly extended into the present (of 1971) by one of my own handwritten notes, so that the flight of the dove is interwoven with the turning of my notebook pages and juxtaposed with a view of opening a window onto the Florentine rooftops.

From the first moment, I am present as an active observer. This is usually shown in clusters of quick camera movements with part of my profile framing the view. The pace develops between searching on location and the central scenes of me writing at the table in front of the window. The notebook is given a filmic form and holds a quantity of visual elements in ever-changing relation like living illustrations on the page.

Finding the present in the past: I was inspired by Leonardo's precepts and his observations on *disegno* and chiaroscuro. As a result, I filmed certain qualities of shadows and their movements. There was time to observe the placid water under the Santa Trinità bridge or to compare the Arno at a more turbulent point with waves of blond hair. Inspired by the freedom and grace of this genial autodidact, I attempted to translate a few isolated elements of his vision into film. It reached a point where I could look into the film camera as a camera obscura, to see the perspective of the image and to place my strips of colored filters in the aperture.

Finding the past in the present: Because this was my first extended encounter with the city, the vestiges of an earlier Florence came to life as I glimpsed them. I saw the window, painted in perspective on the Via Maggio, or the ideal proportions of Alberti's Palazzo Rucellai facade, and each gained a place in the film. The window, with its painted black recesses, suggested new uses for my matte-forms and extended further to that other window in my room, filmed at night. All suggested a search and the incandescence of thought.

There is a distance between my handwritten notes, which are remnants of earlier intentions for filming, and the actual filming as it develops its own direction. The layers of reference are sometimes in sync; more often they simply overlap. The full gamut of these themes, reaching from the past into the present, allowed for productive accidents and later intuitions. The measured rhythm of reading—frequently a quick glimpse of only a few words—is woven into all of the other movements. One passes from the apparent stillness of the notes to the movement in the film's editing. Each new image and sound changes the meaning of the notes as they appear and reappear in the turning of the "matte-pages."

Dividing the frame in half, the matte turns from one side of the screen to the other, and this repetition creates a strong suggestion of perspective, almost a sense of the image turning to its reverse side in a few moments, when the rhythm of the sound encourages this impression.

Remembering the original filming and my more recent reediting of the image and new sound, I see that *From the Notebook of . . .* possesses the youthful energy of my beginning. It is also the film that led to a new dedication and directness.

### Sotiros (1976–1978/1996)

In *Sotiros*, there is an unspoken dialogue and a seen dialogue. The latter is held between the intertitles and the images; the former is moved by the tripod and by the emotions of the filmmaker. Both dialogues are interwoven with the sunlight's movement as it circles the room, touching each wall and corner, detached and intimate.

### Efpsychi (1983/1996)

The details of the young actor's face—his eyebrows, eyes, earlobe, lips, and chin—are set opposite the buildings in the old market quarter of Athens, where every street bears the name of a classical Greek playwright. The nearness of the face and its slightest movements are the means of balancing all of the film, from below street level up to the rooftops. In this setting, an intense stillness is interrupted sometimes by a sudden sound or by a movement in the street. The actor speaks a single word, *teleftea*, meaning "the last one." As he repeats the word, each syllable moves differently over his features, changing with each scene and suggesting the proximity between the erotic, the sacred, and chance.

#### His Image

I found a reality of form in the features of Vangelis's face, in the harmony of light resting upon and within the face, and in certain movements when his features seemed to project beyond themselves.

To recognize the outline of a person's nature in his physical image is not a common experience. It happens at that moment when the habits of seeing open toward a sudden awareness, when the filmmaker can see the other opposite him. Imagine the complex pattern that is made by the eyes' movements when they move away from and directly or indirectly back to the point of attention. Then consider how the movements between the eyes of a filmmaker and actor establish stillness at certain moments. His image may gain distinctness at these moments that will exist in only one film, presenting something near to his essence.

The search is for a reality within the individual physiognomy, for a generous physicality that will not fade, all suggested by the phrase "the outline of a person's nature." The face carries a double sense as direct element within the film frame and as a performance. It is both meaning and mask. When these qualities are present in the image, the face itself will possess a voice and its own lyric.

One looks upon the face and into it. There are an infinite number of different angles between the upper and lower halves or between the profile and full front. Even the smallest detail that might be considered too insignificant to carry expression may for that very reason hold a key to later possibilities in editing the image and sound.

**How the (Filming) Locations Become the Space of One Film**

The small city of Athens remains centered in the few streets that intersect near the main marketplace, the agora, while a new Athens multiplies itself in hundredfold anonymity around it.

The young actor's face equals in its scale these old buildings that line the streets of Evripidou, Aeschylou, Sophocleous, Socratous, and Theatrou. The left side of his face and the left side of the street turn to the right side and back again. The (in)direct view of desire reflected in the face's details balances the direct view of the street angles, the camera movements, and ambient sound.

Parallel to the face is the space of the wholesale stores and workshops below street level. These spaces possess shadows that rise and descend like waves; a space built for escaping the destructive forces of heat and light, the fire of light that slowly dissolves everything. Heat, weight, and light interact to create the sense of movement in still objects. I see how an object, resting its weight and pressing down on the ground, possesses a movement; this invisible gravity is equivalent to quiet desire. It gains serenity through the light, heat, and silence in these spaces.

The pedestrians and the closer view of one foot placed after another on the sidewalk are also seen from below street level. These steps leading down into the shops are near where my actor in real life makes hand brooms; steps that also measure the space between his chin and brow . . . ascending, descending as he sews the brooms. Steps that catch the weight of light and allow us to see the horizontal become vertical.

A theme of numbers develops where one use of number overlaps another. It begins with the house numbers and is followed by the marketplace, the lottery tickets, the bordellos, the candles, etc. Numbers point toward the unseen and unknown, the last one, *teleftea*.

The first three letters of the street signs, ODO, and later the same three letters in the hotel sign, ODO, create a mask for my actor. Details of his face are used like the signs' letters in the film's composition. Each detail of Vangelis's face enters further into the scale of the film and becomes a threshold for the spectator's own sense of sight and hearing.

Another sign: GENIKON EMPORION. The golden letters of commerce are interspersed between views of a bordello and increase in size with each shortening of the word by a syllable . . . EMPORION, PORION, RION, ON.

This stillness and locomotion of material weight are opposed to the images of quantity, as seen in the red fish, the lottery numbers promising millions, and the golden candlewicks that represent the illusion of more.

Another word, OLYMPIAKOS, is written on a wall. Like the close-up of my actor's lips, the first O rests at the center of the frame, then is seen suddenly to one side, at the same angle as the trace of his kiss left on the glass protecting an icon . . . ODOS SOKRATOUS.

Some of the old buildings are surrounded by more modern glass structures that reflect sunlight indirectly over the facades. A lottery vendor's voice offers again a last chance . . . to change your life. *Teleftea*.

### Wingseed (1985)

A seed that floats in the air, a whirligig, a love charm. This magnificent landscape, both hot and dry, is far from sterile; rather, the heat and dryness produce a distinct type of life, seen in the perfect forms of the wild grass and seed pods, the herds of goats, as well as in the naked figure. The torso, in itself, and more, the image that it creates in this light. The sounds of the shepherd's signals and the flute's phrase are heard. And the goats' bells. Imagine the bell's clapper moving from side to side with the goat's movements like the quick side-to-side camera movements, which increase in pace and reach a vibrant ostinato.

### The Stoas (1991–1997)

I sought in these small industrial arcades the spaces that can be seen first from one side and then from the other, a shape of emptiness, then the divinity of the river—this deep sense of appearance—and finally the grasping of the grape. There is no figure, and there are no titles. There are only the hands reaching directly into the space of these small industrial arcades, seen from one end and the other, in a light that can still find proportion and finality. The emptiness of the arcades is transformed into the river's movements, that is again stillness. Through the rhythm of the river's image and its sound, a deeper sense of appearance is projected into the space above it. The full length of the stream gathers in the final clusters of grapes.

### The Ground (1993–2001)

#### Filmmaker/Stonemason

What lives in the space between the stones, in the space cupped between my hand and my chest? Filmmaker/stonemason. A tower or ruin of remembrance. With each swing of the hammer, I cut into the image and the sound rises from the chisel. A rhythm, marked by repetition and animated by variation; strokes of hammer and fist, resounding in dialogue. In this space that the film creates, emptiness gains a contour strong enough for the spectator to see more than the image—a space permitting vision in addition to sight.

## Notes

### PROLOGUE

**1.** A note on source materials: Uncited spoken quotations from Beavers come from interviews with the author and uncited quotations from Beavers's writing come from his unpublished notes in the Temenos Archive. When Beavers's spoken words come from sources other than interviews with the author and when Beavers's written words come from his published writings, those details appear in the notes.

**2.** Paintings introduce potentials to Beavers that continue to evolve in his notes. His 1967 description of the see-through color of Cranach's *Charity* ("pink skin, blue green backgrounds veins of a child—clarity, porcelain . . . the pink and blue tints of the hand") returns shortly thereafter in an idea for a film: "Combine blue and green and pink filters to let figure be tinted by pink and background be tinted blue; cut to pink close-ups." Beavers may or may not heed the specificity of his noted intentions, but he is training himself to mix colored light.

**3.** "I don't usually look through the viewfinder at the moment when I push the button," Beavers said.

**4.** In a manuscript note in *La Boîte de 1914* (The Box of 1914), Duchamp wrote, "On peut regarder voir; On ne peut pas entendre entendre" (One can look at seeing; / one can't hear hearing). See Clement Greenberg's 1961 essay "Modernist Painting," in *Modern Art and Modernism: A Critical Anthology*, ed. Francis Frascina and Charles Harrison (New York: Routledge, 1982).

**5.** Susan Oxtoby, Beavers program notes, San Francisco Museum of Modern Art, October 8, 2009; emphasis added.

**6.** Regarding avant-garde identifications, Beavers said: "I don't want free-floating subjectivity—that's where I depart from [Stan] Brakhage" and "My problem with 1960s structuralism was the complete rejection of narrative." His language of affiliation varies; reflecting on his first encounters with the films of Markopoulos, Ron Rice, Bruce Baillie, and Harry Smith, Beavers said, "I believe in this type of filmmaking and am very happy that by chance I encountered it."

**7.** Marianne Moore, on the occasion of accepting the National Book Award in 1952, in *The Complete Prose of Marianne Moore* (New York: Viking, 1986), 648.

**8.** René Micha, "Robert Beavers or Absolute Film," trans. Noam Scheindlin, in *Robert Beavers*, ed. Rebekah Rutkoff (Vienna: Austrian Film Museum, 2017), 25.

**9.** Tom Chomont, "A Note on *The Count of Days*, a Film by Robert Beavers," in Rutkoff, *Robert Beavers*, 15.

**10.** Jonas Mekas, "Introduction to the Work of Robert Beavers," in Rutkoff, *Robert Beavers*, 20–21.

**11.** Henriette Huldisch and Chrissie Iles, "Frames of Mind: The Films of Robert Beavers," *Artforum*, September 2005, 285.

**12.** For example, when shooting with daylight film under tungsten light.

**13.** In the Bolex reflex camera, the beam-splitting prism deflects approximately 20 percent of light entering through the lens (80 percent reaches the film), projecting the incoming image onto a ground glass screen and causing the viewfinder to present the image right side up.

**14.** Robert Beavers, "La Terra Nuova," in Rutkoff, *Robert Beavers*, 193. "La Terra Nuova," along with four other short essays ("EM · BLEM," "His Image—The Nature of a Filmmaker," "Editing and the Unseen," and "The Senses"), first appeared in the annual Temenos film programs presented in Greece between 1980 and 1986 and in later program notes and publications. Beavers revised and gathered the texts under a single title, *The Searching Measure*, in conjunction with 2004 screenings at the Pacific Film Archive, Berkeley.

**15.** P. Adams Sitney, *Visionary Film: The American Avant-Garde, 1943–1978* (New York: Oxford University Press, 1979), 89.

**16.** Robert Beavers, "Winged Distance," in *My Hand Outstretched: Films by Robert Beavers* (New York: Whitney Museum, 2005), 14.

**17.** See "The Stoas" in the appendix.

**18.** Robert Beavers, "Acnode," in Rutkoff, *Robert Beavers*, 137. "Acnode" is composed of notes Beavers made in the mid-1970s; he edited them for publication at the time of his 2010 retrospective at the Austrian Film Museum.

**19.** Unless otherwise noted, the films discussed in this book are the revised versions. Beavers edited his camera originals in revising; the existence of first versions of Beavers's films today results from the prior acquisition of projection prints by cinematheques and archives including the Austrian Film Museum, Belgian Cinematheque, Munich Film Archive, and Anthology Film Archives.

**20.** Robert Beavers, "A Few Points," in Rutkoff, *Robert Beavers*, 165. Beavers composed "A Few Points" for the brochure that accompanied his 2007 Tate Modern retrospective.

**21.** This line comes from an undated draft of an essay that Beavers never published, "The Senses Create Time and Space."

**22.** Robert Beavers, "Sotiros: A Sequence of Notes," in Rutkoff, *Robert Beavers*, 181. Beavers originally published the text in 1980 as a Temenos imprint booklet; see chapter 6.

**23.** Beavers, "La Terra Nuova," 194. Beavers on the energetic and tactile economy of his process: "I place the pieces of film that are of no further use in one corner of the table. When these have accumulated, I must clear them from the table; their presence alone is an obstacle. They must be out of view to make a space for the next choice in the editing. I memorize the image and movement while holding the film original in hand; the memorizing gains a weight and becomes a source for the editing. To view the film on an editing table would only distract me from this process and create the illusion that editing is done in the viewing." Robert Beavers, "Editing and the Unseen," in Rutkoff, *Robert Beavers*, 198.

**24.** Beavers, "A Few Points," 165.

**25.** Beavers, "A Few Points," 165–166.

**26.** "I am alone when I'm filming . . . not planning. I have my notes and I'm thinking about what I'm doing so I'm not in a trance; but there is a level in which it is not thought out and I think my usage of gesture is happening on that level." Michael Guillén, "Winged Distance / Sightless Measure, Part One: A Conversation with Robert Beavers," *The Evening Class*, October 25, 2009. https://theeveningclass.blogspot.com/2009/10/winged-distance-sightless-measure_5054.html.

27. Robert Beavers, "EM · BLEM," in Rutkoff, *Robert Beavers*, 196.

28. Amy Taubin, "Survival Tactics," *Village Voice*, October 9, 2001, https://www.villagevoice.com/survival-tactics/.

29. Don Daniels, "A Master Motif," in Rutkoff, *Robert Beavers*, 115.

30. Micha, "Robert Beavers or Absolute Film," 25.

31. Paul Valéry, "Poetry and Abstract Thought," *The Art of Poetry*, trans. Denise Folliot (Princeton: Princeton University Press, 1958), 62.

32. Valéry writes: "Poetry is nothing but a formation of words that have resonance. This quality is independent of any meaning. Its presence is manifest. We say: magic." Paul Valéry, *Collected Works of Paul Valéry*, trans. James Lawler (Princeton: Princeton University Press, 2015), 422. My gratitude to Lisa Goldfarb and Don Daniels for pointing me to Valéry's thinking about magic.

33. Valéry, "Poetry and Abstract Thought," 60.

34. Robert Beavers, *Hautprobe for a Spectator* (Milan: Temenos, 1978). Beavers published this short essay to accompany the premiere of his *Sotiros* trilogy at the Zurich Filmpodium.

35. Beavers, "Sotiros: A Sequence of Notes," 184.

36. Robert Beavers, "The Senses," in Rutkoff, *Robert Beavers*, 193.

37. "I'm trying to activate the elements of the apparatus as conscious, to suggest consciousness," Beavers said.

38. Although Mauss ultimately destabilized magic as a sanctified anthropological category and participated in the work of extracting it, ideologically, from the ethnographic field, a one-noted conception of magical otherness persists—codified in teleological sequences of the spirit (first there was magic and then religion, and then God died and there was poetry), mobilized as a defense against mystery (to theorize magic is to patrol the line between the symbolic and the real), shunted to one primitive pole of the human mind. Magic, like every other idea caught in a binary split, asks to be turned over. Marcel Mauss, *A General Theory of Magic*, trans. Robert Brain (New York: Routledge, 2001).

39. Donald Winnicott, "Playing: A Theoretical Statement," in *Playing and Reality* (New York: Routledge, 1989), 63–64.

### CHAPTER 1

1. See a 1975 discussion between Annette Michelson and P. Adams Sitney on Knokke-le-Zoute as "the most important international event in the world of the avant-garde cinema." Annette Michelson and P. Adams Sitney, "A Conversation on Knokke and the Independent Filmmaker," *Artforum*, May 1975, 63–66.

2. At the 1967 Knokke-le-Zoute festival, Beavers saw films by Ernst Schmidt, Hans Jacob Siber, Edward Owens, Birgit and Wilhelm Hein, Paul Sharits, Joyce Wieland, HHK Schoenherr, Gunvor Nelson and Dorothy Wiley, Robert Nelson, James Broughton, Jud Yalkut, Karl-Birger Blomdahl, Stephen Dwoskin, Werner Nekes and Dore O, and Lutz Mommartz. Notably, in his first two volumes of notes from 1967 to 1968, only one film receives commentary, but it registers solely as a warning about intention: "I realized how important the actual filming is and that it must be independent, not guided by ideas of what the filmmaker thinks should be filmed or how." In his notes, Beavers identifies the film as "a short film by Guy LeClercq." LeClercq, a Belgian artist (who had a role in *Plan of Brussels*) did not make any films; it is likely Beavers was referring to a 1967 film in which LeClercq starred: the short Belgian horror film *Les Gardiens,* by Christian Mesnil.

3. René Micha, "Robert Beavers or Absolute Film," trans. Noam Scheindlin, in *Robert Beavers*, ed. Rebekah Rutkoff (Vienna: Austrian Film Museum, 2017), 33.

4. Markopoulos's *Twice a Man* (1963) had been awarded the inaugural $2,000 Prix Baron Lambert Prize at Knokke-le-Zoute in 1963, and Lambert, with a consortium of Belgian businessmen, was financing the completion of his film *The Illiac Passion* (1964–1967).

5. Gregory Markopoulos, "Towards a Complete Order," in *Film as Film: The Collected Writings of Gregory J. Markopoulos*, ed. Mark Webber (London: Visible Press, 2014), 365.

6. Markopoulos's father was born in Lyssarea. The filmmaker first visited the village in 1958 when he was making the film *Serenity* in Greece.

7. Roberta Smith, "Avant-Garde Films 'Repatriated' at Last," *New York Times*, October 21, 2005.

8. Akermark, former director of MoMA's circulating film program, is known for having amassed a vast library of films that reached thousands of U.S. universities, libraries, and museums.

9. In Henry James's novel *The Ambassadors* (1909), Lewis Lambert Strether instructs Little Bilham: "Don't forget that you're young—blessedly young; be glad of it on the contrary and live up to it. Live all you can—it's a mistake not to. It doesn't so much matter what you do in particular, so long as you have your life. If you haven't had that, what *have* you had?" Henry James, *The Ambassadors* (New York: Modern Library, 2012), 181.

10. Gregory Markopoulos, "Inherent Limitations," in Webber, *Film as Film*, 64–69.

11. American artist Leonard Baskin was a model; his Gehenna Press (inspired by William Blake's illustrated books) published books by writers including James Baldwin, Ted Hughes, and Sylvia Plath that featured his own black-and-white prints.

12. Dowd plays Endymion in Markopoulos's *The Illiac Passion* (1964–1967).

13. In the mid-1960s, another filmmaker had passed on a tip to Markopoulos: the Bolex Company, looking to solidify its reputation among filmmakers, was offering cameras on loan—and there was a representative in the New York City office who wasn't strict about following up on returns. Beavers shot his first three rolls of film and *Spiracle* on Markopoulos's infinitely borrowed Bolex, and continued to use it for the next several decades.

14. Tony Pipolo, "An Interview with Robert Beavers," *Millennium Film Journal*, no. 32/33 (Fall 1998): 19.

15. Markopoulos typed his note about Beavers, which followed the main letter, in caps. Konlechner cofounded and codirected the museum with Peter Kubelka. Correspondence, Gregory Markopoulos to Peter Konlechner, September 12, 1967, Austrian Film Museum, Vienna.

16. The film showcase was part of the Festival dei Due Mondi (Festival of Two Worlds), an annual arts event founded by composer Gian Carlo Menotti in 1958.

17. Gregory Markopoulos, "Towards a New Narrative Film Form," in Webber, *Film as Film*, 207. Markopoulos had already incorporated swaths of rapid, single-frame cutting in *Psyche* (1947) and *Swain* (1950) as kaleidoscopic accent marks and short eruptions of narrative recapitulation, but in *Twice a Man*, the technique determined structure and served not to summarize but to capture interiority.

**18.** Markopoulos's hybrid work continued in *Himself as Herself* (1967), *The Illiac Passion* (1964–1967), and *The Mysteries* (1968).

**19.** "A Lecture by Gregory Markopoulos at Kent State University, June 30, 1968," in John G. Hanhardt and Matthew Yokobosky, *Gregory J. Markopoulos: Mythic Themes, Portraiture, and Films of Place* (New York: Whitney Museum, 1996), 92.

**20.** "Interview with Gregory Markopoulos on Radio Free Europe, May 10, 1966, New York City," in Hanhardt and Yokobosky, *Gregory J. Markopoulos*, 86–87.

**21.** Gregory Markopoulos, "The Intuition Space," in Webber, *Film as Film*, 76.

**22.** Gregory Markopoulos, "Eikones Auton," in Webber, *Film as Film*, 379; emphasis in original. Markopoulos's oft-repeated phrase "film as film" signifies the aesthetic/expressive specificity of the medium of film.

**23.** Markopoulos, "The Intuition Space," 77.

**24.** Gregory Markopoulos, "Aei Kalon," in Webber, *Film as Film*, 455; emphasis in original.

**25.** Micha, "Robert Beavers or Absolute Film," 27.

## CHAPTER 2

**1.** Markopoulos wrote "Μικρός Ἔρως," a poem dedicated to Beavers, on Hydra in June 1967. In the final line, he wrote *ρόδα* (wheel) but most likely he meant *ρόδο* (rose). My thanks to Mitsos Triantopoulos and Nicolas Nicolaides for translation.

**2.** The three versions of *Winged Dialogue* (original, revised [silent], and revised [sound]) are discussed in chapter 3.

**3.** Though he had not yet used the compendium, *Winged Dialogue* marks Beavers's first matte use: Markopoulos holds a circular one against his bare abdomen.

**4.** In the late 1960s, Evergreen Book Club, an imprint of Grove Press, began to distribute 8mm films by selling them to club subscribers. Among them was Stan Brakhage's thirty-six-minute *Lovemaking* (1968), which depicts four kinds of sex: heterosexual sex, homosexual sex, canine copulation, and sexual play among nude children. *Lovemaking* was marketed as pornography; Grove Press sold 6,669 copies of the film.

**5.** Beavers said: "When I filmed *Winged Dialogue* I didn't realize what a strongly erotic life I was living. But I'm not looking at an erotic object the way [Markopoulos looked at me in] *Eros, O Basileus* (1967); Markopoulos's film is highly erotic in a more classically cinematic way—it's a closed world, with no daylight."

**6.** The *Winged Dialogue* shot of many-limbed Markopoulos recalls the original eight-limbed human described by Aristophanes.

**7.** The myth accounts for sexuality as well as love: the "matching half" each person longs for is rooted in his or her origin in an originally male, female, or androgynous/combined whole (a man split from an originally male whole would, for example, pursue men). "And so, when a person meets the half that is his very own, whatever his orientation, whether it's to young men or not, then something wonderful happens: the two are struck from their senses by love, by a sense of belonging to one another, and by desire, and they don't want to be separated from one another, not even for a moment," Aristophanes declares. Plato, *Symposium*, trans. Alexander Nehamas and Paul Woodruff (Indianapolis: Hackett Publishing Company, 1989), 26–27.

8. Plato, *Symposium*, 26.

9. Gregory Markopoulos, "10th of July," in *Film as Film: The Collected Writings of Gregory J. Markopoulos*, ed. Mark Webber (London: Visible Press, 2014), 286–287.

10. Markopoulos, "10th of July," 285–286.

11. Gregory Markopoulos, "The Redeeming of the Contrary," in Webber, *Film as Film*, 275.

12. Markopoulos began to use "the Temenos" in his writing in 1969, but the Temenos idea germinated even before it was named. In a set of notes made in 1961, under the heading "DREAMS," Markopoulos writes, "To build a modest home for the Cinema. To build the home step by step just as our films were made. To find the property. To find the funds for its construction." Once he met Beavers, the "our" of the Temenos was exclusively theirs. Gregory Markopoulos, "A Part of the Alphabet," in Webber, *Film as Film*, 96.

13. Gregory Markopoulos, *ERB* (Rome: Temenos, 1972). Markopoulos also referred to Beavers as the Christmas Child and the filmmaker-physician; the latter term is discussed in chapter 6.

14. Robert Beavers, "The Red Ottoman: Memories of a Fraught and Productive Relationship," in *A Trilogy: 50 Years of the Austrian Film Museum*, vol. 2 (Vienna: Austrian Film Museum, 2014), 68.

15. Beavers, "The Red Ottoman," 69.

16. "A Lecture by Gregory Markopoulos at Kent State University, June 30, 1968," in John G. Hanhardt and Matthew Yokobosky, *Gregory J. Markopoulos: Mythic Themes, Portraiture, and Films of Place* (New York: Whitney Museum, 1996), 97.

## CHAPTER 3

1. "The two Bacchi are the child and the phallus," Beavers originally wrote in his notes, but he transferred power to the boy in an addendum: "[The two Bacchi] are the man and the child phallus."

2. "I want to film inside of my own body," Beavers noted in March 1968.

3. As quoted by Gregory Markopoulos, "Bruised by the Critics," in *Film as Film: The Collected Writings of Gregory J. Markopoulos*, ed. Mark Webber (London: Visible Press, 2014), 188.

4. The cycle structure is not determinative; Beavers frequently shows his films individually and in nonchronological groupings.

5. The minuscule frame line on 16mm film renders the splice visible during projection. In "checkerboard" or A/B roll editing, adjacent shots are placed on parallel film strips rather than side by side. Even-numbered shots on the A-roll are spliced to black leader the length of the odd-numbered shots on the B-roll. The black leader hides the welding area, and the projected print produces a continuous, clean image.

6. Beavers and Markopoulos (like many experimental filmmakers) used reversal film, which produces a positive image and makes it possible to edit the camera original; no work copy is required. The reversal film Ektachrome Commercial 7252 was discontinued in 1984; starting with *The Hedge Theater*, Beavers has used color negative film.

7. Beavers characterized these five films in terms of an action/reaction pattern. "In this period, I moved in one direction and then reacted in the other, going against what I had just done," he said.

**8.** The Bollingen Foundation published *Papers from the Eranos Yearbooks*, collected lectures from annual Eranos gatherings in Ascona, Switzerland, devoted to exploring the crossroads of Eastern and Western thought.

**9.** "Markopoulos was not the type to acknowledge influence; he was probably influenced by Deren and all sorts of things. All mixing with Cocteau and Sternberg and Hollywood at a formal level," Beavers added.

**10.** Matthew Yokobosky, "Image, Beauty, and Association: Biographical Notes on the Life and Work of Gregory J. Markopoulos," in John G. Hanhardt and Matthew Yokobosky, *Gregory J. Markopoulos: Mythic Themes, Portraiture, and Films of Place* (New York: Whitney Museum, 1996), 22.

**11.** Richard Poirier writes: "Thinking/writing is different from thoughts/texts; thinking/writing shapes itself as an action that tropes." Richard Poirier, *Poetry and Pragmatism* (Cambridge, MA: Harvard University Press, 1992), 64. I want to acknowledge the impact of Poirier, Stanley Cavell, and Joan Richardson on my understanding of the "textuality" of Beavers's films. Their work emphasizes the poetic roots of the American philosophical tradition that becomes pragmatism. Anchored by Emerson and Thoreau, such a tradition is characterized by self-conscious writing: performative enactment of the labors of reading/writing/thinking in an effort to protect textual speculation from contracting into text. It is worth noting that Beavers is adamant about his identity as an "American artist." Years ago, when I asked him why, he said that he had a "New England mind"—an unwitting allusion to the Americanist Perry Miller's term for the very intellectual heritage that Poirier, Richardson, and Cavell take as their subject. There is indeed an uncanny set of resonances in the interface between Beavers's work and American poetic pragmatism—including Cavell's description of the philosophical tradition as "two-sided"—an image also embedded in Poirier's very notion of "troping" as figurative turning-over and renewal. For reflections on the impact of Cavell on my understanding of Beavers's poetics and the problem of "proving American-ness," see Rebekah Rutkoff, "Mother's Milk: Returning to Stanley Cavell," *Discourse: The Journal for Theoretical Studies in Media and Culture* 44, no. 1 (2022): 78–92. For a study of Beavers's cinema through the lens of Emersonian poetics, see P. Adams Sitney, *Eyes Upside Down: Visionary Filmmakers and the Heritage of Emerson* (New York: Oxford University Press, 2008). For Cavell and Richardson on the American philosophical tradition, see Stanley Cavell, *Emerson's Transcendental Etudes* (Stanford: Stanford University Press, 2003) and Joan Richardson, *A Natural History of Pragmatism: The Fact of Feeling from Jonathan Edwards to Gertrude Stein* (New York: Cambridge University Press, 2007).

**12.** Conversation between P. Adams Sitney and Robert Beavers, Pacific Film Archive, Berkeley, October 13, 2009.

**13.** The twenty individual *Early Monthly Segments* are not titled; phrases in quotes, generated from Beavers's remarks, are included here as identifying tags.

**14.** Beavers had hoped to make a film in Tunis but did not.

**15.** In 1970, Chomont wrote about the film's therapeutic valence in an essay for *Film Culture*: "In one sequence [Sadkowski] is on a red couch reading aloud while images of the dissection of a white rat are interpolated. Then the images of the dissected rat are framed by the pages of the book as though to explain that his writing is a dissection (analysis) just as the film is an analysis (of him). Thus, to some extent the film may be a representation of the author's concept or treatment of himself and the other two." Tom Chomont, "A Note on *The Count of Days*, a Film by Robert Beavers," in *Robert Beavers*, ed. Rebekah Rutkoff (Vienna: Austrian Film Museum, 2017), 15.

**16.** Beavers is uncertain whether the image is connected to the cycle name.

**17.** Beavers generated the voiceover from an improvised session with Gosling in a London sound studio.

**18.** "Still light" is close to the term for an artwork that depicts inanimate subject matter, "still life," thus playfully sending the "inanimate" back to the world of the critic.

**19.** Gregory Markopoulos, "The Filmmaker's Perception in Contemplation," in Webber, *Film as Film,* 356.

**20.** The Amor was named after Beavers's 1980 film. Markopoulos's vision for the design of built structures at the Temenos varies over time in his writings.

**21.** On Beavers's bookshelves: Markopoulos, Rilke, Aristotle, Goethe, Gerard Manley Hopkins, Valéry, Gide, H.D., Elizabeth Bishop, Cavafy, Emerson, Ruskin, Wittgenstein, Marianne Moore, George Santayana, Plato, Kierkegard, Montaigne, Aquinas, Bacon, Wallace Stevens, Bashō, Pasolini. His pages-long list of "Books 1967–77" also includes Horace, Mallarmé, Verlaine, Seferis, Galen, Shakespeare, Eliot, books on artists (Pisano, da Vinci, Watteau, Caravaggio, Cranash, Michelangelo, Balthus), early cinema (by Jean Mitry and Louis Delluc), and essays on mysticism from the *Papers from the Eranos Yearbooks* series. Other elements in Beavers's archive include correspondence (friends, critics, patrons, and foundations); notes on encounters with artworks and music; and documentation of film costs and laboratory work.

**22.** On his attraction to the book form in film, Beavers said: "The relation of the book, the intertitles, the dialogue, and sound effects in this late silent/early sound film has fascinated me ever since I first saw [*Vampyr*]. . . . I noticed the intimacy created for the spectator in these moments of reading a page of a book (seen on-screen)." From an unpublished 2014 interview with Robert Beavers by Francisco Algarín Navarro, Miguel Blanco, Elena Duque, and David Phelps.

**23.** Regarding his revision of films: "There is a whole family of artists who believe in the *nonfinito*," Beavers told a Princeton University film audience in October 2013, identifying himself as a member. He was referring not to Markopoulos, but to other artists who returned to earlier work for reconsideration, including Henry James, William Wordsworth, and Edgar Degas.

**24.** My alertness to the "moving lines" in Beavers's films is informed by Marcel Mauss's tour of the "pharmacy" of magic wherein ordinary ingredients are broken down and reformulated, formed into potent shapes and images. In his description, material representations of linearity stand out: chains, ropes, hair, jets of water, and spools of thread are wound, bound, knotted, and untied. It reads like a protolinguistic scene—a tacit acknowledgment of the associative thought-work behind the scenes of magic that I mention in the prologue. Marcel Mauss, *A General Theory of Magic*, trans. Robert Brain (New York: Routledge, 2001).

**25.** In the film, the red Richter book is visible on Beavers's desk.

**26.** He later added an "N.G." by the second statement.

**27.** Manohla Dargis, "One of the New York Film Festival's Best Movies Isn't at the Main Event," *New York Times*, October 6, 2016, https://www.nytimes.com/2016/10/07/movies/new-york-film -festival-avant -garde-movies.html. Dargis's title refers to the fact that *From the Notebook of . . .* was included in the experimental "Projections" slate when the film screened at the New York Film Festival in 2016.

**28.** Beavers returned to Florence in 1998 to gather new sound. He said, "I took time to make it richer twenty years later. I had the opportunity for more complex sound because I had access to a technician and an editing table—in the early years, sound was always a problem because of financial limitations." Prompted by a conversation with Sam Engel, I asked Beavers about his reliance on "indexical sound": he always returns to original sound sources during the revision process. "Perhaps it's a naive way of thinking about sound. I wasn't going to order it from a catalog," Beavers said. For a detailed study of Beavers's sound craft, see Luke Fowler, "In the Shadow of a Sound," in Rutkoff, *Robert Beavers*, 46–63.

**29.** Michael Guillén, "Winged Distance / Sightless Measure, A Conversation with Robert Beavers, Part Two," *The Evening Class*, October 25, 2009, https://theeveningclass.blogspot.com/2009/10/winged -distance-sightless-measure_3062.html.

**30.** Paul Valéry, *Introduction to the Method of Leonardo da Vinci*, trans. Thomas MacGreevy (London: John Rodker, 1929), 31, 48.

**31.** Leonardo da Vinci, *The Notebooks of Leonardo da Vinci* vol. 1, trans. Jean Paul Richter (London, 1888; Project Gutenberg, 2004), https://www.gutenberg.org/cache/epub/4998/pg4998.html. Beavers's transcription departs slightly from the language of Richter's translation: "If you look at the sun or some other luminous body and then shut your eyes you will see it again inside your eye for a long time."

**32.** da Vinci, *The Notebooks of Leonardo da Vinci*.

**33.** And like the perspectograph (da Vinci's glass and viewing slot contraption), the glass pane in Beavers's camera compendium mediates between eye and observed scene.

**34.** See "From the Notebook of . . ." in the appendix.

### CHAPTER 4

**1.** Jacques Derrida, "The Parergon," in *The Truth in Painting* (Chicago: University of Chicago Press, 1987), 37.

**2.** While making *Ruskin*, Beavers, in his notes, imagined the camera lens, sun, and filmed objects rotating along separate but intersecting axes, together generating "the sphere of the film." He placed himself inside these orbits to conduct structure and subject himself to chance.

**3.** Michael Guillén, "Winged Distance / Sightless Measure: Robert Beavers On . . . ," *The Evening Class*, October 25, 2009, https://theeveningclass.blogspot.com/2009/10/winged-distance-sightless -measure_25.html.

**4.** In *Ruskin*, as soon as the second of two lenses "arrives" (via turret turn) on a single color shot, Beavers cuts immediately to a static black-and-white shot, producing a rhythmic contrast between churning color and black-and-white stillness.

**5.** The book is one of the volumes of *The Stones of Venice*.

**6.** Gustave Flaubert, *Flaubert in Egypt: A Sensibility on Tour*, ed. and trans. Francis Steegmuller (New York: Penguin, 1996), 21. Underline is Beavers's.

7. John Ruskin, *The Stones of Venice*, vol. 2 (London: Smith, Elder, and Co., 1853), 165.

8. Ruskin, *The Stones of Venice*, vol. 2, 171.

9. John Ruskin, *The Stones of Venice*, vol. 1 (London: Smith, Elder, and Co., 1851), 344–346.

10. Tony Pipolo, "An Interview with Robert Beavers," *Millennium Film Journal*, no. 32/33 (Fall 1998): 16.

11. The young man attended a screening of Markopoulos's films at Arnolfini Gallery in Bristol; Markopoulos recommended him to Beavers as his *Ruskin* reader.

12. Pipolo, "An Interview with Robert Beavers," 16. Pipolo interviewed Beavers about his life and films in November 1997 and February and March 1998.

13. Pipolo, "An Interview with Robert Beavers," 16.

14. Pipolo, "An Interview with Robert Beavers," 24.

15. Ruskin, *The Stones of Venice*, vol. 1, 263.

16. Ruskin, *The Stones of Venice*, vol. 1, 19.

17. For analyses of Ruskin's thinking about surface and time, see S. Pearl Brilmyer, "Durations of Presents Past: Ruskin and the Accretive Quality of Time," *Victorian Studies* 59, no.1 (Autumn 2016): 94–97, and Anuradha Chatterjee, "Tectonic into Textile: John Ruskin and His Obsession with the Architectural Surface," *TEXTILE* 7, no. 1 (2009): 68–97.

18. Ruskin, *The Stones of Venice*, vol. 1, 1–2.

19. Leo Bersani, *The Freudian Body: Psychoanalysis and Art* (New York: Columbia University Press, 1986).

20. Beavers learned about Soglio from Rilke's letters to Princess Marie von Thurn und Taxis.

21. John Ruskin, "*Examples of the Architecture of Venice*," in *The Complete Works of John Ruskin*, Library Edition vol. 9, ed. E. T. Cook and Alexander Wedderburn (London and New York: George Allen and Longmans, Green, and Co., 1903), 841.

22. John Ruskin, *Cambridge School of Art. Mr. Ruskin's Inaugural Address* (Cambridge and London: Deighton, Bell and Co. and Bell and Daldy, 1858), 19.

23. Ruskin, *The Stones of Venice*, vol. 2, 41.

24. "Ruskin will be in two texts: the first, from 'The Stones,' is complete; the second will be a reading from 'Unto This Last,' para 61–77," Beavers wrote.

25. Beavers described an experience of aesthetic feeling in his *Ruskin* notes: "A painting which has impressed me expands in memory to the greatest proportion as if a real-life landscape moved between the actual parts of the composition." Reading this note, I realized such imaginative migration was operative in my own reception of *Ruskin*: the acts of book lifting and lowering occur much less frequently in fact than they do in my memory and experience of the film. The gesture belongs, rather, to a *spectrum* of performance: sometimes Beavers's hand on the book is unmoving, or the book appears on the table without the filmmaker, or the book is absent from the filmmaker's table.

26. Pipolo, "An Interview with Robert Beavers," 15.

27. Pipolo, "An Interview with Robert Beavers," 15.

28. Gregory Markopoulos, "The Gathering of Perception and Judgment," in *Film as Film: The Collected Writings of Gregory J. Markopoulos*, ed. Mark Webber (London: Visible Press, 2014), 325.

29. Both images were shot on Portland Place near a building that Ruskin admired: All Saints Church. Ruskin singles it out as a rare example of worthy modern architecture in the conclusion of *The Stones of Venice*.

30. John Ruskin, *Unto This Last* (New York: Penguin, 1985), 27.

31. Ruskin, *The Stones of Venice*, vol. 2, 309.

32. For a study of Ruskin's photographic documentation of Venice, see Thordis Arrhenius, "John Ruskin's Daguerreotypes of Venice," ACIS Conference for Cultural Studies, Norrköping, June 2005, https://ep.liu.se/ecp/015/008/ecp015008b.pdf.

## CHAPTER 5

1. Grayscale grisaille mimics sculpture.

2. Beavers cannot recall if he had seen the triptych in person or only in reproduction at that time.

3. The triptych may have been commissioned for the Church of Saint-Hippolyte, Poligny, his hometown.

4. The story of Hippolytus is a double, too: the Roman Christian poet Prudentius lyricized the martyr's end with the imprint of mythical Hippolytus (son of Theseus), who was dismembered by horses. Markopoulos's *Twice a Man* (1963) concerns the myth of Hippolytus, but Beavers's film is not intended as a reference.

5. The pension imagery was shot during the period when Beavers was making *From the Notebook of . . .* in Florence. The material was produced for one of his *Degeneration* experiments, but Beavers did not include it when he later revised the short films into *Early Monthly Segments*.

6. Erwin Panofsky, *Perspective as Symbolic Form*, trans. Christopher S. Wood (New York: Zone, 1991).

7. Edmund Husserl, *Logical Investigations*, vol. 1 (New York: Routledge, 2001), 168.

8. Tony Pipolo, "An Interview with Robert Beavers," *Millennium Film Journal*, no. 32/33 (Fall 1998): 11.

9. Pipolo, "An Interview with Robert Beavers," 11.

10. Pipolo, "An Interview with Robert Beavers," 11.

11. Pipolo, "An Interview with Robert Beavers," 11.

12. Pipolo, "An Interview with Robert Beavers," 11.

13. The repair of a medieval manuscript was an exception.

14. Pipolo, "An Interview with Robert Beavers," 11.

15. Pipolo, "An Interview with Robert Beavers," 11.

16. In the first film, environmental sound "stays" with its images. Beavers establishes diegetic sync in the first third of the revised film—visual intercutting accompanied by acoustic exchange—before opening the sound design to overlap and abstraction.

17. Rainer Maria Rilke, "Archaic Torso of Apollo," in *Ahead of All Parting: Selected Poetry and Prose of Rainer Maria Rilke*, trans. Stephen Mitchell (New York: Modern Library, 1995), 67.

18. Screening Q&A, Yale University, Whitney Humanities Center, January 29, 2009.

**19.** Gregory Markopoulos, "Stoa Palikari," in *Film as Film: The Collected Writings of Gregory J. Markopoulos*, ed. Mark Webber (London: Visible Press, 2014), 51.

**20.** Gregory Markopoulos, "Gregory Markopoulos Dissociates Himself from Film Archives," *Variety*, June 5, 1974, 7. Markopoulos also demanded P. Adams Sitney remove the chapter about his work from the second (1979) edition of *Visionary Film: The American Avant-Garde*.

**21.** See Erika Balsom's study of Markopoulos's developing Temenos vision in the context of his diverse and robust pursuits of distribution means and commercial support, including via gallery representation and limited editions. Balsom, "A Cinematic Bayreuth," in *After Uniqueness: A History of Film and Video Art in Circulation* (New York: Columbia University Press, 2017), 192–218.

**22.** Gregory Markopoulos, "Towards a Complete Order," in Webber, *Film as Film*, 367.

**23.** The other two are *Wingseed* and *The Ground*.

**24.** Robert Beavers, "La Terra Nuova," in *Robert Beavers*, ed. Rebekah Rutkoff (Vienna: Austrian Film Museum, 2017), 194.

**25.** "EM · BLEM" is the title of an essay Beavers first composed in the early 1980s; it later became one of the short texts included in *The Searching Measure*.

**26.** Marisa Bass, email correspondence with the author, March 18, 2019.

**27.** Beavers, "La Terra Nuova," 193.

**28.** For *AMOR*, Beavers also shot at a tailor shop in Turin.

**29.** Beavers said Dante inspired the film's title. "Amor, ch'a nullo amato amar perdona" (in Canto 5 of the *Inferno*) is translated by Allen Mandelbaum as "Love, that releases no beloved from loving." *The Divine Comedy of Dante Alighieri: A Verse Translation*, trans. Allen Mandelbaum (Berkeley: University of California Press, 1980), 42.

**30.** Regarding the "lost-and-found" ethos, Beavers, in his notes, instructed himself to "examine the hidden (lost) quality of the materials," a reference to the full-frame shots of marble pieces scattered throughout *AMOR*. They were inspired by learning about the historical uses of particular stone types (in ancient Greece, for example, green marble evoked the patina of bronze).

**31.** Robert Beavers, "A Few Points," in Rutkoff, *Robert Beavers*, 166.

**32.** "Find in the way I see the body its bright nature rather than downward violence," Beavers noted while making *AMOR*.

**33.** Dome construction also involved the filmmaker's body. "The head is the dome," Beavers said about his own headless figure under the lens arc in *AMOR*. "The head should return where it was absent in the earlier film," he wrote in his notes while making *The Hedge Theater*.

**34.** Bion, *Poems and Fragments* (Cambridge, MA: Harvard University Press, 2015), 406. In fast pans to and from the *richiami*, Beavers mimics the search for prey. "Camera movement like *la caccia* [hunting]," Beavers wrote in his notes for the film.

**35.** As quoted in Jake Morrissey, *The Genius in the Design: Bernini, Borromini and the Rivalry That Transformed Rome* (New York: Harper Collins, 2005), 132.

**36.** As quoted in Rudolf Wittkower, "Francesco Borromini: Personality and Destiny," *Studies on Borromini*, vol. 1 (Rome: De Luca Editori d'Arte, 1970), 33.

37. Leo Steinberg, *Borromini's San Carlo alle Quattro Fontane: A Study in Multiple Form and Architectural Symbolism* (New York: Garland, 1977).

38. The cycle title, *My Hand Outstretched to the Winged Distance and Sightless Measure*, appears at the start of the first reel; Beavers's name appears at the end of *The Ground*.

39. Anthony Blunt, *Borromini* (Cambridge, MA: Harvard University Press, 1979).

40. "The so-called 'belly' of the *roccolo*." Antonio Fappani, Sandro Fontana, Alberto Fumagalli, and Attilio Mazza, *Architettura Contadina in Valtrompia* (Milan: Silvana, 1980), 63.

41. Raniero Gnoli, *Marmora Romana* (Rome: Edizioni dell'Elefante, 1971).

42. Wagner was, for Markopoulos, a model of aesthetic unification; his *Gesamtkunstwerk*—total work of art—integrates music, drama, and design. Two of Markopoulos's early films are connected to the German composer: *Ming Green* (1966) features the song *Träume* (Dreams) from Wagner's *Five Songs on Poems by Mathilde Wesendonck*; *Sorrows* (1969) is a lyrical portrait of the Swiss chateau that King Ludwig II built for Wagner.

43. Beavers's dates follow European convention: "4.11.86" refers to November 4, 1986. Colons following dates have been added.

44. Beavers received financial support from Swiss art collector Doris Epstein between 1974 and 2005.

45. RAI is the Italian public broadcasting company.

#### CHAPTER 6

1. *Die Fragmente der Vorsokratike*, ed. Hermann Diels and Walther Kranz (Berlin: Weidmann, 1954), B93.

2. Gregory Markopoulos, "Pnoee," in *Film as Film: The Collected Writings of Gregory J. Markopoulos*, ed. Mark Webber (London: Visible Press, 2014), 335.

3. For a study of Markopoulos's reading habits and engagements, see P. Adams Sitney, "Markopoulos and the Temenos," *The Cinema of Poetry* (Oxford: Oxford University Press, 2015), 212–249.

4. Robert Beavers, "Sotiros: A Sequence of Notes," in *Robert Beavers*, ed. Rebekah Rutkoff (Vienna: Austrian Film Museum, 2017), 184. Beavers's many notes on the power of Hellenic art suggest other valences of "the nearness of distant objects seen in Greece." In 1986, he described the gathering of diverse histories (ancient, Byzantine) and exhibition planes in a single view at the Benaki Museum: "Waiting in the hallway, I could see a few of the display cases in the first few rooms, and, from this distance, I had a clearer impression of the color of certain objects—some of the textiles, the small painting of a bird, the color remaining on a small terra-cotta fragment—and further in the distance, an early Christian textile of crucified Christ and twelve apostles. A strength was gained from seeing this—all in calm."

5. Asclepius's mother was a mortal—Koronis—and he was originally a hero before becoming a god.

6. In a book on the healing god that Markopoulos read closely, Hungarian philologist Karl Kerényi frames Asclepian healing as a grand testament to the power of transference: a night in the god's temple provided the sick an "opportunity to bring about the cure whose elements he bore within himself." Kerényi writes, "The purpose of a visit to the sanctuary of Epidauros was to meet this divine power halfway.

This was no visit to a doctor who simply administers medicine; it was an encounter with the naked and immediate event of healing itself." Karl Kerényi, *Asklepios: Archetypal Image of the Physician's Existence* (New York: Pantheon, 1959), 34.

**7.** In the final year of his life, after a decade of editing *Eniaios*, Markopoulos prepared for a new epic work that would centralize the god and ancient healing even more deeply: *Asklepiades*.

**8.** Gregory Markopoulos, "The Complex Illusion," in Webber, *Film as Film*, 360.

**9.** In a 1964 essay footnote, Markopoulos even suggested that film might be physiologically curative. "I believe the motion picture is a sacred art. It is capable of healing. For instance, what would occur if in cases of cerebral palsy the patients were photographed reenacting a puppet play (those who cannot from one moment to another recall what has transpired) and then had the images returned to them, systematically through the medium of motion pictures, i.e., projection—double, triple, projection." Gregory Markopoulos, "Innocent Revels," in Webber, *Film as Film*, 142.

**10.** Gregory Markopoulos, "Unification of the Frame," in Webber, *Film as Film*, 485–488.

**11.** In his study of Markopoulos's film poetics, P. Adams Sitney discusses the contradictory and fluid nature of Markopoulos's Temenos vision and *Eniaios* plans. The eighty-hour film duration, for example, is based on a projection speed of 24fps; but his own notes reveal that Markopoulos planned to alter the speed of projection, and even to run the entire film in reverse after a forward-moving screening, making the total *Eniaios* duration variable. Sitney, "Markopoulos and the Temenos," 214–249.

**12.** Gregory Markopoulos, "In Other Words It Is His Tongue," in Webber, *Film as Film*, 308.

**13.** Erika Balsom, "A Cinematic Bayreuth," in *After Uniqueness: A History of Film and Video Art in Circulation* (New York: Columbia University Press, 2017), 205. See Balsom's chapter for a study of the National Gallery episode and a detailed timeline of Markopoulos's identification of the Temenos site that complicates and corrects earlier accounts.

**14.** Plotinus, *Enneads*, vol. 2, trans. A. H. Armstrong (Cambridge, MA: Harvard University Press, 1966), 38.

**15.** Beavers shot locations close to the Bassae temple on a walk from Stemnitsa but did not shoot the temple itself.

**16.** Tony Pipolo, "An Interview with Robert Beavers," *Millennium Film Journal*, no. 32/33 (Fall 1998): 19.

**17.** Pipolo, "An Interview with Robert Beavers," 19.

**18.** In *Sotiros Responds*, Beavers used a black matte, placed perpendicular to the lens in his compendium, to bisect some images. "The vertical black matte is a passage from the interior binocular fold of the spectator towards the screen and (negative?) force within Sight which unifies the image," he writes. Beavers, "Sotiros: A Sequence of Notes," 183. Beavers uses the term "binocular fold" to refer to the area of overlap between each eye's field of view in depth perception.

**19.** Readers should note the distinction between the unpublished notes Beavers composed during the making of the film *Sotiros* ("his *Sotiros* notes") and the publication *Sotiros: A Sequence of Notes*. Citations for the publication appear in quotation marks ("Sotiros: A Sequence of Notes") because they refer to its subsequent republication in Rebekah Rutkoff, *Robert Beavers* (Vienna: Austrian Film Museum, 2017).

**20.** A few key shots from *Sotiros in the Elements* appear in the second part of the final *Sotiros*.

**21.** Sigmund Freud, "A Disturbance of Memory on the Acropolis," *The Standard Edition of the Complete Psychological Works of Sigmund Freud*, vol. 22, ed. and trans. James Strachey in collab. with Anna Freud (London: Hogarth Press, 1964), 239–248.

**22.** People from the southwest corner of ancient Arcadia.

**23.** Beavers, "Sotiros: A Sequence of Notes," 184.

**24.** Beavers, "Sotiros: A Sequence of Notes," 184.

**25.** Beavers attributes the construction site and kafeneion scene imagery to Greek painter and friend Diamantis Diamantopoulos (1914–1995), known for his politically engaged and dignified depictions of ordinary Greek life. Beavers's inclusion of red frames in *Sotiros in the Elements* may also have been influenced by Diamantopoulos, who sometimes painted red figures or set his subjects against red backgrounds.

**26.** Beavers, "Sotiros: A Sequence of Notes," 181. While he did not shoot the Bern hotel room a third time, he included shots of it in *Sotiros in the Elements*. Of the light transit progressively elaborated across the films, Beavers writes: "The path of light that enters the room and moves along three walls appears only during a few winter weeks, on the infrequently clear days between noon and one o'clock. This movement of sunlight underlies each of the three films and is progressively condensed; [their respective durations are] twenty-five minutes, ten minutes, slightly more than six and a half minutes."

**27.** Beavers, "Sotiros: A Sequence of Notes," 181.

**28.** Beavers, "Sotiros: A Sequence of Notes," 184.

**29.** Beavers, "Sotiros: A Sequence of Notes," 181.

**30.** Beavers, "Sotiros: A Sequence of Notes," 183.

**31.** Beavers, "Sotiros: A Sequence of Notes," 184.

**32.** Beavers, "Sotiros: A Sequence of Notes," 182.

**33.** Beavers, "Sotiros: A Sequence of Notes," 192.

**34.** "The time of year, the place and nature of the body that is being treated." Beavers included this excerpt from Galen's "Commentary on Hippocrates's Book *On Fractures*" (in the Greek) in *Sotiros: A Sequence of Notes*. Galen's text emphasizes Hippocrates's understanding of the variety of factors that impact the duration of healing. My thanks to Sean Coughlin for his translation and analysis of Galen's remark. Beavers, "Sotiros: A Sequence of Notes," 187.

**35.** Beavers, "Sotiros: A Sequence of Notes," 187.

**36.** In *Sotiros: A Sequence of Notes*, Beavers writes of the "psychomachia of dark images and light" in the film. "Psychomachia" (conflict of the soul) is the title of a poem by Prudentius. Beavers, "Sotiros: A Sequence of Notes," 183.

**37.** Beavers, "Sotiros: A Sequence of Notes," 184.

**38.** Pipolo, "An Interview with Robert Beavers," 20.

**39.** Beavers, "Sotiros: A Sequence of Notes," 188.

**40.** Beavers, "Sotiros: A Sequence of Notes," 184.

**41.** Beavers, "Sotiros: A Sequence of Notes," 184.

**42.** Beavers, "Sotiros: A Sequence of Notes," 189.

43. "The reflected light and shadow is held on a piece of paper as a second screen within the frame; when torn and thrown aside, the 'projection' moves to the wall," Beavers writes in "Sotiros: A Sequence of Notes," 189.

44. Beavers, "Sotiros: A Sequence of Notes," 189.

45. *Sotiros* is a film of men: the dialogic "he," Beavers and Markopoulos, elderly men in a kafeneion, young shirtless men on a rooftop construction site, the blind beggar and village fool. In an interview with Tony Pipolo, Beavers identified the *Sotiros* speaker as the healer and the film itself: "The 'he' is left unidentified," Beavers said. "It is the voice of Sotiros without Sotiros being shown in the film. In one way 'he' is the film." Pipolo, "An Interview with Robert Beavers," 19.

46. Constantine Cavafy, "At the Theatre," in *C. P. CAVAFY: Collected Poems*, rev. ed., trans. Edmund Keeley and Philip Sherrard, ed. George Savidis (Princeton: Princeton University Press, 1993), 92.

47. Athens became capital in 1834. King Otto's former residence is now the Museum of the City of Athens.

48. See "Efpsychi" in the appendix. Additional references to masks appear in Beavers's *Efpsychi* filming notes. In October 1982, while looking at a book with images of ancient death masks, *teleftea*, a term used in contemporary commerce, acquired an echo of ancient ritual. "I noticed the ancient Greek word *τελευτᾶν* (*teleftan*) meaning Death," he noted.

49. In a March 1982 note, he continued to explore "emblem" as a figure of bothness, now with respect to sound and image. "The sound of the word is shown in the lips and in the eyebrows: *τε: λευταία* lips: eyebrows."

50. See "Efpsychi" in the appendix.

51. See "Efpsychi" in the appendix.

52. For a Foucault-informed study of Cavafy's poetics of hiding, see Dimitris Papanikolaou, "'Words that tell and hide': Revisiting C. P. Cavafy's Closets," *Journal of Modern Greek Studies* 23, no. 2 (October 2005): 235–260.

53. Paul Arthur, "Between the Place and the Act: *Efpsychi*," *Millennium Film Journal*, no. 32/33 (Fall 1998): 55. Micha expresses a related sentiment with respect to Beavers's early city-based films: "Though we only see a tiny piece" of a given place, "in the instant that we recognize the place, it seems to us that we also seize upon something essential to their being, yet up until now missing from our perception." René Micha, "Robert Beavers or Absolute Film," in Rutkoff, *Robert Beavers*, 25.

54. In 2022, I ran into a friend in Athens and asked where he was going. "I'm going to look for the arcades Beavers shot in *The Stoas*," he said.

55. "Troika" refers to the consortium (composed of the European Commission, the European Central Bank, and the International Monetary Fund) that intervened financially in Greece and other countries following the 2007–2008 financial crisis.

56. "Stoicism" is so-named because Zeno taught philosophy in the Stoa Poikile (Painted Porch) in 300 BCE.

57. Ute Aurand and Robert Beavers, "Conversation about *The Stoas*," in Rutkoff, *Robert Beavers*, 143.

58. Apollo is known as the god of light. Classicist Joshua Billings suggests that "god of appearances" may reflect a Nietzschean understanding of Apollo as god of beautiful appearances.

**59.** Aurand and Beavers, "Conversation about *The Stoas*," 144. Reflecting on the challenges of filming the human body, Beavers said: "I can barely put anyone in my films. It's difficult to work with the figure at this moment in my life. Consumerism and capitalism have used the body in so many ways, it's almost impossible to have a positive way into it . . . maybe young people can do it. There was a brief realization in the 1960s—coming through Gide, Cocteau, Whitman with Youcenar, Pasolini, Markopoulos—all had a utopian vision for sexuality."

**60.** Three months earlier, in April, he had noted, "*δῶρον*—meaning 'hollow of the hand.'"

**61.** For reflections on the role of catharsis in *The Ground*, see Max Goldberg, "In Berkeley, a Master Filmmaker Reflects on His Craft," *KQED*, November 9, 2016, https://www.kqed.org/arts/12318079/bask-in-master-filmmaker-robert-beavers-light-touch-at-bampfa.

**62.** While editing in Switzerland in July 1995, Beavers noted the shift from grief to clarity after reviewing his work copy. "There was a sense of euphoria . . . the tone of the film is bright + clear . . . different . . . than what I expected, since the editing had been difficult and because of the associated sense of the images . . . quite different from this wonderful clearness. It seems all to be carried by the stone cutter."

**63.** Francis Ponge, *Vegetation*, trans. Lee Fahnestock (New York: Red Dust, 1987), 13. Beavers visited Ponge in France in the 1970s; he showed the poet *Work Done* in Paris and the first version of *Ruskin* at the Fondation Maeght, in Saint-Paul-de-Vence.

**64.** See P. Adams Sitney, "Directing and Observing *Wingseed*," *Millennium Film Journal*, no. 32/33 (Fall 1998): 44–51, for an analysis of the complex erotic landscape of the film.

**65.** See "Wingseed" in the appendix.

**66.** Osip Mandelstam, "On the Nature of the Word," in *Complete Critical Prose*, trans. Jane Gary Harris and Constance Link (Dana Point: Ardis, 1997), 80.

### CHAPTER 7

**1.** Beginning with Beavers's first post-cycle film, *Pitcher of Colored Light*, the Georg and Bertha Schwyzer-Winiker Foundation in Switzerland also became a new source of financial support.

**2.** For a study of Beavers's post-cycle films, see Haden Guest, "Of Place and Portraiture," in *Robert Beavers*, ed. Rebekah Rutkoff (Vienna: Austrian Film Museum, 2017), 145–161.

**3.** Anthony Everitt, *Hadrian and the Triumph of Rome* (New York: Random House, 2009), 319.

**4.** Robert Beavers, program notes, Punto de Vista International Documentary Film Festival of Navarra, 2019.

**5.** For an architectural history of the Staehelins' house, designed by Swiss architect Oskar Burri as part of an artists' community, see James MacGillivray, "Tectonics and Space: Architectural Thought in the Films of Robert Beavers," in Rutkoff, *Robert Beavers*, 79–101.

**6.** A. W. Price, *Love and Friendship in Plato and Aristotle* (New York: Oxford University Press, 1989), 227.

**7.** "Each of the two who constitute the couple possesses a body, a face and a name, but their real reality, precisely at the most intense moment of the embrace, disperses in a cascade of sensation which disperses in turn. There is a question that all lovers ask each other, and in it the erotic mystery is epitomized: Who are you? A question without an answer. . . . The senses are and are not of this world. By means of them, poetry traces a bridge between seeing and believing." Octavio Paz, *The Double Flame: Love and Eroticism* (New York: Ecco, 1996), 2.

**8.** Aurand curated the series "Filmarbeiterinnen-Abend," in 1990–1995, and "Sie zum Bespiel," in 1995–1996, at the Arsenal and Babylon Mitte cinemas in Berlin, featuring only women filmmakers.

**9.** An ancient Greek literary theme, *nostos* refers to homecoming, especially by a hero (most famously Odysseus) after a long journey.

**10.** The book Beavers refers to is *Zeami and the Nô Theatre in the World*, ed. Benito Ortolani and Samuel L. Leiter (New York: Martin E. Segal Theatre Center, 1998).

**11.** For a short commentary on the audience response to *AMOR*, see Paul Arthur, "Avant-Garde Retreat," *Film Comment* 32, no. 6 (November/December 1996): 69.

**12.** For details on the *Eniaios* restoration, see Rebekah Rutkoff, "Other Galaxies: The Temenos beyond the Screen," *Framework: The Journal of Cinema and Media* 61, no. 2 (Fall 2020): 158–179.

**13.** Beavers shot this material at the Yale Workshop in the Woods Hole Historical Museum, the summertime workspace of Dr. Leroy Milton Yale Jr., a pediatrician and artist who founded the New York Etching Society.

### APPENDIX

The appendix contains Beavers's short introductory texts and essays about selected films in his *My Hand Outstretched* cycle; his writings on his post-cycle films are included in chapter 7. The texts on *From the Notebook of . . .* and *Efpsychi* in this appendix previously appeared in *Robert Beavers*, ed. Rebekah Rutkoff (Vienna: Austrian Film Museum, 2017) among a larger collection of his writings about filmmaking.

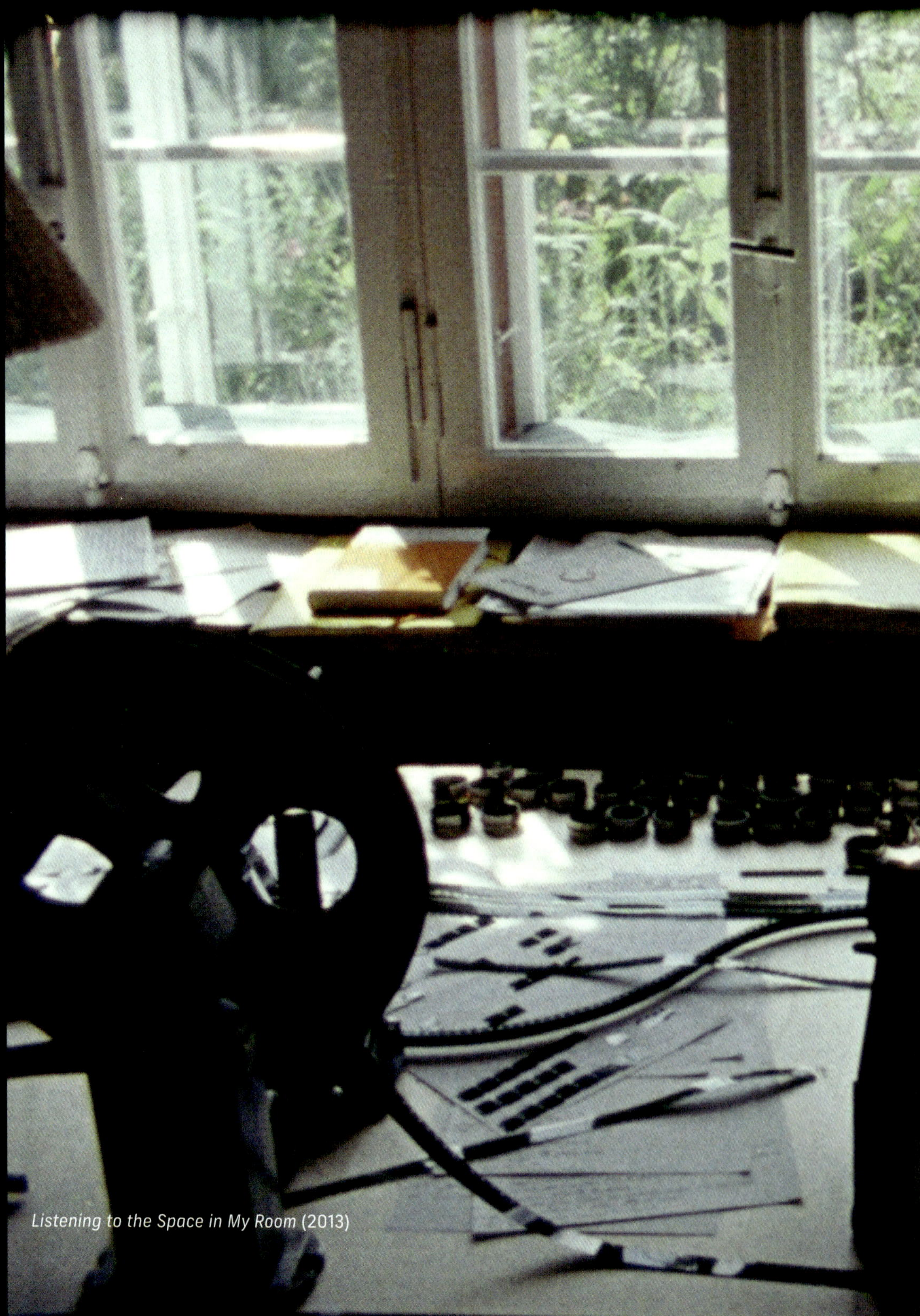

*Listening to the Space in My Room* (2013)

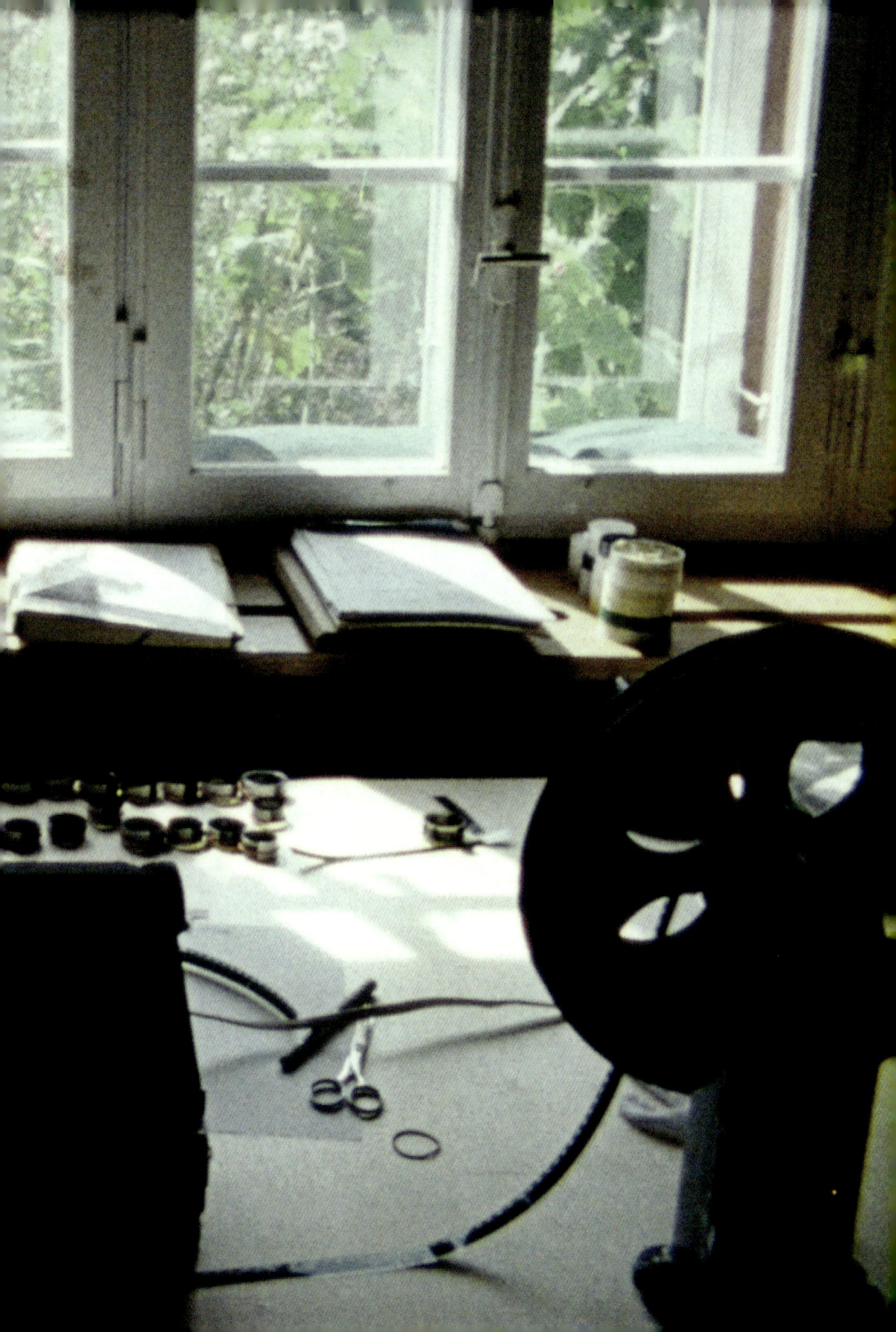

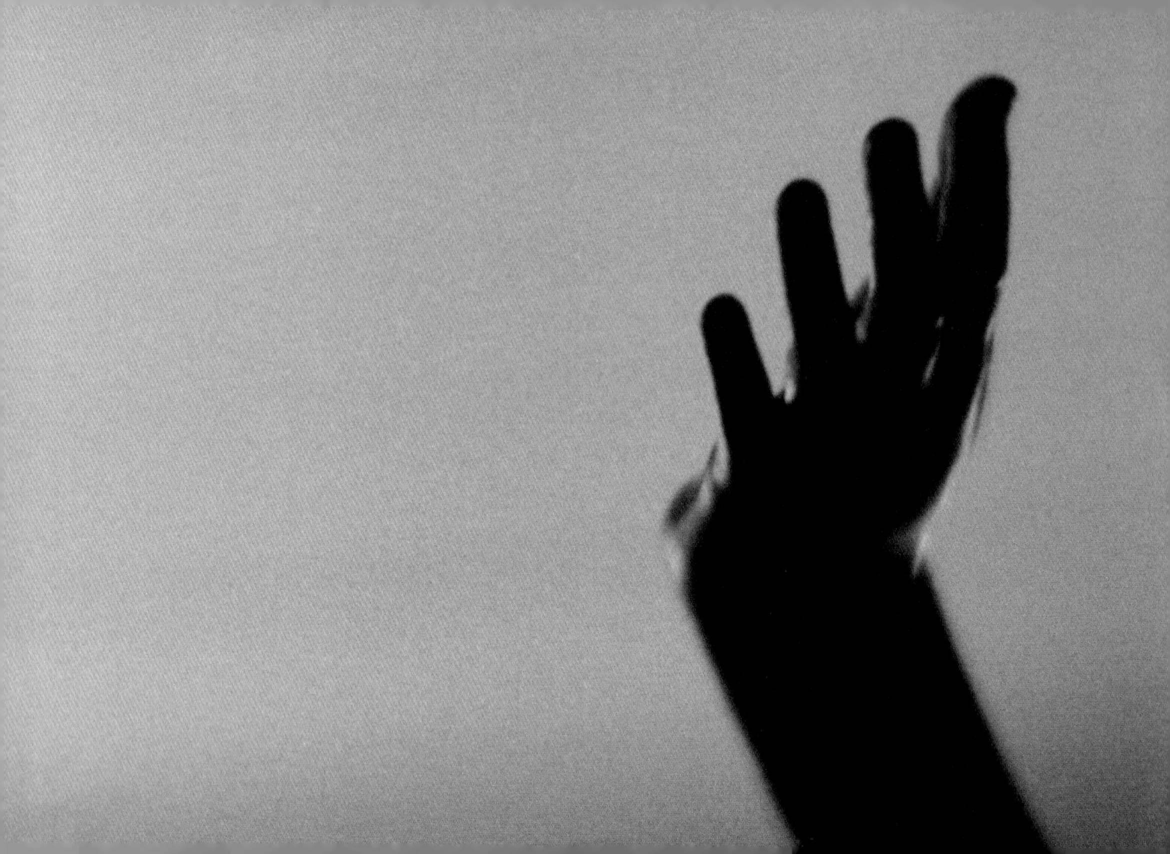